L.F.

D0084759

REVOLUTIONARY
SPARKS

REVOLUTIONARY SPARKS

★★★

Freedom of Expression in Modern America

Margaret A. Blanchard

New York   Oxford
OXFORD UNIVERSITY PRESS
1992

ALBRIGHT COLLEGE LIBRARY

Oxford University Press

Oxford   New York   Toronto
Delhi   Bombay   Calcutta   Madras   Karachi
Petaling Jaya   Singapore   Hong Kong   Tokyo
Nairobi   Dar es Salaam   Cape Town
Melbourne   Auckland

and associated companies in
Berlin   Ibadan

Copyright © 1992 by Margaret A. Blanchard

Published by Oxford University Press, Inc.,
200 Madison Avenue, New York, New York 10016

Oxford is a registered trademark of Oxford University Press

All rights reserved. No part of this publication may be reproduced,
stored in a retrieval system, or transmitted, in any form or by any means,
electronic, mechanical, photocopying, recording, or otherwise,
without the prior permission of Oxford University Press.

Library of Congress Cataloging-in-Publication Data
Blanchard, Margaret A.
Revolutionary sparks : freedom of expression in modern America /
Margaret A. Blanchard.
p. cm.   Includes bibliographical references and index.
ISBN 0-19-505436-9
1. Freedom of speech—United States—History—20th century.
2. Freedom of the press—United States—History—20th century.
I. Title.   JC599.U5B553   1992
323.44′3′0973—dc20   91-16147

Portions of this book have appeared, in a somewhat different form,
in the *William and Mary Law Review* (Spring 1992).

1 3 5 7 9 8 6 4 2

Printed in the United States of America
on acid-free paper

323.443
β639r
1992

238794

For John E. Semonche,
teacher, mentor, and friend

#9.95

230784

——————— ★ ★ ★ ———————

Preface

The governmental pledge to the American people found in the First Amendment reads, "Congress shall make no law . . . abridging the freedom of speech, or of the press; or the right of the people peaceably to assemble, and to petition the Government for a redress of grievances." Written more than two hundred years ago, these words now protect a wide range of expressive activity.

Although much of the expression that finds shelter under the First Amendment is taken for granted today, the battle for the freedom to speak in the United States has been long, and, indeed, still persists as the Bill of Rights enters its third century. As these words are being written, concern has spread across the land about the ability of dissenters to destroy a symbol close to the hearts of most Americans—the flag. More apprehension exists over the bounds of permissible expressive activities connected with the increasingly heated debate over abortion. Medical facilities are picketed; patients and physicians are harassed; residential neighborhoods are disturbed by protesters. And fears increase when in the face of war, American journalists send news of military and political plans around the world almot instantaneously—including into the offices of enemy leaders. Why, ask many Americans, should such forms of expression be allowed? Surely, such types of expression were not meant to be protected under the Bill of Rights!

Such questions, however, go to the heart of the meaning of First Amendment guarantees. For as long as individuals have been allowed to speak, some people have advanced theories that have the potential for turning Americans' known, safe world upside down. Others in society, seeking to protect the status quo, have sought to repress dissident ideas. This conflict between those advancing positions out of the mainstream and those defending existing lifestyles forms the story of freedom of expression in the United States that follows.

These two points of view may be best expressed in the words of two U.S. Supreme Court justices who were responding to one another in a 1925 decision that upheld the conviction of a Communist on charges of attempting to overthrow the government of the state of New York. Sending Benjamin Gitlow to jail for his advocacy of a different form of government was perfectly logical to Edward Sanford, who wrote for the majority, despite the fact that the Communist had committed no overt act of revolution. Even the discussion of such a

change in government was to be suppressed, he wrote, for after all, "a single revolutionary spark may kindle a fire that, smouldering for a time, may burst into
a sweeping and destructive conflagration." The state government had the right
and, indeed, the obligation, "to extinguish the spark without waiting until it has
enkindled the flame or blazed into the conflagration." Justice Oliver Wendell
Holmes, Jr., countered that broader freedom for expression was essential, even
if that speech challenged core values of American society. "Every idea is an incit-
ment," he wrote. "The only meaning of free speech," he added, "is that they
[ideas] should be given their chance."[1]

These two opinions broadly summarize American attitudes toward freedom
of expression. Those who would preserve the status quo generally favor quieting
dissident speech; those who accept change support wider freedom of expression.
The battle lines over freedom of expression stretch back to the early history of
the colonies when religious dissenters sought to practice the Quaker faith in Puri-
tan Massachusetts, through the Revolution where inflammatory speech was a
key to rousing the colonists to revolt against George III, to the days prior to the
Civil War when abolitionists sought to use the printed and spoken word to ignite
the conscience of a nation to overthrow slavery. Each was a truly revolutionary
idea at the time and often much despised by those interested in preserving the
status quo. But the outcomes of these encounters are highly valued today, for
from these revolutionary ideas came religious tolerance, independence from
Great Britain, and the end of slavery. Similar revolutionary sparks came with
the advocacy of such notions as the vote for women, the right of workers to organize into labor unions, and the ability of blacks to exercise their constitutionally
guaranteed rights. In each case, the forces of change battled the forces of the status quo with expressive activities as a major weapon. In each case, after much
travail, the forces of change prevailed and, in the process, significantly altered
the face of American society. Thus we see both the prize to be won in the struggle
and the reason for attempts to curtail the expressive freedom of dissident minorities. Revolutionary sparks can indeed break forth into a sweeping conflagration
capable of substantially changing American life.

Indeed, the one theme that recurs repeatedly in the pages that follow is that
American reaction to efforts to express different political, social, economic, religious, educational, and sexual views is based on how acceptable the idea
espoused is to the prevailing definition of Americanism. At times, when the
nation is beset by internal and external challenges, the definition of what is
acceptably American contracts sharply. This contraction does not always reflect
real danger to the nation but often focuses on changes in society that are perceived to be harmful to the status quo. The ideas that are targets for repression
often advocate some action or change in lifestyle that will take the nation farther
away from a model America and make it more diverse and less homogeneous.
In response to such challenges, certain Americans want to revert to a simpler
time when, they believe, citizens thought alike, dreamed alike, and lived alike in
rustic splendor, isolated from all contaminants. This is a highly idealized version
of the Puritans' city on a hill, but it exists in the hearts and minds of individuals
fearful of challenges to the existing order.

Being able to label one particular group or category of individuals as the primary suppressor of free expression would be comforting. Unfortunately, the urge for conformity and, thus, the effort to suppress ideas comes from all segments of the American population. At some points, different churches have taken the lead in this effort; at other times, various levels of government have served as the prime suppressive force. Business and industrial leaders have aided in this push toward conformity as have conservatives and liberals, blacks and whites, males and females. Generally, the cause for such activity is insecurity— a fear of new ideas and, even more so, a fear of the inability of fellow citizens to make the proper choices among the ideas being presented. The definition of proper, of course, depends more on the group interested in suppression of speech and on the operative definition of Americanism at the time than on any constitutional interpretation of freedom of expression. In such circumstances, the climate greeting free speech very much reflects Alexander Hamilton's discussion in *The Federalist Papers* in 1787. Facing pressures to add a bill of rights to the new Constitution guaranteeing, among other protections, freedom of the press, Hamilton responded that written guarantees were almost worthless. "Whatever fine declarations may be inserted in any constitution respecting it [freedom of the press]," he wrote, "must altogether depend on public opinion, and on the general spirit of the people and of the government."[2]

Particularly insidious in this urge toward conformity is the notion that freedom is being saved via the suppression of dissident speech. In almost every generation, the argument surfaces that revolutionary ideas must be quieted because the existing governmental structure must be preserved. Often accompanying this point is the notion that freedom of speech or of the press must be used responsibly—that individuals must be held accountable for the damage caused by their expressive activities. Perhaps no two thoughts are more alluring to those with suppressive tendencies or more dangerous to the survival of individual rights than these. Much to the dismay of those who wish a peaceful society, the nation has survived hearty, robust, unintimidated, and often unwise debate many times in its past. As a result of such experiences, it has emerged wiser and stronger because of the challenge to the status quo. But yet, many Americans so distrust their fellow citizens that, in the guise of offering protection, they bring repression.

Fortunately for the nation, despite such pressures for conformity, some individuals in every generation pursue a different view of what is best for America. These individuals are largely responsible for expanding the boundaries of what is acceptable in terms of freedom of expression and for creating a society as diverse and as rich as the one that exists today. Without such struggles, many changes considered beneficial today—including the right of workers to organize, the right to discuss birth control and sexual matters, and the right to disagree with wartime policy—never would have been won.

Enabling these individuals to spread their doctrines and to win changes in American society is the ability to spread ideas—or, more basically, information—about their desired goals. Part of the story that follows, then, will focus on the need for Americans to have the raw data upon which to base opinions and to make judgments. Unfortunately, the reverse side—attempts by individuals and groups to keep information from flowing freely—shows itself far more frequently in American society than does the enabling side. The connection between information and the proper functioning of society was recognized early by James Madison, who wrote in 1822, "A popular Government, without popular information, or the means of acquiring it, is but a Prologue to a Farce or a Tragedy; or, perhaps both. Knowledge will forever govern ignorance: And a people who mean to be their own Governors, must arm themselves with the power which knowledge gives."[3] The ability of the American people to gain that needed information waxes and wanes with the nation's perceived self-confidence.

As the twentieth century draws to a close, most Americans have become accustomed to seeing this battle of ideas being played out before the U.S. Supreme Court. Since the late 1930s, the Court has used the guarantees in the First Amendment to protect the expression of civil rights groups, labor union members, journalists, members of fringe and mainline political groups, and others. In fact, Supreme Court opinions largely are the medium through which freedom of expression is defined in the United States today. Viewing the meaning of freedom of expression through the prism provided by the High Bench, however, limits our understanding of this most important freedom. First Amendment interpretation by the Supreme Court is a mid-twentieth-century phenomenon. Focusing solely on these judicial decisions ignores the development of free expression within American society in earlier years. Even more important, the Supreme Court can focus on expressive concerns only in the context of a legal dispute. Although Americans are indeed a litigious people, not all free expression issues have been or can be presented in a court case, nor can all individuals with such interests bring cases.

To understand the place of freedom of expression in American society, then, one must look at its development in terms of the social, political, and economic history of the United States. Within the ebb and flow of the ongoing growth of the nation as a whole comes the development of freedom of expression. The person on the street may not know or understand the language of the First Amendment or how the Supreme Court has interpreted those words in a certain case, but that individual does know the kind of speech that is tolerated in his or her community, regardless of whether legal justification exists for acceptance or rejection of such speech. Perhaps that community standard will be litigated if someone takes offense to it, perhaps not. But in this day-to-day existence outside the courtroom, freedom of expression has developed.

Looking at the evolution of freedom of expression in the United States from a social, political, economic, and legal perspective presents both problems and rewards. The major problem is that such an approach makes almost all of the American experience a candidate for inclusion in a history of free expression. To a large part, the selection of themes for discussion in the pages that follow was based on what the Supreme Court in recent years has said qualifies for First Amendment protection. With those guidelines dealing with associative rights, symbolic speech, political activities, and so on, the search began for situations and individuals that many years ago established the heritage that the Court drew on in making its decisions. Results of the inquiry clearly showed that speech activities placed under the First Amendment by recent Courts were deeply rooted in earlier American experiences. But because such earlier activities were not framed in terms of the First Amendment or in terms of a court case, many such antecedents simply were buried in time and ignored by most later scholars.

Another potential problem in framing this study is the danger that it easily could become solely a review of the development of freedom of the press in this country. Of all of the liberties guaranteed by the First Amendment, freedom of the press has the most organized and most vocal group of supporters. Because of the interest in this guarantee evidenced by the mainline or institutional press, studies of this protection abound, but with these studies come significant difficulties. For instance, many of these works are limited in the time period investigated. The roots of freedom of the press up to about 1800 are popular with researchers caught up in the quest to understand what the framers of the First Amendment really meant when they wrote those words.[4] Then, generally, the study of press freedom jumps to the twentieth century and to the Supreme Court, with little done so far on freedom of the press in the nineteenth century.[5] In addition, students of freedom of the press seldom attempt to tie that freedom to other expressive activities, acting as if one First Amendment value can stand in splendid isolation from all others. Such an approach limits our understanding of the development of First Amendment values and, indeed, undercuts those values themselves.

Moreover, most studies of press freedom ignore the somewhat contradictory role that the press has played in terms of overall freedom of expression. Evidence suggests that the institutional press frequently has aligned itself with the forces seeking to suppress dissident speech in this country. As the press became a larger, more institutionalized force in American society, its leaders have had a greater vested interest in preserving the status quo. Thus journalistic opposition to the rights of workers to organize or anarchists to plead for their cause, for instance, dot the pages that follow. Much more research into this particular subject is needed, but press antagonism toward the expressive activities of dissidents historically has led to substantial problems for the development of divergent opinions in the United States.

Readers of this study will not find an effort to explain historical developments in terms of existing First Amendment theories. Most of the theories in existence today are limited in nature because they focus largely on the way in which the Supreme Court has interpreted First Amendment rights.[6] Although the Supreme Court becomes an increasingly important player in our study of freedom of expression, seldom will we look at the doctrine that the Court's decisions are establishing. Instead, we focus on what the opinions tell us about the stance of freedom of expression in society at that particular time. In addition, much of this study looks at extrajudicial forces and their impact on freedom of expression, with the goal being to place this value in a much broader context. Although omitting existing First Amendment theoretical concepts may lead to criticism, the ultimate decision was based on the belief that reliance on someone else's formulation of how the First Amendment works in American society would require bending information to fit those hypotheses. The goal, instead, was to allow the richness of the American experience with freedom of expression to be experienced without forcing the material into a theoretical model.

Nor will readers of this study find a complete review of freedom of expression as developed through the religion clauses of the First Amendment. Freedom of religion is indeed a vital component of freedom of expression, but the principles and problems involved in the evolution of freedom of religion are too different from those involved in the promulgation of revolutionary social and political ideas to be included in this study. Religious groups are not absent from the following pages. Jehovah's Witnesses and Christian fundamentalists, for example, appear in the pages that follow but more because of their connection with the broader scope of political, social, economic, and legal issues involved in free expression than for their contributions to interpretations of the religion clauses.

To a certain extent, the availability of literature on certain subjects in this study governs the way in which it is put together. Although this reality may limit the exploration of some points, the value in such an approach far outweighs any possible shortcomings. The study that follows brings material together in a way not done before by anyone studying the component parts of freedom of expression. Through such a synthesis, we come to understand—and appreciate—the way in which this value has grown and developed in the United States.

The study itself focuses on freedom of expression after the Civil War and Reconstruction, in what we call "modern America." Although freedom of expression certainly was affected by events in our nation's earlier history, only after the Civil War do more and more Americans start to frame their concerns in terms of their free-speech rights. These years represent a time period in which new and unsettling ideas appeared with great regularity on the American scene—with too great a regularity for some Americans, as the pages that follow will amply illustrate. Indeed, the nation was virtually inundated with revolutionary ideas. So many were floating around during these years that the nation's leaders often joined forces to repress aberrant notions. In response to such suppression, individuals seeking to better their lives through the expression of new ideas began to demand their rights to speak, write, and associate together to advance their points of view. The tumult that this contest for control of the nation's destiny sparked has not yet ended, for those persons who support freedom of speech still must battle others who find certain ideas simply too dangerous for voicing.

The pages that follow show clearly that the urge to suppress continues to be strong in Americans. Faith in one another to make the appropriate decisions to keep the country growing and developing still is lacking. After 200 years under the First Amendment and 350-plus years on the continent, the lesson of the strength provided by freedom of expression still has not been learned. The pages that follow not only show those who try to both express and suppress ideas but also feature the beneficial developments that have followed in the wake of a robust freedom of expression. In large part, the story of freedom of expression in the United States is one of ordinary people who because their beliefs are driven to do or say extraordinary things. It is a story of the conflict between peaceful change and harsh repression, one that many would not associate with the United States. It shows that if revolutionary ideas are not heard peaceably by the larger society, voices of protest will become more strident and that a growing animosity on both sides will often lead to property damage, personal injury, and death, all because of intolerance exhibited toward those voicing revolutionary ideas.

Americans have a short memory when it comes to the consequences of freedom of expression. They condemned the actions of the leaders of the People's Republic of China in 1989, for instance, for their bloody suppression of the Tiananmen Square protest movement, but they forgot the actions of Southern police against black demonstrators and the violence perpetrated by law enforcement and military personnel on all levels of government against antiwar demonstrators less than twenty-five years earlier in the United States. Chinese Communists are not the only ones willing and able to use repressive measures against dissenters; Americans have as long a tradition of repression as they do of speaking their minds on various issues. Indeed, perhaps, violent repression and outspokenness go hand in hand.

The book that follows is far from unbiased. From an inspection of the problems encountered by freedom of expression in the past should come lessons that will help build an appreciation of freedom of expression today. Fear of ideas and of those who express them, no matter how radical, shows national insecurity rather than national strength.

———— ★★★ ————

Acknowledgments

This book would not have been possible without the work of other scholars quoted within its pages. Many of them most likely will be surprised to find their work cited in such a study, for researching freedom of expression was not their goal as they prepared their papers, dissertations, articles, and books. Much research remains to be done to develop our understanding of freedom of expression, and the foundation that these individuals have established for that understanding is crucial. I thank them all for their contributions; any errors in the interpretation of their data are, of course, solely mine.

Others provided assistance at just the right moments along the way. Richard R. Cole, dean of the School of Journalism and Mass Communication at the University of North Carolina at Chapel Hill, supplied a research leave that allowed me to put the majority of this book on paper. He also provided talented research assistants and other aid, for which I am truly grateful. Jane Rhodes and Hosoon Chang, both Ph.D. students in the School, worked on various phases of this book. Their diligence in pursuing information in the library helped to round out the picture that follows. Shannon Martin and David Copeland, also Ph.D. students in the School, were invaluable in the later stages of work.

One person who was instrumental in taking this book from its intellectual inception to the last word on the last page was John E. Semonche, professor of history at the University of North Carolina at Chapel Hill. His enthusiastic support of the project and careful analysis of its strengths and weaknesses were essential. Without his backing, the study that follows may never have come to fruition. Barbara Semonche, Jack's wife, became director of the School of Journalism and Mass Communication's library at a crucial stage in my research. Her work on computerized data bases was especially helpful in the final portions of this study.

I can only say to my friends and colleagues at the University of North Carolina and elsewhere that I appreciate their encouragement during the years that I worked on this project. Special thanks must go to Ruth Walden and Cathy Packer, who kept me in touch with what really was important while I was working on this book. My family probably was more tolerant of the time that I spent on what follows than they should have been. I am especially appreciative of the support that came my way from my parents, Earl and Gladys Blanchard.

Chapel Hill, N.C.   M.A.B.
June 1991

Contents

REVOLUTIONARY
SPARKS

CHAPTER 1

★ ★ ★

Seeking Conformity:
Freedom of Expression
in the Age of Enterprise

Great ferment characterized the last quarter of the nineteenth century in America. These years have been known by various terms—the age of industrialization, the age of urbanization, the age of enterprise, the gilded age. Americans began concentrating in cities, and when the federal government declared the frontier officially closed in 1890, the United States was an urban nation. The country now was joined by transcontinental railroads. Industrialization occurred rapidly in all aspects of business as the pace of invention quickened. Changes in business and industry led to the appearance of a management class and to bureaucratization. An economic revolution fostered the concentration of wealth in the hands of a few and the development of huge trusts that dominated various industries. Labor problems led to unionization and to strikes, many of them violent. These were years of increased immigration, increased concentration of newcomers in cities, and increased worries about alien ideas being carried by these individuals. The fear of anarchism first appeared. And it was a time of reform, with efforts concentrating on purifying American society of its less desirable people and ideas.

Each of these vast changes in American society affected freedom of expression. For the first time, or so it seemed to many Americans, the nation was seething with ideas that, if adopted, could vastly alter its customary, comfortable way of life. Anarchists wanted to topple the government; labor unionists wanted higher wages and shorter hours; freethinkers wanted the right to discuss and practice birth control. New idea after new idea tried to win a place on the country's agenda. The cacophony of voices alarmed those who feared change in the nation's social and political structure. Thus, the conservative classes—business, political, religious, educational—banded together to impose their views of a properly ordered society on the entire nation.

Conformity of opinion and suppression of dissident ideas became the linchpins of the program that these individuals developed to save the United States from concepts that they believed would lead to its destruction. Trying to deter-

3

mine just which idea was most frightening to late nineteenth-century Americans is difficult. Fears developed around so many notions, and emotions became so intertwined that separating one concern from another is almost impossible. Most likely, however, the greatest fears came from two sources: labor unionists and anarchists. Business leaders saw the sources as identical. The labor movement was anarchistic. Workers who joined together in unions wanted to overthrow the business community that had served its leaders and the country so well, thus making the labor movement anarchism in its purest form. Foreigners promoting a stateless society in which all individuals were equal had infiltrated the American working classes. Consequently, the suppression of the worker's right to organize as well as the right of anarchists to speak became top priorities.

Workers had been banding together periodically for years to improve their wages and working conditions. As mechanization increased after the Civil War, the pressure for greater production grew. Safety standards for operating machinery were minimal; sanitary conditions were lacking; and dehumanization of the work force was common. Working women and children created another set of problems. After the Civil War, workers tried to combine forces. In 1866, for instance, workers joined in a loose federation called the National Labor Union, whose goals included an eight-hour workday. This federation did convince Congress to pass legislation mandating shorter work hours for federal employees before it expired. Such laws rarely were effective, however, because workers could always agree to work longer hours, and few of the laws had enforcement provisions. But continued agitation for such measures led to concern within the business community. Adding to employers' fears, the National Labor Union endorsed the abolition of capitalism and its replacement with worker-owned businesses that would treat laborers fairly.[1]

Before employers could justify a wave of suppression, the workers needed a viable national labor union. This appeared in 1869 when the Noble Order of the Knights of Labor organized in Philadelphia. The Knights started as a secret society in order to keep employers from taking reprisals against individuals who joined their ranks. Secrecy was slowly dropped, and in 1879, Terence V. Powderly took over as leader and pushed for a large, national union for all workers. Again, the proposal that the traditional capitalistic system be bypassed in favor of worker-owned cooperatives appeared. But the Knights also advocated education for members and legislation to ameliorate problems. Powderly, in fact, preferred mediation of worker-employer problems.

The labor movement was temporarily derailed in 1873 by a significant depression. In the midst of the depression, workers went on strike in the coal fields of Pennsylvania. Closely following the strike was a wave of violence known as the Molly Maguire riots of 1875 and 1876. For several months, the coal fields were filled with murders, assaults, robberies, and arsons, all attributed to the Molly Maguires. In 1876, twenty-four miners were brought to trial. Testimony against them came from Pinkerton detectives who had been hired by employers to infiltrate the Mollies in order to gather evidence against them. With the testimony came charges that the Pinkertons had stirred the Mollies on to greater acts of violence. Some prolabor voices even contended that the Mollies themselves were a creation of mine owners, who were intent on destroying unionism. All twenty-four defendants were convicted of various crimes; ten were executed. Unionism in mine country was effectively dead for years.

The use of spies within union organizations became common to maintain control of workers who might be tempted to affiliate with unions. These spies, often employees of detective agencies, really had to do nothing more than take down names to be effective. Employers maintained blacklists of members or organizers of unions. Such persons were declared unemployable in that industry. In times of economic hardship, the threat of being placed on the blacklist was highly intimidating. Thus, even meeting together to discuss work-related problems required great bravery. Many labor union infiltrators, however, played more decisive roles. One common assignment was that of *agent provocateur,* a person who promoted violence. Spies also successfully sowed dissent and mistrust within union ranks.

Whether employers had grounds for the fears they evidenced beginning in the 1870s is problematical. They certainly thought they had just cause. For one thing, they pointed to the Paris Commune of 1871, in which workers seized control of the city of Paris and tried to institute a series of socialist changes. And Marxist groups were infiltrating the United States, as evidenced by the formation of the Socialist Workers Party in 1877. The final straw, so far as the employers were concerned, was the railroad strike of 1877. If that was not proof of the un-American intentions of their employees, nothing would be.

The railway strike of 1877 was triggered by a 35 percent cut in wages over the previous three years, by irregular employment, by the high cost of living in railway-owned hotels while working away from home, and by the blacklisting of members of three peaceful railroad brotherhoods. Another round of wage cuts came in spring 1877, and railroad managers began a new round of discharges and blacklistings. In July, a strike spread throughout the country. About two-thirds of the nation's total track mileage was idled by the walkout. Urban workers and farmers, who were also upset by railroad operations, joined the strike. Protests across the country were spontaneous, but business leaders saw the menacing hand of international communism manipulating the workers. Fears arose of a general strike whereby workers would attempt to shut down all industry in the country.

Business leaders appealed to the government for help. President Rutherford B. Hayes threatened to declare martial law in the most distressed areas and authorized the use of federal troops to rout the strikers. State militias also were used to put down the strike; groups of privately armed individuals joined in as well. The strike was broken. In addition to loss of lives and injuries on both sides, quite a bit of railroad property was destroyed. Strikers and strike leaders were arrested on various charges, and many of them spent time in jail. Employers most likely hoped that workers had now learned that any intrusion on employers' property rights would be met by the concerted opposition of both business and government.

Somewhat ironically, after the abortive 1877 railroad strike, the Knights of Labor grew into a strong force. Its goals included an eight-hour workday; government regulations establishing minimum wages, maximum hours, and safety requirements; equal pay for equal work; and child labor laws. Although the Knights wanted changes in the capitalistic system to benefit the workers, they sought to achieve their goals through peaceful political means. Yet because the Knights wished to decrease the benefits accruing to the nation's industrial leadership, its goals were considered disruptive and threatening.

Adding to the fear bred by the Knights was the fact that the organization was growing substantially in the early 1880s. The Knights had around 9,000 members in 1879 but had jumped to 700,000 members in 1886, its peak year after several successful strikes.[2] In addition, its membership included both skilled and unskilled laborers spanning all industries. Strikes called by this union could paralyze the industrial system. The high point of its activities came in 1885, when the Knights launched a successful strike against railroads owned by financier Jay Gould. With the Gould victory, the Knights had engaged in five important railroad strikes between 1884 and 1885 and had won four of them. Such a record could not be ignored long by industrialists.

Employers did not have to try too hard to find ways to destroy the labor movement. The movement almost self-destructed in 1886, the year just after its greatest success. One factor was an ill-conceived strike against railroads in the Southwest that spring. Although workers there had many of the same grievances as workers elsewhere, the Knights had not properly laid the groundwork for this strike; nor was there much public support for the workers' complaints, which had proven important in other work stoppages. The strike collapsed in early May 1886, coinciding with a major disaster in the labor movement.

Another factor in the collapse of the labor movement was the growing anarchist movement, which became inextricably intertwined with the workers' efforts in the early 1880s. Anarchism, as its critics repeatedly proclaimed, was foreign in origin. Stemming at least in part from the growing Marxist movement, anarchists advocated terrorism to gain their goals. Under the Marxist philosophy, which began taking form in pre-Civil War days, capitalism was doomed, a classless society was inevitable, and workers were to be the instrument of the change. While accepting Marxist goals, anarchists saw violence as indispensable to reaching that end. Both Communists and anarchists watched the American labor movement with great interest, and both groups established beachheads in the United States in the 1870s. Americans became preoccupied with the anarchists.[3]

Many of the anarchists' ideas had been present in the United States for years; some even were indigenous. Industrialism had created a variety of forces that wanted to return to a simpler society in which small business and small government was the rule and where all individuals lived together in peace for the benefit of all. Anarchists simply wanted to speed their accomplishment via violence. But first, they had to convince Americans of the efficacy of anarchism. So, their propagandists set to work. Johann Most, the leading anarchist voice in America, was a German by birth who came to the United States in 1882 after spending sixteen months in a British jail for celebrating the assassination of Czar Alexander II of Russia. Most first attracted the attention of concerned Americans when he toured the country promoting anarchism; he continued in the public spotlight when he published a controversial pamphlet on the "Science of Revolutionary Warfare," which told readers how to use various explosives. In 1883, Most joined with Albert Parsons and August Spies to launch the International Working People's Association, popularly known as the Black International. The party's manifesto bypassed traditional American faith in peaceful change through the ballot box, declaring such reliance "futile." If "we must then rely upon the kindness of our masters for whatever redress we have, and knowing that from them no good may be expected," the party manifesto said, "there remains but one recourse—FORCE!"[4]

The organization quickly became known by its symbol, the black flag, which Americans equated with assassination and terror. Anarchism in America existed only in small pockets around the country, but it too grew as the Knights of Labor and other workers' groups increased in strength in the mid-1880s. In the minds of many Americans, particularly those who were not among the working classes, unionists and anarchists were inextricably joined. Both groups wanted to change the American worker's life. The strikes that labor unions called often were marked by violence, and separating the goals of the movements became increasingly difficult. Soon, all groups calling for change in society fell under condemnation.

Labor organizations picked May 1886 for a massive protest in favor of eight-hour workdays. Efforts to achieve such a work schedule through legislation, which was the route preferred by the Knights, were largely unsuccessful. Thus, labor and political groups laid plans for a nationwide strike to promote the shorter workday. In 1886, most workers spent about ten hours a day on the job, totaling 60 hours a week. Some laborers even spent 90 to 100 hours a week at their posts. Shorter work weeks were necessary, they felt, to allow workers a more civilized existence and to solve periodic industrial depressions, which workers thought were caused by overproduction. Fewer hours on the job would mean fewer goods produced and more workers hired for the production that did occur. Industrial leaders disliked the eight-hour movement for numerous reasons, including the fact that most of its supporters wanted the same pay for fewer hours of work as they received for longer days on the job.

May 1, 1886, the date of the demonstration, was peaceful. Some 30,000 Chicago area workers had struck for shorter working hours, and at least twice that number participated in or witnessed various demonstrations. On Sunday, May 2, the city was still quiet; no parades or mass meetings occurred. On Monday, however, violence occurred at the strike-bound McCormick Harvester plant near Chicago. August Spies, a leader of the International Working People's Association, had been asked to address the strikers, who had been out of work since February. His speech focused on shorter hours for workers and contained no revolutionary rhetoric. When strikebreakers arrived to start work, Spies pleaded with them to leave. When they did not, the strikers attacked the scabs with sticks and stones. Police fired warning shots to disperse the crowd; the strikers fired back; and the police called for reinforcements. By the time the ensuing mêlée was over, one striker was dead, several others were seriously wounded, and more were injured. Two or three police officers had been beaten before reinforcements arrived; six others were injured, but none was shot.

Spies, aghast at police behavior, hurried to his newspaper office and wrote what became known as the "Revenge Circular." "Workingmen, to Arms!!!" trumpeted the circular. "Your masters sent out their bloodhounds—the police," Spies wrote, who killed "six of your brothers at McCormick's this afternoon. They killed the poor wretches, because they, like you, had the courage to disobey the supreme will of your bosses." The workers were killed "because they dared to ask for the shortening of the hours of toil. They killed them to show that you *'Free American Citizens'* that you *must* be satisfied and contented with whatever your bosses condescend to allow you, or you will get killed!" Now, he said, the workers must respond. "If you are men, if you are the sons of your grandsires, who have shed their blood to free you, then you must rise in your might, Hercules, and destroy the hideous monster that seeks to destroy you. To arms we call you, to arms!"[5]

Some 5,000 copies of the Revenge Circular were printed, and readers were called to Haymarket Square in downtown Chicago to denounce the latest atrocities by police and employers. Some 1,200 people—men, women, and children—gathered peacefully the night of May 4. Spies talked in noninflammatory terms for some twenty minutes; other speakers also were essentially calm in approach, and the crowd dwindled significantly after a rainstorm. Although police authorities had agreed to allow the meeting to go forward if it was tranquil, a large contingent of officers arrived and ordered the few remaining listeners to disperse as the last speaker was concluding. As words were being exchanged, a dynamite bomb was thrown in the midst of the police. Officers opened fire on the crowd, which fled for cover. The affair was over in a matter of seconds. One police officer was killed in the blast, seven others were killed in the exchange of fire after the bombing, and almost seventy officers were injured. Police claimed that only one person attending the rally was killed while twelve were injured; participants contended that the numbers killed and wounded were several times that total.

Chicago was gripped with fear. Calls went out for retribution for the police deaths and for protection from rampaging mobs of anarchists, labor union members, Socialists, and Communists. Respectable labor organizations, including the Knights of Labor, joined in the denunciations of the Haymarket affair. With the safety of society at stake, anarchists now had to be suppressed. Toleration was no longer possible. The nation, said one critical journal, could no longer be "at the mercy of a few long-haired, wild-eyed, bad-smelling, atheistic, reckless foreign wretches, who never did an honest hour's work in their lives, but who, driven half crazy with years of oppression and mad with envy of the rich, think to level society and its distinctions with a few bombs."[6] Chicago police conducted massive searches and arrested leading anarchists. Eight rally participants were charged with murder, despite the fact that no evidence had been found as to who had thrown the bomb.

All eight defendants were tried together before a jury that was strongly biased against them. Freedom of speech was not an issue, the prosecuting attorney told the jury. Although criticism of the existing government was permissible, anarchy was far from acceptable. The defendants, he said, had tried to launch an "insidious, infamous plot to ruin our laws and our country secretly and in this cowardly way."[7] The judge in the case made sure that the defendants would be convicted, even though the prosecutor had not been able to prove that any of them had actually thrown the bomb. If any of the defendants had conspired together "to take the lives of other persons . . . publicly, by print or speech, advised or encouraged the commission of murder without designating time, place or occasion at which it should be done," then they were guilty of murder, he said.[8] After three hours of deliberation, the jury delivered guilty verdicts. Most of that time was spent deciding the fate of one defendant who was given a fifteen-year term. Death sentences were imposed on the others.

When the state supreme court upheld their convictions, Spies responded, "If the people of this great country are satisfied that free speech should be strangled, then what use for me to complain."[9] As the execution date neared, some liberals around the country argued that violence was not the appropriate answer to anarchy and that the most some of the defendants were guilty of was the use of insurrectionary language. Fourteen labor leaders appealed for executive clemency, arguing that "liberty, free speech and justice impartially and fearlessly meted out to friend and foe, are the only safe-guards and the primary conditions of a peaceable social development in this country."[10] The governor commuted the sentence of two of the defendants. One man committed suicide before the execution date; four were hanged. The remaining defendants later were pardoned by Governor John Peter Altgeld, who said in his pardon message that none of them had received a fair trial.

Fears engendered by the Haymarket affair led to many problems for the labor movement. Business leaders and newspaper editors tied anarchism and labor unions so closely together that few Americans could separate the two. Many state legislatures used the atmosphere of fear to generate new laws that curbed the freedom of labor unions to organize. Courts became more active limiting union activities as well. Employers capitalized on the prevailing emotions as well by beginning widespread anti-union campaigns that included more blacklisting of union members and organizers, increased use of private detectives to subvert the activities of those unions that did exist, lockouts that kept union members from working, and yellow-dog contracts that required workers to promise they were not union members and would not affiliate with a union while employed.

The Haymarket affair marked the end of the Knights of Labor even though its involvement in the eight-hour movement had been limited and despite its refusal to support those accused in the bombing. Out of the rubble of the Knights came a labor union that ultimately would make a difference for American workers. In late 1886, the American Federation of Labor (AFL) evolved out of a labor organization set up earlier by individuals unhappy with the Knights of Labor. Samuel Gompers became the AFL's head and served in that capacity for most of the next forty years. Rather than trying to organize all workers, which threatened employers, the AFL sought to organize skilled workers only. Although still forming a national union, the AFL now dealt with employees that were harder for employers to replace. In addition, the federation abandoned plans to reform society advocated by the Knights and embraced capitalism while seeking reforms that were critical to members but were much less threatening to employers.

Early efforts by AFL member unions met with little success. The first major confrontation with management occurred in 1892, when the Amalgamated Association of Iron and Steel Workers faced the intransigence of Henry C. Frick, manager of the Homestead plant of Carnegie Steel. Andrew Carnegie, the plant's owner, was on record as approving of unions, but Frick opposed them. In the contract offered in 1892, Frick proposed wage cuts and other actions detrimental to workers. The strike that followed actually was more of a lockout, as Frick was determined to break the union. Steel Workers members controlled the town of Homestead and sought to protect the plant from violence during the strike. The company called in strikebreakers from the Pinkerton agency and when the inevitable violence occurred, asked the governor to call out the state militia. Local courts charged union leaders with a variety of crimes, including murder. Prosecutors were unable to obtain any convictions, but the Steel Workers' treasury was drained by the costs of defending its leaders. No charges were filed against the company for its role in inciting the violence. After five months, the strikers gave in, and the effort to unionize the steel industry ended.

Further complicating the Homestead strike was the attack made on Frick's life by Alexander Berkman, a Russian immigrant who was an ardent anarchist. Berkman managed to enter Frick's private office during the strike while carrying both a knife and pistol. Berkman shot Frick in the neck and stabbed him several times before he was stopped. When the assailant was searched after being subdued, he was found to be chewing a fulminate of mercury capsule in an attempt to set off a bomb that would finish the assassination. Frick survived Berkman's attack. Berkman claimed to have attacked the steel plant manager on behalf of the American worker, but he actually did the worker more harm than good. Once again, the specter of the mad anarchist intent on disrupting American society with guns, knives, and bombs became prevalent in the news outlets of the day. Employers successfully used that image to stir up the American people against both anarchists and unionists. Berkman also suffered. The maximum sentence in Pennsylvania for attempted murder was seven years; Berkman was sentenced to twenty-one years for his offense.[11]

Everywhere big business leaders looked in the 1890s they saw efforts to break up their control of the economy. Even the farmers of the Midwest and the South were calling for radical changes in governmental and economic structures. Railroads again provided focus for the farmers' concerns. For instance, railroad firms had offered farmers easy credit terms to encourage settlement that later turned into debilitating mortgages when crops were poor. Farmers also were unhappy about the rates railroads charged to haul their crops to market and about railroad control of crop storage facilities. In addition, the railroad magnates and their colleagues monopolized access to essential items such as clothing, farm equipment, and building materials. Thus, farmers increasingly felt that they were totally at the mercy of distant and disinterested big businesses.[12]

Farmers in both the South and Midwest began banding together to seek redress of their grievances. Most of their proposals were considered subversive by conservative business leaders. They wanted, for instance, government ownership and regulation of railroads, a variety of laws aimed at curbing the increasing power of corporations, cheap money, and tax reforms to aid agriculture. In 1892, agricultural interests formed the People's party, better known as the Populists. The Populist platform declared that "we meet in the midst of a nation brought to the verge of moral, political, and material ruin." They found no hope for reform because "the newspapers are largely subsidized or muzzled; public opinion silenced; business prostrated; our homes covered with mortgages; labor impoverished; and the land concentrating in the hands of the capitalists."[13] Populist candidates captured a variety of offices ranging from governorships to local posts as well as some seats in Congress.

Populists failed to capitalize on their successes because they became enamored with the free-silver issue, which is beyond the scope of this study. Although they disappeared from view, many of their ideas became accepted parts of the American political system. Populists, for instance, supported use of the Australian, or secret, ballot for elections. They advocated taking the right to select members of the U.S. Senate away from state legislatures and making senators subject to popular election. They also sought the vote for women, the use of direct primary elections, and the recall. The success of the Populist platform in the face of great opposition from the establishment proves the importance of minority ideas, despite their revolutionary origins.

Minority ideas brought about independence from Great Britain, created the Constitution, and led to the end of slavery. The notions of the Populists would lead to even greater reform. As one Populist editor put it, the cranks usually win:

> The cranks are those who do not accept the existing order of things, and propose to change them. The existing order of things is always accepted by the majority, therefore the cranks are always in the minority. They are always progressive thinkers and always in advance of their time, and they always win. Called fanatics and fools at first, they are sometimes persecuted and abused. But their reforms are generally righteous, and time, reason and argument bring men to their side. Abused and ridiculed, then tolerated, then respectfully given a hearing, then supported. This has been the gauntlet that all great reforms and reformers have run, from Galileo to John Brown.[14]

Even though Populist ideas eventually were accepted, the pressures placed on party members while their ideas are still considered revolutionary were tremendous. After their ideas were institutionalized, Populists were romanticized for their contributions, and the history of oppression that greeted their ideas initially was forgotten.

Fear of challenges to the established system runs deep in American society, and reactions to revolutionary ideas at times seem excessive. Such an overreaction and denial of basic constitutional rights occurred in the winter and early spring of 1894 when Washington, D.C., was besieged by an army of unemployed workers. The economic depression of 1893 had hit many industries hard; more than two million workers were without jobs by the end of the year. Local relief efforts, minimal at best, were strained to the breaking point. Unemployed men took to the road in search of work, gathering themselves together in informal military-like organizations to seek government assistance. One leader of such efforts was Jacob S. Coxey, a self-made businessman, who endorsed putting the unemployed on the government payroll to construct a national system of roads. Coxey joined with other reformers and with groups of unemployed workers to take his proposal to the nation's capital. Coxey's army was on the march.[15]

Groups of unemployed individuals spread eastward over the early months of 1894 as best they could. At times, they commandeered railroad cars to provide the necessary transportation. In other instances, communities provided food, clothing, and transportation. In all cases, the march was controversial. Many expressed fear over what the marchers would do once they arrived at the capital; others suggested that the army stay at home and work on reform issues. Coxey and his supporters just wanted to dramatize the plight of the unemployed by petitioning the federal government for aid en masse. But no plan could be that simple in the government's eyes, and federal agents infiltrated the movement to keep an ear out for intended violence. Troops were mobilized, and special police officers were sworn in. Some members of the Senate wanted to meet with Coxey's army to hear the workers' grievances in order to show that the American people had the right to petition their government. Critics in the Senate succeeded in labeling Coxey and his supporters as anarchists and defeated any efforts to dignify the march with official recognition.

When Coxey arrived in Washington, he sought a parade permit, which was denied. After declaring his constitutional right to speak and to petition, he said that he and his followers would assemble on the Capitol grounds to express their grievances. On May 1, 1894, the march on the Capitol began as troops stood in wait. When Coxey and two of his colleagues tried to confer about their next move, District of Columbia police arrested them for trampling the Capitol grass. Eventually the three men were found guilty of carrying banners, which carried a twenty-day sentence. Coxey and one other man also were found guilty of walking on the grass and were fined $5. Troops remained on guard to make sure that the army of unemployed did not try to lay siege to the Capitol.

No action was taken against the Capitol or against the congressmen who remained inside the building in fear. The industrial army movement had no intention of committing violence or of trying to overthrow the government. As with most protesters, Coxey and his followers simply wanted the government to work for a wider range of people. To them, the government supported the rich and ignored the poor; a redress of the imbalance was essential. Few in official Washington, however, were willing to listen to the protests of the poor. The unemployed not only were without work, but they were essentially without a political voice. Their ideas were too disruptive of the status quo to be considered, and their presence was too frightening to be evaluated clearly.

Ignoring workers' complaints was customary in these days, and violence marked many encounters between employees and employers. But by the 1890s, employers found that they could protect their property peacefully by obtaining a court injunction that ordered strike-related activities to stop. These court orders soon became the major weapon in the employers' arsenal against strikes, boycotts, and picketing. Injunctions were fairly easy to obtain. An employer faced with a strike situation would go into a state or federal court and swear, either in person or through a written affidavit, that the strike was doing irreparable harm to his business. Sitting as a court of equity, one judge alone would make the decision. If the judge had been suitably convinced, he would issue a temporary restraining order to stop the offensive union activity.[16]

In most cases, union leaders would not even know that the employer had gone into court until after the temporary restraining order had been issued. Hearings, with both parties present, were required to turn a temporary restraining order into an injunction. Labor union representatives, however, seldom persuaded the judge to change his mind. Judges were primarily concerned about the damage the labor union could do to a business rather than the harm an employer could do to the labor movement. Violation of the injunction meant that strikers would be called before the same judge who had issued the order to be tried for contempt of court. Contempt hearings were held without a jury, and judges generally convicted strikers very quickly. Union leaders usually were sent to jail for violating injunctions, and with the removal of strike leaders, the protest collapsed.

The power of injunctions first became apparent during a strike sparked by employees of the Pullman Palace Car Company, which made sleeping, dining, and parlor cars for the nation's railroads. Pullman employees were required to live in a company town and to buy their goods in company stores. By many standards, Pullman, Illinois, was an enlightened community with facilities designed to benefit workers, but the town's prices were set by management, and prices did not fall when wages went down. In addition, Pullman officials kept close watch over their employees' activities; any hint of unionization efforts brought retaliation. The economic panic of 1893 led to severe wage cuts for Pullman employees but did not affect the level of dividends paid to company investors. In fact, profits and dividends remained substantial in 1893 and 1894, and management and supervisory personnel were not hit by wage cuts. For the average laborer, the cuts ranged from a low of 17.5 percent up to 41 percent. In addition, the number of hours worked, which usually averaged almost eleven a day, was reduced, thus further cutting take-home pay. Nor did the slashed wages affect the cost of homes or groceries in the company town. In fact, the Pullman bank, which collected rents, withheld the full amounts from pay envelopes, which often meant employees had little if any money for food and other necessities.[17]

Pullman workers struck when George Pullman not only refused to make concessions but fired the individuals sent to present the workers' grievances. Workers, feeling the need for support, called upon the year-old American Railway Union (ARU) for assistance. Founded by Eugene V. Debs, the ARU brought together all railroad workers in an industrywide union to create a stronger position for dealing with owners and managers. Union leaders wanted to solve differences before strikes, lockouts, and blacklists occurred. The ARU experienced quick success in a strike against the Great Northern Railroad in the spring of 1894, where it won increased wages through arbitration. ARU leaders agreed that unless Pullman changed his attitude, the union would refuse to handle all Pullman Palace Cars. The boycott of Pullman cars was as total as the union could make it. Inspectors were not to inspect those cars; switchmen were not to put them on trains; and engineers and brakemen were not to haul them. If anyone was dismissed for such actions, then all workers were to leave their jobs immediately.

Arrayed against the union workers was the General Managers' Association, an employer-based organization determined to end both the strike and union interference with the railroads. Its goal was to get the federal government involved by claiming that the strike interfered with the mails and with interstate commerce. ARU members had agreed to handle mail cars as long as the Pullman cars were not attached to the trains as well, but the managers refused to make that concession. Complete trains—mail and Pullman cars together—must be hauled, they argued, or no trains would run. The federal government, concerned about growing voices of discontent in the nation in the face of economic disorientation, was receptive to the managers' efforts. Attorney General Richard Olney, who had specialized in railroad law in private life, favored intervening on the managers' side. With a railroad manager as his special adviser, Olney acted. Initially, the Justice Department ruled that a mail train, by definition, had to carry all normal cars—including Pullman cars—and that anyone who detached any car could be charged with obstructing the mail.

Under Olney's urging, the federal court granted an injunction against the leaders of the American Railway Union, ordering them "absolutely to desist and refrain from in any way or manner interfering with, hindering, obstructing or stopping any of the business" of specified railroads. The named individuals, including Debs, were barred from engaging in a long list of activities including "ordering, directing, aiding, assisting, or abetting in any manner whatever, any person or persons to commit any or either of the acts aforesaid."[18] Union leaders were ordered to stay away from railroad yards and to stop trying to win additional support for the strike. They also were told that the injunction forbade any form of communication with workers. Almost any effort to continue or widen the strike would violate the terms of the injunction.

Federal officials would read the injunction to crowds of strikers and their supporters. When the crowds did not leave voluntarily, they were forcibly dispersed. Ultimately, federal troops were used to put the railroad facilities back in the hands of the managers. The situation grew steadily worse despite the presence of federal troops. Supporters of both sides were injured and killed as efforts were made to get the trains running again. Damage from the strike to railroad and other property was extensive, although a special commission assigned to investigate the event blamed much of the damage on rampaging area youths rather than on striking workers. In fact, union officials sought to ensure that the strike was peaceful; they knew that violence would alienate the general public and cause irreparable damage to the union's cause. The strike ended approximately a month after it began.

Debs was convinced that the strike would have continued had he and other ARU leaders been able to stay in touch with union members. But as Debs told the special panel investigating the Pullman strike, "As soon as the employés found that we were arrested, and taken from the scene of action, they became demoralized and that ended the strike. It was not the soldiers that ended the strike. . . . It was simply the United States courts that ended the strike." Debs firmly believed that "our men were in a position that never would have been shaken, under any circumstances, if we had been permitted to remain upon the field among them."[19] The injunction and the contempt citations that followed kept the leaders from functioning.

In fact, Debs and other ARU leaders not only were arrested for contempt of court for violating the injunction, but they were jailed on charges of conspiracy to unlawfully interfere in the delivery of the mail and in interstate commerce. Although the conspiracy case against Debs and other ARU leaders ended in a mistrial, Debs and other leaders were found guilty of contempt of court. Debs received a six-month jail sentence. Union leaders appealed the contempt citation to the U.S. Supreme Court, but the justices unanimously upheld the lower court's determination that Debs and his colleagues had violated a proper injunction. With the Pullman strike, the federal and state courts found just how useful an injunction could be in suppressing strikes. Violence continued to be part of antistrike measures used by employers, but more and more, intimidation came from the court system. As Debs had said, the U.S. court system had ended the Pullman strike, and it would end many more labor disputes in the future.

While the business community, with some governmental aid, suppressed radical political and economic thought, other elements of society were hard at work to return the nation to the purer moral standards of earlier years. Cleaning up the sexual dregs of society definitely was part of the attempt to preserve the status quo. This campaign appealed to individuals who believed that the national moral atmosphere needed to be purified in order to preserve a stable social structure. The era spawned the Young Men's Christian Association (YMCA), the Sunday school movement, the Salvation Army, and the Moody and Sankey revivals. The focus increasingly was on the fate of inexperienced young men, often fresh from the farm, who were employed in the cities and who, if left to their own devices at night, fell prey to temptations provided by billiard parlors, bars, theaters, houses of prostitution, and gambling. The campaign spawned the first great crusader for cleaning up American literature and artwork, Anthony Comstock.[20]

Comstock came to New York City to work in a dry goods store, but soon his strong religious background led him in a different direction. Appalled by his co-workers' reading materials, he became convinced that he must do something to save them and others from falling into irreversible sin. Thus, Comstock appealed to the YMCA for funding to support his campaign against obscene materials, and in 1872, Comstock and the Y joined forces to create the Committee for the Suppression of Vice, with Comstock as its secretary. Listed among the incorporators of that first committee were some of the city's leading citizens: financier J. P. Morgan, mining millionaire William Dodge, and industrialist Samuel Colgate.[21] Each had a stake in protecting the work force from corrupting influences that may have been far different from Comstock's concern for the workers' immortal souls. Together they launched a campaign against obscenity, pornography, and information on birth control and abortion that set a standard for repression of sexually related ideas unseen before that time.

To a certain extent, Comstock's crusade was a confusing one. He did interfere with the progress of American art and literature, but for the most part, he campaigned against fringe materials. Among the books he was responsible for destroying were such little-known titles as *The Lustful Turk, The Lascivious London Beauty,* and the *Beautiful Creole of Havana.* The closest he got to real literature was *Fanny Hill,* and debate continues as to whether *Fanny Hill* constitutes real literature.[22] Others during this era, however, did move closer to the censorship of significant literature that is mistakenly associated with Comstock. Nathaniel Hawthorne's *The Scarlet Letter,* for instance, ran into trouble because of its subject matter. Critics said it endorsed adultery even though the author treated the subject carefully and made sure that the act was punished in the end. And Walt Whitman's *Leaves of Grass* ran afoul of community censors because of its explicit references to anatomy and sexual intercourse.[23]

When Comstock became active, few states had obscenity laws on the books.[24] The federal government had included provisions against the importation of obscene material as part of customs legislation as early as 1842.[25] The first federal legislation came in 1865 when Congress, concerned about obscene materials being sent to Union troops, passed legislation barring such materials from the mails.[26] The statute merely legitimated the postmaster general's removal of materials considered obscene from mail heading to soldiers during the Civil War.[27] In 1868, Congress added information on lotteries to the list of items considered nonmailable.[28] In 1872, Congress expanded the section on obscenity somewhat so that "no obscene book, pamphlet, picture, print, or other publication of a vulgar or indecent character, or any letter upon the envelope of which, or postal card upon which scurrilous epithets may have been written or printed, or disloyal devices printed or engraved, shall be carried in the mail."[29] Comstock, however, "found laws inadequate, and public sentiment worse than dead because of an appetite that had been formed for salacious reading; and especially because decent people could not be made to see or understand the necessity of doing anything in this line."[30]

Soon after beginning work with the Committee for the Suppression of Vice, Comstock sought new legislation to ban obscene materials from the mails. Even though Congress had revised the postal code in 1872, Comstock's campaign in 1873 came at a propitious time because senators and representatives were bogged down in the Crédit Mobilier scandal in which various members of Congress were charged with selling political influence in return for a share of railroad profits. Congress needed an issue that would clean up its much tarnished reputation; Comstock's purity campaign was just the ticket.

Unwilling to leave anything to chance, Comstock personally lobbied for revisions in existing law with the aid of an exhibit of offensive materials. Included were questionable publications, devices to increase sexual potency, and material on birth control and abortion. The problem was immense, Comstock told anyone who would listen to him. Children could purchase "vile books" at their schools for a mere ten cents. In his brief career to date, he had seized obscene photographs, books, and pamphlets, sheet music for impure songs, obscene playing cards, and immoral rubber articles. None of this material should be available to the general public, he said. He estimated that 6,000 people were regularly employed by more than 144 companies producing and distributing obscene materials. "This business," Comstock told congressmen, "is carried on principally by the agency of the United States mails, and there is no law to-day by which we can interfere with the sending out of these catalogues and circulars through the mail, except they are obscene on their face."[31] Proposed revisions in the postal code attracted little debate, let alone criticism. The measure passed at 2 a.m. the morning before Ulysses S. Grant's second inaugural.

Quickly known as the Comstock Act, the new legislation said that "no obscene, lewd, or lascivious book, pamphlet, picture, paper, print, or other publication of an indecent character, or any article or thing designed or intended for the prevention of conception or procuring of abortion, nor any article or thing intended or adapted for any indecent or immoral use or nature . . . shall be carried in the mail." Persons violating the law could be convicted of a misdemeanor and fined not less than $100 nor more than $5,000 for each offense or imprisoned at hard labor for one to ten years.[32] Comstock was named a special agent of Post Office Department, without pay, and began to help enforce the act. By the end of 1873, he reported fifty-five arrests and twenty convictions. Legislative imprecision banned from the mails only materials relating to abortion and contraception. Ordinary obscene publications had slipped through the congressional net. Consequently the Comstock Act was amended in 1876 to declare nonmailable "every obscene, lewd, or lascivious book, pamphlet, picture, paper, writing, print, or other publication of an indecent character, and every article or thing designed or intended for the prevention of conception or procuring of abortion."[33]

The judicial system helped Comstock's battle against obscenity. As of 1868, judges began applying a restrictive rule borrowed from the British to determine whether challenged material was obscene. Using the Hicklin test, judges said the question of obscenity would turn on "whether the tendency of the matter charged as obscenity is to deprave and corrupt those whose minds are open to such immoral influences, and into whose hands a publication of this sort may fall."[34] Judges using this standard condemned books because parts of them might be considered obscene by the young and inexperienced into whose hands they might fall rather than evaluating them by the audience for whom they were intended. Further enhancing the ability to obtain convictions was the refusal of court officials to enter obscene material into the court proceedings for fear of offending jurors and the audience. Nor were jurors allowed to hear so-called expert witnesses on the value of the material being challenged. The court system was fairly well rigged to guarantee that material challenged as obscene would be found to be so.

Comstock carried out his assigned tasks with great vigor. His favorite tactic was to purchase copies of suspect publications and then order—under an assumed name, of course—illicit materials through the mails. Once he had the goods in his hands, he obtained his indictment, and the seller usually was on his way to jail.

In 1873, the anti-vice campaign had become so large—and perhaps so controversial—that it was severed from the YMCA. Most of the supporters of the campaign while it was attached to the Y continued to back the new Society for the Suppression of Vice, which had extensive powers. In its formal papers, careful readers found the clause saying, "the police force of the city of New York, as well as of other places, where police organizations exist, shall, as occasion may require, aid this corporation, its members or agents, in the enforcement of all laws which now exist or which may hereafter be enacted for the suppression" of vice. The vice society was not to help the police; the police were to help it. Furthermore, when the New York State criminal code was changed two years later to include a version of the Comstock law, its provisions allowed society agents to be deputized and to "make arrests and bring before any court . . . offenders found violating the provisions of any" state or federal law regulating the distribution of obscene and indecent materials.[35] Many other states passed so-called little Comstock laws, thus spreading the net widely for persons promoting obscenity, pornography, and birth control information.

Opposition to Comstock's efforts did develop within the ranks of the freethinkers—individuals opposed to the established religious orthodoxy that dominated thought in the late nineteenth century. In fact, before the appearance of anarchists, many conservatives considered freethinkers to be the leading threat to the nation's way of life. In place of organized religion, freethinkers advocated absolute freedom of thought; they trusted the ability of individuals to discover the truth for themselves. Because of their beliefs, freedom of expression on a wide variety of subjects was essential.[36]

The antireligion stance of the freethinkers may not have caught Anthony Comstock's eye, but the willingness of freethinkers to discuss alternative sexual relationships won his attention. In addition, the freethinkers called even more attention to themselves by banding together in July 1876 to form the Liberal League and setting as one of their primary goals the repeal of the Comstock Act. Liberal League members maintained that the act was "diametrically opposed to the fundamental provisions of the American Constitution and subversive of the personal liberties to which every citizen is entitled." Although publishers, booksellers, and artists were affected, the average citizen was kept from "using the mail for such purposes as originally designed by the founders of our government." Said the league resolution of concern: "The mail is an institution for the people and belonging to the people and should by no means be controlled or dominated by any sect, creed or church. No censorship of the mail should be tolerated in this country." According to Liberal League members, "It is far better that some objectionable matter should be carried by it than that the greater evil of the destruction of the personal liberties of the people should be perpetrated."[37]

Comstock found the league resolution distressing, to say the least. He denied abridging freedom of speech: "I accord to every man the fullest scope for his views and convictions. He may shout them from the housetop, or print them over the face of every fence and building for all I care. But the common law and statutes both declare that he must do it in a decent and lawful manner or not at all." Seeing himself as sworn to uphold the law, Comstock said, "A man may think, write, and speak as he pleases by himself, but he must put his public utterances into decent language. The law says no obscene book *shall be published;* therefore if he writes a book he must not make it obscene, as it is unlawful, and if he does so make it, he must take the consequences of his own acts."[38] And Anthony Comstock was pledged to make sure those consequences were felt.

Liberal League members soon began a petition drive designed to obtain repeal of the act. Some 70,000 citizens signed the document submitted to the House of Representatives in February 1878. Proclaiming themselves as "loyal and devoted supporters of the Constitution" and firm believers in "personal liberty, freedom of conscience, of the press, and of the expression of opinion," they asked members of Congress to repeal or modify the obscenity statutes "so that they cannot be used to abridge the freedom of the press or of conscience, or to destroy the liberty and equality of the people before the law and departments of the government, on account of any religious, moral, political, medical, or commercial grounds or pretexts whatsoever."[39]

Efforts to repeal the legislation, according to Comstock, were "backed by one of the basest conspiracies ever concocted against a holy cause."[40] In addition, Comstock contended that the statutes already had been found constitutional by the U.S. Supreme Court. Indeed, a unanimous Court had affirmed the right of Congress to bar lottery information from the mail. In that decision the Court noted that "the right to designate what shall be carried [in the mail] necessarily involves the right to determine what shall be excluded." And the Court, for one of the first times in the nineteenth century, directly addressed First Amendment concerns. "In excluding various articles from the mail," Justice Stephen Field wrote, "the object of Congress has not been to interfere with the freedom of the press, or with any other rights of the people; but to refuse its facilities for the distribution of matter deemed injurious to the public morals." Congress may dictate "that the mail should not be used to transport such corrupting publications and articles, and that any one who attempted to use it for that purpose should be punished." The justices did recognize, however, that "liberty of circulating is as essential to that freedom [of the press] as liberty of publishing; indeed, without the circulation, the publication would be of little value." Thus, "if, therefore, printed matter be excluded from the mails, its transportation in any other way cannot be forbidden by Congress."[41]

Despite Supreme Court backing for the Comstock Act, the Liberal League persisted in its efforts at repeal. Comstock found its tactics repulsive and claimed league members were attempting to "make the writer [Comstock] so odious that he would not be believed."[42] After six weeks of trying, the league won a hearing before a House committee, but league members won little else. The committee reported to the full House that "the Post-Office was not established to carry instruments of vice, or obscene writings, indecent pictures, or lewd books."[43] The law, the committee recommended, should remain unchanged.

Although Comstock had won the battle over the law, his war with freethinkers continued. The individuals who became particularly odious to him in the 1880s were the advocates of free love who encouraged abandoning the traditional bonds of marriage and the family, who supported equality for women, and who, because of other beliefs, favored the dissemination of birth control information. Because free love required the freedom to enter into and end relationships at will, they argued, having children should be a matter of deliberate choice. The first encounter between Comstock and a free-love advocate involved Ezra Heywood and *Cupid's Yokes,* an argument against marriage that Heywood had written in 1876. Comstock personally arrested Heywood in 1877 and took credit for the two-year prison sentence meted out. The judge in the trial considered the offending pamphlet too obscene for the jurors to consider, making the case turn on whether Heywood had put the tract in the mail. Heywood's conviction led to substantial protest around the country and ultimately to a pardon from President Rutherford B. Hayes.

The topic of sexual freedom was growing in importance in the United States, and Anthony Comstock stood astride the road to discussions of sex education and family planning that were at the heart of this issue. And Comstock's encounters with the Liberal League and with Ezra Heywood were beginning to undermine some of his support. He continued to lose adherents as he went after D. M. Bennett, another freethinker who, through the pages of *The Truth Seeker,* regularly took Comstock to task for his narrow-mindedness. Bennett may have eluded Comstock's net had he not advertised Heywood's *Cupid's Yokes* in the pages of his newspaper and had he not responded to a request from Comstock, using a false name and address, for a pamphlet. Once the tract was received through the mail, Bennett was arrested.

In his trial, Bennett tried to win support for a new standard of obscenity that would have, among other things, called upon the jury to consider the challenged language and to review it in the context of the publication and in light of its avowed purpose. Although such an approach later would carry the day, the judge rejected the argument. The trial judge also refused to acknowledge that freedom of the press was involved. "All men in this country, so far as this statute is concerned, have a right to their opinions," the judge told the jury. "They may publish them. . . . Freelovers and freethinkers have a right to their views, and they may express them, and they may publish them; but they cannot publish them in connection with obscene matter, and then send that matter through the mails."[44] Bennett's conviction and thirteen-month jail term were upheld on appeal. This time the president refused to intervene; the sentence was served, but Bennett had made several telling points about the way in which matter considered obscene should be reviewed.

The battle for the right to discuss human sexuality resumed in 1883 when Ezra Heywood again fell victim to Comstock. This time Heywood carried advertisements for a feminine syringe in a magazine he published. Through this trial, Heywood again raised questions about the morality of Comstock's attempts to suppress discussion of certain topics. Serving as his own attorney, Heywood argued that freethinkers insisted "on Free Speech, Free Press and Free Mails *for the proclamation of opinions relative to a syringe as well as for tracts, books, newspapers on all other subjects of human interest."* A plea for increased freedom of expression topped his list of requested instructions to the jury. "Since the Right of Private Judgment in Morals and the . . . right to utter, print and mail opinions thereon are irrevocably assured in those clauses of the Federal Constitution which guarantee Freedom of Conscience and Liberty of the Press," he said, any "interpretation of this statute which excludes opinions from the United States mails, or otherwise restricts their circulation, . . . is subversive of the Constitution itself."[45] The judge refused Heywood's plea for the jury to consider the question of freedom of expression. Jurors refused to find Heywood guilty, leading him to contend that jurors had decided to enlarge the scope of allowable discussion regardless of legal restrictions.

Heywood's acquittal in no way ended Anthony Comstock's reign of terror over the ideas espoused by American citizens. In this case, Comstock had gotten too close to individuals who had the intellectual resources to make a viable argument against his attacks. Generally, as a crusader for increased morality, Comstock stayed away from such individuals. He preferred coarser literature and coarser opponents, but he also conducted campaigns to force legitimate newspapers to stop carrying stories about football and boxing, sports considered far too violent for the type of society that Comstock envisioned. In addition, Comstock and his backers pursued so-called "blood and thunder" publications that carried vivid stories of crime. The dime novel, the functional equivalent of a comic book for an earlier generation of children, also came under Comstock's watchful eyes. To Comstock, these dime novels were leading all youths who read them down the pathway to destruction, for once a child had read such stories, no one could prevent a career of crime and the loss of an immortal soul.[46]

Most of Comstock's campaigns attacked only surface problems in American society. Life was changing too rapidly for some people. By labeling certain ideas as the cause of all of society's woes and by trying to eradicate them, Comstock was attempting to hold back the sands of time. The ideas that were being expounded were unsettling, but newer times demanded newer approaches to problems. Comstock really could wage only a delaying action; change would come.

As societal pressures for change became increasingly pronounced, Comstock's efforts were ridiculed, especially as he ventured into newer areas. He began attacking more of the classics in literature, for instance, and he invaded the world of art in attempt to purge it of depictions of naked women. After he had seized photographs of French masterpieces from a Fifth Avenue gallery, the *New York World* asked, "Has it really been determined that there is nothing wholesome in art unless it has clothes on?"[47] His attack on George Bernard Shaw's play, *Mrs. Warren's Profession,* which dealt with prostitution, led to packed houses and, allegedly, to Shaw's invention of the term "comstockery," which has forevermore been applied to extensive prudery.

The tide was turning on Anthony Comstock, but he remained proud of his accomplishments. In 1913, two years before his death, Comstock recalled that in his forty-one years of work, he had been responsible for the conviction of enough people to fill a passenger train of sixty-one coaches, with sixty of the coaches containing sixty people each and the last one being almost full. He had destroyed almost 160 tons of obscene literature.[48] Perhaps one of Comstock's greatest contributions, however, was his ability to spark the development of an articulate opposition to his censorship. In addition to the efforts of the Liberal League and of Heywood and Bennett, Theodore Schroeder, one of the nation's earliest theorists on the meaning of the First Amendment, challenged the presuppositions upon which Comstock based his activities. Emerging from a variety of journal articles that were later republished in book form was the first substantial defense of the right to print material that many in society would label as obscene.

State and federal laws against obscene literature must be discarded, Schroeder said, because they conflicted with the original intent of the First Amendment. In his view, the framers of the Bill of Rights meant to enlarge the sphere of intellectual liberty for citizens; punishment of alleged obscene materials contracted that liberty. In addition, laws such as those Comstock inspired violated the constitutional guarantee of due process of law in that they were so vague that individuals were not sufficiently forewarned as to what behavior was illegal. Schroeder firmly believed that eventually adverse judicial and public reaction would lead to the elimination of such laws. The campaign against obscenity, Schroeder believed, was marked by the "same passionate 'moral' necessity which once impelled judges to exercise their wits and their might in a crusade against witchcraft and verbal treason."[49] To Schroeder, censorship of ideas, even sexual ones, was part of one individual's desire to tyrannize others. Eventually, he argued, the desire to determine what others could read would reach popularly acceptable materials. In all cases, society would suffer for not having needed information available. Censorship had to be stopped, he contended, and soon.

But the need to conform to standards set by others was great in the late nineteenth century, as college professors could attest. Their offense was relatively simple: they had become interested in and had started teaching a new scientific theory—evolution. By the 1870s, Charles Darwin's theory as set forth in *Origin of Species* had gained acceptance within the scientific community. Teachers began adding discussions of evolution to their lectures, and religious forces began pushing for its elimination. One of the first great battles over academic freedom was developing.[50]

Many institutions of higher education still were tied to religious denominations during these years, making the stakes in the struggle even higher. Scientists on faculties felt the need to explore all avenues of potential knowledge; sectarian forces in charge of the schools felt the need to protect the faith of faculty, students, and the nation by foreclosing dangerous areas of discussion. Faculty members at institutions with strong religious ties soon found that their ability to discuss evolution was nonexistent. Offending faculty members were called before the proper authorities and usually lost their jobs after facing questions about their religious beliefs.

In older, nonsectarian institutions, the ability to discuss evolution was much greater. In fact, professors who lost positions at church-related schools often found their academic careers salvaged by their colleagues in the great public and private institutions. Gradually, academic resentment over the continued intrusion of religious authority led to demands for academic freedom. Professors sought a basic toleration of intellectual inquiry, complete with acceptance of the idea that errors were a natural part of such investigations. They demanded that faculty members be judged on their qualifications by their peers rather than by outside administrators who knew nothing of the subject matter, and they strove to convince administrators and trustees that scientific work had to be separated from the beliefs of the scholar.

Such standards became the foundation on which more modern-day notions of academic freedom were built. In the last quarter of the nineteenth century, however, the standards were mere words, for academic freedom was being buffeted from other sources as well. This challenge came as business leaders, anxious to leave a significant legacy behind, began donating large sums to higher education. As a result, schools became less tied to sectarian interests and more wrapped up in their new benefactors. But these contributions carried important strings. Business leaders, for instance, often wanted to decide how the colleges would spend their contributions. At times, they became active in setting academic policies, in hiring and firing faculty members, and in influencing the subjects taught. Unfortunately for college professors, these intrusions by business leaders coincided with a growing professional interest in the world beyond the campus boundaries. Professors who dared side with labor unions were subject to immediate dismissal at certain institutions. Others who championed restrictions on monopolies or who opposed imperialism likewise faced the imperious disdain of the new collegiate benefactors.[51]

Curiously absent from all of the above discussion is any mention of the press and its role in the dissemination of new ideas. During these years, the institutional press, rather than advocating new propositions, generally called for the suppression of ideas that would change the status quo. To a certain extent, the press was simply continuing its time-honored allegiance with establishment classes, which could be traced far back in American history. If anything, the tendency of publishers to become identified with the conservative business and political establishment was even more pronounced because industrialization affected America's newspaper industry in the age of enterprise just as it had other businesses.

As the turn of the century approached, newspapering was big business. With such changes came new challenges to freedom of the press; only now, charges would emerge that the era's newspapers were undermining that right. As with any other entrepreneur, owners of newspapers sought every new invention available to allow them to produce more attractive newspapers faster and cheaper. In the age of industrialism many such developments coalesced so that large newspapers with circulations unheard of in earlier days became possible. The stereotyping process caught on widely during these years. This process of making papier-mâché impressions of type and then curving those impressions to fit on presses made changes in the design of newspapers and in advertising format possible. Such changes allowed for broader-based financial support from the business community and for more sensational layout designs that brought increased street sales. The first Linotype machine showed up in the offices of the *New York*

ALBRIGHT COLLEGE LIBRARY   238794

Tribune in July 1886. Before that time, all the type had to be set by hand, thus limiting the size of newspapers. Now newspapers could run more pages and produce issues faster. The web-perfecting press, which allowed the newspaper to be printed on both sides simultaneously, became widely used by the 1870s. By the 1890s, presses existed that allowed a publisher to print between 80 and 128 pages daily. Prices for the presses now ran from $40,000 to $80,000. Electricity was used to drive the presses even faster; color was soon added to make the newspapers even more attractive to readers. Wood pulp paper made it possible to print more pages for less money.[52]

The press benefiting from these changes was quite different from that of previous eras. The number of newspapers was increasing to serve a growing reading audience. Between 1870 and 1900, for instance, the United States had doubled its population and tripled the number of urban residents. During these same years, the number of daily newspapers quadrupled, and the number of copies sold each day increased sixfold. The percentage of subscribers among adults rose from 10 to 26 percent, marking the arrival of a major new business. New publishers were needed to build a new journalism for changing times and to find a new meaning for press freedom.

These newer papers were low-priced, aggressive, and easy to read. Their editors believed strongly in the news function of the press; they were independent in political stance; they crusaded in the community to build a base of support; and they appealed to a mass audience through improved writing, better makeup, use of headlines, and popularization of newspaper content. Once again, the common man became the target of newspapers, and once again, freedom of the press was defined in terms of what this particular category of readers would buy.

The audience for these newspapers was quite different. Now people congregated in cities and worked in factories. The work was generally boring, and the readers wanted entertainment in their newspapers. Because more women were reading newspapers, publishers provided details of society life. As the industrial world developed vigorous and aggressive leadership to take advantage of changed conditions, so, too, did the newspaper world. Here two dominant figures were Joseph Pulitzer and William Randolph Hearst. By the time these two publishers were finished with their circulation wars in New York City, freedom of the press had been decidedly dirtied in the public's eyes.

Pulitzer began his journalistic career in St. Louis, Missouri, where he purchased the *Dispatch* in 1878 and three days later bought the *Post*. Pulitzer's aggressive support of the common people and his investigative reporting became the model for enterprising journalists to follow. He moved to New York in 1883 and purchased the *World* for $346,000. While demanding various reforms to aid the working classes, Pulitzer also added a bit of crime, sex, catastrophe, sports, children, and animals to his editorial mix. He used the new technology to develop the use of illustration in newspapers and to initiate color comics and Sunday supplements.

By the end of his first year, the *World*'s circulation was more than 61,000—four times what it had been when Pulitzer bought it. By 1885, after two years under Pulitzer, the circulation was more than 100,000. September 1886 found the circulation at 250,000—the highest level ever achieved by a newspaper until that time. The large circulation meant an increased ability to influence people. His crusades included uncovering bribery of New York aldermen in connection with awarding a Broadway streetcar franchise, seeking prosecution and conviction of a contractor for erecting flimsy tenement houses, and exposing a white slave ring. If Joseph Pulitzer had been the sole founder of the new journalism of the 1890s, the era likely would have been remembered fondly as a high-water mark for what a free press could do in society. But William Randolph Hearst entered the New York market in 1895 by purchasing the *New York Journal.*

By late 1896, the circulation war between Pulitzer and Hearst was on. The figures went up and down daily depending on street sales. The day after the McKinley-Bryant election in 1896, for instance, each publication sold 1.5 million copies to break all existing records. During the first year, the *Journal* was very much like the *World.* Both newspapers liked to present crime news and details of accidents and disasters; both publishers favored large illustrations with stories; and both publications crusaded. Hearst soon offered readers the trademarks of what became known as yellow journalism—fictionalization, melodrama, and human interest—and Pulitzer kept pace.

The sensationalism that resulted from the circulation war was denounced as "yellow journalism," which took its name from the first color cartoon character. Yellow journalism was known for its extreme exaggeration, for its prying into the lives of its subjects, for its efforts to build higher circulations based on increasingly lower ethical standards. The behavior of Pulitzer and Hearst and their imitators around the country was denounced not only by business and community leaders but by the conservative press as well. For instance, E. L. Godkin, editor of the *New York Evening Post* and the *Nation,* said of yellow journalism, "A yellow journal office is probably the nearest approach, in atmosphere, to hell, existing in any Christian state." He added, "A better place in which to prepare a young man for eternal damnation than a yellow journal office does not exist."[53]

If publishers were abusing freedom of the press, their reporters followed in their footsteps. Reporters of the gilded age were overworked and underpaid servants of a newspaper world that devoured their copy and encouraged them to play fast and loose with the truth in order to sell more papers. Salaries for reporters in New York in the late nineteenth century ranged between $40 and $60 a week. But the reporters worked six ten-hour days to earn that money, and often much of their pay was based on piecemeal rates—on how many inches of the copy they produced were printed. Reporters had no job security during these years; hiring and firing were often based on whim.[54]

Such working conditions led reporters to engage in practices that undermined fair and accurate journalism—hallmarks of a free press. Reporters often took payoffs for dropping names in stories or for getting certain stories into print. In other situations, reporters worked to increase the news value of their work because newspapers paid more for sensational stories. The interview, which had developed earlier in the century, was used to extract information from all sorts of news sources. Witnesses to crimes were hired and hidden away from opposition reporters and from the police until an exclusive story could be published.

News events were created on paper, and then reporters would hire someone to swear that the event had occurred should anyone check. Reporters would steal evidence in criminal cases or try to find criminals on their own rather than wait for the police to solve the crime.

Developments in American journalism in these days generally were greeted with disdain by conservative elements in society—and, indeed, all newspapers did not practice the sensationalism that was so roundly condemned. The journals that did deal in sensationalism drew the attention of a pair of young Boston attorneys in 1890. Samuel D. Warren and Louis D. Brandeis combined to produce a *Harvard Law Review* article that sought to create a legal right to privacy— a protection for individuals from intrusions by the press that did not violate existing libel law. Although the exact motivation for their work is murky, Warren and Brandeis denounced "instantaneous photographs and newspaper enterprise [that] have invaded the sacred precincts of private and domestic life." In their view, "The press is overstepping in every direction the obvious bounds of propriety and of decency. Gossip is no longer the resource of the idle and of the vicious, but has become a trade, which is pursued with industry as well as effrontery." Newspapers, in order "to satisfy a prurient taste . . . spread broadcast in the columns of the daily papers" intimate details of private sexual relations. In addition, "to occupy the indolent, column upon column is filled with idle gossip, which can only be procured by intrusion upon the domestic circle."[55]

The press, Warren and Brandeis argued, had clearly overstepped its bounds by its persistent intrusion into the personal lives of Americans. Even Henry B. Brown, an associate justice on the U.S. Supreme Court, took note of press excesses in 1900. While praising journalists for their good deeds, Brown candidly acknowledged that "the press hold[s] our reputations completely at its mercy." He could not understand why journalists felt that invasion of personal privacy was essential in news gathering. "The legitimate field for political discussion, Heaven knows, is broad enough, without invading the privacy of our homes or the sanctity of our domestic life." Nevertheless, men in political life were "confronted by the fact that in this free country, there has grown up a despotic, irresponsible power which holds our reputations completely at its mercy."[56]

To a large extent, the complaints registered about the press were due to changes in the kinds of newspapers being published. No longer were newspapers sold only to the elites; now the lower classes bought them, and these groups wanted to read about their social betters. No aspect of life escaped some of the more obnoxious journals. Even the honeymoon of President Grover Cleveland in 1886 served as fodder for the new journalists, as reporters camped out near the couple's retreat in order to report juicy morsels.[57] In 1890, the *New York Sun* defined the sensational journalist of the day perfectly by saying a reporter "cannot be too depraved to suit the use of his employer. He must possess the arts of the confidence man, the furtive keeness [*sic*] of the practiced thief, and be endowed with all the malodorous gifts of the professional imposter." A journalist must be prepared "to glue his ear to a crack in a door, to consort with blacklegs and burglars, to entice and provoke to crime for the sake of possible exposure, to master the acrobatics of chimneys and the bedroom window, and to penetrate and violate the sanctity of the jury room."[58]

Pushing reporters to such extremes were the owners of new journalism publications who, in turn, were driven both by the need to make as much money as possible to support the massive investment that newspapers now entailed and by the desire to become part of the big business establishment that monetary success would bring. But publishers making such a move ran headlong into an institution determined to calm a society increasingly ruffled by the press's prying: the courts. Libel suits proliferated in the latter part of the nineteenth century as a direct result of popular journalism's emphasis on sensationalism and its carelessness with the facts.[59] As judges heard these cases, they used their decisions to criticize press behavior. The chief justice of the Illinois supreme court, for instance, wrote: "There is probably no other country in the civilized world where private character has so little security against newspaper assault. The conductors of the press . . . are singularly reckless in the exercise of their great power . . . in pandering to the morbid taste of their readers for personal and worthless gossip."[60]

With the increase in libel actions and with the substantial monetary losses that each adverse verdict entailed, newspaper owners sought an effective line of defense. The approach finally taken is still followed today, for newspaper attorneys began to argue for special treatment for the press because of its role as a watchdog on government and other institutions. Such an assignment, they urged, meant that newspapers' news-gathering and publishing functions should be immune from libel prosecutions—or at least face lesser monetary judgments. After all, newspapers were acting in the public interest when they presented the information challenged in lawsuits. In fact, such reporting was a duty imposed upon newspapers; consequently, protection from lawsuits must be available.[61]

Judges of the era, however, generally were unwilling to grant the press special treatment in court. Most judges disliked the way in which newspapers of the day treated public men in particular and felt that reporters, editors, and publishers were too careless in their methods and too lax about the truth to merit exceptions from the rules of libel. Although the watchdog concept of freedom of the press won few converts within the judiciary and saved few dollars in libel judgments in the nineteenth century, newspaper attorneys would continue to argue for special treatment. The campaign for a special institutional privilege for the press soon occupied a leading spot on the agendas of most professional organizations. As time passed, the court system came to accept the argument, with some members of the bench in the late twentieth century even going so far as to assume that the framers of the First Amendment had intended to protect the institutional press when the Bill of Rights was crafted.[62] Thus, out of economic necessity grew a major protection for the press; few journalists would remember its ignoble roots.

The news-gathering practices of the late nineteenth century also gave rise to demands for legislation establishing a journalist's privilege so that a reporter could not be forced to reveal the name of a confidential source of information. The nation's first shield law for reporters was enacted by the Maryland legislature in 1896 and apparently stemmed from an incident in which John T. Morris, a reporter for *The Sun* in Baltimore, revealed details of secret grand jury deliberations. Morris refused to disclose the source of his information, was found in contempt of court, and was sent to jail for the duration of the grand jury's term. He refused to purge himself of his contempt, telling the judge that he was sorry if information had been made public that should have remained confidential. He added that "as a member of an honorable profession," he had to "refuse to violate the confidence reposed in him by making known to any person whomsoever the source of his information."[63] Morris spent two days in jail and another two weeks or so in close confinement at his home before being released from custody. This incident sparked pressure for passage of the law, which went into effect ten years later, thirty-seven years before any other similar legislation in the country.

News gathering was not the only aspect of journalism affected by the changes in newspapering in the late nineteenth century. For instance, bureaucracy hit newspapers during these years. Editors became less likely to own their publications and more likely to be employees of owners, who may or may not have had journalistic careers before becoming publishers.[64] As publishers became more interested in the business aspects of journalism, they concentrated their attention on the problems inherent in the big business that journalism had become. Newspaper owners struggled to win larger circulations and increased advertising, worried over maintaining expensive physical plants, and feared unstable labor relations because one of the oldest and strongest unions in the country, the typographers, ran the machinery essential for printing a newspaper. As with big business, newspapers that failed to keep up competitively were doomed to extinction. In big cities, newspapers had become corporate enterprises because expenses had increased so dramatically. As problems connected with the business of newspapering grew, representatives of leading publications called for the creation of a daily newspaper association to speak for this particular segment of the business community. In 1887, publishers and business managers met to form the American Newspaper Publishers Association (ANPA).[65]

Although the ANPA clearly represented the business interests of the newspaper industry, as time went on, its leaders talked of protecting freedom of the press. In its early years, the ANPA definition of freedom of the press had a decidedly business orientation. By the early twentieth century, this group was promoting a laissez-faire version of the constitutional freedom: newspapers were to be free from interference from any source because a financially sound foundation was essential to a free press. The only government interference that the ANPA encouraged involved second-class mailing rates. Here, the ANPA felt that such lower rates were an integral part of operating a newspaper and that any government attempt to raise the rates constituted tampering with freedom of the press. ANPA representatives regularly testified against such increases after the group's founding.[66] The creation of this group established another prong in the institutionalization of "freedom of the press."

Still other events in the late nineteenth century affected the way in which freedom of the press developed in the twentieth century. One such event was the evolution of the New York Associated Press into the Associated Press (AP), as it is known today. Founded in 1848, the New York Associated Press was a cooperative news-gathering organization set up for the benefit of its members. As the organization became more successful at midcentury, it began selling its news to other newspapers around the country. These clients were not allowed full membership privileges, which remained closely held by the original founders in New York, although they paid at least their fair share of the costs involved. In addition, the news product was tailored to meet the needs of the founding members rather than its growing number of clients. By 1866, clients in the West, who had formed the Western Associated Press, were terming the New York organization a monopoly and making plans for turning the news agency into an organization fairer to all its members.[67]

The Westerners forced the New Yorkers to modify their approach and to provide clients with a greater voice in association affairs. No effort was made to open the news-gathering cooperative up to all newspapers. Members knew too well that competition among papers gave those who had access to the news service an important edge that no publisher would voluntarily surrender. The New Yorkers still tried to manipulate the organization to their advantage, this time by cooperating covertly with a rival news agency, the first United Press. When AP members discovered that their news stories had appeared in United Press newspapers often before AP members had run them, compromise with the New Yorkers was no longer possible. AP members from around the country staged a coup and ousted the founders of the association from office.

New headquarters for the Associated Press were set up in Illinois, and again, the association was a closed national monopoly designed to keep the number of members down. The new charter also continued to forbid AP members to exchange news with other news agencies. This latter point brought the first court challenge to agency's existence after AP leaders tried to exclude the *Chicago Inter-Ocean* from membership because it had participated in just such an exchange. After preliminary court skirmishes, the Supreme Court of Illinois declared in 1900 that the Associated Press was a public utility and that it had no power to prevent members from obtaining news from other agencies or to expel members. In finding in favor of the Chicago newspaper, the Illinois court noted that the AP bylaws would allow the agency "to designate the character of the news that should be published, and, whether true or false, there could be no check on it by publishing news from other sources." The rules, thus, "would be powerful in the creation of a monopoly in its favor, and could dictate the character of news it would furnish and could prejudice the interests of the public. Such a power," the court determined, "is hostile to public interests."[68] The public would be better served if a newspaper had full access to news provided by the Associated Press and by other agencies as well. Then information could be cross-checked for accuracy, and readers would have a choice of news sources.

The Associated Press, upon hearing of the court decision, returned to New York once again, where kinder incorporation laws allowed strict control over membership. The Associated Press was now an official monopoly, as were many business ventures of the day. Concern over the effect such a monopoly would have on the ability to start new newspapers and on the availability of news to the nation as a whole was sporadic through the years. The issue finally came before the Supreme Court in the 1940s, where the justices would measure the news-gathering monopoly against the First Amendment's guarantee of freedom of the press.

In addition to serving as the newspaper industry's monopoly, the Associated Press also contributed further to the standardization of content of newspapers across the country. The marketplace of ideas diminished significantly as cooperative news gathering increased. The development of feature syndicates similarly decreased that marketplace. First started around the time of the Civil War to help small country newspapers fill their columns while writers and editors were off at war, the feature syndicates increased in importance as the nineteenth century drew to a close. Critics charged that by selling similar content to numerous publications, these embryonic feature syndicates were attempting to control the thought processes of an entire state or region. Those newspapers who used the feature material responded that by using so much syndicated material, editors would able to use reporters to provide more local stories for publication. Although the feature syndicate, known then as the newspaper union, became more popular, increased local coverage was more myth than reality.[69]

By the end of the nineteenth century then, many changes that would have far-reaching effects on American journalism were already in place. The notion of a special protection for the press because of the role that it filled in society was already placed on the agenda, albeit for rather selfish motives. Those motives stemmed directly from the press's position as a major business enterprise, a fact of life that would become only more pronounced in the next century. And the desire for success in the business world had led to a substantial contraction of the marketplace of ideas, another phenomenon that would continue in the new century. The press was more aggressive, to be sure, in covering the news, but that energy often was another part of its desire for success. One fact was certain: the institutional press was building a reputation that would make it a prime target of reformers in the twentieth century.

Before the nineteenth century ended, American journalists exercised their freedom in covering another war and, in the process, added fuel to the complaints of abuse of privilege that would rise during the reform movements of the early twentieth century. The Spanish-American War, which Secretary of State John Hay called "a splendid little war,"[70] lasted only six months in 1898. The nation's sensational press had been focusing American attention on Cuba and its problems with its Spanish governors for nearly three years before the outbreak of hostilities. Arguments over the acquisition of an American empire continued for several years after the cessation of fighting. Thus, six months of conflict actually occupied American media attention for many years.

Unrest in Cuba was longstanding. The island was one of the last vestiges of the Spanish empire, and Cubans had tried to oust their despised overlords several times. Each attempt was unsuccessful; by the mid-1890s, Cuban revolutionaries decided that outside support was necessary. Emissaries were sent to the United States to seek official backing for their efforts or, failing that, to build public support within the country that might some day convince the government to intercede on behalf of the revolutionaries. Fortuitously for the Cubans, their public relations venture coincided with calls from business leaders, politicians, and newspaper editors around the country for an expansion of American activity abroad. With the continental United States settled, the time was at hand to make America a world power.

The problems in Cuba and the calls for a stronger American role in international affairs also coincided with the great circulation wars in New York City. This combination made the Cuban situation a favorite newspaper topic. To say that the stories that told many Americans of events transpiring in Cuba were exaggerated may be stating the situation mildly. Reporters for Pulitzer and Hearst were at their competitive best in seeking information on Cuban affairs, and through the vast distribution networks that both men had established, many other American newspapers carried their stories as well. Both New York newspapers were members of the Associated Press at the time, and under the rule allowing the sharing of members' stories with other members, the news association distributed their stories even further. The Spanish government contributed greatly to the amount of misinformation given to the American people by imposing a strict censorship on all news coming from island as of 1895. This shortage of news from Cuba placed increased importance on the Cuban revolutionary junta operating out of New York, which, of course, slanted data to fit its needs.[71]

Correspondents who went to Cuba had difficulty obtaining information. Journalists who tried to report the revolt from the Spanish perspective were limited to information the government decided to give out and to scenes of battle that were accessible by rail lines. Trying to cover the revolt from the rebel perspective was dangerous. Reporters first had to slip through Spanish lines; then they had to wander, sometimes for 50 or 100 miles, before they found the rebel forces. The rebels then had to be convinced to allow journalistic coverage; after that, reporters had to find ways to get their stories back to the United States. Correspondents who did violate Spanish rules against visiting with the rebels faced harsh reprisals if they fell into the military's hands after such excursions.[72]

Despite these difficulties, during the three years before the United States declared war, about seventy-five journalists for American newspapers and magazines went to Cuba. Some fourteen managed to join the rebel forces for varying periods of time. American journalists in Cuba faced varying fates. One, for instance, died while observing a battle; another was executed by the Spanish after having been taken prisoner. Others were arrested for different reasons and imprisoned for varying periods.[73] The plight of one reporter, Sylvester Scovel of the *New York World,* who was arrested in February 1897, became a cause célèbre in American press circles. Spanish military authorities charged Scovel with communicating with the enemy, with passing through Spanish lines without permission, with obtaining a police pass under a false name, and with traveling without a military pass. The *World* mounted a massive campaign on Scovel's behalf, claiming that he was in danger of being court-martialed, that his health was jeopardized due to the surroundings in which he was being held, and that he had difficulty obtaining counsel to defend him. Above all else, freedom of the press was endangered by allowing a foreign government to treat an American reporter this way. Public meetings demanding his freedom were held; groups passed resolutions on his behalf; and the U.S. Senate even supported efforts to obtain Scovel's release. Finally, the secretary of state arranged for his return, but not before this great challenge to freedom of the press had been played prominently in the *World* and other newspapers around the country for days.[74]

Inadvertently, Scovel had become part of the formula that American sensationalistic journals followed for covering the Spanish-American War. The big story, the exclusive, the tragedy that could be followed for days was the goal of most correspondents sent to Cuba. War fever gripped the yellow journals as each development led to calls for American intervention to end Spanish atrocities. At one point, E. L. Godkin complained about the excessive war fervor displayed in the pages of the yellow journals. "The advocacy of war by a newspaper ought to operate as legal notice that the editor-in-chief is willing to serve on shipboard in some capacity," he wrote in 1895. "Nothing is more shocking than the preparation of the public mind for hostilities by persons who do not propose to fight themselves, but do expect to make money out of the spectacle of other men's deaths and destruction."[75] Godkin's opposition to war increased as other newspapers grew more ardent in their support of fighting to free Cuba.

The press magnified and sensationalized many events in Cuba, as a few examples prove. One favorite subject during these years was the brutality of Valeriano Weyler, captain-general of the Spanish occupation force, known as "the butcher." According to the sensational press, Weyler's armies took hospital patients from their beds and executed them while women and children looked on. Bodies of men, women, and children, the victims of famine and disease, were reported to be piled everywhere in Cuba. Correspondents estimated that some 300,000 Cubans had died from famine alone, at least three times the actual figure. Weyler was indeed brutal, and his reconcentration program that forced peasants to leave their villages in an effort to deny rebels support was particularly savage. American journalists made no effort to explain the Spanish side of the controversy or to tell of conditions facing the occupation forces.

Weyler was a target of all newspapers of the day, but some newspapers had their own special causes as well. Pulitzer's *World,* for instance, had advocated Sylvester Scovel's cause with little assistance from other New York publications. William Randolph Hearst's exclusive province was the story of Evangelina Cisneros, niece of the Cuban rebel president. Miss Cisneros, proclaimed to be the most beautiful girl in all of Cuba, was charged with luring a Spanish military officer to her home, where she had him killed. Hearst leaped to defend her honor, carrying story after story about her plight and enlisting the support of leading American women in his campaign for her release, which continued after she had been convicted of sedition in a Spanish court-martial. Her sentence likely would have been confinement to a Spanish penal colony in Africa, which, Hearst said, would result in her death. Even the nine months that she had spent in a Spanish prison in Cuba had left her on the verge of consumption. Mrs. William McKinley, wife of the president, joined those calling for her release. As the story continued to fill the front pages of Hearst's newspapers, one of his reporters miraculously rescued the frail young woman from prison and brought her to New

York for a triumphant welcome—and more coverage by the *New York Journal,* of course. At Hearst's urging, Miss Cisneros was received by the president himself. Here, Hearst clearly went beyond the bounds of what a free press should do. He interfered in the affairs of a foreign country and shamelessly manipulated the American people, including the president of the United States, to achieve his ends—higher circulation.

The third major news event that was played to its height was the reprinting of a personal letter from the Spanish ambassador to the United States, Dupuy de Lôme, to the editor of a Madrid newspaper. The letter, which was stolen by the Cuban junta, received widespread display in American newspapers. In it, de Lôme harshly criticized President McKinley, terming him a "low politician" accustomed to "catering to the rabble."[76] A handwriting expert confirmed that de Lôme had written the letter, and de Lôme soon admitted his authorship and resigned his post. The American president had been libeled by a foreign diplomat, and U.S. newspapers were at their patriotic best in calling for retribution. They virtually ignored that the letter was private correspondence and that it had been stolen.

While the press was cooperating with other forces in American society to encourage U.S. intervention in Cuba, President McKinley tried to avoid the issue. As one of the first presidents to explore the influence of public opinion on politics, he watched the press carefully but refused to be pushed into action by it. In fact, he waited for a lull in the journalistic storm over Cuba before he announced his hopes to negotiate a settlement to the island's problems.[77] Although not as expert at manipulation of the media as many of his successors would be, McKinley's efforts did probably help to delay the war. But events simply overtook his rudimentary information management system.

The event that ultimately brought the nation to war was the sinking of the battleship *Maine* in Havana harbor on January 24, 1898, accompanied by the deaths of 260 sailors. The yellow journals had a field day with the sinking, setting forth their own hypotheses on how the Spanish had managed to plant the explosives that sent the ship to the bottom of the harbor. President McKinley appointed a board of inquiry to investigate. The board worked for six weeks before its official report was ready, but the newspapers had to publish in the interim. Rumor replaced fact, and calls for declarations of war abounded. Hearst even took senators and representatives to Cuba aboard his own yacht to investigate the sinking. The official report, which was leaked to the press before McKinley was ready to distribute it, refused to fix responsibility for the explosion. The sensational press had no such problems: the Spanish clearly were responsible. War was essential. The president, however, still attempted to slow the rush toward war.[78]

Regardless of the sensational press's machinations and despite McKinley's determination not to be forced into action by flamboyant journalism, the president went before both houses of Congress on April 11, 1898, to ask for a declaration of war against Spain. Although the press had been a major factor in keeping large segments of the American public stirred up on the Cuban issue for the previous three years, the decision to go to war was based more on the desire of the United States to assume its rightful place as a world power than on sensational journalism.

The war itself began on April 20, and before the fighting ended six months later, some 500 journalists, photographers, and artists had covered the war in some way. Little of the reporting emanating from the war showered journalists with glory. Animosity between the press and the military and the press and the civilian government had been a substantial problem during the Civil War, and those old feelings resurfaced. The government did put together a censorship program of sorts, but the war was so short that much of the policy was piecemeal and not terribly effective. On McKinley's orders, federal authorities took charge of the telegraph wires leading north from Key West, Florida, end point for the transoceanic cable from Cuba. Military censors were also installed in Tampa and in New York City in an effort to restrict transmission of details about military operations. Key West and Tampa were primary staging areas for missions into Cuba, and New York was an important relay point for the nation's news. The government did not, however, take control of telegraph operations out of Washington, D.C., and the nation's capital provided many news leaks during the conflict.

Censorship in the Spanish-American War was quite different because of advances in technology. Now, transoceanic cables could transmit information to a foe across a vast body of water. The availability of such data could lead enemies to change their plans in order to take advantage of American intentions. The possibility that reporters, especially irresponsible ones in an age of highly competitive journalism, might provide data that could aid the enemy increased significantly. But still the press's approach to war reporting remained unchanged.

Although journalists were told that they were not to write stories about troop ships leaving for Cuba, the first expedition to the island was well reported. Correspondents hired their own boats and set out in pursuit of Navy vessels. In response, the military beefed up its censorship operation in Key West. Journalists loudly protested against increased attempts to restrict the flow of information to the United States. Explained a writer for the *New York Sun,* "Suddenly a man was thrust upon them with the power to 'kill' every word they wrote. Newspaper speculation was cut off. No more theories of war were allowed." Now, said the *Sun* correspondent, "the writer who had been in the habit of directing military and naval operations with his pen found himself held down to facts, and only such facts as had been reported to Washington, and whose publication would not hurt the country's interests." The new policy, the reporter said, "played havoc in more ways than one."[79]

Despite the government's efforts, journalists regularly discovered military plans. When Admiral William T. Sampson took a rather large fleet in search of the Spanish navy, for instance, journalists followed and ultimately discovered his intentions. The plans appeared in print, and when Sampson returned, correspondents were soundly chastised for their breach of security. Efforts to send troops and materials to aid the Cuban rebels, likewise allegedly a secret operation, similarly appeared in print. Reporters again were harshly criticized, and military censors were given even more authority over dispatches. In evaluating such security leaks, it is only fair to note that the military was not very discreet in planning or carrying out such ventures. The attempt to aid the Cuban rebels, for instance, was conducted by using a bright red side-wheeler that was brilliantly lighted in the evening hours and clearly visible for miles.

Eventually, the government tried harder to keep its plans secret. The secretary of the navy, for instance, refused to allow naval personnel to talk with journalists. Any information available for publication simply was posted on bulletin boards and rarely did this reach beyond routine data. The secretary of war adopted this practice as well. Censorship in Florida became successful after the military threatened to bar correspondents who violated the rules from accompanying the army to Cuba. News would be made on the battlefields, and no correspondent wanted to be left behind. Preparations for an invasion went ahead, unhampered by news leaks. But this time, leaks should have occurred because the expeditionary force was poorly organized and equipped. Only one reporter, writing for *Harper's Weekly,* told that story. For his efforts he was denounced by his colleagues and banned from military posts.

Relations between the military and the press in Cuba were less successful. Correspondents almost unanimously disliked General William Shafter, and their stories reflected their feelings. They argued that Shafter had mismanaged his forces and that when in the midst of battle a general was needed on the scene, the 300-pound Shafter had taken to his cot with heat stroke. In addition, the Cuban expedition was using old equipment and was fighting in a climate where disease felled more soldiers than the enemy. As boatloads of sick soldiers returned home, public sentiment began turning against the expedition. With the shift in opinion at home, reporters sent back stories about conditions in Cuba. Such stories appeared just about the time that the government was trying to negotiate an end to the war with Spain; so indirectly, once again, the press may have aided the enemy. The question of when to report problems within military operations and when to keep quiet in order to protect national interests always has been and always would be perplexing for American journalists.

As this splendid little war to liberate Cubans from the tyranny of Spain ended, the United States became a colonial power faced with the problems that such status brings. Through the treaty with Spain, the United States purchased the Philippines, where Americans soon were engulfed in a long guerrilla war against insurrectionaries who had also battled Spanish occupation forces. As the war ended and the Philippine insurrection continued, a number of Americans found the idea of becoming a colonial power unappetizing, and a sizable opposition arose to continued occupation of the Philippines. Anti-imperialists were drawn from the highest levels of society. Former presidents Benjamin Harrison and Grover Cleveland were among their number as were presidential hopeful William Jennings Bryan and a number of senators and representatives from both sides of the aisle. Reformers and political independents such as Jane Addams, E. L. Godkin, and Carl Schurz were included, as were the presidents of Harvard University, the American Federation of Labor, and Carnegie Steel.[80]

Experience had proven that when the country was divided over its government's military operations, dissenters could try to influence national policy with little interference. The breadth of opposition to the creation of an American empire provided just such protection for those who campaigned against the involvement of U.S. troops in the Philippine Islands. The individuals who feared an American empire had varying grounds for doing so, some of which were not too noble. Arguments against continued American involvement included concerns about becoming involved in international power politics, about contradicting the nation's democratic principles, and about corrupting the nation by taking in people of a different color, language, and religion. The anti-imperialist campaign lasted for two years. Anti-imperialist clubs were formed in many cities; mass meetings were held; and imperialism was denounced roundly in newspapers, magazines, pamphlets, and from the speaker's podium. In large part, the anti-imperialist movement derived from the dominant urge of the era to return the nation to the stability and security of the past. Only by the end of the nineteenth century the winds of change were blowing through the nation, and the security of the past was no longer as attractive to many.

Generally, the rights of these individuals to speak and to write against national policy were respected. The only violation of those rights surrounded controversial pamphlets written by Edward Atkinson of Boston, a 72-year-old retired textile manufacturer. The pamphlets were written at a time of growing dissatisfaction among the troops in the Philippines, who were asking why they were fighting in the islands when the war against Spain was over. With the troops' families raising the same questions, Atkinson's pamphlets underlined their concerns. In the spring of 1899, Atkinson sent copies of his three pamphlets to the secretary of war, announcing his intention to send them to soldiers stationed in the Philippines. When he received no reply, he sent copies to top military officers on the islands as a test.[81]

In early May 1899, the postmaster general ordered the postmaster in San Francisco to remove all of the Atkinson pamphlets from the Manila-bound mails. The attorney general followed up by saying that Atkinson was surely guilty of treason and that he faced a heavy fine and prison term for his acts. A firestorm of protest erupted in the face of such comments. The government was harshly criticized for exercising "the mailed hand of the rule of blood and iron which . . . will next fall heavily upon freedom of speech within the old borders of the United States."[82] Most of the nation's newspapers supported imperialism and were critical of Atkinson's actions, but enough outcry was raised to make the government regret having interfered with Atkinson's efforts to send his pamphlets to the Philippines.

Other members of the Anti-Imperialist League spoke out without interference. One of the leading voices was E. L. Godkin, considered by many to be the leading editorialist of his day. Godkin had regularly decried American efforts to take in uncivilized nations and chastised the press for supporting a "pugilist's view" of foreign affairs.[83] Godkin was an intellectual dissenter, and his arguments reached a fairly small audience. The dissident who reached the masses was Martin P. Dooley, bartender extraordinary, who worked in a small pub on Archer Road, Bridgeport, in the heart of the Irish-American settlement of Chicago. Mr. Dooley, as he was known to the millions of people who read of his exploits, was the creation of Finley Peter Dunne, a columnist for the *Evening Post*. Until the Spanish-American War, Mr. Dooley concerned himself primarily with local issues, but with the American effort to build an empire, Dunne had Dooley turn to foreign affairs. With that change came a national audience for the bartender who spoke with a heavy brogue and who discussed the world in terms of his immediate surroundings.[84]

Dooley soon was satirizing American war preparations and shortly became ardently antiwar. To Mr. Dooley, Americans could win if the game was horseshoes, wrestling, chasing a greased pig, a one-legged race, or a tug of war, but Americans would lose the game of diplomacy. Mr. Dooley's stance against imperialism was hardly surprising, given the Irish experience with British imperialism, but Dunne's writing made him an implausible ally with the blue-blooded, old-line Americans represented within the Anti-Imperialist League. Although the campaign was insufficient to stop American activity in the Philippines, such anti-imperialist comments were a major factor in blocking the creation of an American empire.

While disapproval of America's imperialistic bent did not lead to violence against the dissenters, it often led to a questioning of their patriotism. Another opponent of imperialism, Samuel Clemens, who called himself Mark Twain, recalled the situation a year or so after the campaign had ended. During the war and subsequent insurrection, Twain had opposed American military actions, writing that the American flag should have "the white stripes painted black and the stars replaced by the skull and crossbones." He was publicly rebuked by a clergyman who said that "if I had my just deserts I should be . . . dangling from a lamp-post somewhere. . . . He hadn't anything personal against me, except that I was opposed to the political war, and he said I was a traitor." Twain, who was relating the experiences in an after-dinner speech, reflected on the cleric's comments. "It would be an entirely different question if the country's life was in danger, its existence at stake; then . . . we would all come forward and stand by the flag, and stop thinking about whether the nation was right or wrong." The recent situation was quite different. "When there is no question that the nation is any way in danger, but only some little war away off, then it may be that on the question of politics the nation is divided, half-patriot and half-traitors, and no man can tell which from which."[85]

The fact that Twain could indulge in such musings publicly showed that American society had changed substantially. Although many people still were unwilling to allow unlimited discussion on many issues, pressure was building for increased freedom of expression on certain topics. The ideas advocated by outsiders at times were definitely revolutionary. In fact, the notion that outsiders wanted to have access to the nation's political, economic, and social agenda was in itself most unusual. Despite the best efforts of society's leaders in the last twenty-five years of the century, certain ideas simply would not die. In fact, the ferment in ideas started in these years was destined to multiply until new notions no longer could safely be ignored, and conformity of opinion became impossible.

CHAPTER 2

Setting the Stage for Repression:
Freedom of Expression in the
Early Twentieth Century

The dawning of the twentieth century unfortunately did not initiate a new tolerance for freedom of expression in the United States. The nation still faced forces seeking change in society. Political and economic power still was concentrated in the hands of a few, and those without either complained even more loudly about their deprivations. Violence flared across the country, and with each incident came calls for repression. Strangely enough, coinciding with increased efforts to suppress dissidents was one of the most active reform movements in the nation's history. Substantially middle-class in nature and thus socially acceptable, progressive reform affected significant sections of American life, but the suppressive urge still brought repeated efforts to eliminate dissent from the American scene. The first fifteen years or so of the twentieth century laid a firm foundation legally, psychologically, and philosophically for the most repressive wartime experience in the nation's history.

Perhaps such reactions were not so unusual for individuals faced with the assassination of a president. William McKinley had gone to Buffalo, New York, for a September 5, 1901, speech at the Pan-American Exposition. At a reception the following day, a man passing through the receiving line pulled a gun from his pocket and shot the president. McKinley, a basically well-liked chief executive, died on September 14 from complications resulting from the abdominal wound. His assassin, who was captured immediately, represented all that was considered evil in American society—foreignness, radicalism, and domestic discontent. Serving to further inflame public opinion, Leon Czolgosz declared, "I am an Anarchist—a disciple of Emma Goldman. Her words set me on fire."[1] In further explanation, he said, "McKinley was going around the country shouting prosperity when there was no prosperity for the poor man. I don't believe in the Republican form of government and I don't believe we should have any rulers. It is right to kill them."[2]

Most Americans immediately concluded that the assassination was part of an international plot to overthrow the government. Few accepted Czolgosz's contention that he was working alone; they believed his actions were inspired by the anarchists who had been causing trouble for years. The nation's press rehearsed the evils of anarchism including the Haymarket riot of 1886 and the Homestead strike of 1892. After all, did not anarchists teach that all government was evil and unnecessary and that all rulers should be assassinated? For many Americans, no further proof was necessary, and they went on a rampage against anyone with anarchist connections.

Anarchists were jailed just because of their political beliefs; their homes were raided; and their newspaper offices were destroyed. They were beaten, tarred, feathered, and forced from their homes. Leaders of the anarchist community suffered even more intimidation. Authorities in Chicago, for instance, arrested Emma Goldman, "Red Emma" as she was known, on suspicion of being an accessory to the assassination. Long an effective advocate of the anarchist cause, Goldman was held for two weeks before she was freed on bond. She denied participating in any conspiracy to kill the president, and said that although she advocated anarchy, she did not endorse murder. "Am I accountable because some crack-brained person put a wrong construction on my words?" she asked. "Leon Czolgosz, I am convinced, planned the deed unaided and entirely alone. There may be anarchists who would murder, but there are also men in every walk of life who sometimes feel the impulse to kill." Although the assassin "may have been inspired by me," she said, "he took the wrong way of showing it."[3] Charges against Goldman ultimately were dropped after the Buffalo police found no connection between her and the crime.

Johann Most, editor of the *Freiheit,* the leading German-language anarchist publication in the United States, also was arrested. Most had been a target of anti-anarchist forces ever since he arrived in 1882 and helped establish the movement. He had spent time in jail in the late nineteenth century after he had criticized the execution of several of the Haymarket defendants. Now Most was arrested for an article advocating the murder of rulers that appeared on the front page of his newspaper the day after McKinley was shot. The essay, "Murder Against Murder," was written by a German revolutionary in 1849 who contended that since the rulers of the world were essentially despots who got their power through violent means, they deserved killing. Police argued that the piece had contributed to the murder; Most retorted that the police action violated his rights to freedom of speech and of the press. He said that the only reason the article had appeared in print on that particular day was to fill space and that the essay had appeared in the *Freiheit* several times before.

Although Most had withdrawn the edition as soon as he heard about the assassination, he still had been arrested. His $1,000 bond was lowered to $500 when officials figured out that a newspaper printed in New York City on September 7 could not have circulated in Buffalo on September 6, the day of the shooting. Most was tried for printing the old article under a section of the New York code that made it a misdemeanor to seriously disturb the public peace or to openly outrage public decency. Although his attorney presented a free-press argument, Most was convicted and sentenced to a year in prison. His conviction was upheld on appeal, with the state court of appeals ruling that the article "held forth murder as a duty and exhorted his readers to practice it upon their rulers." Courts "cannot shut their eyes to the fact that there are elements in our population, small in number but reckless and aggressive, who are ready to act on such advice and to become the assassins of those whom the people have placed in authority."[4]

Before his arrest, Most actually had denounced Czolgosz, saying that he believed the assassin to be "a crank or perhaps downright crazy . . . no Anarchists in this country want to kill McKinley. He is not a despot, and it is only against the despotic ruler of the Old World that men who are working for better social conditions have an enmity."[5] Some anarchists argued that the assassination really was caused by more establishment newspapers, especially those owned by William Randolph Hearst, who had conducted a vicious editorial campaign against the president after McKinley's initial election in 1896.

Shortly after the assassination of Governor Goebel of Kentucky in early 1901, for instance, Hearst's *Journal* ran a rather shocking bit of verse:

> The bullet that pierced Goebel's breast
> Can not be found in all the West;
> Good reason, it is speeding here
> To stretch McKinley on his bier.[6]

Two months later, Hearst's *Evening Journal* carried an editorial that included the line, "If bad institutions and bad men can be got rid of only by killing, then killing must be done."[7] Such comments perhaps were even worse than the fifty-year-old essay reprinted by Johann Most because they were directed squarely at the sitting president. Despite that fact, Hearst was not charged with complicity in the crime. When news got out that the assassin supposedly had a copy of one of Hearst's editorials criticizing McKinley in his possession at the time of the shooting, the public took its retribution. Sales dropped off as a number of groups boycotted the *Journal;* Hearst himself was hanged in effigy. To salvage his New York publication, Hearst changed its name to the *American* and toned it down considerably. Other so-called yellow journals followed suit, and another sensational period of journalism ended.[8]

Czolgosz was arraigned on murder charges on September 16, two days after the president's death. The trial began on September 23 and lasted two days. After deliberating twenty-seven minutes, the jury found Czolgosz guilty. He had done little to cooperate with his court-appointed attorneys; they, in turn, did little to defend him, and in fact, they spent most of their time complaining about their assignment. Czolgosz was electrocuted on October 29, little more than a month after his conviction. Although few people were swayed by their determination, psychiatrists who examined Czolgosz's personality profile after his execution decided that he was not an anarchist after all. Czolgosz, they said, only claimed affiliation with the anarchists to justify his act.

The events surrounding the murder of the president unleashed a call for repression that seemed unending. Theodore Roosevelt, the new president of the United States, capitalized on public sentiment. He called on Congress to enact legislation forbidding anarchists to enter the United States and to allow the federal government to deport any alien anarchists found within its territory. Congress complied, enacting the requested legislation early in 1903. The legislation also forbade the naturalization of anyone with known anarchistic tendencies and required individuals supervising the process to make careful inquiries as to the political views of prospective citizens.[9]

New York State enacted the nation's first criminal anarchy law in 1902, defining anarchy as "the doctrine that organized government should be overthrown by force or violence, or by assassination of the executive head or of any of the executive officials of government, or by any unlawful means." Advocacy of criminal anarchy by written or spoken word could lead to a felony conviction carrying a prison term of up to ten years and a fine of $5,000. Being a member of any group advocating such activities was equally as bad. In fact, even allowing a group advocating criminal anarchy to assemble in a building that you owned could bring a conviction for a misdemeanor, two years in prison, and a $2,000 fine.[10] Other states enacted similar legislation.

With increased pressure on their right to meet and discuss their philosophy, anarchists decided to build their defense on free-speech grounds, and in 1903, the U.S. government provided them with the perfect test case. English anarchist and trade unionist John Turner had arrived in this country for a series of lectures. He made his first speech about trade unionism and a general strike in which all workers would participate and then was arrested by federal authorities for having entered the country in violation of the new immigration law. Turner was searched, and evidence was turned up connecting him with Johann Most and with protests against the Haymarket executions. After an administrative hearing before a special panel from the Department of Commerce and Labor, he was ordered deported.

Anarchists decided to appeal the case, and with Turner confined to Ellis Island for the duration, the anarchists turned to the Free Speech League, which Theodore Schroeder helped to found. The league hired Clarence Darrow and his partner, Edgar Lee Masters, as Turner's attorneys. The issue, said a league statement, was "Shall the Federal Government be a Judge of beliefs and disbeliefs?" The statement added, "Tyranny always begins with the most unpopular man or class and extends by degrees: it should be resisted at the beginning."[11] Darrow and Masters continued the free-speech argument in their brief before the U.S. Supreme Court, saying, "The fundamental basis of free opinion demands that convictions shall be freely spoken to the end that the truth shall be known. Upon this freedom all progress depends."[12]

The Supreme Court rejected the notion that anarchists had a right to freedom of speech. A majority of the Court believed that Congress had the right to declare that an alien anarchist was deportable. Turner's speeches were evidence enough of his belief in anarchism; in fact, his statements were incitements to violence that could legitimately be quieted. The Court added that the American people should not read the decision as "depreciating the vital importance of freedom of speech and of the press," for the justices failed to find such values involved. Instead, the case underlined the fact that "as long as human governments endure they cannot be denied the power of self-preservation."[13]

With the passage of the new immigration laws and their ratification by the Supreme Court and with the enactment of various state provisions aimed at outlawing anarchism, the nation's leading citizens likely felt that they had saved the nation from a horrible fate. That conclusion was not true, however, as forces beyond the reach of most existing legislation were starting to stir. Soon, anarchism would be replaced as the primary doctrine to be feared. These new movements, through the strength of their ideas and their willingness to place individual lives on the line for those beliefs, would challenge the American system as never before and would evoke some of the most violent reactions that the nation has ever seen.

Radical labor organizations that seemed as much dedicated to violence as to reforming the economic structure of the United States posed the greatest threat. The first group to attract attention in the twentieth century was the Western Federation of Miners (WFM). Laboring in the silver mines of the Far West, these workers were highly skilled and much in demand. Most WFM members were either native-born or naturalized American citizens, and they had a long history of banding together to seek eight-hour workdays, higher wages, and better working conditions. The workers were fairly successful until the price of silver fell in the late nineteenth century and increased mechanization affected their jobs. A nasty strike ensued in 1893, and even more violence followed in its wake.[14]

By the early twentieth century, the WFM was the most radical and militant group in American labor. As the mine owners grew stronger and less willing to negotiate, violent encounters increased. Employers wanted the freedom to hire and fire individuals and to set wages and working conditions based solely on market demands. Workers wanted unions to negotiate with the employers to win job stability and better working conditions despite fluctuations in the silver market. Another major and violent strike in the Colorado silver mines in 1903 brought state authorities to the aid of the owners. Martial law was declared, and the WFM was defeated. Union members were deported from Colorado, often being forced to leave family and property behind. They were warned never to return.

Such repression further radicalized the miners. When efforts to find allies within other political and labor forces in the nation uncovered few likely supporters, the miners issued a call for a secret conference in Chicago in 1904. There radical labor leaders discussed the formation of a new union, the Industrial Workers of the World (IWW).[15] For the next twenty years, the IWW was the chief villain in the lives of conservative American business leaders, regardless of its involvement in labor unrest. With its arrival, most Americans forgot their fears of anarchism and focused their attention on this organization, which would hold the spotlight until replaced by the Communist party.

The IWW presented a distinct challenge to the American business community. As an industrial union, the IWW organized workers regardless of their level of skill. Allegedly this meant the IWW could cripple an industry by calling all of its workers out on strike at one time. Because of its structure, the IWW attracted primarily unskilled workers, who had the greatest grievances. And the times made grievances great. By the early twentieth century, about 2 percent of the population held 60 percent of the nation's wealth, and to at least one-third of the nation, starvation was a daily companion.[16] Because of these harsh realities, employers, government, and courts systematically exercised their powers to keep workers in their places.

IWW leaders, however, wanted to change the place of workers in American society. Union goals included ending what its leaders called wage slavery and establishing worker cooperatives. The rhetoric was Marxist and revolutionary, heightening fears within the ruling classes. At its organizational meeting in 1905, the IWW went on record as favoring political action rather than violent over-throw of the government, but organizers also inserted inflammatory language in its constitution. The preamble said, for instance, that "the working class and the employing class have nothing in common. There can be no peace so long as hun-ger and want are found among the millions of working people, and the few, who make up the employing class, have all the good things of life." Further, the pre-amble said, "Between these two classes a struggle must go on until all the toilers come together on the political, as well as on the industrial field, and take and hold that which they produce by their labor, through an economic organization of the working class without affiliation with any political party."[17]

This language was the equivalent of a declaration of industrial warfare to many business leaders. All of the techniques used so effectively against other sus-pect organizations once again were employed to keep these workers from asso-ciating together. IWW organizers had difficulty contacting workers, and they were in constant physical jeopardy. Workers who joined the union were fired and banned from further employment. Spies infiltrated the organization, and the courts issued orders to impede strikes and organizing activities. Violence flared, and establishment newspapers willingly inflamed the minds of middle-class America against the IWW. If the IWW wanted industrial war, the business community was ready.

With William D. Haywood, who had been a leader of the Western Federation of Miners, as its head, the IWW stood ready for the confrontation. The organi-zation advocated direct action in labor disputes of which peaceful strikes and picketing were the mildest forms. General strikes, in which workers tried to pull all their colleagues in a community off the job, slowdowns in production, passive resistance, sabotage, and, some said, revolution were the more extreme activities that the union backed. The IWW was strongest west of the Mississippi where it organized loggers, mine workers, and migratory farm laborers with relative ease. Thus, to the business community, even the IWW's clientele was on the disrep-utable side. The union had to be stopped—and quickly.

When the former governor of Idaho, who had cooperated in breaking silver mine strikes in Coeur d'Alene, was assassinated, IWW leaders were implicated on the flimsiest of evidence supplied by the alleged killer. Although none of the union's leadership had been in Idaho at the time of the slaying, Haywood and two other men were ordered extradited to stand trial. In order to prevent efforts to release the men on writs of habeas corpus, the suspects were arrested on a Saturday night. At dawn Sunday morning, they were placed aboard a special train that deposited them in Boise, Idaho, where they were held incommunicado for days. Haywood and one other man were acquitted; the state, convinced that the union had intimidated the jurors, dropped the charges against the third defendant.

Almost immediately after Haywood's acquittal, the final radicalization of the IWW occurred. In the organization's 1908 convention, individuals advocating direct action as opposed to working through the political system took control. Whereas the preamble to the original IWW constitution endorsed political as well as economic action, the 1908 meeting changed that approach. The revised preamble now read: "Between these two classes a struggle must go on until the workers of the world organize as a class, take possession of the earth and the machinery of production and abolish the wage system."[18] The new leadership of the organization, which again chose Haywood as president, believed that any worker who thought that change could be achieved through the political system was simply a tool of those who sought to dominate workers. Direct action and sabotage were specifically endorsed to change society. IWW leaders wanted a nonpolitical revolution that would destroy the existing system and erect in its place a society fairer to their constituents, who were the outcasts of American life. Dues were kept purposefully low enough to bring in unskilled workers as well as immigrants, including Asian-Americans, Mexicans, and blacks.

Despite their image as violent revolutionaries IWW leaders advocated non-violence, including passive resistance, to contrast the worker's behavior against the employer's. Workers were advised to adopt the work slowdown, to tamper with but not to destroy equipment, and to harass the employer in any way possible. This approach was ignored by most union critics, who focused instead on IWW participation in the destruction of property, adulteration of products, and, perhaps, the injury of other workers. The IWW became identified with various syndicalist movements that were springing up in Europe. In such movements, labor unions sought to overthrow the capitalist system by direct action rather than through participation in the political process. To most American business leaders, the IWW was the personification of syndicalism.

Fears of radicalism ran rampant. A 1907 strike by members of the Western Federation of Miners and the IWW in Goldfield, Nevada, brought a firm reaction. This time, President Theodore Roosevelt sent federal troops in to end the work disruption rather than leave the matter solely in the hands of the owners or the states as in previous strikes. The troops remained for three months despite reports from the president's own investigators that they were not needed and that the employers were using the troops' presence to break the union.

While labor's concerns remained high because of the president's intervention in Nevada, the Supreme Court dealt two body blows to union activities within a week in early 1908. In *Adair v. United States,* the Court found that Congress had no right to protect workers' efforts to join together to seek better working conditions.[19] In reaching that decision, the Court declared the Erdman Act of 1898[20]—which made it illegal for an interstate carrier to dismiss employees for union membership—an unconstitutional abridgement of the liberty of contract guaranteed by the Fifth Amendment. William Adair, an agent of the Louisville and Nashville Railroad Company, had fired an employee because he held membership in the Order of Locomotive Engineers. Under the act, workers could not be fired for such membership, nor could they be forced to sign so-called yellow-dog contracts that made them pledge not to join unions while employed, nor could they be blacklisted or barred from all future railroad employment for participating in union activities. Ignoring the gross inequities in the bargaining positions of employee and employer, six members of the Court agreed that the statutory requirement "is an invasion of the personal liberty, as well as of the right of property, guaranteed by that Amendment. Such liberty and right embraces the right to make contracts for the purchase of the labor of others and equally the right to make contracts for the sale of one's own labor."[21]

About a week after the Adair decision, the Supreme Court found another way to suppress labor unions within the Sherman Antitrust Act of 1890,[22] a piece of legislation enacted to restrain the rapid growth of large financial monopolies known as trusts. This case, popularly known as the Danbury Hatters case,[23] grew out of a strike called by the United Hatters of America against Loewe and Company in 1903. The company had resisted union efforts to organize its employees. To the union, which had organized seventy of the eighty-two plants in the country that made fur hats, winning the Loewe plant was crucial. Since the union was part of the American Federation of Labor, its leaders sought to ensure victory by getting the federation's 1.4 million members to boycott Loewe's products. Dietrich Loewe, a partner in the company, brought suit on the grounds that the boycott violated the Sherman Act's provisions against restraint of interstate trade. Loewe sought treble damages against the 240 members of the hatters' union in Danbury and collected $240,000 in damages after the Supreme Court unanimously found in his favor. The homes of union members were attached in order to pay the fine, and Samuel Gompers asked all AFL members to donate one hour's worth of their wages to help the Danbury workers.

Despite the success of court action against labor unions, the nation felt no more secure. Several murders in different places in the country were linked to the almost nonexistent anarchist movement. In response to this alleged recurrence of anarchy, the federal government announced plans to help local authorities round up undesirable aliens for deportation. Roosevelt also authorized the banning of *La Question Sociale,* an anarchist newspaper published in New Jersey, from the mails. The action against the newspaper had no legal base; the president simply announced that "those who write, publish and circulate these articles stand on a level with those who use the mails for distributing poison for the purpose of murder; and convictions have been obtained for the distribution of poisons."[24] The anarchists were likewise distributing poison and should be stopped. When staff members of the banned newspaper tried to rent a hall to protest the president's action, they found none available. When they tried to hold the session inside their own offices, police swinging clubs broke it up. Said the editor of *La Question Sociale,* "This is worse than Russia or Italy. There the officers attend the anarchist meetings and if the speaker uses language they think is improper they speak to him and make him change his tone, but they don't prevent peaceful assemblies. And yet you call this a free country."[25]

Roosevelt was not yet finished with his efforts to cleanse the mails. On April

8, 1908, he sent a special message to Congress asking for an amendment to the postal code to allow the postmaster general to bar anarchist materials from the mail. "The anarchist is the enemy of humanity, the enemy of all mankind," the president told Congress, "and his is a deeper degree of criminality than any other. No immigrant is allowed to come to our shores if he is an anarchist; and no paper published here or abroad should be permitted circulation in this country if it propagates anarchistic opinions."[26] The result of the president's plea was the addition of a new definition of the term "indecent" in Anthony Comstock's law. According to congressional action in 1908, "indecent" now included "tending to incite arson, murder, or assassination."[27] This marked the first time that political criteria were used to define material that could be excluded from the mails.

Although the anarchist scare of 1908 was brief, it heightened the nation's fears of alien people and ideas. In the hands of radicals even such traditional American values as freedom of speech seemed foreign, as IWW members soon discovered. Beginning in 1909 and continuing sporadically through 1912, IWW members became involved in a number of free-speech fights up and down the West Coast. Starting in Spokane, Washington, and moving to Fresno and San Diego, California, IWW members used the soap-box to claim their right to freely address the citizens of any community. Spokane city fathers sparked the protest by passing an ordinance banning all speaking on the street in an area where most of the community's workers congregated. To make matters worse, the ordinance was amended to allow religious groups including the Salvation Army to speak there. The law was discriminatory, and IWW members took to the streets to say so.

Their technique was simple. A union member would stand on a street corner and attempt to address a crowd; the police would arrest the member, generally for disorderly conduct. Another member would immediately replace the arrested individual, and so on. Police officers paid no attention to what the IWW members were saying—one was even arrested for reading the Declaration of Independence. All that was needed for the police to spring into action was for one IWW member to try to speak in public. IWW members saw these encounters as full-fledged challenges to those in authority. American liberals, however, saw the free-speech fights as civil liberties issues; union members should have the right to stand on the street corner to recruit new members.

Free-speech fighters filled the jails in various cities, but still more IWW members came to address crowds. After filling the jails, the Wobblies would clog the court systems by demanding separate jury trials and the right to manage their own defenses. Beleaguered city governments conceded, and IWW members won the right to hold organizational meetings in various communities without police interference. The free-speech fights were moderately successful until they were mounted in San Diego in 1911. There, IWW members were not arrested; they were simply taken over the county line. Anyone who returned to resume the protest was greeted with vigilante justice. The nonviolent technique lost its effectiveness in the face of officially sanctioned and publicly supported violence against the speakers. No higher authority intervened on behalf of the Wobblies, and the free-speech fight in San Diego was lost.

Community dislike of labor unions did not end with the persecution of IWW members. In 1912, the AFL discovered that only its ability to pursue a case through the court system saved its president, Samuel Gompers, from a jail term. Gompers, as editor of the *American Federationist,* had placed Buck's Stove and Range Company on the union's "Unfair" and "We Don't Patronize" list when the union and the company failed to reach an agreement on work hours. The president of the company, who also headed the American Manufacturers Association, brought suit against Gompers for injury to his business as a result of the listing. The district court issued an injunction ordering Gompers to cease "abetting, aiding or assisting in any such boycott" and to stop "printing, issuing, publishing, or distributing through the mails, or in any other matter . . . printed or written newspaper, magazine, circular, letter or other document . . . which shall contain . . . the name of the complainant, its business or its product in the 'We Don't Patronize,' or the 'Unfair' list."[28]

The AFL continued to include Buck's Stove on the "Unfair" list, and Gompers and other union officials were convicted of contempt of court. The Supreme Court reluctantly overturned the conviction because of substantial irregularities during the contempt hearing. The Court refused to look at the defendants' claims that injunctions like the one issued against Gompers interfered with fundamental rights of free expression. To the justices, speech and press questions simply were not involved. The issue at hand was "the power of a court of equity to enjoin the defendants from continuing a boycott which, by words and signals, printed or spoken, caused or threatened irreparable damage." The law, said the Court, "recognizes the right of workingmen to unite and to invite others to join their ranks, thereby making available the strength, influence and power that come from such association. By virtue of this right, powerful labor unions have been organized." So powerful were the unions that "the individual may be helpless" before them. By placing the Buck's Stove Company on the "Unfair" and "We Don't Patronize" list, union members acted in concert, giving the statements "a force not inhering in the words themselves, and therefore exceeding any possible right of speech which a single individual might have." Consequently the union had engaged in " 'verbal acts,' as much subject to injunction as the use of any other force whereby property is unlawfully damaged."[29]

AFL leaders most likely would have admitted that verbal acts were precisely what they intended, for only by combining voices would the lone worker have any chance of being treated fairly by an employer. Although the court system regularly refused to listen to pleas from union members, the imbalance between workers and their employers did attract the attention of Congress. The AFL helped encourage this interest by publicizing labor's concerns and by selectively endorsing candidates. In 1912, Congress created a Commission on Industrial Relations to investigate the nation's working conditions. Its report, issued in 1916, confirmed all of the problems highlighted by labor, endorsed the right of workers to organize into unions, and advocated increased freedom of speech for workers.[30]

Commission members seemingly feared the results of preventing the organization of workers into unions more than the results of their combining. The worker's right to organize, said the commission, was fundamental to improving the lot of all workers in an age in which huge corporations dominated the business scene and exercised tremendous power. The report ridiculed employers who preferred an open-shop arrangement in which both union and nonunion workers would be employed. Commissioners refused to believe that the two categories of workers would be treated equally, and they noted that collective action to win basic rights was not possible in such a situation. Even though employers who refused to deal collectively with their workers stressed that they were willing to hear workers' complaints, the commission found those reassurances hollow. "One is repelled rather than impressed by the insistence with which this idea has been presented," responded the commission. "Every tyrant in history has on stated days granted audiences to which his faithful subjects might bring their complaints against his officers and agents." But the justice obtained from royal audiences was capricious at best, said the commission, adding, "it is equally sure that in industry justice can never be obtained by such a method."[31]

Nor was the commission impressed by employers who said that they were willing to deal with local unions while finding national combinations of laborers unacceptable. "The underlying motive of such statements," said the commission, "seems to be that as long as organizations are unsupported from outside they are ineffective and capable of being crushed with ease and impunity by discharging the ringleaders."[32] Employers knew from their own experiences that business operated best when organized on a national level, commissioners said. In fact, not only were the businesses organized nationally, but their managers belonged to special national organizations designed to further their special interests. The commissioners believed that workers deserved the same opportunities.

In the final analysis, said the commission, "the fundamental question for the Nation to decide . . . is whether the workers shall have an effective means of adjusting their grievances, improving their condition, and securing their liberty, through negotiation with their employers, or whether they shall be driven by necessity and oppression to the extreme of revolt." An examination of past disputes showed that "where men are well organized, and the power of employers and employees is fairly well balanced, agreements are nearly always reached by negotiation." If unorganized individuals protest, "there is no hope of achieving anything except by spontaneous revolt." In the latter situation, "without strike funds or other financial support the unorganized must achieve results at once; they can not afford to wait for reason and compromise to come into play. Lacking strong leaders and definite organization, such revolts can only be expected to change to mob action on the slightest provocation."[33]

Thus, to the commission, the inability of workers to organize was one reason why violence attended certain labor disputes. Another major reason was the systematic suppression of the speech of union organizers and members by the police. The commission found no section of the country immune from police interference with the right of individuals to assemble and to discuss union business. "In many instances such interference has been carried out with a degree of brutality which would be incredible if it were not vouched for by reliable witnesses," said the commission. Police interference, the report said, "undoubtedly is the result of a belief by the police or their superiors that they were 'supporting and defending the Government' by such an invasion of personal rights." To commission members, "There could be no greater error. Such action strikes at the very foundation of government. It is axiomatic that a government which can be maintained only by the suppression of criticism should not be maintained. Furthermore, it is the lesson of history that attempts to suppress ideas result only in their more rapid propagation."[34]

Commissioners asked Congress to protect the rights of workers to organize, bargain, and speak. The act intended to affect the worker's condition the most was the Clayton Antitrust Act of 1914. Offended by the way in which courts had used the Sherman Antitrust Act as a weapon against unions, the authors of the Clayton Act wrote language specifically barring judicial misuse of this law. In section six, for instance, Congress said, "the labor of a human being is not a commodity or article of commerce." Consequently, antitrust laws shall not "be construed to forbid the existence and operation of labor . . . organizations, instituted for the purposes of mutual help." Nor shall these organizations "be held or construed to be illegal combinations or conspiracies in restraint of trade, under the antitrust laws." In an effort to stop the continuing use of injunctions against union activities, the legislation said in no uncertain terms that "no restraining order or injunction" may be granted by a federal judicial official that would interfere in the employee-employer relationship. Unfortunately, Congress qualified the prohibition with the words "unless necessary to prevent irreparable injury to property, or to a property right, of the party making the application,"[35] which allowed judges to continue issuing injunctions against labor unions.

Although from the current perspective, actions by judges in the pre-World War I era seem repressive, they fit the tenor of the times perfectly. The Commission on Industrial Relations represented a minority view; most individuals clearly favored the suppression of disruptive forces in American society—especially labor unions of all varieties. AFL unions largely tried to play a conservative role in society during these years, working hard to make and consolidate gains as quietly as possible. Even the Socialist party, established in 1901, amended the party's constitution in 1912 to require the expulsion of any individual calling for societal change through violent means. The constitution already called for the expulsion of anyone who disavowed the use of political action to obtain change. The 1912 language said, "any member of the party who opposes political action or advocates crime, sabotage, or other methods of violence as a weapon of the working class to aid in its emancipation shall be expelled from membership in the party."[36] Among those turning in their resignations was Bill Haywood, president of the IWW, against whom the amendment was specifically aimed. The goal was to insulate Socialists from increased criticism, an effort that essentially was futile.

When society tries to protect itself from change, all sorts of people and activities become targets. In the early twentieth century, complaints focused on immigrants. In part, this concern was connected to the changing nature of immigration. No longer were new residents coming from the British Isles or northern Europe. Now, southern and eastern Europeans predominated, bringing with them very different languages, social customs, and beliefs. Difference became undesirable; alien became subversive. The federal government slowly increased its bars against so-called subversives entering the country and made it increasingly difficult for them to obtain citizenship if they managed to enter. Nativists still wanted to keep foreign ideas away from American citizens in the expectation that they would not develop certain notions on their own.

Other members of society eagerly sought to restrict errant thoughts. The dawn of the new century brought renewed interest in the distribution of information about birth control, and the old censors were ready and waiting to halt such ideas from circulating. The Comstock Act, and indeed Anthony Comstock himself, still closed the avenues of communication to this information—even if it came from medical sources and was both accurate and safe. In 1912, Margaret Sanger began a campaign to publicize accurate sexual information that ultimately led to the first breaches in the law. Sanger's campaign started with two articles for the *New York Call.* The first, "What Every Mother Should Know," ran without difficulty. The second, "What Every Girl Should Know," riled Comstock so much that the issue containing it was barred from the mails. The next issue of the newspaper carried the notice, "What Every Girl Should Know: 'NOTHING! By Order of the Post Office Department.'" The objectionable article contained no information on birth control; instead Comstock disliked Sanger's accurate discussion of venereal disease and her use of such words as gonorrhea and syphilis.[37]

Having run afoul of the Comstock law once, Sanger determined to attack it again. This time, she planned to use her own publication, *The Woman Rebel,* as an offensive weapon. The first issue of the newspaper in March 1914 and six out of the first eight editions were stopped by the post office for violating the Comstock law. Again, Sanger had provided no specific information about birth control but had talked generally about related topics such as how much it cost to raise a large family, how prevalent abortions were in the United States, and how harmless birth control was. She also carried a philosophical essay on the efficacy of assassination as a cure for political problems, apparently much like the one that Johann Most had carried. Sanger was arraigned on nine counts of violating the Comstock Act in August 1914; one of those counts was for the publication of the essay on assassination.

Sanger did not object to going to jail to serve the cause of birth control; she did not want to be imprisoned for publishing basically innocuous materials. She asked the prosecuting attorney if she could change the charges on which she would be tried. She wanted to send a copy of her pamphlet "Family Limitation" through the mail and be charged for violating the Comstock Act for it. The pamphlet, which clearly discussed and described birth control techniques, would provide an ample test case for the viability of the Comstock Act when it came to discussing such information. The authorities refused, and Sanger, rather than face charges that would provide less of a showcase for her views, fled to Europe.

The trial on "Family Limitation" came when Sanger's estranged husband, William, sold a copy of the pamphlet to a young man who begged for information on contraception. The young man, of course, had been sent by Anthony Comstock, who turned up an hour or so later in person to arrest William Sanger for violating New York State laws against the sale of such materials. William Sanger based his defense on the notion that freedom of the press allowed the mailing of the publication. Although contributions poured in for a defense fund, William Sanger defended himself on free-press grounds. He was convicted and sentenced to thirty days in jail and given a $150 fine.

Upon his conviction, Margaret Sanger returned to the United States to face the charges pending against her. After several postponements, the government decided not to prosecute her in February 1916. Although Margaret Sanger continued to speak on birth control topics, the issue of disseminating sexual information essentially was sidetracked until after the war. By then, the cause of honesty in the use of sexual language, at least, had been aided, strangely enough, by the federal government itself. Substantial problems with syphilis among soldiers during the war led to a massive federal educational campaign on the disease among the military and civilian populations. Language that Anthony Comstock had considered indecent in 1914 had been made socially acceptable by the government.[38]

Government intervention of a different kind led to the tightening of restrictions in a new area of communication that had caused a great deal of concern from its inception. The first motion pictures appeared in the late nineteenth century and soon thereafter came the first incidents of censorship. In 1895, for instance, a kinetoscope parlor on the boardwalk at Atlantic City, New Jersey, pulled a short film called *Dolorita in the Passion Dance* to avoid offending local authorities. The next year, complaints arose about a prolonged kiss in *The Widow Jones,* a film version of a hit Broadway play. And in 1897, authorities in New York City registered disapproval of *Orange Blossoms,* a short film showing a young bride taking off her clothes and revealing a bit of skin. Crime and violence joined sex on the list of complaints against motion pictures when *The Great Train Robbery* was released in 1903. Objections were fairly alike in all instances. Community leaders were concerned about the effect that such depictions would have on the impressionable minds of immigrants, the working classes, and young people.[39]

Community concerns led almost immediately to calls for censorship. Civic groups, churches, reform organizations, police, and some segments of the press demanded that restrictions be placed on motion pictures. In 1907, a *Chicago Tribune* editorial explained the nation's fears about this new form of entertainment. Movies were "schools of crime where murders, robberies, and holdups are illustrated. The outlaw life they portray in their cheap plays tends to the encouragement of wickedness. . . . Not a single thing connected with them has influence for good." The editorial concluded, "The proper thing for city authorities to do is to suppress them at once."[40]

City officials were fairly quick to heed such calls for suppression. The first municipal censorship ordinance went into effect in Chicago in 1907; under its provisions, the superintendent of police was required to issue permits before films could be shown. He was to bar the showing of all films that he considered immoral or obscene. Neither term was well defined, leaving motion-picture censorship based almost totally on the personal whim of the licensing official, a trait that was characteristic of almost all provisions. The Chicago ordinance allowed an appeal to the mayor, but after that, the ruling stood. Film distributors challenged the licensing program in court but lost.[41] Other municipalities enacted similar restrictions, and by 1911, Pennsylvania instituted the first statewide licensing program.

Most early efforts to regulate the showing of motion pictures were based on the power of local governments to regulate businesses that operated within their domain. In December 1908, the mayor of New York City revoked the licenses of every motion-picture theater within his jurisdiction. The charges focused on the safety standards of the theaters themselves as well as on the allegedly indecent character of many of the films shown there. The mayor's action in closing this large market to the growing film industry led almost immediately to the establishment of a local censorship committee. The movie houses were allowed to reopen after this civic group approved the films to be displayed. This municipal effort soon became transformed into the National Board of Censorship of Motion Pictures, which was sanctioned by the motion-picture producers as the official clearinghouse for all films.

The National Board of Censorship created the pattern for most future efforts at self-censorship. The goal was to set up an organization that would gain credibility throughout the nation so that its stamp of approval would be accepted in place of local or state review of films. Producers would send films to the board for clearance prior to release and promise to make the cuts recommended by its censors. Eventually, the Motion Picture Patents Company, the monopolistic organization that controlled the making of most movies in the United States at the time, agreed not to send films to theaters that showed unapproved movies, thus giving the board's sanction even more power. To further enhance its credibility, the board enlisted representatives of various charitable organizations, women's clubs, churches, and similar groups to serve as reviewers. The board issued weekly bulletins to mayors, police chiefs, and censoring boards around the country giving the results of its reviews. By 1913, the National Board of Censorship issued a list of standards used to evaluate films, which included the prohibition of obscenity, vulgarity, certain representations of crime, elaborate depictions of violence, blasphemy, and libel.[42] In all of their actions, said the board, the goal was to apply national standards rather than local.

Movie censorship sponsored by the film industry inevitably enjoyed only limited success and acceptance. Organizations that had joined the effort initially soon dropped out after charging that the National Board of Censorship was a tool of the industry and was more interested in circulating movies than in cleaning them up. Community leaders were increasingly upset by the contents of films. Reformers argued that despite the board's existence, more and more children were being exposed to depictions of crime and immorality. Some 500,000 to 600,000 children a day were said to see motion pictures that inevitably would corrupt their values and certainly lead to the degradation of the United States as a nation. In 1910, a committee in Cleveland, Ohio, reviewed some 250 films and declared that 40 percent of them were unfit for children because they focused on crime, drunkenness, and loose morals. The national board countered that influences other than motion pictures shaped a juvenile's life choices, but as in the arguments about dime novels before and about comic books and rock music later, reality had no influence on exaggerated views of the medium's influence. Although the National Board of Censorship was correct in its evaluation of the effect movies had on individuals, its critics were right about the board's subservience to the industry. Comparisons of films found objectionable by the review board and those rejected by municipal or state censors found the industry-related critics much more lenient. Of 228 films reviewed by both the Pennsylvania State board of censorship and the National Board of Censorship, the state censor called for 1,464 deletions while the national board asked for only 47.[43]

Unpersuaded by the industry's efforts to clean itself up, critics continued to seek governmental regulation of the movies. In some areas, the critics were successful. In 1912, Congress barred films of prize fights from interstate commerce.[44] The action was based less on concern about the brutality of the sport than on concern about the circulation of a film that showed black heavyweight champion Jack Johnson defeating white former champion Jim Jefferies. Racial unrest was feared in certain parts of the country if the newsreel had wide distribution. More along the lines of the concerns of those who would censor movies was the 1913 tariff act that allowed the secretary of the treasury to censor films before allowing them to enter this country.[45] And in 1914, Congress considered establishing a national censorship board to regulate movies.

Although Congress did not enact such legislation, the Supreme Court did enter the censorship fray in 1915. The case involved the efforts of Mutual Film Corporation, a Detroit-based film distribution company, to avoid submitting its movies to the Ohio licensing commission prior to displaying them in that state. The company argued that the state's regulation was an impermissible burden on interstate commerce, that it did not provide clear standards for evaluation, and that it violated free-speech clauses in both state and federal constitutions. Before the Supreme Court, the company's counsel had described motion pictures "as graphic expressions of opinion and sentiments, as exponents of policies, as teachers of science and history, as useful, interesting, amusing, educational and moral."[46]

Justice Joseph McKenna, writing for a unanimous Court, however, was unwilling to consider film as a medium of communication similar to speech or press. "They, indeed, may be mediums of thought, but so are many things. So is the theatre, the circus, and all other shows and spectacles, and their performances may be thus brought by the like reasoning under the same immunity from repression or supervision as the public press." To the Court, only rights of property were involved. "It cannot be put out of view that the exhibition of moving pictures is a business pure and simple, originated and conducted for profit, like other spectacles, not to be regarded, . . . we think, as part of the press of the country or as organs of public opinion." Movies, McKenna wrote, were "mere representations of events, of ideas and sentiments published and known, vivid, useful and entertaining no doubt, but, as we have said, capable of evil, having power for it, the greater because of their attractiveness and manner of exhibition."[47] The Supreme Court could find no reason to intervene in state regulation of motion pictures.

Just because the Supreme Court had declined to place motion pictures within the protections offered to freedom of expression on the state and national levels did not mean that individuals stopped arguing for these safeguards. For instance, one of the major themes running through the struggles of D. W. Griffith to obtain clearance for the display of his controversial movie, *The Birth of a Nation,* in 1915, was the idea that motion pictures were a form of expression worthy of constitutional shelter. The movie, which dealt with the Civil War and Reconstruction years and featured the rise of the Ku Klux Klan, encountered opposition on many fronts, including the National Association for the Advancement of Colored People, which protested its demeaning portrayal of blacks.[48]

In defense of his masterpiece, Griffith wrote a tract, "The Rise and Fall of Free Speech in America," in which he argued for identical protection for motion pictures and the printed press. "The moving picture," he wrote, "is simply the pictorial press," which, he said, "claims the same constitutional freedom as the printed press." To Griffith, such protection meant "unjustifiable speech or publication may be punished, but cannot be forbidden in advance." Censorship and its effect on the emerging motion-picture industry was of primary concern for the great film-maker. Continued restrictions, he claimed, are "seriously hampering the growth of the art." The Supreme Court's reasoning when it declared movies outside the protections granted free expression was worthless, Griffith argued. "It is said the motion picture tells its story more vividly than any other art. In other words, we are to be blamed for efficiency, for completeness. Is this justice? Is this common sense? We do not think so." Griffith denied that he wished to "offend with indecencies or obscenities"; all he wanted was the "right, the liberty to show the dark side of wrong that we may illuminate the bright side of virtue—the same liberty that is conceded to art of the written word—that art to which we owe the *Bible* and the works of Shakespeare."[49]

Strangely enough all of the foregoing suppression of ideas and of individuals espousing them occurred during one of the most reform-minded periods in American history. But the reformers were primarily middle-class people with goals suited more toward their station in life than that of the working class. Consequently the problems of the lower classes were left primarily to the radicals, even though the reformers had to know of the lower classes' difficulties. To be sure, reformers of the Progressive era attacked the incursions that big corporations made on American life, but much of their concern focused on the fact that a concentration of wealth made it harder for the middle class to obtain its appropriate share. But not only were the reformers concerned about the problems caused by big business; they also worried about what would happen to their middle-class world should the leftist population of the United States—the Socialists, the members of the IWW, and even those who belonged to the AFL—gain control. If the Progressives sought to help the lower classes it was primarily to keep the radical fringes from gaining a stronger hold and upsetting society with their revolutionary ideas.[50]

Although the Progressive period in the early twentieth century may not have been designed to truly deal with revolutionary ideas, the ideas that were dealt with were substantial. For whatever their reasons, Progressives were interested in the unsafe tenements that housed millions of immigrants, in the tainted supplies of food and medicine that all Americans ingested, and in political corruption. Helping to raise the American consciousness to these problems was a new breed of journalist, the muckraker. The muckraking period of journalism, which ran from about 1902 to 1912, combined the reform movement and investigative journalism in a way never before seen. To some observers, the activity of the press during these years served as the epitome of freedom of the press. Here journalists were using their abilities and the freedoms granted them to focus on the ills of the nation. Although the journalists of the period are much to be praised, their critics would also note that the muckraking phenomenon was also driven by commercial interests. Muckraking journalism was essentially practiced by American magazines that were seeking even more readers and higher profit margins.

Their targets included food adulteration, unscrupulous practices by finance and insurance companies, false and misleading advertising for patent medicines, destruction of natural resources, prison conditions, mistreatment of child labor, and corruption within city government. Famous articles included Lincoln Steffens's "The Shame of the Cities" and Ida Tarbell's "History of Standard Oil." During the ten to twelve years that these investigative journalists were active, they contributed significantly to major reforms including the Pure Food and Drug Act and changes in the life insurance industry. They also gave impetus to the movement for direct election of senators that had been backed by the Populists, to investigations of vice at all levels of government, to prison reform, and to changes in the way in which railroads were operated.

The muckrakers inevitably turned their attention to the newspaper industry in an attempt to evaluate the performance of those who claimed the protection of freedom of the press. Most of the criticism centered on problems caused by journalism's transformation into a big business.[51] Hamilton Holt, managing editor of the *Independent,* a leading muckraking magazine, for instance, levied his criticism directly against advertising's influence on freedom of the press: "Commercialism is at present the greatest menace to freedom of the press."[52]

The financial interests of the publisher and the effect those interests had on journalism also caught the attention of Will Irwin. His fifteen-part series, "The American Newspaper," written for *Collier's,* is the most well-known muckraking attack on the journalism of the day. Newspaper publishers, Irwin said, viewed a newspaper as a private enterprise with its proprietor responsible solely to his own conscience. "They forget, probably, that the extraordinary freedom granted our press is a tacit franchise; and that the payment expected by American society for this franchise is leadership by means of light."[53] Rather, newspaper publishers served wealth, preferring to guard the owners' sources of revenue and social position. As a result, the system suppressed news that would assist progress if it created problems for the publisher's friends and business associates. "Publicly, the controlled newspaper assumes to exercise its ancient office of tribune of the people," Irwin said. "Privately, it serves wealth. Publicly, that it may keep subscribers, it pretends to favor progress; privately, that it may guard its owner's sources of revenue and social position, it suppresses and denatures news which would assist that progress. The system is dishonest to its marrow."[54]

Some critics of the press believed that professionalism among journalists—specifically college training and a written code of ethics—would eliminate most of the problems. Irwin was not so sure. Possibly, he said, legislation was needed—especially to protect the privacy of individuals, which newspapers so freely invaded. "Law," he said, "is the last resort of society, the ultimate social corrective when all others have failed."[55] At some point, he seemed to be implying, the legal system might be called upon to put the press back on the right path if the owners of newspapers were unable or unwilling to take that step for themselves.

The reasons for the attacks were many. Prime among them was the practice of running advertisements that looked like news stories or editorials. These reading notices were preferred by advertisers who felt that the notices were more likely be read. Consequently, readers would be exposed to what they thought was a news story about a miraculous cure for disease that, in reality, was a disguised advertisement for a patent medicine. Some publishers even openly promised a reading notice for every regular advertisement purchased. In the early part of the twentieth century, businesses began using reading notices to shape public opinion on sensitive issues, and publishers were willing participants in this effort to subvert public opinion. Not only did they reap substantial financial rewards for their efforts, but they often pledged not to publish anything detrimental to the industry that advertised as well.[56]

Reading notices finally disappeared as the result of action by the federal government, which gave ammunition to reformers convinced that government intervention was necessary to improve press performance. In 1912, Congress attached a rider to the post office appropriation bill called the Newspaper Publicity Act. The law required that paid reading notices be labeled as advertisements and that ownership of the newspaper and accurate circulation figures be publicly disclosed.[57] The American Newspaper Publishers Association (ANPA) challenged the constitutionality of the law, bringing suit on First and Fifth Amendment grounds. ANPA attorneys joined counsel for the Lewis Publishing Company, publishers of several New York newspapers, in charging that the law was an attempt "*to regulate journalism*" and that exclusion from the mails, which was the punishment for noncompliance, was "*a means of enforcing this censorship of the press.*"[58] Government attorneys, of course, denied any attempt to violate the First Amendment; the law, they said, was only an attempt to establish criteria for use of cheaper second-class mailing rates. Congress, in fact, had argued that second-class mailing rates, which were financed largely by the people, placed additional responsibilities on those who used them.

The Supreme Court, in unanimously upholding the law, said the justices had difficulty believing that the publishers intended "to generally assail as an infringement of the constitutional prohibition against the invasion of the freedom of the press the legislation which for a long series of years has favored the press by discriminating so as to secure to it great pecuniary and other concessions and a wider circulation and consequently a greater sphere of influence."[59] The new law, the Court said, was a constitutional regulation of a privilege that the government saw fit to grant the press. The Lewis Publishing case marked the first attempt of the ANPA to argue an issue on freedom of the press grounds, with the ANPA defining that freedom in terms of the financial interests of the newspaper owners.[60]

Another financial interest of the American press caught the attention of reformers during these years as well. American journalism, James Edward Rogers claimed, had followed in the footsteps of American business and had become concentrated in the hands of a few: "This country is the home of large concentrated enterprises and along with all the rest the press has become centralized." Such concentration concerned Rogers. "The trust tendency among our newspapers is marked," he wrote. "A good many of these owners of our large newspapers possess them not only for the material gain but also for the prestige and power they give. Backed by a newspaper, politically and socially, a man wields immense power in his community."[61]

Rogers was talking about the growth of newspaper chains, a phenomenon well known in the late twentieth century, and the effect the development would have on the independence of the press. The modern chain first appeared in 1880 when E. W. Scripps and his family began purchasing newspapers in the Midwest. As costs for running a newspaper—and possible profit margins—increased, more newspaper owners began to appreciate the economies of scale so well understood by their counterparts in other industries. Newspapers under one owner could share reporters, photographers, advertising, and feature material, and supplies could be purchased in bulk at lower prices. A chain newspaper's fate depended on who owned the chain. If the owner was E. W. Scripps, the newspaper had a fair amount of autonomy. But if the owner was William Randolph Hearst, the newspaper was expected to support the owner's positions on various matters.

As this buying and selling of newspapers continued into the twentieth century, the number of newspapers in the United States dwindled. Starting a new newspaper became almost impossible, and only individuals with millions of dollars could purchase an existing newspaper. Access to the newspaper marketplace of ideas was becoming more restricted. In addition, efforts were ongoing to further standardize the contents of newspapers. The ANPA was pushing for similar page sizes and column widths nationwide to make the interchange of advertising simpler, and feature syndicates were increasing, further reducing the amount of locally produced copy for reader consumption. At a time when the number of ideas that needed discussion had significantly increased, the number of outlets for those ideas had begun to contract. Many outlets that did exist practiced the kind of journalism so decried by their critics. Only establishment views were presented; serious treatment of radical opinions was impossible. Thus, denied access to the public through the pages of respectable newspapers, radical ideas were expressed through acting them out, as with the IWW free-speech fights. The pattern had occurred before and would occur again.

While the newspaper industry was busy trying to fend off intervention in its affairs, one aspect of the communications industry sought minimal regulation in an attempt to avoid further restrictions. Fraudulent advertising had been the target of muckraking journalists for a number of years. Especially vulnerable was advertising for patent medicines that made claims far in excess of their potency and that formed a large percentage of advertising for American newspapers and magazines. Samuel Hopkins Adams started off the war against misleading advertising with a series of articles in *Collier's* called "The Great American Fraud" in October 1905. In his first article, Adams told readers, "Gullible America will spend this year some seventy-five millions of dollars in the purchase of patent medicines. In consideration of this sum it will swallow huge quantities of alcohol, an appalling amount of opiates and narcotics, a wide assortment of varied drugs ranging from powerful and dangerous heart depressants to insidious liver stimulants; and, far in excess of all other ingredients, undiluted fraud." According to Adams, "Fraud, exploited by the skilfulest of advertising bunco men, is the basis of the trade." The way to stop these individuals from preying on the American was public was simple, Adams said. "Should the newspapers, the magazines, and the medical journals refuse their pages to this class of advertisements, the patent medicine business in five years would be as scandalously historic as the South Sea Bubble, and the nation would be the richer not only in lives and money, but in drunkards and drug fiends saved."[62]

Adams's work was followed by an anonymous article in *Collier's* entitled, "The Patent Medicine Conspiracy Against Freedom of the Press." Written by lawyer Mark Sullivan, this article detailed how patent medicine manufacturers had inserted special clauses in contracts with newspapers that called for cancellation of lucrative advertising arrangements should the state in which the newspaper was published enact any laws interfering with the sale of patent medicines. With this clause in place, the manufacturers were able to pressure newspapers into using their editorial clout against proposed legislation.[63]

Such articles led to concern in the growing advertising industry. The profession was relatively new, and its practices were suspect at the outset. To help secure its place in American society and to upgrade its image, advertising practitioners professionalized their ranks. And in 1911, the Associated Advertising Clubs of America proposed a form of self-regulation as token of good faith to the American people and, incidentally, to fend off outside efforts to regulate the business. About the same time, the magazine *Printer's Ink* proposed enactment of a statute aimed at making deceptive advertising a misdemeanor. Although the statute was limited in scope, it was an attempt to clean up the profession. The model statute was introduced in fifteen states by 1913; twenty-three states had adopted it by 1921.[64] Through the *Printer's Ink* Statute and increased efforts of local professional groups, advertising was kept generally free of government regulation despite some support for a national truth-in-advertising statute and the creation of the Federal Trade Commission in 1914.

Old problems appeared right next to new ones during the first part of the twentieth century. One of the least welcomed featured another bout with seditious libel, which had reached its high point in the late eighteenth century with the Alien and Sedition Acts. Attacks on government had been plentiful in the nineteenth century, but few attempts had been made to hold the press responsible for decreasing the esteem in which the people held its officials. But Theodore Roosevelt, one of the first presidents to claim journalists as friends and to attempt to use them to promote his positions, changed all that. For most of his administration, Roosevelt had carefully courted reporters, allowing face-to-face encounters and founding the modern press conference.[65] He had displayed his unhappiness with journalists when a series written by an investigative reporter on corruption in the Senate led to the president's labeling the magazine journalists of the era "muckrakers." That displeasure was mild compared with his anger over stories appearing in the nation's press about the acquisition of land for the Panama Canal. When charges of corruption were connected to the president's brother-in-law and to the brother of Roosevelt's hand-picked successor, presidential candidate William Howard Taft, Roosevelt could no longer contain himself. In a magnificent fit of pique, the president attacked two newspapers for seditious libel.

Americans had long been fascinated by the idea of a canal across Central America. After the Spanish-American War, interest in a canal perked up since the nation now was a Pacific power and needed to move its ships from one ocean to the other with relative ease and quickness. The ideal site was across the isthmus of Panama, but that land was Colombian territory. A French corporation had purchased the rights to use the Panamanian land for a canal in 1889, but by the early twentieth century, the firm had gone bankrupt. The French owners wanted to sell their rights to the United States, but the Colombian government balked at the terms. Representatives of the French interests joined with American financiers to plan the perfect solution: helping Panama secede from Colombia and make its own deal with Americans.[66]

The Panamanian revolution occurred on schedule in November 1903. Within an hour of receiving news that Panama had declared itself an independent nation, the United States recognized the new country and began making plans for building the canal. Problems arose only after some Panamanians began to complain that they had not gotten a fair share of the monetary rewards stemming from the revolution. The Panamanian government had received $10 million for permitting the construction; $40 million went to investors in the bankrupt French company. Later information revealed that much of that $40 million ended up in the pockets of American investors who had pushed the Panamanian site to the exclusion of all others. Joseph Pulitzer's *New York World* ran the first stories charging corruption in the Panama Canal deal but failed to follow up on the allegations. The most critical early commentary on the canal deal came from the *Indianapolis News,* owned by Vice President Charles W. Fairbanks, who Roosevelt had bypassed in endorsing Taft as his successor. The question of the day became "Who got the money?" The answer, the *News* suggested, might not be available until after the election, if at all. The president, enraged at indications of wrongdoing, denied any improprieties and struck back the newspaper carrying the charges.[67]

Roosevelt's response failed to stop the growing tide of criticism. The *New York World* called for an immediate congressional investigation of alleged improprieties.[68] The *World's* editorial blast sent Roosevelt to even further extremes. He soon wrote Henry L. Stimson, U.S. attorney in New York, saying, "I do not know anything about the law of criminal libel, but I should dearly like to have it invoked against Pulitzer, of the *World.* . . . Would you have his various utterances of the last three or four months . . . looked up?"[69] The president also asked state authorities about suing Pulitzer under New York libel laws.

In fact, Roosevelt was so irate that he sent a special message to Congress about the affront to his honor and the dignity of the nation caused by comments in the *Indianapolis News* and the *New York World.* "These stories," the president told Congress, "need no investigation whatever . . . they are in fact wholly and in form partly a libel upon the United States Government." The real culprit in the case, according to Roosevelt, was Joseph Pulitzer, publisher of the *World.* "While the criminal offense of which Mr. Pulitzer has been guilty is in form a libel upon individuals, the great injury done is in blackening the good name of the American people. It should not be left to a private citizen to sue Mr. Pulitzer for libel. He should be prosecuted for libel by the governmental authorities." In fact, said the president, he believed it was "a high national duty to bring to justice this vilifier of the American people, this man who wantonly and wickedly and without one shadow of justice seeks to blacken the character of reputable private citizens and to convict the government of his own country in the eyes of the civilized world of wrong-doing of the basest and foulest kind" without justification or proof.[70]

Pulitzer was unimpressed with the president's challenge. In an editorial the day after Roosevelt's message to Congress, the *World* noted that for the first time a president had "proposed in the absence of specific legislation the criminal prosecution by the Government of citizens who criticized the conduct of the Government, or the conduct of individuals who may have had business dealings with the Government." Roosevelt seemed undeterred by the lack of statutory support for his position, the newspaper said, and "officially proposes to use all of the power of the greatest government on earth to cripple the freedom of the press on the pretext that the Government itself has been libelled—and he is the Government." The editorial closed on a personal note: "So far as the *World* is concerned, its proprietor may go to jail, if Mr. Roosevelt succeeds, as he threatens; but even in jail the *World* will not cease to be a fearless champion of free speech, a free press and a free people. It cannot be muzzled."[71]

Despite its efforts to foreclose the actions on free-press grounds, the *World* did face legal proceedings. In February 1909, a District of Columbia grand jury indicted Joseph Pulitzer, two *World* officers, and the Press Publishing Company, the newspaper's corporate body, on five counts of criminally libeling six men including Theodore Roosevelt himself, financier J. P. Morgan, Douglas Robinson, the Roosevelt's brother-in-law, and Charles P. Taft, the president-elect's brother. Two representatives of the *Indianapolis News* were indicted on seven counts. In March 1909, on the day Roosevelt left office, a federal grand jury in New York indicted the *World* and two of its editors for having circulated twenty-nine copies of the offending publication on the grounds of the military reservation at West Point and for passing it through U.S. post offices. The charges were based on an 1825 statute, as amended in 1898, that required the government to protect its reservations from malicious injury. The U.S. attorney argued that each issue of the offending newspaper constituted a new offense and could merit adding another count to the indictment. The portents were grim for newspapers if circulation on any of the nation's military outposts could open the way for prosecution on criminal libel charges.

With the indictments delivered, Theodore Roosevelt went off to Africa for a round of big-game hunting. The prosecutions continued. The first break in the case came in October 1910 when a federal judge in Indianapolis threw the charges against the *News* out of court on the grounds that the government could not constitutionally indict persons in the nation's capital for a crime allegedly committed in Indianapolis. Judge A. B. Anderson, in dismissing the charges, noted that the Panama Canal scandal involved "a great public question" about which "there are many very peculiar circumstances." The American people "were interested in the construction of a canal. It was a matter of great public concern. It was much discussed." Thus, said Judge Anderson, "we have this situation: Here was a matter of great public interest, public concern. I was interested in it. You were interested in it. We were all interested in it. Here was a newspaper printing the news, or trying to. Here was this matter up for discussion."[72] The newspapers, then, were simply trying to do their jobs as facilitators of public debate. Roosevelt, upon hearing of Judge Anderson's decision, denounced him as "a jackass and a crook."[73] Other law enforcement officers apparently agreed with Anderson's assessment. The U.S. attorney for Indianapolis resigned rather than continue the case against the newspaper and its editors. The state district attorney in New York City already had declined to bring action against the *World* in state court.

With the case against the *News* over, attention turned to the *New York World*. In January 1910, a U.S. district court judge quashed the indictment against the newspaper and its top management on the grounds that the federal statute relied upon was inapplicable. If the case were pursued, said the judge, the application of the act would be found unconstitutional. Although Pulitzer had won, he would not be satisfied until he had gained the sanction of the U.S. Supreme Court. The government appealed the decision, only to be told in January 1911 that the district court judge was correct. If Roosevelt wanted to pursue Pulitzer, said the Court, action under state libel laws was the only permissible avenue.[74]

Pulitzer was delighted with the decision. The *World* termed the Supreme Court decision "the most sweeping victory won for freedom of speech and of the press since the American people destroyed the Federalist party more than a century ago for enacting the infamous Sedition law." The statement was rather far-reaching because the Court did not engage in any side comments on the role of the press and made no comment about freedom of the press in its restricted opinion. Nevertheless, the *World* proclaimed that the decision "is so sweeping that no other President will be tempted to follow in the footsteps of Theodore Roosevelt, no matter how greedy he may be for power, no matter how resentful of opposition."[75] Theodore Roosevelt refused to comment on the decision.

Although the picture of society painted in the foregoing pages is one of basic intolerance to ideas that might challenge the basic order, by the late nineteenth and early twentieth century, signs began appearing that a greater understanding of freedom of expression was emerging in various parts of the country. In part, these changes were initiated by increasing numbers of dissident groups who were demanding their fundamental right to speak. Repeated denial of that right slowly became less acceptable as concern for minorities and their needs started to appear. In part, these changes were also due to numerous challenges from the institutional press, which had the money and the social standing to demand that state and federal protections for freedom of the press mean something more than a safeguard against prior restraint. Slowly, individuals in municipal and state governments, on courts in various jurisdictions, and in law schools began to argue that a greater freedom of expression not only was consonant with our constitutional guarantees but was absolutely essential for national development.[76]

By the late nineteenth century, courts had addressed few free-speech issues and had provided almost no guidance in the interpretation of constitutional guarantees. The U.S. Supreme Court had been preoccupied with other matters, and the idea that the Bill of Rights protected individuals was years in the future. The Court, in fact, had had the opportunity to apply the Bill of Rights to the states in 1833. The case, *Barron v. Baltimore,* involved a claim that the city of Baltimore had violated the Fifth Amendment's prohibition against the taking of private property for public use without just compensation to the owner. Chief Justice John Marshall disagreed, and in one of his last opinions, wrote that state residents must depend on state bills of rights for protection. Of the federal Bill of Rights, Marshall wrote for a unanimous bench: "These amendments contain no expression indicating an intention to apply them to the state governments."[77]

State courts, however, were active in the free-speech area, but our understanding of just how these jurists functioned in this important arena still is limited. State judges relied on decisions from other jurisdictions, on the few legal treatises in existence that touched on free-speech issues, on history, and often on common sense as bases for their decisions. In the area of freedom of the press, many of their decisions were governed by what they determined to be the "good motives" and "justifiable ends" of the publication involved. These terms had been introduced into the law of libel by Alexander Hamilton in 1805 and had become popular yardsticks over the years. Unfortunately, these terms protected only a narrow range of expression. With other expressive activities, state court judges were guided by the prevailing attitude that majority interests should triumph over individual or minority interests. This, too, led to restrictive interpretations of permissible activities when minorities sought protection.[78]

To a large extent, these state court judges were limited by their teachers. Sir William Blackstone still influenced court decisions, and his 1765 view that freedom of the press "consists in laying no *previous* restraints upon publications, and not in freedom from censure for criminal matter when published"[79] continued to dominate legal thinking. American legal commentators adapted Blackstone's restrictive interpretation to the new national experience. Thus, James Kent, chancellor of the state of New York, talked of how the "liberal communication of sentiment, and entire freedom of discussion, in respect to the character and conduct of public men, and of candidates for public favour" was "essential to the judicious exercise of the right of suffrage, and of that control over their rulers, which resides in the free people of these United States." Even so, he cautioned, Americans had accepted as a constitutional principle the idea that "every citizen may freely speak, write, and publish his sentiments, on all subjects, being responsible for the abuse of that right."[80]

Another leading commentator on American law during these years, Supreme Court Justice Joseph Story, voiced similar beliefs. The idea that the First Amendment "was intended to secure to every citizen an absolute right to speak, or write, or print, whatever he might please, without any responsibility, public or private, therefor [*sic*], is a supposition too wild to be indulged in by any rational man," he said. Rather, the protection of freedom of expression "imports no more, than that every man shall have a right to speak, write, and print his opinions upon any subject whatsoever, without any prior restraint, so always, that he does not injure any other person[,] . . . disturb the public peace, or attempt to subvert the government."[81]

Consequently, the available scholarship and much of the immediate history of freedom of expression provided restrictive precedents for courts to use in adjudicating free-expression matters. These materials were applied to cases involving labor union organizers and members, anarchists, Socialists, religious minorities, editors and publishers, movie distributors, government employees, and candidates for office. The majority of the decisions rejected the free-speech claim no matter how it was presented. In many cases, judges would specifically ignore the issue, refusing to even comment on the argument.

Even so, these state court opinions made several common points. Prime among them was that the free-speech provisions of state and national constitutions did not protect the abusive use of speech. Courts, for example, could restrict obnoxious speech in public places and issue injunctions to stop labor union threats to the business's well-being. Judges also were willing to hold newspapers responsible for libel and contempt of court with little regard for the impact those decisions had on freedom of the press.

One of the most important concepts emerging from state court adjudication was the willingness of the judicial system to allow infringements of expressive activities based upon the police power of state and local governments. This police power allowed governmental authorities to limit activities deemed to be harmful to a citizen's health, safety, and moral well-being. Under the police power, governments were permitted to engage in a wide range of repressive functions. Courts allowed the regulation of motion pictures and of obscenity under this concept. Police power also justified forbidding speakers from addressing audiences in public places. Unauthorized parades in public streets also could be banned, as could picketing in labor disputes and distributing circulars. State courts routinely determined that public property was for the use of the entire public and not for the use of disgruntled minorities who wanted to upset the peace of mind and ease of transit of majorities.[82] For instance, Oliver Wendell Holmes, Jr., sitting on the Massachusetts supreme court, upheld the decision of officials to bar preaching on Boston Commons in 1895, saying, "For the Legislature absolutely or conditionally to forbid public speaking in a highway or public park is no more an infringement of the rights of a member of the public than for the owner of a private house to forbid it in his house."[83]

Public streets, however, were important to minorities who could not afford to hire a hall to present their messages. Oftentimes, even if the group had the money, a hall would not be available to individuals of their peculiar interests. And, frankly, minority groups needed to come in contact with the general public in order to win converts. Speaking in a hall usually meant speaking to persons who already were adherents to the cause. Numerous decisions denying access to public places led to repeated calls from religious and political minorities, attorneys, and some judges for the development of a doctrine that would allow the use of public highways, parks, and other facilities for the communication of ideas. Slowly, the idea that the out-of-doors could serve as a public forum appeared. Or, perhaps more correctly, the idea reappeared. Americans during the colonial and revolutionary periods strongly believed in outdoor public activities to win public support for their causes. As meetings grew more disruptive in the abolitionist period, they fell into disfavor.

Movement toward opening up public facilities to minority interests depended almost entirely on the social acceptability of the group seeking permission to communicate. The greatest strides at the end of the nineteenth century were made by the Salvation Army, which at first was considered a fringe religious group. Initially, the Army was barred from parading and playing music in the streets because people and horses were upset by the sounds. As the Army gained acceptance, it won permission to hold functions on the city streets. A Michigan court in 1886 discussed the importance of the streets for the Salvation Army's effort to communicate, saying, "It has been customary, from time immemorial, in all free countries, and in most civilized countries, for people who are assembled for common purpose to parade together, by day or reasonable hours at night, with banners and other paraphernalia, and with music of various kinds." Such activities are designed to keep "unity of feeling and enthusiasm, and frequently to produce some effect on the public mind by the spectacle of union and numbers. They are a natural product and exponent of common aims, and valuable factors in furthering them." Because the goal was to win new adherents, spectators were absolutely essential. And because of the long history of public demonstrations, municipal governments had dealt with them without any special repressive legislation, the court said. Consequently, special rules to restrict access to public streets now were impermissible.[84] The Salvation Army had won a major case that would lead to other victories around the country. But the success of the Salvation Army did not lead to success for anarchists or union members to parade; the latter groups were still socially unacceptable.

Arguments persisted that the streets and parks of a community could be used for communication. As the public-forum notion picked up supporters, advocates argued that demonstrations could be limited solely by reasonable and non-discriminatory restrictions on the time, place, and manner of meetings. Courts did begin to become less tolerant of efforts to stop the use of public facilities when it was clear that the police power had been exercised solely as a means of suppression. The use of nondiscriminatory time, place, and manner restrictions became the favored standard of evaluation of the Supreme Court and still is used to determine the reasonableness of regulations affecting public demonstrations today.

Confusing the issue where activities concerning the public forum are concerned, however, was the developing judicial attitude on the right of individuals and businesses to have their freedom to conduct business unencumbered by outsiders. Many actions in this area focused on the activities of labor unions that were striving for recognition and reform in the workplace. In case after case, courts decided that the rights of business owners to enjoy the fruits of their property—past, present, or future profits, or community goodwill—outweighed the rights of workers to inform the public about work-related grievances. The workers' cases, by the way, generally were not argued on expressive grounds. A worker's right to picket simply was less important in the scheme of things than an employer's right to enjoy his property.

State court judges also began dealing with what could, in nineteenth- and early twentieth-century terms, be regarded as dangerous speech. Presentations by anarchists generally fell into this category. The doctrine that was used to justify suppression of such speech was whether the words used had the tendency to bring about unacceptable behavior. Bad tendency, in these cases, was defined as the possibility, however remote, that something awful might happen as a result of the speech. The evil did not have to be imminent; all that was necessary was for the fear to exist. This bad tendency doctrine was used in federal courts to suppress speech of dangerous individuals as well. Well into the twentieth century, judges could be found who sent people to jail on the grounds that their speech might at some time in the future lead individuals to behave in socially unacceptable ways. Arguments that there should be a close connection between speech and action were made to no avail.

Some state courts considered a number of issues decades before the U.S. Supreme Court heard similar cases. And in many cases, these precursors to Supreme Court decisions at least considered the role of speech and press in society. State courts, for instance, dealt with prior restraint, which did not reach the Supreme Court until 1931;[85] with the extent to which obscene material would be protected by free-speech guarantees, which did not reach the Supreme Court until 1957;[86] with the extent of excusable falsehood in libelous stories about public officials, which did not reach the Supreme Court until 1964;[87] and with journalist's privilege, which did not reach the Supreme Court until 1972.[88] In other cases, state courts explored the relationship between free speech and political rights, nondiscriminatory business regulation of newspapers, symbolic speech, offensive language, and the right to a fair trial. Many of the early First Amendment cases heard by the U.S. Supreme Court are filled with references to state court decisions on the same issues.

The Supreme Court was essentially silent on free-expression issues prior to 1917. One scholar has analyzed the Court's case load and determined that justices heard twelve cases involving speech and press issues between 1791 and

1889 and fifty-three cases on those topics between 1890 and 1917.[89] We have already accounted for the major reasons for this lack of cases, but in 1868, a new amendment was added to the Constitution that might have changed the situation. The Fourteenth Amendment, ratification of which was required for Southern states to rejoin the Union after the Civil War, read in part, "No State shall make or enforce any law which shall abridge the privileges or immunities of citizens of the United States; nor shall any State deprive any person of life, liberty, or property, without due process of law; nor deny to any person within its jurisdiction the equal protection of the laws."[90]

Exactly what the phrasing of that amendment meant was significantly in doubt. Immediate attention focused on language granting citizenship to freed slaves. But within the language preventing states from abridging the privileges and immunities of citizens of the United States might have been found a way to make the guarantees of the Bill of Rights applicable to the states,[91] where much of the suppression occurred. The Supreme Court stifled such speculation when it ruled in 1873 that citizenship in the United States and citizenship in a state were quite different things. The Fourteenth Amendment applied solely to whatever rights accrued to national citizenship.[92] Through this decision, the Supreme Court virtually stripped the privileges and immunities clause of any meaning.

With the use of the First Amendment as a bar to state infringement on speech and press out of the question, the question became whether the First Amendment provided any protection when laws of the United States were concerned. The Supreme Court once again showed that individuals in these years could have little hope for help from the federal government when it came to free-speech rights. In 1876, a group of free blacks in Louisiana attempted to assemble to plan political action, and a group of whites launched a campaign of intimidation to bar such activity. The Supreme Court ruled that the Fourteenth Amendment did not protect individuals seeking to exercise their rights to associate from private individuals seeking to halt their activities. Constitutional guarantees applied only to official actions by the state against individuals.[93]

Where questions of federal governmental power were properly presented, as in the right of Congress to exclude lottery materials from the mails, the Supreme Court upheld these possible incursions into freedom of expression.[94] The Court also upheld the right of Congress to impose a variety of restrictions on members of the Church of Jesus Christ of the Latter Day Saints (the Mormons) in order to stamp out the hated practice of polygamy.[95] And the Supreme Court also approved of congressional efforts to reform the system under which federal employees worked. Included in the reform measure were provisions barring most workers from participating in political activities and thus denying them their rights of political speech. Congress, the Court said, was within its power to enact such legislation.[96]

Although Supreme Court justices had not dealt with many free-expression cases prior to World War I, parties in the cases continued to bring the issues before the high court, hoping, perhaps, to present just the argument that would win judicial protection for expressive activities. Even though no protection was forthcoming in these cases, the argument that the First Amendment had some meaning was being placed before the Court with increasing frequency. From time to time, the cases even required the justices to address the issue. In *Patterson v. Colorado*,[97] two members of the Supreme Court squared off against one another in discussing the possible meaning of the protections provided by the First Amendment. The case involved contempt of court, the second greatest threat to the ability of newspapers to report the news after libel. In contempt cases involving journalists the issue usually did not involve misbehavior within the courtroom; rather, the issue was indirect or constructive contempt—offenses that occurred outside of the courtroom that judges believed had an impact on the conduct of a trial over which they were presiding. With journalists, the offense generally consisted of a news story or an editorial that was deemed prejudicial.

The federal government had attempted to limit the ability of judges to cite journalists for indirect contempt in 1831, when Congress enacted a statute designed to restrict the judge's power over contempt of court to actions that occurred "in the presence of the said courts, or so near thereto as to obstruct the administration of justice."[98] The law was the result of an attempt to impeach a federal judge who used his contempt power indiscriminately to quiet opponents of his actions in the community. After failing to remove the judge, Congress limited a judge's power over contempt to actions occurring within the courtroom.[99] Many states copied the language of the federal statute, and for many years, contempt of court citations against journalists almost disappeared.

With the rise of more intrusive journalism, contempt cases reappeared. In the Patterson case, the newspaper publisher claimed that he was simply fulfilling his public obligation by criticizing the court's behavior. Judges sitting on the case decided that the articles and cartoons that Patterson published tended to lower the community's respect for the judicial system and adversely affected the administration of justice. The U.S. Supreme Court agreed, upholding the state court's decision in 1907. The fact that a seven-man majority of the Court decided to vindicate the honor of the judicial system is not what makes *Patterson* so interesting; the decision was almost a foregone conclusion given the understanding of the law at the time.

The most important aspect of *Patterson* rests in an argument between members of the Court on the meaning of the First Amendment. Justice Oliver Wendell Holmes, Jr., writing for the majority, refused to look at the idea that the First Amendment might be applied to the state through the Fourteenth Amendment. Change was in the wind, however, as the dissent of Justice John Marshall Harlan indicated. Harlan, for some time a vigorous dissenter on civil liberties issues, saw the need to make the protections of the Bill of Rights applicable to the states. His vehicle for accomplishing this end was the Fourteenth Amendment, and he would turn these guarantees into attributes of national citizenship that could not be abridged by states: "It is, I think, impossible to conceive of liberty, as secured by the Constitution against hostile action, whether by the Nation or by the States, which does not embrace the right to enjoy free speech and the right to have a free press."[100] Harlan was some sixteen years ahead of his time when it came to the application of free-expression guarantees in the Bill of Rights to the states. The Court would make that move, finally, in 1925. Protection for journalists to comment on pending court cases would be far later in coming, with the first real breaches in the impenetrable shield that protected judges from criticism coming in the 1940s.[101]

In the meantime, efforts continued to win support for expressive activities on a variety of fronts. Among those contributing to an increased understanding of the value of freedom of speech were a number of legal scholars who argued that open debate would benefit a growing society. Writing primarily around the turn of the century, these scholars, who included Thomas Cooley, Theodore Schroeder, and Ernst Freund, took somewhat different paths toward the same objective: greater freedom of expression.[102]

Cooley, who was the earliest writer, began his career as a judicial commentator at mid-century. His study of the law of torts or civil wrongs soon became a standard citation in state court cases. One of his goals was to free the press from the limited Blackstonian definition of its freedoms. "Freedom of discussion [must] be permitted," he wrote, "but there must be exemption afterward from liability for any publication made in good faith, and in the belief in its truth, the making of which, if true, would be justified by the occasion."[103] In his study on constitutional limitations, Cooley argued that greater freedom was essential for the press because of expectations placed on that medium by the public. Readers demanded that the publisher "shall daily spread before his readers a complete summary of the events transpiring in the world, public or private, so far as those readers can reasonably be supposed to take an interest in them; and he who does not comply with this demand must give way to him who will." In addition, readers "demand and expect accounts of every important meeting, of every important trial, and of all the events which have a bearing upon trade and business, or upon political affairs. It is impossible that these shall be given in all cases without matters being mentioned derogatory to individuals."[104] Because of the new standing of the press, new approaches must be found to dealing with it.

To Theodore Schroeder, who argued repeatedly with Anthony Comstock about the need for free speech in sexually related matters, society had become so complex that greater freedom of expression in all realms was necessary. The crux of freedom of speech to Schroeder was "that every idea, no matter how unpopular, so far as the law is concerned, shall have the same opportunity as every other idea, no matter how popular, to secure public favor." To support his ideas, Schroeder began historical research, and from his studies he deduced "that the unabridged freedom of speech guaranteed by the Federal Constitution implies a guarantee of impunity even in the advocacy of resistance to our Government as a whole and by a necessary implication it guarantees impunity in the fruitless and harmless advocacy of lesser crimes."[105] This historical investigation brought Schroeder to the conclusion that radicals must be allowed to speak—even if they advocated the abolition of government as it then existed.

In supporting his conclusion, Schroeder looked to the Declaration of Independence, which, he noted, "affirms that 'whenever any form of government becomes destructive of these ends [liberty, justice, etc.,] it is the right of the people to alter or to abolish it.'" He combined this clause from the Declaration of

Independence with the constitutionally guaranteed right to bear arms, right to free speech, and difficult-to-prove treason clauses to conclude that the Constitution "was designed to maintain an equality of intellectual opportunity between those who might wish to uphold and those who would overthrow the government."[106] Should that evidence be insufficient, Schroeder quoted Thomas Jefferson, who wrote in 1787, "I hold it that a little rebellion now and then is a good thing, & as necessary in the political world as storms in the physical. . . . And observation of this truth should render honest republican governors so mild in their punishment of rebellions, as not to discourage them too much. It is a medicine necessary for the sound health of government."[107] Jefferson kept his faith in citizens' rising against unjust governments later that year when he wrote: "What country before ever existed a century & a half without a rebellion? & what country can preserve it's [*sic*] liberties if their rulers are not warned from time to time that their people preserve the spirit of resistance?" In fact, said Jefferson, "Let them take arms. The remedy is to set them right as to facts, pardon & pacify them. What signify a few lives lost in a century or two? The tree of liberty must be refreshed from time to time with the blood of patriots & tyrants."[108] Although Schroeder agreed with Jefferson on the need to allow citizens to resist governments considered unjust, he seemed to stop short of encouraging violence. Instead, he would give individuals "the right to say with impunity anything and everything which any one chooses to say, and to speak it with impunity so long as no actual material injury results to any one, and when it results then only to punish for contribution to that material injury and not for the mere speech as such."[109]

Others writing during this time began to agree with this position. Ernst Freund, for instance, in his study on the police power, noted that "freedom of political discussion is merely a phrase if it must stop short of questioning the fundamental ideas of politics, law and government. Otherwise every government is justified in drawing the line of free discussion at those principles or institutions, which it deems essential to its perpetuation." Even czarist Russia could agree with that interpretation, Freund noted. Instead, "it is of the essence of political liberty that it may create disaffection or other inconvenience to the existing government, otherwise there would be no merit in tolerating it." Toleration, he stressed, "is not based upon generosity, but on sound policy: on the consideration, namely, that ideas are not suppressed by suppressing their free and public discussion, and that such discussion alone can render them harmless and remove the excuse for illegality by giving hope of their realisation by lawful means." While permitting the free discussion of numerous ideas currently being suppressed by government and society at large, Freund drew the line at incitement to crime and violence. The problem, though, rested in how to determine whether crime and violence came from the ideas espoused or from "morbid brooding over conditions which are the cause of social discontent." Great care needed to be taken lest in suppressing crime and violence government also quieted ideas that should be heard.[110]

Greater discrimination among ideas and greater toleration for dissident thought, however, were decades off. As World War I approached, American society had been beset by forty-odd years of concerted efforts to make all elements in the nation conform to more conservative standards. Fear was a key weapon used in this attack on different individuals and unusual ideas. The unknown was a cause of apprehension; to calm the nerves, repression was the order of the day. The idea that revolutionary ideas should be given a chance to be heard, discussed, disputed, and accepted or rejected simply was unacceptable. An honest evaluation of society just before World War I, though, would show a nation far more diverse ever before—despite efforts to eliminate nonconformist ideas and individuals. Attempts to limit the diversity present in the country would continue throughout World War I, with society becoming even more repressive, if possible, as the nation entered the fighting. Despite or perhaps because of these repressive activities, the variety of ideas present in America would continue to grow.

CHAPTER 3

Making the World Safe for Democracy: Freedom of Expression during World War I

The American descent into World War I was long in the making. Between 1914, when the war started in Europe, and 1917, when America entered the fray, Woodrow Wilson worked to keep the nation out of the conflict that had overwhelmed the European continent. His goal, he told Congress in August 1914 shortly after the fighting began, was to keep the United States "neutral in fact as well as in name during these days that are to try men's souls. We must," he said, "be impartial in thought as well as in action, must put a curb upon our sentiments as well as upon every transaction that might be construed as a preference of one party to the struggle before another."[1] Despite his best efforts, the United States slowly was drawn into the conflict; American policy tipped more and more toward the Allies, and intermittent crises with Germany cemented that bond.[2]

Almost three years passed before war finally engulfed the United States, and when it did, the nation was badly divided. Between 1914 and 1917, a strong opposition to American involvement had developed. With each step that Wilson took to aid the Allies or to encourage American military preparedness, the opposition grew even stronger, although it never managed to win majority support. In like manner, backing for American entry increased, capturing national allegiance along the way. As the war drew nearer, Wilson knew that U.S. entry would cause substantial problems for Americans who disagreed with the decision, but he had exhausted his options. "Once lead this people into war," he said, "and they'll forget there ever was such a thing as tolerance." Speaking just days before the congressional declaration, he added, "To fight you must be brutal and ruthless, and the spirit of ruthless brutality will enter into the very fibre of our national life, infecting Congress, the courts, the policeman on the beat, the man in the street."[3] The nation was not well known for its tolerance before 1917; the coming of war on April 6, 1917, only heightened those feelings.[4]

Perceptive Americans had watched the war clouds gathering. Criticism of governmental actions mounted with each presidential decision that made American entry more likely. Many of those opposed to Wilson's course were convinced that the nation was being manipulated into war by expert British propaganda and by bankers and munitions makers who stood to profit handsomely by American participation. Others argued a more traditional pacifist line, stating that war itself was a crime and should be outlawed. Conscription, which became the way in which the army was raised, was heartily despised in some quarters. Still others doubted the validity of the unannounced war aims of the Allies; many dissenters felt that Americans would simply be fighting to preserve a corrupt European system in which empire, hegemony, and secret alliances predominated. Some opponents of war claimed that their opinions represented the national view and that any declaration of war should be placed before the people on a national referendum. Even before war was declared, those demanding that the United States stay out of the conflict were criticized for their opinions. After war was declared, opponents were seen as national enemies who should be firmly suppressed.

Wilson's desire to stifle criticism of his wartime plans and programs was born out of necessity. If he wanted to lead a united country into war, Wilson knew that voices of discontent had to be silenced. He used all the powers available to him—his own considerable rhetorical abilities, legislation enacted by Congress and augmented by measures passed by states, and the general fervor of the American people—to accomplish his ends. His targets included the already familiar Socialists and members of the Industrial Workers of the World; with the coming of war, the list of individuals, groups, and ideas to be suppressed expanded to include pacifists and hyphenated Americans—particularly German-Americans and Irish-Americans.

Pacifists might seem to be the most unusual dissident group to merit presidential condemnation, but the espousal of peace in wartime was dangerous. Although peace organizations had been active in the United States for generations, until the start of the European war in 1914, they had posed little threat to national interests. Prior to 1914, however, the peace movement had gained respectability. Among its leading proponents was steel magnate Andrew Carnegie, who as its leading financier had established the Carnegie Endowment for International Peace to endorse the abolition of war as a means for solving international disagreements. Elihu Root, who had served as secretary of war for Presidents William McKinley and Theodore Roosevelt and as secretary of state for Roosevelt, had won the Nobel Peace Prize in 1912 for his efforts to establish the International Court of Justice.[5]

But pacifists encountered difficulties when the war started in Europe. As with other opponents of war, many pacifists quickly became caught up in the nationalism of the moment and supported the president in light of the deepening world crisis. Other American pacifists maintained their opposition to war and joined together to form the American Union Against Militarism (AUAM), which published thousands of pieces of literature against the war and sent speakers out to denounce Wilson's efforts to build up American military power. Prior to American entry into the war, the AUAM worked against all preparedness efforts, campaigned against plans to impose conscription to build an army, and argued for the United States to remain neutral. Although Wilson had proclaimed his intentions to keep the United States out of the European conflict, pacifists were not so sure that he would be able to keep his word. Thus, they did everything they could to help him. In 1915, for instance, automobile maker Henry Ford sent a peace delegation to Europe in an attempt to mediate the differences among the warring nations. And William Jennings Bryan, who served as secretary of state, lobbied the president and his advisers to take all steps possible to remain out of the conflict. When he failed to moderate the president's response to the *Lusitania* crisis in 1915, Bryan resigned and became involved in an active peace campaign.[6]

When America actually entered the war, the peace movement fragmented once again. One section, perhaps the largest, was captured by Wilson's vision of world affairs and supported the war effort, pledging to work for a new international order after the conflict that would make further wars unnecessary. AUAM leaders announced that the organization would cease opposition to the war and would drop its unequivocal opposition to military conscription. They pledged instead to seek the most liberal draft bill possible, especially in terms of exemptions for conscientious objectors. The day after the Selective Service Act was passed, AUAM staff member Roger N. Baldwin organized a Bureau of Conscientious Objectors to assist those seeking CO status. After AUAM members voiced fears that Baldwin's activities could hurt the parent organization's reputation, Baldwin changed the name of his group to the Civil Liberties Bureau and sought to help anyone caught in the net of wartime repression. Finding the project still unpopular, Baldwin led a number of sympathetic AUAM members from that organization in October 1917 to set up the National Civil Liberties Bureau, the immediate forerunner of the American Civil Liberties Union.

Other pacifists working with COs likewise encountered difficulty. In 1915, the Anti-Enlistment League began, forerunner of the War Resisters League, which was started in 1923. Its members pledged not to enlist during the war. The Anti-Enlistment League did not survive the passage of the Selective Service Act and disbanded in 1917. The Fellowship of Reconciliation, likewise founded in 1915, became the major pacifist organization during the war years and beyond. Many of its members endured imprisonment for refusing induction into the military service and for counseling others to behave similarly.

Although the influence of the peace movement was slight after the declaration of war and the enactment of the Selective Service Act, President Wilson maintained his criticism of it. In his Flag Day speech of June 14, 1917, the president equated the advocacy of peace and pacifism during wartime with treason. The peace movement, he said, was a "new intrigue," and its supporters were tools of German masters. These individuals could "make no headway" in the United States, he said, because "this is a People's War, a war for freedom and justice and self-government amongst all the nations of the world, a war to make the world safe for the peoples who live upon it and have made it their own." Opponents of the war were doomed, the president said. "Woe be to the man or group of men that seeks to stand in our way in this day of high resolution when every principle we hold dearest is to be vindicated and made secure for the salvation of the nations."[7]

Nor was Wilson overly committed to the rights of immigrant Americans. He was particularly harsh on two groups during the war years—Irish-Americans and German-Americans. The problems encountered by the former are less known than those of the latter, but they were substantial. Irish-Americans were particularly suspect because of the hatred that many of them had for Great Britain. The 1910 census reported that of 92 million people counted, some 4.5 million residents were either Irish immigrants or their first-generation children; the total number of Americans that could claim Irish ancestry was between 15 million and 20 million. Consequently, when Wilson contemplated joining Great Britain in a war against Germany, he faced a potentially sizable resistance. He once pointedly criticized Irish-Americans as individuals who "need[ed] hyphens in their names because only part of them has come over."[8]

Wilson's criticisms of the Irish-Americans meshed well with the nativist sentiment that captured a great number of Americans in the early twentieth century. As the nation became involved in World War I, Wilson turned his attention to German-Americans. The 1910 census placed the total number of residents with close blood ties to Germany at more than 8 million—26 percent of the total white foreign stock. Most second-generation German-Americans considered themselves more American than German, but that fact made little difference to the president. When the war broke out in Europe, many German-Americans felt obliged to support Germany, if only to counter British propaganda. As a result, by fall 1915, a full-fledged campaign was under way against hyphenism as exemplified by the German-Americans. President Wilson, for instance, in a December speech on preparedness, talked about hyphenated Americans "who have sought to bring the authority and good name of our Government into contempt, to destroy our industries wherever they thought it effective for their vindictive purposes to strike at them, and to debase our policies to the uses of foreign intrigue."[9] Former President Theodore Roosevelt, an unabashed nativist, joined in the condemnation of German-Americans in June 1916, saying that "the professional German-Americans . . . are acting purely in the sinister interest of Germany. They have shown their eager readiness to sacrifice the interests of the United States whenever its interest conflicts with that of Germany. They represent that adherence to the politico-racial hyphen which is the badge and sign of moral treason."[10] The hyphen was the sign of un-Americanism, pure and simple. One could be American or one could be German; one could not be German-American.

American Socialists also faced the problem of divided loyalties as war approached. While only Europe was embroiled, most Socialists were united in denouncing the war and in calling for President Wilson to negotiate an end to the fighting. The war, said the Socialists, was started by the ruling classes of Europe for the sole purpose of further mistreating the working classes. As the war came closer, American Socialists split. A sizable minority, primarily the intellectuals, abandoned the party's traditional antiwar position and supported the war effort. Although war was to be opposed generally, these intellectuals reasoned that once the United States finally endorsed Allied interests, Americans should support the government until German militarism was destroyed. Finding the right response to the war was difficult for the majority of Socialists. They reacted to each new crisis, but they had no plan to rely on should the United States actually declare war. American Socialists had watched in horror as the Socialist parties of Europe, similarly unprepared, had abandoned their antiwar principles to become ardent patriots serving national interests. Not wanting to face such a situation, American Socialists called a national convention for April 7, 1917, to establish a position on which they could all agree. The convention met the day after war had been declared, and the product of its labors placed the Socialist party near the top of the list of organizations to be suppressed.[11]

Heading the list of groups to be repressed during the war, however, was the Industrial Workers of the World. Throughout its history, the organization had taken strong positions against militarism and patriotism. Members did not change their approach as the crisis deepened in Europe; if anything they stepped up their rhetoric in an effort to counter the growing patriotism of other Americans. IWW leaders advised members to stay at home to fight the only worthwhile war—the one against their employers. This language increased as Wobbly leaders saw European workers caught up in patriotic fervor much as the European Socialists were. At their 1916 convention, IWW members adopted a resolution against all wars. Although no official action was taken, talk at the convention was heated. Members suggested a massive protest, perhaps even a general strike, should war be declared. Fearful of governmental retribution, IWW leaders took a more cautious official line, recommending, for instance, against a formal statement on whether members should report for the draft. In fact, 95 percent of those Wobblies who were eligible for the draft registered, and most of those who were called served. But the rhetoric was remembered—and when it was buttressed by strikes in essential food, lumber, and copper industries in the spring and summer of 1917, the radical union became the prime target for repression.[12]

As war approached, the Wilson administration began putting in place a comprehensive internal security program. By the end of the war, more than 1,900 prosecutions had been inaugurated for speeches, newspaper articles, books, and pamphlets seen as opposing the war. More than 800 individuals were convicted under various wartime statutes, and most of them remained in prison well after the war ended in 1918. In addition, more than 100 publications were barred from the mails by the postmaster general, the most extensive such interference in American history.

Each suppressive act was built on fear. Concern for the president's physical well-being, for example, led Congress to enact the Threats Against the President Act, which punished individuals who "knowingly or willfully" made "any threat to take the life of or to inflict bodily harm upon the President of the United States."[13] Some sixty cases were prosecuted under this act before June 1918, with at least thirty-five people being convicted—mostly for expressive activities. Apprehensive about possible dangers posed by foreigners in the United States, the president issued a Proclamation Regarding Alien Enemies, which was based on the Alien Enemies Act of 1798. Its provisions included restrictions on their right to criticize the American government or its policies. The Justice Department registered these individuals; more than 6,000 alien enemies were arrested, with more than 2,000 people being interned by the military as being potentially dangerous to national security.[14] Fears about the loyalty of federal employees led to a confidential executive order that authorized department heads to discharge any employee considered a loyalty risk because of "his conduct, sympathies, or utterances, or because of other reasons growing out of the war."[15]

Despite these moves, President Wilson remained obsessed by the possibility that the Germans might try to build support for their cause in the United States. Even as Wilson asked Congress to declare war, he showed apprehension about the activities of German agents who have "filled our unsuspecting communities and even our offices of government with spies and set criminal intrigues everywhere afoot against our national unity of counsel, our peace within and without, our industries and our commerce." He feared disloyalty within the country and promised, "if there should be disloyalty, it will be dealt with with a firm hand of stern repression." But the president hoped that "if it lifts its head at all, it will lift it only here and there without countenance except from a lawless and malignant few."[16] The suppression of the malignant few was the goal of the Espionage Act of 1917.

Much of the language of the Espionage Act deals, quite naturally, with the work of spies passing sensitive information to the enemy. But hidden within its provisions was the language that led to most of the prosecutions under the act. Individuals, for instance, could not "make or convey false reports or false statements with intent to interfere with the operation or success of the military or naval forces of the United States or to promote the success of its enemies." In addition, the act affected anyone who, while the country was at war, "shall willfully cause or attempt to cause insubordination, disloyalty, mutiny, or refusal of duty, in the military or naval forces of the United States, or shall willfully obstruct the recruiting or enlistment service of the United States." The punishment upon conviction was a fine of not more than $10,000, imprisonment for not more than twenty years, or both.[17] This language led to the prosecution of various critics of the war, including those who counseled conscientious objection. More than two thousand people were prosecuted under this act and its later amendments, including the Sedition Act, for expressive activities. More than half of the cases resulted in convictions. According to scholars who have studied this period, not one spy or saboteur was caught within its net.

Another provision of the Espionage Act gave the postmaster general a substantial amount of power by declaring "every letter, writing, circular, postal card, picture, print, engraving, photograph, newspaper, pamphlet, book, or other publication, matter, or thing, of any kind, in violation of any of the provisions of this Act . . . to be nonmailable matter." In addition, any material "containing any matter advocating or urging treason, insurrection, or forcible resistance to any law of the United States" was also declared nonmailable. Anyone who attempted to use the mails to send such materials could be subjected to a fine of not more than $5,000, a prison term of not more than five years, or both.[18] This language gave Albert Burleson, the postmaster general, a powerful commission to purge the mails of all materials that he considered subversive to the war effort, and he wielded his power with great enthusiasm.

Burleson's power was augmented by provisions in the Trading with the Enemy Act, which became law on October 6, 1917. This law forbade the publication, in a foreign language, of "any news item, editorial or other printed matter, respecting the Government of the United States, or of any nation engaged in the present war, its policies, international relations, the state or conduct of the war, or any matter relating thereto." If a foreign-language publication wanted to discuss the war, it had to submit a certified English-language translation of these articles when the publication was entered in the mail. Violation of this portion of the act carried a fine of not more than $500, a prison term of not more than one year, or both.[19] Congress felt that the large number of foreign-language newspapers and magazines published in this country at the start of the war made this act essential. Many of these publications served the German-American community, and Burleson moved against these periodicals with great vigor.

Despite the repressive pieces of legislation already in place, Wilson and his advisers remained dissatisfied. Attorney General Thomas Gregory complained that disloyal statements still were being made and that the speakers were not being punished. In addition, Gregory noted, "these individual disloyal utterances" were causing problems around the country where they irritated and angered residents to the point that "unfortunate violence and lawlessness [occurred] and . . . dissatisfaction with the inadequacy of the Federal law to reach such cases" was heard.[20] Wilson and Gregory wanted to stop this kind of speech. In May 1918, more than a year after war had been declared, Congress passed amendments to the Espionage Act that are commonly known as the Sedition Act of 1918. Its provisions reached anyone who "shall willfully utter, print, write, or publish any disloyal, profane, scurrilous, or abusive language" about the American form of government, its Constitution, military forces, or flag. Also a target was any person who tried to "incite, provoke, or encourage resistance to the United States, or to promote the cause of its enemies." The list of offenses was long, and few of them were intimately connected with the war effort. Punishment upon conviction for violating these provisions was a fine of not more than $10,000, a prison term of not more than twenty years, or both. The act further enlarged the activities of the postmaster general as well, granting him the power to refuse to deliver mail to any individual or business who used the mails to violate the statute.[21]

Proponents of the act, such as Gregory, contended that its passage was essential to stop vigilante action against dissenters. Senator Joseph France, Republican of Maryland, however, found the Sedition Act too extreme. He tried to amend it to say that "nothing in this act shall be construed as limiting the liberty or impairing the right of any individual to publish or speak what is true, with good motives, and for justifiable ends."[22] The language was borrowed from most libel statutes of the day and was designed to protect a limited amount of criticism of the government. Attorney General Gregory forcefully opposed the amendment, arguing, "some of the most dangerous types of propaganda were either made from good motives, or else their traitorous motives were not provable."[23] France's amendment, he said, would undermine the intent of the act. The amendment was defeated, with Senator France remarking that the Western world had seen "no such repressive a criminal statute since the dark ages."[24]

One more piece of legislation, enacted October 16, 1918, about a month before the end of the war, completed the mosaic of repression. The Alien Act was designed to rid the nation of individuals who had anarchistic or similar tendencies. Under its provisions "any alien who, at any time after entering the United States, is found to have been at the time of entry, or to have become thereafter" a member of an unacceptable organization was immediately deportable. Falling within the law's reach were aliens who were anarchists or who advocated the overthrow of the government by force and violence.[25] Previous acts aimed at aliens with unacceptable political views had established a time limit after which the alien would no longer be at risk for deportation, but the new act carried no similar restrictions. By October 1918, the Bolshevik Revolution was a year old, and the Alien Act became part of an increasing effort by Congress to exclude Communists.

Only one small aspect of all of the oppressive legislation outlined above caused any great outcry or led to debate about the effects such measures would have on American life. The controversial element was a section of the Espionage Act of 1917 that would have gone beyond imposing restrictions on fringe publications and would have allowed the president to censor all newspapers, including mainline publications. The proposed section of the law would have made it a crime for anyone "in time of war, in violation of regulations to be prescribed by the President, which he is hereby authorized to make and promulgate," to "collect, record, publish, or communicate or attempt to elicit any information" about troop movements or dispositions, planned military operations, "or any other information relating to the public defense or calculated to be or which might be useful to the enemy." Violation of this provision would have been punishable by a fine of not more $10,000, a prison term of not more than ten years, or both. The proposal carried a special caveat saying "nothing in this section shall be construed to limit or restrain any comment or criticism of the acts or policies of the Government, or its representatives, or the publications of the same; provided, no discussion, comment or criticism shall convey information prohibited under this section."[26]

Although the act was proposed by his administration, Wilson quickly told the American people, "I shall not expect or permit any part of this law to apply to me or any of my official acts, or in any way to be used as a shield against criticism."[27] The president's reassurances did little to calm the fears of the American press, which saw within the proposal attempts to stifle both the gathering and dissemination of news and the criticizing of governmental actions. Few newspapers questioned the need to restrict the freedom of pro-German speakers, for, as the *New York Times* commented, "The newspaper or the individual who publishes or seeks to obtain information about the policies or military operations of the Government with the intent to communicate to the enemy to his benefit and to our harm ought to be made to smart for treason." The loyal newspaper, however, merited different treatment. "But the newspaper or the individual who criticizes or points out defects in policies and preparations with the honest purpose of promoting remedial action and warning against danger is not a public enemy," said the *Times*.[28]

Congressional leaders, picking up on newspaper opposition, debated this proposed section of the Espionage Act rather fully, with much of their attention focusing on whether the war-powers language in the Constitution took precedence over guarantees of the First Amendment. The administration's position was clearly stated by Senator Lee S. Overman, Democrat from North Carolina, who responded to questions by asking, "What is it worth to have a Commander in Chief of the Army and Navy and to appropriate $7,000,000,000 if we can not stop comment that is useful to our enemy and against our own country?"[29] The war powers granted Congress, Overman and his supporters argued, authorized restrictions on the press. Why would the founding fathers have given Congress the power to make war if they intended to cripple the war effort by allowing the press to interfere? In addition, supporters of the censorship provision believed that governmental self-preservation surpassed all other rights.

Other senators believed that the First Amendment stood as a firm bar against such a provision, even in wartime. Senator Frank B. Brandegee, Republican of Connecticut, for instance, believed that the measure would be declared unconstitutional if challenged in court. The provision, he said, gave the president authority "to make any regulations he sees fit about what people shall say to each other, what sort of inquiries they shall make, what information newspaper reporters shall obtain, what they may ask the departments." The president could make "one of his regulations that no newspaper reporter shall visit any of the departments . . . to make an inquiry about the state of our troops or how the enlistments are going on, or whether the supplies are coming forward rapidly," Brandegee said. This language, he contended, would restrict the dissemination of important information and undercut fundamental constitutional guarantees. "If this provision does not abridge the freedom of the press and the freedom of speech, as inhibited by the first amendment to the Constitution, I confess that the English language has lost its meaning to me," he said.[30]

Nor could Senator Charles S. Thomas, Democrat of Colorado, find any defensible rationale for the measure. The proposal, he contended, "is not justice . . . is not liberty." It is, instead, "the suppression of every field of legitimate inquiry in time of war." "Which is best," he asked of his colleagues, "the despotism of Germany, which we are to-day, in common with the other nations of the earth, engaged in destroying, or the greater despotism in a free republic which a law of this kind, enacted in a period of stress and excitement, will impose upon the American people"? To Thomas, First Amendment protections were even more necessary in wartime. "It is only in time of war that these great constitutional limitations upon despotism are put to the test," he said. Only in wartime do they "become effective and their value is priceless. Consequently, it is at such times that we must see to it that they are preserved, lest when peace does return we shall realize that some of the most important safeguards of liberty have been swept away in the torrent of the conflict." To Senator Thomas, the proposed censorship provision was a reversion to the hated Sedition Act of 1798 and should be rejected.[31]

A similar historical study led Senator William E. Borah, Republican of Idaho, to oppose the censorship proposal as well. In fending off defenders of the provision who argued that the war effort would benefit from such restrictions, Borah noted, "We must take into consideration that there has never been an attack made upon the press in the history of the press in which the attack has not been based upon public welfare. The king, in the first place, believed it was detrimental to the public welfare for anyone to publish anything without his consent." Dictators behaved in similar fashion, he said, and the United States was involved in a struggle to preserve democracy: "In this crusade for free institutions, let us hold fast among ourselves to those great underlying principles of freedom and liberty without which we may be a Republic in name, but could never be one in fact. Without an unfettered press, without liberty of speech, all the outward forms and structures of free institutions are a sham, a pretense—the sheerest mockery." Freedom of expression was vital in wartime, he argued, for "if the mind is shackled or made impotent through fear, it makes no difference under what form of government you live[;] you are a subject and not a citizen. Republics are not in and of themselves better than other forms of government except in so far as they carry with them and guarantee to the citizen that liberty of thought and action for which they were established."[32]

In fact, said Borah, "I think one of the greatest services we can render the cause of democracy just now is to demonstrate to the world that a Republic can carry on war, defend itself effectively and triumphantly without recurring to the practices and procedures of absolute governments." One of "the saddest features of this war," he said, "has been the haste with which the freer, more liberal governments have adopted the arbitrary and dictatorial policies and practices of the most absolute of governments. There are no democracies at this hour in this conflict, whatever may be the outward form or whatever the fact was before the war, and whatever the fact may be after the war." If the danger to the United States became greater, Borah was sure that the press would become even more vigilant in its self-censorship: "I think the individual citizen will measure up to the occasion. I at least want to try out this situation to the end and see if a Republic may not be a Republic in war as well as a Republic in peace."[33]

In the end, Congress refused to grant the president power to censor mainline newspapers. Having lost the battle for a statutory censorship program, the administration turned to efforts to promote a voluntary censorship program through the Committee on Public Information. With mainline publications safe from government incursion, these newspapers became strong supporters of efforts to curtail the rights and freedoms of fringe outlets. No matter how significant the suppression of expressive rights throughout the war, few cries of outrage were heard from the establishment journals. With their home front secured, repression became part of their wartime patriotism. The need to preserve democracy at home in the face of a war against autocracy disappeared once establishment organs had been protected. Total war now included action against any who would dissent from the goals set by the majority.

The nation's primary goal during World War I was, quite naturally, to win the war. To do so, military forces had to be gathered, equipped, trained, and deployed. As the laws cited above indicate, any interference with these activities brought quick government action. Unfortunately, the method chosen to raise the army—the draft—was controversial, meaning that vehement opposition was likely. To some opponents of the draft, conscription represented everything they had fled Europe to avoid. To others, fighting a war that they thought had been instigated by business and financial interests was an abomination. To still others, any fighting was a violation of their religious principles. Thus, opposition to the draft brought together a variety of individuals—members of the Industrial Workers of the World and the Socialist party, pacifists, and adherents of a relatively new religious sect, the Jehovah's Witnesses. While criticism of the concept of a draft while Congress was still debating the legislation had to be accepted; continued comment after the conscription measure became law on May 18, 1917, was something else altogether. The freedom to campaign for the repeal or alteration of legislation disappeared during the war.

Socialists went on record early as opposing both the draft and the war. In the statement adopted at its St. Louis convention, which began the day after war was declared, American Socialists pledged "unyielding opposition to all proposed legislations for military or industrial conscription." Should "such conscription be forced upon the people, we pledge ourselves to continuous efforts for the repeal of such laws and to the support of all mass movements in opposition to conscription." The Socialists also vowed "to oppose with all our strength any attempt to raise money for payment of war expense by taxing the necessaries of life or issuing bonds which will put the burden upon future generations." The capitalists who were responsible for the war should pay the cost, they said. "Let those who kindled the fire, furnish the fuel."[34]

Individuals got into trouble with authorities for making speeches or writing material advising others not to register for the draft and for failing to register themselves. Although the latter was a punishable offense, the former raised fundamental questions regarding freedom of expression. Especially critical here was whether the speeches or writings caused anyone to evade the draft or led to desertions from or insurrections in the military. No causal links between speech and actions were made in any of the cases involving those who protested the draft, but, then, the court system did not require such connections. All that the government had to prove was that the person charged had made statements against the draft. The courts then assumed that the person intended to disrupt the Selective Service program and that was sufficient for conviction.

The first weeks after the passage of the Selective Service Act were especially hard on draft opponents. Meetings were regularly broken up by crowds that included private detectives, police, and military personnel. Fearing a recurrence of the Civil War draft riots, authorities silenced anyone who might so inspire draft-aged men. Although the national sign-up day on June 5 was peaceful, the government continued to suppress draft opponents. Even a New Yorker who had the audacity to circulate a copy of the Declaration of Independence on July 4 accompanied by the question "Does your Government live up to these principles?" was arrested.[35] The more vivid and more persuasive the dissent, the more likely the speaker, writer, or distributor would find himself in trouble with the law.

A graphic description of the horrors of war written by prominent Episcopalian clergyman Irwin St. John Tucker and distributed by the Socialists, for instance, led to problems. "Conscription is upon us: the draft law is a fact!" Tucker wrote. "Into your homes the recruiting officers are coming. They will take your sons of military age and impress them into the army. . . . Then they will be shipped thru the submarine zone by the hundreds of thousands to the bloody quagmire of Europe." Once there, "Into that seething, heaving swamp of torn flesh and floating entrails they will be plunged, in regiments, divisions and armies, screaming as they go. Agonies of torture will rend their flesh from their sinews, will crack their bones and dissolve their lungs; every pang will be multiplied in its passage to you." Finally, "black death will be a guest at every American fireside. Mothers and fathers and sisters, wives and sweethearts will know the weight of that awful vacancy left by the bullet which finds its mark." Despite the finality of such death, Tucker warned, "still the recruiting officers will come; seizing age after age, mounting up to the elder ones and taking the younger ones as they grow to soldier size; And still the toll of death will grow."[36] This depiction of war could be devastating to the recruiting effort government officials said as they seized copies of the pamphlet and arrested individuals attempting to distribute it. A few judges protected Tucker's work as a legitimate attempt to win changes in the draft law. In most locales, however, judges considered the material designed to obstruct the recruiting effort, making its distributors liable for prosecution under the Espionage Act.

Other political arguments against the draft also ran afoul of courts eager to enforce the Espionage Act. New York City Socialists, under the direction of Charles T. Schenck, prepared 15,000 copies of a circular against the draft. One side of the handbill was entitled "Long Live the Constitution of the United States. Wake Up, America. Your Liberties Are in Danger." One of the most objectionable sections of this essay compared conscripts to convicts. A draftee, said the Socialists, "is deprived of his liberty and of his right to think and act as a freeman. A conscripted citizen is forced to surrender his right as a citizen and become a subject. He is forced into involuntary servitude. He is deprived of the protection given him by the Constitution of the United States. He is deprived of all freedom of conscience in being forced to kill against his will." The other side of the handbill was entitled "Assert Your Rights" and reminded readers that the government was designed to serve the people rather than the people to serve the government. "Their wages comes [*sic*] from the expenses of government which you pay. Will you allow them to unjustly rule you?" Here, the Socialists contended that "no power was delegated to send our citizens away to foreign shores to shoot up the people of other lands, no matter what may be their internal or international disputes." American citizens, the Socialists argued, must deny the government the right to become involved in such activities.[37] Despite the fact that this publication essentially reminded Americans that they controlled their government and allegedly had the power to change it should its leaders make unacceptable decisions, Schenck and four other leaders of the New York party were arrested.

The grand old man of socialism, Eugene V. Debs, had long opposed war and conscription. After watching many of his friends go to jail for protesting against the war, Debs decided that he should not remain free. In a highly publicized speech on June 16, 1918, Debs publicly supported the Socialists' antiwar stance, praised the Industrial Workers of the World, called the Bolsheviks of the Soviet Union comrades, and chastised the government for its treatment of war critics. When it came to commenting on the duty of American citizens to oppose the war, however, his language was somewhat restrained, and he avoided any specific call for avoiding the draft.

In the audience were a number of federal agents and representatives of private vigilante organizations, who were taking notes and checking to see if draft-aged men were present. Speeches against conscription became more damaging if they were made to audiences of young men who could be induced by the words to avoid their patriotic obligation. Not only were such men in attendance, but some fifty-five of them had failed to register with the appropriate authorities and were immediately arrested. Debs was not arrested until he repeated virtually the same talk two weeks later. At that point, he was charged with violating the Espionage Act.

His conviction was a foregone conclusion, but Debs used the courtroom as a forum for advancing his antiwar views: "I have been accused of having obstructed the war. I admit it. Gentlemen, I abhor war. I would oppose the war if I stood alone. When I think of a cold, glittering steel bayonet being plunged into the white, quivering flesh of a human being, I recoil with horror. I have often wondered if I could take the life of my fellow man, even to save my own." To Debs, there were no good wars. "I am perfectly willing to be branded as a disloyalist," he told the court, "and if it is a crime under the American law, punishable by imprisonment, for being opposed to bloodshed, I am perfectly willing to be clothed in the stripes of a convict and to end my days in a prison cell." He freely admitted saying that "men were fit for something better than slavery and cannon fodder." In fact, he said, "I meant exactly what I said. . . . I can hear the shrieks of the soldiers of Europe in my dreams. I have imagination enough to see a battlefield. I can see it strewn with the legs of human beings, who but yesterday were in the flush and glory of their young manhood. I can see them at eventide, scattered about in remnants, their limbs torn from their bodies, their eyes gouged out." He said he could also see "the mothers who are bowed in the shadow of their last great grief—whose hearts are breaking. And I say to myself, 'I am going to do the little that lies in my power to wipe from this earth that terrible scourge of war.'"[38]

Jurors found Debs guilty on three counts—for attempting to incite insubordination in the military, for obstructing and attempting to obstruct recruiting and enlistments, and for encouraging resistance to the U.S. government and support of the enemy. He was sentenced to ten years in prison on each charge, with the terms to run concurrently. With the prosecution and conviction of Debs, the federal government had eliminated the leading spokesman for the Socialist cause, albeit rather late in the war.

The leading voice of the remnants of the anarchist movement also was removed from the scene for opposing the draft. Although anarchists, as other dissidents, had split over the war, Emma Goldman continued to follow a strong anarchist line. With the passage of the Selective Service Act, Goldman set up a No-Conscription League to fight the law on moral and legal grounds and to provide support for individuals who refused induction. According to Goldman, league members opposed conscription "because we are internationalists, antimilitarists, and opposed to all wars waged by capitalist governments. We will fight for what we choose to fight for. We will never fight simply because we are ordered to fight." In addition, the league believed that "the militarization of America is an evil that far outweighs, in its anti-social and anti-libertarian effects, any good that may come from America's participation in the war. We will resist conscription by every means in our power, and we will sustain those who, for similar reasons, refuse to be conscripted."[39]

Goldman planned a mass meeting in New York City for the day that the measure became law. About 6,000 people, including police stenographers, heard her denounce a conspiracy by Wall Street bankers as the cause of the war. She held additional public meetings, making essentially the same statements until she discovered that the gatherings served as convenient places for the authorities to trap draft-aged men who had failed to register. She then turned to printed materials.

Police finally arrested Goldman and her co-worker Alexander Berkman on June 17, 1918, and charged them with conspiracy to induce men not to register for the draft as required by law. The two anarchists refused legal counsel, and both addressed the jury personally. Goldman contended that she had opposed war for years and was involved in no conspiracy against the present encounter. Rather, she considered her opposition patriotic. She told jurors that she loved "America with open eyes. Our relation toward America is the same as the relation of a man who loves a woman, who is enchanted by her beauty and yet who cannot be blind to her defects." That love, she said, "must not make us blind to the social faults of America. That cannot make us deaf to the discords in America. That cannot compel us to be inarticulate to the terrible wrongs committed in the name of patriotism and in the name of the country."[40] The jury was unmoved by Goldman's claims of patriotism. After deliberating a mere thirty-nine minutes, the jury found both Goldman and Berkman guilty as charged. They were sentenced to two years in prison and maximum fines of $20,000 each. The jury also made the recommendation that the prison terms and fines be waived on the condition that the pair be deported to the Soviet Union.

Also encountering difficulties for allegedly discouraging enlistments were the Jehovah's Witnesses. By World War I, the sect was not quite fifty years old, and few Americans understood the intricacies of its beliefs. Fundamental tenets included the notion that all members were ministers and that, if a member of the sect killed another person, the believer's immortal soul would be destroyed. Years later, these religious beliefs would win exemption from service, but in the First World War, the government sought to induct members into the military. The Witnesses responded by using their famous publishing service to denounce the war and the draft and by circulating these materials not only to sect members but more widely to draft-aged individuals.

The language in the Witnesses' publications was just as vivid as that produced by the Socialists, but the former's imagery was strongly religious. A tract entitled

"The Finished Mystery" said: "Standing opposite to those Satan has placed three great untruths, human immorality, the Antichrist and a certain delusion which is best described by the word Patriotism, but which is in reality murder, the spirit of the very Devil." Governments exploit these feelings, the publication said, for "under the guise of Patriotism the civil governments of the earth demand of peace-loving men the sacrifice of themselves and their loved ones and the butchery of their fellows, and hail it as a duty demanded by the laws of heaven."[41] This pamphlet and others issued by the Watch Tower Bible & Tract Society led to indictment of the sect's leaders for violating various provisions of the Espionage Act. The jury found them guilty, and the maximum sentences were imposed on seven of eight defendants, with the eighth being given only ten years in jail. The conviction was reversed on appeal due to a technicality, but the understanding of the Witnesses' special needs was clearly absent in the judicial system and in the government that it represented.

In fact, the government was quite unsympathetic to all those with conscientious objections to fighting in the war. Part of the problem here was that, perhaps for the first time, the government was faced with individuals with all sorts of objections. Military officials were familiar with and somewhat ready to deal with problems presented by members of the historic peace churches such as the Quakers and the Mennonites. In World War I, additional religious groups claimed exemptions, and individuals with humanitarian and political objections to the war caused additional problems. The Selective Service Act allowed objector status only for those who belonged to religious groups that opposed the war. Applicants for CO status had to prove their claims to military officials and then accept assigned noncombatant service. No provisions were made for individuals who opposed the war on nonreligious grounds, nor, for that matter, were provisions made for individuals who belonged to religious groups other than the historic peace churches with objections to war.

Almost 21,000 men were granted CO status; only about 3,500 of them maintained their CO status after being placed in the hands of the military, which actively discouraged their pacifism. Although assigned to noncombatant work, the military officers who supervised COs had difficulty understanding how anyone could object to fulfilling his patriotic duty during wartime. Some military men might be able to understand religious objectors, but the political dissenter was totally beyond their ken. The latter were the equivalent of cowards. The duty of the military officer then became to shape these misbegotten individuals into real men.[42] Stories, which were later proven true, surfaced about the gross mistreatment of objectors who refused to conform to army discipline. Physical abuse was fairly common. Objectors were fed less than other troops; they were awakened in the middle of the night for no reason; and they were subjected to cold showers at any time of the day or night. Anything that could help convince them to forgo their beliefs and to take a regular army assignment was tried.

Further confounding the army were objectors who took an absolutist position and refused to obey all military authority, including the order to wear uniforms. Many of these resisters refused to do any assigned work. Their sole goal was to irritate the army so much that military officials would be forced to discharge them. Because of fears that this noncooperation would spread, the military court-martialed some 540 COs during World War I; only one was acquitted. Seventeen COs received death sentences, and 142 were sentenced to life terms. Seventy-three others were given twenty-year terms. Only fifteen men got sentences of three years or less. Apparently all of the death sentences were altered after review; but 450 men went to jail because they opposed military service during the war. They spent their jail time in some of the nation's worst prisons. At least seventeen conscientious objectors died while incarcerated. Finding COs placed in solitary confinement was not uncommon; their diet often was bread and water. On other occasions, they were kept in dark cells and were handcuffed or chained to the cell walls for hours at a time. They were forced to wear uniforms, beaten, and otherwise mistreated.

Although few Americans worried about conscientious objectors, the National Civil Liberties Bureau, under the direction of Roger N. Baldwin, kept watch. NCLB officials repeatedly complained to Secretary of War Newton Baker about this mistreatment, and as a result of their efforts, Baker ordered changes made. The instructions, however, were so loosely written that many military officials continued to mistreat absolutists. Eventually the bureau publicized the information it had gathered on the mistreatment of COs. The War Department responded by roundly criticizing the bureau rather than by admitting that it, too, had discovered similar problems. Baldwin and the NCLB were accused of defending traitors and were warned that prosecution under the Espionage Act might be forthcoming.

Life was hard for radicals during the war as conservative business and government leaders found just the leverage needed to launch major attacks on their enemies. Soon after the war began, IWW-sponsored strikes hit copper mines, lumber camps, and certain agricultural fields. Employers refused to believe that these strikes were caused by any work-related grievance. To employers, IWW members were German agents in disguise, and the strikes were designed to undermine the war effort. Government at all levels mobilized to suppress radical labor. If governmental support for suppression was unavailable, local citizens often acted on their own.[43]

The worst instance of vigilante justice occurred in Bisbee, Arizona, where a bitter strike against the owners of copper mines led to patriotic reprisals. Some 2,000 Bisbee residents sealed the town off from outside interference in mid-July 1917 and began a search for IWW members. About 1,200 men who were considered subversive were picked up and shoved into cattle cars on a waiting train. The train then took them to the middle of the desert in New Mexico, where the alleged subversives were forced off. The U.S. Army took charge of the deportees; its officials discovered that almost half of the men were American citizens, most of whom had registered for the draft. In addition, most of the deportees had families, property, and bank accounts back in Bisbee.

Events in Bisbee led to an outcry from IWW leaders and from the few liberals still willing to speak out. Although President Wilson was convinced that the IWW was a treasonous organization, he eventually set up a special commission to evaluate wartime labor disturbances. The commission investigated the Bisbee deportations and recommended that action be taken against the vigilantes who had participated in the IWW roundup. The Justice Department unenthusiastically pursued the case and found, to its dismay, that the vigilantes had been armed and financed by the major employer in the area. Indictments against specific vigilantes were thrown out of court on the grounds that the vigilantes had broken no federal laws.

Nor were there any prosecutions after similar problems in Butte, Montana. Here, vigilantes picked up Frank Little, an IWW organizer, and hanged him. State and local authorities took no action; federal officials said that no federal law had been broken and that they could not interfere. Outraged at atrocities perpetrated on members of his union, IWW president Bill Haywood raised the level of rhetoric dramatically. Unless the government intervened to help union members, Haywood threatened to call a general strike of metal miners and agricultural workers, which would cripple the war effort. Haywood's attempts to protect his followers backfired as Wilson, now convinced that the IWW was a substantial threat, ordered the full authority of the federal government unleashed on the union.

On September 5, 1917, agents of the Bureau of Investigation and members of local police forces staged massive raids on IWW offices and the homes of various leaders. Anyone on the premises was arrested. Authorities confiscated almost everything found in the offices, including equipment, although their main target was anything committed to paper. Federal officials argued that IWW publications showed that the union had opposed various government actions in support of the war; that it had encouraged its members to evade the draft; that it had supported and encouraged insubordination in the armed services; and that it had conspired to interfere with the ability of employers working for the war effort to fulfill their government contracts. Many of the words used to characterize the union's attitudes were taken out of context, and most of the statements quoted also were taken out of the time period in which they had been committed to paper.

Although IWW leaders had carefully avoided encouraging members to evade the draft, paper rhetoric indicated a lack of support for the draft and other wartime efforts. Based upon this evidence, federal prosecutors obtained indictments against 166 union leaders. All those charged, including the top leadership, surrendered to authorities in the belief that a jury would vindicate them. Among those awaiting trial in Chicago was Bill Haywood. IWW attorneys argued that the charges should be dismissed because they were based on evidence that had been obtained illegally. The argument was rejected, and in April 1918, 101 Wobbly leaders stood trial in Chicago before Judge Kenesaw Mountain Landis.

Further raids followed in an effort to deprive the union of effective leadership and to hamper efforts to help defend members facing charges. When the National Civil Liberties Bureau tried to publicize the trial and to build support for the union by arguing that the IWW was a legitimate trade union and that it did not advocate treason or sabotage, the bureau ran afoul of the authorities. Postal officials suppressed a pamphlet defending the Wobblies, and the Justice Department ordered express companies not to circulate it. The Civil Liberties

Bureau tried to publish advertisements to raise defense funds for the union leaders but found publications either unwilling philosophically to carry the ads or too frightened of repercussions to do so. The IWW leaders on trial in Chicago were essentially on their own.

In normal times, the charges against the union probably would not have persuaded a jury. Government prosecutors were unable to prove them guilty of any actual crime. Instead, they had to rely on written material to prove a conspiracy that simply had not yet born fruit. After five months of testimony, the jury took only slightly less than a hour to find the defendants guilty on all counts. Since each defendant was charged with four separate counts, the jury, in effect, returned more than 400 verdicts involving more than 10,000 crimes in record time. Two weeks later, Judge Landis levied more than $2 million in fines and meted out lengthy prison terms. Haywood was given the maximum possible sentence—a $10,000 fine and twenty years in prison. As he imposed punishment, Judge Landis explained the limits of free speech in time of war: "When the country is at peace it is the legal right of free speech to oppose going to war and to oppose even preparation for war. But when once war is declared this right ceases." Even after the declaration of war, it was permissible to oppose the draft—until the Selective Service Act was passed. "But once that law was passed free speech did not authorize a man to oppose or resist that law. The man that opposes it or resists it violates it, and men who conspire to aid another man to oppose or resist it violate the statute penalizing conspiracy."[44] Trials in other parts of the country had similar endings. The top union leadership was decimated by the government's attacks.

The government's basic approach to most grievances during the war was to ignore them and, if possible, to prosecute individuals audacious enough to bring problems to the public's attention. One of the groups feeling the government's sting was the Nonpartisan League, an organization of farmers in North Dakota and adjoining states who were disgruntled about economic conditions. The league, set up in 1915, was a philosophical heir of the Populist party in that it opposed the control that bankers and business leaders had over agriculture. Like the Populists, the Nonpartisan League became an effective political organization and gained political power throughout the region.[45]

When the war in Europe started, rural Midwesterners generally opposed American involvement. The league was among those against American entry, in part because many of its leaders had connections with the Socialist party and in part because many farmers felt U.S. participation would hurt agricultural interests. As American involvement became more likely, the league became more supportive of it, but bones of contention still existed. Cries that the league was unpatriotic increased in 1917 as Joseph Gilbert worked to establish the organization in Minnesota, where a special state commission watched for seditious speech. Gilbert provided commission members with plenty of reasons to suspect him when he drafted a series of statements on the war for the Minnesota Nonpartisan League to adopt.

Although the position paper said, "Whatever ideas we as individuals may have had, as to the wisdom of our nation engaging in this war, we realize that a crisis now confronts us in which it becomes necessary that we all stand unreservedly pledged to safeguard, defend and preserve our country," it also included comments that cast doubt on league loyalty. For instance, the statement called for allied governments to renounce intentions to seek territory or indemnities from Germany at the end of the war, for an end to secret diplomacy and agreements, for the U.S. government to announce its war aims, and for the conscription of wealth. "Patriotism demands service from all according to their capacity," said the league. "To conscript men and exempt the bloodstained wealth coined from the sufferings of humanity is repugnant to the spirit of America and contrary to the ideals of democracy." The organization also declared its belief in freedom of expression: "We declare freedom of speech to be the bulwark of human liberty. . . . A declaration of war does not repeal the Constitution of the United States, and the unwarranted interference of military and other authorities with the rights of individuals must cease."[46]

Few members of the establishment believed that the Constitution still mandated such freedom. Rumors spread that the Nonpartisan League in Minnesota was advocating un-American ideas, and efforts to interfere with members' freedom of expression grew. Finding places to meet became harder; organizers found themselves in danger of physical violence including tarring and feathering, and the property of league sympathizers was not only vandalized but, at times, was painted yellow to symbolize the cowardice that critics attached to league members. Finally, Minnesota officials indicted Gilbert and other league leaders for harming the war effort. One piece of evidence was a pamphlet entitled "The Nonpartisan League; Its Origin, Purposes, and Methods of Organization," which included the war resolutions. Gilbert also was indicted under the Minnesota sedition act for a speech in which he said, "We are going over to Europe to make the world safe for democracy, but I tell you we had better make America safe for democracy first."[47] Gilbert went to jail for his comments, and the Nonpartisan League never really recovered from the wartime onslaught against its patriotism.

Success in suppressing dissident speech only led to more attempts, and the federal government decided the time was ripe to attack the National Civil Liberties Bureau. After certain bureau publications, including one supporting the IWW, were barred from the mail because they were allegedly subversive, a postal inspector reviewed all bureau materials entered into the mails. He found them filled with subversive comments, noting, "The NATIONAL CIVIL LIBERTIES BUREAU seems never to have considered that . . . in times of great danger it may be necessary to suspend the constitutional right of free speech; obviously it is more important that freedom be saved than it indefinitely be allowed to chatter to its heart's content."[48] Fourteen bureau publications were declared nonmailable despite the fact that they did not violate any portion of the Espionage Act. The Justice Department ordered a full-scale investigation of the NCLB, but department officials could find no violation of law. Bureau leaders took the post office to court and forced it to accept all fourteen of its publications for mailing, becoming one of the few organizations to challenge the postmaster general and win.

Another group of protesters that was harshly suppressed during the war years eventually turned out to be big winners as well. The critics in this case were suffragists who were tired of peacefully advocating a constitutional amendment allowing women to vote. Nothing had happened by being ladylike, so just as the war was getting started, militant suffragists decided new tactics were needed. They turned to picketing, parading, and burning Wilson in effigy—all in downtown Washington, D.C., and sometimes right next to the White House. Silent sentinels posted by the National Woman's party took up their positions at the White House in January 1917. With the nation's entry into the war in April 1917, criticism of these women increased substantially, with their loyalty coming into question. They were also physically attacked, and the banners that they carried were ripped from their hands and destroyed.[49]

By June 1917, women were being arrested for doing exactly the same thing that they had done with impunity a few months earlier. The picketing continued as did the jailings. The crowds greeting the women became increasingly hostile, particularly when the women termed the president "Kaiser Wilson." Some congressmen became so concerned about the suffragists' campaign that they tried to suppress expressive activities still further. Senator Henry L. Myers, Democrat of Montana, for example, introduced a bill in August that would have made it illegal, when the nation was at war, for any person "to carry, hold, wave, exhibit, display, or have in his or her possession in any public road, highway, alley, street, thoroughfare, park, or other public place in the District of Columbia, any banner, flag, streamer, sash, or other device having thereon any words or language with reference to the President or the Vice President."[50] Senator Myers explained that his proposal was intended "to prevent the infamous, outrageous, scandalous, and I think, almost treasonable actions that have been going on around the White House for months past, which have been a gross insult to the President of the United States and to the people of the United States." The suffragists had deeply offended Myers by "the so-called picketing of the White House, branding the President of the United States as comparable to the Kaiser of Germany, the greatest autocrat, the worst despot, the most tyrannical ruler in the world, and a murderer, who has brought upon the world the greatest scourge that has ever been known in the history of all time."[51]

The idea that behavior could be a form of expression was not widely accepted during these days, and so the suffragists had additional problems to overcome. At least the Socialists and members of the Nonpartisan League and other obnoxious groups were carrying on recognizable expressive activities—speeches, distribution of written materials, and the like. But a suffragist standing or walking before the White House served as a message of protest. Granted, the women generally did wear sashes or carry banners, but the communication was personal and was occurring in the president's back yard. Picketing turned to burnings in effigy and to the lighting of watch fires to encourage congressmen to vote for the suffrage amendment. And more women went to jail.

Interestingly, the women never were charged for violations of the Espionage Act, even though most of their activities could easily have been categorized as interfering with the war effort just as much as those of the IWW. Instead, they were arrested for obstructing traffic, unlawful assembly, or some other minor offense. Indeed, the charges against them for the same basic activity seemed to change regularly, and the suffragists never really got a good explanation of how their behavior broke the law. Despite their ongoing legal problems, the suffragists continued their picketing until Congress finally ratified the Nineteenth Amendment in 1919; women cast their first ballots in the 1920 presidential elections. The change that was so detested during the war years had become part of the fundamental scheme of government, and the women who had helped to win it proudly wore their battle scars.

The scars inflicted on another segment of American society during the war were less proudly worn. In fact, a whole subculture in American society was virtually destroyed because of irrational fears. Although they had generally supported the German cause before American entry into the conflict, once the United States declared war, German-Americans rallied behind the flag. Yet the American people were so frightened of and so enraged at anything German that almost all vestiges of that heritage were systematically eliminated in the United States. Individuals and communities with German sounding names Anglicized them in order to avoid community-sponsored retribution. The German language was all but outlawed; German music could no longer be played; and sauerkraut was renamed liberty cabbage. The German-language press, which probably was the strongest of the ethnic presses at the start of the war, suffered terribly. No German-language newspaper was suppressed during the war, but several did lose second-class mailing privileges or, in a few cases, all access to the mail. Most of them also lost subscribers and advertisers and were as permanently crippled as the community they had served.[52]

As the war drew to a close, the casualty figures within radical organizations were high. With its leaders in prison, the Industrial Workers of the World was near extinction. The Socialist party was badly wounded by wartime prosecutions, and its membership was so split that it fell prey to further disintegration as the Communists began to organize. The Nonpartisan League never regained its prewar vigor in the Midwest, once again leaving farmers at the mercy of bankers, business leaders, and railroads. On the other hand, several persecuted groups survived and prospered. The peace movement, decimated during the war years, enjoyed a significant revival in the 1920s and 1930s. Suffragists obtained their goal soon after the war, with their leaders entering other reform areas. And the National Civil Liberties Bureau changed its name to the American Civil Liberties Union in 1919 and moved on to defend unpopular causes in future generations.

Although most of the nation's attention was focused on deviant organizations and persons, some mainline individuals and groups also came in for close scrutiny. Of particular concern during World War I were members of the American Federation of Labor (AFL). As union president, Samuel Gompers was just as worried about the loyalty of his members during the war as outsiders were. With many members having strong pacifist leanings and ties with Socialists, Gompers feared that they could be lured into opposition by rhetoric about the war being one to make the rich richer while doing nothing to better the condition of the working class. To offset that propaganda, Gompers and his close associates set up the American Alliance for Labor and Democracy, a strongly prowar organization designed to support President Wilson. Although some labor problems occurred during the war, Gompers generally kept federation members in line.[53]

For his efforts, Gompers won a degree of recognition for the labor movement that had never before been granted by the federal government. For instance, in 1917 Woodrow Wilson became the first American president to address an AFL convention. In return for labor's cooperation during the war, its leadership won seats on a number of important federal boards and agencies. Most important was its representation on the War Labor Board, which kept war-related industries running smoothly. The War Labor Board granted many of labor's goals including recognition of the right of workers to bargain collectively with employers through representatives of their own choosing. Dismissals based on union membership or organizing activities were not allowed. Wages and hours came more in line with longtime labor demands, including the implementation of eight-hour days. Employers were not happy with the accommodations that they were forced to make during the war, however, and as soon as the conflict was over and the government was out of the picture, they began to renege on their agreements with labor.[54]

American educators had no one to stand up for them during the war as Gompers did for union members. Teachers had fairly accurately mirrored society in general in the years before the war, with a fair number of them opposing American entrance into the conflict. When Congress declared war in 1917 most teachers quickly muted their opposition. In the public schools, employment often depended on open support of the war in the classroom. Individuals who tried to be impartial about the war or who attempted to show both sides of the picture jeopardized their jobs. On the college and university level, the position of professors who opposed the war was not much better. Professors had banded together in 1915 to establish the American Association of University Professors (AAUP), which supposedly was to defend academics who lost their jobs for political reasons. But the patriotism generated by the war was simply too powerful for the AAUP. Higher education had weathered attacks by various religious groups and by big business interests, but patriotism was overwhelming.[55]

Various states set up special committees to investigate professors' loyalty. A Nebraska committee, for example, submitted a list of twelve suspect teachers to the University of Nebraska Board of Regents. These individuals, the regents were told, "assumed an attitude calculated to encourage among those who come under their influence, within and without the university, a spirit of inactivity, indifference, and opposition towards this war and an undesirable view with respect to the several fundamental questions inseparable from the war."[56] A regents investigation showed that three of the professors supported internationalism, interfered with the sale of Liberty Bonds, and criticized their more patriotic colleagues. The three were dismissed.

Columbia University set up the first program in a private institution to investigate faculty loyalty. University president Nicholas Murray Butler believed professors should not object to this questioning, for academic freedom simply did not exist in wartime. As Butler explained in 1917, "So long as national policies were in debate, we gave complete freedom, as is our wont, and as becomes a university—freedom of assembly, freedom of speech, and freedom of publication to all members of the University who in lawful and decent ways might wish to inform and to guide public policy." Such freedom is necessary in a university community, he explained: "Wrongheadedness and folly we might deplore, but we are bound to tolerate." The declaration of war changed all that. "What had been tolerated before becomes intolerable now," he said. "What had been wrongheadedness was now sedition. What had been folly was now treason." He added: "This is the University's last and only warning to any among us, if such there be, who are not with whole heart and mind and strength committed to fight with us to make the world safe for democracy."[57] At least one Columbia professor was fired, and others were interrogated by the loyalty committee.

Few segments of American society protected dissident speech. In fact, if some individuals had had their way, no dissident speech would have been left to seek protection. With all of the legislation available, the natural assumption would be that the U.S. Department of Justice was the main suppressor of expressive activity during the war. Indeed, the Justice Department had a significant role in such repression, but it was not alone. Another leading player was Postmaster General Albert J. Burleson, a man who sought to quiet all criticism of the war effort with a missionary's zeal. Burleson's attack on publications was authorized by several pieces of wartime legislation and by his statutory power to regulate materials using the cheaper second-class mailing privileges.[58]

Burleson wasted no time in beginning his attack. Local postal officials were told to exclude publications from the mails if certain articles violated wartime statutes. Burleson ordered local postmasters to carefully check "unsealed matter, newspapers, etc., containing matter which is calculated to interfere with the success of any Federal loan . . . or to cause insubordination, disloyalty, or mutiny, or refusal of duty in the military or naval service, or to obstruct the recruiting, draft or enlistment services . . . or otherwise to embarrass or hamper the Government in conducting the war."[59] Local postmasters were told to send any suspicious material to Washington for review. With this broad charge guiding local actions, postal inspectors in the nation's capital soon were inundated with material that had been considered unpatriotic on the local level. Much of the material forwarded for review did not meet Burleson's criteria for suppression but instead reflected local concern about the overall tone of publications and about the possibility that some gullible individual might be led astray by reading suspect pages.[60]

Once the postmaster general had been officially informed that a publication contained material that could impair the war effort, he ordered its publisher to explain why the publication should not be excluded from the second-class mails. A hearing would be held immediately, with a determination coming at its conclusion. Decisions could be appealed through the court system, and some publishers even sought President Wilson's intervention on their behalf. Second-class mailing rates were beneficial, and no publisher would risk losing them without doing everything possible to overturn the administrative decision. In most cases, the publication could continue using the mails if it were placed in a sealed envelope and sent under first-class postage, which, of course, cost much more. Few publications could afford to send material at the higher rate. Some publications were found so offensive that authorities banned them from using first-class postage, and some publishers were barred from even receiving mail. Imposition of either or both of the latter two punishments usually meant the publication's death.

Burleson exercised his extensive authority with vigor and relish. Within a month after he received authorization, he had acted against close to fifteen major publications. Most of these publications were Socialist, including the party's leading voices—the *Masses,* the *International Socialist Review,* the *Appeal to Reason,* the *American Socialist,* and the *Milwaukee Leader.* The publications, he said, carried material that could interfere with the war effort. When chastised for suppressing publications that were critical of the administration's policies, Burleson's response was brusk. The post office, he said, had never done anything to "suppress free criticism, right or wrong, of the Government, nor has the department attempted in any way to interfere with the legitimate expression of views which do not coincide with those of the Government."[61] Strangely, though, the publications that were suppressed all seemed to be strong critics of administration policy, and in some cases, their offenses against the war effort seemed slight or even nonexistent.

After the passage of the Trading with the Enemy Act, the last piece in the postmaster general's arsenal against the radical press, Burleson was pushed to explain the standards that he used to guide his censorship. No publication, he said, could "say that this Government got in the war wrong, that it is in it for the wrong purposes, or anything that will impugn the motives of the Government for going into the war. They can not say that this Government is the tool of Wall Street or the munitions makers. That kind of thing makes for insubordination in the Army and Navy and breeds a spirit of disloyalty through the country. It is a false statement, a lie, and it will not be permitted." Although he repeated his intentions not to suppress legitimate criticism, he stressed that "nothing can be said inciting people to resist the laws. There can be no campaign against conscription and the Draft Law, nothing that will interfere with enlistments or the raising of an army. There can be nothing said to hamper and obstruct the Government in the prosecution of the war."[62] When all of those exclusions were put together, almost all of the reasons that radical groups had for opposing the war constituted grounds for barring from the mails.

Burleson's powers were virtually unchecked. Although some cases were appealed to the courts, the post office invariably won. Even if a publication won the right to mail a contested issue, Burleson could challenge other issues or, even more likely, block the future use of second-class mails because the magazine or newspaper had failed to circulate issues regularly, which was one qualification for maintaining second-class mailing privileges. Appeal to the president was of little use. Only twice did Wilson intervene on behalf of a banned publication. Once was on behalf of the *Nation,* edited by Oswald Garrison Villard, who knew both the president and his secretary, Joseph P. Tumulty. Villard demanded to see the president about the ban; Wilson refused to meet with the editor, but he did order the magazine released. The offending publication had carried an attack on the attorney general's efforts to round up draft dodgers and a critical essay on Samuel Gompers.

In the other case in which Wilson intervened, the publication involved was the *World Tomorrow,* the magazine of the pacifist Fellowship of Reconciliation. The offense here apparently was criticism of American intervention in Russia. This appeal to the president was handled by the brother of the president's son-in-law; in addition, the editor of the magazine had been a student of Wilson's at Princeton. That combination overwhelmed Burleson, who allowed the publication to re-enter the mail but not at second-class rates. Another attempt to circumvent Burleson by appealing to the president failed, as the postmaster general threatened to quit if Wilson disliked the way in which the censorship was being conducted. The president withdrew his questions, and Burleson continued unabated.

Burleson acted only against small, inconsequential publications while ignoring comments in establishment outlets. The Hearst newspapers, for example, regularly criticized Wilson's policies, often making the same points that got radical publications banned, but nothing happened to them. The *New York Evening Post* published secret agreements and treaties among the allies in January 1918 without repercussions. And in September 1918, the *New York Times* used its editorial page to suggest that peace negotiations should begin. Such a suggestion in a Socialist publication would have merited immediate banning from the mails. With this record, Villard charged that Burleson was interested only in "terrifying helpless fry who could not strike back."[63]

Whatever his rationale, Burleson's actions were effective. By the time the war was over, most radical newspapers had lost their second-class mailing privileges, and many had gone out of business. After the war, an emerging class of civil libertarians argued that never again should one man or one department of government be given the power to ride roughshod over the communication of ideas. The critics had forgotten, however, that censorship of political ideas was a long-standing tradition in the post office. The British had tried to keep revolutionary ideas from spreading; Southerners had tried to ban abolitionists' ideas from their territory; and Northern officials tried to keep pro-Southern opinions from circulating. Postmasters would continue to use their power over the second-class mail classification to regulate the reading materials of American citizens. As long as the Congress, the courts, and the postmaster general agree that the use of the mails to disseminate ideas is a privilege rather than a right, restrictions may be imposed, and ideas out of the mainstream of American society will continue to be the primary targets.

Postmaster General Burleson was not the only member of the Wilson administration actively engaged in the suppression of dissident speech. Attorney General Gregory was an active participant in the crusade as well. The coming of war had frightened Gregory, who was convinced that German agents were omnipresent. In the years before American involvement, Gregory felt he needed more personnel to investigate a broader range of offenses, but Congress would not cooperate. Eventually, in 1916, Congress allowed Bureau of Investigation agents to investigate matters that were not actual violations of federal law upon the request of the secretary of state. Although now better equipped to protect the national security, Gregory still was unhappy with the resources at his disposal.

Thus, in the early months of the conflict, Gregory asked all loyal Americans to serve as volunteer detectives, and he promised that law enforcement agencies on all levels would investigate citizen suspicions. The Justice Department even placed advertisements in newspapers telling the American people of their patriotic responsibility to ferret out evil forces. By May 1917, the attorney general reported that he was receiving 1,000 accusations of alleged disloyalty a day. A year later, the total had reached 1,500 a day. The average American, apparently, was as concerned about loyalty as the attorney general, although Gregory had to admit that most of the information came from "hysterical women and . . . men, some doubtless actuated by malice and ill-will, and the vast majority utterly worthless."[64] Still, he was impressed with the willingness of Americans to spy on each other and to submit their suspicions to the government for verification.

Finding such private surveillance useful, Gregory entertained an offer to set up a massive volunteer spy-catching organization. The proposal to establish the American Protective League (APL) came in February 1917, two months before the declaration of war. The volunteer spies came from the best ranks of American society, with a high percentage of political conservatives signing up. Persons who became APL agents agreed to pay their own expenses and provide their own transportation, thus placing membership beyond the reach of most average Americans. In return, they were given credentials that looked almost like those of real government agents, which they flashed in the faces of offenders with all the authority of actual agents.[65]

Although Gregory originally had wanted the volunteer spies to protect the country from sabotage, the lack of such problems left the volunteers with nothing to do. So, with Gregory's blessing, ideas and the dissidents who advocated them became APL targets. APL agents/community business leaders shadowed IWW leaders, infiltrated meetings, and helped to disrupt the organization in any way possible. APL members even went along on the government raids of IWW headquarters that netted the materials used to prosecute the union's leaders. Volunteer agents looked for draft dodgers and turned them in for prosecution. Here, they staged mass roundups of draft-aged men in which all those picked up had to prove that they were either ineligible for the draft or that they were registered. Those who could prove neither were turned over to military authorities.

As complaints reached the department about the excessive zeal of some APL agents, Gregory tried to distance the department from the organization. For example, he warned APL members that they should not view wartime legislation as a means "whereby efforts are made to suppress honest, legitimate criticism . . . or discussion . . . nor . . . for personal feuds or persecution." In fact, said the attorney general, "protection of loyal persons from unjust suspicion and persecution is quite as important as the suppression of actual disloyalty." APL members should take care "to avoid unjustified arrests and prosecutions."[66] In addition, APL members were ordered to return their official-looking badges and were told to stop making arrests. The APL, however, made few, if any, changes in the way in which it operated despite Gregory's comments and orders, and the department continued to recognize it as an official auxiliary.

Events conspired to keep the APL as an important Justice Department adjunct. When the new Bolshevik government ratified the treaty of Brest-Litovsk in March 1918 and ended the war between Germany and Russia, a new spy scare swept the country. Now the allies faced the full force of the German military, making the war situation precarious. About the same time, fears rose about the dangers posed by Bolshevik sympathizers in the United States, and anxiety about Communists, which would haunt this country for the next seventy years, began. APL agents again became important in internal security plans, but problems with APL agents also increased.

Control of these agents was almost impossible, and APL members often used intimidation to obtain desired results. Public school teachers were watched for any signs of disloyalty. The organization tried to get undesirable books removed from library shelves. The privacy of thousands of ordinary Americans was violated as APL agents obtained access to medical, legal, and bank records and were able to convince a number of individuals, including ministers, to serve as confidential sources of information. APL agents shadowed suspicious individuals and through their connections were able to wiretap telephones and bug homes and offices. Federal and state prosecutions of radicals benefited from any information the APL obtained because courts refused to exclude it. The evidence may have been gotten illegally, but federal agents had not broken any laws to obtain it.

Despite repeated violations of what we today would consider basic civil liberties, the APL probably would have continued as an auxiliary to the Department of Justice indefinitely—if not for the organization's excesses in fall 1918. A need for men for the army combined with a governmental bounty on the head of each deserter led to a joint effort to pick up deserters and nonregistrants. The most obnoxious of the so-called slacker raids occurred over Labor Day weekend in New York City. Thousands of draft-aged men were picked up and held until they could prove that they were appropriately registered. Holding the detainees was not easy; facilities became overtaxed; and crowds outside the buildings became restive as family members were denied access to the men held within. Despite the problems, the raids continued.

The raids were finally called off on the Thursday after Labor Day, and the Justice Department launched an investigation. Complaints were particularly strong about the role that the APL had played in the raids, especially in that APL members, who lacked the requisite authority, had actually arrested many of the men. Gregory, although still supportive of the league, stressed that the APL was a voluntary group assisting the department and that it had no formal status or power. The immediate effect was to deprive league members of much of the information that they had been able to obtain due to their semi-official status. The group continued to function through the end of the war, when it finally disbanded.

The APL was not the only organization seeking to enforce patriotism during the war years. The National Security League, which had been established before the war in an attempt to boost military preparedness, also promoted 100 percent Americanism while the fighting lasted. One of the organization's primary targets was the educational system, which members felt was not teaching a proper understanding of national values.[67] Groups with lesser prestige also carried on the patriotic struggle. Overall, super-patriots sought to make sure that each Liberty Loan campaign was oversubscribed. Often, they would visit individuals who they felt had not pledged sufficiently, inform them of their unacceptable behavior, and almost force them to donate additional money. Individuals who were not considered suitably patriotic could awake one morning to find their houses painted yellow, a symbol of cowardice. In more obnoxious situations, the individual himself could be doused with yellow paint or covered with tar and feathers to indicate unacceptable behavior. Patriotic citizens also would force those whose devotion was suspect to kiss the flag or to sing the "Star Spangled Banner" in public as testimony to their loyalty. Americans could find themselves in trouble for criticizing the Red Cross, the YMCA, or the quality of knitting by volunteer sock makers.

Eventually, mob violence even concerned Woodrow Wilson, who for months had ignored the growing national intolerance. After a German living in the United States had been lynched for alleged unpatriotic acts,[68] Wilson spoke out. He told Americans that if they claimed to be "the champions of democracy," they must behave suitably. "I say plainly that every American who takes part in the action of a mob . . . is no true son of this great democracy, but its betrayer, and does more to discredit her by that single disloyalty to her standards of law and right, than the words of her statesmen or the sacrifices of her heroic boys in the trenches can do to make suffering peoples believe her to be their savior." The president asked, "How shall we commend democracy to the acceptance of other peoples if we disgrace our own by proving that it is, after all, no protection to the weak?" Indeed, "every mob contributes to German lies about the United States, what her most gifted liars cannot improve upon by the way of calumny. They can at least say that such things cannot happen in Germany except in times of revolution, when law is swept away!"[69] The president's comments, however, were too little and too late to stop vigilante action against those who disagreed with the war effort. His earlier comments about the intolerance that war would bring were far more accurate.

Wilson, in fact, had been the originator of most of the nation's psychological preparation for war. His public comments generally were designed to build the greatest possible support for the government's efforts. In addition, through creating the Committee on Public Information (CPI), the president set up an effective propaganda agency that carried the government's message throughout the nation. Agency head George Creel believed that the CPI was fighting for control of the minds of American citizens and that the battle lines ran through the center of every home in the country. His task was that of "holding fast the inner lines," of making sure that America was united on war-related issues.[70] In the process of creating support, Creel built on the existing intolerance and helped to structure a society incapable of accepting dissent.

The Creel Committee, as the CPI also was known, attracted the most talented individuals in a variety of fields to the task of promoting America. Top artists of the day, including Charles Dana Gibson, signed on to create posters promoting everything from liberty gardens to donating blood. Advertising experts prepared publicity campaigns for Liberty Loan drives and other patriotic endeavors that were widely distributed. Patriotic ideas were sent to cartoonists for use in political and other cartoons. Special publications were aimed at school children to enlist them in the war effort. Displays of captured German equipment were sent around the country so that the people could get a firsthand look at the war machinery of the terrible Huns. Through such efforts, Creel's employees attacked the American psyche on all sides.

In addition to propagandizing the war, the CPI's assignment was to ensure that the American press both supported the war effort and kept material that could be helpful to the Germans from being printed. In a strange contrast with previous wartime experiences, the Creel Committee encountered little difficulty with the press on either count. After protesting the censorship clause in the Espionage Act, few newspapers raised questions about the war, and almost no mainstream newspaper challenged other repressive legislation. The *New York Times* was fairly typical when it commented, "The time has come for strict interpretation and prompt enforcement of the laws of this country relating to treason, sedition and conspiracy against the Government. . . . It is the duty of every good citizen to communicate to the proper authorities any evidence of sedition that comes to his notice."[71] This enforcement, of course, did not extend to criticism of government actions in mainline newspapers, for, as the *New York Tribune* said, "Nobody seriously believes that a sane government would ever undertake to suppress proper criticism in this country, or that such an attempt, if made, could possibly succeed."[72] But there were no attacks on mainline newspapers.

The support of the war evidenced by the lack of criticism of repressive legislation and the calls for the prosecution of disloyal citizens carried over, for the most part, to the reportage of news. With mandatory censorship eliminated after the rejection of the provision in the original Espionage Act that would have authorized presidential action in that area, Creel was left with the responsibility of selling the press on a voluntary system of censorship. Fortunately for Creel, and unfortunately for a nation that probably needed more honest information than it received, the press was inclined to cooperate.[73]

Creel proclaimed that he was trying to balance the need for the maximum possible public disclosure of information with the need for national security. He publicly endorsed the right of newspapers to report events fully and to criticize the government where justified. By May 28, 1917, Creel had issued what the CPI termed a preliminary statement to the press on the need for cooperation. The statement divided news into three categories: dangerous, questionable, and routine. Dangerous news, which newspapers were asked to suppress voluntarily, focused on military operations in progress, on the movement of troops or of the president, and similar materials. Questionable news dealt with information focusing on training missions or the development of new weapons; in this situation, editors were asked to obtain CPI clearance before publication. Routine news, which Creel believed was the largest category, could be carried without approval, although the CPI did encourage editors and reporters to contact officials should there be any question. Newspapers were counseled about the dangers of carrying too much information about the war. "Reckless journalism, regrettable enough in times of peace, is a positive menace when the Nation is at war," the CPI statement said. "In this day of high emotionalism and mental confusion, the printed word has immeasurable power, and the term traitor is not too harsh in application to the publisher, editor, or writer who wields this power without full and even solemn recognition of responsibilities."[74]

Despite the care with which the CPI advised newspapers, arguments still developed over what news could be printed without endangering the war effort. CPI officials, for instance, were unhappy when journalists named a ship and its master while praising the exploits of armed merchant ships that attacked and sank German U-boats. Not that they objected to praise for heroes, but committee members remembered the case of a British officer who was captured, tried, and executed because he had been publicly commended for similar heroism. Complaints were on sounder ground when newspapers carried stories about the way in which mines were laid to prevent U-boats from reaching American shipping or about the efforts of the Renault company to develop a new tank. Such violations merited only a sharp letter of rebuke. Nor did Creel protest if journalists exposed inefficiency in the war effort or criticized wartime restrictions on food, fuel, or prices. The bottom line with the CPI head was always whether the publication was fundamentally loyal to the war effort; if loyalty had been proven, Creel essentially looked the other way when offenses occurred.

The record of cooperation between newspaper editors and the government during the World War I was exemplary. Few secrets were leaked, little information of value to the enemy was published, and most of the American press was wholeheartedly behind the war effort. After the war, however, critics charged that Creel had blown American fears of foreigners out of proportion and had set in motion a series of postwar repressions. In addition, said some of his critics, he had prepared the nation so well for war that the people had no way to deal with the possibilities of peace. Journalists of the day could well stand accused with Creel, for they were eager participants in selling of the war. To a certain extent, the government did not have to take away the journalists' First Amendment freedoms; the journalists put those freedoms aside voluntarily for the duration of the war. The question that emerges from this experience is just how do journalists best serve the nation during war? Should they mindlessly follow the government line? Or should they ask hard questions about government policy and objectives—behavior that could lead to them being labeled as traitors? The debate over which approach better serves the national interest still rages.

Just because the Committee on Public Information did not flex its muscles within the United States to prevent the publication of certain information did not mean that censorship did not exist. Transatlantic communication was regulated by military officials who reviewed all messages designated for transmission via underwater cable. In addition, newspapers and periodicals leaving the country were closely examined to make sure that they contained nothing that would antagonize allied or neutral countries or give harmful impressions of the United States. Even establishment publications such as the *New York Tribune,* the *Baltimore Sun, Scientific American,* and the *Saturday Evening Post* ran afoul of these censors. Stories stopped at the border included criticism of Mexican authorities, details of strikes and labor unrest in the United States, and information on the invention of a machine that allowed gun barrels to be straightened. The most important story stopped dealt with a U.S. Senate investigation into the aircraft industry, which focused on profiteering and waste in aircraft manufacture and revealed that $640 million had produced no airplanes for the front. These stories and others, though barred from circulating abroad, did make the pages of publications available within the United States.[75]

Although broadcasting was in its infancy and posed no real problems during World War I, censors did have to deal with the motion picture, and they used both formal and informal methods of persuasion to make sure that movies supported the war effort. Prior to American entrance into the war, movies with a peace theme were popular, but they disappeared with the U.S. declaration of war. Movie producers were warned that the government would take action against any movie that undermined the war effort. Producers needed only to witness the plight of Robert Goldstein in 1917 to learn that lesson thoroughly. Goldstein had worked with D. W. Griffith on *Birth of a Nation* and wanted some of the success that Griffith earned with his controversial production. Looking to history for the topic of his film, Goldstein decided on the Revolutionary War and made his movie, *The Spirit of '76,* which was released in 1917. The film was completed before the United States entered the war but was first viewed after American entrance. It was almost immediately suppressed, and charges were brought against Goldstein under the Espionage Act. As a depiction of the Revolution, the film was strongly anti-British; one of its featured scenes was the Wyoming Valley Massacre in which the Redcoats were seen killing women and children. The film was critically praised for condensing eight years of war into two-and-a-half hours of film with remarkable historical accuracy. Unfortunately, 1917 was not the time to accurately recall British atrocities. Goldstein was found guilty of attempting to foment disloyalty through the film. He was forced into bankruptcy because of the various court actions against him; his film was confiscated; and he was sentenced to ten years in the penitentiary.

Journalists attempting to report history in the making from the battlefields of Europe also faced censorship. At the front, the military controlled the information that could be sent back home, and the armed forces apparently had learned from their mistakes in earlier wars. This time, correspondents had to be accredited by the War Department. Journalists had to swear to write only the truth and not to reveal information that might aid the enemy. In order to reach the front, journalists also had to post a $10,000 good behavior bond that would be forfeited upon any violation of the rules. Stories were to be reviewed and cleared by military censors before being sent back to the United States for publication.[76]

Some correspondents ran into difficulty with the censors as they tried to tell readers exactly what was happening to American troops in Europe. The military censors, of course, wanted to release as little information as possible, and then only that information that could be considered favorable to the American cause. The conflict peaked over attempts to write stories about problems in properly supplying the American Expeditionary Force. Only after Heywood Broun left his assignment in Europe and returned to the United States was the *New York World* able to detail the problems. The War Department withdrew Broun's accreditation and declared his $10,000 bond forfeited. Westbrook Pegler tried to send out a story detailing the rate of illness among American troops in Europe and telling how more soldiers were dying from pneumonia than from enemy bullets. The military intercepted that story and had him recalled. Despite these examples, the press and the military apparently got along quite well during World War I. The accrediting process, which had begun during the Spanish-American War, apparently was the key, for reporters were not allowed to accompany military units without permission of the government. Misbehavior, including the sending of stories that military officials disliked, merited withdrawal of accreditation and immediate return home. Accreditation remains the military's main way to control reporters today.

The journalist's task in Europe was not completed when the fighting ended in November 1918. Indeed, many reporters thought their biggest story was still ahead, for President Wilson had announced plans to go to Paris to help negotiate the peace. Journalists planned to be right there with the president, covering the treaty negotiations much the way that they covered city council meetings. Wilson himself was responsible for raising press hopes about the peace conference. In January 1918, the president had finally announced his agenda for peace, and in an address to Congress, Wilson had presented his famous Fourteen Points. Point one promised the world that henceforth there would be "open covenants of peace, openly arrived at, after which there shall be no private international understandings of any kind but diplomacy shall proceed always frankly and in the public view."[77]

By 1918, the whole world knew that the war had been caused by secret alliances that, once triggered, had brought all of Europe into the conflict. Those secret agreements had been a major target of many dissident groups in the United States; now Wilson was publicly disavowing the continuation of such diplomacy. To journalists, Wilson's speech meant that they would have full access to all of the deliberations involved in establishing the peace. Wilson's definition of "open covenants openly arrived at," however, was quite different. He firmly believed that the press could release too much information to the public before agreements were finally settled; diplomacy was far too delicate to be conducted in the spotlight. Rather, Wilson believed that his point one would be served if the public knew of the general topics of discussion and was told of agreements after they were finished. With such disparate definitions of "open covenants openly arrived at," trouble loomed.[78]

American journalists arrived in Paris ready to attend all peace conference sessions, to interview attending diplomats, and to let the world know what was transpiring. Instead, they were barred from all but the most formal occasions and restricted to daily briefings by the press attaché. The fear of censorship pervaded the conference; American journalists also believed that the British and the French would keep unfavorable information from leaving Europe. But Wilson did ask British and French censors to leave American news dispatches alone because censorship would cause him great problems at home. Regardless of Wilson's efforts, charges that news was censored by the British and the French did emerge during the conference, although the incidents apparently were few. What did occur, though, was a tremendous overtaxing of available cable facilities, which led to a slowdown in transmission and to reporter complaints.

American journalists, irate over the circumstances surrounding coverage of the conference, tried to convince reporters from other countries that they should jointly demand greater access to sessions. Instead of winning their point, the American reporters confronted, possibly for the first time, the fact that the phrase "freedom of the press" meant different things not only for politicians and reporters but also for journalists from various countries. American journalists wanted to be admitted to all working sessions, or at least to have a pool of reporters admitted to those sessions. The British would not go that far and would have accepted fuller briefings from press attachés. The French liked things as they were because newspapers in France were closely tied to the government, and reporters obtained as much information as they desired. After hours of argument, the reporters decided to ask for as complete a communiqué as possible each day, for continued informal contacts between reporters and delegates, and for the abolition of censorship in all Allied countries. Since the reporters were not united on the demands little was achieved.

But the heads of state present did take note of the press complaints and sent British Prime Minister Lloyd George to explain the importance of secrecy in diplomatic negotiations to journalists. Among his points was the idea that their discussions were so sensitive that early release of information might excite the emotions of the people at home, thus making it impossible for the delegates to reach an agreement. In addition, if each item was debated in the press, negotiations would be prolonged and peace delayed. If deliberations were publicized, George continued, delegates would have a harder time compromising because the news accounts could put their political careers at risk if they made concessions. The democratic system, George said, must allow for the confidential exchange of opinions while holding leaders responsible for the decisions made. American journalists found those arguments sadly wanting in light of the Fourteen Points. The reasons for confidential diplomacy given at the Paris Peace Conference in 1919 would remain the rationale for shrouding future negotiations in secrecy. American journalists would protest at such later events as well but to no avail.

To a certain extent, American reporters are responsible for their exclusion from the discussions. Little remains secret once it falls into the hands of U.S. journalists, and American allies have more than once complained about the way in which the press broadcasts national secrets. As a result, foreign diplomats are more than likely to demand extra secrecy from their American counterparts. In addition, American journalists often have been found guilty of pursuing special interests in their reporting. Many correspondents attending the Paris Conference, for instance, went prepared to support or oppose President Wilson's plans for peace without even knowing the details of his proposals. Their decisions were based on political alliances that existed back in the United States.

The Paris Peace Conference found certain members of the press pushing for special privileges as well. Leaders of the major U.S. news services wanted provisions in peace treaties to open up the continent more fully to American reporters. Prior to the war, the world had been split into spheres of influence politically and journalistically. Each major nation had its own news service with exclusive jurisdiction over the news occurring in certain territories. Through an international cartel arrangement, that news then was shared with other national news agencies. The Associated Press (AP) was the American news agency participating in this arrangement, but with the advent of war, AP officials began to lobby for the dissolution of the news cartels and for permission for American reporters to wander freely throughout the world gathering news. Continuation of prewar news practices, the AP argued, would foment further misunderstanding among nations. The Associated Press believed one cause of World War I was the biased news that most European countries had been fed for years. Since the European agencies were closely tied to their national governments, they spewed forth the patriotic line both at home and abroad. The Associated Press, of course, had no ties to the United States government and was pursuing the opening of additional territory to its reporters as a business venture. Rather than talking in terms of dollars and cents, however, AP officials used the rhetoric of freedom of the press.[79]

Such demands made no headway with the peace negotiators at the end of World War I. In truth, the demands presented at least two delicate problems. First, few foreign governments wanted American journalists prying into their affairs. U.S. reporters with their arrogant investigations and boastful proclamations about freedom of the press were not well liked or well respected abroad. Second, any demand for language in peace treaties opening up new territories to American news agencies required governmental intervention on behalf of the press. Many journalists believed that the government should stay as far away from the press as possible and that even intervention to aid the press should be discouraged. Despite the inherent problems that the demands raised, they would reappear with greater intensity after World War II.

Just why American journalists thought that their government would intervene on their behalf is unclear. Certainly the performance of most reporters at the peace conference was not sufficient to merit favorable consideration. Offended at what they perceived to be unfair treatment at the Paris conference, American journalists, by and large, sent negative stories back to the United States. Even those journalists normally predisposed to support Wilson fell into this trap. Coverage of the Paris Peace Conference was to be the crowning achievement of many careers, and their disappointment was reflected in their stories. Wilson, of course, could have changed the way in which the conference was portrayed in the press, but the president never had liked the press and did little to ensure a positive response to his endeavors in Paris. The state of the president's health may well have contributed to his unwillingness to cope with the press, but whatever the reason, his failure to win journalistic support was costly. Opposition to the centerpiece of the president's peace proposal, the League of Nations, was building in the United States, and Wilson failed to create a groundswell of public opinion to counter that opposition. Ultimately, the League was lost when the Senate refused to sanction American participation. The League may well have been lost much earlier than the Senate vote—perhaps when press hopes for reporting on the Paris Peace Conference were dashed or perhaps even back in 1917 when Wilson decided to seek legislation allowing the censorship of the press. Regardless of the exact time that the League was lost, it surely was a victim of Wilson's wartime policies.

Wilson's efforts to suppress dissent in wartime had a lasting impact on American history. Because of the legislation that his administration was responsible for placing on the books and because of the numerous prosecutions for differences of opinion based on that legislation, his wartime presidency must be considered one of the most repressive in American history. Despite the effect that his efforts to win total support from the American people had on the ability of individuals to speak freely, Wilson's repressive tendencies had one positive outcome. The numerous prosecutions that resulted from those repressions ultimately forced the Supreme Court to investigate the possible meaning of First Amendment protections for freedom of expression.

Convictions abounded and so, too, did appeals. Sometimes, attorneys argued for overturning the conviction on technical grounds; other times, they raised First Amendment issues in the hopes of forcing the judicial system to examine the meaning of those guarantees. For the first time, many of the cases were framed in terms that allowed little room for maneuvering around the First Amendment. Congress had passed the laws under which federal officials had arrested individuals who then were tried and convicted in federal courts. Federal appeals courts, then, were asked to decide whether the statement "Congress shall make no law" really meant that or whether those words in effect had an asterisk next to them leading to a footnote that read "except under certain circumstances."

When the Supreme Court started ruling on cases under the Espionage Act of 1917 and the Sedition Act of 1918, the justices found little speech worthy of First Amendment protection. The Court established this stance in 1919 when it handed down its decision in *Schenck v. United States.* The case centered on Charles T. Schenck's distribution of a handbill calling for resistance to the draft. The question was whether comments by Schenck, a Socialist, threatened the nation's ability to raise an army. A unanimous Court, speaking through Oliver Wendell Holmes, Jr., upheld Schenck's conviction. "In many places and in ordinary times the defendants in saying all that was said in the circular would have been within their constitutional rights," Holmes wrote. "But the character of every act depends upon the circumstances in which it was done." In Schenck's case, "the question . . . is whether the words used are used in such circumstances and are of such a nature as to create a clear and present danger that they will bring about the substantive evils that Congress has a right to prevent." The standard for evaluation was one "of proximity and degree. When a nation is at war many things that might be said in time of peace are such a hindrance to its effort that their utterance will not be endured so long as men fight and that no Court could regard them as protected by any constitutional right."[80]

The possibility that Schenck's circular *could* cause problems for the government in raising an army was sufficient for Justice Holmes and his colleagues. There was no need to prove that the circular had fallen into the hands of draft-aged men nor to prove that anyone had taken action based on its words. The possibility of such eventualities was all that was necessary. In this case, Holmes established the famous clear-and-present-danger test for deciding when the government could suppress free expression. The meaning of Holmes's catch phrase has long been debated on and off the Court. Although Holmes later seemed to indicate that he favored a close linkage between words and actions, the Court in the postwar period endorsed a much more remote connection between the two.

Within a week, the Court returned to the issue of free speech in wartime. In *Frohwerk v. United States*,[81] the justices looked at several articles published in the *Missouri Staats-Zeitung* on the constitutionality of the draft. The publishers of the newspaper made no special effort to reach men of draft age nor were they advocating obstruction of the draft; they simply wanted to discuss the issues involved. But Justice Holmes, writing again for a unanimous Court, affirmed the convictions. The same day, the Court looked at the conviction of Socialist Eugene V. Debs for attempting to cause insubordination in the ranks of the military and to obstruct recruiting.[82] Although Debs had said nothing about resisting the draft, he was convicted of that offense. After his conviction was upheld, Debs began serving a ten-year sentence for violation of the Espionage Act.

These three cases were brought under the Espionage Act of 1917—a law that required the government to prove that an individual intended to commit specific offenses that would interfere with the war effort before conviction was possible. All three cases found the Supreme Court upholding the convictions of individuals involved even though evidence, viewed at a safe distance from the war itself, seemed weak. The next major case, *Abrams v. United States*,[83] involved the Sedition Act of 1918, the amendment to the Espionage Act that was aimed at silencing dissenting speech. *Abrams* involved an effort by Russian Jews to condemn the American incursion into the Soviet Union in the waning days of the war. The individuals involved printed leaflets opposing this military action and distributed them in August 1918—by throwing many of them from the rooftops of buildings in New York City. They were arrested and charged under the Sedition Act with making comments designed to undermine the American war effort. They were convicted, and on appeal, the case came to the Supreme Court.[84]

This case is worth special attention because the Supreme Court split for the first time on First Amendment issues, with Holmes and his colleague, Louis D. Brandeis, emerging as eloquent dissenters in the cause of freedom of expression. Holmes, the writer for a unanimous Court in the three earlier cases just a few months earlier, had changed his mind on the value of freedom of speech. He had been lobbied strongly by friends and colleagues over the summer to reconsider his opinion, and, with the decision in *Abrams*, this effort had paid off.[85] His eloquent voice and that of Brandeis would be heard often in succeeding years. Said

Holmes, dissenting from a seven-man majority that upheld the convictions of Abrams and his colleagues, "Persecution for the expression of opinions seems to me perfectly logical. If you have no doubt of your premises or your power and want a certain result with all your heart you naturally express your wishes in law and sweep away all opposition." But in wartime, circumstances change, Holmes said, for "when men have realized that time has upset many fighting faiths, they may come to believe even more than they believe the very foundations of their own conduct that the ultimate good desired is better reached by free trade in ideas—that the best test of truth is the power of the thought to get itself accepted in the competition of the market, and that truth is the only ground upon which their wishes safely can be carried out."[86] Here Holmes brings back the Miltonian concept of the marketplace of ideas and begins presenting the argument that even in wartime, free trade in ideas—all ideas, including those opposed to war— should be allowed. The notion won few adherents.

The next case on the docket, *Schaefer v. United States,* brought the Court face to face with convictions of five officers of the corporation publishing the *Phila-delphia Tageblatt,* a German-language newspaper. The five had been charged with treason for publishing fifteen articles that allegedly glorified Germany while denigrating the United States. They were acquitted of the treason charges but were immediately recharged with violations of the Espionage Act, were tried and found guilty. In 1920, the Supreme Court upheld the convictions of three of the defendants by a six-three vote. The majority in *Schaefer,* led by Joseph McKenna, began to look at the action of wartime dissenters in terms of the much more restrictive bad tendency test rather than the clear-and-present-danger test first advocated by Holmes. Wrote McKenna: "The tendency of the articles and their efficacy were enough for offense. . . . The incidence of its violation might not be immediately seen, evil appearing only in disaster, the result of the disloy-alty engendered and the spirit of mutiny."[87] The bad tendency test, which would dot Supreme Court decisions for years to come, permitted a much more relaxed standard for the suppression of speech. The connection between speech and action was gone; in its place was the idea that if the speech might possibly pro-duce unwanted behavior at some unspecified time in the future, then it could be suppressed.

The Schaefer case brought Brandeis's first dissent on behalf of freedom of expression. Commenting for himself and Holmes, he invoked First Amendment grounds in citing his disapproval of the Court's decision. The language of the dissent reflected his concern over the suppression of speech during the Red Scare that followed the war as well. "In peace, too, men may differ widely as to what loyalty to our country demands; and an intolerant majority, swayed by passion or by fear, may be prone in the future, as it has often been in the past, to stamp as disloyal opinions with which it disagrees," Brandeis said. "Convictions such as these, besides abridging freedom of speech, threaten freedom of thought and of belief."[88]

Brandeis continued to dissent in the next Espionage Act case before the Court, *Pierce v. United States.* In this case, three Socialists were prosecuted for distrib-uting "The Price We Pay," a pamphlet against the war written by a prominent

Episcopalian clergyman. Seven members of the Court voted to uphold the conviction in an opinion that criticized the views expressed in the pamphlet. Brandeis, for himself and Holmes, argued against punishing opinion. By permitting the suppression of these comments, the Court "would practically deny members of small political parties freedom of criticism and of discussion in times when feelings run high and the questions involved are deemed fundamental," he said. Brandeis worried about the effect that the Court's decisions would have on those arguing for change in government if it became apparent that First Amendment protections would be denied "merely, because the argument presented seems to those exercising judicial power to be unfair in its portrayal of existing evils, mistaken in its assumptions, unsound in reasoning or intemperate in language."[89]

Intemperate speech was the focus of *Gilbert v. Minnesota* as well. The case stemmed from the efforts of Joseph Gilbert to organize the Nonpartisan League in Minnesota. His efforts were condemned as violating a Minnesota law designed to stop the spread of antiwar sentiments. The Minnesota law could be violated even if no person was actually discouraged from enlisting and if the speaker had no intent to hinder the operation of the draft. The Supreme Court, in a seven-two vote, upheld Gilbert's conviction as a valid exercise of the state's police power. Holmes, content here to give the states greater discretion in the area, concurred in the result although not in the Court's reasoning. Brandeis dissented on First Amendment grounds, arguing prematurely that free speech was protected against state action by the federal Constitution. "I cannot believe," he wrote, "that the liberty guaranteed by the Fourteenth Amendment includes only liberty to acquire and enjoy property."[90] The fact that the Court accepted the case at all was a hint that, perhaps, John Marshall's embargo against application of the federal Bill of Rights to the states was about to be breached.

The final major wartime case, *United States ex rel. Milwaukee Social Democratic Publishing Company v. Burleson,* involved the postmaster general's efforts to ban dissenting publications from the mails during wartime. In the case of the *Milwaukee Leader,* a Socialist publication, Burleson had revoked second-class mailing privileges for future issues based on what had been printed in the past rather than evaluating each issue as it was presented. The Supreme Court, in a seven-two decision, upheld the postmaster general. Holmes and Brandeis dissented, contending that the law did not give the postmaster general power to bar future issues from the mail and arguing that the right of circulation via the mails was critical to the existence of newspapers. Said Brandeis, if the postmaster general had the power to ban all future publications because of past offenses, "he would, in view of the practical finality of his decisions, become the universal censor of publications."[91]

To those few Americans who wanted to support freedom of expression, the Supreme Court's decisions were disappointing. The justices, with Holmes and Brandeis often dissenting, came down solidly behind the repressive policies of the Wilson administration. Yet expecting a different performance from the Court was unrealistic. Supreme Court justices are products of their times, and the times at the end of World War I were definitely repressive. The major accomplishment in these cases was that the Court finally was addressing First Amendment arguments in a forthright manner. Even more important, perhaps, was that by their eloquent dissents, Justices Holmes and Brandeis were planting the seeds for future, more emancipating decisions.

In fact, the entire wartime experience can be viewed in much the same terms. The repression of these years was monstrous. But because of its excesses, individuals and groups started to argue for greater freedom of expression. Eventually, Americans would become ashamed of the way in which their country had behaved during wartime, and then the seed that would guarantee freedom of expression would begin to grow. Such a development, however, was to be delayed by another round of repression and super-patriotism.

CHAPTER 4

Facing New Challenges:
Freedom of Expression in the 1920s

Although the fighting in World War I ended, the repression of individuals with differing opinions in the United States did not. In fact, the suppression of dissidents increased in the months immediately after the armistice as a great wave of fear, known as the Red Scare, swept the nation. Behind this renewed effort to bring the nation into conformity with "American" ideas was the Bolshevik revolution in the Soviet Union and the beginning of Communist parties in the United States. But the causes of the Red Scare go much deeper than the emergence of new political parties. War's end brought substantial economic dislocation. Soldiers were ready to re-enter the work force; prices went up appreciably; and organized labor, which generally had honored its no-strike pledge during the war, began to agitate for higher wages to keep up with inflation. Once again, the nation's business leaders felt significantly threatened by unsettled conditions. But rather than take action to force a return to prewar standards themselves, business leaders relied on government-inspired fear of radicals and on numerous state and federal statutes against dissident activity to handle the situation for them. The year or so of repression that resulted was widespread, violent, and excessive. Strangely enough, out of the excesses of this period emerged the nation's first true understanding of the value of freedom of expression and the right to dissent.[1]

Woodrow Wilson was largely responsible for the excesses of the postwar period even though he was incapacitated due to a stroke for much of the time. The climate of super-patriotism established during the war years was not easily dissipated. Still looking for scapegoats for their problems, Americans simply substituted Communists for Germans. Wilson helped to breed the fear of the Bolsheviks that many Americans soon exhibited. The toppling of the czar had led to great hopes for democracy in Russia, but within months, the Communists had taken control. Soon after their takeover, the Bolsheviks signed a treaty with Germany and pulled out of the war, leaving the United States and the Allies to fight a united German army in a one-front war. Shortly after the Communist takeover, American troops entered Russia on the pretext of helping to extricate Allied forces stranded in a hostile land. The troops stayed on after the end of the war and supported efforts to topple the new regime.

As Americans surveyed the world scene after the war, their apprehension of communism only increased. In March 1919, the Bolsheviks set up the Third International, which was dedicated to exporting the Soviet revolution. Governments in Germany, Poland, Italy, and Hungary seemed susceptible to Communist intrigues. When rumors spread that the United States was a target of revolution, fears mounted. In addition, many Americans felt abandoned by their government in the face of a rising crisis. With the end of the war, the federal government had dropped hundreds of Espionage Act cases, had ordered the American Protective League to disband, and had stopped investigating the loyalty of many individuals. Clearly, the way had been left open for a resurgence of radicalism.

American radicals who were not in jail due to war-related offenses fed these apprehensions. Most of them praised the Communist revolution, seeing within it an opportunity for workers to obtain their fair share of the nation's wealth, and many American radicals called for importation of these ideas to the United States. Such endorsements largely came from the Socialist party, which, though debilitated by wartime prosecutions, began to grow once more with the end of the fighting, and from the remnants of the Industrial Workers of the World. Conservative concern focused initially on the Socialists, who in 1919 split over the issue of the Russian revolution. The right wing remained true to the party's long-held trust in change through the ballot box. The left wing endorsed the revolutionary ideas of the Soviet Communists and abandoned the Socialist party. The latter contingent then split again, with the native-born left-wingers forming the Communist Labor party, with about 10,000 members, and the foreign-born establishing the American Communist party, with about 60,000 members. The parties merged later in the 1920s, but earlier, factionalism prevailed. Even with the membership of both parties combined, avowed Communists in the United States totaled less than one-tenth of 1 percent of the nation's adult population in 1919. But the nation did have its share of Communist sympathizers as well, with the conservatives becoming particularly incensed about the so-called "parlor pink," the liberal, often well-to-do, native-born American who gave moral and financial support to Communist causes. The total number of Communists and their supporters came to about one million in 1919.[2]

In addition, radicalism seemed to be infecting the labor movement. Samuel Gompers, head of the American Federation of Labor (AFL), had kept union members loyal during the war years. Now the AFL called for government ownership of public utilities, regulation of corporations, and public financing of low-cost housing. Conservative business leaders had tolerated an increased governmental presence during the war, but now they wanted government to leave business alone. Republicans in Congress worked hard to accomplish this end, trying, for instance, to roll back many prewar reform measures and to end war-related business regulations. The AFL, on the other hand, wanted an increased governmental presence. To end this threat, business leaders sought to tar the legitimate labor movement with the Bolshevik label, and accomplishing that end was not difficult.

The Industrial Workers of the World helped bring the wrath of the nation down on labor unions in 1919 when it participated in a massive strike in Seattle, Washington. The work stoppage started in the shipyard, but it soon spread throughout the city as the union called a general strike. More than 60,000 workers left their jobs, paralyzing the entire city. Union members continued to provide essential services such as garbage collection and food deliveries. But Mayor Ole Hanson became convinced that the strike was the first stage of the Bolshevik revolution in the United States. He asked for federal troops to force the union members back to work. The strikers made that request unnecessary because, fearing public opinion, they called off the strike and resumed work on their own. Hanson, however, built both a political career and a national reputation as a red basher based on *his* stopping the strike.

Labor union members now were labeled as radical, and employers discovered that they no longer had to act against unions. State and municipal governments, upset by the rise in radicalism, took up the cause. By 1920, thirty-five states had statutes on the books restricting radical activity. All went beyond the prohibition of violence against the state in order to punish speech designed to promote discontent with the existing system of government. Many of the acts specifically barred speech designed to change the industrial as well as the governmental system. And many states enacted red-flag statutes that made it illegal to display any flag or banner that symbolized opposition to organized government. The fight against radicalism became socially acceptable and politically popular. Business leaders and politicians took up the cause as did the establishment press, and the American people believed allegations that the Communists were inspiring massive unrest. A campaign to stamp out all domestic radicals soon was under way.

Many events in 1919 combined to inflame the antiradical campaign. In late April 1919, a number of bombs were found in post offices around the country. One had been sent to Mayor Hanson, but it was discovered before delivery. Another was delivered to former Georgia Senator Thomas Hardwick, whose maid opened the package. Her hands were blown off, and Mrs. Hardwick was badly burned. The post office found thirty-four other bombs addressed to such notables as Supreme Court Justice Oliver Wendell Holmes, Jr., Postmaster General Albert Burleson, Attorney General A. Mitchell Palmer, and business leaders John D. Rockefeller and J. P. Morgan. None of the packages had been delivered because of insufficient postage. Although no perpetrator was found, most Americans seemed convinced that the Bolsheviks were behind the planned bombings.

Fears rose again on May 1, 1919, when riots broke out in many American cities. Radicals celebrating International Labor Day marched through major cities carrying their red flags and banners and calling for changes in government and industry. Generally, the marches occurred without the proper permits, and in many locations, police joined with bystanders to put a bloody end to the marches. Riots ensued in Boston, New York City, and Cleveland, convincing Attorney General Palmer that radicals would go to any end to accomplish their goals—even though the riots were caused by police and bystanders rather than by the marchers. Only protesters were arrested, in compliance with the legal theory that made them guilty for inspiring violence in others.

More bombs went off in early June. Two people were killed, and several public and private buildings were damaged. The most important bombing, in terms of long-range effects on the nation's radicals, occurred in front of Attorney General Palmer's home. The attorney general and his family had just gone to bed when a bomb destroyed the front of his house. Authorities found pieces of the body of at least one person and theorized that the bomb had gone off prematurely. They identified the bomber as an anarchist on the basis of copies of a pamphlet found in the neighborhood.[3]

Pressure had been mounting on Palmer to act against radicals; now he was ready. First he had to retool the Department of Justice. Many of its key wartime personnel had left public service, and some of those still on the job were suspected of harboring sympathies toward liberal causes. New personnel were named, and a reorganization that had a long-term impact on civil liberties in the United States began. William J. Flynn, a former Secret Service agent, was named to head the Intelligence Bureau, whose task was to protect the nation from radicals. Even more important, Palmer set up a General Intelligence Division (GID), or Radical Division, within the department itself and named J. Edgar Hoover as its head. Hoover immediately began to accumulate files on alleged radicals in the United States. Soon he had more than half a million names in his ever-growing index of possible subversives and had fairly full files on some 70,000 other potential troublemakers.[4]

Whether there really was a chance for a Communist revolution in the United States in 1919 is doubtful. Communist presses were busy and their speakers talked a good deal, but they had no plans for or means to carry out any revolution. Despite the Soviet Union's attempt to finance efforts to overturn the U.S. government, the conditions that made the Soviet Union ripe for revolution simply did not exist in the United States. In addition, American radicals traditionally wanted to change their system of government to make it fairer and more representative rather than to overthrow it. The facts of the situation, however, made little difference to conservatives. The Communist label was readily employed to repress dissent and to tarnish the reputations of those calling for change in society. For a while, the use of that label was highly successful.

All of the gathering forces of conservatism and fear were energized in fall 1919 as the nation was rocked by a number of strikes. Boston police officers were the first to leave their jobs. The strike was triggered by traditional workers' complaints—low pay, long hours, and poor conditions—and by the firing of officers attempting to organize the police for the AFL. The National Guard was called in to maintain order and to protect property. Samuel Gompers urged the police to return to work, but the police commissioner refused to take the strikers back. Governor Calvin Coolidge backed the commissioner and began his road to the White House by announcing, "There is no right to strike against the public safety."[5] The image of the AFL was badly damaged by the strike, as business and government leaders depicted it as a radical organization. In addition, due to the police strike, many Americans became convinced that the Bolsheviks had infiltrated the nation's police forces and that the nation would be left helpless in the face of revolution.

Compounding these fears was a nationwide strike of steelworkers, called two days after the police walkout had begun. About half of the workers employed by the industry labored under deplorable conditions, working twelve-hour days and seven-day weeks. The unskilled worker took home less than the minimum amount needed to support a family of four. Organizing efforts by a non-AFL-related union had been under way for only about a year, but the strike was judged to be 90 percent effective. The industry was closed down, and violence erupted. Once again, the strikers were portrayed as harbingers of the Bolshevik revolution in the United States. Police raids in Gary, Indiana, uncovered radical literature, which the officers then connected to the strikers. Later investigations found little or no radical infiltration of the strike and blamed the industry's problems on the oppressive policies of the owners. The strike ended in January 1920, and the workers, who had won no concessions from their employers, were lucky to still have jobs.

A third major strike simply confirmed the growing national suspicion. This time, the United Mine Workers (UMW) called its members out of the mines in November 1919. The mine owners had made a good deal of money during the war, but employees' wages had not risen. The workers simply wanted a share in the profits, but their demands were considered radical—communistic. President Wilson had sought an injunction to prevent the walkout, but the court order only stopped UMW leaders from calling the strike; the miners left their jobs anyway. UMW leaders were ordered to call the strike off, which they did. Many miners, though, remained off the job as the nation's coal supplies reached a dangerous low point with winter approaching. Since coal was the nation's major source of heat, schools and factories were closed. Transportation by railroad, the primary means of traveling any distance, was limited. The strike ended only after President Wilson forced mine owners to implement a wage increase and after he had set up a special panel to settle other grievances. Because the miners had remained off the job in the face of a legal order to return, the nation once again saw the red hand of Bolshevism at work.

Members of Congress were among those convinced that the nation was at risk. After several days of debate, the Senate asked the attorney general to "advise and inform" members as to "whether or not the Department of Justice has taken legal proceedings—and if not, why not; and if so, to what extent—for the arrest and punishment of the various persons within the United States who, during recent days and weeks" have worked to bring about the forcible overthrow of the government. The senators were concerned about individuals who "have advised the defiance of law and authority, both by the printing and circulation of printed newspapers, books, pamphlets, circulars, stickers, and dodgers, and also by spoken word" and who have "advised and openly advocated the unlawful obstruction of industry and the unlawful and violent destruction of property, in pursuance of a deliberate plan and purpose to destroy existing property rights and to impede and obstruct the conduct of business essential to the prosperity and life of the community."[6]

As criticism mounted, Palmer prepared to act. Palmer had presidential ambitions, and a lack of decisive action would definitely jeopardize his chances for the nomination. With prosecutions under most wartime legislation impossible,

Palmer used the only measure available to him—the Alien Act of 1918.[7] He believed that 90 percent of the nation's radicals were foreign-born. Most of these people were Southern and Eastern Europeans, already targeted by nativist groups as the least desirable of all aliens. The attorney general was convinced that removing these foreign-born radicals would end all problems. Under provisions of the act, any alien anarchist could be deported no matter how peaceful his views might be. In addition, any alien who advocated the use of violence against government, property, or public officials could be deported. Any alien who simply belonged to an organization advocating such things likewise was subject to deportation. The reach of the law was wide indeed.[8]

Under the legislation, the departments of justice and labor had to cooperate on any moves against aliens. The Justice Department was to supply the names of individuals to be arrested; the Labor Department was to issue the appropriate warrants. Then, Justice Department agents would arrest the suspects, and Labor Department officials would hold the hearings necessary for deportation. The two departments decided to move first against the Union of Russian Workers, a nationwide organization to which some 4,000 Russian immigrants belonged. Although all of its members were not necessarily Bolsheviks, the union itself had issued a manifesto advocating violent revolution. Many immigrants associated with the union simply for companionship of like-speaking individuals, but the bare fact of membership made them deportable. The law did not require that they adhere to the union's stand or, for that matter, that they even know about the manifesto. Despite the government's targeting of the organization, officials had no evidence that its members had ever participated in violent actions against established authority.

Government agents chose a symbolic date for their raids on the Union of Russian Workers—November 7, 1919, the second anniversary of the Bolshevik revolution. Justice Department agents raided Russian Workers' meeting places in twelve cities almost simultaneously, arresting everyone in the buildings regardless of whether the individuals were connected with the union. Reports surfaced that police involved in the raids manhandled many of the people arrested. In addition, Justice Department agents had only twenty-seven warrants for New York City, but they arrested more than 200 men and women. Despite explicit orders to the contrary, many of those picked up were American citizens; others had no connection with the union. Similar problems occurred elsewhere. Reported civil liberties abuses included arrests without warrants, illegal searches of individuals and property, and physical violence. The detention centers to which these people were taken were often overcrowded and unsanitary. Most of the nation, however, ignored these problems and praised the attorney general. The adulation grew even greater when the *Buford,* nicknamed the Soviet Ark, left New York harbor on December 21 taking 249 anarchists to Russia.

Shortly before the first Palmer Raid, Senator Thomas Sterling, Republican of South Dakota, introduced the first major peacetime sedition bill in Congress. Dozens of similar proposals were placed in the hopper, but only four of them, including Sterling's proposal, won serious consideration. According to the bill's provisions, it would be "unlawful for any person to advocate or advise the overthrow . . . by force or violence, or by physical injury to person or property of the Government of the United States." The measure proscribed the advocacy of any "change in the form of government or the Constitution of the United States." Its provisions also forbade the display of red flags and other emblems of the radical movement and declared printed material prepared by such groups nonmailable.[9]

Representative Martin L. Davey, Democrat of Ohio, introduced another peacetime sedition bill on November 17, 1919. Said to be the measure backed by Attorney General Palmer, the Davey bill was aimed at anyone who intended "to levy war against the United States, or to cause the change, overthrow, or destruction of the Government or of any of the laws or authority thereof. . . [by] any act of terrorism, hate, revenge, or injury." The targets of the measure were individuals who actually spoke in favor of overthrowing the government, who advised it, advocated it, taught it or justified it, or who joined any organization involved in promoting like action. Aliens convicted under the act would be deported after they had served their jail sentences; any naturalized citizens convicted under the provisions would lose their citizenship and likewise be deported after serving any jail sentences.[10]

While action was beginning on a peacetime sedition law, members of the House of Representatives found another way to preserve national security. Their work focused on the ouster of one of their own members, Victor L. Berger, a Socialist who represented the city of Milwaukee. Berger, long an active Socialist, had served one term in Congress beginning in 1911. While out of office during the war years, he edited the *Milwaukee Leader,* a Socialist publication whose mailing privileges were removed by the postmaster general because of the newspaper's antiwar articles. A signatory of the Socialist party's St. Louis Platform, Berger also had been convicted under the Espionage Act for interfering with the war effort. The conviction occurred in January 1919; in May, he reported to Congress to begin his second term.

Members of the House, who have the constitutional power to pass upon the qualifications of their colleagues, refused to seat him. A special committee set up to hear his case based the ouster on the language of the Fourteenth Amendment that excluded any person who had once sworn to uphold the Constitution but who then had provided aid and comfort to the enemy from Congress. The provision was a loyalty test inserted just after the Civil War to keep former Confederates from regaining their seats in Congress. The committee, not surprisingly, found that Berger "did obstruct, hinder, and embarrass the Government of the United States in the prosecution of the war and did give aid and comfort to the enemy."[11] On November 10, 1919, the House voted to exclude Berger from membership. Their victory over Berger was only temporary, for his constituents reelected him to the seat from which he had been ousted. He was again kept from taking his seat. Nominated again, he lost the 1920 election in a Harding victory. He ran again in 1923, was elected, and finally was seated. In the interim, the Supreme Court had overturned his Espionage Act conviction on a technicality.[12]

The day after Berger was first ousted from the House of Representatives, Armistice Day 1919, residents of Centralia, Washington, acted against local radicals. After a patriotic parade through the center of town, members of the American Legion and other townspeople launched a bloody attack on the Industrial Workers of the World meeting hall. Several Legionnaires were shot during the battle, and the Wobblies were, of course, blamed for the entire affair. IWW members were rounded up and jailed; during that night, one of the men charged was spirited away, beaten, emasculated, hanged three times on a rope that was too short, and finally pumped full of bullets. Said the coroner, "Everest broke out of jail, went to the Chehalis River bridge, and committed suicide. He jumped off with a rope around his neck and then shot himself full of holes."[13] Immediately after the Centralia Massacre, IWW halls up and down the West Coast were raided in a final attempt to eliminate the hated union. Those members who managed to stay out of jail went underground, and the union, for all intents and purposes, dissolved. The defendants in the Centralia case were convicted of second-degree murder and given prison terms ranging from twenty-five to forty years. Many observers felt that if the defendants had not been Wobblies, they likely would not have been convicted because the situation surrounding the shooting was so confused that it was hard to pinpoint responsibility.

To many Americans, the blame for everything bad that happened could be laid directly at the feet of radicals. Attorney General Palmer accurately reflected popular opinion as he planned another series of raids, this time against the Communist and the Communist Labor parties. Secretary of Labor William Wilson was reluctant to approve 3,000 warrants, but he finally did and the raids went ahead. Palmer planned for quick hearings before Labor Department functionaries and rapid deportation of those aliens swept up in the raids. On January 2, 1920, government agents swooped down on Communist party headquarters in thirty-three major cities in twenty-three states. Undercover agents had prepared the groundwork for the assault by engineering party meetings for that day. More than 4,000 people were arrested, often without matching individuals and warrants. Individual rights were again violated by illegal searches, and once more, brutality was a major problem. Victims of these arrests again were housed in overcrowded, unsanitary holding facilities. Agents also picked up literature, letters, and other possible documentary evidence.

Generally, the public supported the Justice Department's actions. The popular press was among the strongest backers of Palmer and his raids. The *New York Times,* for instance, said, "The more of these dangerous anarchists are arrested, the more of them are sent back to Europe, the better for the United States."[14] Editors of the *Washington Post* concurred, commenting, "The time has come when foreign enemy propaganda must be prevented from utilizing freedom of speaking and printing in America for the purpose of destroying America itself. The abuse of free speaking and printing must be defined and punishment provided." According to the *Post,* "The right of free speech, printing and assembly in the United States should not include the right to preach bolshevism directly or indirectly."[15]

Not all newspapers supported Palmer's policy. The *St. Louis Post-Dispatch,* for example, noted that "the right and duty of our government to protect itself and to guard our institutions against revolution and unlawful action and propaganda are unquestioned." Palmer's methods, however, were questionable. "Let us clean up the revolutionists and the propagandists of disorder, lawlessness, and violence. But let us do it in a sane, legal, orderly manner," the *Post-Dispatch* said. "Free government cannot be saved by the destruction of the pillars upon which it stands—free speech, free assemblage, and freedom from official oppression in any form."[16] While the *San Francisco Examiner* approved of deporting "trouble making aliens who come to war upon American institutions," it had problems with the nationalism that led to the raids. "We do not think the obnoxious aliens are more dangerous than the tendencies of some American statesmen," it commented. "These officials are trying to change our laws so that any American citizen who DISAGREES WITH THEIR IDEAS or advocates a change in government may be sent to jail for twenty years."[17]

Other opposition developed as well. Various Protestant churches attacked the excesses of nativism, with the Interchurch World Movement investigation of the steel strike of October 1919 disproving the popular notion of radical instigation. Some members of the legal community spoke out against the suppression of individual opinion as well. Zechariah Chafee, Jr., one of the most outspoken critics, wrote his first article on a First Amendment topic, "Freedom of Speech in War Time," for the June 1919 *Harvard Law Review*. His criticism of the Justice Department earned Chafee a place on the department's list of suspicious characters. Further essays and his signature on a petition asking for amnesty for political prisoners of World War I won him the enmity of conservative Harvard Law School alumni and led to a strong, but unsuccessful, attempt to have him fired in 1921.[18] Some scholars even suggest that one factor contributing to U.S. Supreme Court Justice Oliver Wendell Holmes, Jr.'s new position on free speech was the excesses of the fall of 1919. The Abrams decision was handed down in November 1919.

Opposition picked up with the January 1920 raids, although it was still insufficient to halt the persecution of individuals for their political opinions. Francis Fisher Kane, the U.S. attorney for Philadelphia, resigned rather than prosecute individuals picked up in the raids. He sent copies of his letter containing his objections to the arrests to Palmer, to President Wilson, and to the press. And a Department of Labor official unexpectedly thwarted most of Attorney General Palmer's plans to deport those arrested in the January raids as undesirable aliens. Secretary of Labor William Wilson had become ill, and Assistant Secretary Louis F. Post filled that position temporarily.

Rather than rush the deportations through, Post examined each case carefully. A number of aliens were released because of insufficient evidence or because their arrests were based on illegally seized material. Members of the Communist Labor party, the native-born branch of the party, were released immediately because the warrants had authorized action only against the foreign-born Communist party. Post also had problems with the kind of aliens arrested in the Justice Department's dragnet. "As a rule, the hearings show the aliens arrested to be working men of good character who have never been arrested before, who are not anarchists or revolutionists, nor politically or otherwise dangerous in any sense." After thoroughly reviewing each case, Post allowed the deportation only of persons clearly shown to be members of the Communist party regardless of their understanding of party doctrine.[19]

Post's strictness in interpreting the rules of evidence and the instructions to arresting officers distressed many members of the Department of Justice. At the urging of the Justice Department, the acting secretary of labor was called before a House committee to explain his actions. Talk spread about impeaching Post for misconduct. The hearings dragged along, with the committee actively considering a resolution to censure him for being too lenient. After Post appeared before the committee in early May and offered a powerful defense of his behavior, the entire issue was dropped.

By May 1920, most Americans were ready to forget about the Red Scare, but that January, few thought the fear would ever abate. In addition to the second round of raids, January brought discussions on enacting a peacetime sedition bill in Congress to a new height. Three measures caught the greatest attention: the Sterling and Davey bills mentioned above and a proposal introduced by Representative George S. Graham, Republican of Pennsylvania. The Graham bill was particularly harsh because under certain circumstances it would have allowed the imposition of the death penalty on those convicted of sedition in peacetime.[20]

Debate focused on the loose language used to frame most of the legislation and on the delegation of powers inherent in the proposals. A major criticism of the Sterling bill related to provisions that would make material advocating the overthrow of the government nonmailable. Senators distressed about Postmaster General Burleson's behavior during the war questioned placing so much authority in the hands of one man. Language suggesting that individuals who promoted nonviolent change in the government could fall within the snare laid by the legislation raised other concerns. The Graham bill, for instance, could be applied against anyone who sought to speak or write in a way designed to bring about the "overthrow or change of the Government of the United States or the Constitution, laws, and authority."[21] Senator Robert L. Owen, Democrat of Oklahoma, said that with such language, "advocacy of an amendment to the Constitution of the United States in favor of prohibition, which would be a change of the Constitution, would be a criminal act under this proposed law." Likewise, advocacy of an income tax or a woman's suffrage amendment could be forbidden.[22]

Senator Owen was exaggerating somewhat because the Graham bill said changes must be imposed by force and violence, but the language of legislation can be perverted or, in times of stress, enlarged to make even the peaceful advocacy of change illegal. As Senator Owen said, "I do not want any bureaucrat in this Government having arbitrary power to lay a rough hand upon a man who is expressing his honest opinion and his belief as to what is the good thing and the better thing for his fellow citizens." The senator from Oklahoma believed, "It is freedom of opinion, it is freedom of speech, it is freedom of the press, it is freedom of religion and freedom of education which have combined to make this country the greatest free nation in the world." In addition, Owen strongly believed that supporters of a peacetime law were "the stupid friends of vested interests, who would like to use the powers of the Government to put a bayonet through everyone who balks against vested interests." Restrictions on discussion and advocacy "would be pursuing a policy like that of chaining down the escape valve on a steam boiler. . . . To do this under the false pretense of suppressing bolshevism and anarchy is Prussianism and not Americanism."[23]

Other senators held different views of permissible speech. Senator Thomas J. Walsh, Democrat of Montana, for example, believed governmental self-preservation was paramount. At one time in American history, he said, the nation might have "allow[ed] the loud-mouthed anarchist freely to express his views and purposes in public, depending upon the general good sense of the people of this country and their attachment to the principles of our Government to counteract whatever possible evil there might be in the assertion; but that time has gone by." Now, Walsh contended, "we have in our midst here a vast multitude of people who have no appreciation whatever of our institutions. . . . They came here poisoned with political ideas that they have absorbed in the midst of some oppressive, autocratic system of some country in Europe . . . and fired with a purpose to . . . overthrow all governments." Attitudes bred in the tyranny of Europe now threatened the United States, and Congress must protect the nation, Walsh argued.[24]

Essentially, the argument over a peacetime sedition act was as old as the debates over the Alien and Sedition Acts of 1798. One side argued that trust in the people and in the free discussion of issues would provide the only true security for the nation; the other side stressed that the nation must first and foremost take steps to protect itself from threats from outside forces. The Senate did pass an amalgamation of the Sterling and the Davey bills. House action got caught up in the furor over the Palmer raids and related Red Scare activities, with the measures eventually dying in committee as the life went out of the scare itself.

Several factors contributed to the end of the Red Scare in early 1920. The excesses of the January raids and the actions of Louis F. Post were, of course, instrumental in nudging the American public into distrusting red bashing. Another major factor was an action of the New York State legislature in January, shortly after the second round of Palmer Raids. Recently elected legislators were in Albany to begin a new session when the speaker of the state house refused to allow five representatives to be seated. The five were all Socialists, duly elected by voters in New York City, but Speaker Thaddeus C. Sweet accused them of having been "elected on a platform that is absolutely inimical to the best interests of the State of New York and of the United States."[25] A committee was formed to decide whether the five men should be permanently excluded from the assembly. No charges of improper behavior were brought against them; none of them had been charged or convicted under the Espionage Act as had Victor Berger. Their only crime was membership in the Socialist party, a legally recognized political party in the state.[26]

The ouster of the five men brought an immediate critical outcry. Among those leading the protest was Charles Evans Hughes, a Republican who had served as governor of the state, as a justice on the U.S. Supreme Court, as his party's candidate for president in 1916, and who later would become chief justice of the United States. Hughes rounded up support from the New York City Bar Association, an organization filled with establishment attorneys, the majority of whom were outraged at the speaker's action. With the bar's blessing, Hughes led a committee to Albany to denounce the action. The speaker, contending that the state constitution, as the national, gave each house the right to seat its own members, would allow the New York City attorneys only to submit a written statement.

The heart of Speaker Sweet's case rested on the principle of guilt by association. The men themselves may not have done anything wrong, but they associated with others who did violate the law. One of the prosecutors in the case, John B. Stanchfield, said that the men had admitted being members of the Socialist party, an organization "embarked upon a program that calls for the overthrow of our form of government, some assert by constitutional means, other[s] by violence." Stanchfield continued that every person "who upholds those claims, who supports those principles, who stands upon that platform, is bound by the speeches, the sentiments, the writings, the books, the publications of every other man affiliated with that association, whether they were present at the time when it was made or they were uttered, or whether they were absent."[27]

With such a broadly based rationale for seeking the exclusion of the men, the outcome was a foregone conclusion. The five were ousted, but, as with Victor Berger, they were reelected in a special election called to fill their seats. By that time, public ridicule of the New York assembly for cowering in fear before five Socialists had been severe, and the assembly members decided to seat two of the five while expelling the other three, who supposedly had made questionable speeches. The two who were seated resigned immediately out of sympathy for their colleagues. When two of the five won reelection again, they were seated when the legislature convened in 1921. The Red Scare in New York State was over.

Also helping to end the Red Scare nationally was the emergence of a coalition of liberals who were determined to stand firm against the abuses of the Justice Department. The National Popular Government League, whose membership included Zechariah Chafee, Jr., Felix Frankfurter, and Roscoe Pound, all of the Harvard Law School, and Ernst Freund of the University of Chicago Law School, investigated the Palmer Raids. The organization's findings charged the Justice Department with violating numerous sections of the Bill of Rights in its eagerness to suppress radical thought. "It has always been the proud boast of America that this is a government of laws and not of men. Our Constitution and laws have been based on the simple elements of human nature," they said. "Free men cannot be driven and repressed; they must be led. Free men respect justice and follow truth, but arbitrary power they will oppose until the end of time. There is no danger of revolution so great as that created by suppression, by ruthlessness, and by deliberate violation of the simple rules of American law and American decency."[28] The time had come to stop oppression based on political views. The National Popular Government League report was issued toward the end of May, a month that had begun with Assistant Secretary of Labor Louis F. Post defending his refusal to deport hundreds of aliens caught in Attorney General Palmer's raids.

The final blow against the Red Scare was struck by Judge George W. Anderson, who was serving on the U.S. District Court in Massachusetts. In June 1920, after months of testimony, Anderson handed down a decision in a case involving eighteen aliens entrapped in Palmer's snare. In finding for the defendants, Anderson entered a scathing indictment of the Justice Department's behavior on the record. Although he restrained himself from making "any extended comment on the lawlessness of these proceedings by our supposedly law-enforcing officials," Judge Anderson did note, "a mob is a mob, whether made up of government officials acting under instructions from the Department of Justice, or of criminals, loafers, and the vicious classes."[29]

By June 1920 the great postwar Red Scare was essentially over. The nation was ready to stop searching out radicals and to get on with the business of enjoying life in what would become known as the Roaring Twenties. Remnants of the great fear lingered in the corridors of government. In 1920, Congress amended statutes to allow the deportation of any alien convicted of violating wartime legislation[30] and to expel any alien who had lent or given money to a proscribed organization.[31] In 1921, Congress began amending immigration laws to limit foreign nationals allowed to enter the United States,[32] and by 1924, Congress established the quota system that allowed individuals to enter the country based upon the percentage of persons of their national origin who were in the United States in 1890.[33] Through this legislation, Congress hoped to favor the safer immigrants of northern and western Europe, who were here in greater numbers in 1890, and reduce the number of newcomers from southern and eastern Europe who allegedly were more likely to be radicals.

The remnants of the Red Scare permeated the Supreme Court, where it left a lasting legacy for freedom of speech. When the justices heard the appeal of Benjamin Gitlow, a New York Socialist who had moved over to the new Communist party and was arrested for violating the state's 1902 criminal anarchy law, few imagined that the case would long be remembered. Gitlow was picked up in a state raid on party headquarters in November 1919; he had served as business manager of the party's publication, *Revolutionary Age.* The charges were based on the publication of the "Left Wing Manifesto," a document criticizing capitalism and defending the revolutionary ideas of Marx.[34]

Clarence Darrow, one of the nation's leading defense attorneys, developed two lines of defense for Gitlow. First, he intended to argue that the manifesto did not call for a violent revolution and thus was not within the terms of the 1902 act, and second, that the statute was unconstitutional in that it violated both state and federal guarantees of freedom of speech and of the press. Darrow's line of defense proved ineffective with various state courts. On appeal, he argued that the Supreme Court should overturn Gitlow's conviction by using the clause in the Fourteenth Amendment that barred the states from infringing on anyone's life, liberty, or property without due process of law. In the latter instance, he had mixed results.

On the point most important to future generations seeking federal intervention on behalf of civil liberties impaired by state action, Darrow won. Justice Edward Sanford, speaking for seven members of the Court, noted, "for present purposes we may and do assume that freedom of speech and of the press—which are protected by the First Amendment from abridgment by Congress—are among the fundamental personal rights and 'liberties' protected by the due process clause of the Fourteenth Amendment from impairment by the States."[35] In that one sentence, the Court majority sanctioned the doctrine known as incorporation, meaning that they saw within the due-process clause of the Fourteenth Amendment a way to make the Bill of Rights applicable to state action.

Claims that the Bill of Rights provided protection against state action had been specifically denied by Chief Justice John Marshall in 1833. Some Supreme Court justices, attorneys, and legal scholars had argued that the Fourteenth Amendment, ratified in 1868, bypassed Marshall's objections. That notion, however, had never won a majority of the Court. But more and more lawyers had been arguing the point because of a perceived need to find greater protection for speech and press than that offered by state courts. Finally here, in an offhanded manner, the Court accepted the idea. In fact, the entire Court approved of incorporation because the two dissenters, Oliver Wendell Holmes, Jr., and Louis D. Brandeis, also supported incorporation.

Although Darrow managed to have this principle accepted by the Court, he lost the case. The seven-man majority upheld Gitlow's conviction. Justice Sanford, for the majority, approved the idea of a state protecting itself from overthrow. "That utterances inciting to the overthrow of organized government by unlawful means, present a sufficient danger of substantive evil to bring their punishment within the range of legislative discretion, is clear," he said. "Such utterances, by their very nature, involve danger to the public peace and the security of the State. They threaten breaches of the peace and ultimate revolution. And the immediate danger is none the less real and substantial, because the effect of a given utterance cannot be accurately foreseen." Governments cannot be too careful, Sanford said. "A single revolutionary spark may kindle a fire that, smouldering for a time, may burst into a sweeping and destructive conflagration."[36] States consequently were justified in extinguishing any revolutionary sparks before they could ignite.

Disagreeing with the majority's contention that the manifesto would incite action against the government, Holmes replied for himself and Brandeis: "Every idea is an incitement. It offers itself for belief and if believed it is acted on unless some other belief outweighs it or some failure of energy stifles the movement at its birth. The only difference between the expression of an opinion and an incitement in the narrow sense is the speaker's enthusiasm for the result. Eloquence may set fire to reason." Holmes did not believe that the ideas set forth by the Communists had any chance of acceptance, but he was firmly committed to allowing the words to be spoken. "If in the long run the beliefs expressed in proletarian dictatorship are destined to be accepted by the dominant forces of the community, the only meaning of free speech is that they should be given their chance and have their way."[37]

A free rein for revolutionary ideas did not come about as a result of Gitlow's case, even though New York Governor Alfred E. Smith pardoned Gitlow soon after the Supreme Court's decision. Nor were the doors opened wide for radical speech as a result of the second important decision emanating from the Red Scare. Charlotte Anita Whitney, a patrician social reformer with impeccable family credentials from California, ran afoul of a 1919 state law that made it a felony to advocate force and violence to change the industrial or political order. Her offenses were twofold. She had participated in the transformation of her unit of the Socialist party into a unit of the Communist Labor party, and she had spoken publicly on race relations. California authorities were zealous in her prosecution, in large part because of her political and social standing. She was, for instance, the niece of former U.S. Supreme Court Justice Stephen J. Field. Many considered her a "parlor pink" who should be punished for the bad example that she set.[38]

The Whitney case reached the Supreme Court in 1927, and the justices upheld the conviction unanimously. Because they found the case, as presented, could have convinced jurors that a sufficient danger existed to merit conviction, Justices Holmes and Brandeis concurred with the result. But Brandeis turned his concurrence into a ringing endorsement of the right of free speech as he offered his particular interpretation of original intent. "Those who won our independence believed . . . that freedom to think as you will and to speak as you think are means indispensable to the discovery and spread of political truth," he said. The founding fathers believed "that without free speech and assembly discussion would be futile; that with them, discussion affords ordinarily adequate protection against the dissemination of noxious doctrine; that the greatest menace to freedom is an inert people; that public discussion is a political duty; and that this should be a fundamental principle of the American government."[39]

In addition, the founding fathers knew, Brandeis said, "that it is hazardous to discourage thought, hope and imagination; that fear breeds repression; that repression breeds hate; that hate menaces stable government; that the path of safety lies in the opportunity to discuss freely supposed grievances and proposed remedies; and that the fitting remedy for evil counsels is good ones." Brandeis believed that "those who won our independence by revolution were not cowards. They did not fear political change." They remembered the repressions of the British and colonial periods and the problems that fear created. "Men feared witches and burnt women," Brandeis said. The founding fathers, in drafting the Constitution and then by adding the Bill of Rights, meant for such an occurrence never to happen again.[40] Although 1927 was far removed from the immediate turmoil of the Red Scare, Justice Brandeis could not save Miss Whitney. California Governor C. C. Young quoted Justice Brandeis's words profusely as he pardoned Miss Whitney for her offenses.

Although the Red Scare ended in 1920, problems for individuals trying to express deviant ideas continued. In general, the nation was tired of war and of the constant edginess connected with it and its aftermath. Thus, the 1920s were times of change and complexity, of challenge and conformity, of confusion and certainty. The decade saw a tying up of loose ends left over from the war, new challenges to old lifestyles, efforts to reinstate past values, and a greater understanding of the right to be different and to express dissident ideas.

The 1920 election brought a resounding defeat for the Democrats and, many analysts claim, a repudiation of the Wilsonian ideals that had carried the nation through the war. The administration of Warren G. Harding confronted several problems left over from the war. The major question for a growing number of liberals was when would the individuals imprisoned as a result of speech-related offenses in World War I be freed. The American Civil Liberties Union (ACLU) and other organizations, including the American Federation of Labor, began calling for the release of those they termed political prisoners with the armistice. Within a year of that time, most Europeans who had been jailed for opposing the war in their homelands had been released, but most Americans jailed for similar offenses remained in prison. The Wilson administration refused to acknowledge that anyone had been jailed for differing with wartime policies. Rather, those individuals who were in jail were there because of specific violations of valid legislation and deserved no special consideration. If any clemency was to be awarded, consideration would go to individuals who had shown true repentance and not to those who continued to hold that their old ideas were correct. As a result, campaigns to obtain the release of political prisoners, and especially Eugene V. Debs, whose cause became a symbol for many amnesty workers, were greeted with great hostility.[41]

Congress formally ended the nation's state of war on July 2, 1921. After that, the campaign for amnesty picked up significantly. Harding's attorney general, Harry Daugherty, finally recommended that Debs be released for Christmas 1921—because of his age and his ill health. Although released, Debs was not given a full pardon, and his citizenship rights were not restored. Slowly, the Republican administration began releasing others who had been jailed for their opinions. All were finally freed by mid-December 1923. Harding's postmaster general, Will Hays, returned the mailing privileges of publications that had been banned from the mails during the war. A number of those publications, however, had gone out of business after having lost their mailing privileges.

Although the nation's conservatives generally approved of efforts to reverse the social and political reforms of the Wilson era, they found the campaigns to free traitors totally unacceptable. Numerous groups combined during the early 1920s to reestablish 100 percent Americanism in the United States and to quash any individual or organization that tried to argue for diversity and tolerance. Leaders of the movement included the American Legion, the Daughters of the American Revolution, and the Ku Klux Klan. For their efforts, they were labeled, in a derogatory manner, as super-patriots.[42] Little escaped their attention, and many efforts were made to re-form society in an early nineteenth-century image.

Leaders of the 100 percent Americanism movement focused at least part of their attention on the educational system. Great concerns arose that the nation's children, especially those from immigrant backgrounds, were not being properly indoctrinated in the American value system. Part of the problem was that a number of these children were allowed to attend private schools run either by religious or national-origin groups where they learned allegedly subversive doctrines. Consequently, efforts were made to force all children under a certain age to attend public schools where the correct patriotic attitudes would be taught. A 1919 Nebraska law, for instance, made it illegal to teach children in any language other than English until after those pupils had completed an eighth-grade education. In 1922, the residents of Oregon approved an initiative backed by the Ku Klux Klan that required parents to send their children to public schools.[43]

The laws were challenged and ultimately wound up on the Supreme Court calendar. Writing for a seven-man majority in the Nebraska case, Justice James McReynolds acknowledged that the state had great latitude in establishing its educational system. But, he said, individuals also had certain fundamental rights that had to be respected. "The protection of the Constitution extends to all, to those who speak other languages as well as to those born with English on the tongue," he said. "Perhaps it would be highly advantageous if all had ready understanding of our ordinary speech, but this cannot be coerced by methods which conflict with the Constitution—a desirable end cannot be promoted by prohibited means."[44]

Trying to force immigrants to use the English language or requiring their children to learn it in school refused to die. In the 1980s, it would again become popular in areas where large Hispanic populations congregated. The underlying concern in both eras was the need to make residents of the United States alike in language, thought, and action. The inconvenience that large populations speaking foreign tongues creates for others is, of course, one reason behind the effort to require the use of English. Beneath these arguments rests the fact that Americans continue to harbor a substantial fear of foreign people, foreign languages, and foreign ideas. The Supreme Court decision in 1923 turned back that era's effort to require English-language instruction, but it did little to defuse that fear.

The Supreme Court's decision in the case stemming from the Oregon law against the use of private schools led to its being declared unconstitutional as well, this time on the grounds that parents had the right to decide how they preferred to educate their children.[45] National reaction to the case fell into two diametrically opposed positions that would have great future impact. Liberals viewed the unanimous decision as a restatement by the Court of the basic principle that parents were to decide what was right for their children in the education area and that states were to play a secondary role. Conservatives, on the other hand, read the part of the decision that permitted states to set guidelines as empowering governments to make a variety of rules affecting education. Among those citing the ruling as favorable to conservative interests was William Jennings Bryan, who used the decision as a line of offense in one of the most famous court cases of the decade, the trial of John Scopes for teaching evolution to high school students.[46]

Several factors coalesced in the 1920s to bring the evolution issue to the forefront. Reformers, concerned about the number of children who were leaving school at an early age for employment, demanded compulsory school attendance legislation that would keep more young people in school longer. This policy meant that more of the nation's youth could be exposed to such doctrines. In addition, religious fundamentalism grew substantially in the 1920s as a revival movement accompanied efforts to return the nation to its more conservative roots. And in 1921, Bryan, known as one of the last of the great orators, adopted opposition to the teaching of evolution as his final crusade. Bryan denounced Darwin's theory of evolution as just that—a theory that was being taught to schoolchildren as truth.

The target, of course, was the teaching of Charles Darwin's theory of evolution, which had first been put forth in his 1859 book, *Origin of Species*. Once a dangerous theory to teach, evolution slowly had moved into science texts and into high school science lectures. But by the mid-1920s the teaching of evolution once again became controversial. Many of Darwin's ideas directly countered biblical statements and were considered as heresy by individuals who believed in the literal truth of the Bible. Darwin taught that humans had evolved from lower species, which conflicted with the idea that God had created man and woman in His image. In Darwin's discussion of evolution, he placed the time span needed for the development of man in the millions of years, far more than the six days that literalists believed. The teaching of these ideas, religious fundamentalists argued, undermined a child's faith in God, which, they believed, would have a significant impact on the survival of the nation.

Bryan agreed, arguing that the removal of God from the center of national life would cause many problems. He soon began advocating that state legislatures should protect children from indoctrination in Darwin's theory in the public schools. He did not advocate the presentation of the biblical creation doctrine on an equal basis with the theory of evolution; he would have eliminated both from the curriculum. To a certain extent, Tennessee's law did just that by forbidding teachers to tell students about the idea that man might be descended from a lower form of animal. The 1925 law made it "unlawful for any teacher in any of the Universities, Normals and all other public schools of the State which are supported in whole or in part by the public school funds of the State, to teach any theory that denies the story of Divine Creation of man as taught in the Bible, and to teach instead that man has descended from a lower order of animals."[47] A fine of $100 to $500 was attached upon conviction for this misdemeanor.

As soon as the Tennessee statute went on the books, liberals made plans to challenge its constitutionality. The American Civil Liberties Union, which had widened its field of interest considerably since the war, sought a friendly test case in which the teacher would not risk unemployment as a result. Residents of Dayton, Tennessee, a small mining and farming community, laid plans to host the case. Scopes agreed to be the person against whom the charges were brought. Unmarried, popular, and not particularly religious, Scopes was a high school science teacher and coach, and in spring 1925, he had substituted for the regular biology instructor. On the syllabus during that time was the section of the textbook that dealt with evolution.

Even though the school year was over, authorities arrested Scopes, and his trial was set for July 1925. To make sure the case got the appropriate attention, both sides called in top attorneys. Bryan agreed to be the special prosecutor; Clarence Darrow followed as defense counsel. More than one hundred newspaper reporters poured into the small Tennessee community for the trial, which often seemed more of a circus than a legal proceeding. To the nation at large, the case became the "great monkey trial," and its participants were transformed into defenders of progress or retrogression. Bryan had a simple view of the issues. He did not necessarily object to the presentation of many ideas in school, but he firmly believed that if schoolchildren were told of other theories of creation then they should be told the biblical version as well. Darrow, on the other hand, was concerned about state legislation proscribing certain fields of inquiry from the public schools. If you allowed this trend to continue, Darrow argued, "at the next session [of the legislature] you may ban books and the newspapers. Soon you may set Catholic against Protestant and Protestant against Protestant, and try to foist your own religion upon the minds of men."[48]

The two views represented in the 1925 trial are still present when issues of creation and evolution are discussed today. The evolution argument made little headway in the Scopes trial itself, however, although it dominated the pages of many of the nation's newspapers. The judge limited the issues discussed in the case by ruling that state law made it unlawful to teach evolution; all the jury had to decide was whether Scopes had violated that law. With his decision, the judge made most of Darrow's case, which had leaned heavily on proving that evolution was a viable theory that could and should be taught in the classroom, useless. Despite the ruling, Darrow remained undaunted. He and his supporters in the ACLU had, in fact, anticipated that Scopes would be convicted on the local level. Their hope rested in appealing the case until the U.S. Supreme Court declared laws against the teaching of evolution as unconstitutional as laws against the teaching of foreign languages.

Jurors quickly convicted Scopes of violating the law, and the judge imposed a $100 fine. On appeal, the conviction was vacated, but not on the grounds hoped for by the ACLU. The judge had erred in imposing the $100 fine, the state supreme court ruled; under Tennessee law, any fine in excess of $50 had to be levied by the jury. Because the state supreme court had found in favor of Scopes, the ACLU could not appeal the issue, and the case ended. The decision, which came in January 1927, was anticlimactic. William Jennings Bryan had died in his sleep a few days after the trial, most likely from exhaustion brought on by the trial and by extensive speaking engagements in the midsummer's heat. John Scopes had left high school teaching to begin graduate work in geology at the University of Chicago—on a scholarship funded by sympathetic scientists and professors. As a final blow, Scopes had confided to a reporter shortly after the trial that he had skipped the lesson on evolution because he had been ill and had too much other material to cover. His admission received little publicity. The great monkey trial of 1925 lived on in legend as a major confrontation between God-fearing Christians and secular forces seeking to undermine the central place of the Christian religion in American life. Whether the trial ever really presented a clash between the forces of good and evil is debatable. The trial certainly did present a debate over the right to teach revolutionary ideas in the classroom.

Just how the Supreme Court would have viewed efforts to ban evolution from the classroom in the 1920s is unknown. When presented with a question of the constitutionality of a 1925 Arkansas statute forbidding the teaching of evolution in 1968, the Court found its restrictions to be an unconstitutional invasion of the First Amendment's religion clauses.[49] In 1925, the backlash against attempts to interfere with scientific subject matter taught in the classroom was so great that most states halted consideration of similar laws. Those states with such regulations on the books stopped enforcing them. Limitations on the teaching of science simply were not permitted in a nation that desired to be progressive.

As the 1920s progressed, American willingness to allow others to decide what they should read or see or listen to decreased significantly. Even the federal government reflected this change in attitude when Harlan Fiske Stone was named attorney general to clean house in the wake of Harding administration scandals. He limited the Bureau of Investigation's activities to the pursuit of criminals, dissolved the bureau's antiradical division, and abolished the department's General Intelligence Division. These agencies had for years been keeping files on numerous Americans including Harvard Law School professors Zechariah Chafee, Jr., and Felix Frankfurter, and ACLU head Roger Baldwin.[50] In explaining his moves, Stone said, "There is always the possibility that a secret police may become a menace to free government and free institutions because it carries with it the possibility of abuses of power which are not always quickly apprehended or understood." Consequently, the Bureau's range of activities must be restricted. "The Bureau of Investigation is not concerned with political or other opinions of individuals. It is concerned only with their conduct and then only with such conduct as is forbidden by the laws of the United States. When a police system passes beyond these limits," he noted, "it is dangerous to the proper administration of justice and to human liberty, which it should be our first concern to cherish."[51]

Stone, who would move to the Supreme Court in 1925 and become chief justice in 1941, was a committed civil libertarian who was concerned with protecting freedom of expression. Unfortunately, he himself undermined his efforts to eliminate the Bureau of Investigation's intelligence gathering on radical groups, for Stone named J. Edgar Hoover as the bureau's new head. Hoover, who knew the value of confidential information on domestic radicals, bided his time until the nation again became concerned about internal security matters and political dissenters. When that happened in Franklin Roosevelt's administration, Hoover easily revived his intelligence-gathering operation. From that point until after the Watergate affair in the 1970s, the Federal Bureau of Investigation kept close watch on almost all dissident groups and individuals in the United States.

The campaign against labor unions finally died out in the 1920s as well but not because of public acceptance of unions and their goals. Instead, employers had gained almost total control of their relationship with their employees, and union membership hit an all-time low. One reason for the employers' success was the adoption by most business leaders of the so-called "American Plan." A form of welfare capitalism, this approach undercut many of the traditional demands of labor unions by having the employers voluntarily improve working conditions and pay scales. The other side of this coin, however, was an increased use of the traditional weapons against individuals involved in unionization.

Employers developed a wide-ranging blacklist against individuals considered to be union agitators. The yellow-dog contract, in which employees pledged as a condition of maintaining their jobs not to become involved in unionization, was widely used. Injunctions once again played a prominent role in the relationship between employer and unionized employees. Industrial espionage also resumed, with employers once again using *agents provocateurs* to report on all suspicious actions and to disrupt as many activities as possible. And if strikes could not be prevented, employers came to rely even more on strikebreakers to fill empty jobs and on private police forces to break up union demonstrations. These private police forces were as well equipped as any military force, for employers stockpiled arms and munitions for use in case of violence.[52]

Once again the federal government was influential in helping employers to extinguish the union movement. In fact, thanks to the U.S. Supreme Court and the Department of Justice, the union movement was dealt such severe blows in 1921 and 1922 that only the Great Depression saved it from extinction. Early in 1921, the Supreme Court finally interpreted the Clayton Act, the measure enacted in 1914 that included provisions allegedly protecting union organizing efforts.[53] The Duplex Printing Press Company in Battle Creek, Michigan, manufactured printing presses, with workers employed under an open-shop policy that allowed for the hiring of both union and nonunion members, but the International Association of Machinists wanted a closed shop in which only members of the union could work. To force Duplex Printing to adopt such a policy, the machinists' union instituted a secondary boycott that called on individuals who were not union members to avoid purchasing or using Duplex products. The lower court, after reviewing the Clayton Act, refused to grant an injunction against the union; the Supreme Court ruled the other way.

The key in the case was the secondary boycott, which, if successful, was a powerful union weapon. Here, the machinists sought to exercise the secondary boycott throughout the country, but they particularly brought pressure to bear in New York City, which was highly unionized. The machinists told Duplex customers not to purchase any more products from the company or else they would face the loss of business from other union members and from as many members of the general public as could be convinced to cooperate. The Supreme Court, with Justice Mahlon Pitney writing for six members, found the pressure so intense that it violated both the Sherman and Clayton antitrust acts. The Clayton Act, Justice Pitney said, required that actions to convince others of the rightness of the union's cause had to be "peaceful and lawful," which the machinists' efforts certainly were not. The machinists' secondary boycott was aimed at businesses that were not parties to the dispute between Duplex and its employees and was illegal. An injunction ordering the machinists' union to cease the secondary boycott was upheld.[54] That injunction effectively killed the secondary boycott as a union weapon.

The Court continued to ride roughshod over the rights of union members. In December 1921, it handed down two decisions, both written by the new chief justice, William Howard Taft, who had come to the Court with a reputation of being strongly anti-union. The first case again involved the Clayton Act, with the seven-man majority agreeing that injunctions could be used to stop picketing regardless of the law's provisions. The strike against the American Steel Foundries plant in Granite City, Illinois, had been called because the company had reduced its workers' wages. Pickets were posted outside the plant to inform workers and other passers-by of the situation. The restraining order issued by a federal district court "perpetually restrained and enjoined [the union] from in any way or manner whatsoever by the use of *persuasion,* threats, or personal injury, intimidation, suggestion of danger or threats of violence of any kind, from interfering with, hindering, obstructing or stopping, any person engaged in the employ of the American Steel Foundries" plant from going to work. The injunction also specifically banned picketing "*at or near the premises of the complainant, or on the streets leading to the premises of said complainant, any picket or pickets.*"[55]

In handing down his decision in favor of the manufacturer, Chief Justice Taft looked at section 20 of the Clayton Act, which not only called for peaceful and lawful means of persuasion but which allowed property to be protected if the danger of irreparable injury loomed.[56] Taft found the three or four groups of pickets around the plant, each containing four to twelve members, threatening and intimidating. "They could not be otherwise," he said. "It is idle to talk of peaceful communication in such a place and under such conditions. The numbers of the pickets in the groups constituted intimidation. The name 'picket' indicated a militant purpose, inconsistent with peaceable persuasion. The crowds they drew made the passage of the employees to and from the place of work, one of running the gauntlet." Under such conditions, "persuasion or communication . . . was anything but peaceable and lawful."[57] Thus, the legal system was correct in protecting the employer. Taft allowed the union to station a single picket at each entrance or exit to the plant—while restraining those pickets from any so-called threatening or abusive communication with those who entered.

But the chief justice did not decide that labor unions were illegal. In fact, he specifically noted that unions allowed "laborers [an] opportunity to deal on equality with their employer." Strikes even had value "in a lawful economic struggle or competition between employers and employees." And unions had the right to extend their memberships beyond one business. "It is helpful to have as many as may be in the same trade in the same community united, because in the competition between employers they are bound to be affected by the standard of wages of their trade in the neighborhood." In addition, unions had the right to engage in propaganda to win others to their way of thinking.[58] But, to the chief justice, the activities of the union had to be peaceful and nonthreatening.

Taft did not say how peaceful tactics could counter the employer. Unions whose activities had been restricted were far from equals in the bargaining situation, and their voices would not be heard if used only in moderation. The demand, though, that union activities be peaceful would continue throughout most Supreme Court decisions, even in those rulings favorable to labor's cause.

Union members and other dissidents advocating different propositions learned that peaceful demonstrations were doomed to failure. In an increasingly complex and busy world, the only way some causes come to the attention of the larger public is through actions and increasingly high-pitched voices.

The ability of unions to oppose employers took another body blow in a decision handed down about two weeks after the American Steel Foundries case. Here, the Court, again through the pen of Chief Justice Taft, showed that it was no more tolerant of state efforts to protect unions from injunctions than it was of federal attempts. Arizona had enacted legislation regulating the use of injunctions in labor disputes, which was challenged under the Fourteenth Amendment's provisions that prevented states from depriving individuals of their property without due process of law. The case involved efforts of cooks and waiters employed by the English Kitchen in Bisbee, Arizona, to encourage community residents to boycott the restaurant because of its treatment of union members. As a result of the boycott, the restaurant's daily income was cut in half, posing the possibility of irreparable damage to the business. Taft, and four other members of the Court, found the boycott and the picket line designed to enforce it abusive and unlawful. The picket line, he said, "was compelling every customer or would-be customer to run the gauntlet of most uncomfortable publicity, aggressive and annoying importunity, libelous attacks and fear of injurious consequences, illegally inflicted, to his reputation and standing in the community." Peaceful picketing, said the chief justice, "was a contradiction in terms."[59]

Labor's woes were multiplied in the summer of 1922 when nearly 400,000 railway workers walked off the job in response to a 12 percent wage cut ordered by the Railway Labor Board, which was dominated by management personnel. This was the largest strike of the decade, and increasing public hostility dogged its participants. On September 1, Attorney General Harry Daugherty went to James H. Wilkerson, an ultraconservative federal district judge in Chicago, for an injunction to keep union officials from heading up strike efforts. The product of Wilkerson's intervention was an injunction far more broadly worded than that issued against Eugene V. Debs in the Pullman strike some thirty years earlier, which had long stood as the high-water mark of the judicial system's intolerance of the labor movement. Under Wilkerson's order, union leaders were barred from encouraging, directing, or commanding striking workers "by letters, printed or other circulars, telegrams, telephones, word of mouth, oral persuasion, or suggestion, or through interviews to be published in newspapers or otherwise."[60] In addition, union leaders were told to stay off of railroad property and to refrain from trying to keep people from working for the railroads. In fact, they were ordered not to say anything to anyone that could be construed as supporting the strike or the right to strike. Picketing, of course, was not allowed.[61]

The expansive wording of the injunction drew immediate criticism. Not only did liberal supporters of the rights of the workers, including the ACLU, protest, but so, too, did American newspapers, who considered the phrasing a possible infringement on their rights. The *Brooklyn Eagle,* for instance, said that "if the spokesmen for the strikers can be enjoined from writing about the strike or from talking about it for publication, newspapers can also be enjoined from publishing interviews and statements which have any color favorable to the strikers or adverse to the railroads."[62] *Editor & Publisher,* a newspaper trade publication not known for its liberal tendencies, also complained: "The constitutional guarantees of a free press and free citizenship . . . were taken away last Saturday when the First Amendment to the Constitution was abridged by Federal Injunction."[63] Protests led to calls for a congressional investigation of Daugherty's intrusion on First Amendment rights. The inquiry was referred to committee, but nothing ever came of it because the strike was settled soon thereafter.

Conservatives, of course, lauded Daugherty's decisiveness. State governors equipped with the appropriate legislation issued their own orders to bar picketing and other support for the strikers. In Kansas, for example, William Allen White, editor of the *Emporia Gazette,* was ordered to remove a poster supporting the strike from the window of his newspaper office because the poster was deemed a form of picketing. When he refused to do so, he was arrested for violating orders against picketing and for conspiring with the strikers. White, who was more conservative than liberal, protested that his arrest violated his freedom of speech. The ACLU and other civil libertarians made plans to defend him, but the charges against the editor were dropped before the case got to court. Out of the episode came a Pulitzer Prize-winning editorial entitled "To an Anxious Friend." In that commentary, White said, "You say that freedom of utterance is not for time of stress, and I reply with the sad truth that only in time of stress is freedom of utterance in danger. No one questions it in calm days, because it is not needed. And the reverse is true also; only when free utterance is suppressed is it needed, and when it is needed, it is most vital to justice."[64]

By the mid-1920s, then, the labor movement, although not destroyed, was fairly well intimidated and deprived of its most potent weapons. One positive effort by Congress was the enactment in 1926 of the Railway Labor Act, which institutionalized collective bargaining, mediation, and arbitration for workers employed on the railroads.[65] But that was about the only bright spot on the horizon for workers during this era. Union membership dropped from about 5 million workers in 1920 to about 3.6 million in 1923, where it remained for the rest of the decade. Only about 10 percent of the nation's 30 million nonagricultural workers were union members. William Green assumed the AFL presidency in 1924 after the death of Samuel Gompers and launched a campaign designed to show that union members were conservative, supportive of the capitalistic system, and ardent opponents of Communists. The effort had slight impact on anti-union employers and did little to help union leaders carve out an image that would attract new members.

Few Americans were interested in the unions' plight as they concentrated on the challenges presented by societal changes that were having revolutionary effects on the nation's lifestyle in the 1920s. The Roaring Twenties' problems included automobiles, motion pictures, radio, prohibition and speakeasies, modern dancing, liberated women, and freer discussion of sexual matters. The excesses of the decade fed on a growing disillusionment about the nation's involvement in World War I that stemmed from revelations about how the United States became involved in the conflict coupled with a burgeoning disapproval of the way European nations were reverting to their prewar attitudes. Disenchantment with the political side of life led even more Americans into the contest against longstanding personal taboos. Before the decade was over, the system of censorship of ideas established by Anthony Comstock was badly shaken although not totally destroyed. Due to these battles, freedom of expression on sexual matters in particular was decidedly expanded. In addition, these encounters led to an increased understanding of the value of freedom of expression generally.

The most successful struggle dealt with the right of Americans to decide what they wanted to read for themselves without having a censor interfere in the selection process. Comstock's vice society movement had survived his death and at the end of World War I was still strong in New York City, Boston, and other communities. Before the war, in fact, a conspiracy of sorts existed to keep offensive literature from contaminating American society. The reputable publishing houses refused to print controversial material. Booksellers, fearing visits from local censorship agents and possible prosecution, declined to sell such works. If any controversial manuscripts managed to get printed, librarians restricted their purchases in light of what they thought patrons should read. Theodore Dreiser's experience with *The Genius,* his fifth novel, was a case in point. The book had been in circulation for some nine months before anyone brought it to the attention of John Sumner, Comstock's successor as head of the New York Society for the Suppression of Vice. Sumner complained about its contents to the publisher, and postal inspectors expressed concerns about mailing the volume. In the end, the publisher recalled all copies of the book, and Dreiser managed to obtain the printing plates just before the publisher destroyed them. H. L. Mencken, who headed the Authors' League of America at the time, unsuccessfully tried to get his fellow authors to take a stand against the censorship of Dreiser's book.[66]

With the new decade came a change in faces and attitudes. New publishing houses were run by hungry executives who not only were unafraid of challenging existing mores but who were often convinced that such attacks were necessary in order to win customers. With the growing disillusionment with the war and the values for which it stood, these new publishers had many excellent books to choose from. Even with the changes, efforts to promote freer distribution of literature may not have progressed far had Sumner and his allies not tried to obtain a revision of the New York State obscenity law. Supporters of the vice society movement decided in 1923, as had Anthony Comstock's supporters fifty years earlier, that the major problem rested in poor legislation. A tighter law would make it easier to prosecute offenders and to ban books. But this time, the society's "clean books" campaign ran into substantial opposition. For the first time, the legislative proposals sparked substantial debates among authors, booksellers, and librarians. Many professional groups split over the issue, but out of each discussion came strong support for greater freedom of choice for the reading public. The measure went down to a resounding defeat in 1925, taking with it, for all intents and purposes, the New York Society for the Suppression of Vice. The society did not go out of business immediately, of course, but successful suppressions of literature were few after the legislation's defeat.

The next target in the war against restrictions on access to literature was the U.S. customs service, which used tariff acts to keep certain books produced by foreign publishers from entering the country. This review of literature was uneven and idiosyncratic. Books banned by inspectors at one port, for instance, might be allowed to enter the country at another location. Censorship was exercised by individuals who read few books, who had little experience with great literature, and who often boasted about how many books they personally had excluded. The problem came to a head in the 1920s because these functionaries were systematically excluding some of the great classics of Europe—works by such authors as Balzac, Boccaccio, Rabelais, and Casanova. In spring 1929, Congress began debating a tariff bill that not only would have perpetuated the ban on allegedly obscene books but would have extended the prohibition to material that advocated the overthrow of the U.S. government. The latter provision was designed to bring the tariff bill in compliance with legislation denying such publications access to the mails.

A new tariff bill containing both provisions passed the House of Representatives while protest increased about the exclusion of political material. In the Senate, Bronson Cutting, Republican of New Mexico, decided to attack both censorship provisions. Spurring Cutting's concern were complaints from a constituent whose efforts to bring in a personal copy of D. H. Lawrence's *Lady Chatterley's Lover* had been thwarted by customs officials. The senator wisely based his protest on customs action against Erich Remarque's *All Quiet on the Western Front,* a critically acclaimed volume that was strongly antiwar. The book was available in the United States in an expurgated form because Remarque's material allegedly was too realistic for American audiences. Cutting used the issue to raise the vital question of who should decide what Americans could read.

The debate on Cutting's proposal to eliminate both the political and obscenity exclusions from the tariff bill occupied four days of the Senate's time in October 1929 and March 1930, the first time that either house of Congress had ever discussed the ramifications of censorship at length. Comstock's original measure was enacted after a perfunctory discussion. The news media provided substantial coverage of the 1929–30 debate, thus educating the general public on the censorship issue. The measure that finally passed removed the obscenity clause and most of the vague political references. All that was left was a ban on material calling for forcible resistance to the law or threatening the life of the president. Further provisions called for books to be judged in their entirety, for the secretary of the treasury to issue blanket rulings allowing the admission of known classics and books of literary or scientific merit, and for individuals who were upset by customs rulings to have access to the federal courts for redress.[67]

Provisions of the new law immediately liberalized the practices of the customs service. In 1931, for example, the Treasury Department removed bans on *The Arabian Nights,* Casanova's *Memoirs,* and Boccaccio's *Decameron.* When Franklin Roosevelt took office in 1933, his secretary of the treasury appointed a special legal adviser to handle challenges to decisions by customs officials. By 1935, almost every book published by a reputable European firm was freely admitted to the United States. Appeals were quickly decided, and books with any possible merit were allowed to enter. The whole process was speeded along by two court decisions in 1933 and 1934 that ruled that one of the most controversial books of the era, *Ulysses* by James Joyce, could enter the country uninhibited. The federal judges hearing that case read the entire book and weighed its allegedly obscene passages against the merit of other sections. In the end, jurists sitting on both the district and circuit courts decided that the book had enough merit to allow it into the United States and to be read by any Americans who wanted to read it. In the process, the judges firmly established the standard whereby the whole work had to be considered and its effect had to be evaluated by the reactions of an average person.[68]

This new standard was a far cry from decades of obscenity decisions in which isolated passages of the book could be charged as obscene, in which the jury was kept from even reading the contested passages, and in which the material's effect on the most susceptible individual in society was the measuring stick for declaring a work obscene. Such changes did not mean that obscenity was dead as an issue, for Americans continued to be concerned about obscenity and its effect on its readers and viewers. Nor, unfortunately, did Cutting's victory over the customs operation mean that that agency stopped interfering with the flow of information reaching the American people, but judged by the standards of the late 1920s and early 1930s, Cutting's accomplishment was, without a doubt, quite significant.

Buoyed by his success against customs officials, Senator Cutting decided to try to restrict the ability of the post office to exclude materials from the mails. That effort failed legislatively, but the court system toppled another of Anthony Comstock's major legacies. The case involved a pamphlet by Mary Ware Dennett, a mother of two boys and an activist in the birth-control movement. Mrs. Dennett had written a pamphlet for her sons explaining the facts of life. The pamphlet, "The Sex Side of Life," was well written, thorough, and tasteful, and soon was being distributed by the YMCA and similar organizations. Attempts to circulate the publication through the mail under the cheaper mailing rates available to printed material were stopped cold in 1922 by postal officials who termed the publication nonmailable because of its indecent contents.[69]

For the remainder of the decade, Mrs. Dennett asked the post office to change its position on her booklet. She carried on an extensive correspondence with postal officials trying to find out just what part of "The Sex Side of Life" was so objectionable. The publication did not deal with birth control nor did it discuss abortion, yet the material was still termed indecent and, under Comstock's law, nonmailable. As Mrs. Dennett told one postal official in 1925, "So far as I know, you are the only individual in the country who considers anything in this pamphlet indecent. . . . If your single opinion is to outweigh theirs, must you not at least let them and me have the opportunity to know on what you base your willingness to utilize the power of the law to enforce your individual view?"[70] Departmental Solicitor Edgar M. Blessing simply responded that he had reviewed the publication and found it indecent under terms of the law. The term still was not defined.

Even as Mrs. Dennett carried on this correspondence with postal officials, she continued to send "The Sex Side of Life" through the mail. Because she was forbidden use of the cheaper mail classifications, she filled orders for single copies by placing the material in sealed envelopes and using first-class postage; bulk orders went by express. Her continuing effort to force postal authorities to explain their actions led to problems. In January 1929, Mrs. Dennett was indicted for inserting into the U.S. mails "a pamphlet, booklet and certain printed matter enclosed in an envelope, which said pamphlet, booklet and certain printed matter were obscene, lewd, lascivious, filthy, vile and indecent, and unfit to be set forth in this instrument and to be spread upon the records of this Honorable Court."[71] Using the best of Anthony Comstock's tactics, a copy of "The Sex Side of Life" had been ordered by a decoy for the sole purpose of providing the evidence necessary to prosecute Mrs. Dennett for sending obscene material through the mails.

The liberal community, joined by a healthy representation from the scientific and religious communities, rushed to Mrs. Dennett's aid. Despite such support, Mrs. Dennett was convicted in a trial in which the judge allowed no testimony on the value of the pamphlet to be entered into evidence. The only issue, he said, was whether it had been placed in the mail. The post office had already decided that such material was nonmailable. The guilty verdict was overturned on appeal, with the court noting that "an accurate exposition of the relevant facts of the sex side of life in decent language and in manifestly serious and disinterested spirit cannot ordinarily be regarded as obscene."[72] With the Dennett case, the mails became more available for the dissemination of information related to sex education.

The campaign to send such material through the mails was accompanied by a similar effort to promote freer public discussion on birth control. Mrs. Dennett and Margaret Sanger were the main protagonists in this effort, and they often took different paths toward accomplishing the same goal. Mrs. Dennett argued for the dissemination of birth-control information as part of her total free-speech campaign. Mrs. Sanger moved to a more conservative position and sought state and federal laws to protect doctors who discussed birth control with their patients. Both efforts moved forward in the 1920s, with Mrs. Dennett's program apparently scoring the major success.

Although Mrs. Sanger did get legislation protecting the medical discussion of birth control introduced in Congress and in some state legislatures, it was not enacted. By the mid-1930s, most individuals active in the birth-control movement believed that even though the Comstock laws remained on the books, they were no longer being used to bar the dissemination of birth-control information through the mails. Also, there was no proof that physicians were running into legal difficulties if they talked about or prescribed birth-control devices. Thus, the legislative effort died. By the 1940s, the movement to promote the discussion of birth control had evolved into the Planned Parenthood Federation of America, which still exists today.[73] Despite the gains made by Mrs. Dennett, Mrs. Sanger, and others in the area of promoting freedom for the discussion of sex education and birth control, those issues continued to present problems. The U.S.

Supreme Court finally entered the battle in the late 1960s by ruling generally that the dissemination of information about birth control was a permissible First Amendment activity with which neither the state nor federal government could interfere.[74]

The urge to censor runs deep in American souls, and the newer the medium of communication or the more pervasive its perceived influence, the more Americans want to curb its dangerous tendencies. Motion pictures, which had faced the repressive urges of a substantial segment of the American public ever since they first appeared, encountered even greater difficulties in the 1920s. Church workers, teachers, physicians, and parents all joined the campaign to blunt the impact of movies, especially on the young. The silver screen was seen as the cause of most of the nation's problems during the decade ranging from liberated women to disrespectful children.[75]

Motion-picture producers, in fact, helped to bring the 1920s censorship campaign on themselves. As the decade began, the producers found themselves briefly facing a business slump. To keep their profits high, they turned to more sensational fare. The era also marked the beginnings of the star system and the press agent. The everyday lives of the stars, which were not worth emulating according to many in middle America, became common fare not only in fan magazines but in the daily newspapers. As scandals rocked the movie community, reformers sought governmental censorship of motion pictures. In 1921 alone almost 100 bills designed to censor motion pictures were introduced in thirty-seven state legislatures.[76] During that same year, the U.S. Senate considered a congressional investigation of the industry. And in the winter of 1921–22, bills calling for federal censorship of movies were introduced into the U.S. House of Representatives.

Industry forces decided to act before the federal government intervened. With the National Board of Censorship discredited as a reviewing mechanism, the producers decided to try self-regulation. After creating the National Association of the Motion Picture Industry in March 1921, they issued the Thirteen Points, a statement pledging members to avoid certain controversial topics in their films. Sensitive topics included those that "emphasize and exaggerate sex appeal or depict scenes therein exploiting interest in sex in an improper or suggestive form or manner," those that "unnecessarily prolong expressions or demonstrations of passionate love," or those that are "predominantly concerned with the underworld of vice and crime, and like scenes, unless the scenes are part of an essential conflict between good and evil." Stories that made gambling and drinking attractive or that emphasized crime were to be treated with care.[77] Unfortunately for the leaders of the Hollywood community, their pledge existed only on paper; business continued as usual behind the cameras.

With more calls for federal intervention in the film-making process, the Hollywood producers decided to try another tactic. Professional baseball had just hired a "czar" to clean up its image in the wake of a terrible scandal; motion-picture producers decided to do the same. They settled on Will H. Hays, who at the time of his hiring was serving as postmaster general under Warren G. Harding. Hays was a nonsmoker, a teetotaler, an elder in the Presbyterian church, a power in the Republican party, and the image of civic rectitude—just what the industry needed. After assuming the directorship of the Motion Picture Producers and Distributors of America, better known as the Hays Office, Hays worked to clean up the movie capital's image. He persuaded the studios to put morals clauses in stars' contracts so that they would lose their jobs if accused of moral turpitude. And he got the studios' publicity operations to tone down descriptions of the stars' lifestyles and salaries.

For many years, his activities were primarily in the public relations realm, and he staved off additional legislative regulation. As he worked to improve the industry's image, Hays also worked to improve the product that producers turned out. In 1924, his office took the first significant step toward self-regulation with the issuance of a statement known as "The Formula." Hays and his staff had decided that counseling before work on a picture began was better than trying to revise the finished product. "The Formula" tried to prevent stage plays, books, or stories that had unacceptable themes from being considered for motion-picture adaptation. Adherence to "The Formula" again was strictly voluntary.

Still not satisfied with motion-picture standards, the Hays Office issued the "Don'ts and Be Carefuls" in 1927. This list of eleven forbidden subjects and twenty-five topics on which producers had to be careful was designed to quiet frequent complaints. The "Don'ts" included profanity, nudity, drug trafficking, and miscegenation. The "Be Careful" list touched on respect for the flag, treatment of international sensitivities, details about crime and criminals, and sex-related topics such as "first-night scenes" and "man and woman in bed together."[78] Once again, however, agreement to follow the "Don'ts and Be Carefuls" was voluntary. Not until the early 1930s would the Hays Office have authority to punish producers who violated its standards.

The campaign against the motion-picture industry contradicted efforts to win greater freedom for other forms of expression. Many people still believed that movies exerted a bad influence on their audiences. As a result, despite efforts to win greater freedom for printed materials, few voices called for freedom of expression for movie producers. With their repeated attempts at self-censorship, the motion-picture producers, in fact, were not even calling for freedom of expression for themselves. Just putting inhibitory rules on paper showed that the producers were willing to bargain away much of their freedom of expression in order to be free from the constant threat of censorship. Financial exigencies demanded that producers turn out movies that could be shown nationwide with little local interference. This need to make a profit would soon lead producers to a greater willingness to sacrifice their claims to freedom of expression.

The 1920s brought another new form of mass communication on the scene, but the appearance of radio created a different set of problems. In the early 1920s, the airwaves were filled with stations offering programming on political, religious, educational, and social issues. Although many of these stations were on the air for only a few hours a week and appealed to narrow audiences, the new medium was an excellent vehicle for the presentation of different ideas. Technical problems involved in radio transmission, however, were insurmountable without governmental limitations on programming times and station power. The electromagnetic spectrum was limited and the equipment primitive. Only through governmental involvement could the American public benefit from this new medium and could opportunities for its use be properly distributed.[79]

Government participation in broadcasting in the postwar period was not without precedent. Federal officials had intervened legislatively during the medium's infancy with varying degrees of effectiveness. The Wireless Ship Act of 1910, which was enacted before anyone anticipated a commercial use of the airwaves, required the installation of wireless devices and the hiring of operators for all seagoing vessels.[80] Unfortunately, the act did not require operators to be on duty twenty-four hours a day, an omission that had to be rectified after the *Titanic* disaster of 1912, in which 1,500 persons died. The Radio Act of 1912 showed some inkling of radio's potential. Lawmakers divided the frequencies among shipping, coastal, amateur, and commercial interests. The act also gave the secretary of commerce and labor power to assign wavelengths and time limits to stations, but it denied him the authority to refuse to issue a license.[81] This act remained in force until 1927, and because of its numerous weaknesses, the law was the major cause of many early difficulties.

Problems inherent in the legislation did not emerge until the 1920s because the government had banned commercial activity during World War I. The first commercial station, KDKA in Pittsburgh, Pennsylvania, used the airwaves in November 1920 to report the election of Warren G. Harding to a limited audience. Neither the audience nor the programming remained limited for long, for broadcasting became one of the hottest crazes of the 1920s. By 1922, at least 1.5 million receivers were reported in homes across the country with more than 550 radio stations to serve those listeners. Such growth brought problems. The secretary of commerce and labor received repeated complaints about poor reception and interference in broadcasts by other stations. In addition, more stations wanted to be licensed, and others wanted to be heard for longer hours and on frequencies that would interfere with preexisting outlets. Broadcasters were complaining, and so were listeners.

In an attempt to find solutions, Secretary of Commerce and Labor Herbert Hoover called the first of four national radio conferences in 1922. The goal here, as with all of the conferences, was to push Congress into enacting legislation regulating the airwaves, but measures proposed by delegates attending the first conference made no headway.[82] By 1923, Hoover's problems with broadcasting had increased substantially. The secretary had been regularly exceeding the powers given him legislatively in an effort to provide the American people with improved radio services. Early that year, a federal court ruled that, under the Radio Act of 1912, Hoover had to issue a license to anyone who sought one.[83]

While Hoover waited for Congress to act, a new threat to radio's development loomed. The patents necessary for the equipment required for station operation were held by a few companies, and in 1923, the Federal Trade Commission reported that such a concentration could mean problems for the industry. In 1924, one of the major patent holders, the American Telephone and Telegraph

Company (AT&T), accused WHN, a New York City radio station, of patent infringement. In response, the radio station accused AT&T of wanting to hurt the American people by monopolizing the airwaves.

The case confirmed Hoover's fears that radio might become a monopoly. In response to a question from a radio industry magazine in 1924, for instance, Hoover said, "I can state emphatically it would be most unfortunate for the people of this country to whom broadcasting has become an important incident of life if its control should come into the hands of any single corporation, individual, or combination. It would be in principle the same as though the entire press of the country were so controlled."[84] Any censorship imposed on the medium should come from the people most directly affected—the listeners, Hoover said. "These stations naturally are endeavoring to please their listeners and thus there is an indirect censorship by the public," Hoover told a radio audience in 1924. "This is the place where it belongs. What we must safeguard is that there shall be no interference with free speech, that no monopoly of broadcasting stations should grow up under which any person or group could determine what material will be delivered to the public."[85]

AT&T, of course, denied any plans to monopolize the air. Any operator could use its patented equipment, if the station would just pay an appropriate fee or if it would initially purchase the needed equipment from the manufacturer. The Commerce and Labor Department essentially ignored the AT&T attempts to protect its patents and continued to issue licenses without inquiring into the source of the equipment used. WHN eventually paid the fee that AT&T had demanded, and because of bad publicity, the manufacturer dropped its pursuit of other stations allegedly violating its patents.

The issue of censorship, however, refused to go away. The 1924 presidential election revealed another aspect of the problem when candidates wanted to use the new medium to communicate with voters. The question soon became who would have access to the airwaves during the campaign. Democrats, for example, worried about access because most station operators were Republicans. Essentially the fears of mainline politicians were groundless. Broadcasters presented the campaign as fairly as possible and provided candidates with equal access to facilities at the same cost regardless of political party.[86] The ability of fringe political figures to gain access to radio time was a different issue altogether, but few individuals supported their cause. The needs of establishment politicians, on the other hand, always headed the agenda of members of Congress who ultimately would rewrite broadcast legislation.

Although legislation was debated for years, nothing was enacted. Through additional radio conferences, Hoover sought to further refine the issues, to promote self-regulation within the industry until he obtained statutory powers, to answer the concerns raised by the American people about the fate of this new medium with which they had become so enamored, and to pressure Congress. The 1925 conference touched on freedom of speech on the air, with conferees again stressing that the public should censor what radio carried by turning their sets on or off. Hoover believed this freedom would be enhanced by legislation allowing government regulation of the airwaves. As he explained after the conference, "Freedom cannot mean a license to every person or corporation who wishes to broadcast his name or his wares and thus monopolize the listener's set. We do not get much freedom of speech if 50 people speak at the same place at the same time. . . . The ether is a public medium, and its use must be for public benefit."[87]

Chances that the public would benefit from radio continued to recede. In April 1926, a federal court stripped Hoover of any remnants of power to regulate broadcasting.[88] Hoover complained that if, because of the court decision, "stations proceed to select their own wavelengths and choose their own time, considering only their selfish advantage, effective public service will be at an end."[89] Hoover sought a contrary opinion from the attorney general but was told that the court had interpreted the extent of his powers correctly. As the problems of radio deepened, calls for federal intervention increased. Strangely, many of the calls came from broadcasters themselves. Although publicly proclaiming the importance of free speech on radio, they believed that the medium would be nothing but a muddle without federal intervention.

The broadcasting world became more complicated in the fall of 1926, when the National Broadcasting Company (NBC) became the first network. In fact, NBC established two networks, both of which worked under the auspices of the same parent company. Now the fear of monopoly became greater as individuals began to picture the existence of one or two monster networks that stretched across the country and dominated programming with little regard for the diverse needs of the American people. To fend off complaints, NBC set up an advisory council on programming. Through this and other means, chain broadcasting remained safe from government intervention into the 1940s. Its appearance led to even more concern about the fate of broadcasting in American society.

Secretary Hoover pushed Congress even harder for action. After President Coolidge joined in the request in December 1926, Congress began the process of enacting the Radio Act of 1927.[90] After six years of effort the legislation was approved in a little more than a month. One sticking point in the process centered on where to house the regulatory authority. Democrats in Congress feared granting too much power to Hoover, who was soon to be the Republican candidate for president. To solve this dilemma, they created the Federal Radio Commission (FRC), an independent regulatory board.[91] Another political issue also caused problems. Democrats wanted to make sure that radio stations owned by Republicans would not exclude them from the airwaves during election campaigns.[92] The answer here was the so-called "equal-time provision," which said that if any legally qualified candidate for public office was given an opportunity to use broadcasting facilities, then that opportunity must be made available to all other qualified candidates. In addition, the broadcasting station was to have no power to censor what the candidates said.[93]

Although little discussion about philosophical matters intruded into debates on the act, the history of radio regulation indicates that federal intervention was based on the belief that the electromagnetic spectrum, as a scarce natural commodity, had to be preserved for public use. The goal was to distribute radio service as equally as possible around the country and to allow those best qualified to run the stations. Licenses were to be allocated among applicants based on "public convenience, interest, or necessity,"[94] with those terms open to definition by the Federal Radio Commission.

Little attention was paid to free-speech issues that might be involved with the regulation of the medium. The goal was to bring some order to the airwaves by having the government regulate the frequencies and hours used by broadcasters; otherwise the industry was to decide its own future. The first year of the Federal Radio Commission's existence was quite difficult. Two of the president's nominees failed to win confirmation by the Senate, and Congress neglected to authorize an operating budget. The legislation establishing the commission provided only a one-year life span, so commissioners used their time trying to accommodate existing stations through time-sharing and other innovative arrangements. Only when Congress renewed the commission's lease on life in 1928 did the commissioners begin to make decisions that significantly reshaped American broadcasting.[95]

The philosophy that would govern radio evolved as the FRC decided which stations could stay on the air. Within the first year or so of actual regulation, the commission began defining what the "public convenience, interest, or necessity" meant in terms of license allocation and renewal. But public interest did not include the right to use the airwaves to advocate particular points of view. In 1929, commissioners used a case involving WCFL, a station operated by the American Federation of Labor in Chicago, to indicate that propaganda programming was not acceptable. The station wanted to increase its power and number of hours of operation, but the FRC denied the request because the station served too narrow a group of listeners. Said the commissioners in what was known as the Great Lakes Broadcasting case, the broadcasting system had no room "for every school of thought, religious, political, social, and economic, each to have its separate broadcasting station, its mouthpiece in the ether. If franchises are extended to some it gives them an unfair advantage over others, and results in a corresponding cutting down of general public service stations."[96]

Broadcasters, the FRC said, were given licenses to serve the entire public and not just small sections of it. Because the FRC had decided that propaganda stations were bad, the Great Lakes Broadcasting case became the first in a series of attempts to drive special-interest stations off the air.[97] The effort to homogenize broadcasting would pick up in the Depression years, and before long, a medium that had offered great opportunity for expanding the marketplace of ideas in the United States was turned into an avenue for communication by majority interests. The challenges that these decisions presented to free speech would be debated, but the die was cast early. In exchange for clear and uninterrupted communication channels, the medium sacrificed its right to offer the nation a multitude of voices. Soon, broadcasting, as newspapers, became an operation in which only the well-financed could participate, and the ideas of the minorities in society became even less likely to be heard.

Thus, by the end of the 1920s, both the broadcasting and the motion-picture industries were firmly in the hands of establishment interests. Such a direction had long been visible within the newspaper industry, and efforts to place access to the press outside the reach of most dissident groups continued in the 1920s. Financial trends in the industry heightened the criticism of journalism from concerned individuals both in and out of the profession. Some of the forces that turned newspapers into even bigger businesses with greater establishment-related interests during these years were beyond the control of the publishers. Newsprint, for example, jumped considerably in price. The cost of equipment necessary to run newspapers also increased, in part due to the demands that circulation wars placed on the publications to produce bigger, more attractive newspapers.[98]

Few new newspapers were started, and the money involved when newspapers changed hands was staggering. In 1930, for instance, the selling price of the *Philadelphia Inquirer* was $18 million. Even providing a new home for a newspaper that stayed under the same ownership was costly. In 1935, the *Los Angeles Times* moved into a new building that cost $1.65 million to build; when the value of the land and the equipment was added to the total, the new plant was worth some $4 million.[99] Long gone were the days when a person with a dream or a mission could gather a few thousand dollars together and publish a newspaper. Just as lost were the opportunities for using newspapers to challenge the system. Now, the newspaper business was as big as many other industries around the country. The conservatism that infiltrated the business leadership class at large also affected newspaper publishers. Even if the publishers had proven immune to the conservative mentality, they likely would not have opened their newspapers to deviant views because such news did not sell. With substantial investments riding on the contents of each newspaper, controversy had to be avoided.

The increasing battle for advertising dollars also contributed to the medium's problems. Many advertisers would buy space only in the largest newspapers in a community. This practice led to devastating circulation wars and to the deaths of many newspapers unable to attract advertising dollars. The importance of advertising to the survival of a newspaper is demonstrated by the fact that in 1919, advertising accounted for about two-thirds of a publication's total income. By 1926, advertising accounted for about three-quarters of the budget.[100] As the amount of income from advertising increased, so too did the demand for space in the nation's newspapers. According to one study of newspaper space distribution, in 1900 about 32 percent of the publication was filled with advertising; by 1925 that total had reached almost 61 percent of the total space available.[101] The influence of the advertiser increased in proportion to the percentage of the bill he paid, and the room for information available to the public declined in an inverse relationship.

Newspapers caught up in this financial crunch became part of a merger mania that led to consolidation in larger cities and to the disappearance of many well-known publications. In Chicago, the number of morning newspapers dropped from seven to two. In the early 1890s, when New York had a population of four million, it had eleven morning newspapers; in the 1920s, with a population of six million, only seven general circulation publications remained, and five of those were owned by chains.[102] Nationwide, the loss of newspapers during these years was impressive, and the implications of these losses for access to channels of communication were overpowering. In 1910, the nation had 2,200 English-language general circulation dailies; in 1930, the total was down to 1,942. In 1910, 509 of the nation's cities were one-daily cities; in 1930, the number of cities with only one daily newspaper was 1,002. In 1910, 689 cities had competing dailies; in 1930, only 288 cities had competing dailies.[103]

Not only were the number of outlets available for communication decreasing, but the variety offered by the existing outlets dropped as newspapers that did survive were swallowed up by burgeoning newspaper chains. Virtually unknown in the nineteenth century, chain newspapers accounted for about 37 percent of the nation's total daily circulation by 1933.[104] In some of these instances, individual publications were remade in the image of the parent company, thus further lessening chances for diversity of opinion. In many chain operations, owners became involved in economies of scale that were so popular with other big businesses. Rather than sending multiple correspondents to the nation's capital, for example, all the newspapers in the chain would use the information provided by a single reporter.

The Associated Press (AP) continued its stranglehold on the transmission of news. Attempts by the newly formed International News Service (INS) to distribute foreign news available solely through the AP because of its relationship with news organizations abroad were rejected by the U.S. Supreme Court. The INS had wanted to distribute the information after it had been published by AP-member newspapers so that its clients, who were excluded from AP membership, would have some international news for their readers. The Supreme Court held that the AP maintained a sufficient property interest in the news, even after the news had been printed, to keep other news services from distributing AP dispatches.[105] As a result, readers of newspapers that were not members of the Associated Press had little access to certain kinds of information.

Although readers of the nation's leading newspapers generally had unimpeded access to a great deal of information, much of the data was biased. In 1920, for example, Walter Lippmann and Charles Merz published a study of *New York Times*'s coverage of the Russian revolution of 1917 and related events running through March 1920. In instance after instance, the two men found that *Times* stories, headlines, picture captions, and editorials were biased and incorrect. They concluded that the journalists had purposely shaped the news to prejudice the American people against the Bolsheviks—and that the effort had succeeded. These practices, Lippmann and Merz warned, were dangerous in a society that depended on information for the shaping of public opinion.[106]

Apprehension about the journalistic standards of the 1920s was not limited to the incidents cited above, for newspapers raised new concerns about their behavior during the Jazz Age. These years featured another round of sensationalism and more challenges to the right of newspapers to serve as the caretakers of freedom of the press. The new form of journalism, appropriately named jazz journalism, once again became identified with the common people, using their interests, heroes, and needs as a focal point. Once again, however, the medium for this new form of journalism—the tabloid—sank into the depths of sensationalism. A writer for the magazine *The Independent* found the tabs to be "an unholy blot on the fourth estate—they carry all the news that isn't fit to print." Another critic concluded that these new journalists "reduce the highest ideals of the newspaper to the process of fastening a camera lens to every boudoir keyhole." Oswald Garrison Villard, editor of *The Nation,* added, "No journalist of the 90's ever sank to quite such depths of vulgarity, sensationalism and degeneracy as do the tabloids in New York today."[107]

Simply a mirror of the times, the tabloid was part of the Roaring Twenties—bathing beauties, movie stars, big-time sports, speakeasies, jazz, and jazz journalism. The format had its roots in the penny press of James Gordon Bennett and the yellow journalism of Joseph Pulitzer and William Randolph Hearst. The leading papers again were in New York—the *Daily News,* started in 1919 by Joseph Patterson, and the *Mirror,* started in 1924 by Hearst. An ideal size for reading in the subway, the tabloid devoted its space to beautiful girls, sensational murders, and serialized fiction. Says author Jim Bishop, who got his first newspaper job on the New York City tabs, the editors had a formula for success: "A man who betrayed an innocent girl was a story. If he was rich, it was a better story. If he beat her with Arabian whips or wrote his name on her abdomen with a lighted cigarette, it was a nine-day wonder."[108]

The behavior of such journalists was exacerbated by advertisers who disliked tabloids in the first place and who would reward only those publications with the highest circulation figures with their patronage. To reach new circulation heights, tabloid newspapers engaged in even more outrageous conduct. Contests were popular, syndicated columnists became a must, and a sensational story a day was essential. If a sensational story did not exist on a particular day, reporters and editors invented one, as when on a slow day at the *New York Evening Graphic* a reporter was assigned to fire a shot into the newsroom ceiling from a fire escape outside the building. The headline on the next edition read: "UNDERWORLD TRIES TO INTIMIDATE THE GRAPHIC."[109]

The forces that drove the tabloids to excess—the dynamics of the economic marketplace—were beyond their control. As these problems continued, the influence of advertisers on American journalism became a prime target for critics of the press during the 1920s. Author Upton Sinclair opened the decade by comparing American journalism to prostitution, claiming "American newspapers as a whole represent private interests not public interests." The newspapers, he charged, would pass up stories of legitimate public value if those stories offended the private interests to which they were beholden. Sinclair believed that the American people had little respect for the press. In fact, they "thoroughly despise and hate their newspapers; yet they seem to have no idea of what to do about it, and take for granted that they must go on reading falsehoods for the balance of their days!"[110] His remedy was legislative: laws to require source approval of a story before its printing, to force mandatory retraction of errors, to break up the Associated Press monopoly, and to forbid the faking of news.

Also concerned about the functioning of the press was journalist Walter Lippmann. In addition to his study on news about the Soviet Union, Lippmann wrote about the connection between a free press and the preservation of democracy. "The newspaper," he wrote in 1920, "is in all literalness the bible of democracy, the book out of which a people determines its conduct. It is the only serious book most people read. It is the only book they read every day." Yet, Lippmann said, the newspaper has not been fulfilling its role in society. Lies were printed; privacy was invaded; international relations were jeopardized, and the public had no recourse. He worried that "the next generation will attempt to bring the publishing business under greater social control. There is everywhere an increasingly angry disillusionment about the press, a growing sense of being baffled and misled; and wise publishers will not pooh-pooh these omens." Lippmann feared that "if publishers and authors themselves do not face the facts and attempt to deal with them, some day Congress, in a fit of temper, egged on by an outraged public opinion, will operate on the press with an ax."[111]

The question remained: who would reform the profession? The major effort to protect journalism from its critics in the 1920s came from newspaper editors who, irritated by repeated attacks, established the American Society of Newspaper Editors (ASNE) in 1923. One of its first orders of business was the adoption of a code of ethics for the newspaper profession, known as the Canons of Journalism.[112] The code of ethics was controversial from its inception. After all, who had the right to set up ethical standards for this individualistic group?

Each editor was firmly committed to freedom of the press, but each defined that freedom alone, without interference from other editors. The only thing that made the editors willing to even consider a code was the increasing amount of criticism of the press. A written ethical code might just cool some of the critics' ardor. When H. J. Wright of the *New York Globe* presented the committee's report on the canons, he said, "I think all members of the Committee agree that the chief weakness of American journalism is its failure to take itself seriously." The committee hoped that by editors joining together to declare the "purposes and practices" of the profession, "there will come to be, first of all, a better understanding on our own part of the seriousness of our own profession, its enormous obligations, and that the public itself will come to a better recognition of the standing which we think we should have."[113]

As presented, the canons intruded into many areas considered sacred by the American press. One of the most controversial sections said that journalists had no right to publish statements taken from private conversations with a source or comments overheard by reporters without first gaining the speaker's permission. After a hot debate, the provision was voted down. The remainder of the code was adopted, but its last proviso contained a telling statement: "Lacking authority to enforce its canons, the journalism here represented can but express the hope that deliberate pandering to vicious instincts will encounter effective public disapproval or yield to the influence of a professional condemnation."[114] The debate over a code of ethics designed to increase public confidence in journalism had been emotional and heated. But the product of that interchange specifically ruled out any enforcement of its provisions. If journalists abused their privileges, the only hope of correcting their behavior was to resort to the much maligned recourse of public criticism. They were essentially back where they had started.

Journalists did not have to wait long to see just how ineffective the canons were. In November 1922, two ASNE members were accused—and rightfully so—of taking money to suppress details of the Teapot Dome scandal. ASNE leaders investigated the affair but declared the organization helpless to act. No provision had been made for disciplining members. In addition, the offenses had occurred before the canons had been ratified. Consequently, application of the code would be retroactive and illegal. Critics of the newspaper profession complained loudly but to no avail. Debate over the issue dragged on for several years, and the accused individuals finally resigned their memberships without any formal action being taken against them. For the next several years, society members debated whether they should insert a disciplinary mechanism into the organization's constitution. Finally, in 1932, the ASNE amended its constitution to allow for the expulsion of members for "due cause," with no definition of that term provided. Criticism of the media did not end with the adoption of the Canons of Journalism. As the decade wore on, in fact, complaints became even stronger. Much of the hostility was aimed at newspaper owners who became increasingly powerful, arrogating unto themselves such a variety of privileges that the next wave of critics would label them lords of the press and call for legislation to curtail their influence. By the 1930s, an all-out war would be raging over freedom of the press and who should serve as its trustee for the American people.

The upheaval in the ranks of the press would be typical of the changes affecting freedom of expression in the Depression years. The 1920s had set the stage for massive changes. Slowly the American people learned that freedom of expression was an important right. In the 1920s, conservative business leaders still controlled large segments of the community, and freedom of expression remained limited. With the coming of the Depression, all basic values were questioned— including the implicit trust the nation had placed in its business leaders. Then, Americans were willing to listen to numerous voices in their eagerness to find answers to the economic problems of the day. And then, those individuals, including newspaper publishers, who impeded free communication of information would become the targets of the sharpest barbs yet thrown.

CHAPTER 5

Inching toward a Marketplace of Ideas: Freedom of Expression in the 1930s

The stock-market crash of 1929 and the Great Depression that followed in its wake caused severe dislocations in American society. Millions of people were thrown out of work; millions more barely earned enough to survive. Confidence in the basic institutions of society and the nation's longtime leadership was badly shaken. The American people, dissatisfied with the solutions offered by those in control, looked for new ways to respond to new situations. As a result of this great economic disaster, Americans became more willing to hear and try new ideas. Perhaps for the first time in its history, the United States was moving toward the establishment of a true marketplace of ideas. No notion was too far-fetched for a desperate people to try; no proposal was too revolutionary. Radical ideas came from all segments of society. Americans had decided, for a change, that the solutions they wanted could be found not in the safety of the past but in free discussion about the future.

Herbert Hoover's administration ended with one of the largest demonstrations of the right of free assembly ever seen in the nation's capital and with one of the most brutal repressions of that right in our history. The protesters were veterans demanding the immediate payment of a bonus for the time they had served during World War I. The campaign for a lump-sum payment to veterans—a bonus—was not a product of the Depression. Complicated and emotional, the bonus issue had been around for years. The American Legion began asking for these concessions in 1919, and although the character of the request changed often, the demand remained constant. Several times Congress acceded to pressures from the veterans' lobby and enacted such legislation, but Presidents Harding, Coolidge, and Hoover vetoed those measures. In 1924, Congress overrode the presidential veto to establish a trust fund that would pay each veteran about $1,000 in 1944. Still the veterans wanted more and, with the Depression, demanded immediate payment of the bonus. President Hoover refused their requests, in large part because the country could not finance the expenditure.[1]

With Congress scheduled to discuss the issue once again, many veterans decided to march on Washington in 1932. The veterans' plans were made in the midst of increasing apprehension in Washington. A small group of Communists had picketed the White House in late October 1931 demanding unemployment insurance and payment of the bonus. Although the demonstrators left peacefully, rumors spread that the Communists were planning to launch their long-awaited attempt to overthrow the government. Despite these concerns, when some 4,000 Communists arrived in Washington in December 1931, the government worked to ensure a peaceful protest, which it was. Similar provisions were made for a Catholic priest who brought about 12,000 unemployed workers to the nation's capital in January 1932. President Hoover accepted a petition from the Communists and met with the priest.

But the president believed that the Bonus Expeditionary Force (BEF), as the unemployed veterans called themselves, presented different problems. They were an organized pressure group coming to cause trouble. He had refused to discuss immediate payment of the bonus with lobbyists and vowed not to talk about the issue with any marchers. The administration made no plans to cooperate with participants in what turned out to be the largest demonstration the capital had ever seen. As the number of marchers far exceeded the president's expectations, Hoover covertly authorized housing, food, and medical supplies. About 20,000 people—soldiers and their families—occupied some twenty-seven encampments near the Capitol. When the tent cities filled, demonstrators moved into old federal office buildings that were due to be demolished and set up housekeeping.

Bonus Army members were mainly middle-class people who were after what they considered theirs by right. They were certainly not seeking radical changes in the government. As their numbers grew, rumors once again spread that Communists would infiltrate the march, take it over, and use the soldiers to foment revolution. Many Americans believed the fanciful tales because, in traveling to the capital, veterans had commandeered railroad cars, forced businesses to feed them, and behaved in other allegedly un-American ways. In addition, members of the Bonus Army looked scruffy and dangerous. Contingency plans were made to bring in the U.S. Army if the outnumbered District of Columbia police force encountered problems. To defuse any potential danger, the government made marchers relocate outside the city in order to obtain food.

While the marchers were testing the will of the federal government, members of Congress debated bonus legislation. The bill passed in the House but with a majority short of the number necessary to override a presidential veto. The Senate defeated the measure. Despite the presence of thousands of veterans near the Capitol, no riot occurred when the defeat was announced; the men returned peaceably to their camps. When Congress adjourned, the veterans planned to transfer their protest to the White House. This move led to efforts to rid the nation's capital of all veterans. To encourage their departures, the government offered the veterans loans to finance their transportation home. By the July 24 deadline, all but 8,000 to 10,000 veterans had abandoned the protest.

The next step was to evict veterans who remained in government-owned buildings. The first eviction was fairly peaceful, but soon BEF members from the outlying areas arrived to prevent additional removals. Fears rose; violence occurred; and injuries were incurred on both sides. The police commissioner of Washington appealed to the president for help. Federal troops under the command of General Douglas MacArthur, the army chief of staff, drove the Bonus Expeditionary Force out of the capital using a full range of military force. Over the protests of his staff aide, Dwight D. Eisenhower, MacArthur used machine guns, tanks, infantry, cavalry, tear gas, and bayonets to disperse the veterans, most of whom were unarmed.

Although initially critical of MacArthur's techniques, Hoover eventually adopted the idea that the BEF had threatened the continued existence of organized government. Furthermore, the president remained adamantly opposed to capitulating to the demands of an unruly mob. "There is no group, no matter what its origins, that can be allowed either to violate the laws of this city or to intimidate the Government," he said. "Government cannot be coerced by mob rule. . . . There can be no safe harbor in the United States of America for violence."[2] As time passed, criticisms of the administration's actions increased as did efforts by the president and his officials to rebuff and suppress such commentary. While the White House became increasingly enamored of the idea of Communist domination of the marchers, the District police commissioner released a report saying that only about 200 Communists were among the veterans and that these individuals had been controlled easily by District police and by BEF military police.

Hoover's handling of the veterans' constitutional protest haunted him into the election. Just how mass protest should be handled would similarly worry future presidents. Dealing with thousands of people who decide to assemble in the nation's capital in order to petition for a redress of their grievances in person is a daunting challenge. The fear always exists that within the ranks of these assembled people lurk individuals who intend to assassinate the president and members of Congress, burn the city to the ground, and establish a dictatorship. Lost in the wave of apprehension, however, is the fact that Americans are guaranteed the right to petition their government. If petition from afar is unsuccessful, the Bill of Rights poses no bar to personal petition at the seat of government. Nor does the Bill of Rights say that only a certain number of individuals may gather at one time to seek solutions to their problems. Masses of people seeking redress are naturally intimidating, but the responsibility for protecting the constitutional rights of these individuals remains with the government.

Perhaps presidents need to learn a lesson from the way Franklin D. Roosevelt handled later bonus marches. The issue of an immediate cash bonus for veterans continued to be debated during Roosevelt's first administration, and the president opposed it, as Hoover had done before him. His stance led to three marches by veterans on the capital. These marches had much clearer connections with the Communists, but in each instance, the federal government publicly fed and housed the veterans. Arrangements were made for representatives of the groups to present their grievances to members of the president's staff. One delegation of protesting veterans met with the president himself, and Eleanor Roosevelt had dinner with the veterans on another occasion. Special provisions were made to place the unemployed veterans in the Civilian Conservation Corps as well. Each march drew less publicity than the previous one. In each case the participants—Communist or not—were viewed as citizens with grievances to be heard, regardless of whether their petitions were to be granted.[3]

The Great Depression tested American democracy in many ways. Disillusioned with Hoover's attempts to deal with economic chaos and unwilling to wait for Franklin Roosevelt to prove himself, radicals of all varieties built mass movements on ideas for economic and social cure-alls. The demagogues of the depression sought power about the same time that Adolf Hitler was taking over the leadership of Germany. Some say that through the American demagogues the United States flirted with its own fascist dictatorship. Another possibility is that the mythical marketplace of ideas finally was at work in the United States—that these demagogues were putting forth their proposals but that Americans simply were not buying.

One group of demagogues appeared more in the mainstream than most, but these individuals lost whatever chance they had to influence government as Roosevelt's New Deal successfully attacked the economic problems caused by the Depression. Another set of demagogues, who indeed were closer to the fascist view, remained on the fringes of society throughout the decade. Most of the so-called demagogues were dominant personalities who were adept at using radio. Each carefully identified scapegoats who were charged with responsibility for the American plight. The more mainstream demagogues joined with many New Dealers in blaming the plutocrats—wealthy individuals who used their money for selfish ends. Fringe demagogues often chose the Jews and, in the process, gave rise to a virulent wave of anti-Semitism. Binding these demagogues together was their belief that individuals could seize control of their own destinies.

Two names head the list of such demagogues during these years: Huey Long, the political boss of Louisiana, and Father Charles Coughlin, a Catholic priest with a radio ministry that reached millions of listeners.[4] Long became a Louisiana senator in 1932 and immediately began arguing for a redistribution of the nation's wealth as the way to end the Depression. A spellbinding speaker, Long often complained about the concentration of the wealth in the hands of a few. His goal was to ride his monetary campaign right into the White House. Although he had supported Franklin Roosevelt in 1932, Long discovered that, despite the president's reassurances, Roosevelt was not going to introduce the far-reaching economic reforms that Long desired. These rebuffs did not quiet the senator. His speeches were filled with calls to limit the size of personal fortunes and restrict both personal incomes and inheritances. He regularly introduced bills to implement his plans, and as Long discussed his financial programs, he won the public attention that he so craved.

Long broke with the president in late 1933. As he worked, Long feared that Roosevelt would try to stop his efforts to build a new political movement. In fact, the president did deny federal patronage to Long, and he encouraged the Internal Revenue Service to reopen investigations into the tax returns of Long and some of his political associates. Despite this blatant abuse of presidential power to silence a critic, Long shored up his support back home and continued opposing Roosevelt. Emerging from Long's efforts was the Share Our Wealth Program, which was designed to guarantee each American citizen a fair portion of the nation's wealth. His financial scheme allegedly would bring in enough money for the government to provide each Depression-bound individual with a house, a car, a radio, and a guaranteed annual income sufficient for a decent standard of living. As Long's program attracted more followers, some Roosevelt advisers feared that Long would set up a third-party movement in 1936 and try to seize the presidency. Long did not have the opportunity to challenge Roosevelt in 1936, however, for an assassin, upset about a Louisiana patronage matter, killed him in 1935.

A more persistent critic of Franklin Roosevelt, and perhaps an even more dangerous one, was Father Charles Coughlin, a Catholic priest who had begun his radio ministry in the 1920s as a way to help meet parish expenses. By 1930, Coughlin, another spellbinding speaker, was devoting most of his sermons to political and economic issues. Millions of people listened each week, and he allegedly received more mail than movie stars, sports heroes, and the president of the United States. As the Depression deepened in 1930, Coughlin's weekly sermons were carried over CBS, and his Radio League of the Little Flower was in full bloom. His criticism of Herbert Hoover and of other men and institutions became so strong that in 1931 CBS dropped his program. Coughlin protested in vain that the network had censored his right to free speech. An effort to move the weekly broadcasts to NBC was spurned by that network, and Coughlin strung together his own ad hoc network that resulted in his reaching even more people than before.

As with Long, Coughlin had supported Franklin Roosevelt in 1932. The president invited Coughlin to Washington for the inauguration, and the priest assumed that he and Roosevelt agreed on plans for economic recovery. But by late 1932, Coughlin began making specific suggestions for reform that were far more radical than Roosevelt was considering. Father Coughlin centered his curative ideas on money and banking. He believed that there simply was not enough money to go around and that, consequently, if more currency were put in circulation, the nation's financial woes would be solved. To accomplish this reform, Coughlin suggested that the country back its money with silver, an idea long rejected by American political leaders. He also wanted control of banking shifted from private bankers, whom he distrusted, to the federal government. Most of his ideas were based on the belief that plutocrats manipulated the nation's money supply to the detriment of the common people. As with Long, Coughlin was winning national support for his ideas, which reached at least 10 million radio parishioners each Sunday.

In fact, the radio priest was becoming so popular nationwide that the president's advisers believed that any public repudiation of Coughlin's ideas would endanger Roosevelt's own plans for economic recovery. Although a frontal attack on the radio priest was considered unwise, presidential advisers did make sure that Coughlin had as little contact with Roosevelt as possible as they sought other ways to end the menace they believed Coughlin posed. By 1934, Coughlin realized that his ability to influence the administration was minimal at best, and he looked for new ways to put his ideas into action.

About the time that Coughlin's criticisms of Roosevelt heated up, the administration attacked the priest through persons who worked with him. Officials revealed, for instance, that Father Coughlin's personal secretary had invested heavily in silver on behalf of the Radio League of the Little Flower while the priest was advocating that the government back the nation's currency with silver. A conflict of interest at the least, charged his critics; an attempt to manipulate the national economy for personal profit at worst, they added. Government officials also explored ways to force broadcasters to stop carrying Coughlin's weekly messages and attempted to get the Catholic leadership to stop the radio broadcasts. This latter approach failed when the president's advisers discovered that Coughlin's immediate superior strongly supported the priest's message. Although the administration's campaign against Coughlin was just beginning, the priest was undaunted.[5]

In November 1934, Coughlin set up an organization that was designed to bring about changes in the government—the National Union for Social Justice. Within two weeks, 200,000 people joined. When Coughlin encountered difficulty in lobbying the existing government, he moved toward the establishment of a third party to challenge Roosevelt in 1936, which greatly concerned presidential advisers. If Coughlin and Long found a way to join forces, they worried, Roosevelt could have a difficult time winning reelection. In many ways, the president's advisers were correct in linking the threats posed by Long and Coughlin. The priest and the politician had many things in common. Merging the Share Our Wealth movement and the National Union for Social Justice seemed to be on the horizon.

After Long's death, the Share Our Wealth movement fell into the hands of Gerald L. K. Smith, who had been the senator's chief assistant. Although he was equally as spellbinding a speaker as Long, Smith did not have Long's political skills nor the backing of Long's political machine. As part of a deal worked out to get back in Roosevelt's good graces after the senator's death, the Long machine sought to dismantle the Share Our Wealth movement and began by making Smith unwelcome in Louisiana. In order to preserve the movement, Smith combined efforts with Coughlin in 1936 and the Union party was born.

Joining Union party efforts to unseat Roosevelt in 1936 was Dr. Francis E. Townsend, developer of the Old Age Revolving Pension Plan, which advocated financial security for senior citizens. Townsend's demands were only partially met by Roosevelt's Social Security program, and so he, too, sought more change through the political process. Rounding out the party's leadership was Congressman William Lemke of North Dakota, leader of the Nonpartisan League, who brought agricultural interests into the alliance. Their platform combined their individual goals and was based largely on a major redistribution of the wealth. The party was established less than five months before the election and ran into trouble almost immediately when Socialists and Communists called its members fascists. Lemke, an uninspiring figure at best, was named as the Union party's presidential candidate. The campaign's leading orators were Coughlin and Smith, but they often disagreed with each other and with the other members of the party, including Lemke.

The Union party received only 2 percent of the national vote total as Franklin Roosevelt swept to victory. After the election, leaders of the movement went their separate ways, which, to a certain degree, they had done all along. Although labeled demagogues, Long, Coughlin, Smith, Lemke, and Townsend had put forth their ideas for saving the nation and had attracted substantial audiences. Because of that support, Franklin Roosevelt had had to pay attention to some of their proposals, and thus Union party leaders could claim credit for some of the social legislation that the president ultimately put forth. And because they were so successful, they also had become targets of Roosevelt's ire. They had, however, survived the presidential temper and efforts to quiet their voices of dissent. Had they been perceived as greater threats or had the president unleashed more of the power of the federal bureaucracy against them, they might not have been able to launch a third party campaign in 1936. But as it was, they added to the ferment of ideas brewing in the United States during these Depression years.

Neither Father Coughlin nor Gerald L. K. Smith disappeared from the American scene after 1936. Both became involved in right-wing political activities that had been developing in this country for years. Many of these groups advocated 100 percent Americanism, an idea that had been popularized during the Red Scare after World War I. Liberalism was a target for these arch-conservatives—anything liberal. Churches, labor unions, colleges and universities, blacks, immigrants—and especially Jews—were all viewed as dangerous to the continuation of American society in its purist form.

Many of these right wingers had long considered Jews responsible for a variety of evils in American life, especially when the problems were economic in origin. The Depression roused the fears of Jewish influence in the nation's economic structure once again; blaming America's financial woes on the manipulations of international bankers of Jewish heritage became easy. The liberalism of Roosevelt and the number of Jews among his advisers aggravated those fears, for many conservatives perceived a dangerous alien force at work within the administration. When the president broke with tradition and extended diplomatic recognition to the Soviet Union, the Jews advising the president were blamed, just as Jewish Bolsheviks had been blamed for orchestrating the overthrow of the czar in 1917. The list of problems that could be attributed to Jews grew, aided in no small way by the inflammatory anti-Jewish rhetoric emanating from Nazi Germany. The increasingly virulent American strain of anti-Semitism raised fears in the hearts of many American liberals who worried that European fascism might find roots in an American society rent by economic disorder.[6]

Leaders of the anti-Semitic movement were many. Most tried to set up an organization, often paramilitary in nature, and each sought to offer answers to the problems afflicting America. None of their solutions was as far-reaching as those suggested by Long, Coughlin, or Townsend, but the existence of such organizations led liberals to call for suppressing the speech of these representatives of the political fringe.[7] One of the favorite targets of liberal criticism was William Dudley Pelley, the son of a minister and a former journalist, who set up his Silver Legion in 1933. A mystical experience in 1931 had led Pelley to see demon spirits in the bodies of Jews and had turned him into an arch anti-Semite and a fervent supporter of Adolf Hitler. He condemned a variety of groups including the Congress of Industrial Organizations, the American Medical Association, the American Civil Liberties Union, the League of Nations, and the Church of Jesus Christ of the Latter Day Saints as being dominated by Jews.

To join Pelley's Silver Legion, you had to be a white Christian, which was proven in part by the questions asked on the membership form and in part by the picture that had to accompany the application. Although a paramilitary organization, members did little more than wear uniforms to meetings. The emotional boost that participating in a paramilitary organization provided to men on the brink of financial disaster was not lost on Pelley. "Men in Little Towns are suddenly galvanized by the piercing tocsins of the Silver Bugles," he wrote. "Rippling flags go past foggy windows where they've viewed the world with increasing sullenness during this highly successful Jewish Depression. . . . They deploy upon the sidewalks and behold the finest specimens of American manhood DOING something to reli[e]ve mass resentment. . . . They want to play their parts."[8] At its peak in 1934, the Silver Legion had about 15,000 members relieving their resentment and suffering. That total made the legion considerably smaller than the organizations of Long or Coughlin. In addition, Pelley's estimation of the dangers facing the United States was far-fetched at best. He predicted, for example, that the Jews would replace Franklin Roosevelt with someone even worse in 1935 and that the Silver Shirts would step in to protect constitutional liberty by establishing a Christian commonwealth. This new order would make jobs available to all, limit the total income accruing to any one person, and provide a livable minimum wage for each American.

Federal and state governments handled Pelley's dissident views by investigating his organization's finances. In 1934, the state of North Carolina, where the Silver Legion was headquartered, indicted Pelley for selling stock that was unregistered in the state and for advertising an insolvent company. He was fined $1,000 on the first charge and was granted a prayer for judgment continued on the second charge, which allowed him to remain free for five years under the supervision of the court. And the federal government, on orders of Franklin Roosevelt himself, inquired into whether Pelley could be prosecuted for criminal libel because of some of the criticisms of the president that Pelley was printing in the official Silver Legion newspaper. The president, however, did not follow up on his inquiries.

Another right-wing leader of the 1930s, Gerald B. Winrod, established his Defenders of the Christian Faith to promote fundamental Protestant values in 1925. As Franklin Roosevelt attempted to cure the economic dislocations brought on by the Depression through governmental action, Winrod made his organization more active politically. Of special concern to Winrod were the twin possibilities and later realities of the recognition of the Soviet Union and the repeal of Prohibition. Winrod finally became convinced that all of the problems afflicting the United States were caused by an international Zionist plot, and he became a violent anti-Semite. In 1938, he entered the Republican primary as a candidate for U.S. senator from Kansas. The same year, his publication, *The Defender,* reached its peak subscription total of 110,000. Rumors circulated that his campaign had been funded largely by the Nazi party, and Winrod finished third in the primary balloting.

The third person who had difficulties because of his anti-Semitic views was Gerald L. K. Smith, the heir to Huey Long's Share Our Wealth program. His hatred for Franklin Roosevelt and support of the Union party led to Smith's being labeled an anti-Semite and a native fascist. A rabble-rousing speaker, this former minister set up his Committee of One Million in April 1937. Subjected to more subtle censorship than that exerted against others of his ilk, Smith found halls for speeches generally closed to him. When he did appear in public, he was the target of massive picketing. Those people who sought to silence Smith believed they were upholding constitutional values. Smith, said his political opponents, endangered free speech because he sought to subvert the social stability necessary for that freedom to continue.

Changes in European governments helped to revive nativism in the United States and to focus fears on Americans of Italian or German descent. The term fascist became loosely used to condemn anyone who said anything favorable about an Axis power. By the mid- to late 1930s, demands increased for laws to suppress alleged fascist activities in the United States, even though it was often hard to distinguish between real support for fascist causes and legitimate criticism of government. Individuals making these calls for repression often had impeccable liberal credentials, but they were convinced that, given the country's unsettled economic condition, the nation was in grave peril of falling under a right-wing dictatorship. Thus, liberals, who usually supported freedom of expression, used the national security argument, so traditionally a part of the conservative's arsenal, to demand the repression of right-wing groups and individuals.

Although Americans of Italian extraction raised the first fears, attention soon switched to German-Americans in general and to members of the German-American Bund in particular. Americans of German extraction still comprised the largest single ethnic group in the United States, and the Nazis actively sought to win the loyalty of individuals of German blood regardless of their citizenship status or of how many generations had passed since they had left the mother country. By focusing on blood rather than place of birth, the Nazis hoped for even more adherents. German propaganda agents were well financed in their efforts to win German-American support.[9]

The German-American Bund served as the main organization for mobilizing support for the Nazi regime between 1936 and 1942. Fritz Kuhn led the Bund, which became another paramilitary organization, complete with the slogan of "Free America," which was shouted in "Heil Hitler" fashion at meetings. Although the size of the Bund was hard to establish, best estimates place it at under 10,000; most members were loyal Americans who believed they were just showing pride in their heritage. Attempts to organize the Bund encountered constant government harassment. Kuhn was not allowed to rent buildings for meetings, and his organization was infiltrated by police officers. After an intensive investigation, authorities discovered Kuhn had diverted Bund money for his own purposes, and he wound up in jail for his crime. Perhaps more precisely, he wound up in jail for the political beliefs he was advocating, for Kuhn and the Bund never would have been pursued so intensely had they not been perceived as a distinct threat to the American way of life.

Fears of native fascism led to a variety of repressive measures at all levels of government. Perhaps the most ominous effort of all began in the U.S. Congress in 1933 with Samuel Dickstein's campaign for a special House committee to investigate subversive activities. A liberal Democrat and a Jew from a strong Jewish district in New York City, Dickstein feared that fascists might gain a foothold in the United States during the Depression and that Jews then would be persecuted here as they were in Germany. Dickstein was especially alarmed by the reactions of some American businessmen who, early in the reigns of Mussolini and Hitler, praised the two dictators for straightening out business and industry in their homelands. Could a strongman come to power in the United States? Fearing that possibility, Dickstein wanted the House to investigate right-wing propaganda activities to find a way to stop such organizations. In January 1934, Dickstein won his special investigation of Nazi activities in the United States.

Dickstein was denied the privilege of chairing the committee because he was deemed too emotionally involved in the issue. He served as vice chairman under John McCormack, Democrat of Massachusetts. The New Yorker's displeasure with the committee's progress was evident from the beginning as he continued his own personal legislative campaign against fascists. In 1935, for instance, Dickstein advocated banning material from the mails that promoted "racial or religious hatred, bigotry or intolerance."[10] Still concerned over the lack of action, in 1937 he asked Congress to investigate all organizations trying to spread religious or racial hatred throughout the United States. Dickstein, however, made little headway in the House, where his proposals generally were rejected. State governments, on the other hand, seemed more willing to restrict activities designed to promote race hate. In 1935, New Jersey enacted a law that made it a misdemeanor to make any statement "in the presence of two or more persons . . . which in any way incites, counsels, promotes or advocates hatred, abuse, violence or hostility against any group or groups of persons residing or being in this state, by reason of race, color, religion or manner of worship."[11]

Congress could not long ignore increasing demands that it act. In 1937, on the same day that it refused to support Dickstein's proposal on un-American propaganda, the House also rejected an effort by Martin Dies, Democrat of Texas, to establish a special committee to investigate the sit-down strikes that were plaguing industry at the time. Three months later, Dies asked for a committee to investigate subversive and un-American propaganda. Seeing within that effort some hope of obtaining the legislation he so desired, Dickstein worked for its passage. The result was the creation of the first of several Dies committees—the first House Committee on Un-American Activities.[12]

Similar congressional concern about changes abroad was manifested in the enactment of the major piece of legislation recommended by the McCormack-Dickstein Committee, the Foreign Agents Registration Act of 1938. Under this act, individuals conducting propaganda activities financed by foreign governments had to reveal who was underwriting their efforts. Persons failing to register were subject to a $1,000 fine, not more than two years in jail, or both.[13] Although individuals forced to register complained that the legislation impaired their right to speak, the U.S. State Department rejected those claims: "The Act is broad in its terms and imposes the duty to register on many American citizens, companies and organizations whose work is of a wholly unimpeachable character." Nor did registration cast aspersions on anyone's patriotism. "The mere fact of registration under the Act affords no ground for assuming that any person so registered is engaged in unpatriotic activity."[14] All registration meant was that a foreign government was paying the bills.

The Foreign Agents Registration Act was the first of several pieces of legislation enacted within a two-year span to suppress subversive groups. In 1939, Congress approved the Hatch Act, which, among other things, required the dismissal of federal employees who advocated the forcible overthrow of the government or who were members of an organization believing in the forcible overthrow of the government. The legislation required the federal government to begin making lists of organizations to which its employees could not belong and maintain their jobs.[15] The government's list-making activities were aided in 1940 by the Voorhis Act, which was designed to force nativist groups that advocated hate, fear, and persecution of certain groups to register with the attorney general.[16] The practice of maintaining lists of proscribed organizations begun with these laws soon would become all-pervasive in state and federal governments obsessed with employee loyalty during the cold war.

The major law stemming from concern about fascist subversion in the United States was the Alien Registration Act of 1940, better known as the Smith Act. This repressive statute was so popular that only four members of the House voted against it, while forty-five representatives abstained. Under its provisions, millions of aliens were registered and fingerprinted so that the government could keep better track of them. The law included provisions to protect the military from efforts to undermine the loyalty of its members by making it a felony "to interfere with, impair, or influence the loyalty, morale, or discipline of the military or naval forces of the United States" by advising or counseling such insubordination or by distributing written materials encouraging that behavior. Even more important was the fact that the Smith Act contained provisions establishing the first peacetime sedition law since 1798. This language was based on the New York Criminal Anarchy Act of 1902 and made it a felony "to knowingly or willfully advocate, abet, advise, or teach the duty, necessity, desirability or propriety of overthrowing or destroying any government in the United States by force or violence, or by the assassination of any officer of any such government." The production and distribution of these materials could be punished, as could the organization of a group designed to pursue that end.[17]

Consequently, by 1940, a series of repressive measures, much like those enacted during World War I, was in place. The goal was to suppress the fascist influence in the United States, for the nation was caught in another spasm of great fear. Few Americans reflected on the impact that the legislation would have on all speech even though Roger Baldwin, executive director of the American

Civil Liberties Union (ACLU), had warned, "Any restrictions on freedom of speech, press or assembly, regardless of whom they affect, lay down the precedents by which those rights are generally injured."[18] With such legislation, members of Congress showed little faith in the ability of their fellow Americans to reject fascist ideas. This same fear of native fascism led Franklin Roosevelt to order the Federal Bureau of Investigation (FBI) to launch an inquiry into pro-Nazi groups in 1934. The German-American Bund was J. Edgar Hoover's first target, but the wily bureau director soon warned the president of the dangers that domestic Communists posed to the national security, and by 1936 he had won approval to watch both groups.[19]

Strangely enough, the repression evidenced in the 1930s was not aimed at the Communist Party of the United States of America (CPUSA), which for the first, and perhaps only, time in its history was accepted as a legitimate part of the nation's political structure. The decade did not begin well for the party, which had only started its climb out from the underground into which it had fled during the Red Scare. Mired in another intraparty feud, the party had been unable to capitalize on the stock-market crash when it occurred.[20] Communists also faced a congressional inquiry headed by Representative Hamilton Fish of New York at the beginning of the decade. After holding hearings in various parts of the country, the committee announced, without explaining the source of its statistics, that between 500,000 to 600,000 Communists and Communist sympathizers existed in the country. Only 12,000 of these people, however, were dues-paying members of the party. Many organizations, including the ACLU, were listed as connected with Communist attempts to subvert the nation.[21] The committee made numerous restrictive recommendations, which found few supporters on Capitol Hill, perhaps because the minority report of Representative John E. Nelson of Maine convinced congressmen that toleration was the best approach. "Freedom should be the rule in America rather than restrictive legislation," Nelson wrote, "and we should approach with reserve the consideration of any criminal statutes that seek to fetter the operation of the human mind or to encroach in the slightest degree on those rights guaranteed in our Constitution to the lowliest individual in the United States."[22]

The Supreme Court added to the room provided Communists in 1931 when it held that a California law against the display of a red flag, the symbol of the Communist party, was an unconstitutional infringement of First Amendment rights. Yetta Stromberg had raised the flag daily as part of her duties at a party-sponsored summer camp and was arrested for her actions. Chief Justice Charles Evans Hughes, writing for seven members of the Court, denounced the law: "The maintenance of the opportunity for free political discussion to the end that government may be responsive to the will of the people and that changes may be obtained by lawful means, an opportunity essential to the security of the Republic, is a fundamental principle of our constitutional system."[23] The California law interfered with such free discussions. For the first time the Court had declared a law unconstitutional on free-speech grounds.

Even as various forces in the United States moved toward giving the Communist party room in which to operate, Moscow was slowly altering its perspective on American party life. Part of the reason for the change in Soviet plans for the United States focused on the unique character of the American Communist movement. Contrary to expectations, American Communists enjoyed very little success among the unemployed, the group allegedly most susceptible to prose-lytizing during times of economic dislocation. Instead, the CPUSA enjoyed its greatest popularity among liberals, intellectuals, and the middle class. In addition, the Roosevelt administration extended diplomatic recognition to the Soviet Union in 1933, and in response, the Comintern began a series of moves designed to improve relations with the administration, including telling American Communists to support Roosevelt-sponsored reform programs. Now CPUSA members were instructed to build coalitions with liberal groups in order to advocate mutually acceptable changes in society. Although these changes warmed the climate in which the CPUSA functioned during most of the 1930s, these new policies led to personal problems for individual American Communists who had been bitter critics of Roosevelt one day and who found themselves cooperating with the president the next day. But such was the lot of American Communists, and compliance was forthcoming as Earl Browder led CPUSA members into a period of coexistence and cooperation with American liberals. With these changes, the era of the popular front had arrived.

Through these coalitions, popular fronts against fascism, against racism, and for trade unions were established. Communists liked this approach because the front was nominally non-Communist. Liberals liked the arrangement because of the fervor that Communists brought to any cause. CPUSA leaders promoted that enthusiasm and used party participation to take over many of the front organizations that they helped set up. Large numbers of party members would attend meetings and thus assume key leadership positions simply because of their willingness to work. Their ultimate goal was to draw the non-Communist front members closer to the party line on various issues. Although their allies were wary of their relationships with Communists, generally the causes were seen as so important that these apprehensions disappeared, and cooperation became the norm. The American League Against War and Fascism, for instance, became a favorite popular front during the mid-1930s as Soviet policy and the interests of American liberals coalesced to fight both war and the advance of fascism.

As a result of the popular front movement, the Communist party in the United States began to grow slowly. About 26,000 members were on the books in 1934; probably at least twice as many people had signed up for membership but then withdrew. One reason for erratic membership figures was the fact that party life was thoroughly unpleasant for American liberals. Meetings, which usually were boring, were held several times a week, and members were expected to drop everything when the party called on them to protest some wrong or to hand out literature. The difficulties of party life served as only a partial reason for fluctuating membership levels. Many individuals who might have joined still feared legal difficulties if they took that step. Thirty-five states, for example, still had criminal syndicalism acts on the books ready to use against Communists, and numerous foreign-born individuals feared deportation if they became party members.

With the popular front movement, the party moved into several areas of American life in which it had enjoyed little previous success. Now, CPUSA members were accepted activists in the labor movement. Party members, in fact, were instrumental in helping the Congress of Industrial Organizations (CIO) organize several key industrial unions. The party contributed organizers and leadership to the movement as well as members who would not flinch in the face of management intimidation. Their bravado then would encourage other workers to stand firm, and the industry would be organized. Because of these efforts, party members wound up in the CIO's inner councils. CPUSA members also ended up spending more time on union activities than on party functions, which helped to weaken the overall party. Party involvement with labor unions, however, led to problems later when conservative forces again gained control of the government. Then, for labor unions to hold the gains made during the Roosevelt years, party members had to be purged from union leadership positions.

Young people proved to be another fertile ground for Communist activity. In fact, college students and members of the middle class formed the core of the party's membership in the thirties. Although initially distrusting these young people, the party eventually welcomed college students and embraced a variety of student-oriented concerns, including the student antiwar movement. Students were participating in the first great wave of rebellion to strike college campuses, which made party causes attractive. Although memories of the Red Scare were still fairly fresh, the fear that another and larger Red Scare would trap those people who flirted with party membership in the 1930s seemed remote to American youth. Party membership during one's college years in the 1930s became a primary cause for individuals being called before various investigatory bodies in the cold war.

Another cause that attracted individuals to the Communist party during the 1930s was its advocacy of civil rights. The Comintern was particularly interested in black members and for a while promoted the idea that Southern blacks, as an oppressed people, should secede from the United States and set up a separate nation. This idea drew little support and was abandoned. The party found a far more popular way to attract interest to the civil rights cause when it moved into celebrated criminal cases involving Southern blacks. When the Scottsboro Boys were arrested and charged with raping two white women in 1931, party leaders took control of the case. Unfortunately, they were more interested in political gains than legal tactics. When the defendants were found guilty, the CPUSA attributed the verdict to the inadequacies of the American legal system rather than to its inept handling of the case. Even worse, when one of the alleged victims wanted to change her story, party members tried to bribe her to remain silent. The convictions were overturned only when the National Association for the Advancement of Colored People (NAACP), the American Civil Liberties Union, and other groups joined in the defense. The Communists, although still involved, were relegated to a minor role.

Despite their behavior in the Scottsboro case, the party still was perceived as having the right attitude on race in a badly racist country. Because of this image, Communists were able to establish a popular front organization on racial issues. In 1935, the National Negro Congress brought together leaders of the NAACP, the Urban League, and other groups, as well as Communists, in an attempt to secure racial equality. A. Phillip Randolph, founder of the Brotherhood of Sleeping Car Porters, was elected president. Although most of the delegates were certainly not Communists, they were prepared to cooperate with party members to achieve their goals. Since the Communists were exerting no revolutionary demands upon the blacks participating, the coalition worked for a while. But this momentary joining of interests led to problems for the civil rights movement in later years when Southern conservatives recalled the alliance between Communists and civil rights leaders of the 1930s. Such an affiliation then, opponents of integration argued in the 1950s and 1960s, surely meant that the later drive for racial equality was motivated by Communist goals.

Another fertile field for Communist organizers was the movie colony in Hollywood. Stars, screenwriters, and producers who became involved in the party did not do so out of affection for the Soviet Union or because they wanted to overthrow the government; civil liberties issues were the attraction. Over time, some three hundred or so movie people ranging from artists and screenwriters to back-lot and front-office personnel joined the party. Hollywood members were prized because they were heavy contributors to party coffers and because their names lent prestige to party gatherings. As with others who flirted with communism in the 1930s, Hollywood's actors and writers would come to rue the day that they had decided it was safe to associate with Communists. By the 1940s, the House Committee on Un-American Activities was investigating residents of the film community who had been tarred by the Communist brush.[24]

Popular fronts of all kinds existed up through August 1939. But August 23 brought the carefully constructed popular front façade crashing down upon the heads of the American party leaders. On that day, representatives of Nazi Germany and the Soviet Union signed a nonaggression pact between the two countries. A week later, the Germans invaded Poland from the east and the Soviets entered from the west. Three months later, the Soviet army invaded Finland. Now the Comintern wanted to keep the U.S. government out of European affairs.

The CPUSA had made significant gains during the height of the popular front movement. In spring 1936, the party claimed 41,000 members; before the Nazi-Soviet Pact, the figure was said to have hit 100,000.[25] Whether those figures are accurate is unknown. The party had a great turnover in membership, and the figures released may have simply included every person who had at some time signed a membership card. Party leaders continually stressed that names on the roster actually underestimated their strength because many people did not become formally aligned with the party.

With the Nazi-Soviet Pact, liberals left the popular front movement in droves. Many became ardent non-Communists or anti-Communists depending on their degree of alienation. Few liberals could understand how American Communists could be antifascist and for all of the causes that liberals espoused on one day and how, on the next day, these same Communists if not actively profascist at least opposed measures to hinder Germany's advance. In addition, American Communists were ordered to stop cooperating with their former allies in popular fronts because those individuals no longer espoused ideologically pure ideas. The betrayal of American liberals by American Communists led the liberals to form new organizations, most of which included strongly anti-Communist statements in their constitutions or bylaws.

Rocked by international events, the American Civil Liberties Union became one of those groups adhering to anticommunism in the 1940s. An internal power struggle pitted ACLU counsel Morris Ernst and his supporters against members who still defended the rights of Communists to speak freely. One of Ernst's goals was to rid the organization of the pro-Communist stigma that governmental investigations had given it in the 1930s. Another goal was to remove Elizabeth Gurley Flynn, an admitted Communist, from the board of directors.[26] After Miss Flynn was purged in 1940, the ACLU board explained that it was "inappropriate for any person to serve on the governing committees of the Union or on its staff, who is a member of any political organization which supports totalitarian dictatorship in any country, or who by his public declarations indicates his support of such a principle."[27] Totalitarian dictatorships included supporters of the Soviet Union and fascist nations. Even the organization most devoted to the maximum possible extension of freedom of speech in the United States found that protecting the rights of Communists to speak was no longer possible.

The political atmosphere became tense where Communists were concerned. Part of this change had to do with shifts in Congress, for conservatives began trying to reclaim control of the government in 1938 in order to halt Roosevelt's efforts to change society. One way to reverse the president's programs was to label those social changes as Communist-inspired. And the best way to accomplish this end was through highly publicized congressional hearings. Thus in 1938, Martin Dies, as chairman of the House Committee on Un-American Activities, began hearings into the Communist party.

By 1939, the Dies Committee was summoning party leaders to testify. These individuals were especially vulnerable after the Nazi-Soviet Pact had been signed. Now, said the anti-Communists, the connection between the Soviet Union and American Communists could be proved because domestic Communists had come in line with the Russians so quickly. Earl Browder, CPUSA general secretary, was called to testify about the connection between the two parties. In the course of his testimony, he revealed that he had traveled to the Soviet Union on a false passport. As a result of that testimony, Browder was convicted on charges of falsely obtaining a passport and was sent to prison. Browder also invoked the Fifth Amendment as he refused to answer certain questions, becoming the first Communist to do so. His testimony further proved to American liberals that the Communist party was not indigenous to the United States and that it did not act with the nation's welfare in mind.[28]

Dies also used the hearings to try to embarrass the Roosevelt administration by showing that the Communist party counted federal employees among its members. Communists did indeed work for the federal government during the 1930s. Scholars have shown that party members were hired after Franklin Roosevelt took office, but no proof exists that they were hired because of their political beliefs. Fewer than one hundred Communists worked for the federal government during these years. The total number of government employees then was around half a million. The highest concentrations of Communists in government apparently occurred in the Department of Agriculture, on some congressional committees, and on the staff of the National Labor Relations Board. Although these individuals could obtain information of relatively minor importance and pass it on to Soviet officials, they did not make policy decisions. And in all cases, non-Communists eliminated any threat that party members may have posed as soon as their presence was revealed.[29]

The same basic statement could be made about Communists in almost every aspect of American life. Although they were present, seldom, except perhaps for some labor unions, were they in a position to change the course of history. But in a way, their very existence instigated those changes. The anti-Communist panic that swept the country after World War II began after the Nazi-Soviet Pact. No longer were Communists simply liberals with whom other liberals could work to better American society. Now they were seen clearly as puppets of a foreign government, as representatives of evil incarnate. Moves began to outlaw the party. Measures such as the Foreign Agents Registration Act, the Smith Act, and the Hatch Act, which allegedly were enacted to prevent profascist forces from gaining a foothold in this country, were ready to be used against Communists. And any liberals who refused to disavow publicly past connections with popular fronts or with the party itself soon were caught up in a massive inquisition. Only the intervention of World War II kept the great purge from happening sooner.

Members of the Communist party were not the only social outcasts whose presence and opinions became respectable during the 1930s. The labor movement won constitutional protection for workers to organize and picket employers during the Roosevelt years. As with the Communists, the decade did not begin well for unions. More than 4 million workers were out of jobs as 1930 began. In the face of staggering economic problems, union membership dropped significantly, and union leaders sought simply to maintain a solid core of members rather than try to expand. The few strikes that were called during the Hoover years were sparked by employers' efforts to cut wages.[30]

Out of the furor that surrounded strikes in the early 1930s came the first major piece of legislation in almost twenty years designed to help workers to organize and to protest their working conditions. The Norris–La Guardia Act of 1932 was designed to ensure governmental neutrality in labor-management quarrels by ending the ability of federal courts to issue injunctions in labor disputes. The measure's preamble explicitly labeled such injunctions as against public policy as defined by Congress, and the law's authors made it clear that fundamental rights of free association were at stake. "Whereas under prevailing economic conditions . . . the individual unorganized worker is commonly helpless to exercise actual liberty of contract and to protect his freedom of labor," the law read, "it is necessary that he have full freedom of association, self-organization, and designation of representatives of his own choosing."[31]

Franklin Roosevelt built upon growing public concern about the plight of the nation's workers early in his administration when he tried to meet the needs of both business and labor in 1933 through the National Industrial Recovery Act (NIRA). To promote recovery, the law insulated businesses from the operation of the laws and made each industry write a code that would establish principles of fair competition. Those codes were to include provisions that recognized the primary demands of labor unions. Section 7(a), one of the most controversial portions of the law, said that "employees shall have the right to organize and bargain collectively through representatives of their own choosing, and shall be free from the interference, restraint, or coercion of employers of labor, or their agents, in the designation of such representatives or in self-organization or in other concerted activities for the purpose of collective bargaining or other mutual aid or protection." That same section forbade employers from requiring workers to join company unions or forcing them to promise not to affiliate with a union on pain of losing their jobs. Section 7(a) also required industries to establish maximum hours to be worked for a minimum level of wages.[32]

While this law was making its way through Congress, the economy showed a slight improvement, and business leaders, many of whom had been willing to participate to speed recovery, became less cooperative. Particularly abhorrent to business leaders was the government's attempt to force the recognition of the rights of workers to organize. Strangely enough, the American Federation of Labor (AFL) was not overly pleased with the law either. The federation was organized along craft lines, meaning that it focused on individuals with specialized talents and organized them across diverse industries. Machinists, for instance, could be organized in public utilities, automotive plants, and steel mills. Under the NIRA, however, whole industries would have to be organized; skilled and nonskilled workers would join the same union. The AFL was unequipped for and uninterested in such a task. Thus, when the nation's business leaders challenged the NIRA in court, many AFL members likely were not too upset.[33]

A small group of AFL leaders, led by United Mine Workers president John L. Lewis, however, feared the implications of a court decision finding the NIRA unconstitutional. Lewis and his colleagues had a vision of a new kind of unionism—an industrial unionism that would organize workers according to where they worked rather than by what they did. By 1935, the industrial unionists had established a Committee for Industrial Organization within the AFL, but by 1938, the two groups split, with the industrial unionists forming the Congress of Industrial Organizations (CIO), the era's major organizing force.

Just as the industrial unionists were winning recognition, the Supreme Court struck a massive blow in favor of the conservative status quo in business and against Roosevelt's economic improvisations. In 1935, the Court, which still was filled with conservatives left over from a decade of Republican, business-oriented government, declared the NIRA unconstitutional.[34] Congress, anticipating the Court's action, once more stepped into the breach, this time with the National Labor Relations Act of 1935, better known as the Wagner Act. The act set up the National Labor Relations Board and was specifically designed to ensure basic civil liberties to anyone who wanted to organize or join unions. Once again "the policy of the United States" was declared to be the promotion of interstate commerce by "encouraging the practice and procedure of collective bargaining and by protecting the exercise of workers by full freedom of association, self-organization, and designation of representatives of their own choosing, for the purpose of negotiating the terms and conditions of their employment and other mutual aid or protection."[35] As expected, the Wagner Act was immediately challenged in court.

With the court challenge under way, the Senate launched an attack on those persons whom Roosevelt supporters termed economic royalists—individuals of great wealth and conservatism who tried to block social reform. The vehicle for the assault was the La Follette Civil Liberties Committee, a subcommittee of the Committee on Education and Labor chaired by Senator Robert M. La Follette of Wisconsin. The committee's precise target was the barrier that business and industrial leaders had erected to prevent individuals from organizing into labor unions and to create problems for existing unions in the areas of recruiting membership and collective bargaining. At the core of the investigation was the emerging understanding that employers were infringing the First Amendment rights of their employees, who had a constitutional right to band together to better their lot.[36]

The La Follette Committee had been founded in the wake of complaints that business leaders were ignoring the requirements of the Wagner Act, perhaps on the assumption that it, too, would be declared unconstitutional. The resolution authorizing the special subcommittee called on its members to "make an investigation of violations of the rights of free speech and assembly and undue interference with the right of labor to organize and bargain collectively."[37] While the Senate was setting up the committee, the Supreme Court invalidated additional New Deal legislation, making union supporters increasingly fearful that the Wagner Act would be next. The need for public education on labor-related issues was imperative, and the La Follette committee was assigned that task.

Through its meetings, the committee aired four longstanding employer practices that created problems for employees attempting to organize into unions: the use of labor spies to infiltrate unions and disrupt their activities, the use of strikebreakers to intimidate union members and deprive them of their jobs, the use of armed private police to break up strikes and demonstrations, and the stockpiling of munitions for use in violent attacks on union members who tried to strike. Although each of these employer techniques had been practiced by business for years, committee members never looked at both sides of the problem. Conspicuously missing from the investigation, for example, was a discussion of the intimidation of nonunion employees by union members, strikers, or organizers. While the committee was holding its hearings and putting the union case before the American people, the Supreme Court, in a dramatic turnabout, began validating New Deal economic measures. The first legislation to receive the Court's stamp of approval was the National Labor Relations Act.[38]

The Court's decision did not end labor unions' problems. When management resistance to unionization was probed, the La Follette Committee discovered alleged fears of communism. Unions, said management representatives, were filled with Communists, and no business could operate if Communists were given any power. In this popular front era, Communist party members were stalwarts in organizing efforts. This fear of Communist infiltration was played upon by Martin Dies, whose special House Committee on Un-American Activities represented the conservative response to those persons defending the rights of labor in the Senate. Ignoring those fears, La Follette Committee members proposed legislation to bar the use of labor spies, strikebreaking, armed guards, or munitions such as tear gas or automatic weapons in strike situations. Although that bill did not pass, the investigations did lead to the creation of a civil liberties unit within the Department of Justice in February 1939, which brought the federal government into the business of protecting individual civil rights.

While the La Follette Committee was holding its hearings and the National Labor Relations Act was being tested in court, the industrial union movement took its fate into its own hands. The mid-1930s were marked by more strikes involving more workers than had ever been seen in the nation's history. The primary issue in these strikes was union recognition, which employers refused to grant until the Supreme Court so ordered. These strikes also saw the beginning of a new kind of behavior by union organizers. Rather than having protesting workers leave their jobs to set up picket lines outside the factory and thus allowing owners the opportunity to bring in strikebreakers to keep the business operating, workers would sit down in the factory until their demands were met. The tactic was nonviolent, and the workers took care to protect equipment from damage. The technique was highly successful and led to more rapid capitulation by employers than any approach ever tried.

Ultimately, the Supreme Court included many union activities within the protection offered by the First Amendment. The first major case came in 1939, when the Court upheld the rights of CIO workers to hold meetings on the streets of Jersey City, New Jersey, despite efforts by Mayor Frank Hague to oust them. Hague was an old-time big-city boss who believed that he controlled whatever was said or done in Jersey City. When union organizers tried to invade his province, Hague often had them picked up and taken outside the city limits. In other instances, their meetings were interrupted, and their literature was confiscated. The organizers asked the Court to recognize the right of individuals to hold public meetings, in the streets if necessary, in order to win support for their cause. The right that the union organizers were seeking directly infringed upon the police power of a municipality. For years, the court system had been most considerate of those powers. Now, said the Court, the need to communicate ideas was greater than the need to protect citizens. Justice Owen Roberts, in writing for a badly fragmented bench, put the idea that cities could keep their streets free from the influence of disruptive ideas to rest. "Wherever the title of streets and parks may rest, they have immemorially been held in trust for the use of the public and, time out of mind, have been used for purposes of assembly, communicating thoughts between citizens, and discussing public questions," Roberts said.[39]

The Supreme Court continued to provide protection for union activities, and in 1940, in *Thornhill v. Alabama,* reached its high-water mark by deciding that picketing was a form of free speech. An Alabama law prohibited anyone from loitering around or picketing the business of another person. Byron Thornhill, an AFL organizer, was charged with violating that law when he tried to encourage workers at a plant in Tuscaloosa to participate in a strike. Justice Frank Murphy, writing for eight members of the Court, decided that the time had arrived to extend the full protection of the First Amendment to speech on economic disputes. "In the circumstances of our times," he wrote, "the dissemination of information concerning the facts of a labor dispute must be regarded as within that area of free discussion that is guaranteed by the Constitution." In fact, said Murphy, "free discussion concerning the conditions in industry and the causes of labor disputes appears to us indispensable to the effective and intelligent use of the processes of popular government to shape the destiny of modern industrial society."[40] Any laws that limited that discussion simply could not be tolerated.[41]

Court members did not give labor carte blanche for picketing in all situations. *Thornhill* marked the outer limits of the protections and may have been the product of Frank Murphy's longstanding interest in promoting the cause of labor. Within a year or so, limitations on picketing would be imposed.[42] In these later rulings, the Court considered picketing as speech-plus, meaning that picketing was an amalgam of speech and action. The speech portion would be protected; the more that action became involved, however, the less willing Court members were to provide First Amendment protection.[43] Despite the changes that lay ahead, labor had come a long way from the days in which persecution was expected and in which fortitude was essential for membership.

Pacifists were another group advocating revolutionary ideas that finally won public acceptance during the 1930s. In fact, the years after World War I led to a great change in the way war was viewed in American society. For the first time in American history, it became popular to be a pacifist. The world had not been made safe for democracy despite American efforts and the promises of Woodrow Wilson; the same old corrupt powers ruled in Europe. Americans, ever suspicious, believed that world leaders were simply taking a few years off from war in order to prepare for the next one, and Americans fully intended to sit the next conflict out.[44]

Revisionism became the byword as war was no longer glorified. A new wave of fiction showed the horrors of war and turned public opinion against aggression. Academicians studied the impact of propaganda on society and convinced Americans that they had been manipulated into going to war by their leaders and by their European allies who were intent on preserving colonial empires. In addition, Congress studied the causes of World War I and concluded that financial interests and munitions manufacturers had played a primary role in the American decision to enter the conflict. Peace became a great concern in schools, churches, and government. Groups involved in the effort differed in tactics and goals, but the ultimate idea was the same: to end the use of war as the means of solving disagreements among nations. Some individuals worked for international agreements such as those pacts resulting from the Washington Conference in 1922 in which the United States, Great Britain, Japan, France, and Italy agreed to limit their respective naval forces. Also highly praised was the Kellogg-Briand Pact, signed in 1928, in which the signatories renounced war as an instrument of national policy to settle disputes.

The only major governmental institution that seemed out of step with this new interest in peace was the Supreme Court. In 1929 and again in 1931, the Court refused to allow individuals who were avowed pacifists to become naturalized citizens because the Constitution required all citizens to be willing to bear arms in defense of the nation. In 1929, the Court split six to three and denied citizenship to Rosika Schwimmer, a 49-year-old pacifist who lectured and wrote on the subject, because she refused to swear that she would take up arms to defend the United States should war be declared. Justice Oliver Wendell Holmes, Jr., dissenting for himself and Louis D. Brandeis, called the Court's refusal of this educated, motivated applicant for citizenship a reflection of the majority's dislike for pacifism. Mrs. Schwimmer was too old to be called to defend the nation, Justice Holmes noted, and besides, the United States did not draft women. "Some of her answers might excite popular prejudice," he wrote, "but if there is any principle of the Constitution that more imperatively calls for attachment than any other it is the principle of free thought—not free thought for those who agree with us but freedom for the thought that we hate."[45] Toleration of pacifism was not forthcoming two years later either when the Court, by a five-four vote, refused to accept Douglas C. Macintosh as a citizen. Macintosh, a seminary professor, stated that he would be willing to join the nation in fighting a just war. The Supreme Court majority found it improper for potential American citizens to decide which wars might command their loyalty. The majority decided that Macintosh did not merit citizenship. Chief Justice Charles Evans Hughes disagreed, finding the majority's decision an invasion of an individual's First Amendment right to religious freedom.[46]

Nor could the Court find any validity in an appeal from University of California students who wanted to graduate without taking the mandatory courses in military science and tactics. The young men involved were sons of Methodist ministers and members of a denomination that had taken a strong stance against militarism and war. They argued that their beliefs constituted a form of conscientious objection that should exempt them from the required classes. A unanimous Court rejected their contentions, with Justice Pierce Butler writing that "government, federal and state, each in its own sphere owes a duty to the people within its jurisdiction to preserve itself in adequate strength to maintain peace and order and to assure the just enforcement of law. And every citizen owes the reciprocal duty, according to his capacity, to support and defend government against all enemies."[47] The state's imposition of these requirements on students who chose to attend a public university, the Court said, was reasonable. If the students did not want to fulfill such requirements, they should have attended another institution.

These Supreme Court decisions clearly ran against the growing national sentiment toward pacifism, which included proposals to limit the constitutional power to declare war. The amendment would have forbidden the government to enter a war without voter approval. Thirty-one war referendum measures were introduced between 1914 and 1935. Another thirty-three were introduced between 1935 and 1941. A chief sponsor of these proposals was Representative Louis Ludlow, Democrat from Indiana. His 1935 proposal read: "Except in the event of attack or invasion the authority of Congress to declare war shall not become effective until confirmed by a majority of all votes cast thereon in a Nation-wide referendum."[48] The Ludlow Amendment stood its greatest chance of passage in 1937 as war clouds hung over Europe and Asia. The Japanese invasion of China gave it a considerable boost, but the Roosevelt administration waged an all-out effort to keep the House from formally considering the proposal. The president's forces successfully blocked the amendment, which eventually was lost in increasing concern about events abroad.

The single greatest success for the peace movement in the 1930s occurred on college campuses. This campaign became the first major student movement to sweep the United States, serving as a precursor to the student activism of the 1960s. Peace caught the imaginations of thousands of students and bound them together behind one national cause. Students were disillusioned about the state of the economy and about the problems they would face getting jobs after graduation. They were concerned about the manner in which World War I had been prosecuted—and they became increasingly angry about the way their universities and professors had supported the war. Overall, the students opposed compulsory military training, American participation in further foreign wars, and financial gains by munitions manufacturers and others involved in producing war material. Just how to demonstrate those concerns became the issue.[49]

Initially, American students followed the lead of fellow students in Great Britain, where a similar disillusionment was prevalent. British students had developed a pledge against war, known as the Oxford Oath, and swearing to it became the first move in opposition to war. The oath came to the United States in 1933, and students across the country soon had the opportunity to sign its Americanized version. Signees noted their belief "that war is futile and destructive and should be abandoned as an instrument of international action"; "that it is to the best interests of the United States and other nations that peace be maintained"; "that peace can be maintained only by open opposition to the selfish interests that promote war"; and "that increasing militarism and nationalism in the United States must be opposed by united action." Based on these beliefs, the students pledged themselves "not to bear arms, except in cases of the invasion of the mainland of the United States, and to work actively for the organization of the world on a peace basis."[50] College newspapers around the country reprinted the oath, and students held formal ceremonies in which they solemnly signed the pledge.

American peace activists protested visits by fascists to campus, arguing that the latter's rights of free speech should be curtailed, and they complained so much about compulsory military training for all males that participation in the Reserve Officers Training Corps eventually became voluntary. Many student demonstrations against war were criticized as being in bad taste, and super-patriotism developed on campus in response to the antiwar movement. Nevertheless, student opposition to war continued, reaching a peak between 1934 and 1936. In 1934, for instance, the first nationwide student protest against war led at least 25,000 students to leave their classrooms and march for peace. A year later, on the anniversary of the American declaration of war in 1917, up to 175,000 students left classes to strike against war.

Unfortunately for the students in later life, Communists were involved in the student peace movement. They helped to set up the American Student Union (ASU) in 1935, which united students of Communist, Socialist, and liberal persuasions much the way that their elders combined efforts on similar issues. ASU leaders organized successful antiwar strikes among college students in 1936 and 1937. Problems for the campus peace movement began when the Spanish Civil War broke out in July 1936. This conflict between the Loyalists, who were backed by the Soviet Union, and the Rebels, who were led by Francisco Franco and who were considered fascists, laid the groundwork for World War II. This war and the growing issue of fascism led to the abandonment of the Oxford Oath and to a movement toward collective security rather than isolationism. The ASU eventually was torn apart by debates over the proper stand on a possible war against fascism. The Nazi-Soviet Pact of August 1939 was the final blow to the ASU as it was to all other popular front activities.

The peace movement of the 1930s set the stage for the much stronger effort launched in the 1960s. In the 1930s, the idea of popular protest against the nation's foreign policy was relatively new. As late as World War I, individuals who opposed national policy had been arrested for violating laws written primarily to enforce allegiance to international goals. The protests of the 1930s were a backlash against such restrictions. Although there were some attempts to quiet pacifists, antiwar activists essentially were unmolested. The movement died for several reasons, most of which were out of the control of peace activists. As the fascists in Europe moved closer to war, a broadly based coalition against war was simply impossible. Some antiwar activists wanted to continue to oppose all wars; others wanted to fight good wars, which the battle against fascism surely was. By the time America became involved in the war, the same hard core of pacifists who opposed World War I stood against World War II. These people formed the core of the conscientious objector class during World War II, and they, or their philosophical heirs, would lead the anti–Vietnam War movement in the 1960s.

Although more voices were heard during the 1930s than ever before, the era was not without its conservative critics nor without efforts by the administration to limit the range of dissent. In fact, during Franklin Roosevelt's presidency much of the federal bureaucracy was first used against persons disagreeing with the administration. Although many of the movements discussed above touched on Roosevelt's plans for economic recovery, none presented as strong a threat as the American Liberty League, which brought together the forces of American conservatism in a concerted effort to block administration programs.[51]

The Liberty League grew as the economy started to strengthen, as business people, who had at first agreed to work with Roosevelt, began abandoning his administration, and as the president, in response to efforts by Long, Coughlin,

Townsend, and others, began to push his more liberal proposals through Congress. The league, started in August 1934, sought to "awaken in the hearts and minds of our people an appreciation of the necessity of cherishing, protecting, defending, and fighting for the liberties and rights which are guaranteed by the Constitution."[52] From such noble aims, the league created one of the most powerful pressure groups ever seen in American politics. Many of its supporters, who charged the president with leading the nation into the arms of communism through his liberal proposals, were criticized for sounding like fascists. Indeed, some league members did advocate the removal of both the president and the Congress and the installation of a dictatorship similar to Mussolini's in Italy. The Liberty League's rhetoric so concerned some members of the government that the McCormack-Dickstein Committee included the league in its investigation of possibly un-American organizations.

Drawing its leadership from conservative elements of the Democratic party as well as from the Republicans and its financing from a few staunchly conservative members of the business community, the league busied itself by denouncing New Deal legislation as unconstitutional and by helping to arrange court challenges to overturn such measures. The Liberty League reached its high point in 1936—the year in which Roosevelt scored his biggest electoral victory. As a prelude to that campaign, the Roosevelt administration took on individual members of the league and managed to successfully tarnish the entire organization by revealing the excesses of a few. Results of various congressional investigations also hurt the league's reputation. By the time Democratic National Chairman James Farley told the 1936 convention that the Liberty League had "financed every undercover agency that has disgraced American politics with their appeals to race prejudice, religious intolerance and personalities so gross," the league was on its way to extinction.[53]

A powerful weapon in all of Roosevelt's battles with conservatives was public opinion, which the president skillfully manipulated. Roosevelt may well have been the first president to succeed at news management. Other presidents had tried controlling information about government with mixed results. Efforts to manipulate public opinion during the administration of Theodore Roosevelt caught the eye of Congress, which then forbade the hiring of publicity agents by the executive branch without express congressional approval.[54] Various executive branches continued to hire such personnel, however, hiding them under euphemistic job titles. The greatest effort to mold public opinion before FDR, of course, came during World War I when Woodrow Wilson set up the Committee on Public Information to build support for the war. The backlash against presidential manipulation of public opinion was significant because of fears that the people would not have enough information to make informed decisions about the policies of their government. This issue goes to the heart of First Amendment values, but neither Franklin Roosevelt nor his successors seemed too concerned about these problems.[55]

Part of Roosevelt's plan to win public backing for his programs focused on gaining the support of the American press. In that effort, the president faced a formidable foe in the American Newspaper Publishers Association (ANPA) and in Colonel Robert R. McCormick, publisher of the *Chicago Tribune* and arch political conservative. For years the ANPA had concerned itself primarily with the business needs of the press, but in the late 1920s, the organization had become involved in traditional free-press issues. In 1928, the ANPA established a Freedom of the Press Committee with McCormick at its head.[56] The first case to attract committee attention involved Minnesota legislation aimed at quieting scandal sheets that attacked individual reputations and invaded citizens' privacy. Using the law, attorneys obtained a permanent injunction forbidding the *Saturday Press* to print any further issues without governmental approval. The newspaper had been labeled a "nuisance," meaning that it published "obscene, lewd, and lascivious" or "malicious, scandalous, and defamatory" materials.[57] When the colonel heard about the Minnesota action, he sought to help the *Saturday Press* fight off this state incursion on freedom of the press despite the publication's well-deserved reputation. With the backing of McCormick and the ANPA, Jay Near's complaint against Minnesota authorities was on its way to the Supreme Court.[58]

Chief Justice Charles Evans Hughes used the case as a vehicle for finally placing a constitutional blessing on Sir William Blackstone's concept that freedom of the press forbade the imposition of prior restraints on publication. "The fact that liberty of the press may be abused by miscreant purveyors of scandal," the chief justice wrote for five members of the Court, "does not make any the less necessary the immunity of the press from previous restraint in dealing with official misconduct." If the abuse was bad enough, he said, "subsequent punishment for such abuses as may exist is the appropriate remedy, consistent with constitutional principle."[59]

If Hughes simply had banned prior restraint against the *Saturday Press,* the opinion would have erected a First Amendment barrier to future attempts to stop a publication before distribution. But, since *Near* marked the first time that the Court had used the press clause of the First Amendment to declare a state law unconstitutional, Hughes went farther. He explained under what conditions prior restraint might be appropriate. "No one would question but that a government might prevent actual obstruction to its recruiting service or the publication of the sailing dates of transports or the number and location of troops," he said. "On similar grounds, the primary requirements of decency may be enforced against obscene publications. The security of the community life may be protected against incitements to acts of violence and the overthrow by force of orderly government." That list of exceptions, which seemed reasonable in 1931, would come back to haunt the press some forty years later.[60]

Although ANPA leaders gained a reputation for defending a broadly based freedom of the press, they still had a distinctly fiduciary interest in that constitutional protection. The First Amendment, they argued, exempted a newspaper's business activities from all government regulation. Under this banner, they denounced a 1930 bill that would have allowed the government to review advertising claims as a form of censorship.[61] The association maintained its campaign against business legislation throughout the New Deal years to the detriment of its role as a protector of freedom of the press. As Americans came to believe that most institutions needed to change in order to meet new economic and social conditions, newspaper publishers continued to seek special privileges. They seldom were successful in explaining how government regulation of the business aspects of the press could so injure the financial stability of a newspaper that it might die. Rather than showing the American people the very real connection between financial independence and freedom of the press, the newspaper publishers revealed themselves as self-centered and unwilling to adapt to changing conditions.

The ANPA's stance on financial matters, when combined with several decades of harsh criticism of the publishers' overwhelming interest in monetary rewards to the detriment of national well-being, played right into Franklin Roosevelt's hands. Throughout the 1930s, one of the president's favorite foes was the American press—or, more particularly, the publishers of American newspapers. He would claim repeatedly that 85 percent of the nation's newspapers displayed outright antagonism toward the New Deal. Ignoring the support that he had within the nation's journalistic community and overexaggerating the opposition, Roosevelt labeled the owners of these publications as "the Tory press." The President roundly chastised them for being too interested in their own financial affairs. Although he got along quite well with reporters, Roosevelt considered them as pawns in the hands of manipulative publishers who twisted journalists' copy to suit the publishers' political and financial ends. Never, he said, could he count on the leaders of the nation's press to understand the true ramifications of freedom of the press and its obligations to its readers. Thus, the president believed, the greatest danger to freedom of the press in the United States came from the publishers' greed.[62]

Given the attitudes of the publishers and the president, a monumental clash was inevitable. That battle came over efforts to have the newspaper industry write a code of good practices under the National Industrial Recovery Act. Although many other businesses in the United States were accustomed to being subjected to various codes, the newspaper industry was peculiarly unwilling to agree on much of anything. The ANPA, for instance, had been trying for years to standardize newspaper size to facilitate the interchange of advertising and syndicated materials. But publishers displayed an idiosyncratic individualism that cherished diversity in newspaper size as a matter of freedom of the press. Members of the American Society of Newspaper Editors, who largely just observed the 1930s battles, could not obtain agreement on their Canons of Journalism either, for many of the group's members felt that freedom of the press included the right to set one's own ethical standards. So, when the president asked for a newspaper code, he was walking into a buzz saw called freedom of the press.[63]

The publishers, who were the major negotiators with the National Recovery Administration (NRA), objected to writing a code on several grounds. Section 4(a) of the law required the setting of maximum hours and minimum wages and the recognition of the right of employees to form unions to bargain collectively with their employers. Most of the back-shop personnel who often caused the publishers a great deal of difficulty were already highly unionized. Walkouts that shut newspapers down for weeks were not uncommon, and the technicians who kept the presses running and who set the type were among the highest paid employees on a newspaper's payroll. Publishers could do little about the back-shop situation, but they greatly feared unionization of their reporters, who were being urged to join the new American Newspaper Guild. If publishers agreed to a code under the National Industrial Recovery Act, they would have no way to stop Guild organizing efforts. Publishers wanted to classify reporters and similar personnel as professionals who were exempt from wage and hour and unionization provisions and who could work as long as possible for as little as possible.[64]

Section 4(b) of the act was even worse as far as the publishers were concerned. This section contained the so-called licensing provision, which allowed the president to prescribe a code of good practices for any industry unable to develop one on its own. American newspaper publishers immediately had visions of earlier government efforts to control the press—including the Stationers Company, the Star Chamber, the Stamp Act, John Peter Zenger, and the Alien and Sedition Acts—each of which was cited as a reason to oppose the measure. Thus financial concerns meshed with legitimate fears about incursions on freedom of the press. The publishers dared the president to act against the newspaper industry.

Despite his personal feelings, Roosevelt was not ready to force the nation's newspapers into even greater opposition to his efforts. Besides, he needed the newspapers to serve as a role model and as publicity vehicles for his programs. Negotiations conducted with the publishers' committee, which was headed by McCormick and ANPA counsel Elisha Hanson, over the contents of the newspaper code were hardly conciliatory. The publishers drafted several versions of their code before coming up with acceptable language. In each one they included language along the lines of a statement in their first draft: "Nothing in the adoption and acceptance of this code shall be construed as waiving, abrogating or modifying any rights secured under the Constitution of the United States or of any state, or limiting the freedom of the press." Furthermore, "It is mutually understood that because of the limitations of the First Amendment to the Constitution of the United States nothing in this code shall be construed as authorizing the licensing of publishers and/or newspapers or as permitting injunction proceedings which would restrain the publication of newspapers."[65]

By December 1933, the publishers and the NRA had come to terms on a newspaper industry code. The publishers had included their language about nothing in the code interfering with freedom of the press as guaranteed by the Bill of Rights, which NRA head Hugh Johnson declared unnecessary. The administration, he said, had no intention of infringing on anyone's freedom of the press, stressing that the newspaper code was no different from workers' compensation laws and similar measures from which no publisher had claimed exemption. When President Roosevelt approved the newspaper code six weeks later, he allowed the language protecting First Amendment rights to remain in, but he criticized the publishers for that section. "It is pure surplusage," said the president as he approved the code. "While it has no meaning it is permitted to stand merely because it has been requested. . . . Of course, nobody waives any constitutional rights by assenting to a code. The recitation of the freedom of the press clause in the code has no more place here than would the recitation of the whole

Constitution or of the Ten Commandments." To further irritate the publishers, Roosevelt added, "The freedom guaranteed by the Constitution is freedom of expression and that will be scrupulously respected—but it is not freedom to work children, or do business in a fire trap or violate laws against obscenity, libel and lewdness."[66]

Roosevelt's gratuitous criticism of the newspaper industry raised the hackles of the nation's publishers, who denounced the president's language and called for an immediate apology. No words of conciliation, however, came from either side. On paper, the newspaper publishers had agreed to limits on wages and hours and to accept collective bargaining on behalf of any and all employees. But because the publishers had stressed the First Amendment as a bar to unwanted interference with their business practices, the government was left with few weapons to use in enforcing the code. The president had won at least surface allegiance from the publishers on the issue, but the eight months of arguing over the contents of the code gave way to three-plus years of increased sniping between the president and the publishers.

FDR's unhappiness with the press gave impetus to another wave of criticism of that institution from journalists, politicians, and public figures. This time, the press critics were far harsher, and most of them believed that only through governmental intervention could the press become more responsive to the needs of the American people. To the press critics of the 1930s, publishers were "malefactors of great wealth" and "economic royalists," and the American Newspaper Publishers Association was "America's House of Lords." George Seldes, liberal critic of the press and one-time foreign correspondent for the *Chicago Tribune,* noted, "Newspapers, like kings, pretend they can do no wrong. I wish they were right."[67]

Harold L. Ickes, Roosevelt's secretary of the interior and a former journalist himself, also placed most of the blame for the nation's irresponsible press on publishers. "With rare exceptions," he wrote, "the attitude of that newspaper is unsocial whose publisher belongs to the moneyed class and whose primary objective is to make profits." As he explained, "The press, being an essential organ of a free society, must not be a servant of special interests nor . . . a purely profit-making business. . . . A free and enlightened society cannot afford the dangerous luxury of a press that is eager for privileges for itself . . . while at the same time it is indifferent to its obligations."[68] Although greatly concerned about the irresponsibility of the press, Ickes did not suggest government control of newspapers. The closest he could come to recommending legal intervention was to suggest that newspapers be required to offer individuals criticized in their columns an immediate chance to respond.

Other critics were not so hesitant to call for legal remedies for journalistic abuses. Some congressmen issued calls for laws making editors and publishers criminally responsible for the publication of lies. Morris Ernst, the attorney for the American Newspaper Guild, offered the most far-reaching suggestions for limiting the excessive influence of publishers in American society. He would have forbidden horizontal concentrations within the newspaper industry such as a newspaper publisher owning paper mills. He also would have kept newspapers from obtaining licenses for radio stations, imposed extra taxes on news-paper chains, and granted tax breaks to individuals trying to start new communications outlets.[69] All of these proposals for increased governmental intervention in the activities of the nation's press were coming at a time when press suppression was occurring around the world, thereby raising great fears within newspaper publishers. Although none of the suggestions came near fruition, Roosevelt and his supporters continued their efforts to make the press of the nation more nearly resemble their image of a truly free press.

Strangely enough, the instrument of government that ultimately forced publishers to comply with at least a modicum of the New Deal's definition of freedom of the press was the court system, which was emerging as a major defender of First Amendment rights. When the National Labor Relations Act was challenged, the Associated Press (AP) was one of the businesses contesting the protection it offered to labor organizers. The AP had fired Newspaper Guild organizer Morris Watson in 1935 for his efforts on behalf of the union. The Guild appealed to the National Labor Relations Board, and the AP was told to reinstate Watson with back pay and other benefits. The Associated Press refused, and the NLRB sought a court order to force compliance.[70]

The Associated Press argued that it served newspapers of all political persuasions. Having a union organizer as an employee would taint the AP's news with bias; hence, Watson had to be dismissed. The Associated Press and its backers within the publishing community undoubtedly felt that its argument would win the day. The Supreme Court had been discarding New Deal economic regulations for several years; the National Labor Relations Act would simply be next on the list. But the news agency and its supporters had not counted on a shift in Court priorities. When the Court upheld the National Labor Relations Act, one of the cases involved in that holding was Morris Watson's.[71]

Not only was the Associated Press told to put Watson back to work, but the agency was roundly chastised for having fired him in the first place. Justice Owen Roberts, in writing for a five-man majority, noted that the AP contended that Watson had been fired because his prolabor views had contaminated the news. The news agency had provided no evidence of bias in Watson's work. "The actual reason for his discharge, as shown by the unattacked finding of the Board," said the Court, "was his Guild activity and his agitation for collective bargaining." A firing on that ground simply was not allowed. In addition, Justice Roberts punctured the newspaper industry's claims for special treatment under the First Amendment. "The publisher of a newspaper has no special immunity from the application of general laws," Roberts wrote. Publishers were responsible in libel and contempt of court actions; they were subject to nondiscriminatory taxes and to the antitrust laws; and they had to respect the privacy of others. The NLRB order "in nowise circumscribes the full freedom and liberty of the petitioner to publish the news as it desires it published or to enforce policies of its own choosing with respect to the editing and rewriting of news for publication, and the petitioner is free at any time to discharge Watson or any editorial employee who fails to comply with the policies it may adopt."[72] But Watson could not be fired for union organizing.

Other court cases followed. ANPA members denounced the Fair Labor Standards Act of 1938,[73] on free press grounds. Here, ANPA attorney Hanson argued that forcing newspapers to limit the number of hours certain employees could work and to pay a minimum wage for that labor could mean the difference between a newspaper staying in business and a newspaper dying. The Supreme Court ruled that all businesses, including newspapers, were subject to the law. Wrote Justice Wiley B. Rutledge, "Coloring almost all of petitioners' positions, as we understand them, is a primary misconception that the First Amendment knocks out any possible application of the Fair Labor Standards Act to the business of publishing and distributing newspapers." The Court would have none of that, Rutledge said, stressing, "The Amendment does not forbid this or other regulation which end in no restraint upon expression."[74]

The biggest blow to the press's campaign for a special protection for its business interests came with an antitrust case that was aimed at opening membership in the Associated Press to all comers. Interestingly, the case was a direct result of the personal animosity between Franklin Roosevelt and Robert McCormick. The president felt that Chicago needed a liberal morning newspaper to compete with the colonel's conservative *Tribune,* and Marshall Field III obligingly established the *Chicago Sun* in 1941. Field's application for membership in the Associated Press was blocked by McCormick, who, based on the organization's charter, held veto rights over admitting direct competitors. That action launched a major antitrust action that wound up in the Supreme Court in 1945.[75]

Members of the Court's majority wrote three separate opinions as five justices joined in declaring the organization's bylaws an unacceptable infringement on freedom of the press. The plurality decision, written by Hugo Black, said the news agency was "engaged in business for profit exactly as are other business men who sell food, steel, aluminium, or anything else people need or want. . . . The fact that the publisher handles news while others handle food does not . . . afford the publisher a peculiar constitutional sanctuary in which he can with impunity violate laws regulating his business practices." Justice Black, one of the strongest First Amendment supporters to sit on the Court, could find nothing in the Bill of Rights to exempt an agency of the press from the application of the nation's antitrust laws. "It would be strange indeed . . . if the grave concern for freedom of the press which prompted adoption of the First Amendment should be read as a command that the government was without power to protect that freedom," Black said. "The First Amendment, far from providing an argument against application of the Sherman Act, here provides powerful reasons to the contrary."[76]

According to Black, the foundation of the First Amendment rested on the public's need for information. "That Amendment rests on the assumption that the widest possible dissemination of information from diverse and antagonistic sources is essential to the welfare of the public, that a free press is a condition of a free society," he said. "Surely a command that the government itself shall not impede the free flow of ideas does not afford non-governmental combinations a refuge if they impose restraints upon that constitutionally guaranteed freedom." Black also told the newspaper community just what freedom of the press did mean under the nation's constitutional system: "Freedom to publish means freedom for all and not some. Freedom to publish is guaranteed by the Constitution, but freedom to combine to keep others from publishing is not. Freedom of the press from governmental interference under the First Amendment does not sanction repression of that freedom by private interests."[77] With this decision, the century-old Associated Press practice of limiting access to its daily news report ended. Fears that unlimited membership would create problems for the news agency's continued existence proved groundless, as the Associated Press grew stronger and today dominates the field.

The audacity of American newspapers in the 1930s, combined with their perceived and often demonstrated insensitivity to a changing society, significantly affected the level of support available to them. By the end of the decade, their repeated claims that freedom of the press was being threatened by various actions of government or of a competitor began falling on deaf ears. Most Americans simply were unwilling to accept the press's definition of that freedom nor were they willing to grant journalists any greater leeway in society. In many respects, public reaction to free-press claims during this era were similar to those that appeared in the late 1970s and 1980s, when Americans once again were disgusted with the excesses of the American media and called for restrictions on journalistic activity. Both the 1930s and the 1980s, then, prove the truth of Alexander Hamilton's belief, stated during the battle for ratification of the Constitution, that "whatever fine declarations may be inserted in any constitution respecting it, [freedom of the press] must altogether depend on public opinion, and on the general spirit of the people and of the government."[78]

Perhaps, though, the "general spirit of the people and of the government" is a bit harder to gauge in the twentieth century than it was in the late eighteenth century. Media manipulation, although in its infancy during the Roosevelt years, has become a prime tool for influencing public opinion, the bedrock on which freedom of expression rests. When such engineering of public opinion takes place, the ability to make sound judgments is seriously jeopardized. In most cases, individuals with the most radical ideas are kept from disseminating their views, and only establishment-oriented opinions are formed. The Roosevelt administration, as seen above, used every avenue within its power to influence the ideas put before the American people. Despite his efforts, Roosevelt still believed that newspapers were not treating him fairly. Because of these concerns, the president turned increasingly to radio to send his message directly to the people without the intervention of journalists.

The airwaves that captured the president's attention were increasingly establishment-oriented. The Federal Radio Commission (FRC) had been busy closing down stations that represented minority viewpoints. According to the FRC, the elimination of fringe groups from the airwaves and the promotion of commercial broadcasting encouraged freedom of speech and a balanced presentation of views. Stations operated by fringe groups more often than not, argued the commission, offered propaganda rather than balance and failed to serve the general public. Commercial stations provided sufficient exposure to varying views; besides, if a listener did not like the information presented on one channel, all that listener had to do was to change stations.[79]

Not all segments of American society, however, were satisfied with the FRC approach. Vocal minorities, including a coalition of educators who wished to use radio and the American Civil Liberties Union, protested that the commission was censoring ideas by removing minority stations from the air. Private interests, they maintained, could limit the range of ideas available for informed decision making just as effectively as the government. As radio became more dependent on advertising for its financial well-being, the willingness of broadcasters to present dissident views decreased because the costs of offending businesses purchasing commercial time could be substantial.[80]

Complaints about the inability of special interests to obtain meaningful amounts of air time went before the FRC. A Senate-ordered investigation resulted in reiterating that commercial broadcasters provided all ideas sufficient access to the airwaves. Commercial broadcasters even provided educational interests time to present their programs, according to the FRC report, which ignored complaints from educational broadcasters that no one wanted to buy the times offered to noncommercial programming because no one listened to the radio during those hours.

Opponents of the commercial system had another chance to make their arguments when Franklin Roosevelt sought to combine the regulation of all forms of electronic communication under one super agency. To a certain extent, his interests in the radio industry rested almost solely in creating a new agency that could be staffed with Democrats since Hoover's appointees would not resign their FRC positions. How much attention he actually gave to the problems of broadcasting during this reorganization is unknown. What is known is that Roosevelt was unwilling to antagonize commercial broadcasters, who he felt held the key to undiluted access to the public. Although the Communications Act of 1934[81] essentially repeated the provisions of the 1927 law where radio was concerned, the president was not unaware that some groups in society had significant concerns about the development of American radio.

Members of the National Committee on Education by Radio, a coalition of educators seeking an alternative to commercial broadcasting, had made the connection with free speech clear. Group chairman Joy Elmer Morgan argued that "genuine freedom of thought is impossible when the machinery thru which thought must flow on a national scale is in the hands of monopoly groups supported by competitive business enterprises who have an immediate interest in keeping the facts from the people." Experience had shown, Morgan said, that "the very points at which facts are most needed if the people are to govern themselves wisely are the points at which freedom of speech is most certain to be denied."[82]

The American Civil Liberties Union also was concerned about the status of American broadcasting and the inability of minority views to be heard on the air. Bethuel M. Webster, Jr., chairman of the ACLU Radio Committee, condemned the national broadcasting policy that allowed the industry to develop "as a purely private enterprise for private gain." Because of this arrangement, Webster said, "the tendency, if not the deliberate policy, of the licensing authority has been to crystallize the status quo. This, together with the operation of prevailing economic forces, has had the effect of vesting the control of the most desirable facilities in a very few private agencies." As a result, he said, "broadcasting has become a profitable and powerful business for those few in control. It has been and is a discouraging business to those to whom the less desirable facilities have been given and the public to whom the commercialized aspects of broadcasting are offensive."[83]

Such protests had little effect on lawmakers, who simply ordered the new Federal Communications Commission (FCC) to conduct another survey on the matter. After holding hearings in the fall of 1934, the FCC announced it could find no reason to interfere with commercial broadcasting. Commercial broadcasters were, after all, good citizens, who would represent the multitude of voices present in the United States and who would provide time for educational programming. No governmental intervention was necessary to guarantee freedom of speech over the airwaves.

As the radio system settled into the pattern that is now so familiar, the dialogue over freedom of speech on the airwaves continued, but now the terms were defined differently. Supporters of commercial broadcasters began to defend the free-speech rights of those using the airwaves. Louis Caldwell, who had been the first general counsel for the Federal Radio Commission and who headed the ABA communications committee, led the effort to obtain First Amendment rights for radio stations. "Broadcasting is at present far and away the most impressive claimant for protection under the constitutional guaranty of the freedom of speech, just as the newspaper is the principle claimant for protection under the sister guaranty of the freedom of the press," Caldwell said. "The scope of freedom of speech by radio should be no whit less than the scope of freedom of the press."[84] This new line of reasoning argued that any governmental interference in broadcasting would violate the First Amendment. The analogy between newspapers and radio was played upon regularly, and the broadcasters' choice of programming, which critics denounced as censorship of differing ideas, was labeled an exercise of editorial judgment. Someone had to pick and choose among the voices clamoring to be heard, Caldwell said. That someone was the station licensee, who was functioning much the way as an editor or publisher did in determining what was carried in the limited confines of a newspaper.

The ACLU took issue with the suggestion that radio licensees were simply functioning as editors. "The radio companies deny that there is any basis for interfering with what they call their right of 'editorial selection.' They compare the radio to the newspaper and invoke the right of free press. But they forget that private editorial rights can hardly apply in a field where the channels are limited in number and publicly owned," said the ACLU. "The author who can find no publisher can always publish on his own account, but the speaker who is barred from radio has no appeal. His chances on the air in any one locality are limited to a few stations. Thus the radio companies do not exercise the right of 'editorial selection,' but a pretty absolute censorship."[85]

The argument over the extent of free speech available to radio seemed never-ending. As long as the spectrum was limited and the holders of licenses were unimpeded in deciding who would have access to the air, charges that licensees were censoring ideas would be heard. As long as controversial minority view-

points were excluded from the air in favor of commercially profitable programming, those charges would increase in magnitude, especially since those persons
advocating special interests were not allowed the licenses necessary to start their
own stations—even if they could afford to do so. Further complicating the
broadcasting picture was the presence of the federal government as the ultimate
arbiter as to which applicant received a license to broadcast. As long as the government held that power, the fear remained that, at some point, the government
would tell licensees how to run their stations.[86]

In fact, Franklin Roosevelt and his successors often came perilously close to
that interference. Roosevelt liked to use the radio for messages to the American
people, and members of his administration used the radio waves for similar purposes. Seldom were such requests refused even though problems arose around
election time when Roosevelt's opponents questioned whether the air time was
being used for political purposes.

Roosevelt appreciated the way in which radio could reach the American people. Broadcasting, he said, was "one of the most effective mediums for dissemination of information. It cannot misrepresent or misquote."[87] But he also had
great fears about the influence of his arch-enemies, the newspaper publishers, on
the medium. By 1940, newspapers owned or controlled more than one-third of
all the nation's stations. In ninety-eight communities across the country, the
only newspaper in town owned the only radio station. The president feared that
his administration would be jeopardized if the ownership of newspapers and
broadcasting facilities became even more intertwined. This led to his famous
message to FCC Chairman James L. Fly that said, simply, "Will you let me know
when you propose to have a hearing on newspaper ownership of radio stations?"[88]

Fly took his cue and announced an inquiry into the wisdom of allowing newspapers and broadcasting stations to have the same owners. The goal, of course,
was to keep anti–New Deal publishers from monopolizing the airwaves. One
problem with that goal was that any ruling made by the FCC would affect pro–
New Deal publishers—and despite what Roosevelt claimed, some did exist—as
well. In addition, any ruling against cross-ownership of facilities would affect
AM licensees who held or wanted to hold licenses for FM facilities. Among those
jumping into the fight against such a rule, quite naturally, was the American
Newspaper Publishers Association. The FCC finally dropped its effort to forbid
cross-ownership of communications facilities.[89]

FCC members, however, did not abandon their efforts to change one important essential in the development of American broadcasting. In 1941, the commission issued a report on chain broadcasting, in which it outlined the control
that the National Broadcasting Company (NBC) and the Columbia Broadcasting System (CBS) had over radio. According to the report, the dominance of
NBC and CBS was almost total: 50 of the nation's 52 clear-channel stations were
owned by the two networks; 85 percent of the total night-time power in the
nation was at their disposal; 45 cities of 50,000 or more residents had no competition for the networks. In addition, NBC had two networks—the more dominant red network and the less prominent blue network, which, claimed the

FCC, was used primarily to fend off competition. The commission took direct aim at the NBC tandem by releasing an order that stated, "No license shall be issued to a standard broadcast station affiliated with a network organization which maintains more than one network."[90]

The networks, of course, fought the ruling in court, but in 1943, the Supreme Court found against them. Shortly after the decision, NBC divested itself of its blue network, which became the American Broadcasting Company. The Court ruling, in addition to upholding the FCC's ability to make the order, addressed the question of whether the First Amendment applied to the licensed medium of radio. Felix Frankfurter, writing for a five-man majority, rejected suggestions that the FCC's regulations must fall because they abridged the networks' freedom of speech. "If that be so, it would follow that every person whose application for a license to operate a station is denied by the Commission is thereby denied his constitutional right of free speech," he said. "Freedom of utterance is abridged to many who wish to use the limited facilities of radio. Unlike other modes of expression, radio inherently is not available to all. That is its unique characteristic, and that is why, unlike other modes of expression, it is subject to government regulation." Frankfurter rejected arguments, prevalent since the late 1930s, that radio licensees had the same right to freedom of speech as newspaper publishers had to freedom of the press. Government regulation, on the grounds spelled out in the Communications Act of 1934, was perfectly constitutional and acceptable. "Denial of a station license," he said, "is not a denial of free speech."[91]

Even as broadcasters encountered an irate public, motion pictures became even more susceptible to pressure. At the onset of the Depression, movie producers still were operating under a voluntary code of self-regulation. As audiences dwindled, producers again tried to lure them back by offering more violent and more sensational material than ever before. Calls for increased restrictions on motion pictures followed. This time, demands for motion-picture censorship were augmented by the results of studies by social scientists of the effects that movies had on the American viewing public. The studies painted a glum picture for movie producers, who were told that American young people in particular spent far too much time in theaters and learned many bad habits from what they saw on the silver screen.[92]

Aware of the national concern about the influence of motion pictures, the U.S. Senate called for an investigation of the motion-picture industry in February 1932. To fend off such intervention, in 1933 motion-picture producers restated their interest in the production standards that the Hays Office administered, but they still refused to make the standards mandatory. Soon, however, the producers were without options. The final push toward a mandatory production code came from the Roman Catholic Church. In October 1933, an emissary from the pope attending a Catholic charitable function in New York announced that "Catholics are called by God, the Pope, the Bishops and the priests to a united and vigorous campaign for the purification of the cinema, which has become a deadly menace to morals."[93]

From that call came the Legion of Decency, an organization sponsored by the

National Conference of Catholic Bishops, which was established in November 1933. Between seven and nine million American Catholics signed the legion pledge, which called upon them to boycott any films declared objectionable by the church hierarchy. The church now had a strong voice at the box office, and its leaders exercised that voice loudly and clearly. Church leaders at times ordered parishioners not to attend certain films on pain of committing sin, and they also encouraged boycotts of theaters that continued to show objectionable movies.

An immediate response to the Legion of Decency was renewed emphasis on the Hays Office and the production code. Now a system was set up so that films required a certificate of approval prior to release, with member studios agreeing not to circulate any film that did not have a certificate. In addition, the producers agreed to impose a $25,000 fine on anyone who produced, distributed, or exhibited a motion picture without this seal of approval. The Hays Office became heavily involved in the censoring of scripts before films were made and in reviewing pictures before release. No fines were ever collected, but the motion pictures of the era were substantially changed. Great emphasis was placed on an overall set of principles guiding film production. According to these standards, "No picture shall be produced which will lower the moral standards of those who see it. Hence the sympathy of the audience will never be thrown to the side of crime, wrong-doing, evil or sin." In addition, "correct standards of life, subject only to the requirements of drama and entertainment, shall be presented." And finally, "law, natural or human, shall not be ridiculed, nor shall sympathy be created for its violation."[94] Although the standards may sound noble to a more modern movie viewer who is satiated by the sex and violence that permeates many motion pictures today, the code and its enforcement created great problems for producers who viewed the screen as a medium for artistic expression and who believed that their speech should be unfettered. Their arguments for freedom of artistic expression were much the same as those made by D. W. Griffith as he argued for more latitude to screen *The Birth of a Nation.*

Indirectly, the federal government helped disgruntled producers find outlets to display their more controversial efforts through a series of antitrust actions brought against the motion-picture industry. As with the broadcasting industry initially, the motion-picture industry long had been dominated by monopolies. In the beginning, the technology necessary to make movies was tightly controlled, with access to the means of production reaching a greater number of individuals only after court action. The next control point was the means of distribution and exhibition. Here, producers would either wholly own or have long-term contracts with distributors of films and the theaters that exhibited movies. Through these arrangements, the major production companies dictated what movie houses would show what films and for how long in more than three-quarters of the nation's cities. Independent theaters had a hard time obtaining films to show, and independent producers had difficulty finding theaters to display their work.[95]

A series of Supreme Court decisions beginning in 1930 chipped away at the monopoly arrangements that so restricted freedom of exhibition in the motion-picture industry.[96] The monopoly was finally broken up in 1948, when the Supreme Court once again found antitrust violations and ruled against the industry.[97] As a result, the producers divested themselves of any theaters that they owned and thus opened the way for competition among individual exhibitors for films. Major movie producers could no longer retaliate against exhibitors who displayed productions offered by independent companies. These so-called independents generally were not adherents to the Hays Office production code, and soon portions of the silver screen were open to experimentation that never would have been possible had the major studios still dominated the means of exhibition.

The case that brought about these changes also offered an interesting insight into the changing view of the Supreme Court about movies and the First Amendment. In 1915 the Supreme Court had definitely placed movies outside of the First Amendment by labeling them part of the entertainment business and hence not worthy of protection.[98] In writing the majority decision in the Paramount Pictures case, Justice William O. Douglas opened up the possibility that movies might be included within the First Amendment. In response to concerns raised about the effect that such a monopoly might have on freedom of speech, Douglas wrote, "We have no doubt that moving pictures, like newspapers and radio, are included in the press whose freedom is guaranteed by the First Amendment."[99] The case, however, offered no room for such speculation since it focused only on interpretation of the antitrust laws. Before too many years had passed, the Supreme Court would be faced squarely with a case that asked for First Amendment protection for expression on the motion picture screen.

The 1930s, then, were important years in the evolution of freedom of expression for the American media. Actions begun during those years substantially changed the nature of freedom of expression available through the major media of the day. Perhaps the Supreme Court cases, all of which culminated in the 1940s, were the most important vehicles for advancing First Amendment rights in each instance. Through the Associated Press case in 1945, newspapers throughout the country were provided access to an important source of news that could make or break a publication. Through the NBC case of 1943, the Court made room for another radio network and for more voices over the airwaves. And through the Paramount case of 1948, the silver screen was opened indirectly to independent producers through the elimination of the major studios' control over exhibition halls. Whether the opening of these avenues of communication would multiply the number of voices heard was another question. In the end, only the changes in the motion-picture industry really provided any increased access to different, nonestablishment views. In the broadcasting and newspaper industries, business continued fairly much as usual, and dissident voices still had difficulty being heard. Part of the reason for this lack of change, however, was the fact that these decisions opening up the mediums came during times of war, both hot and cold. The dissidents seeking to display their wares in the motion-picture industry often were peddling sex and violence rather than disturbing political ideas, which often were targeted for distribution through newspapers or radio. As the cold war intensified, no establishment medium would be willing to give dissident political opinions room for exposition.

Media outlets were not the only beneficiaries of the breathing space provided freedom of expression via Supreme Court decisions. The justices had displayed their interest in deciphering the meaning of the First Amendment for a number of years by the time the Depression rolled around. The issue was first squarely addressed in a number of cases stemming from World War I prosecutions, and then, beginning in 1925, the Court began using the due process clause of the Fourteenth Amendment in order to make the First Amendment reach state action.[100] By 1931, the Court invalidated state laws on speech[101] and press[102] grounds. In 1937, the Court invalidated a state law based on the rights of assembly and petition.[103] Slowly but surely, the members of the Supreme Court were beginning to move into the areas of adjudication that would characterize the modern Court.

For years the Court had spent its time blocking legislative efforts at economic reform. The Court's reaction to the efforts of workers to join unions and to picket their employers show just one part of this effort to support the conservative economic structure. The justices continued on this track well into the 1930s, thwarting most of Franklin Roosevelt's attempts at economic reform along the way. Unwilling to allow "nine old men" sitting on the Supreme Court to destroy his recovery program, Roosevelt attempted to use his landslide victory in 1936 to change the Court's complexion. His opponents called it court-packing, but the plan essentially was to add a justice for each elderly member who refused to retire, up to a total bench of fifteen. In this way, Roosevelt hoped to obtain a majority that would uphold his legislative proposals. The court-packing plan exploded in the president's face, becoming one of the worst political disasters of his career.[104] Even while the plan was being debated in Congress, the Supreme Court in 1937, because of the movement of two justices, began consistently upholding legislative determinations dealing with economic issues. Soon thereafter, the older, more conservative members of the Court began retiring, and Roosevelt had a liberal majority that turned its attention to the interpretation of the Bill of Rights.

What the justices then needed was a philosophy on which to base their decision making in Bill of Rights cases. The first inkling of what that philosophy would be came in a decision involving a murder case. While the Supreme Court denied the appeal of a defendant who claimed to have been placed in double jeopardy, Justice Benjamin N. Cardozo talked about the Bill of Rights and about need to deal selectively with the guarantees in the first ten amendments. Certain rights were so much "the very essence of a scheme of ordered liberty" that states should be held responsible for their protection. "Freedom of thought, and speech," Cardozo wrote, form "the matrix, the indispensable condition, of nearly every other form of freedom,"[105] and these rights obviously should be protected by the Court. Jurists saw within Cardozo's language the creation of an "honor roll of superior rights," or a listing of liberties so critical to the maintenance of free government that Supreme Court intervention was essential to protect them.[106]

From that point, the Court moved on to accept the approach offered by Harlan Fiske Stone in 1938. The opinion in a case that involved the regulation of milk stated that the Court would essentially accept the constitutionality of commercial legislation unless the facts provided proved otherwise. Then, in one of the most famous footnotes ever written to a Supreme Court decision, Stone specifically said, "There may be narrower scope for operation of the presumption of constitutionality when legislation appears on its face to be within a specific prohibition of the Constitution, such as those of the first ten amendments, which are deemed equally specific when held to be embraced within the Fourteenth."[107] From that footnote stemmed the preferred-position doctrine, which meant that in cases involving liberties contained in the Bill of Rights—and especially those protections in the First Amendment—state action would not be presumed to be constitutional and that the Court would carefully evaluate claims put before it.

The preferred-position doctrine, which gave the judicial edge to individuals claiming the protection of the First Amendment, would regularly gather majority votes in the 1940s, especially during the years that Stone served as chief justice. Under its terms, members of the Supreme Court carefully examined the substance of local, state, and federal laws charged with violating essential First Amendment rights. Through its careful application, the late 1930s and early 1940s became some of the most fruitful years in the Court's history for enlarging the ability of dissidents to be heard.

By the end of the 1930s, then, the stage essentially was set for the blossoming of freedom of expression in the United States. Although some problems still existed, more people talked about more things of significance during the Depression years than ever before. Ideas from left, right, and center were put forth, with the nation accepting the best from each while discarding the rest. Efforts by demagogues such as Huey Long and Father Coughlin, for instance, pushed Franklin Roosevelt into more far-reaching social reforms. Similar efforts from the left wing raised important issues dealing with labor unions, the rights of blacks, and the place of peace movements in society. But no one accepted the idea of finding an American version of Hitler or Stalin to run the country. Still, the decade had its dark side as well. Well-meaning individuals concerned about fascists fashioned some very repressive legislation, and Franklin Roosevelt, equally concerned about political dissent, began using the Federal Bureau of Investigation to spy on political dissenters.

The question that remained at the end of the decade was whether freedom or repression would win the nation's loyalty. If the question had been answered toward the middle of the decade, the marketplace of ideas most likely would have been preferred. At the end of the 1930s, war clouds loomed dark on the horizon, and fears increased. Suppression of dissident ideas once again was gaining in popularity. Thus, the 1930s marked the beginning and the end of the American experiment with the marketplace of ideas. A cold war would follow a shooting war, and freedom to dissent would virtually disappear for more than two decades.

CHAPTER 6

★ ★ ★

Fighting the Good War: Freedom of Expression during World War II

As active U.S. involvement in World War II drew ever more likely, some Americans became more concerned as to just how the right to dissent would fare in another war. The World War I experience had been dismal, and the possibility existed for a resumption of restraint stemming from a new conflict. But the country had come a long way in its understanding of freedom of expression since the First World War. A cacophony of voices had emerged in the 1930s, with most of these speakers being greeted with tolerance, if not with acceptance. In addition, the U.S. Supreme Court was providing increased protection for First Amendment activities. On the other side of the coin was Franklin Roosevelt's growing concern that certain individuals and groups would undermine his ability to respond to threats to national security. The president had not hesitated to use the governmental bureaucracy against real or perceived foes in the 1930s. How would he react to criticism in time of war?

Roosevelt's support for opponents of Hitler in the late 1930s led to the rise of several groups dedicated to preventing further American involvement. Militant peace groups such as the Fellowship of Reconciliation and the War Resisters League joined to form the Keep America Out of War Congress after events served notice that the world was on the brink of war. Organization leaders wanted to keep American forces away from locations where they might become involved in armed conflict; they also opposed plans for conscription and supported an antiwar amendment to the Constitution. As war approached, the Congress's membership split over the proper attitude to take during the war. The strongest pacifists maintained their principled resistance to war and worked to protect any individuals who chose to become conscientious objectors.[1]

Although Roosevelt obviously noticed the pacifistic Keep America Out of War Congress, his attention was more focused on the isolationist America First organization. Members of America First also tended to be conservative opponents of other Roosevelt programs, and many of them had supported the Liberty League a few years earlier. The America First Committee served as an umbrella

189

organization for many opponents of war between September 1940 and December 7, 1941. Even the Keep America Out of War Congress had tenuous ties to this broader based and more financially stable organization. America First's foundation rested on a firm distrust of Great Britain, and its propaganda stressed that America was not responsible for solving European problems or for policing the world.[2]

Well-financed and articulate opponents of the path chosen by the president, members of the America First Committee increasingly became targets of interventionists who charged that the conservative committee's members were, in reality, agents for fascist governments. The American Legion condemned the organization for supporting ideas harmful to the United States, and the president asked the Federal Bureau of Investigation (FBI) to keep track of individual members. Surprised by the vehemence of opposition to their efforts to keep the nation out of war, organization leaders tried to deflect the attacks. "We regret very much that you are not in accord with our policies," they usually responded to critics, "but feel that although our approach is different our ultimate aim is the same, namely, the preservation of American Democracy."[3] When the assault on America First escalated to the point that efforts were made to keep their speakers off the airwaves, committee representatives tied their efforts to traditional American reverence for freedom of expression.

Even the president of the United States was reminded of the importance of dissent. Roosevelt, said Philip La Follette, "urged a campaign of 'shaming' opposition to silence, and even bluntly made the unveiled threat of force to suppress those who did not agree." In his speeches, the president had used "words like 'slacker', 'troublemaker', 'appeaser', and the like. . . . Instead of smearing or wrecking," La Follette said, "let us encourage and build character, in ourselves and others. Argue—hit as hard as you please *on the issues,* but refuse to villify individuals simply because they do not agree. That kind of people will make our democracy stronger. The other kind might destroy it."[4]

Unfortunately for the America First Committee, its activities were praised by the German propaganda machine, thus shrouding its work in an aura of disloyalty. In fact, the Dies Committee investigated America First, and after the war started, a federal grand jury included the organization in its probe of groups that had tried to impair the war effort. As war came closer, members of America First sought even more dramatic ways to show their opposition to U.S. involvement. But as they considered an increased role in the 1942 campaign, Pearl Harbor was bombed. The organization dissolved quietly and quickly, with its leaders urging members to support the war effort.

Although prowar groups eventually built support for the idea that the United States should aid those nations fighting Hitler, the pacifist and isolationist groups still controlled American hearts. In fact, public opinion polls revealed that few Americans endorsed U.S. entry into the war itself. To Roosevelt, opponents of his foreign policies were, if not Nazis, certainly strong supporters of the fascist cause. At times, he freely accused his critics of being fifth columnists who ate away at the American spirit.[5] The more upset he became over his opponents' attitudes, the more he sounded ready to restrict severely the rights of Americans to dissent from official policy. After the 1940 election, for instance, Roosevelt warned those individuals who opposed his policy: "No one can tell the exact character of the emergency situations that we may be called upon to meet." Because of this uncertainty, "the Nation's hands must not be tied when the Nation's life is in danger." The best way to prevent such an occurrence, he said, "is, first, to shame them by patriotic example, and if that fails, to use the sovereignty of Government to save Government."[6]

To protect government, Roosevelt sought a special unit within the Department of Justice to keep watch on his political opponents. When that idea failed to come to fruition, he set up an ad hoc group within the White House to accomplish the same task. In setting a pattern for future presidential intimidation, Roosevelt tried to use the entire federal bureaucracy to attack dissidents. He attempted to have the Internal Revenue Service review the tax-exempt status of organizations offering the greatest challenges. Although that effort met with little success, the FBI willingly kept track of presidential opponents. To facilitate its operations, the bureau cooperated with the American Legion, which had volunteered to watch allegedly subversive individuals. Although complaints did not arise from this program, many of the Legionnaires' activities were similar to those of the American Protective League that had so terrorized dissenters during World War I. The agreement with the legion, however, kept its members out of investigatory work and limited their sources of information to data observed in everyday activities.[7]

Although plagued by these concerns, Roosevelt proposed no lengthy list of repressive legislation as war neared. In fact, no legislation was needed because the statutes enacted during the fascist scare of the 1930s stood ready for use. World War II saw far fewer prosecutions than did World War I largely because of Francis Biddle, who became acting attorney general in June 1941 and assumed the job permanently three months later. Soon after his confirmation, Biddle, a liberal with a strong concern for civil liberties, told the California Bar, "We do not lose our right to condemn either measures or men because the country is at war."[8] Shortly after that, he was quoted in the *New York Times* as saying, "In so far as I can, by use of the authority and the influence of my office, I intend to see that civil liberties in this country are protected; that we do not again fall into the disgraceful hysteria of witch hunts, strike breakings and minority persecutions which were such a dark chapter in our record of the last World War."[9] To further underline his position, he told a Bill of Rights commemoration shortly after the attack on Pearl Harbor that "every man . . . who cares about freedom must fight for it for the *other* man with whom he disagrees."[10]

In addition to rhetorical responses, Biddle acted wherever and whenever possible. He forbade the institution of prosecutions for sedition without his personal written authority, for example. "I announced," he said, "that freedom of speech should be curtailed only when public safety was directly imperiled." At times, Biddle's reluctance to initiate prosecutions collided with FDR's desire to punish persons who still criticized his policies. In early 1942, Roosevelt campaigned for the indictment of right-wing opponents of the war. Biddle recalled that Roosevelt "began to go for me in the Cabinet. His technique was always the same.

When my turn came, as he went around the table, his habitual affability dropped. He did not ask me as usual, if I had anything to report. He looked at me, his face pulled tightly together. 'When are you going to indict the seditionists?' he would ask; and the next week, and every week after that."[11] The president's approach remained unchanged until Biddle procured the desired indictments; after that, the president resumed his cordial attitude toward his attorney general.

Roosevelt's attitude on freedom of expression, as with most presidents, was confusing and contradictory. Although his encounters with conservative newspaper publishers raised the level of mistrust, his public rhetoric still placed him firmly on the side of those supporting broader freedom of expression. In his State of the Union address of January 1941, for example, he announced that his vision of the world was filled with international adherence to four basic freedoms, which he considered essential to the maintenance of a free society. As he told Congress, "The first is freedom of speech and expression—everywhere in the world."[12]

Despite these fine statements about the importance of freedom of expression, Franklin Roosevelt still had his private demons. In the 1930s, his focus was on the likes of Huey Long and Father Coughlin. With the coming of war, his concern for national loyalty led him into the nation's worst single episode of intolerance. Within months after the bombing of Pearl Harbor, at least 112,000 persons of Japanese heritage, two-thirds of whom were native-born or naturalized American citizens, were forcibly relocated into poorly equipped internment camps. Significant doubts about the loyalty of such individuals was the official reason given for the relocation. Racial prejudice, long endemic on the Pacific Coast, was the underlying cause of the mass action.[13]

Traditional opponents of war also emerged despite what seemed to be overwhelming public support of the American effort. Only one member of Congress voted against American entry into World War II; fifty had cast negative votes against participation in World War I. The declaration of war in 1917 had come after a week of debate; in 1941, war was declared against Japan the day after the attack on Pearl Harbor.[14] Except for the hard-core pacifists, the antiwar movement virtually collapsed after Pearl Harbor. Fewer opponents of war appeared, and fewer conscientious objectors registered during World War II than during World War I. Some 34 million men signed up for the draft; only about 72,000 applied for CO status. Of the 10 million men inducted, only about 43,000 actually sought conscientious exemption from service.[15]

Pacifists were constantly pressured to change their attitudes in order to maintain their jobs, and any attempt to spread pacifistic doctrines encountered community disapproval. Despite such opposition, pacifist organizations remained strongly attached to their fundamental principles. On December 9, 1941, the executive committee of one of the nation's leading pacifist groups, the Fellowship of Reconciliation, which was led by Rev. A. J. Muste, reiterated its belief that war could not solve international problems: "The fact that our beloved country has now again been openly and fully drawn into war does not alter our opposition to all war or our refusal, in so far as we are free to determine our own course, to take part in war measures."[16]

Unfortunately for most male pacifists, they needed to cope with the draft. The selective service act that was passed in 1940 offered little hope for conscientious objectors to war.[17] Only those men from a sect with a tradition of pacifism would even have the possibility of winning CO status. Court rulings eventually widened these definitions, but individuals with political or philosophical objections to war were denied this status. Once CO status was granted, the problem became what to do with men so classified. The government preferred to assign them to noncombatant work in the military such as driving ambulances and serving in hospitals. About 12,000 COs refused these tasks because they aided the war effort. Most of these men were assigned to Civilian Public Service Camps, where they engaged in a variety of conservation-related activities. Although the camps were administered by the historic peace churches, thus avoiding the World War I problem of placing the COs directly under the control of the military, restiveness grew. Pacifists during World War II were well educated, and although they did not object to working for the government as an alternative form of service, they disliked the type of work they were given. Many of them thought that the government would make use of their talents, or at least allow them to work in civilian hospitals or in other humanitarian endeavors rather than assign them to physical labor.

Selective service officials were totally unsympathetic. As one official said in 1942, "The program is not being carried on for the education or development of individuals to train groups for foreign service or future activities in the postwar period. . . . There is no obligation to provide an assignee with work for which he has been particularly prepared, wishes to do, or regards as socially significant."[18] Adding to the problem was the fact that, unlike those men who were serving in the military, the men in the camps received no pay. Public support existed for paying the COs, but selective service officials rejected such proposals on the grounds that payment would make CO status too appealing.

Military officials eventually assumed stronger roles in camp administration, and when military rules were imposed, discontent grew. Some of this dissatisfaction took the form of nonviolent disobedience to orders. If COs were told to chop a tree down, for instance, they demanded separate orders for each blow that was landed. The men reported sick regularly, and they began fasting. Some even sat down on the job and refused to work, adopting the techniques used with great success by the labor movement in the 1930s and by Mohandas Gandhi in India. Soon they simply walked out of the camps. Similar techniques were being learned by pacifists who were jailed for their beliefs. These men often had been unable to win classification as religious objectors or were so opposed to war that they refused all forms of cooperation with the system, including seeking CO status. While in jail, the pacifists participated in antiwar demonstrations and campaigned for better treatment of black prisoners.

In all instances, pacifists were honing techniques that would become invaluable in both the civil rights and the antiwar movements of the 1960s. Some thoughtful Americans believed the COs were being mistreated because of their deeply held beliefs, and that seemed wrong. But in World War II, COs were still seen as almost as much of an enemy as the Germans, the Italians, or the Japanese. Their crime was not the covert bombing of the American fleet at anchor in a Pacific harbor. It was much worse: they had questioned using military might to solve the world's problems. Because of their offenses, COs in the camps and in the prisons remained out of circulation for months after men serving in the military forces were demobilized. Pacifism was simply too dangerous an idea to have running loose in the country.

In addition to their other misdeeds, American pacifists were accused of trying to convince other citizens to support a negotiated peace with Germany. The movement, which began in 1942, drew its strength from the remnants of the America First Committee and the radical pacifists. Both sought to capitalize on lukewarm American support for the war against Germany. The president labeled these individuals divisionists and told J. Edgar Hoover to investigate the movement. Hoover in turn told his agents to find out whether the remnants of the America First Committee were being "used by foreign interests, or by individuals cooperating with foreign interests, in such a manner as to interfere with the national defense effort."[19]

Other supporters of the effort to split American support from its European allies included the isolationist newspapers run by Colonel Robert R. McCormick and his family and by William Randolph Hearst. Although the president had long campaigned against the likes of McCormick, attacking conservative newspaper publishers without just cause would have been foolhardy. Roosevelt tried to find links between the isolationist press and Nazi propaganda. Failing that, he bided his time until one or all of the offensive newspapers overstepped the line. The impact of the divisionists on American public opinion declined toward the end of 1942 as the probability of an Allied victory increased.

As that movement faded from the scene, People's Peace Now picked up steam. Organized by radical pacifist David Dellinger, who later would be a leading figure in the anti–Vietnam War effort, People's Peace Now pressed for an immediate end to the war. The protest was spurred on by American saturation bombing—and destruction—of European cities and by American demands for the unconditional surrender of its foes. People's Peace Now advocates ran into multiple problems. Attempts to picket in Washington, D.C., were disrupted; its leaflets were confiscated; individuals participating in its activities were picked up for selective service violations; and its members were investigated by the Dies Committee. The idea that the people could tell the government to stop a war because they did not like the way in which the battle was being fought was simply beyond the understanding of the individuals who lived in the 1940s. The People's Peace Now movement lived for little more than a year; its successors in the 1960s would struggle for nearly a decade before they brought another war, which started out as unpopular with a small group, to a standstill.

Although patriotism was not forced on Americans during World War II to the same degree that it was in the First World War, the pressure to conform and to display loyalty to one's country still existed. In the 1940s, much of the attention was focused on a small group of religious dissenters, the Jehovah's Witnesses, and upon the refusal of their children to salute the American flag. By 1940, a substantial majority of the nation's children began each day by saluting the American flag, which school officials firmly believed was the best way to teach children to love their country. For most of the children, the salute was no more than a routine ritual. For children of Jehovah's Witnesses, however, pledging allegiance to the flag was an act that jeopardized their immortal souls. Such actions violated portions of the Ten Commandments that forbade God's people to pay homage to graven images, and Witnesses' children refused to participate.[20]

Believing as they did that all organized religions were fraudulent, Witnesses were known for their highly intrusive and objectionable evangelistic efforts. When Witness children refused to salute the flag on religious grounds, public officials tended to reject their claims, writing the protests off as just another example of the sect's intransigence rather than considering the possibility that matters of conscience were truly involved. Punishments for failure to salute the flag were stiff. In almost all cases, Witness children were expelled from school. In some instances, the children were declared delinquent, and their parents were charged with contributing to the delinquency of minors. If the children were allowed to enroll in private schools where the salute was not required, the parents, who generally were of modest means, had difficulty meeting the costs of their education. One additional trait of the Jehovah's Witnesses made it unlikely that they would accept this treatment of their children with equanimity. Absolutely convinced of the correctness of their stance, the Jehovah's Witnesses were strong advocates of using the court system to establish the rightness of their position.[21]

By 1940, when the Supreme Court heard the first flag salute case, the Witnesses were already familiar to the justices. The first of some eighteen or so Witnesses cases to come before the Court in a little less than a decade presented itself in 1938 when Alma Lovell complained that a city ordinance in Griffin, Georgia, infringed on her First Amendment rights to distribute literature promoting her faith. The city fathers wanted all persons handing out materials to obtain permission first; Mrs. Lovell said she "regarded herself as sent 'by Jehovah to do His work' and that such an application would have been 'an act of disobedience to His commandment.'" A unanimous Court found the ordinance invalid, with Chief Justice Charles Evans Hughes noting that "it strikes at the very foundation of the freedom of the press by subjecting it to license and censorship." Through Alma Lovell's efforts to distribute her literature without government intervention came a freedom for thousands of others to follow in her footsteps.[22]

The freedom to distribute information was broadened the next year, when Jehovah's Witnesses challenged city ordinances that forbade the distribution of leaflets on public streets. "To require a censorship through license which makes impossible the free and unhampered distribution of pamphlets strikes at the very heart of the constitutional guarantees," Owen Roberts wrote for an eight-man majority. Although fraudulent appeals might well be made and although some people might litter the city's streets with the material, neither problem justified a restraint on the free distribution of information.[23]

And the Jehovah's Witnesses won another important battle when a unanimous Supreme Court decided that their speech could not be restrained just because it was likely to raise the ire of listeners. One of the Witnesses' favorite evangelizing techniques called for them to visit neighborhoods that were heavily

Roman Catholic. There the Witnesses would play phonograph records attacking the Catholic Church and distribute literature describing the faults of that faith. When Jesse Cantwell behaved in that manner in New Haven, Connecticut, he was arrested on several charges, including causing a breach of the peace. With Justice Roberts writing once again, the Court decided that a city could not stop a Jehovah's Witness from proclaiming his faith on a public street simply because of the possibility of a breach of the peace. Such a restriction, Roberts wrote, would hamper the full discussion of ideas: "In the realm of religious faith, and in that of political belief, sharp differences arise. In both fields the tenets of one man may seem the rankest error to his neighbor. To persuade others to his own point of view, the pleader, as we know, at times, resorts to exaggeration, to vilification of men who have been, or are, prominent in church or state, and even to false statement." These problems were familiar, he said, and did not merit restrictions. "The people of this nation," Roberts said, "have ordained in the light of history, that, in spite of the probability of excesses and abuses, these liberties are, in the long view, essential to enlightened opinion and right conduct on the part of the citizens of a democracy."[24]

Despite these early victories, hard times lay ahead for the Jehovah's Witnesses, especially as the flag salute cases began working their way through the judicial system. The first case reaching the Supreme Court came out of Minersville, Pennsylvania, where two children of Walter Gobitis had been expelled from public school for refusing to salute the flag. In the course of the trial, the children testified that they believed themselves to be loyal Americans but that they considered saluting the flag to be the equivalent of paying homage to a graven image. The Jehovah's Witnesses triumphed in both the federal district court and the court of appeals. The case reached the Supreme Court in 1940, a few years after the justices had begun talking about the First Amendment as a preferred freedom. Even more important for the Gobitis children, the case reached the justices as war was already raging in Europe.

In an eight-to-one decision, the Supreme Court overturned the lower court decisions and found that Jehovah's Witnesses' children could be forced to salute the flag. The majority decision was written by Felix Frankfurter, the only member of the Court who had immigrated to this country and the only Jew then sitting as a justice. Frankfurter argued that although religious beliefs were important, they did not relieve individuals of the need to support their government. "National unity is the basis of national security," he wrote, adding that "the ultimate foundation of a free society is the binding tie of cohesive sentiment. Such a sentiment is fostered by all those agencies of the mind and spirit which may serve to gather up the traditions of a people, transmit them from generation to generation, and thereby create that continuity of a treasured common life which constitutes a civilization."[25] Parents, he wrote, were responsible for a child's religious training; school authorities were to guide the child's attitude toward his or her country. Thus school officials were within their rights to require children, regardless of their religious beliefs, to salute the flag.

Justice Harlan Fiske Stone, who had enunciated the preferred freedoms doctrine in 1938, sharply rebuked Frankfurter and those justices who joined with him. To Stone, the state was seeking "to coerce these children to express a sentiment which, as they interpret it, they do not entertain, and which violates their deepest religious convictions." Stone believed that the state could find ways to teach the children patriotism that did not violate religious beliefs. The Bill of Rights protected "the very essence" of liberty, and that, at a bare minimum, had to include the right of individuals to believe as they saw fit. The Court, he warned, needed to be careful because most infringements on personal liberty were justified "in the name of righteousness and the public good" and most were directed "as they are now, at politically helpless minorities."[26] The Court's role was to protect such minorities.

The Gobitis decision let loose a wave of anti-Witness behavior around the country. Witness evangelists had an increasingly hard time in spreading their message. Their children became the targets of additional state and local legislation requiring them to salute the flag. More than 2,000 Witness children were expelled from school by 1943. The Supreme Court added to the Witnesses' problems when it handed down three more rulings against them in fairly rapid succession. In 1941, for instance, the Court decided unanimously that communities were justified in demanding that Jehovah's Witnesses obtain a permit if they intended to parade on public streets. "Civil liberties, as guaranteed by the Constitution, imply the existence of an organized society maintaining public order without which liberty itself would be lost in the excesses of unrestrained abuses," wrote Chief Justice Hughes. "The authority of a municipality to impose regulations in order to assure the safety and convenience of the people in the use of public highways has never been regarded as inconsistent with civil liberties but rather as one of the means of safeguarding the good order upon which they ultimately depend."[27]

In 1942, the Court reduced the amount of freedom granted Witnesses who made upsetting comments in public. Walter Chaplinsky, a Witness active in Rochester, New Hampshire, had been presenting the typical Witness appeal on the streets. In a complicated series of interactions, Chaplinsky was arrested for causing a disturbance. When informed of his arrest, Chaplinsky allegedly said to the city marshal, "you are a God damned racketeer" and "a damned Fascist and the whole government of Rochester are Fascists or agents of Fascists." Chaplinsky denied only using the Lord's name, and the case reached the Supreme Court. A unanimous bench upheld the right of communities to prevent a breach of the peace caused by language such as Chaplinsky's.[28]

"There are certain well-defined and narrowly limited classes of speech, the prevention and punishment of which have never been thought to raise any Constitutional problem," said Justice Frank Murphy. "These include the lewd and obscene, the profane, the libelous, and the insulting or 'fighting' words—those which by their very utterance inflict injury or tend to incite an immediate breach of the peace." According to the Court, "It has been well observed that such utterances are no essential part of any exposition of ideas, and are of such slight social value as a step to truth that any benefit that might be derived from them is clearly outweighed by the social interest in order and morality."[29] With his opinion, Justice Murphy wrote the concept of "fighting words" into Supreme Court precedent.

In the wake of the flag salute case, the Court also took a giant step away from continued protection from license fees. Five members of the Court joined in 1942 to uphold a license fee imposed on Witnesses who sold their literature. Nondiscriminatory requirements such as a flat tax on those persons who sold literature, the majority said, were acceptable under the Constitution. Stone, who was now chief justice, denounced the majority for undermining First Amendment guarantees in a scorching dissent. To Stone, Roscoe Jones had the right to distribute his literature without paying the fee imposed by the city of Opelika, Alabama. "The constitutional protection of the Bill of Rights is not to be evaded by classifying with business callings an activity whose sole purpose is the dissemination of ideas, and taxing it as business callings are taxed," he said. Freedom of speech and of religion, he added, are "in a preferred position. Their commands are not restricted to cases where the protected privilege is sought out for attack. They extend at least to every form of taxation which, because it is a condition of the exercise of the privilege, is capable of being used to control or suppress it." To the chief justice, it was "fairly obvious that if the present taxes, laid in small communities upon peripatetic religious propagandists, are to be sustained, a way has been found for the effective suppression of speech and press and religion despite constitutional guaranties." That Stone simply could not accept.[30]

Nor could Justices Hugo Black, William O. Douglas, and Frank Murphy accept such an interpretation. They joined in Stone's dissent and in a separate dissent written by Murphy. They also added a special comment at the end of the official opinion. "The opinion of the Court," the trio said, "sanctions a device which in our opinion suppresses or tends to suppress the free exercise of a religion practiced by a minority group." It followed in the footsteps of the Gobitis decision, they said, and "since we joined in the opinion in the Gobitis Case, we think this is an appropriate occasion to state that we now believe that it was also wrongly decided."[31] The justices were reacting in part to the increasing persecution of Witnesses around the nation. Treatment of the sect was becoming a national disgrace, and the Supreme Court soon tried to end such behavior.[32]

In the winter and spring of 1943, the Supreme Court decided eight Jehovah's Witnesses cases, with the victory in each case going to the religious sect. The justices returned to their earlier position that streets had to be opened to Witness proselytizing without restriction when a Dallas, Texas, ordinance prohibiting the distribution of handbills on the city's streets was declared unconstitutional. Justice Hugo Black found the city's contention that "it has the power absolutely to prohibit the use of the streets for the communication of ideas" unpersuasive. Rather, he wrote for seven members of the Court, "one who is rightfully on a street which the state has left open to the public carries with him there as elsewhere the constitutional right to express his views in an orderly fashion. This right extends to the communication of ideas by handbills and literature as well as by the spoken word."[33] The licensing law of Paris, Texas, fell before a unanimous Court that decided its provisions were too broad. Said Justice Stanley Reed, "The mayor issues a permit only if after thorough investigation he 'deems it proper or advisable.' Dissemination of ideas depends upon the approval of the distributor by the official. This is administrative censorship in an extreme form."[34]

To show that the Supreme Court was not above rehearing cases and changing its mind, in May 1943, it overturned its year-old decision in *Jones v. Opelika.* Roscoe Jones was now free to sell his literature without paying the fee that the Court had earlier sanctioned.[35] In another case decided the same day, a badly divided Court explained the rationale for the change. "The mere fact that the religious literature is 'sold' by itinerant preachers rather than 'donated' does not transform evangelism into a commercial enterprise," Justice William O. Douglas wrote for the five-man majority. "It is plain that a religious organization needs funds to remain a going concern. But an itinerant evangelist, however misguided or intolerant he may be, does not become a mere book agent by selling the Bible or religious tracts to help defray his expenses or to sustain him." No, said Douglas, "freedom of speech, freedom of the press, freedom of religion are available to all, not merely to those who can pay their own way."[36]

Nor was the tenor of the literature involved a just cause for taxation. "Considerable emphasis is placed on the kind of literature which petitioners were distributing—its provocative, abusive, and ill-mannered character and the assault which it makes on our established churches and the cherished faiths of many of us. . . . But those considerations are no justification for the license tax which the ordinance imposes." To Douglas, "a community may not suppress, or the state tax, the dissemination of views because they are unpopular, annoying or distasteful. If that device were ever sanctioned, there would have been forged a ready instrument for the suppression of the faith which any minority cherishes but which does not happen to be in favor. That would be a complete repudiation of the philosophy of the Bill of Rights."[37]

A hard-core majority of the Court—Stone, Black, Douglas, Murphy, and Rutledge—now were intent on removing any roadblocks to Witness evangelizing. Even regulations designed to protect individuals in the privacy of their homes from the intrusion of religious zealots could not stand. As Hugo Black explained, "For centuries it has been a common practice in this and other countries for persons not specifically invited to go from home to home and knock on doors or ring doorbells to communicate ideas to the occupants or to invite them to political, religious, or other kinds of public meetings." For all of this time, Black said, "whether such visiting shall be permitted has in general been deemed to depend upon the will of the individual master of each household, and not upon the determination of the community." He saw no reason to change that approach. The dissenters, on the other hand, saw no problems with an ordinance. "If the citizens of Struthers desire to be protected from the annoyance of being called to their doors to receive printed matter," said Justice Stanley Reed, "there is to my mind no constitutional provision which forbids their municipal council from modifying the rule that anyone may sound a call for the householder to attend his door."[38]

The problems that the Jehovah's Witnesses caused during their evangelizing were detailed in a dissent to yet another decision rejecting a community's attempt to regulate their activities. Justice Robert Jackson, who dissented in several of these cases, explained that resting at the heart of each of his opinions was "the problem of those in local authority when the right to proselyte comes in contact with what many people have an idea is their right to be let alone." In the instant case, Witnesses descended on the industrial city of Jeannette, Pennsylvania, population about 16,000, and systematically knocked on every householder's door to sell Witness tracts. Complaints arrived at city hall, and the mayor sought out the man in charge of the Witnesses' activities. They could distribute their literature in the streets, and they could give their materials away for free, the mayor said, but residents disliked being pestered at home to buy tracts, especially on Sunday. The zone servant, or Witness in charge of the operation, told the mayor "that he would bring enough Witnesses into the City of Jeannette to get the job done whether the Mayor liked it or not." On Palm Sunday, 1939, more than 100 Witnesses showed up to distribute materials. Complaints again came in, and Witnesses were arrested as they "called at homes singly and in groups. . . . Some of the homes complained that they were called upon several times." Twenty-one Witnesses were arrested that day. The literature that they distributed was highly antagonistic to Roman Catholics as were their personal talks.[39]

Such evangelizing caused real problems for Jackson, a Roman Catholic. "These Witnesses, in common with all others, have extensive rights to proselyte and propagandize," he said. "These of course include the right to oppose and criticize the Roman Catholic Church or any other denomination. These rights are, and should be held to be, as extensive as any orderly society can tolerate in religious disputation. The real question is where their rights end and the rights of others begin." To Justice Jackson, "The First Amendment assures the broadest tolerable exercise of free speech, free press, and free assembly, not merely for religious purposes, but for political, economic, scientific, news, or informational ends as well." But there were limits, he said, asking, "Does what is obscene, or commercial, or abusive, or inciting become less so if employed to promote a religious ideology?" He wondered how the Court could "hold it a 'high constitutional privilege' to go to homes, including those of devout Catholics on Palm Sunday morning, and thrust upon them literature calling their church a 'whore' and their faith a 'racket'." In addition, Jackson remained unconvinced that freedom of religion required "denying the American's deep-seated conviction that his home is a refuge from the pulling and hauling of the market place and the street. For a stranger to corner a man in his home, summon him to the door and put him in the position either of arguing his religion or of ordering one of unknown disposition to leave is a questionable use of religious freedom."[40]

Despite Jackson's concerns about the acceptability of the Witnesses' evangelistic techniques, he had no doubts about their right to exercise their religious faith in another way. On Flag Day, 1943, Jackson delivered the decision that the earlier 1943 decisions had been pointing to: an overturning of the Gobitis ruling that required Witness children to salute the flag. The decision, which contains some of the most profound statements about the meaning of patriotism ever written by the Court, remains controversial even today. Six members of the Court, including several who had voted with the majority in *Gobitis,* specifically overturned that earlier decision and established the principle that no governmental authority had the right to require its citizens to salute the flag.[41] The new decision took the unusual approach of refuting the three-year-old precedent point by point. Jackson based his majority decision on the individual's right to freedom of thought. "There is no doubt that, in connection with the pledges, the flag salute is a form of utterance," Jackson wrote. Indeed the salute was a powerful form of symbolism, which, he added, "is a primitive but effective way of communicating ideas." In fact, "the use of an emblem or flag to symbolize some system, idea, institution, or personality, is a short cut from mind to mind."[42] No state should have that much authority over the minds of men, he said.

Although national unity was important, the state must find other ways than compulsory flag salutes to develop these feelings. Enforced uniformity of opinion, Jackson believed, could lead only to disaster. "Those who begin coercive elimination of dissent soon find themselves exterminating dissenters. Compulsory unification of opinion achieves only the unanimity of the graveyard," he wrote. In preferring diversity to uniformity, Jackson added, "If there is any fixed star in our constitutional constellation, it is that no official, high or petty, can prescribe what shall be orthodox in politics, nationalism, religion, or other matters of opinion or force citizens to confess by word or act their faith therein. If there are any circumstances which permit an exception, they do not now occur to us."[43]

With these words, Justice Jackson established the principle that no American could be forced to salute the flag and warned generations to come that forced obeisance to any object, even if it is the American flag, could be more dangerous than allowing dissenters to follow their consciences. By the 1980s, however, national loyalty had become thoroughly enmeshed in a willingness to affirm publicly one's allegiance to a piece of red, white, and blue cloth bearing thirteen stripes and fifty stars. Robert Jackson knew that true loyalty was based on something far different and that compelled rituals endangered the principles on which the nation was founded. Although the Supreme Court's 1943 decision in *West Virginia State Board of Education v. Barnette* still remains the law, it continues to be controversial. At the height of World War II, the issue of the flag also was emotional, but the Supreme Court decided that the nation was strong enough to allow children not to salute the flag. The revolutionary idea advocated by the young Jehovah's Witnesses was not seen as undermining the Republic; rather, permitting such deviance was viewed as strengthening fundamental values. When *Barnette* is combined with the other hotly disputed Jehovah's Witnesses decisions of the war years, the Supreme Court can be seen clearly as carving out a secure place for religious dissidents in American society. Through these cases, political and religious dissenters of later generations would also find a safe harbor.

The question of whether dissent was undermining the war effort or strengthening the nation's fabric also surfaced in the government's relationship with the black press. Newspapers serving the black community had been considered as somewhat less than loyal during World War I, and they were tarnished with the same brush during World War II for basically the same reason. The fundamental problem during both wars was that these newspapers insisted on writing about racial discrimination during wartime. In the Second World War, black editors advocated a greater black presence in the military and increased responsibility for blacks serving in the armed forces. A first objective was a black presence in the military equal to the percentage of blacks in the country; when that was won, they campaigned for an end to segregation in the armed forces. They also reported all violence against blacks serving in the military, which, unfortunately, was not inconsiderable especially when the blacks were assigned to Southern posts.[44]

To the nation's white majority, however, pointing up the nation's flaws during wartime was close to treasonous. As black newspapers inaugurated their "Double V" campaign to symbolize a call for victory over racism at home and victory over the Axis powers abroad, demands surfaced for the suppression of the black press. Some critics immediately labeled the campaign as either Communist-inspired or a propaganda line coming straight from the Japanese. The idea that blacks had reasonable criticisms of an American society that still was racist and segregated apparently did not occur to these white critics. Nor could they cope with the idea that a battle against racism in America was just as necessary as the effort to quash the Axis powers. Disaffection within the black community was automatically the fault of black newspapers. Actually, the black press was simply trying to keep pace with its readers, who were becoming increasingly upset with inequities in society. By advocating the "Double V" campaign, editors and publishers were trying to ensure that the black community would support the war effort and seek social changes at the same time.

One person most concerned with the attitudes of the black press was J. Edgar Hoover, whose reputation for racism increased substantially in later years. During World War II, Hoover had the FBI keep track of the black press. At various times, he would send copies of news stories or editorials to Justice Department officials to encourage prosecution of the individuals involved for sedition. Invariably the response to his requests would be that the material presented amounted only to expressions of opinions and was not actionable. Failing to have black publishers prosecuted, Hoover tried intimidation and sent his agents to black newspaper offices to ask questions and to make their presence known.

Complaints about the loyalty of the black press led to a June 1942 confrontation between Attorney General Biddle and John Sengstacke, publisher of the Chicago *Defender,* one of the nation's largest black newspapers. Biddle, who was a strong supporter of both racial equality and civil liberties, labeled several articles printed in black newspapers as harmful to the war effort. He threatened to take action against black publications if this material continued to appear. Realizing the furor such action would raise among liberal white newspapers in the North, Sengstacke essentially challenged Biddle to try to close the newspapers down. The encounter resulted in a compromise whereby black newspapers became more supportive of the war and efforts to suppress those publications disappeared.[45]

In reality, questions about the war disappeared from black newspapers as the needs of their readers changed. Their constituents, for instance, were finally getting good jobs in defense industries, and blacks were not only winning commissions in the military services but were showing themselves to be fine fighting men. And government public relations officers began providing positive information about black contributions to the war effort for use in the newspapers. In addition, black newspapers were beginning to benefit from increased wartime advertising, which made them less willing to criticize the American effort.

Despite these events, J. Edgar Hoover did not end his surveillance of black publications; throughout the war he continued to seek indictments of certain publishers for what they had written. Attorney General Biddle, after his confrontation with Sengstacke, became supportive of the black press, commenting in a 1943 speech, "The Negro press throughout the country, although they very properly protest, and passionately, against the wrongs done to members of their race, are loyal to their government and are all out for the war."[46] Thus, although Hoover continued to bluster about the black press, his complaints were never acted upon.

Although prosecutions for opinions during World War II were far fewer than during the First World War, several did occur. Franklin Roosevelt took the opportunity that the war afforded to prosecute several of his longtime foes. Some cases were brought under the Espionage Act of 1917[47] and the Alien Registration Act of 1940, better known as the Smith Act.[48] The most significant effort was aimed at critics on the right, with the first major prosecution targeting William Dudley Pelley, who stood trial in 1942 for violation of the Espionage Act.

As leader of the Silver Shirts, Pelley was charged with making statements designed to undermine the loyalty and morale of the armed services. Pelley could find "not the slightest enthusiasm anywhere in all America for this war—with the sole exception of the Jewish ghetto sections of our swollen cities. And those ghettos will not fight. Gentile boys from factory and farm must do the fighting." Nor was he impressed with the president's Four Freedoms, which Pelley claimed effectively said, " 'We propose to impress the American Way of Life upon you whether you like it or not.' Hitler expresses the same sentiment when he is alleged to declare: 'We propose to impress the Nazi Way of Life upon you whether you like it or not.' What's the difference between the two, excepting that one is ours and the other Germany's." He also opposed the draft, commenting that its existence showed "one of three things—The mass of the citizens disapprove of such war; The nation has suffered a decadence of morale prompting its males not to concern themselves with the public interest; or—The populace senses that settlement of differences could be arrived at by some other course than a destructive resort to arms."[49]

His offensive comments were published in the *Galilean,* the official publication of the Silver Shirts. Between 3,000 and 5,000 copies of the magazine were printed regularly, another 6,000 copies of particular articles may have been circulated through reprints. Seeking to prove that Pelley's comments followed the official Nazi line, the government called Dr. Harold Lasswell, a propaganda expert, to the stand. According to the appeals court, Lasswell proved "that of the total 1,240 statements in the 157 articles of the Galilean, *1,195* statements were consistent with and suggested copying from the German propaganda themes, and only *45* were not in harmony with them." The appeals court accepted the jury's decision. "It is hardly conceivable that a writer or speaker would have written such propaganda, at a time when his country was at war, save as he entertained the hope of weakening the patriotic resolve of his fellow citizens in their assistance of their country's cause," said the court. "No loyal citizen, in time of war, forecasts and assumes doom and defeat and futility of his country's fight, when his fellow citizens are battling in a war for their country's existence, except with an intent to retard their patriotic ardor in a cause approved by the Congress and the citizenry of this nation."[50]

The first prosecution under the Smith Act was the only wartime case involving individuals on the left of the political spectrum. Its targets were not Communists, who now were allies against Hitler, but dissident leftists—Trotskyites—who were active union members in Minneapolis. Set up in 1937, party principles called for members to work toward overthrow of the government, but the party abandoned that pledge in 1940 after the Smith Act was enacted. The party's main strength in Minneapolis rested in Teamsters Local 544, and by 1941, FBI agents had infiltrated that local. Soon, twenty-nine members of the Socialist Workers party, as the Trotskyites were officially known, were charged with advocating the overthrow of the U.S. government through word and publication.

Although the Trotskyites argued that the First Amendment protected their comments, the appeals court upheld the convictions and the constitutionality of the Alien Registration Act. A challenged section of the act did not "limit expressions of opinion or of criticisms of the Government or of its policies (civil or military) or of any officials or officers (civil or military) or of their actions," said the court, "so long as such expressions are not made with intent to bring about the unlawful things and situations covered by the section [or] . . . have a natural tendency and a reasonable probability of effecting these forbidden results." In addition, said the court, "the Nation may protect the integrity of its armed forces and may prevent the overthrow of the Government by force and . . . may, as a means to those ends, punish utterances which have a tendency to and are intended to produce the forbidden results."[51] The Supreme Court refused to review the decision.[52]

Despite the Trotskyite case, supporters of fascism in the United States remained the major targets of efforts to silence dissent. Some of the old demagogues of the Depression—including Pelley, who had already been convicted on other charges, and Gerald P. Winrod—were among the thirty defendants in the case that became known as *United States v. McWilliams.* Missing from the lineup was Father Charles Coughlin, who finally had been silenced by the Roman Catholic hierarchy, and Gerald L. K. Smith, against whom, said officials, no evidence could be found that would stand up in court.[53] The prosecution grew out of Franklin Roosevelt's increasing resentment over the attacks by American fascists.

Attorney General Biddle was unenthusiastic about the effort, although he realized the problems posed by domestic fascism. Some people, perhaps even the president, believed that the American fascists were being told what to do by foreign governments. "The 'line' was all about the same, and was taken directly from or closely related to official German propaganda," he recalled. "America, not Japan, was guilty of starting the war in the Pacific; American aid to Britain was a Jewish plot, and Roosevelt (Rosenfeldt) was a Jew; American boys were being killed to support a tottering British and French imperialism; the secret manipulations of the new money power and the munition makers had brought about the war; fighting was useless against the new order, and we should retire from the war." Roosevelt began sending Biddle memoranda outlining reasons for suppressing right-wing speech. Biddle responded by explaining his belief in "the unwisdom of bringing indictment for sedition except where there was evidence that recruitment was substantially being interfered with, or there was some connection between the speech and propaganda centers in Germany." Such a stance brought the president's constant taunting question of "When are you going to indict the seditionists?"[54] and Biddle finally brought action against leading right-wing representatives.

Government prosecutors charged thirty individuals with being part of an international conspiracy "to impair and undermine the loyalty and morale of the military and naval forces of the United States of America and of other countries" and to bring a Nazi-style government to power in the United States. Among other things, the defendants were charged with printing and distributing publications that supported the Nazi cause, including *Mein Kampf* and a variety of newspapers, magazines, and pamphlets. Their most offensive statements termed President Roosevelt "a warmonger, liar, unscrupulous, and a pawn of the Jews, Communists and Plutocrats," said the U.S. government was "controlled by Communists, International Jews, and plutocrats," and charged that "the acts, proclamations, and orders of the public officials of the United States and the laws of Congress are illegal, corrupt, traitorous and in direct violation of the Constitution of the United States."[55]

As *McWilliams* was being tried in 1944, the Supreme Court handed down a decision that indicated that the legacy the justices would leave after this conflict would be far different from that left after World War I. *Hartzel v. United States* involved an anti-Semite who had sent materials directly to members of the armed forces that denounced the British and the Jews and that had criticized the president's patriotism. In overturning Hartzel's conviction for violating the Espionage Act of 1917, Justice Frank Murphy said, "We are not unmindful of the fact that the United States is now engaged in a total war for national survival and that total war of the modern variety cannot be won by a doubtful, disunited nation in which any appreciable sector is disloyal. For that reason our enemies have developed psychological warfare to a high degree in an effort to cause unrest and disloyalty." Although recognizing that "much of this type of warfare takes the form of insidious propaganda in the manner and tenor displayed by the petitioner's three pamphlets," Murphy noted that while Hartzel's commentary might be socially unacceptable, "the mere fact that such ideas are enunciated by a citizen is not enough by itself to warrant a finding of a criminal intent to violate §3 of the Espionage Act." Indeed, he said, "unless there is sufficient evidence from which a jury could infer beyond a reasonable doubt that he intended to bring about the specific consequences prohibited by the Act, an American citizen has the right to discuss these matters either by temperate reasoning or by immoderate and vicious invective without running afoul of the Espionage Act of 1917."[56]

Of all of the defendants in war-related cases, including those persons who faced the Supreme Court after World War I, Hartzel was probably the one individual whose activities most closely fit the description of behavior that would violate the provisions of the Espionage Act. According to the Court, Hartzel's materials showed "the war as a gross betrayal of America." He also denounced "our English allies and the Jews and assail[ed] in reckless terms the integrity and the patriotism of the President of the United States."[57] The materials were sent directly to military officials in an attempt to win their support. Granted, few high-ranking military officers would be persuaded to abandon their posts based on Hartzel's arguments, but Schenck, Abrams, and others were convicted for doing far less during World War I.

The McWilliams defendants naturally argued that they had done nothing more than Hartzel had done; thus the Supreme Court decision, which reflected the fact that the end of the war was in sight, should free them. But the presiding judge rejected that interpretation after the government argued that it had evidence that the defendants in *McWilliams* had foreign connections lacking in *Hartzel* and that they had had the specific intent to disrupt the armed forces. In late November 1944, the presiding judge suffered a fatal heart attack, and a mistrial was declared. The Justice Department was not anxious to retry the case, especially after the Supreme Court freed members of the German-American Bund charged with making statements designed to promote draft evasion. Here by another five-to-four decision, the justices decided that Bund members were opposing a rider to the conscription bill of 1940 that denied employment in defense industries to Bund members rather than voicing disapproval of the draft itself.[58] This decision made it even more unlikely that any conviction of the defendants in *McWilliams,* if obtained, would survive the scrutiny of the Supreme Court. In November 1946, the indictments were dismissed because the defendants had not been granted a speedy trial.

Members of the Supreme Court continued their liberating decisions when confronted with cases involving speech critical of the war effort. In many instances, the Court seemed to stretch its principles to protect defendants. In the case of George Sylvester Viereck, five members of the Court found that the German propagandist was not guilty of failure to register all his activities as an agent of a foreign government under the Foreign Agents Registration Act. Chief Justice Stone, writing for the majority, found that the act was intended to force individuals to report only those activities financed by a foreign government. Although Viereck definitely was a German propaganda agent, he also had the right to speak on his own, which the majority said was exactly what he was doing in the instances that led to his conviction.[59]

The Court also heard cases involving government attempts to revoke the citizenship of two German-Americans on the grounds that they were not properly devoted to the Constitution at the time that they took their oaths. In the case of Carl Wilhelm Baumgartner, a unanimous panel found that his support of Hitler, which included speaking out at work and in Sunday school classes and encouraging his family, which was visiting Germany at the outbreak of war, to stay put, provided insufficient grounds for the revocation of his citizenship. Just because Baumgartner talked about Germany in flattering terms did not mean that he had falsely pledged his loyalty to the United States.[60]

"One of the prerogatives of American citizenship is the right to criticize public men and measures—and that means not only informed and responsible criticism but the freedom to speak foolishly and without moderation," said Justice Felix Frankfurter. "Our trust in the good sense of the people on deliberate reflection goes deep. For such is the contradictoriness of the human mind that the expression of views which may collide with cherished American ideals does not necessarily prove want of devotion to the Nation."[61] The problems for naturalized citizens in time of international upheaval, Frankfurter said, were great, but Baumgartner's behavior was insufficient to cost his citizenship.

Paul Knauer was less fortunate when the Court decided his case in 1946. Before examining Knauer's history, Justice William O. Douglas cautioned that "great tolerance and caution are necessary lest good faith exercise of the rights of citizenship be turned against the naturalized citizen and be used to deprive him of the cherished status. Ill-tempered expressions, extreme views, even the promotion of ideas which run counter to our American ideals, are not to be given disloyal connotations in absence of solid, convincing evidence that that is their significance." Indeed, he said, "Any other course would run counter to our traditions and make denaturalization proceedings the ready instrument for political persecutions." But Knauer was different from Baumgartner. Not only had Knauer talked about the appropriateness of German behavior prior to the war, but he had put action behind his words. He had been, for instance, a visible and important member of the German-American Bund. His activities, Douglas ruled for seven members of the Court, clearly indicated that Knauer had falsely sworn loyalty to the United States. His citizenship was ordered revoked.[62]

Sedition was one type of objectionable speech during wartime, and, as noted, prosecutions for such offenses generally were few and unsuccessful. World War II also gave rise to several prominent treason prosecutions. As one of the few offenses specifically described in the Constitution, the crime was carefully circumscribed because of the framers' memories of British abuses. "Treason against the United States," says the Constitution, "shall consist only in levying War against them, or in adhering to their Enemies, giving them Aid and Comfort. No Person shall be convicted of Treason unless on the Testimony of two Witnesses to the same overt Act, or on Confession in open Court."[63] These restrictions made proving the crime difficult.

Nevertheless, the government did pursue several individuals for treason as a result of World War II activities. Three of the cases focused on American citizens who used the airwaves to promote the Axis cause during the war. The trio—a woman who worked for Hitler, another woman whom the government claimed was Tokyo Rose, and the poet Ezra Pound—was charged with treason for their broadcasts. Both Mildred Elizabeth Gillars and the woman accused of being Tokyo Rose were convicted and spent time in prison for their offenses. Pound was declared mentally incompetent and spent more than a dozen years in a federal mental institution.

In the German case, Gillars was convicted for her part in a broadcast made prior to the D-Day landings in France called "Vision of Invasion," which allegedly portrayed the attitudes of American parents toward the invasion. Gillars read the mother's part and reportedly said, "But everyone says the invasion is suicide. The simplest person knows that. Between seventy and ninety percent of the boys will be killed or crippled for the rest of their lives." When asked by the father what could be done to stop the killing, Gillars responded, "Bah. We could have done a lot about it. Have we got a government by the people or not? Roosevelt had no right to go to war." Gillars and her attorneys tried to argue, among other things, that her speech had been protected by the First Amendment. The appeals court reviewing her conviction disagreed.[64]

"While the crime is not committed by mere expressions of opinion or criticism, words spoken as part of a program of propaganda warfare, in the course of employment by the enemy in its conduct of war against the United States, to which the accused owes allegiance, may be an integral part of the crime," it said. The case demonstrated that Gillars was involved in "a course of conduct on behalf of the enemy in the prosecution of its war against the United States. The use of speech to this end, as the evidence permitted the jury to believe, made acts of words. The First Amendment does not protect one from accountability for words as such." Free speech, the judges said, depends upon the use to which the words are put. The First Amendment "protects the free expression of thought and belief as a part of the liberty of the individual as a human personality. But words which reasonably viewed constitute acts in furtherance of a program of an enemy to which the speaker adheres and to which he gives aid with intent to betray his own country, are not rid of criminal character merely because they are words."[65]

The Tokyo Rose case provided unique challenges because of the lack of proof that the woman charged, Iva Ikuko Toguri d'Aquino, an American citizen of Japanese ancestry who was in Japan at the start of the war, was the one and only Tokyo Rose. Nor was there any proof that she had broadcast anything that had harmed the morale of American troops in the Pacific. In fact, military and civilian authorities shortly after the war had decided to drop the charges against her for lack of evidence. Then, with the onset of the cold war, demands increased to punish persons who had been disloyal during the shooting war, and d'Aquino was brought to trial. The overt act on which her conviction was based was a statement broadcast after a typhoon had caused heavy American naval losses in fall 1944. Two witnesses testified that they watched her as she said, "Now you fellows have lost all your ships. You really are orphans of the Pacific. Now how do you think you will ever get home?"[66] Her ten-year prison term was upheld.

Ezra Pound, who fancied himself an expert in economic and political matters, ran into trouble for making outrageous statements while in the employ of the Italian fascists. Once, for instance, he said that Mussolini and Hitler "are your leaders, however much you think you are conducted by Roosevelt or told up by Churchill. You follow Mussolini and Hitler in every constructive act of your government."[67] Whether his comments had any effect on American troops is questionable, but Pound eventually was brought back to the United States to face charges of treason.

The poet contended that he was simply exercising his right as an American to freedom of expression. In a letter to Attorney General Biddle after his indictment, Pound declared, "The whole basis of democratic or majority government assumes that the citizen shall be informed of the facts. I have not claimed to know all the facts, but I have claimed to know some of the facts which are an essential part of the total that should be known to the people." Pound added that "I have for years believed that the American people should be better informed as to Europe, and informed by men who are not tied to a special interest or under definite control." Since he believed "the freedom of the press has become a farce, as everyone knows that the press is controlled, if not by its titular owners, at least by the advertisers," he sought another avenue of communication, the radio. "Free speech under modern conditions becomes a mockery if it does not include the right of free speech over the radio."[68]

Pound's effort to win First Amendment protection failed, and plans were made to proceed with the trial. Only the fact that he was found incompetent to face the charges stood in the way of his conviction. Many scholars have argued that Pound himself engineered his insanity plea and put on an outstanding display of aberrant behavior to convince authorities of his condition. He stayed in St. Elizabeth's Hospital for thirteen years—until his lawyers were sure that the government would not attempt to prosecute him upon his release. A campaign by leading writers helped lead to his release in the late 1950s, after which Pound returned to his beloved Italy, where he lived until his death in 1972.[69]

The questions that these cases raised are significant. By World War II, broadcasting had become an important tool in circulating ideas. With the right equipment, programs could be heard over wide territories. In each instance, expatriate Americans—none of whom had surrendered his or her citizenship—conducted radio broadcasts capable of reaching American troops. In their broadcasts, Pound and Gillars, at least, provided information designed to undercut the faith the troops had in their government. Had the comments been made in the United States, the trio likely would have been ignored by authorities given the approach taken to allegedly seditious utterances during the war. But each defendant had worked for the enemy, and because of that relationship, each was considered a traitor.

Few federal agencies are willing to allow information favorable to the enemy to circulate in wartime. During World War II, the post office proved no exception to that general rule. Run by Frank Walker, the post office flexed its muscles, although its efforts did not match those of Albert Burleson in World War I. While praising freedom of expression, Walker gathered information about right-wing publications, the black press, and the foreign-language press. By mid-1942, he began to take action, primarily against the right-wing publications. As he revoked the second-class mailing permits of several publications, Walker said that he believed that "no publisher need have difficulty in conforming to the injunctions of the Espionage Act in time of war. If he has doubt whether an utterance may violate the law, then his good conscience, his sincere regard for the Nation, for the Constitution and for his fellow-countrymen will invariably lead him to resolve the doubt in favor of the United States." Such an approach was not censorship, he said, and was "in no way . . . restrictive of the boldness of the press in thought and speech."[70]

In his annual report for 1942, Walker noted that his office was investigating several hundred publications for possible violations of the Espionage Act. According to his interpretation of that legislation, the post office could ban publications designed to undermine the nation's war effort, and he intended to make sure that his subordinates obeyed the full extent of the law. Just how expansive his suppression of material was is one of those aspects of the World War II experience that is shrouded in obscurity due to the reputation that conflict has as "the good war" in which the entire nation supported the government's efforts.

World War II was far more popular than World War I, and disruptions of wartime activities by dissenters were fewer during World War II. Once again, for instance, labor unions cooperated with employers to bring a time of relative peace in the workplace. In late 1940 and early 1941, however, before this agreement was in place, a number of strikes—most likely caused by rapid unionization and a rise in the cost of living—hit key defense industries. Many Americans blamed the Communists for the work stoppages, claiming that the strikes were part of a Soviet plot to keep the Americans from building their defenses and aiding Great Britain. Communists were involved in the strikes, but whether the walkouts were called for an evil purpose is another matter. Worrying primarily about the effects that the strikes had on defense production, President Roosevelt set up a special mediation board to handle disputes in defense plants. Neither labor nor management was required to accept the mediation board's help, but the president could seize a plant considered essential if it remained crippled by strikes. Another version of this board was established in 1942, after American entry into the war.[71]

The start of the war led to a no-strike pledge from union leaders that was good for the duration of the conflict. In fact, strike activity did drop significantly, although disagreements between labor and management continued almost unabated, keeping the president's War Labor Board busy. Conservative business community opposition to Roosevelt administration policies favoring labor organizations continued to grow. In 1943, with a more conservative Congress in place, business leaders achieved their first success against organized labor in more than a decade when Congress enacted the Smith-Connally Act over the president's veto. Known more formally as the War Labor Disputes Act,[72] the legislation was a reaction to a growing number of work stoppages called despite the War Labor Board and the no-strike pledge. None of these work stoppages involved a diabolical plan to subvert the war effort or to disrupt the stability of the home front. Almost all of the strikes stemmed from understandable desires to share in increased business profits brought on by the war. Regardless of the reasons for the disruptions, reaction to the walkouts was almost unanimously adverse. National endorsement of labor union activities, which had reached its high point with the National Labor Relations Act of 1935, had turned a corner.

Under the provisions of the War Labor Disputes Act, all interference with the war effort was illegal. Unions were required to give thirty days' notice of threatened work stoppages in industries involved in defense work; after that cooling-off period, the workers were to be polled about whether they wanted to strike. Workers assumed that strikes then would be permissible; the government, business leaders, and much of the nation, however, still considered strikes to violate the act's provisions. No major confrontation occurred over this issue because most workers found that strike votes alone brought about desired changes. The War Labor Disputes Act expired six months after the war ended, but the restrictions on union activity built into the measure proved popular with employers who sought to have them enacted permanently after the war.

Members of the Supreme Court soon reflected this changed attitude toward labor unions as well. By 1941, the justices were beginning to backtrack on their precedent-making decision in *Thornhill v. Alabama,* which had been handed down the preceding year.[73] Under the pen of Felix Frankfurter, a six-member majority decided that when violence accompanied picketing, First Amendment protection was sacrificed. Establishing the speech-plus doctrine, in which speech closely related to illegal conduct could lose its protection, Frankfurter wrote, "Back of the guarantee of free speech lay faith in the power of an appeal to reason by all the peaceful means for gaining access to the mind. It was in order to avert force and explosions due to restrictions upon rational modes of communication that the guarantee of free speech was given a generous scope." Speech, however, took on a different meaning when accompanied by violence. "Utterance in a context of violence can lose its significance as an appeal to reason and become part of an instrument of force. Such utterance was not meant to be sheltered by the Constitution."[74]

Although Hugo Black argued that the strike was not so marred by violence as to necessitate state action to stop picketing, the majority stood firm. A series of rulings followed that chipped away at earlier decisions that had expanded the ability of labor unions to communicate with their members, with other workers, and with the general public.[75] Although tying Supreme Court decisions to public opinion is almost impossible, a convincing case can be made here that the rulings were in tune with an increasing public dismay at labor unions' behavior.[76]

As the war years signaled a change in the fortunes of labor unions in the United States, so, too, did they indicate a new direction for the Communist Party of the United States of America (CPUSA). With the Nazi-Soviet Pact of 1939, Americans began to refer to Communazis, an epithet used against individuals who still were attached to the Communist cause. Investigation of American Communists was encouraged in liberal circles. The fall of France magnified fears that a fifth column, a group of traitors in high places ready to turn strategic installations over to the enemy, was in place in the United States. Communists were prime suspects. The pressure on the party increased from all corners of the nation. Individuals who signed petitions to place Earl Browder's name on the presidential ballot in 1940 faced discrimination. Communist publications went out of business because of harassment. And a movement developed within organized labor to oust all Communists within its ranks.[77]

On June 22, 1941, the position of the American Communist party underwent another major change in status not of its own making. Hitler violated his pact, which was less than two years old, and invaded the Soviet Union. The Russians now were allies of Great Britain in combating fascism. Thus, they were also friends of the United States, which began sending aid to the brave Red Army that only days earlier had been depicted as an aggressive force. American Communists, again under orders of the Moscow-based Comintern, became patriotic Roosevelt supporters. In labor unions, where they still held positions of power, the Communists announced a no-strike pledge that they rigidly followed, even to the point of criticizing workers who did walk off the job. Politically, they offered unwavering support for almost any Roosevelt initiative. The goal now was to win the war, to protect Mother Russia from German brutality. Any means directed toward that goal were acceptable.

This new relationship led to a spurt of pro-Communist activities. The success of the Russian army in holding off Hitler's forces in the battle of Moscow only increased American admiration for the Soviets. Books, magazine articles, and motion pictures focused on the bravery of the Russian people. Alliances between American Communists and the nation's liberals once again became politically acceptable, with one of the most popular activities focusing on civilian relief efforts. Franklin Roosevelt commuted Earl Browder's prison term for violating the nation's passport laws because, according to the White House, the American Communist party chief's freedom would "have a tendency to promote national unity and allay any feeling. . . that the unusually long sentence in Browder's case was by way of penalty upon him because of his political views."[78] Always the consummate politician, Roosevelt, an ardent anti-Communist during the days of the Nazi-Soviet Pact, now, once again, supported Soviet efforts. He would not live long enough to see the time when wartime support of the Soviet Union would backfire on numerous individuals.

American Communist males volunteered to serve in the armed forces. A number of them had seen combat in the Spanish Civil War, and they were anxious to begin fighting anywhere in order to provide relief for the Soviet Union. Although the American military accepted their enlistments, Communists were given less than an enthusiastic welcome. For months, the armed forces kept them in nonessential, stateside assignments for fear that their allegiances would change once again. In addition, the Communists in the armed forces were subjected to a variety of harassments, including searches of their lockers and review of their mail by military intelligence officers. Other service personnel serving with them often were questioned about their loyalty. Only after liberal journalists investigated Browder's charges of discrimination did the mistreatment stop. Then, party members won the right to participate in the military action that they had so sought.

Ironically, the desire of Communist males to participate in the American war effort led to a significant weakening of the party in the United States. With more than 15,000 male Communists serving in the American military during the war years, the party was stripped of its experienced leadership. As in many other areas, women stepped into party offices, but they were inexperienced leaders. Party discipline weakened, and the ranks became more susceptible to infiltration by government informers, who would play an important role in the cold war. In addition, simply by serving in the armed forces, male members of the Communist party had their horizons significantly broadened. When they returned, many of these veterans would assume leadership positions in the party where they would challenge the way in which the party operated. They asked questions about how to make the party accessible and attractive to Americans and how to better shape its goals for an American rather than a Soviet society. This development, too, would have a significant impact on the postwar structure of the Communist party in the United States.

For the war period, the Soviets still decided how the American party responded to events. Since the Soviet leadership perceived that at least part of the American distrust of the CPUSA rested on its susceptibility to foreign manipulation, the Russians publicly abolished the Comintern in 1943. Ostensibly American Communists now were free to function in their own country as their leadership thought best. Browder took the Soviet leadership's statement at face value and launched a major campaign to open up the party to debate its future. The goal, according to the American general secretary, was to make the party a legitimate political institution. To that end, Browder convinced the American party leadership in 1944 to abolish the organization and to create in its place the Communist Political Association, which would serve as a political action group supporting various liberal causes. By 1945, the Soviet leadership sent a distinct signal that Browder was taking the American party too far away from its desired path. Browder was purged from the party, and William Z. Foster, a longtime party leader, who had no interest in accommodating party needs to the American environment, took control. Under Foster's direction, the party moved further to the left just as American society became less tolerant of such activity.

Before its cold war defeats, however, the party won two major victories in the U.S. Supreme Court. Both cases involved attempts to deport individuals allegedly connected with the CPUSA. The first case, decided by a five-to-three margin, involved William Schneiderman, an immigrant from Russia and a high-ranking party official in California, whose naturalized citizenship had been revoked some twelve years after it had been granted. Justice Frank Murphy, the author of the majority decision, said the Court decided to hear the Schneiderman case because of "its importance and its possible relation to freedom of thought."[79] Revocation was based on the belief that Schneiderman had not been suitably attached to the principles of the U.S. Constitution prior to his taking the oath of allegiance required of all new citizens. That judgment was based on his longtime Communist party activity, which was considered to be inherently anti-American and prima facie evidence of lack of the necessary devotion to American principles.

In an elaborate opinion, Murphy traced Schneiderman's involvement with the Communist party and noted that, throughout his party activities, Schneiderman never had thought that he was participating in anything that was incompatible with his American citizenship. Individuals seeking his denaturalization and deportation argued that party membership meant adherence to the goal of overthrowing the U.S. government. Murphy, in response, stressed "that under our traditions beliefs are personal and not a matter of mere association, and that men in adhering to a political party or other organization notoriously do not subscribe unqualifiedly to all of its platforms or asserted principles." Thus, Schneiderman could not be said to hold a belief in the violent overthrow of the American government simply because other members of the Communist party held such a belief. In addition, said Murphy, "whatever attitude we may individually hold toward persons and organizations that believe in or advocate extensive changes in our existing order, it should be our desire and concern at all times to uphold the right of free discussion and free thinking to which we as a people claim primary attachment."[80]

Murphy's decision placed the most benign interpretation on much of the party's line. Chief Justice Harlan Fiske Stone, writing in dissent, strongly disagreed. To Stone, the man who had enunciated the preferred freedoms doctrine in the late 1930s, the issue did not focus on freedom of belief or on the nation's relationship to the Soviet Union or on concern as to what the Communist party's actual purpose was. "Our concern," said Stone, "is only that the declared will of Congress shall prevail—that no man shall become a citizen or retain his citizenship whose behavior for five years before his application does not show attachment to the principles of the Constitution."[81] Historical evidence proved that the Communist party in 1927, the year that Schneiderman became a citizen, clearly believed in the violent overthrow of governments as the way to achieve its goals. This history meant that Schneiderman's citizenship could be revoked. Only Owen Roberts and Felix Frankfurter agreed with Stone; consequently, Schneiderman was allowed to maintain his citizenship and remain in the United States. The party viewed the decision as a major step toward obtaining legitimate status within the American political system.

The second major victory for the Communist party in the Supreme Court came in 1946 in another deportation matter. This case involved Harry Bridges, an immigrant from Australia who had risen to leadership in the longshoreman's union on the West Coast. A powerful labor leader, Bridges had been exceedingly lax about obtaining American citizenship. He had filed papers indicating his intention to become a citizen but had not completed the process. In the interim, he had made many enemies among business and political leaders on the West Coast. Whether he actually was a member of the Communist party is open to question, but he did have strong connections to party members. Political pressure led to two investigations by hearing officers for the Immigration and Naturalization Service (INS) that reached diametrically opposing views. In the first inquiry, Bridges was found not to be a Communist; and even if he were one, the hearing officer said, there was no indication that the Communist party supported the violent overthrow of the government. These findings led to the dismissal of deportation proceedings. Then the INS moved from the Department of Labor to the Department of Justice, and the Justice Department ordered the INS to hold another hearing. This investigation found that the Communist party was as dangerous as everyone thought it was and that Bridges was a Communist who should be deported. The orders were cut, and Bridges took the case into the court system.[82]

The Supreme Court, by a five-to-three majority, found that Bridges was a militant trade unionist who sought allies wherever they were available, including from within the ranks of the Communist party. The Court, however, did not find him to be a Communist and rescinded the order for his deportation. Justice Douglas, in writing for the majority, noted, "The associations which Harry Bridges had with various Communist groups seem to indicate no more than cooperative measures to attain objectives which are wholly legitimate. The link by which it is sought to tie him to subversive activities is an exceedingly tenuous one, if it may be said to exist at all."[83]

In concurring, Justice Murphy, a strong supporter of organized labor, noted, "The record in this case will stand forever as a monument to man's intolerance of man. Seldom if ever in the history of this nation has there been such a concentrated and relentless crusade to deport an individual because he dared to exercise the freedom that belongs to him as a human being and that is guaranteed to him by the Constitution." Law enforcement agencies, veterans' groups, and business and political leaders campaigned against Bridges. All ignored the fact, said Murphy, that aliens had First Amendment rights. Murphy believed that the case involved far more than the right of Harry Bridges to remain in the United States. "The liberties of the 3,500,000 other aliens in this nation are also at stake," he said. "Many of these aliens, like many of our forebears, were driven from their original homelands by bigoted authorities who denied the existence of freedom and tolerance. It would be a dismal prospect for them to discover that their freedom in the United States is dependent upon their conformity to the popular notions of the moment." Murphy did not believe that this was the case. "The Bill of Rights belongs to them as well as to all citizens," he said. Indeed, "it protects them in the exercise of the great individual rights necessary to a sound political and economic democracy. . . . Only by zealously guarding the rights of the most humble, the most unorthodox and the most despised among us can freedom flourish and endure in our land."[84]

The Bridges case, which was decided in June 1945, when the Soviet Union was still an American ally, was the high-water mark of American tolerance of the Communist party and of individuals who had strong relationships with Communists. The cold war was about to begin, and individuals who had been caught in the web of communism during the years when it was acceptable to be a party member or to associate with popular fronts soon would pay the price. The rhetoric of the Supreme Court decisions of the 1930s and the early 1940s in which communism was treated as just another political doctrine to be accepted or rejected by the American people represents great confidence in the ability of the people to receive information, evaluate it, and make proper decisions. With such confidence, even the most revolutionary ideas could be discussed because the people were seen as intelligent, rational, and trustworthy—as able to exercise the decision-making powers granted to them under the Constitution. Soon, however, such trust in the wisdom of the people withered.

To a certain extent, this lack of trust in the American people was present even before Pearl Harbor. The country was awash with propaganda for and against American participation in the war. All participants in this great debate told highly partial and slanted versions of the truth to the American people, leading to distinct problems for any citizens who hoped to make their decisions based on facts. A major player in the debate, of course, was Franklin Roosevelt. The president had long believed in the manipulation of public opinion, and his years in office left a trail of alphabet-soup agencies designed to help manipulate the American people. But Roosevelt hesitated before setting up an official propaganda agency related to the wartime emergency. The legacy of the Committee on Public Information of World War I still loomed forebodingly over the capital. Many Americans opposed to involvement in World War II remained firmly convinced that the nation had been manipulated into the earlier war by propaganda and pointed an accusing finger at the Creel Committee for its role in promoting the war and the intolerance that accompanied it. In place of one agency designed to promote public acceptance of American involvement, FDR tried several approaches to winning that support, each of which failed. The beginning of the war solved Roosevelt's dilemma. The bombing of Pearl Harbor brought interventionists and isolationists together in a grand orgy of patriotism that never could have been achieved by any propaganda agency.[85]

War, however, brought additional problems. Now, obviously, there was a need for information control and for the development of a successful propaganda operation to keep the American people supportive of the war effort. Again because of the World War I experience, Roosevelt decided to separate the two functions. On December 19, 1941, he established the Office of Censorship (OC), which was to deal with the information that was allowed to circulate within the United States during the war. In June 1942, Roosevelt authorized the Office of War Information (OWI). To head both agencies, he selected outstanding journalists. Byron Price, executive news editor of the Associated Press, was named to direct the censorship operation. Elmer Davis, a well-respected radio commentator, headed the OWI.

Price ran the simplest of the two operations. Although his charge from the president involved the censorship of international mail, cable, and wireless operations, most of his efforts were concentrated on the domestic news media. Military and postal officials, under Price's supervision, ran the other operations. In announcing the creation of the censorship office, Roosevelt acknowledged that "all Americans abhor censorship, just as they abhor war. . . . But the experience of this and of all other nations has demonstrated that some degree of censorship is essential in wartime, and we are at war." The goal, said the president, was "that such forms of censorship as are necessary shall be administered effectively and in harmony with the best interests of our free institutions."[86]

Just what the Office of Censorship's role would be during the war was unclear. In the year or so before the war, journalists had been sent mixed signals from the administration as to what its policy might be. At the end of 1940, for instance, Secretary of the Navy Frank Knox sent a confidential letter to all editors and broadcasters asking them not to mention the U.S. Navy in any way unless the Navy asked for or authorized the coverage. The only activity that could be discussed was recruiting. Although editors questioned the need for such restrictions, they acceded to his request, but they refused to obey another appeal from Knox in March 1941. This time, he wanted information about British ships in American ports not to be reported. The nation's journalists felt that the presence of British ships in American ports was obvious to any resident of the affected community, and they refused to ignore the ships' presence.

Whether limitations on information would become commonplace was a question that sparked much debate within journalistic circles. President Roosevelt confused the picture in April 1941 when he told members of the American Society of Newspaper Editors, "Suppression of opinion and censorship of news are among the mortal weapons that dictatorships direct against their own people and against the world. As far as I am concerned there will be no government control of news unless it be of vital military information. . . . It would be a shameful abuse of patriotism to suggest that opinion should be stifled in its service." The coming of war, of course, changed everything, as both the president and the nation's journalists knew it would. Within hours of the attack on Pearl Harbor, Secretary of War Henry L. Stimson used the Espionage Act of 1917 to label as secret "all information relative to the strength, location, designation, composition, and movement of U.S. troops or Army transports outside the continental limits of the United States."[87]

By mid-January 1942, censorship of news stories was firmly in Price's hands. Once again, censorship was to be voluntary, and once again, journalists were intimately involved in making and enforcing the voluntary code.[88] An OC document, which was circulated to all news outlets, reminded editors that "the outcome of the war is a matter of vital personal concern to the future of every American citizen" and that "the security of our armed forces and even of our homes and liberties will be weakened in greater or less degree by every disclosure of information which will help the enemy." Editors were left fairly well on their own to determine what information should be published. As the code said, "a maximum of accomplishment will be attained if editors will ask themselves with respect to any given detail, 'Is this information I would like to have if I were the enemy?' and then act accordingly."[89]

Although the war would mean "some sacrifice of the journalistic enterprise of ordinary times," Price believed "it will not mean a news or editorial black-out. It is the hope and expectation of the Office of Censorship that the columns of American publications will remain the freest in the world, and will tell the story of our national successes and shortcomings accurately and in much detail."[90] The code concluded with suggested restrictions on the reporting of the disposition of troops, ships, planes, and fortifications, as well as warnings against revealing details on war production that might aid saboteurs. If journalists had questions, a staff member at the Office of Censorship was available twenty-four hours a day for consultation. Save for a few exceptions, members of the press and representatives of the Office of Censorship generally agreed on what could be safely disclosed.

Problems often centered more on gathering information than on disseminating data once obtained. The Office of War Information was to procure and distribute reports from the nation's military leaders. Unfortunately, early in the war much of the news was far from encouraging, and military leaders were reluctant to release details of repeated defeats. Hard facts about Pearl Harbor, for example, were difficult to obtain. Although reporters tried to get information out of Hawaii as the attack was in progress, their communications with the mainland were quickly terminated by military authorities.[91] The first official communiqués from the islands indicated that only one old battleship and a destroyer had been sunk, that other ships had been damaged, and that American forces had inflicted heavy losses on the Japanese.

Since Radio Tokyo was reporting the full extent of the damage to the Pacific fleet, the military censorship was designed to keep the enormity of the loss from the American people rather than from the enemy. Shortly after the attack, Secretary of the Navy Knox visited Pearl Harbor and, in a press conference after his return, gave the impression that he was fully disclosing American losses. He announced that the battleship *Arizona* had been lost and that the battleship *Oklahoma* had capsized but could be righted; the rest of the Pacific fleet was fine. In reality, the *Arizona,* the *Oklahoma,* the *California,* the *Nevada,* and the *West Virginia* were all at the bottom of Pearl Harbor. A year later, another version of the disaster was given; this time the Navy said five battleships had been lost but failed to provide details. Full disclosure of the Pearl Harbor disaster awaited the end of the war.[92]

To a certain extent, navy officials were reacting logically to repeated disasters. The Japanese swept across the Pacific taking Singapore, Hong Kong, and Manila. By May 6, Corregidor had fallen. The military response was to cover up the bad news and to highlight individual heroism. Stories of such heroics made for good reading but kept much of the truth from the American people. When the War Department released specific details about the fall of Bataan, the public had not been prepared for the event. The stories of the defenders' individual bravery that had filled the news for weeks had led the public to believe that the Japanese had no chance of taking the fortress.

Elmer Davis faced an almost impenetrable ring of military opposition to disclosure of information. The only standard that Roosevelt had imposed on the dissemination of information was that "war news, to be released, must be true, and must not give aid and comfort to the enemy."[93] Secretary of the Navy Knox, however, told his public relations officers to "do their utmost to secure press cooperation in toning down the gruesome details of sinkings particularly the news regarding tankers."[94] To Davis, the military's approach was at best foolish and at worst counterproductive. "These gentlemen, by temperament and training, were fully and properly aware of the requirements of military security," Davis said. But "they appeared to be less aware that a democracy fighting a total war will fight it more enthusiastically and effectively if it knows what is going on, if it feels that its leaders trust it with as much information as can possibly be given without giving aid and comfort to the enemy."[95]

Only after the navy began winning battles did it become freer with its information, but by then, Davis said, the public had begun to distrust the data it received. By 1943, fewer instances of bad news had to be covered up, and public trust in the military was on the rise. Debates over concealing information recurred after World War II. Military officers would argue that details needed to be kept secret in order to provide room to maneuver and to maintain civilian morale. Members of the press would respond, as had Elmer Davis, that the American people were strong enough to carry on a war despite bad news; that, in fact, they would be more likely to make the necessary sacrifices if told the truth than if fed sugar-coated lies. American political and military leaders, however, have never been willing to take a chance on the fundamental loyalty of their fellow citizens.

On the other hand, few journalists disagreed with keeping some news out of circulation during the war. The press generally agreed to downplay stories about the success of Nazi U-boat raids off the Atlantic coast. The Office of Censorship was active here in trying to keep the information suppressed. Many of the ships, often heavily laden merchant vessels, went down in sight of land; survivors frequently made it to shore. But the U-boat captains, argued the OC leadership, could not be sure how successful they had been—how many ships were sunk, how much tonnage was lost, how many lives were taken. Since the submarines could remain offshore for hours trying to pick up hints of their success from American broadcast stations, the simplest news stories could provide the enemy with data that could be collected in no other way. Although they did not like toning down coverage of these disasters, most journalists cooperated with the Office of Censorship. These problems occurred only in the early months of 1942; what the journalistic attitude would have been had they been more long-lasting is unknown.[96]

Journalists, not surprisingly, were not always cooperative with authorities, and at times they became quite incensed by government censorship tactics. Perhaps one of the most unpleasant encounters between the government and the nation's journalists came over the trial of ten German saboteurs. The saboteurs had been dropped off near Jacksonville, Florida, in June 1942. They were equipped with explosives, forged documents, cash, and the layouts of several industrial plants. The mission was disclosed because of several miscues by similar saboteurs who had landed off the coast of New York. Within two weeks, the ten men had been picked up by the FBI. The story of the capture was released, and journalists were hot on the trail of additional information. The men were charged with entering the country in disguise for the purpose of waging war against the United States. The case was considered so important that Attorney General Biddle handled the prosecution himself before a military court. Journalists smelled a story and were waiting to cover the trial.[97]

The order came down rather quickly that the trial was to be closed to the press. American journalists protested loudly, and OWI head Davis jumped into the fray. Officials at the War and Justice departments believed that press coverage of the trial would disclose secret counterespionage methods that had helped bring about the arrests. Although Davis believed that position "deserved consideration;" still, he stressed, "it seemed that a limited coverage, with reporters excluded when certain secret techniques were under discussion, would satisfy the legitimate public interest in a story which had been blown up far beyond its real value by some of those who were now trying to bury it." Concerned about the wild speculation that the trial was engendering in the press, Davis appealed to Roosevelt, who agreed to allow photographers limited opportunities to take pictures and to have the president of the court issue a summary of each day's proceedings.[98] At one point, the trial proceedings were suspended, and eleven carefully chosen journalists were allowed into the courtroom for fifteen minutes to observe the defendants and to see some of the exhibits. They were then ushered out, and the trial resumed with the press on the outside once more.

Journalists had difficulty reporting one of the war's major naval battles as well, again because of governmental action. The story dealt with the tremendous American naval victory at Midway, which occurred in June 1942. One reporter, Robert J. Casey of the *Chicago Daily News,* was on the scene of the battle and sent in an eyewitness account, but military censors held the story up for more than two weeks. When the story did break, it was on the front page of the *Chicago Tribune,* which was run by President Roosevelt's most hated foe in the journalistic world, Colonel Robert R. McCormick. The *Tribune* was immediately chastised for its coverage by the Office of Censorship, and before long, the Justice Department leveled charges under the Espionage Act.[99]

Governmental reaction to the *Tribune*'s coverage of the story led most other American newspapers to discount the information altogether. The problem, however, was not with the fundamental data about the victory; the bone of contention was a sidebar story. The headline over that secondary article read, "Navy Had Word of Jap Plan to Strike at Sea, Knew Dutch Harbor Was Feint." The story, written by Chicago-based correspondent Stanley Johnston, appeared with a Washington, D.C., dateline and began by saying, "The strength of the Japanese forces which the American Navy is battling somewhere west of Midway Island in what is believed to be the greatest naval battle of the war, was well known in American naval circles several days before the battle began, reliable sources in naval intelligence disclosed here tonight."[100] Government officials alleged that if the Japanese saw that story they would be able to deduce that American naval intelligence officers had broken the secret Japanese code. Then the enemy would change the code, leaving American forces at a distinct disadvantage.

The *Tribune* responded that Johnston had recently returned from assignment aboard naval vessels in the South Pacific and that he had written the story based on knowledge gained there and on his familiarity with *Jane's Fighting Ships,* an encyclopedic volume that describes in detail the world's navies. Putting the two factors together, Johnston was able to deduce which Japanese ships had participated in the encounter and their actual line of battle. Johnston's effort was quite an accomplishment, according to government officials, because he had not been present at the battle, and even if he had been present, he would not have been able to gather such information because the Battle of Midway was fought primarily by naval air power with neither side seeing the ships of the other. In actuality, Johnston was lying.

During his time in the Pacific, he had been aboard the USS *Lexington,* which had been heavily damaged at the Battle of the Coral Sea. He and other survivors were picked up by other ships for transportation back to safety. His efforts to win the confidence of the officers and men aboard the USS *Barnett* was facilitated by Johnston's bravery in helping to rescue sailors trapped below decks on the burning *Lexington*. In fact, some naval officers wanted to cite Johnston for his valor. Thus, while on board the *Barnett,* Johnston was quite a celebrity. He and the officers and men aboard the ship shared a great deal of information; Johnston even managed to see a secret dispatch from Admiral Chester Nimitz that itemized the strength of the Japanese fleet that was near Midway. The navy knew the number and kinds of ships present in the Japanese armada through intercepted and decoded messages. Johnston's story was based directly on this dispatch and even included misspellings that had been in the admiral's message. The story was even more dangerous, said the military, because it carried a false Washington dateline that made it seem as if the facts had come from government officials. Johnston exacerbated the situation by attributing his information to "reliable sources in naval intelligence."

Although the actual prosecution of the *Tribune* rested on Johnston's story, its roots went back to the 1930s battles between Roosevelt and McCormick. Government attorneys believed their case to be airtight. As the *Tribune*'s employees moved closer to their date with the grand jury, the newspaper charged that the "administration which for years has been seeking by one sly means or another, but always with complete futility, to intimidate this newspaper has finally despaired of all other means and is now preparing criminal prosecutions." In fact, the publication said, "We take pride in the knowledge that the administration was moved to this action because of its previous failures to scare us or cajole us into surrender of our independence."[101]

In the end, the *Tribune*'s pride remained intact, and the president was once again frustrated in his desire to punish Colonel McCormick. At the last minute, the navy decided not to allow its cryptography experts to testify. Naval intelligence had decided that the Japanese had not read Johnston's story; the enemy was still using the same code that it had before the Battle of Midway. Testimony before the grand jury and in a trial, especially one in which employees of the *Chicago Tribune* served as defendants, would have given the Japanese information that they did not already have. Colonel McCormick viewed the dropping of charges as a great victory for his publication, and the navy suffered considerable public embarrassment as it was unable to explain why the prosecution had been begun in the first place and why it had been dropped. The only real change that resulted from the encounter came in the Office of Censorship's list of prohibited subjects for discussion. Before the Johnston incident, journalists had been allowed to comment upon the movement of enemy forces; now, the code was changed to forbid reporting on the movement of both Allied and enemy forces.

The Office of Censorship's voluntary code, of course, applied only to materials obtained and printed within the United States. Correspondents attached to military forces overseas had their stories carefully screened by military censors attached to the various theaters of operation. Coverage of the war again was uneven. One of the problems, quite naturally, rested in the global nature of the conflict. No newspaper, broadcasting network, or news agency could afford to have correspondents everywhere. So, Americans got much of their news through official communiqués funneled through Elmer Davis's OWI. When reporters were on the scene, they often fell prey to the traditional belief that battles made news while behind-the-lines information was not terribly useful. This behavior left American audiences at home unaware of misbehavior by their troops, including the massive black market operations that a number of military personnel ran. The need to stay on the good side of commanding officers also led to the suppression of certain harmful information. The most outrageous example of such repression centered on the acquiescence by accredited correspondents to a request from General Dwight D. Eisenhower that they not transmit information about General George C. Patton's striking an enlisted man. Eisenhower said releasing the information would harm the morale of soldiers in the field. The incident finally was reported stateside when columnist Drew Pearson found out about it from a soldier who had returned home.[102]

As might be expected, the role of a war correspondent abroad still was not clear during World War II. Perhaps General Eisenhower best explained the military's view of the correspondent when he said, "Public opinion wins war. I have always considered as quasi-staff officers, correspondents accredited to my headquarters."[103] Reporters who were treated in this way certainly did become arms of the military information machine in reporting the war. In addition, many reporters found military censorship helped their work. A *New York Times* reporter who covered World War II and Vietnam, for instance, is on record as saying that censorship facilitated information gathering. "As long as all copy was submitted to censors before transmission, people in the field, from generals down, felt free to discuss top secret material with reporters," said Drew Middleton. "On three trips to Vietnam I found generals and everyone else far more wary of talking to reporters precisely because there was no censorship."[104]

In later wars, the relationship between the press and the military would become more adversarial and would be patterned more after press-government relations in the civilian sector. When considered strictly from the standpoint of the need to provide information to the American people so that they can properly exercise their roles in democratic government, the adversarial attitude of the press seems more appropriate. When considered solely from the military's perspective of the need to maintain morale and to keep information out of enemy hands, however, press support of the government seems more appropriate. But maintaining morale is often a spurious reason for seeking blind obedience from the press and the people. As Elmer Davis tried to explain early in World War II, such an approach greatly underestimates the ability and the willingness of the American people to support their government when told the truth. And, as the experience of World War II showed, when the military provides slanted information to the public, distrust increases; when honest data is provided, more support is generated.

During World War II, media cooperation was the rule rather than the exception. Byron Price had few complaints about the way in which the press performed during the war years. Especially noteworthy was the way in which the government was able to keep the development of the atomic bomb out of the news. This scientific project was so secret that the Office of Censorship did not know of its existence until late March 1943. Even then, only the bare facts were passed along because newspapers in areas where construction projects related to the bomb were under way had started to write about those activities. Army officers demanded a blackout of all news relating in any way to the bomb's development. Office of Censorship officials replied that they simply did not work that way. Much of the information being reported locally came from official public records dealing with land transactions and related matters. One of the primary rules under which the office had operated since its beginning was that if the reporter had obtained information from an "official" source, the data could be printed. Public records certainly fell into that category.[105]

Office of Censorship officials, however, had a solution to the problem. They sent a special memorandum to all media outlets requesting "that nothing be published or broadcast about 'new or secret military weapons. . . . experiments.'" In particular, the memo asked for no circulation of information relating to "production or utilization of atom smashing, atomic energy, atomic fission, atomic splitting, or any of their equivalents." Journalists were not to write about "the use for military purposes of radium or radioactive materials, heavy water, high voltage discharge equipment, cyclotrons." And their stories were to exclude any mention of "the following elements or any of their compounds: polonium, uranium, ytterbium, hafnium, protactinium, radium, rhenium, thorium, deuterium."[106] The memorandum aroused no undue interest among journalists; little was written or broadcast about any of the forbidden topics. On occasion, slips occurred. A radio commentator, for example, featured a story on atomic energy one day. OC officials discovered that he knew little about the subject but wanted to talk about something that would scare the Germans into surrendering. In another instance, the comic book hero Superman became involved in an adventure that called on him to survive a bombardment of electrons emitted by a cyclotron. That story line quickly ceased after the Office of Censorship talked to the artist. As research on the bomb continued, news stories that touched at least on the fringes of the subject appeared. Although army officials in charge of the Manhattan Project worried about the slightest leak, the Office of Censorship, generally speaking, thought the press had kept the development of the bomb a secret.

Secrecy was maintained even after the army set off a test blast in the New Mexican desert in July 1945. In case anyone asked about the explosions, military officials released a cover story saying that an ammunition dump had blown up with no loss of life or significant property damage. After the bomb was first dropped on Japan on August 6, the Office of Censorship rescinded its request that the media refrain from discussing atomic energy. The office did ask for continued restraint in stories involving specifics about scientific formulas, construction of the bomb, research sites, and the like.

The success that the Office of Censorship enjoyed in maintaining a virtual news blackout on the bomb's development led to a variety of problems after the war. Almost as soon as the first bomb was dropped, a movement appeared within the country to ban the future use and development of atomic weapons. Individuals active in that movement later would claim that America's love affair with the bomb, which lasted for years after the war, was directly due to the Office of Censorship's energetic cooperation in keeping details about the bomb's development and the ramifications of its use confidential. Data about the effects of fallout and the long-term impact of such explosions on people and places, for example, were concealed from the American public, thus, antinuclear forces would claim, rendering Americans unable to make an informed decision about proceeding with the development of nuclear weapons. That debate between freedom of expression and atomic energy advocates rested in the future. As the war drew to a close, the Office of Censorship's activities in relation to the development of the bomb clearly were acceptable.

Although most of the Office of Censorship's work during World War II focused on hard news events as described above, its officials did, on occasion, move into less familiar territory. Radio broadcasts, for instance, posed new and unusual challenges. Information carried over the airwaves would travel for long distances, and censors feared that enemy agents could use those broadcasts to transmit messages. Such concerns led to unusual restrictions on programming. Prior to the war, stations played certain songs upon the request of listeners, and impromptu interview shows were popular. Interview shows virtually were banned for the duration of the war because of the possibility that an enemy agent might include a message and because service personnel home on leave might let some important information slip inadvertently. Music request shows could no longer respond to appeals by telephone or telegraph; now the requests had to come in by mail, and the stations could not promise to broadcast songs at any given time on any specific day.[107]

The Office of Censorship also had limited responsibility for material that came out of the Hollywood studios. As far as motion pictures were concerned, OC officials were to keep films that they considered harmful to the American war effort from leaving the country. The term harmful, in this context, was broadly defined. "Labor, class or other disturbances since 1917 which might be distorted into enemy propaganda generally are prohibited for export," said the official rules. If the scenes were only "incident to the main theme of a picture" that was otherwise considered "not harmful to the war effort," then permission for export might be granted. The OC was also concerned about lawlessness in motion pictures and said "likewise scenes of lawlessness or disorder in which order is restored and the offenders punished may be approved if lawlessness is not the main theme and is not the major part of the production." The image that the motion pictures presented of allies was the focus of another restriction, which said, "United Nations armed forces should not be burlesqued, held up to ridicule or shown as unworthy representatives of their government as the main theme or major part of any dramatic production."[108] An official board of review inspected each film before certifying it for export.

The life of a Hollywood producer might have been much easier had he been responsible only to the Office of Censorship during the war. Unfortunately, the

Office of War Information, because its mandate included the maintenance of public morale, also played a role in the production of wartime motion pictures. The heads of the movie studios entered the war after years of being buffeted by international events. A hefty percentage of their income from each motion picture stemmed from foreign distribution, and as the war developed, foreign restrictions on film production had mounted. Germany, for instance, imposed rules forbidding the showing of films that included Jewish actors and generally limited the number of foreign films that could be displayed in the country annually. For several years, Hollywood attempted to comply with the vicissitudes of the foreign film market and produced fairly innocuous films. By 1940, however, only the British Commonwealth remained as a major foreign market, and Hollywood turned its attention to making movies that would sell there.[109]

Films supporting intervention soon began appearing, much to the dismay of isolationists. From this era come such classics as *Yank in the R.A.F., International Squadron,* and *Confessions of a Nazi Spy.* These productions led Congress to investigate the propaganda content of Hollywood films in 1941. After Pearl Harbor, prowar films were desired, and the OWI began displaying interest in the content of American motion pictures. Few films considered to have a war-related theme in the six months immediately after Pearl Harbor were acceptable to OWI representatives in Hollywood. Films, said the OWI, should help advance American war aims, should present a true view of the enemy, and should depict the American people properly abroad. Having Tarzan defeat a group of Nazis who had invaded his jungle simply was not acceptable.

By the summer of 1942, the OWI issued an information manual for the motion-picture industry. The first question that the government officials said producers should ask themselves when they began a new film was "Will this picture help win the war?" If the film was not war-related, producers should ask "Will it harm the war effort by creating a false picture of America, her allies, or the world we live in?"[110] To forward its goals, the OWI wanted powers similar to those held by the Motion Picture Production Code Office. OWI representatives wanted script approval and wanted to intervene in the production of movies whenever they felt it appropriate or necessary. OWI representatives soon became too demanding, and producers became irritable and uncooperative. In addition, the OWI lacked statutory authority to enforce its demands. In order to accomplish its ends, OWI representatives joined forces with OC personnel, who were charged with approving films for export. In this manner, the OWI film crew implemented many of its goals for motion-picture production. The producers, although they heartily disliked OWI intervention, wanted and needed the foreign markets that the OC controlled. This fact, then, became a powerful weapon in turning the motion-picture industry into a major cog in the nation's propaganda machinery.

To a large extent, the OWI picture of America was one in which everyone was happy, brave, trustworthy, and loyal. Support of the war effort was universal in the OWI's world, and all Americans were strongly behind the liberal policies of the Roosevelt administration. In addition, American allies had similar noteworthy characteristics. One film that personified the OWI image was the Acad-

emy Award–winning *Mrs. Miniver,* in which citizens of a close ally were shown
as withstanding incredible pressure while upholding all the good values in life.
Among the allies that the OWI encouraged film makers to praise in their films
were the Russians. Unfortunately, World War II–era films that met this request
became targets of committees investigating subversive activities after the war.
Among the films that were later criticized for being pro-Communist were *Action
in the North Atlantic,* starring Humphrey Bogart, which was so labeled because
the Soviets were depicted as heroic and friendly, and *Mission to Moscow,* which
also showed the Russians in a positive light and was based on a best-seller by the
former U.S. ambassador to the Soviet Union. In addition to promoting certain
kinds of films, OWI/OC personnel worked hard to discourage certain movies.
High on the list of special targets of OWI/OC workers were films that made light
of the war effort or that showed America and Americans in a bad light. The former category included wartime comedies and light-hearted romances; the latter
included gangster movies, which were always popular with movie audiences but
not with OWI/OC reviewers.

Using American feature films to cast the United States in a favorable light was
just one small part of a growing American propaganda machine. When World
War II began, the United States was the only major player without a full-time
propaganda ministry. Propaganda activities had always been looked upon with
great suspicion in the United States, and Franklin Roosevelt had hesitated before
setting up such an operation. In establishing the Office of War Information, however, he created that program under the cover of dispensing information. The
director of the Office of War Information was told to "formulate and carry out,
through the use of press, radio, motion pictures and other facilities, information
programs designed to facilitate the development of an informed and intelligent
understanding, at home and abroad" of various wartime activities and policies.[111] The role of information dispenser came naturally to Davis, a former journalist, but shaping domestic public opinion was out of his realm of expertise.[112]

Domestic propaganda operations almost immediately became troublesome.
The question soon became one of whether telling Americans the unvarnished
truth was the way to build morale or whether the public had to be sold on the
war. Before the United States entered the war, Archibald MacLeish's Office of
Facts and Figures had assembled a handpicked group of writers and scholars
who turned out intelligent, sophisticated materials arguing for American intervention. With the establishment of the OWI, these writers came under new leadership, and they soon found that the official approach to the war had changed.
Rather than continuing to appeal to the American people as intelligent adults,
the writers claimed that material aimed at twelve-year-olds was being turned out
by former advertising copywriters who were trying to sell the war as they would
soft drinks. The writers, appalled at this approach, resigned en masse, complaining publicly that the domestic operations of the OWI were now controlled by
"high-pressure promoters who prefer slick salesmanship to honest information."[113]

The quarrel within the OWI's domestic operation became public about the
time that Congress grew increasingly interested in the agency's activities. The

1942 elections had put more Republicans and anti-Roosevelt Democrats into office, most of whom were determined not to allow the OWI to deify the president or to establish the groundwork for a fourth try for the White House in 1944. In the summer of 1943, Congress greatly decreased the agency's domestic budget, leaving only enough staff to serve as a conduit for news from government agencies. The ability of the OWI to reach the American people was eliminated because, according to Davis, "it was contended by some Congressmen that the government had no right to use the taxpayers' money for a statement of views with which some taxpayers disagreed."[114] With the congressional budget-cutting action, the OWI was essentially out of the domestic propaganda business.

While the domestic branch of the OWI was foundering, the agency's foreign propaganda program went forward with little interruption. This effort consisted primarily of broadcasts sent into enemy-held territories by shortwave transmitters. The goal was to lead listeners to react positively to the United States and negatively to the enemy. Most individuals involved in the foreign operation believed that transmitting news was the key to winning friends. Generally, the focus remained on news throughout the war, although in certain instances the information provided was selectively biased. At the close of the war, government officials debated the appropriateness of attempting to influence foreign opinion. Any hope of abandoning the foreign propaganda battle disappeared with the onset of the cold war.

Despite American involvement in a full-scale propaganda effort, the United States actively promoted international freedom of information at the close of World War II. The campaign was launched at the behest of American newspaper editors who had long believed that one of the major problems in the world was the inability of nations to truly communicate with one another. The topic of breaking down barriers to the gathering and dissemination of news had come up at the end of World War I, but nothing had been done to promote the cause. World War II was still raging when members of the American Society of Newspaper Editors launched their crusade to promote international freedom of information. The editors argued that if governmental barriers to freedom of expression were lowered, the world's people would not again be led into war because they would know each other better. Their goal was to see clauses incorporating freedom of the press included in postwar peace treaties and in the charter for the United Nations.[115]

The crusade for international freedom of the press continued for several years after the war. The period immediately after the war was a heady one for Americans, many of whom agreed with the editors that the world could be spared future conflict if American values were made universal. Against this background, government leaders, who were strong promoters of the idea of remaking the world in America's image, cooperated with journalists in their particular campaign. The alliance between the two parties often was uneasy, given the history of mistrust that had been built up between newspapers and government officials during the Roosevelt presidency. Making the joint effort somewhat easier was the fact that the journalists involved were editors rather than publishers, who often had incurred the president's wrath. The crusade met with some initial success, most of which may have been based on the fact that foreign leaders saw cooperation with the campaign as necessary to obtain American reconstruction money. As time passed and the cold war deepened, most nations of the world, including America's closest allies, decided that the system of freedom of the press practiced in the United States simply was not for them. American journalists were too disrespectful, too intrusive, and too obnoxious. In addition, many nations believed that American journalists were far too irresponsible to serve as role models. Any effort to turn the world's journalists into carbon copies of U.S. reporters was unacceptable. Nor were other nations willing to accept the other part of the American plan—the opening of their territories to unimpeded news gathering by American journalists. At best, some nations offered limited acceptance of some portions of the editors' plans—if the Americans, in turn, would agree to an international code of ethics that would have limited some of the more disagreeable practices. American editors would accept no such restrictions, and the international campaign collapsed.

Their efforts would come back to haunt the editors in later years as Third World nations in particular began to campaign for international agreements that would restrict journalistic behavior. Once again the primary targets were American correspondents, who leaders of other nations considered were hostile to their national interests. Opposition to what became known as the New World Information Order was quick in developing, with American reporters denouncing it as restrictive, reprehensible, and totally unacceptable. Some editors could almost be heard asking how foreigners could presume to tell Americans how to run their journalistic enterprises, while forgetting the American effort to tell other countries how to run their programs after World War II. These experiences revealed the culture-bound nature of freedom of the press. The American system is unique and can flourish only in the United States, where it has developed over the years. When even American business, political, and community leaders often are unsure about whether they want the free press to continue in its present mode in this country, how U.S. journalists ever thought they could transplant their notions of a free press to foreign countries remains a great mystery.

The only solution to the questions raised by the U.S. campaign is that the experiences of World War II were so positive for American journalists that they wanted to share their rich heritage. Indeed, anyone who lived through the Second World War would have been compelled to agree that freedom of expression had finally taken its rightful place in the hierarchy of values to which Americans paid honor. The Supreme Court of the United States under Charles Evans Hughes and Harlan Fiske Stone was greatly responsible for the esteem now accorded freedom of expression. When coupled with the determination of Attorney General Francis Biddle to block a recurrence of the World War I atrocities against dissidents, the nation did indeed experience a glorious period for freedom of expression in the war years.

Unfortunately, the positive impact of the 1930s and early 1940s on freedom of expression was not destined to survive the war. Even before the fighting stopped, Franklin Roosevelt had died. To his successor, Harry S. Truman, would go the task of naming the next chief justice of the United States. Fred M.

Vinson, who took over the post in 1946, had quite a different attitude on freedom of expression than his predecessors. When faced with a burgeoning cold war, Vinson's belief in the need for government to survive at the expense of freedom of expression moved to the fore. Thus, the Supreme Court, which might have been the only government agency capable of stopping much of the anti-Communist fervor of the next fifteen years or so, joined local, state, and federal officials to stamp out the menace of communism. The result was that recent advances in the area of freedom of expression all but disappeared.

CHAPTER 7

★ ★ ★

Combating the Red Menace:
Freedom of Expression
in the Cold War

Although freedom of expression survived World War II relatively unscathed, the right to voice dissident beliefs disappeared along with many other traditional American values soon thereafter. Exactly when the cold war began is hard to pinpoint. For our purposes, the fact that the relationship between the United States and the Soviet Union began cooling in the closing days of the shooting war will do. As World War II wound down, the Soviets occupied much of Eastern Europe and gave every indication that they intended to establish Communist governments there. Even the hint that the Soviets had plans for territorial expansion and spreading communism was sufficient to rouse the foes of communism in the United States. As the Soviets sent more signals of their postwar ambitions, American anti-Communists propelled the nation into a frenzy of suspicion, fear, hatred, and retribution. Before long, all three branches of the federal government, as well as state and local governments and numerous voluntary associations, competed to show the depth of their patriotism.

The targets of this loyalty fever, which consumed the nation for almost ten years, were American Communists, or at least so this generation's super-patriots said. In reality, the quarry was anyone who had ever been connected in any way with the Communist Party of the United States of America (CPUSA). Using this broad definition, investigators on all levels of government flushed out both card-carrying Communists and individuals who had participated in popular front organizations in the mid-1930s when communism was socially acceptable and politically tolerable. Before the nightmare was over, the dragnet had swept up individuals who had simply signed petitions supporting causes that Communists also backed. Trade unionism, racial integration, and international coexistence became forbidden subjects. Even liberals without Communist affiliations found themselves fighting to survive this onslaught. Only a vocal and active anti-Communist stance could provide protection. Because the danger was so great and liberals were so concerned with survival themselves, persons caught up in the anti-Communist inquiries pretty much had to fend for themselves. The period ended with hundreds of people jailed and with careers, families, and relationships in ruins.

Often termed the McCarthy era after Senator Joseph McCarthy, Republican of Wisconsin, the attack on Communists in the United States began long before the senator started his crusade in 1950. Martin Dies, Democrat from Texas, had kept the House Un-American Activities Committee (HUAC) alive and well during World War II. In many ways, the anti-Communist campaign of the postwar period was closely tied to efforts by conservatives to discredit many Roosevelt reforms. Showing that the administration had been infiltrated with and influenced by Communists seemed the surest way to accomplish this end. One of Dies's favorite techniques, which was copied by innumerable Communist fighters who followed, was the generation of lists of names of people and organizations that he considered subversive. He once sent a list of more than 1,000 names of suspect federal employees to Attorney General Francis Biddle only to have the attorney general report that just two persons had been fired and one disciplined as a result. In addition, the attorney general chided Dies for spending federal money on unproven charges. Dies condemned Biddle's remarks and continued to produce his lists, which usually were culled from the mailing lists of suspect organizations.[1]

Those lists played an integral part in Dies's most sensational and successful attack on alleged Communists in government during the war. Rebuffed by Attorney General Biddle in 1943, Dies sought to remove individuals on his lists from their jobs via legislative action. His proposals did not call for their firing but demanded that Congress specifically refuse to authorize the expenditure of money for their salaries. That year, the House amended its version of the appropriations bill to ban the use of government funds to pay three employees. When the Senate balked, the House agreed to a compromise that required the president to appoint the three men to their jobs and to have the Senate confirm them in office after an investigation of their loyalty. Franklin Roosevelt, who needed the money in the measure, signed the bill, although he denounced the rider. The case ultimately made its way to the Supreme Court, where Justice Hugo L. Black, writing for the majority, declared the law a bill of attainder because Congress had declared individuals guilty of an offense without a judicial trial.[2]

Although the effort to rid the national government of allegedly disloyal individuals failed during the war, conservatives watched for opportunities to continue the anti-Communist crusade. The furor over the *Amerasia* papers as the war was winding down provided one such occasion. In March and April 1945, agents from the Office of Strategic Services, the precursor of the Central Intelligence Agency, surreptitiously entered the magazine's offices and copied government documents that were in the publication's files. Some of the papers were marked "Top Secret" and dealt with American policies and plans for the Far East. *Amerasia,* a magazine that focused on developments in that area of the world, was founded in 1936, just as popular front interest in China began. Its connection with Communists was hazy at best, but the government was concerned about the classified documents found in the magazine's files. Arrests were made on June 6, 1945. The government wanted to prosecute *Amerasia* editors for espionage, but no proof could be found that the documents had been given to the Soviets. In addition, almost all of the government's evidence had been gathered through illegal searches and was inadmissible in court. Charges eventually were lowered to unlawful possession of government documents, and minimum fines were imposed.[3]

The *Amerasia* case, however, had grave implications. Top secret government documents had been found in the possession of a suspect magazine. How could the United States know that other secrets had not been passed to the Soviets? In addition, a State Department employee, John S. Service, was implicated in the affair. Service's involvement became especially important for anti-Communists after China fell to the Communists; he and other so-called China hands at the State Department were blamed for failing to keep the United States abreast of events in that country. The House of Representatives so feared the burgeoning red scare that, in 1945, it made the Committee on Un-American Activities a regular standing committee.

By 1946, fears about Soviet intentions and American security escalated. In February 1946, for instance, Canadian officials charged twenty-two people with trying to steal atomic secrets for the Soviets. About the same time, J. Edgar Hoover told President Harry S. Truman that Elizabeth Bentley and Whittaker Chambers, two former Communist agents, were telling the Federal Bureau of Investigation (FBI) about Soviet espionage in the United States. And in March 1946, former British Prime Minister Winston Churchill, speaking at a small college in Missouri, announced that "from Stettin in the Baltic, to Trieste in the Adriatic, an iron curtain has descended across the Continent."[4] With these developments, the pressure increased on President Truman to fight Communist infiltration.

The most ardent red hunters argued that Communist organizations, at the least, should be registered, that unions with Communist officers should be punished, that public employment should be denied to Communists, and that the immigration and naturalization laws should be revised to exclude Communists. Before long, these demands would become law, but Truman, for the moment, moved slowly. He initiated more screening of federal employees and authorized increased surveillance of the American people. Diplomatically, he became increasingly inflexible toward the Soviets. Truman's growing hostility toward the Soviet Union led Secretary of Commerce Henry A. Wallace to resign in September 1946 and to launch what would turn into both a third-party candidacy for the presidency in 1948 and the last gasp of public liberalism for the better part of a decade.

Truman helped to push the nation into another great red scare after the 1946 elections. Republicans, campaigning against the Roosevelt reforms and for an intensive attack on domestic communism, captured both houses of Congress. The president, stung by charges that he was not concerned enough about the Communist threat, responded with an executive order establishing a temporary commission on employee loyalty on November 25, 1946. The commission was to create standards for investigating persons employed by the government or seeking such employment and for dismissing individuals who were "disloyal or subversive."[5]

Although the focus of the commission's work was the federal employee who had connections, past or present, with the Communist party, individuals with aberrant ideas or certain personal characteristics also attracted attention. Neither was there much consideration as to whether a person could maintain a non-sensitive job regardless of possible loyalty problems. Commission members also tended to consider personal weaknesses such as drunkenness, homosexuality, and womanizing as dangerous. Individuals opposed to the peacetime draft, the Truman Doctrine, the Marshall Plan, or the Berlin Airlift, or who favored peace or integration of the races fell under suspicion just as quickly as persons who had Communist connections. As a military intelligence officer on the president's special commission said, "A liberal is only a hop, skip, and a jump from a Communist. A Communist starts as a liberal."[6] Before this red scare was finished, anyone holding dissident views had learned to be extremely careful in expressing them.

Truman's special commission of November 1946 gave way to a permanent executive branch loyalty program in March 1947. According to the executive order establishing it, the United States must be protected "against infiltration of disloyal persons into the ranks of its employees, and equal protection from unfounded accusations of disloyalty must be afforded the loyal employees of the Government." Individuals were to be investigated prior to employment and as a necessary condition for continued service. Standards for dismissal were established, and provisions for appeals were created. Grounds for dismissal included participating in sabotage, espionage, treason, sedition, advocacy of sedition or revolution, and disclosure of confidential information. In addition, a person could be fired for "membership in, affiliation with or sympathetic association with any foreign or domestic organization, association, movement, group or combination of persons" designated by the attorney general as "totalitarian, fascist, communist, or subversive, or as having adopted a policy of advocating or approving the commission of acts of force or violence to deny other persons their rights under the Constitution of the United States, or as seeking to alter the form of government of the United States by unconstitutional means."[7]

Regardless of whether the nation's loyalty program stemmed from political expediency, irrational fear, or actual danger, it was in place. Soon the national operation would be copied on state and local levels, and public employees' beliefs on numerous subjects would be examined closely. Conformity again became important for maintaining government employment. And as with previous experiences, some thoughtful members of society wondered about the effect of this program on the quality of public employees, but such concerns, if raised, were disregarded in the rush to protect the government from Communist infiltration.

Administration of the loyalty program was a nightmare. After several months of training workers and setting up guidelines, the first inquiries began in October 1947. In many ways, the system was prejudiced against the employee. The identity of individuals who raised questions about a co-worker's loyalty, for example, generally remained confidential. Most loyalty inquiries focused on the employee's thoughts and associations rather than on his or her actions. If the worker had at one time been a member of the Communist party or of a Communist-front organization, loyalty board members assumed continuing association and required the employee to disprove that belief. Even facing a loyalty hearing served as a significant blot upon an individual's reputation. In the beginning, if an employee was fired on loyalty grounds, potential employers seeking background information would be told. If the employee left government work before the investigation was completed, prospective employers would be told that as well. Thus, loyalty investigations not only plagued the workers within the federal bureaucracy but followed them outside as well.

What was even worse, perhaps, was that few cases were brought on the basis of treason, sedition, or advocacy of the overthrow of the government. Most of the investigations were initiated because of the employee's connection with an organization on the attorney general's list. This ubiquitous list had been instrumental in deciding the fate of undesirable individuals at least since World War I. Originally, the list of organizations whose members were simply too dangerous for American society to tolerate was a threat only to aliens. As World War II approached, the list became legislatively mandated and included native fascist and Communist organizations. Truman's executive order establishing a loyalty clearinghouse for federal employees led to the creation of the most comprehensive of attorney general's lists.[8]

Criteria for inclusion on the list were not revealed, but the list appeared to be primarily a compilation of groups condemned by other organizations. The 1947 list, for instance, had headings for totalitarian, fascist, Communist, and "subversive" groups, as well as for organizations that have "adopted a policy of advocating or approving the commission of acts of force and violence to deny others their rights under the Constitution of the United States" and organizations that "seek to alter the form of government of the United States by unconstitutional means." More than 175 organizations, not counting subsidiary groups or repeated mentions under different subheadings, eventually appeared on that list.[9] In addition to the attorney general's list, which was the most famous, the House Committee on Un-American Activities maintained its own list, as did the FBI. The lists drew from each other, and all grew substantially as the period progressed.

As the loyalty program developed, the organizations listed became less likely to take action against the United States and more likely to advocate unacceptable ideas. List making was shrouded in secrecy or, perhaps, confusion. Agencies of government used each other's lists so often that no one could tell who made the original decision to include a particular organization. Errors occurred, and excising an incorrectly listed group was almost impossible. All that was certain was that any connection with a named organization could lead to a loyalty inquiry. As time passed, a family connection with a listed organization was sufficient to cause the employee trouble as well. The cold war's overriding concern about loyalty almost destroyed the inherent right of Americans to form voluntary associations to accomplish desired ends.[10]

Fundamental to these persecutions was the firm belief that the nation's survival was at stake. In the face of such a threat, all other claims faded to insignificance. The right to maintain employment, for instance, was minor in light of the perceived Communist challenge to American society. As the Loyalty Review Board said in its first official statement, "No person has an inherent or Constitutional right to public employment. Public employment is a privilege, not a right."[11] And governments could condition this privilege as they chose. By March 1952, the board reported that 4 million employees had been checked. Charges had been brought in slightly more than 9,000 instances. Just under 3,000 hearings had been held since late 1947. With all of that work, only 378 people had been fired or had not been hired.[12]

The country, however, was in a frenzy over the danger posed by Communists. J. Edgar Hoover, who helped to fan the flames of intolerance, told Congress in 1950 that the FBI estimated CPUSA strength at that time at 54,000 members. But, he stressed, card-carrying, dues-paying membership was not a true indication of Communist strength. "Party leaders themselves boast that for every party member there are ten others who follow the party line and who are ready, willing, and able to do the party's work," Hoover said. "In other words, there is a potential fifth column of 540,000 people dedicated to this philosophy."[13] To confirmed anti-Communists, the magnitude of the threat required action.

To the few critics of the Communist hunters who were brave enough to comment publicly, such fears were exaggerated and unsubstantiated. Even if 540,000 people could be enlisted in the Communist cause, they would easily be swallowed up in the total population. In addition, internationally, Communists seized power only in a time of great national unrest and instability, which did not then characterize the United States. Any action by Communists and their adherents against the nation could easily be put down by police and military forces, liberal critics argued, contending that only after the deed had taken place—if it ever took place—should the government move against the Communists. Then, the laws of treason could logically and reasonably be enforced, and the nation would be spared the stifling of dissent that accompanied attempts to flush out Communists. Although there was a certain logic to these arguments, few bona fide red hunters listened, and few liberals were courageous enough to voice their concerns.

Even as the president's loyalty program got under way in 1947, the House Committee on Un-American Activities became a major force in American life. In spring 1947, the committee, now under the direction of J. Parnell Thomas, Republican of New Jersey, started its investigation into that hotbed of disloyalty and danger to the United States—the movie community in Hollywood. Motion-picture industry workers had indeed participated in many popular fronts during the 1930s, a time of great political activism in Hollywood. The movie community even included some card-carrying Communists, although most persons who flirted with party membership in the 1930s had dropped out. Some individuals, primarily film writers, remained firmly committed to the party, and the Communist hunters of Washington feared that movie scripts served as subtle propaganda that would turn the American people into Communist sympathizers. Congressional concern completely ignored the number of reviews that each script underwent before it became a movie. The Motion Picture Production Code was still in effect, and the chance of anything even slightly pro-Communist getting through those censors was slight indeed. But the concern persisted as the committee began its inquiry.[14]

The film community had been badly split by the signing of the Nazi-Soviet Pact in 1939, and liberals had pulled out of various Communist-front activities. Communism had enjoyed a resurgence in Hollywood during the war as it did throughout the country, and Communist film writers notched a number of top film credits including *Destination Tokyo, Action in the North Atlantic,* and *Thirty Seconds Over Tokyo.* Some films showed the Soviets as noble allies, which was the national attitude toward Stalin at the time. But the war years also saw the emergence of a strong conservative faction in the movie capital. The Motion Picture Alliance for the Preservation of American Ideals, filled with anti-Roosevelt conservatives, protested films seen as spouting the Communist line. Begun in 1944, the alliance attracted both screenwriters and actors, the latter group included Gary Cooper, John Wayne, Ward Bond, and Robert Taylor, all of whom were vigorous anti-Communists. Alliance members invited the House Committee on Un-American Activities to investigate Hollywood.

When the committee finally reached Hollywood in 1947, the movie capital had changed significantly. Labor troubles, which had afflicted the nation as a whole immediately after the war, had upset Hollywood as well, leading to charges that the unions were dominated by Communists. In addition, box office receipts were down, making studio heads even more reliant on obtaining government permission to send their films abroad. This desire for export licenses, when combined with an increasingly conservative American audience, made movies more conventional and studio heads reluctant to do anything that could affect the studios' profits. Thus, when the House Committee on Un-American Activities came to Hollywood, few individuals were ready to defend anyone whose loyalty fell under the committee's scrutiny.

In May 1947, two HUAC members visited Hollywood and heard testimony from fourteen friendly witnesses, each of whom talked broadly about the problems Communists posed in the motion-picture industry. Each witness also identified persons considered to be Communists. The committee then called forty-three members of the film community for further hearings, including nineteen who were strong anti-Communists and nineteen persons considered to be dangerous left-wingers. Of the dangerous nineteen, sixteen were or had been screenwriters, and most of them had been or currently were members of the Communist party. These targets of the investigation hired lawyers and prepared to argue that no congressional committee had the right to inquire into the political beliefs of American citizens. The point was essentially based on the First Amendment's protection of freedom of expression. To support their colleagues who were facing the congressional inquisition, many liberal stars formed the Committee for the First Amendment (CFA), which, though refusing to back the accused individuals, supported the right of Americans to freedom of choice in their political beliefs. William Wyler and John Huston were among the CFA founders, and Humphrey Bogart, Lauren Bacall, and Danny Kaye were among the stars who trooped to Washington to support freedom of expression. To neutralize the impact of the Committee for the First Amendment, HUAC brought forth an equally impressive list of stars to detail the dangers that Communists posed to the movie industry and to the country. Gary Cooper, Robert Montgomery, George Murphy, Ronald Reagan, and Robert Taylor filled the latter roles.

Although the massing of conservative stars did not force the CFA to back down, the behavior of the first suspect witness undermined CFA support for freedom of expression. John Howard Lawson, a screenwriter who was a party member, asked to read a statement before he was questioned. Even though friendly witnesses had all been allowed to do this, committee members refused his request. Questioning was narrowly based, and Lawson was allowed only to respond to the precise point raised and not to elaborate on his answers. Lawson refused to respond to the traditional question, "Are you now or have you ever been a member of the Communist Party?" He was cited for contempt and removed from the witness table. Immediately thereafter, a committee investigator entered into the record the evidence that had been gathered against the screenwriter. Lawson, who was still present, shouted his defiance at the committee and its evidence. His behavior alienated the stars who were present to support the First Amendment. The same day that Lawson testified, Eric Johnston, who had taken over Will Hays's job, appeared before the House committee and carefully supported the investigation while criticizing some of its tactics. With the producers now supporting anti-communism, members of the Committee for the First Amendment abandoned their cause in favor of their careers. The nineteen suspect members of the Hollywood community stood alone.

Eventually ten of the nineteen testified and were cited for contempt of Congress for refusing to discuss their affiliations with the Communist party. All of the recalcitrants were writers. The Hollywood Ten, as they became known, soon encountered a form of double jeopardy that was typical of the era. While they were awaiting trial on the contempt charges, the writers were blacklisted—fired and barred from future employment in the motion-picture industry. The studio heads had met with the East Coast financiers who funded their work to discuss the industry's image soon after the hearings. The result was the Waldorf Statement of December 3, 1947, in which the studio heads placed themselves four-square behind the anti-Communist crusade. Although the statement said the studio heads did not "desire to prejudge their legal rights," the Hollywood Ten were denounced as having done "a disservice to their employers" that impaired "their usefulness to the industry." The Ten were fired or suspended without pay until they were acquitted in court or had purged themselves of contempt by declaring under oath that they were not Communists. In addition, the studio heads pledged to "not knowingly employ a Communist or a member of any party or group which advocates the overthrow of the Government of the United States by force or by illegal or unconstitutional methods."[15]

In many respects, their anti-Communist declaration was a model of contradiction. The studio heads, for example, pledged themselves not "to be swayed by hysteria or intimidation from any source." The policy that they were adopting, they said, "involves dangers and risks. There is the danger of hurting innocent people. There is the risk of creating an atmosphere of fear." Admitting that "creative work at its best cannot be carried on in an atmosphere of fear," the studio heads vowed to "guard against this danger, this risk, this fear." To so protect creative work, the studio bosses pledged to "invite the Hollywood talent guilds to work with us to eliminate any subversives, to protect the innocent, and to safeguard free speech and a free screen wherever threatened."[16]

How eliminating Communists from their jobs on Hollywood's movie stages would safeguard freedom of speech and eliminate fear remained unexplained. One thing was clear: the studio heads intended to carry out their promises. The basis for dismissing the screenwriters was that they had violated the morals clause of their contracts, in which the employee promised to "not do anything which will tend to degrade him in society or bring him into public disrepute, contempt, scorn, or ridicule, or that will tend to shock, insult, or offend the community or public morals or decency or prejudice . . . the motion picture industry."[17]

The Hollywood Ten were cast adrift from the movie community. Denied their request for a joint trial, which would have saved money, all agreed to abide by the verdict reached in the first case. When John Howard Lawson and Dalton Trumbo were convicted of contempt of Congress, the others likewise stood convicted. Although an appeal was launched, the Ten had little hope that they would triumph. Indeed, in June 1949, the appeals court upheld the right of Congress to inquire into their political beliefs especially since motion pictures, "beyond dispute," play "a critically prominent role in the molding of public opinion." Furthermore, "motion pictures are, or are capable of being, a potent medium of propaganda dissemination which may influence the minds of millions of American people." Because of their impact, "it is absurd to argue . . . that questions asked men who, by their authorship of the scripts, vitally influence the ultimate production of motion pictures seen by millions, which questions require disclosure of whether or not they are or ever have been Communists, are not pertinent questions. Indeed, it is hard to envisage how there could be any more pertinent question."[18]

After the Supreme Court refused to review the case, Lawson and Trumbo began serving their one-year sentences. The other defendants spent about an hour each in court, were convicted, and were given identical sentences. Nine of the Hollywood Ten remained blacklisted; one, Edward Dmytryk, went back before the committee where he provided names of persons he considered to be Communists in Hollywood. He was reinstated; for the remaining members of the Hollywood Ten, life was uncertain. The more talented writers sold scripts to television under false names. By the mid-1950s, the most talented of the blacklistees were writing once more for Hollywood, again under pseudonyms. Dalton Trumbo, in fact, won the Academy Award for screen writing in 1956, but the film credits went to Robert Rich. Trumbo announced his authorship in 1959 after the Motion Picture Academy of Arts and Sciences rescinded its rule that had disqualified individuals who had refused to testify fully before any investigating committee from eligibility for awards. In 1960, Otto Preminger announced that Trumbo had written *Exodus* and that his name would appear on the screen. Kirk Douglas then announced that Trumbo would receive screen credit for his authorship of *Spartacus*. The blacklist finally was broken, more than ten years after it had begun. Individuals who had been forced out of Hollywood because of their political affiliations made their way back, but only about 10 percent of them were able to restore their careers to previous levels.

The Hollywood Ten's experience with the House Committee on Un-American Activities was similar to that of many individuals called before that and similar committees. Cooperative witnesses, defined as those individuals who agreed to tell all that they knew about Communist infiltration of a particular area of American life and who were willing to name others whom they suspected of being Communists, were treated with great deference. Uncooperative witnesses, defined as individuals who refused to tell the committee about their activities or the actions of others, were treated with equal hostility. As the various investigatory hearings progressed, many witnesses became willing to talk of their own personal experiences with the Communist party but refused to name others that they may have met during those experiences. Committee members found that attempt to find a middle ground unacceptable. Other witnesses would discuss their present status with regard to party membership but would refuse to say whether they had been members earlier. That, too, was unacceptable. Some witnesses contended that the First Amendment prevented Congress from inquiring into political beliefs and associations, but court decisions seemed to indicate that any reliance on First Amendment protection was misplaced.[19] With that defense disabled, witnesses were left with the Fifth Amendment and hope that resting on the constitutional protection against self-incrimination would protect them from contempt citations and jail terms.

Although HUAC members preferred to have witnesses answer questions, members were not displeased with the number of "Fifth Amendment Communists" uncovered. Appearing before the committee and using the constitutional privilege against self-incrimination was more damning than actually testifying. Most Americans assumed that no one would "take the Fifth" unless he or she had something to hide. In later years, even being called before an investigating body could damage an individual's reputation or career. Indeed, one of the committee's goals was the exposure of individuals who then could be punished through professional and social ostracism. As one of the committee's earliest reports explained, "While Congress does not have the power to deny to citizens the right to believe in, teach, or advocate communism, fascism, and nazism, it does have the right to focus the spotlight of publicity upon their activities."[20] Later the committee proclaimed its intent to protect "our constitutional democracy . . . by pitiless publicity."[21]

No one should conclude, however, that all of the committee's activities were ephemeral. Committee members were, for instance, active in the Alger Hiss case. Through this investigation, Richard M. Nixon, then a Republican congressman from California, first came to national attention. Nixon pursued the former Roosevelt appointee until ultimately, with the help of ex-Communist Whittaker Chambers, he caught Hiss in the lie that sent him to prison for perjury. Whether Nixon proved that Hiss had been a Soviet agent is still being debated by historians. The statute of limitations had expired on potential espionage charges, and so that issue never was tried in court.

But HUAC encountered few Hiss cases. If statistics could reveal how many dangerous Communists the committee had flushed out, then an evaluation of its work might be possible. A study of its hearings would provide the number of witnesses who took the Fifth Amendment to avoid revealing present or past associations. How many of those people posed tangible threats to national security is unknown. But Americans tended to ignore reality as they worried about Communists during these postwar years, and based on external events, that concern seemed to be soundly grounded. But as with the Japanese-Americans during World War II, the FBI knew of any potentially dangerous individuals, had them under surveillance, and could have picked them up at a moment's notice, if necessary. As with the Espionage Act cases that emanated from World War I, the highly publicized hearings of the House committee and similar bodies around the country netted no real spies. More often than not, these sessions were designed to justify rolling back political and social changes rather than stem the tide of godless communism. Many legislative inquisitors, however, could not differentiate between the two.

Similar difficulty in differentiating among causes of concern manifested itself in the development of a changed national policy toward labor unions in 1947. The National Labor Relations Act of 1935 had drastically altered relationships between employers and employees. The relative positions in the bargaining arrangement were not equalized; rather, the employee negotiating through a union was given a decided edge. With the nation's economy stabilized, employers wanted to regain some of their power. In addition, labor unions under the National Labor Relations Act had become powerful political organizations. Although the War Labor Disputes Act of 1943 had barred union contributions to political candidates, the law led the Congress of Industrial Organizations (CIO) to organize what may have been the first political action committee (PAC) in the country, which evaded the legal barrier against direct contributions by unions. Through CIO-PAC efforts, union money and workers helped Franklin Roosevelt win a fourth term in 1944 and carried a number of Democratic senators and representatives into office.[22]

Compounding these basic difficulties was an unprecedented wave of strikes after the war. In the year that followed victory over Japan, the country experienced more than 4,600 work stoppages, involving more than 5 million workers, and costing the nation some 120 million days of work. Many factors led to the work stoppages. The no-strike pledge that had kept workers on the job during the war had expired. Workers who had been accustomed to pay checks padded with overtime money soon found that a forty-hour week lowered their standard of living. Collective bargaining had fallen into disuse during the war years, so when labor union negotiators and management reached an impasse, the workers simply walked off the job, further disrupting the reconversion process. In addition, unions feared mass unemployment as industry tried to absorb the millions of service personnel re-entering the job market; consequently, union leaders adopted a policy of striking before they lost strength. But the walkouts disrupted American life. A strike of oil refinery workers, for example, led to a shortage of gasoline when the days of limited fuel supposedly were over. Workers at General

Motors walked off the job for 113 days, meaning a delay in the production of much-desired civilian automobiles. Massive strikes hit the steel industry, where 750,000 workers were idled in January 1946. Workers at coal mines and railroads also struck. In the latter two instances, President Truman ordered government seizure in order to keep these essential industries operating.[23]

In addition, charges mounted—as they had during the red scare immediately after World War I—that the strikes were the result of Communist domination of the unions. CIO unions were especially vulnerable to such accusations because Communists had helped to organize many of the mass-production industries in which postwar strikes occurred. Most CIO member unions, however, had purged Communist officers before World War II began.[24] But the unions' efforts to cleanse their ranks of Communists went unnoticed. A nation displeased by the inconveniences caused by postwar strikes was easily persuaded by strong anti-union forces within the business and political communities to support legislation designed to redress the imbalance between labor and management created in 1935. The Labor Management Relations Act of 1947, better known as the Taft-Hartley Act,[25] was the result of this intermixture of anti-unionism and anti-communism.

Provisions of the Taft-Hartley Act drastically altered the relationship between labor and management. Congress directly attacked some fundamental union practices that had been used in labor disputes for years and that were strongly disliked by employers. For instance, unions could no longer require employers to establish a closed shop where only union members were hired. Upon the vote of the workers affected, a union shop could be set up in which nonmembers were hired on the condition that they join the union. The act also outlawed the secondary boycott in which strikers picketed businesses with an indirect relationship to the employer with whom the workers had a grievance. Provisions were made to guarantee the employer freedom of speech in labor disputes, which many business leaders said had been preempted by interpretations of the National Labor Relations Act that viewed employer speech as coercive.[26] Conservatives made another attempt to dry up union money directed into liberal campaign coffers by making it illegal for unions to make expenditures or contributions to any national primary or general election.[27] Unions, however, continued to maintain their political action committees by altering the way in which those committees collected money. And the act contained a clause that required all union officials to sign an affidavit annually declaring that they were not members of the Communist party. If any official refused to sign the statement, that union lost its rights to use the services of the National Labor Relations Board.

President Truman vetoed the Taft-Hartley Act when it reached his desk, but Congress overrode that veto. Labor unions immediately launched a campaign to have the act repealed or at least modified, but the fear of unions and their power remained too great. In addition, repeated propaganda about the prevalence of Communists within their ranks did little to help unions win the support of either the American people or members of Congress. In fact, the climate of hostility against unions increased in the 1950s, as charges of communism continued to swirl around union leadership and as congressional hearings revealed corruption within some of the nation's unions. In 1955, the Congress of Industrial Organizations and the American Federation of Labor (AFL) put aside old differences to form the AFL-CIO, in part to better combat the growing attack on unions fostered by the latest red scare.

In 1959, reacting to repeated charges of communism and corruption, Congress enacted even more stringent legislation restricting union freedom. The Labor-Management Reporting and Disclosure Act, better known as the Landrum-Griffin Act, showed even greater distrust of unions on the part of both Congress and the nation. Provisions of the Landrum-Griffin Act revealed a belief that union officers were coercing their members into action. The new law required unions to protect the free-speech rights of their members and to allow members to dissent from leaders' policies without fear of retribution. The legislation's anti-Communist provisions barred members of the Communist party from union office for five years after the termination of their membership.[28] Although many individuals believed the postwar red scare was over by the late 1950s, in the eyes of Congress, labor unions still were suspect.

When Congress began its attack on unions—and on communism in unions—in 1947, the cold war was still in its infancy. But even as Congress put the finishing touches on the Taft-Hartley Act, President Truman announced his Truman Doctrine, which called for helping Greece and Turkey combat communism, and his containment policy, which called for limiting communism to its existing geographical limits. Later that year, a massive program to finance the physical and economic recovery of war-torn Europe, known as the Marshall Plan, was introduced. The goal here, too, was to win European support for democratic institutions and to halt the expansion of communism. In 1948, the Soviets blocked the access of the British, French, and Americans to Berlin, a city that the four powers had agreed to administer jointly at the end of the war. The Americans launched the dramatic Berlin Airlift, which lasted 321 days, to counter the Soviet land blockade. Almost simultaneously with the beginning of the blockade, President Truman signed legislation establishing the first peacetime draft in the nation's history. The Communist juggernaut added another Eastern European nation to its total in 1948 as Czechoslovakia moved behind Winston Churchill's iron curtain. Domestic dangers seemed to increase as well. In August 1948, revelations in the House Committee on Un-American Activities hearings about the relationship between Alger Hiss and Whittaker Chambers left the impression that the highest echelons of government were riddled with Communist spies.

The news grew even worse in 1949. In September, President Truman revealed that the American monopoly on nuclear weapons, in which the nation had placed great trust for its security, no longer existed. The Soviets had exploded their first atomic bomb. In December, the Communists under Mao Tse-tung finished driving Chiang Kai-shek from the Chinese mainland. American fears led the nation irrevocably into the international arena through membership in the North Atlantic Treaty Organization. Inflamed by such external realities, the domestic search for Communists intensified. HUAC continued its investigations unabated; if anything, its role in maintaining the security of the country had been greatly enhanced by its role in the Hiss affair. Investigating committees sprouted in other areas of Congress and throughout the United States. The president's loyalty program was in high gear by this time, and similar programs were under way at the state and local levels. As with other times of great fear, no moderating force was present.

Although individuals did speak out occasionally against the violence done to freedom of expression and individual liberties during these years, there was little concerted effort to help persons accused of having CPUSA connections. The American Civil Liberties Union was strangely silent during the cold war. The broader liberal community was badly split among those who wanted to find a way to live with the Soviets and those who were strongly anti-Communist. The latter group coalesced into the Americans for Democratic Action in 1947, and although its members had concerns about the loyalty frenzy of the cold war, they said little. Liberals' survival demanded that they remain inconspicuous and voice few complaints about the anti-Communist persecution occurring all around them. Liberals who violated these tenets found themselves in great difficulty as the cold war progressed. Individuals who had spoken out in defense of Alger Hiss, for example, later became targets of conservative red-baiters such as Richard Nixon and Joseph R. McCarthy. To insulate themselves from attack, many liberals became as strongly anti-Communist as some of the conservatives they disdained.[29]

The CPUSA did little during the early cold war to deflect concern. The party had changed its position so many times in the previous twenty years at the command of Soviet political leaders that most Americans believed that it constituted a viper in the heart of the nation ready to strike at any time. Although the party was small in number, its members were militant. Most of the moderate faction had been purged at the end of the war with Earl Browder. Now, an old hard-liner, William Z. Foster, was chairman. Eugene Dennis, who was more of a centrist, served as general secretary, but Dennis constantly was on guard against charges of being ideologically unsound. With Foster and Dennis sharing the leadership, the party was essentially split and probably would have self-destructed without the intervention of outside forces. Internal debates raged over what policies to follow and whose voice served as that of the party. Efforts by the Soviets in 1947 to further centralize control over Communist parties in other countries added to the uneasiness within the CPUSA and the nation. In addition, Foster had been told to prepare the American party to go underground to evade persecution. These actions helped to create the impression that the party was indeed subversive and should be extinguished.[30]

Into this growing atmosphere of hostility and apprehension moved the Justice Department. HUAC had chided Attorney General Tom Clark during one of his appearances for lack of initiative against Communists. Although the Justice Department had used immigration and naturalization laws against foreign-born Communists with a fair degree of success, the committee wanted more. The attorney general responded by bringing the first charges against members of the Communist party under the Alien Registration, or Smith, Act. Twelve top party leaders, including Foster, Dennis, and *Daily Worker* editor John Gates, were charged with advocating the overthrow of the United States by force and violence.[31]

The arrests were a mixed blessing for the Truman administration, for they came just as it was trying to demonstrate support for freedom of expression. The reason for this sudden backing of freedom of speech was, of course, political. Harry Truman wanted to be reelected, and he faced a fractured Democratic party that was not quite sure whether it wanted him to carry the standard of Franklin Roosevelt. Further complicating matters, Southerners had walked out of the convention to form the Dixiecrat party and to run a national ticket headed by Strom Thurmond of South Carolina. In addition, many left-wing liberals had abandoned the party in favor of a third-party challenge by former vice president and former cabinet officer Henry A. Wallace. Although the nation's conservatives and many anti-Communist liberals would welcome the arrest and indictment of the Communist party's leadership, other liberals, whose votes Truman needed to be reelected, were sure to be unhappy.[32]

One of Wallace's main reasons for running for president was his disagreement with Truman over the Communist threat. To Wallace, Soviet-American cooperation was more likely to build a prosperous and peaceful postwar world than Soviet-American antagonism. As head of the Progressive party ticket, Wallace offered the nation an amalgam of old-time liberalism and popular-front trust in the Communists, which was at least ten years out of date. When attempts were made to smear his candidacy because Communists supported him, Wallace refused to reject Communist backing. "God bless 'em; let 'em come along," he would say as he defended the rights of Communists to freedom of expression and criticized the red-baiting that was so prevalent in the country.[33] Actually, Truman had no need to worry about the threat that Wallace posed on the left. The Progressive party received only about 2 percent of the popular vote, less than the total received by the Dixiecrat candidate.

With victory in hand, the Truman administration was ready to move vigorously against Communist party leaders. The indictments had come sufficiently early in the cold war that they had triggered some objections within the liberal community, but protests were negligible in the face of overwhelming support for the government's actions. Although the issue may have been misunderstood at the time, the first Smith Act defendants were charged not with actually taking action to overthrow the government but with conspiring together to teach and advocate the revolutionary doctrine of communism. Few people were willing to draw precise lines between talk, which should be permissible on any subject in a country that honors freedom of expression, and action, which might be punishable. Indeed, the first Smith Act trial, which became known as the Dennis case because Foster was dropped due to ill health, was a political trial in which precise definitions of terms and care about traditional constitutional guarantees were absent.

In fact, the government's case was weak. Prosecuting attorneys, for instance, had no proof of actual illegal acts performed by the eleven defendants. To prove that they had conspired to teach and to advocate the overthrow of the government, prosecutors spent much of their time entering Communist propaganda into the record. Books cited for contributing to the conspiracy included *The Communist Manifesto,* by Karl Marx and Friedrich Engels, *State and Revolution,* by V. I. Lenin, *Foundations of Leninism,* by Joseph Stalin, and *History of the Communist Party of the Soviet Union,* edited by the party's central committee, most of which were in the nation's leading libraries. Material from pamphlets and articles from the *Daily Worker* also were read into the record to show the defendants' intention to advocate the overthrow of the government. The indictment covered activities between 1945 and 1948, but much of the material introduced had been written earlier. In addition, the prosecution offered into evidence only selected excerpts from the material. No effort was made to put the quotes in context or to provide non-incriminating selections from the same materials. The defense, of course, objected to such a selective use of evidence; Judge Harold L. Medina overruled their objections.

The trial was a circus as the Communists tried to prove that the U.S. government was persecuting them for their political beliefs. Pickets and noisy demonstrators outside the courthouse led to calls for legislation forbidding picketing near federal courts and to fairly widespread condemnation of extrajudicial attempts to influence the outcome of a court case. Charges of professional misconduct were levied against both sides. Jurors were out for just about a day before delivering guilty verdicts against all eleven defendants. Ten defendants were given the maximum five-year prison terms and $10,000 fines; the eleventh man received reduced prison term because of his military record.

The Dennis defendants were convicted in October 1949. Early in 1950, an aide in the Department of Justice, Judith Coplon, and a Soviet attaché, Valentin Gubitchev, were brought to trial on charges of spying for the Soviet Union. Events soon became bleaker for Americans concerned with communism at home and abroad. In February 1950, the British arrested Klaus Fuchs, a physicist who had worked on the Manhattan Project, and charged him with passing secrets about the atomic bomb to the Soviets. During his interrogation, he named several Americans, including Julius and Ethel Rosenberg, as Communists who also had passed information about the bomb to the Russians. Now Americans knew how the Soviets had been able to develop the bomb so quickly.

Into this deepening fear strode a politician looking for an issue to ride to reelection victory. In February 1950, the junior senator from Wisconsin told a group of Republican women gathered in Wheeling, West Virginia, "I have here in my hand a list of 205—a list of names that were made known to the Secretary of State as being members of the Communist Party and who nevertheless are still ... shaping policy in the State Department."[34] With those words, Joseph R. McCarthy burst on the scene as a Communist fighter without equal. McCarthyism, the blind, mindless persecution of essentially innocent individuals for their political beliefs, had begun. From that point, charges against individuals would become more sensational, more irresponsible, and even less grounded in fact than ever before. McCarthy had no such list in his hand or in his possession. At best, he had a copy of a 1946 letter from Secretary of State James F. Byrnes to Representative Adolph Sabbath that had appeared in the *Congressional Record.*

In that letter, Byrnes talked about the investigation of some 3,000 employees who had transferred to the State Department from wartime agencies and who were seeking permanent government employment. As a result of the screenings, officials had recommended against the continued employment of 285 individuals but not all necessarily for loyalty reasons. By the time the letter had been written, seventy-nine people already had been fired for various reasons. With a little sloppy math, 205 people with questionable backgrounds remained employed by the State Department—in 1946.[35] McCarthy spoke in 1950. How many of these individuals still were employed was unknown, and a different secretary of state was in office.

McCarthy went along on his speaking tour, drawing an increasing number of reporters at each stop. He refused to release the names of the alleged Communists employed by the State Department, acting at all times as if he had such a list in his possession. He soon decided that he had two lists. One enumeration talked of 205 bad risks employed by the State Department; the second version gave the names of fifty-seven card-carrying members of the Communist party still at work in the department. Then, McCarthy began talking only about the fifty-seven, a number that apparently came from a House Appropriations Committee investigation in 1948 that had found 108 government employees about whom questions could be raised concerning loyalty and security matters, fifty-seven of whom still were employed by the State Department in March 1948, two years before McCarthy's charge.[36]

With these speeches in early 1950, McCarthy began his career of playing fast and loose with statistics, facts, and people's reputations. His rise to power was aided significantly by the nation's journalists who repeated his wild accusations verbatim. Few demands were made for proof. Later in his career, when McCarthy started spouting charges against specific individuals on the Senate floor or in official committee meetings, where he was protected by senatorial immunity from the possibility of libel charges, few journalists sought out the accused individuals to print their sides of the story. Nor did journalists, at least early in his career as the nation's chief Communist hunter, point out the inconsistencies in McCarthy's remarks or the errors that he made in crucial facts when he stated his cases against various individuals. McCarthy knew that the press was his best weapon in his personal crusade against communism, and he knew how to use that weapon to his advantage. Few politicians surpassed his ability to manipulate the nation's journalists.

The handful of reporters who tried to deflate McCarthy's crusade found themselves labeled as Communist sympathizers and often bore the brunt of McCarthy-originated campaigns to convince advertisers to boycott them. Newspaper columnist Drew Pearson, for instance, lost a key sponsor for his radio broadcasts because of his continued attacks on McCarthy. If journalists noticed criticism of their coverage of the Wisconsin senator, they responded that they were simply reporting McCarthy objectively. Some journalists believed that serving as a conduit between McCarthy and the people without asking any hard questions about the information being so conveyed was a profound public disservice. As Alan Barth, editorial writer for the *Washington Post* and thoughtful commentator on the McCarthy period, once said, "I do know the American people are being fooled and that the American press is being used, deliberately, to fool them. Maybe we have a responsibility that goes beyond objectivity."[37]

McCarthy gave the press little opportunity to decide on how to deal with his allegations. Soon after his Wheeling speech, he repeated a variation of his charges on the Senate floor, and his colleagues authorized an investigation of his allegations. As these hearings progressed, McCarthy continued to run amok, issuing additional charges against the State Department and challenges to the Truman administration. Many Senate Republicans appreciated his efforts, for he had taken on the State Department, which was considered responsible for many of the multiplying cold war problems, as his own personal devil. In addition, he had brought the spotlight that accompanied the anti-Communist hunt to the Senate. And, frankly, McCarthy provided his Republican colleagues in the Senate with a coarse, rough infighter who liked dirtying his hands in the battle against communism.

Not all senators were pleased with McCarthy's behavior. Democrats on a special committee assigned to look into his charges issued a report in July 1950 that called his accusations "a fraud and a hoax perpetrated on the Senate of the United States and the American people. They represent perhaps the most nefarious campaign of half-truths and untruth in the history of this Republic." The committee found that "for the first time in our history, we have seen the totalitarian technique of the 'big lie' employed on a sustained basis. The result has been to confuse and divide the American people, at a time when they should be strong in their unity, to a degree far beyond the hopes of the Communists themselves whose stock in trade is confusion and division."[38] Although the words were accurate, they were costly as well. The head of the special committee investigating McCarthy's charges, Millard Tydings, a Democrat from Maryland, lost his Senate seat after McCarthy and his supporters launched a major drive to oust him from office.

Nor were all Republicans satisfied with McCarthy's activities. In early June 1950, for example, Senator Margaret Chase Smith of Maine denounced senators who were "abusing our individual powers and privileges." Senators must remember that the Constitution "speaks not only of the freedom of speech but also of trial by jury instead of trial by accusation," she said. To Senator Smith, the problem was clear. "Those of us who shout the loudest about Americanism in making character assassinations are all too frequently those who, by our own words and acts, ignore some of the basic principles of Americanism—The right to criticize. The right to hold unpopular beliefs. The right to protest. The right of independent thought." Exercising these constitutional rights "should not cost one single American citizen his reputation or his right to a livelihood nor should he be in danger of losing his reputation or livelihood merely because he happens to know some one who holds unpopular beliefs. Who of us does not? Otherwise none of us could call our souls our own. Otherwise thought control would have set in."[39]

According to Mrs. Smith, "The American people are sick and tired of being afraid to speak their minds lest they be politically smeared as Communists or

Fascists by their opponents. Freedom of speech is not what it used to be in America. It has been so abused by some that it is not exercised by others." Americans were being "psychologically divided by the confusion and the suspicions that are bred in the United States Senate to spread like cancerous tentacles of 'know nothing, suspect everything' attitudes." Although she knew that Republicans hoped the Communist issue would lead them to the White House, Senator Smith had little use for a political triumph based on "the Four Horsemen of Calumny—fear, ignorance, bigotry, and smear."[40] She followed her attack on McCarthy by issuing what became known as the "Declaration of Conscience," a statement signed by seven Republican senators condemning the rampant anticommunism sweeping the country.[41]

The campaign against McCarthyism, however, was doomed. On June 25, 1950, the army of the People's Republic of Korea crossed the 38th parallel that divided the Communist North from the free South and began the Korean War. With a shooting war in progress, anti-communism rose to new heights. Harry S. Truman, following his policy that communism must be contained within its postwar boundaries, on June 26 authorized the U.S. Navy and Air Force to help South Korean troops below the 38th parallel, without a formal congressional declaration of war. On June 27, the U.N. Security Council, with the Soviet Union absent, passed a resolution calling on members of the United Nations to help protect the national sovereignty of South Korea. Acting on American commitments to the United Nations, Truman sent ground troops into South Korea on June 30 and authorized air force attacks on targets in the North.

This war was destined to be an oddity in the nation's military history. Congress never did declare war against North Korea, but thousands of American service personnel saw duty, bore injury, and encountered death on the peninsula. Fearful of nuclear war, the conflict was limited to that Southeast Asian country, a decision that proved increasingly controversial in the United States. American armed forces, accustomed to winning wars, soon encountered a determined enemy that almost pushed them off the tip of the continent by September 1950. Only a spectacular amphibious landing saved American troops from that ignominy. At home, opposition to the war appeared, but, strangely, the criticism was coming primarily from conservative Republicans. With the cold war raging, liberals were afraid to say anything that might be construed as favoring a Communist cause anywhere in the world. To the Republicans, often joined in Congress by conservative Southern Democrats, the war offered the perfect opportunity to further chastise liberals for foreign policy decisions dating from the Roosevelt presidency.[42]

While the war was just getting under way, Congress enacted a major piece of repressive legislation aimed at making the further existence of the CPUSA almost impossible. The passage of the Internal Security Act of 1950[43] capped four years of debate over how to control the dreaded red menace. The quarrel in Congress was not so much of whether the Communist party ought to be severely limited legislatively but over how draconian the measure should be. The cold war left members of Congress feeling as if they had no legislative weapons to rely on. Wartime legislation allowed close control of and punishment for espionage and sedition; without a declaration of war, such measures were useless. Still on the books, of course, were the pre–World War II laws, including the Smith and Hatch acts, as well as immigration and naturalization laws that were aimed directly at individuals who espoused the violent overthrow of the government. But still, conservative lawmakers wanted more. Heeding a warning from J. Edgar Hoover that outlawing the party would only force members underground and make it far more difficult for the FBI to watch them, congressional leaders stopped short of outlawing the party in the Internal Security Act. Instead the law contained multiple provisions forcing public exposure of the party, in the hopes that support would disappear.[44]

Members of Congress justified the measure on fifteen grounds, beginning with a statement of their belief that a world Communist movement existed "whose purpose it is, by treachery, deceit, infiltration, . . . espionage, sabotage, terrorism, and any other means deemed necessary, to establish a Communist totalitarian dictatorship in the countries throughout the world." With such a dictatorship, Congress said, political opposition would be suppressed, the rights of the individual would disappear, and fundamental liberties, including freedom of speech and press, would be denied. American Communists were simply lying in wait until a time when the nation "may be so far extended by foreign engagements, so far divided in counsel, or so far in industrial or financial straits, that overthrow of the Government of the United States by force and violence may seem possible of achievement."[45] Rather than allow the Communists to recruit new members to prepare for that opportunity, Congress decided to act first.

The Internal Security Act was aimed at both "Communist-action" and "Communist-front" organizations. Seeking to reach the party itself, the law defined a "Communist-action" group as any organization that is "substantially directed, dominated, or controlled by the foreign government, or foreign organization controlling the world Communist movement." In an attempt to reach the popular front, the law defined a "Communist-front" organization as one that was "substantially directed, dominated, or controlled by a Communist-action organization" or was "primarily operated for the purpose of giving aid and support to a Communist-action organization, a Communist foreign government or the world Communist movement."[46] In either event, the attorney general could initiate proceedings to require the suspect organization to register with the Subversive Activities Control Board, which the act created. Should the group be ordered to register after a full hearing and court appeals, it must provide the attorney general with financial statements and lists of officers, and in the case of a Communist-action organization, with lists of members as well.

Penalties for belonging to a registered organization ranged from a bar on employment in certain industries to a ban on foreign travel. Registered organizations were to be denied tax benefits normally provided to public-interest groups. Failure of an organization to register after receiving final orders to do so carried a $10,000 fine for the organization and a maximum five-year prison term for individuals who had the responsibility for filing the papers. The Internal Security Act stiffened regulations pertaining to immigration and naturalization, and as a direct outcome of the Dennis trial, the law forbade picketing and parading near a federal courthouse in an attempt to influence federal judges, juries, and court officers. In addition, the act required any material sent through the mail by a registered organization to carry a warning on the outside of the container saying, "Disseminated by --, a Communist organization." Broadcast material sponsored by Communists had to be labeled similarly.[47]

Finally, the act also set up provisions for the detention of Communists in the event of invasion, declaration of war, or "insurrection within the United States in aid of a foreign enemy."[48] This section of the act legalized internment similar to that experienced by Japanese-Americans during World War II. Some critics denounced the provision as allowing the creation of concentration camps in the United States. Ironically, the emergency detention provisions were proposed by liberal Democratic senators including Hubert Humphrey of Minnesota, Frank Porter Graham of North Carolina, and William Benton of Connecticut. The liberals had suggested the detention program as a way to make the Internal Security Act so distasteful that Congress would refuse to adopt it. When Congress accepted the act, detention provision and all, several of its liberal sponsors voted against the bill.[49]

Harry S. Truman found the entire package intolerable. He vetoed the Internal Security Act and issued a stinging message charging, among other things, that the law "would put the Government of the United States in the thought control business." Truman believed that existing legislation reached all of the activities that the bill sought to punish. In addition, he charged, "the language of the bill is so broad and vague that it might well result in penalizing the legitimate activities of people who are not communists at all, but loyal citizens." He was particularly concerned about definitions of Communist fronts. According to Congress, any group with positions substantially similar to those ideas advocated by Communists were liable to such categorization. This classification, the president said, was particularly dangerous to groups of loyal Americans that advocated social reforms unacceptable to conservative political leaders. The registration requirements for Communist fronts, he said, "can be the greatest danger to freedom of speech, press and assembly, since the Alien and Sedition Laws of 1798." The president reminded the Communist hunters that "in a free country, we punish men for the crimes they commit, but never for the opinions they have." The reason for this freedom, he said, "is not, as many suppose, that it protects the few unorthodox from suppression by the majority. To permit freedom of expression is primarily for the benefit of the majority, because it protects criticism, and criticism leads to progress."[50]

Limiting espionage and sabotage was one thing, said Truman. "But we would betray our finest traditions if we attempted, as this bill would attempt, to curb the simple expression of opinion. This we should never do, no matter how distasteful the opinion may be to the vast majority of our people. The course proposed by this bill would delight the communists, for it would make a mockery of the Bill of Rights and of our claims to stand for freedom in the world." In addition, the bill would have devastating effects on the nation. "If this law were on the statute books," he said, "the part of prudence would be to avoid saying anything that might be construed by someone as not deviating sufficiently from the current communist propaganda line. And since no one could be sure in advance what views were safe to express, the inevitable tendency would be to express no views on controversial subjects." This hostility to freedom of expression, the president said, would undermine the nation's heritage: "Let us not, in cowering and foolish fear, throw away the ideals which are the fundamental basis of our free society."[51] Congress ignored the president. The House voted 286 to 48 to override the veto; the vote in the Senate was 57 to 10 to override. The Internal Security Act of 1950, one of the most oppressive pieces of legislation ever aimed at a political group in American history, was on the books.

One more piece of the repressive puzzle was yet to fall into place. Congressional leaders active in the campaign against Communists had to have been wondering how the U.S. Supreme Court would react to their efforts. The Court had a mixed record on communism. In its early rulings on First Amendment topics, the Court had found communism to be a sufficient menace to permit legislative sanctions.[52] During the 1930s and early 1940s, however, when communism was not seen as quite as great a danger and while the Court was beginning to expand the protections offered to freedom of expression, Communists were allowed to meet and to advocate their cause.[53] The Court revealed its cold war attitude in 1950.

In *American Communications Association v. Douds,* five members of the Court upheld the section of the Taft-Hartley Act that required union officers to file affidavits attesting that they were not members of the Communist party and that they did not believe in the violent overthrow of the government. Chief Justice Fred Vinson wrote a majority opinion that reflected the confusion of the period. "Beliefs are inviolate," the chief justice said as he defended the right of Communists to carry on legitimate political activities. On the other hand, he said, evidence existed to validate the congressional conclusion that "Communists, unlike members of other political parties, and persons who believe in overthrow of the Government by force, unlike persons of other beliefs, represent a continuing danger of disruptive political strikes when they hold positions of union leadership."[54]

Because of these findings, Vinson said, Congress was justified in acting against Communists who might be officers of labor unions—even though its actions might infringe on protected First Amendment values. After all, First Amendment freedoms "are dependent upon the power of constitutional government to survive. If it is to survive it must have power to protect itself against unlawful conduct and, under some circumstances, against incitements to commit unlawful acts. Freedom of speech thus does not comprehend the right to speak on any subject at any time." As the chief justice wrote, he enunciated the test for freedom of expression that would prevail in many cold war era cases. Gone was the notion that freedom of expression merited a preferred position in the hierarchy of the nation's values. Now, expressive values were to be weighed against the nation's need to survive. "In essence," he wrote, "the problem is one of weighing the probable effects of the statute upon the free exercise of the right of speech and assembly against the congressional determination that political strikes are evils of conduct which cause substantial harm to interstate commerce and that Communists . . . pose continuing threats to that public interest when in positions of leadership."⁵⁵ The balancing test in which First Amendment freedoms would be placed on one side of a scale and the government's interest in self-preservation would be placed on the other side had been born.

Any doubts about the Supreme Court's allegiance in the fight against communism were eliminated in 1951 with the justices' first decision on a Smith Act case. By a vote of six to two, the Court upheld the convictions of the Dennis defendants. Chief Justice Vinson, writing for four members of the Court, temporarily abandoned his new test for First Amendment cases and reverted to the old clear and present danger test. In so doing, the chief justice so redefined the test that clear and present danger came perilously close to the bad tendency standard. "Overthrow of the Government by force and violence is certainly a substantial enough interest for the Government to limit speech," Vinson said. "Indeed, this is the ultimate value of any society, for if a society cannot protect its very structure from armed internal attack, it must follow that no subordinate value can be protected." With such words, the chief justice established the clear portion of the clear and present danger test. When moving to the present aspect of the test, Vinson argued that clear and present danger "cannot mean that before the Government may act, it must wait until the *putsch* is about to be executed, the plans have been laid and the signal is awaited. If Government is aware that a group aiming at its overthrow is attempting to indoctrinate its members and to commit them to a course whereby they will strike when the leaders feel the circumstances permit, action by the Government is required." No overt act was required before speech could be suppressed. "Certainly," he said, "an attempt to overthrow the Government by force, even though doomed from the outset because of inadequate numbers or power of the revolutionists, is a sufficient evil for Congress to prevent."⁵⁶

Just as political oppression had brought forth the magnificent dissents of Justices Oliver Wendell Holmes, Jr., and Louis D. Brandeis after World War I, Justices Hugo L. Black and William O. Douglas emerged in *Dennis* as the leading supporters of the First Amendment rights of Communists. Black had dissented in *Douds,* while Douglas had not participated in the case. Here, they began arguing for freedom of speech—even in times of great uncertainty like the cold war. Black, for instance, called the indictment in the Dennis case "a virulent form of prior censorship of speech and press, which I believe the First Amendment forbids." Always realistic, Black noted that "public opinion being what it now is, few will protest the conviction of these Communist petitioners." But he also was an optimist, hoping "that in calmer times, when present pressures, passions and fears subside, this or some later Court will restore the First Amendment liberties to the high preferred place where they belong in a free society."⁵⁷

Douglas was amazed at the books that had been instrumental in obtaining the convictions. "Those books are to Soviet Communism what *Mein Kampf* was to Nazism. If they are understood, the ugliness of Communism is revealed, its deceit and cunning are exposed, the nature of its activities becomes apparent, and the chances of its success less likely." The Court's decision did not outlaw the books and made the crime rest "not on what is taught but on who the teacher is. That is to make freedom of speech turn not on *what is said,* but on the *intent* with which it is said. Once we start down that road we enter territory dangerous to the liberties of every citizen." Douglas also found it difficult to believe that a majority of the Court considered the Communist threat substantial. Personally, he doubted that the Communists' arguments had won many converts. "In days of trouble and confusion when bread lines were long, when the unemployed walked the streets, when people were starving, the advocates of a short-cut by revolution might have a chance to gain adherents," he said, but no such conditions currently existed. "How it can be said that there is a clear and present danger that this advocacy will succeed is, therefore, a mystery," he said. The greatest danger, he believed, rested in the Court's failure to abide by the nation's fundamental principles: "Our faith should be that our people will never give support to these advocates of revolution, so long as we remain loyal to the purposes for which our Nation was founded."[58]

In the early 1950s, few Americans were willing to grant Communists any fundamental protections at all. The level of fear, already great, increased regularly as events were magnified by demagogues who built their reputations on red-baiting. Hit and run attacks on alleged Communists increased at all levels of government and in the private sector as well. Many persons accused of being Communists had had transitory connections with the party in the 1930s. Now their youthful indiscretions caught up with them. In order to save careers, reputations, and families, many people gave in to the demands of investigatory bodies. Out spilled the names of individuals that they had known ten, fifteen, twenty years earlier, who they vaguely identified with their earlier Communist activities. Only by a full disclosure of activities, including implicating others, and a contrite apology did individuals stand a remote chance of salvaging anything from their runins with the red hunters. The legislative sniping usually was augmented by the testimony of professional witnesses, former Communists who had seen light, left the party, and became government informers. At times, these professional ex-Communists-turned-witnesses provided useful information, but before the cold war was over, a number of them had confessed to embellishing the facts in order to build personal images and fees for their testimony. Reputations of innocent people, thus, were destroyed by purposely perjured testimony.

Some people who lived through the cold war would argue that the dangers that communism posed to the nation mandated incursions on individual rights. They would cite the loss of the nuclear monopoly and various spy episodes as justifications for such actions. True, the Soviets did explode a nuclear device far earlier than Americans thought possible thanks in part to the willingness of some individuals to pass secrets to Russian agents. Equally true, some spies were found in the American government; most likely, American spies were discovered in the Soviet government as well. But the American reaction to these problems was a massive witch hunt; the British reaction to a similar world situation and to spies within their government was far more restrained and less damaging to civil liberties.

Perhaps American lack of toleration in the cold war was based, once again, on a society that was changing too rapidly. With World War II, the nation had moved irrevocably into the international arena. Now, whether Americans concurred or not, the nation had become the police officer for the world. In addition, total annihilation cast a dark specter over civilization. As usual, the nation looked for a scapegoat. The need to blame the Communists for all that was evil in the world simply increased as time went on. The war in Korea heightened American awareness of Asian Communists and created still another source of fear.

Although only conservatives safely opposed the newest military encounter, all Americans were not pleased with the limited land war in Asia. Many dissidents remained silent, however, for fear that vocal opposition would brand them as pro-Communist in an era when that label was almost suicidal. Despite this silence, many scholars believed that the depth of public dissatisfaction with the Korean War was similar to that expressed far more overtly during the Vietnam era. The war started out positively for the Americans. In the early fall of 1950, when it looked as if the United Nations forces, led by Americans, were winning, support was high, and debate in Congress and in journalistic circles was focused on whether to accept the 38th parallel as the dividing line between the two Koreas or whether to push for the reunification of the country militarily. After the Chinese Communists entered the war in November 1950, the argument shifted to whether Americans should stay in the war until it was won—regardless of the dividing line—or whether the nation should push for a negotiated peace. Soon the conflict settled down into a stalemate, and casualties began to mount. Public opinion polls, which were the great anonymous barometer of national sentiment, began to reflect increasing discontent, making the handling of the war a major issue in the 1952 elections.[59]

Despite the negative climate greeting antiwar sentiment, opposition grew. Protests came from such mainline pacifist groups as the Catholic Worker and the American Friends Service Committee. Late in 1951, a group calling itself the Peacemakers advocated tax resistance, in the tradition of Henry David Thoreau, to end the war. Members pledged not to pay their income taxes because they found it "impossible to support policies and activities of this kind with our allegiance or with our money. We must, therefore, refuse to give money for such purposes of conquest and massacre, and must give it instead to causes which build understanding and world community."[60]

Supporters of the war believed discontent stemmed in large part from the way in which the war was reported. Despite such beliefs, the American press largely supported the war, and stateside editors systematically toned down stories sent by battlefield reporters that revealed problems in Korea. Correspondents accompanying the troops, for instance, soon discovered that few of the men knew why they were fighting and that both defeats and stalemate had demoralized American forces. Their reports of corruption within the South Korean government and of the way in which the South Koreans treated political prisoners did little to build support for that country. Likewise, their accounts of how unprepared United Nations forces were to face North Korean and Chinese troops probably undermined American support for the war effort. Reporters in Korea faced only voluntary censorship for the first six months or so of the war. In December 1950,

General Douglas MacArthur, irked by a continual stream of critical stories, imposed mandatory censorship similar to that in World War II. Reporters were hurting the morale of his soldiers and providing aid and comfort to the enemy with their stories, the general said, and such irresponsibility had to stop.[61]

Correspondents protested battlefield censorship attempts. Their reporting from Korea was truly patriotic, they said. "So long as our government requires the backing of an aroused and informed public opinion . . . it is necessary to tell the hard bruising truth," said veteran correspondent Marguerite Higgins. "It is best to tell graphically the moments of desperation and horror endured by an unprepared army, so that the American public will demand that it does not happen again."[62] Hostility between the two factions grew as military officials labeled "retreats" as "withdrawals" and provided such high body counts of enemy dead and wounded that reporters said the figures indicated that the entire North Korean population had been eliminated. The festering sores resulting from these unpleasant encounters were not revealed back home, where the domestic political scene mandated editorial intervention. The mistrust between the press and the military that was bred on the battlefields of Korea, however, became more pronounced and very public during the Vietnam War.

During the hysteria that marked these years, just about the only individuals who called attention to themselves were Communists and Communist sympathizers, for they had little to lose and much to gain from their attempts to build sympathy. Their goal, of course, was to force Americans to recognize the national preoccupation with political persecution. Thus, they constantly appealed to the First Amendment's protections for speech, press, and assembly. American Communists often pursued their campaign through the court system. Cases involving Communist claims to traditional American freedoms regularly wound up before the Supreme Court between 1950 and 1965. In other instances, the confrontation was played out totally within the private sector.

Teachers on all levels of the educational system, for instance, underwent regular loyalty screenings. No one wanted a Communist on the staff; the nation's academy was to be populated only by the ideologically pure. By some estimates, close to 20 percent of all persons called before various investigating committees were teachers. In many cases, the only punishment that these individuals faced came from their employers. Failure to respond to committee questioning would inevitably lead to dismissal; failure to answer fully also likely meant loss of employment. To most members of the academy, the cold war years meant that safety rested solely in being inconspicuous and noncontroversial. For a profession that generally had more than its share of outspoken members, the cold war led to a self-imposed silence that deprived the nation of some of its most thoughtful critics.[63]

Although the Senate Internal Security Subcommittee believed that "world communist leaders have made schools and colleges of the United States a target of infiltration and activity as part of their program to destroy the United States,"[64] its members preferred to allow the leaders of the institutions involved to conduct their own purges. In most cases, elaborate hearings and appeals were part of the process, which generally ended in dismissal on grounds of incompetence or insubordination. Few individuals dismissed in this way could find employment in the academic world, for an informal blacklist of Communists and Communist sympathizers quickly developed to ban them from future academic employment. The state university systems in Washington, California, and New York were among those rocked by purges of left-wing professors. Private schools including Harvard and Yale also were targets of red hunters. In the early stages of the purge, colleagues in the academic world would come to the aid of the accused individuals. As the cold war deepened, little help appeared. The American Association of University Professors, considered a bastion of academic freedom, generally ignored appeals for help despite the fact that it had never retracted its public stance against the firing of Communist teachers. The pressure for conformity on campus was irresistible—if one hoped to stay employed.

A number of individuals so dismissed sought redress in the court system. At the Supreme Court level, the justices debated the role of academic freedom and the danger posed by Communist infiltration of the schools. In 1952 the first case reached the Court, and six justices upheld the dismissal of a teacher accused of advocating the violent overthrow of the government or of belonging to an organization advocating the same. School administrators had to be careful in deciding who worked with impressionable children, Sherman Minton wrote for the majority. "A teacher. . . . shapes the attitude of young minds towards the society in which they live. In this, the state has a vital concern," he said. Consequently, school authorities must "screen the officials, teachers, and employees as to their fitness to maintain the integrity of the schools." Fundamental to any review was "one's associates, past and present, as well as one's conduct," Minton said. He found no problems with such scrutiny, noting, "from time immemorial, one's reputation has been determined in part by the company he keeps."[65] Teachers were not exempted from that truism.

Justices Black and Douglas, in dissent, could find one excellent reason for stopping the state's investigation of a teacher's associates: the First Amendment. The New York law, said Douglas, was a perfect example of guilt by association. He and Black would often argue during these trying years that guilt was personal—that an individual had to do something illegal rather than belong to an organization that might talk about doing something that might be illegal should it occur. But guilt by association was then prevalent, despite its harmful effects on society. The New York law, Douglas said, was more appropriate for a police state than for a democracy: "Teachers are under constant surveillance; their pasts are combed for signs of disloyalty; their utterances are watched for clues to dangerous thoughts. A pall is cast over the classrooms. There can be no real academic freedom in that environment." In this situation, "fear stalks the classroom. The teacher is no longer a stimulant to adventurous thinking; she becomes instead a pipe line for safe and sound information. A deadening dogma takes the place of free inquiry. Instruction tends to become sterile; pursuit of knowledge is discouraged; discussion often leaves off where it should begin."[66] Learning is badly damaged in such circumstances, Douglas argued, but without success.

From time to time, the Court would find in favor of a distressed professor, often on procedural grounds. This was the rationale in the case of Paul Sweezy, a guest lecturer at the University of New Hampshire, who was quizzed about his political beliefs by the state's attorney general. In 1957, a Supreme Court with different personnel, by a six-to-three vote, overturned Sweezy's conviction for contempt of a legislative committee based on his refusal to answer questions. In the course of his plurality opinion, Chief Justice Earl Warren noted that freedom of expression was especially important in the university environment. "No one should underestimate the vital role in a democracy that is played by those who guide and train our youth. To impose any strait jacket upon the intellectual leaders in our colleges and universities would imperil the future of our Nation," he said. Freedom of inquiry, which was part of freedom of expression, was essential. "No field of education is so thoroughly comprehended by man that new discoveries cannot yet be made. . . . Scholarship cannot flourish in an atmosphere of suspicion and distrust. Teachers and students must always remain free to inquire, to study and to evaluate, to gain new maturity and understanding; otherwise our civilization will stagnate and die."[67] Few individuals, however, were looking to what they perceived to be the not too certain future. The challenge was to survive the present day with its threat of violent overthrow of the government ever at hand. The sacrifice of academic freedom—and a few professors along the way—was a small price to pay to ensure the survival of the nation.

Fears of communism also made Americans willing to invade the mass media. The House Committee on Un-American Activities returned to the movie capital in 1951, at another time of extreme vulnerability for the industry. Television had just appeared, and box office receipts had sharply declined. This time a number of witnesses, including Edgar G. Robinson, asked to testify in order to dispel rumors about their loyalty. Former party members including writer Budd Schulberg and actor Sterling Hayden named numerous residents of the movie community as one-time party members. In all, more than 300 people were listed as having connections with the Communist party as a result of the 1951 incursion. These individuals were punished in the now traditional manner—by loss of job and blacklisting from future employment.[68]

Entertainers involved in radio and television also had careers destroyed during the cold war. The agent of destruction, although purely private, was as effective as any governmental body. As early as 1947, *Counterattack,* a weekly newsletter published by American Business Consultants, began exposing communism in various areas of American life. The three former FBI agents who formed American Business Consultants published *Red Channels* in 1950, which listed 151 radio and television workers allegedly connected with the Communist party or Communist-front organizations. The names cited in *Red Channels* had been drawn from previous state and federal lists, supplemented by the former agents themselves. *Red Channels* also included a list of 192 suspect organizations, some 70 more than on the most recent attorney general's list. The former agents' goal was to rid the nation's entertainment industry of Communists and thus to deprive the party of the money that these highly paid individuals provided.[69]

Radio and television were, of course, dependent on advertising, and advertisers were very sensitive to public concerns. Complaints about performers sent advertisers into frenzies of terror about the effect on sales. A blacklist, containing the names of actors, producers, directors, writers, and other personnel considered unemployable due to their political beliefs, was constructed.[70] To keep embarrassing situations from recurring, the networks instituted loyalty oaths and began checking the political backgrounds of their employees.

Perhaps even more insidious was the appearance of so-called clearance agencies. If an accused individual went to one of these agencies, hat and money in hand, and was willing to write a sufficiently full statement on his or her political background and to make an abject apology for any past transgressions, the individual's career would be rehabilitated. Such intercession by private groups was almost as beneficial to one's career as a soul-bearing confession before a government investigating body. Often persons and agencies involved in rehabilitating careers were the same ones who had created the problems in the first place.[71]

Radio, television, and motion pictures were not the only media to feel the red hunter's wrath. Even the newspaper industry fell under suspicion. Senator Joseph McCarthy began the probe of journalists in 1953 when he called James A. Wechsler, editor of the *New York Post,* before him. Wechsler had been a member of the Young Communist League in the late 1930s but had publicly renounced his affiliation and had been a strong anti-Communist ever since. He fell into McCarthy's investigatory net allegedly because some books that he had written had appeared in overseas libraries funded by the government. More likely, McCarthy was after Wechsler because of a series of articles carried in the *Post* that were highly critical of McCarthy's campaign against Communists.[72]

Wechsler contended almost from the beginning that McCarthy was attempting to intimidate the press into cooperating with him. "I was called because the newspaper I edit has been fighting Joe McCarthy," he said at a May 7, 1953, news conference. "Subsequent to my hearings McCarthy had announced that he had broadened his inquiry to cover alleged subversives in all media." A number of leading newspapers agreed with Wechsler. As the *Washington Post* noted, "Senator McCarthy has now put editors and other newspapermen on notice that criticism of him in the press may subject the writer to a summons and a star chamber grilling."[73] In the face of such a perceived threat, Wechsler asked the American Society of Newspaper Editors (ASNE) to review the whole episode.

When the ASNE committee reported in August 1953, the majority decided that McCarthy had not endangered freedom of the press by summoning Wechsler. A minority, headed by committee chairman Russell Wiggins of the *Washington Post,* voiced its strong disagreement. "Freedom of the press in these United States, as it has been understood since the adoption of the Constitution, could not long survive the repeated exercise by Congress of unlimited inquiry into the conduct of newspapers," said the minority. Congressional inquiries "if frequently repeated, would extinguish without the passage of a single law, that free and unfettered reporting of events and comment thereon, upon which the preservation of our liberties depends." Minority members believed the danger of intimidation was great: "A press that is under the continuing necessity of accounting to government for its opinions is not a free press—whether the government be a good or bad government."[74]

McCarthy, however, was less of a threat to freedom of the press than the relatively new Senate Internal Security Subcommittee, chaired in 1955 by Senator James Eastland, Democrat of Mississippi. Eastland's target was the *New York Times,* chosen, said many contemporary critics, because of its support of the Supreme Court's 1954 decision abolishing segregation in the public schools. The inquiry began with the testimony of Winston M. Burdett, a reporter for the Columbia Broadcasting System, who had been a Communist while working on the Brooklyn *Eagle* in the 1930s. Burdett identified a number of individuals as having belonged to the party when he did, including a number of *Times* employees. Based on that data, Eastland brought his inquiry to New York City and heard testimony from thirty-eight witnesses, eighteen of whom had past or present connections with the *New York Times.* Twenty-two witnesses took the Fifth Amendment and refused to answer questions about the Communist party. Six of those witnesses standing on the Fifth Amendment's protection against self-incrimination were journalists, three of whom were employed by the *Times.* All six lost their jobs immediately. Four journalists based their efforts to avoid testifying on the First Amendment. All of these individuals were cited for contempt of Congress. One, an employee of the *Daily News,* lost his job; the *New York Times* kept the other three men at work pending disposition of the case.[75]

The *Times* felt more than justified in dismissing the individuals who had taken the Fifth Amendment. Publisher Arthur Hays Sulzberger said that "like any other citizen, a newspaperman has the undoubted right to assert his Constitutional privilege not to incriminate himself." But, he added, "invocation of the Fifth Amendment places upon him a heavy burden of proof of his fitness to continue to hold a place of trust on the news or editorial staff of this newspaper. And it lays upon the newspaper an obligation to consider whether in view of all the facts, including the stand he has taken, he is still qualified to hold his position." According to Sulzberger, "Nowhere is it written that a person claiming protection against self incrimination should be continued in these sensitive departments where trust and confidence are the tools of a good workman."[76]

The dismissals sparked a debate about the propriety of the Eastland investigation and the response of the employers involved. The *New York Post,* where James Wechsler still licked the wounds inflicted by both Senator McCarthy and the ASNE, was critical of the entire journalistic community: "The areas of caution, silence and doubletalk remain large. . . . The Eastland committee . . . has unwittingly exposed the cowardice and submissiveness which afflicts large segments of journalism."[77] Columnist Walter Lippmann, writing in the *New York Herald-Tribune,* also took the *Times* to task for allowing the Eastland Committee to dictate its employment practices: "If we who are connected with newspapers acquiesce in the right to Congress to censor on any grounds whatever newspaper employment, we shall have opened the way to a grave invasion of the freedom of the press."[78] Few journalists adopted the stance taken by Wechsler or Lippmann; most agreed with the analysis of the matter offered by the *Wall Street Journal.* "The First Amendment safeguards a free press and thus the right of anyone to go into the business," the *Journal* commented. "But it does not guarantee that the man is unanswerable for what he prints." Nor, said the newspaper, did the First Amendment protect journalists from exposure of their political beliefs: "For newspapers to claim such a privilege when they themselves are in the daily business of exposing what other people do and say is ludicrous, indeed."[79]

While the firing of the journalists who took the Fifth Amendment was generally sanctioned by the nation's press, the fate of the journalists who stood on the First Amendment remained unsettled for years. The judicial system had regularly rebuffed similar claims, forcing persons who did not wish to testify to rely on the Fifth Amendment. When the journalists' case finally reached the Supreme Court in 1961, their convictions for contempt of Congress were overturned on procedural grounds. While the majority refused to reach the First Amendment issue, William O. Douglas, concurring in the decision, found the case rife with First Amendment implications. Few of those issues, however, related to the right of the defendants to protect their freedom of expression. Rather, Douglas did something that much of the newspaper industry refused to do—he labeled the investigation into the alleged Communist infiltration of the press as totally unconstitutional. Congressional investigations, according to Douglas, were limited to subjects on which legislation was possible or likely. The First Amendment stood as an absolute bar to any legislation affecting the press; hence, the entire inquiry was illegal. "Since the editorials written and the news printed and the policies advocated by the press are none of the Government's business," he wrote, "I see no justification for the Government investigating the capacities, leanings, ideology, qualifications, prejudices or politics of those who collect or write the news."[80]

But Douglas was writing his concurring opinion in 1961, light years, or so it seemed, away from the turmoil of the most intense days of the cold war. The early 1950s, which brought about the inquiries into education and newspapers and featured the height of blacklisting in the entertainment industry, marked the depths of the postwar Communist scare. Much of the scare was motivated by conservatives who were restive about the changes that had been instituted by Franklin Roosevelt and perpetuated by Harry Truman. With Dwight D. Eisenhower assuming the presidency in 1953, the target in the White House was eliminated. Following a dramatic trip to Korea in December 1952, Eisenhower brought an end to the Korean War in July 1953. Also in 1953, Joseph Stalin died, concluding one of the most oppressive eras in Soviet history and removing another target of conservative red-baiters. The Eisenhower administration talked tough about the Communists, threatening "massive retaliation," for instance, in case of nuclear attack, but the president also was the first to sit down with Soviet officials since the Potsdam meetings in July 1945. That summit occurred in 1955. Balancing these moves to decrease tensions, however, was Eisenhower's continued pursuit of Communists in government. Even so, the cold war definitely was thawing during the first Eisenhower administration, but before that change could affect Americans' basic rights to freedom of expression, national paranoia increased substantially.

When Republicans won the White House in 1952, they also captured both houses of Congress. Their ascendancy in the Senate meant that committee chairmanships would go to Republicans, including Joseph R. McCarthy of Wisconsin. McCarthy avoided the high-powered committees, choosing instead the low-profile Committee on Government Operations because that committee had a permanent subcommittee on investigations with wide-ranging discretionary powers. From that base, McCarthy launched a reign of terror that lasted well into 1954. When he began his investigations into the State Department, the army, and the Defense Department, McCarthy was feared by his colleagues. He had campaigned long and hard against certain liberal Democratic senators in 1952, and his power apparently had been shown at the polls when those liberal titans lost their seats. More likely, the liberal Democrats were ousted due to Eisenhower's long coattails, but since McCarthy claimed the credit for their ousters, few Republicans disagreed with him publicly. Even Eisenhower trod gingerly in McCarthy's neighborhood.

But McCarthy's behavior in his investigations was becoming increasingly erratic and irritating. By fall 1953, when he launched his campaign against disloyalty in the army, much of his support within the Senate had disappeared. His lack of respect for army officers appearing before him and his wild accusations about Communist infiltration of the military led to further defections. Ultimately, a political struggle began that was to lead to McCarthy's downfall, not because of his violation of the civil liberties of American citizens but because of his disregard for the dignity of the Senate. The movement against McCarthy began early in 1954, when Senator Ralph E. Flanders, 73-year-old Republican from Vermont, rose to introduce a resolution against his colleague from Wisconsin. "Resolved, That the conduct of the Senator from Wisconsin, Mr. McCarthy, is unbecoming a Member of the United States Senate, is contrary to senatorial traditions, and tends to bring the Senate into disrepute, and such conduct is hereby condemned."[81] He called for McCarthy to be removed from his committee chairmanships until he answered questions about his behavior raised in an earlier Senate investigation of his activities. Shortly thereafter, Flanders told his colleagues in the Senate, "Were the Junior Senator from Wisconsin in the pay of the Communists he could not have done a better job for them."[82]

In the face of pressure from other senators, Flanders changed his resolution to call for McCarthy's censure, and in December 1954, the Senate, by a vote of 67 to 22, formally censured McCarthy, making him only the fourth senator in that body's history to be so treated. Although McCarthy remained in the Senate until his death in 1957, he was ignored by other senators and by the media; his career as the nation's leading red-baiter was over. His credibility in the nation had been destroyed as well—not because of senatorial investigations but because of a thirty-minute television program called "See It Now." The program, hosted by Edward R. Murrow and appearing on CBS in March 1954, featured film clips of McCarthy that brought his antics dramatically and distastefully into the living rooms of many Americans.

While offering McCarthy time to respond to his critique, Murrow proceeded to destroy the senator over the air. The respected commentator concluded his presentation with one of the most powerful discussions about the responsibility of individual citizens for the preservation of freedom of expression ever heard over the air. "This is no time for men who oppose Senator McCarthy's methods to keep silent, or for those who approve. We can deny our heritage and our history, but we cannot escape responsibility for the result," Murrow said. "We proclaim ourselves—as indeed we are—the defenders of freedom, what's left of it, but we cannot defend freedom abroad by deserting it at home." To Murrow, McCarthy bore a fair amount of responsibility for the sad state of freedom in the United States, but McCarthy was not solely to blame. "The actions of the junior senator from Wisconsin have caused alarm and dismay amongst our allies abroad and given considerable comfort to our enemies, and whose fault is that? Not really his. He didn't create this situation of fear; he merely exploited it, and rather successfully. Cassius was right: 'The fault, dear Brutus, is not in our stars but in ourselves.'"[83]

Although the cold war was on the wane, no one was quite ready to abandon the crusade. Even while the Senate was considering its censure of McCarthy, Congress enacted the Communist Control Act, which formally outlawed the CPUSA. Under its terms, anyone who was a party member could be subjected to fines and jail sentences upon conviction of such membership.[84] Some conservatives feared that the measure could undermine the effectiveness of the Smith Act and the Internal Security Act of 1950. Registration provisions of the latter law in particular might be voided by the courts because registration could be considered self-incrimination under the Fifth Amendment.[85] Nevertheless, the measure was enacted, becoming the third major piece of anti-Communist legislation to go on the books in four years.

The new law had been preceded by the Internal Security Act of 1950 and the Immigration and Nationality Act of 1952. The latter measure, also known as the McCarran-Walter Act, was a complete recodification of the country's immigration policy, which also had been vetoed by Harry Truman. The act played upon decades of nativist feelings and was designed to keep the nation ideologically and racially pure. The law substantially tightened provisions for entering the United States and for becoming a citizen, while loosening restrictions on deportations of current, former, and alleged Communists.[86] The Communist Control Act was the last major piece of legislation against Communists. By 1954, that struggle was being waged in a new forum—the Supreme Court—and the justices had their hands full evaluating the laws already on the books.

The Court's record in the Communist cases is best described as mixed. Many early cases, decided in the depths of the cold war, tended to go against the Communists, while later cases, which often presented similar situations, saw the justices carefully differentiating the information presented and deciding for those persons convicted for having Communist connections. Pinpointing the reasons for such changes is difficult. Although almost impossible to prove, the climate of public opinion obviously played some role. Public antipathy toward communism had lessened by the mid-1950s, and many Court decisions reflected these attitudes. New justices who took their places on the Court during the Eisenhower administration also contributed to the changed rulings. Foremost among these appointees, of course, was Earl Warren, who became chief justice in 1953 after the death of Fred Vinson.[87] For a while, Warren joined the minority dissents of Hugo L. Black and William O. Douglas, but before long, the dissents became opinions of the Court. Freedom of expression was on its way back to its pre-eminent place in the Court's hierarchy of values.

But in the early 1950s, the Court had a long way to go before those changes could occur. In the process, convictions of individuals for their political associations were upheld, and people went to jail for their beliefs. In 1951, for instance, the Court, in the Dennis case, upheld the constitutionality of the Smith Act and blessed its use against Communist defendants. To show the unpredictability of the Supreme Court in cases relating to Communists, the same Court, in a case decided just shortly before *Dennis,* indicated that it was not ready to abandon legal niceties in the face of the anti-Communist onslaught.

In *Joint Anti-Fascist Refugee Committee v. McGrath,* five members of the Court restrained Attorney General J. Howard McGrath's eagerness to place new names on the attorney general's list of subversive organizations. The refugee committee, which was most active during World War II, devoted its efforts to aiding the refugees from the Spanish Civil War. By logical extension, the committee then worked to aid the Communist survivors of that conflict since the war essentially was between the Communists and the fascists loyal to Francisco Franco. Regardless of that background, the Court found that McGrath had placed the committee on the list without granting a hearing or stating his reasons. The Court decided that the attorney general had acted arbitrarily and that hearings must be held. Placing an organization on that list, said Justice Harold Burton, essentially labels it as Communist, which "cripple[s] the functioning and damage[s] the reputation of those organizations in their respective communities and in the nation." Thus, the attorney general must take greater care in placing organizations on the list.[88]

The first encounter between the Court and the efforts of the Subversive Activities Control Board authorized by the Internal Security Act of 1950 also ended in a setback for the government's anti-Communist efforts. The party had been ordered to register as a Communist-action organization under the provisions of the law after the board had followed all of the necessary legal steps, including holding a substantial hearing. Party lawyers, however, argued in 1956 that the process was flawed because the board had placed a great deal of reliance on ex-Communist witnesses who worked as professional informants for the government. Three of these witnesses had publicly announced that they had committed perjury. Six members of the Court decided that the Communist party had a valid argument and ordered the Subversive Activities Control Board to reopen its hearing against the party in order to consider the fact that several witnesses had lied under oath.[89]

When the Subversive Activities Control Board next ordered the party to register, the Supreme Court reaction was quite different. In a case that was decided in 1961, five members of the Court upheld the board's order that the party register. Among the claims that the majority justices rejected was that the Internal Security Act violated various First Amendment rights of expression, belief, and association. The majority, in an opinion written by Felix Frankfurter, advocated deference to the legislative determination that communism was dangerous to the continued well-being of the country and that the party in the United States should be exposed by registration.[90]

Taking his traditional place among the dissenters was Hugo L. Black, who used these cases to delineate his own interpretation of the First Amendment. Harlan Fiske Stone had put forth the preferred position; the Vinson Court had generally advocated balancing; and Felix Frankfurter deferred to legislative judgment on most issues. Black advocated an absolutist view of the First Amendment. To him, the words "no law" meant exactly that—Congress could pass no law whatsoever that infringed on expressive activity. The Internal Security Act certainly violated that proscription. "The question under that Amendment [the First] is whether Congress has power to outlaw an association, group or party either on the ground that it advocates a policy of violent overthrow of the existing Government at some time in the distant future or on the ground that it is ideologically subservient to some foreign country," Black said. The answer was obvious: "In my judgment, neither of these factors justifies an invasion of rights protected by the First Amendment. Talk about the desirability of revolution has a long and honorable history, not only in other parts of the world, but also in our own country." Indeed, he said, "this kind of talk, like any other, can be used at the wrong time and for the wrong purpose. But, under our system of Government, the remedy for this danger must be the same remedy that is applied to the danger that comes from any other erroneous talk—education and contrary argument." Black was willing to take the consequences of allowing such freedom: "If that remedy is not sufficient, the only meaning of free speech must be that revolutionary ideas will be allowed to prevail."[91]

Black's faith that the American people would reject communism was obviously not shared by the majority of his colleagues on the high bench or in government. The party was ordered to register with the Subversive Activities Control Board as a Communist-action organization. When it refused to provide the attorney general with a list of its members in compliance with the order, the attorney general asked the Subversive Activities Control Board to require individual party members known to him to register. The board agreed, as did the Court of Appeals for the District of Columbia. The Supreme Court, notwithstanding its approval of the board's earlier order to register, refused to permit the attorney general to force individual members to reveal themselves. This requirement, said a unanimous Court, constituted self-incrimination because it made members subject to a variety of prosecutions, and thus it violated the Fifth Amendment.[92]

Court majorities voided other sections of the Internal Security Act as well. In 1967, for example, six members of the Court invalidated provisions that barred party members from employment in a defense facility. The case involved a party member who worked as a machinist at a shipyard that the secretary of defense had placed on the list of work sites from which Communists should be excluded. Chief Justice Warren noted that the government claimed the act's language was designed "to reduce the threat of sabotage and espionage in the Nation's defense plants." To Warren, the law infringed on an individual's First Amendment rights because it "put appellee to the choice of surrendering his organizational affiliation, regardless of whether his membership threatened the security of a defense facility, or giving up his job." Although the majority was "not unmindful of the congressional concern over the danger of sabotage and espionage in national defense industries," Warren said the provision was too broad, "indiscriminately trapping membership which can be constitutionally punished and membership which cannot be so proscribed."[93]

Justices also reviewed provisions regulating foreign travel in the Internal Security Act and the Immigration and Nationality Act. Officials in the passport office at the Department of State had informally exercised such restraints even before the legislation mandated them. As a result, Communists had great difficulty obtaining permission to travel abroad because government officials believed such trips involved planning the violent overthrow of the American government.[94] The first chink in this protective curtain around the United States came in 1958, when a five-member majority refused to find within the Immigration and Nationality Act permission for State Department officials to require applicants to file affidavits concerning membership in the Communist party before granting passports.[95] In 1964, five justices determined that similar provisions banning travel by party members in the Internal Security Act were unconstitutional. Justice William O. Douglas concurred in the decision but rested his logic on the close relationship of travel to freedom of expression. "Freedom of movement is kin to the right of assembly and to the right of association," he said. "This freedom of movement is the very essence of our free society, setting us apart. Like the right of assembly and the right of association, it often makes all other rights meaningful—knowing, studying, arguing, exploring, conversing, observing and even thinking. Once the right to travel is curtailed, all other rights suffer."[96]

Toleration of travel by Communists, however, was limited. In 1972, in one of the last Communist-related cases to come before the Court, six justices decided that the government could use the Immigration and Nationality Act of 1952 to keep Dr. Ernest Mandel, a revolutionary Marxist scholar who had been in the United States twice before, from entering the country for a speaking tour. The government said that on a previous visit Mandel had gone places and done things for which he had not had prior permission. The case was brought by American citizens who argued that the government's decision violated their First Amendment rights to hear Mandel speak. Although Justice Harry Blackmun, writing for the majority, acknowledged that First Amendment rights were indeed implicated, he noted that if such an argument were successful, almost any alien could be allowed to enter the country because "there are probably those who would wish to meet and speak with him."[97]

William O. Douglas, in dissent, charged that in keeping Mandel from fulfilling his speaking engagements "the Attorney General stands astride our international terminals that bring people here to bar those whose ideas are not acceptable to him." That behavior, Douglas argued, is unconstitutional because "thought control is not within the competence of any branch of government."

Justice Thurgood Marshall dissented on similar grounds, contending "that government has no legitimate interest in stopping the flow of ideas. It has no power to restrict the mere advocacy of communist doctrine, divorced from incitement to imminent lawless action." In Marshall's view, "If Americans want to hear about Marxist doctrine, even from advocates, government cannot intervene simply because it does not approve of the ideas. It certainly may not selectively pick and choose which ideas it will let into the country."[98] The dissenting justices were fighting a losing battle. Such exclusionary practices have a long history in the United States, and in more contemporary times, they have affected advocates of ideas other than communism.

But communism was the abiding concern of justices on the 1950s Court. The other major piece of legislation encountered by the high court in these years was the Smith Act, whose validity had been upheld in 1951. By 1957, however, a substantially new Court was sitting, and the justices had begun cooling the ardor of the nation's remaining red hunters. That year, the Court handed down a decision involving the so-called second-string leaders of the Communist party. Much like its campaign against the Industrial Workers of the World, the federal government was intent on peeling layer after layer of leadership off the party in order to leave the rank and file without guidance or the will to assume control of the party. Since the convictions of the Dennis defendants had been upheld so resoundingly, government officials had little concern about the fate of those involved in the Yates case in 1957.

A six-member majority of the Court surprised the nation as Justice John Marshall Harlan II redefined terms in the law to free the Communist defendants. Essentially the Communists had been charged with doing exactly what their comrades in *Dennis* had spent time in jail for doing—speaking about and advocating the violent overthrow of the government. But in *Yates,* Justice Harlan decided that the defendants were advocating an abstract doctrine rather than teaching that individuals should take action to achieve their goals. The advocacy of action was indeed punishable; the advocacy of an abstract doctrine was not.[99]

Several other major decisions that favored Communist defendants were announced on the same day with *Yates.* With Justice Harlan writing, the Court found that the State Department had been unfair to John Stewart Service, the employee caught up in the *Amerasia* case of the mid-1940s. Although Service had been cleared for continued employment by numerous loyalty review boards, Secretary of State Dean Acheson had dismissed him. Harlan said the firing was illegal.[100] In a case involving the House Committee on Un-American Activities, Chief Justice Earl Warren, writing for five members of the Court, overturned the conviction of a union official who refused to talk about the past membership of certain individuals in the Communist party. The defendant, John T. Watkins, had objected that the inquiry was not related to any clear legislative purpose, which was a requirement for all congressional investigations. Warren agreed and in the process denounced the committee's tendency to "expose for the sake of exposure."[101] In addition, the Court sharply undercut the ability of state governments to conduct free-wheeling investigations of individuals.[102]

Decision Monday, June 17, 1957, also known as "Red Monday," immediately was denounced on Capitol Hill. When that day's opinions were added to other recent opinions protecting the rights of Communists, conservatives demanded action. Pushing for curtailing the Court's jurisdiction was a combination of longtime red-baiters, who were irate about various Communist-related decisions, powerful Southern conservatives, who were equally upset by Court decisions that began to dismantle the segregation system, and supporters of law and order, who feared new directions taken by the Court in protecting the rights of criminals. Among the numerous anti-Court bills introduced were several designed to curtail the Court's right to hear cases dealing with allegedly subversive activities. After much debate, members of Congress left the Court's jurisdiction intact. Even without such legislation, the message from Congress was clearly heard in the Supreme Court's chambers. Some of the less committed justices prudently backed off their precedent-shattering decisions until the furor died down.[103]

Although anti-Communists could count as a victory the Court's determination in 1961 that the Communist party had to register with the Subversive Activities Control Board, there were few additional triumphs. The only other instance in which a significant piece of legislation was upheld also came in 1961, when five members of the Court upheld provisions in the Smith Act that forbade knowing membership in any organization that advocated the violent overthrow of the government.[104] The political winds obviously were changing, and by 1974, a unanimous Court ruled, although for differing reasons, that the state of Indiana had acted unconstitutionally in keeping the Communist party off its 1972 ballot.[105]

Thus the status of the Communist party had undergone another major change. By the 1970s, it was, once again, a political party within the American political system. To a large extent, however, the party granted protection by the Court in 1974 was a mere shadow of its former self. By the early 1950s, membership dropped off significantly due to government persecution. Those individuals who remained in the party were so concerned about the presence of government informers that they, too, set up loyalty purges to rid themselves of traitors. Slowly, the Communist party lost members among the middle-class, black, industrial, and intellectual communities. After Stalin's death, repeated revelations about purges under his rule discouraged still more members. Disclosures about anti-Semitism in the Soviet Union disenchanted Jewish members, who had long been among the most faithful. The forceful way in which the Soviet Union suppressed anti-Communist uprisings in Poland and Hungary led even more members to desert the American party. If external events were insufficient to reduce the party to near-rubble, the party also went through another wrenching internal battle. This time, some younger members, especially ones who had been in the military during World War II or who had escaped party discipline while in prison for subversive activities, sought to turn the party into an institution that would advocate peaceful movement toward socialism. The hard-liners under William Z. Foster won, and by summer 1958, the Communist party had a membership of between 3,000 and 6,000 members.[106] By 1962, well-informed estimates reported that one party member in six was an FBI informer, thus further cutting the threat posed by the party.[107]

By the early 1960s, those individuals tarnished by the Communist stain a decade earlier began to pick up the pieces of their broken lives. Punishment for affiliation with the Communists had been all-pervasive with subway conductors,[108] nuclear physicists,[109] and entertainment personalities affected. In addition, legislative bodies enacted a variety of regulations designed to further punish persons with Communist affiliations. Amendments to legislation, for instance, excluded Communists from certain housing built with government financing[110] and denied old age benefits to Communists.[111] With such a sweeping attack on the perceived evil of communism, legislators occasionally ensnared groups and individuals innocent of Communist connections. At times this sweeping attack was purposeful, as in the case of Southern attempts to turn tried and true Communist-fighting techniques against the burgeoning civil rights movement.

Segregation in the South was doomed after the 1954 Supreme Court decision in *Brown v. Board of Education,* which outlawed separate schools for blacks and whites. For the next decade or so, white Southerners fought a bitter and brutal battle to stave off the inevitable. One of the major targets of their ire was the National Association for the Advancement of Colored People (NAACP), whose legal arm was responsible for the court cases that brought Southern practices to federal attention. By 1956, political leaders across the South sought to outlaw the NAACP in their states much the way national leaders tried to outlaw the Communist party. By 1957, NAACP lawyers were fighting for the organization's very existence in Arkansas, Georgia, Florida, Louisiana, South Carolina, Tennessee, Texas, and Virginia.[112]

Methods of attack were fairly dissimilar, but all had the same objective. In Alabama, for example, the state's attorney general began a lawsuit against the NAACP for failure to register with the state as an out-of-state corporation. The state obtained an injunction to keep the organization from operating in Alabama. The injunction also required the NAACP to give state officials a list of its Alabama members as well as other records and correspondence. The NAACP closed down its operations while it filed appeals in the federal courts. In Florida, the legislature set up a special committee to investigate abuses against the "peace and dignity of the state." One of the targeted groups, of course, was the NAACP, with committee members again demanding membership and financial records. A special committee of the Louisiana legislature began hearing testimony in 1956 aimed at showing that the association was in league with the Communists, even though the NAACP's anti-Communist stance was a matter of public record. In South Carolina, legislators passed a statute declaring membership in the NAACP "wholly incompatible with the peace, tranquility and progress that all citizens have the right to enjoy." Schools and government agencies were prohibited from employing organization members.[113] And in Virginia, the state legislature enacted a series of laws aimed at keeping the NAACP from soliciting plaintiffs for school integration suits.

The techniques of exposure adopted by many Southern states were just as deadly for the NAACP as they were when applied against Communists by the House Committee on Un-American Activities. NAACP officials kept the names of members in Southern states confidential because of the real fear that once an individual's affiliation became known, that person would be subjected to economic pressure and physical violence. As a result of these threats of exposure, NAACP membership in the South dropped sharply. In 1955, Southern membership had accounted for 45 percent of the organization's total; by 1957, the South accounted for only 28 percent of the total membership.[114] As the NAACP took to the courts to win back its right to operate in the South, other organizations stepped into the void left by its departure. Southerners may have rid themselves of the legally pesky NAACP and its cadre of lawyers; they got in their stead new leaders freed from the confines of the legal system who would take the struggle for equality into the streets.

Efforts by NAACP lawyers to secure the organization's right to operate in the South won the blessing of the U.S. Supreme Court. The justices' decisions were ringing endorsements of the rights of Americans to join together to pursue goals unattainable to individuals working alone. Alabama's effort to learn the names of NAACP members was the first case to reach the high court, which unanimously rejected the state's attempt to eliminate an irritation from its borders. Said Justice John Marshall Harlan II, "Effective advocacy of both public and private points of view, particularly controversial ones, is undeniably enhanced by group association, as this Court has more than once recognized by remarking upon the close nexus between the freedoms of speech and assembly."[115]

In reviewing the facts of the case, Harlan determined that history proved that "compelled disclosure of affiliation with groups engaged in advocacy" may be as effective a "restraint on freedom of association" as other government actions aimed at the right of association. The NAACP, said Harlan, "has made an uncontroverted showing that on past occasions revelation of the identity of its rank-and-file members has exposed these members to economic reprisal, loss of employment, threat of physical coercion, and other manifestations of public hostility." Given the circumstances, compelled disclosure of membership lists "is likely to affect adversely the ability of petitioner and its members to pursue their collective effort to foster beliefs which they admittedly have the right to advocate, in that it may induce members to withdraw from the Association and dissuade others from joining it because of fear of exposure."[116]

A somewhat different effort to discover the associational ties of individuals in Arkansas was struck down by the Court in 1960. State law required every teacher in a state-supported school or college to annually file an affidavit listing every organization that the employee had belonged to during the previous five years. Justice Potter Stewart, writing for five members of the Court, determined that the measure was aimed at ferreting out members of the NAACP, who then would be subjected to retribution. Forcing a teacher "to disclose his every associational tie is to impair that teacher's right of free association, a right closely allied to freedom of speech and a right which, like free speech, lies at the foundation of a free society," Stewart wrote. "Even if there were no disclosure to the general public, the pressure upon a teacher to avoid any ties which might displease those who control his professional destiny would be constant and heavy."[117]

The NAACP convinced the Court to declare Virginia's attempts to keep it from soliciting plaintiffs for court cases unconstitutional. Five members of the Court agreed with Justice William J. Brennan that legal action was a constitutionally protected form of expression and association. "In the context of NAACP objectives, litigation is not a technique of resolving private differences," Brennan wrote. "It is a means for achieving the lawful objectives of equality of treatment by all government, federal, state and local, for the members of the Negro community in this country. It is thus a form of political expression." Acknowledging that the NAACP was not a political party in conventional terms, Brennan noted, "the litigation it assists, while serving to vindicate the legal rights of members of the American Negro community, at the same time and perhaps more importantly, makes possible the distinctive contribution of a minority group to the ideas and beliefs of our society. For such a group, association for litigation may be the most effective form of political association."[118]

Supreme Court members also derailed Florida's effort to investigate alleged Communist infiltration of the NAACP. Theodore R. Gibson, president of the Miami branch of the NAACP, had been ordered to appear before a special investigatory committee with its membership records. When he agreed to testify but declined to produce the records, he was cited for contempt. Justice Arthur Goldberg, speaking for five members of the Court, repulsed Florida's attempt to intimidate the association. "There is no suggestion that the Miami branch of the N.A.A.C.P. or the national organization with which it is affiliated was, or is, itself a subversive organization," he said. "Nor is there any indication that the activities or policies of the N.A.A.C.P. were either Communist dominated or influenced. In fact, this very record indicates that the association was and is against communism and has voluntarily taken steps to keep Communists from being members." Goldberg discounted the legislative committee's production of a witness who claimed that the Miami branch had fourteen alleged Communists as members. Protection of the NAACP and similar organizations was especially important, Goldberg said, because "the challenged privacy is that of persons espousing beliefs already unpopular with their neighbors and the deterrent and 'chilling' effect on the free exercise of constitutionally enshrined rights of free speech, expression, and association is consequently the more immediate and substantial."[119]

Throughout these cases runs a strong commitment to associational rights almost totally lacking in similar cases involving individuals allegedly connected to the Communist party. The Court's decisions in the NAACP cases surprised many Southerners who considered civil rights advocates equally as dangerous as the Communists.[120] But the Supreme Court felt differently. The justices obviously had pledged themselves to ensure integration in the South, and they knew that goal could not be accomplished if the NAACP was kept from functioning there by discriminatory state laws. Conversely, supporting the rights of Communists to advocate unpopular ideas apparently served no useful purpose and found few supporters other than Justices Black and Douglas, who repeatedly stressed that First Amendment rights belonged to both blacks and Communists without distinction between the ideas being advocated.

Despite the Court's rulings in civil rights cases, few Americans were willing to open society to a variety of ideas. In fact, the more common reaction during the cold war was to erect additional protective barriers around broad expanses of national life. During these years, for instance, the first great battles over the availability of government information were fought. In 1951, President Truman issued an executive order establishing the system of classification of documents so well known today. No such program had existed outside of wartime, and permission for the executive to restrict access to information was not sought from the Congress. Truman based his order primarily on an ancient piece of legislation, the Housekeeping Statute of 1789, which made each executive department the custodian of its own records,[121] and on the Administrative Procedure Act of 1946, which allowed government agencies to keep information "confidential for good cause found."[122] Truman's executive order, which established the now-familiar categories of top secret, secret, confidential, and restricted, was issued "in order to protect the national security of the United States."[123]

Given world conditions, Truman found it necessary to protect "official information the unauthorized disclosure of which would or could harm, tend to impair, or otherwise threaten the security of the nation." The president assumed that the classification system would facilitate the disclosure of information by clearly identifying data that must be kept secret.[124] Dwight Eisenhower, a former military man, continued the classification system. Although he believed that citizens should have information about their government, he also was convinced that "the interests of national defense require the preservation of the ability of the United States to protect and defend itself against all hostile or destructive action by covert or overt means, including espionage as well as military action."[125]

Although President Truman's executive order was accepted with relative calm by Congress, members of the press reacted differently. Journalists had had a rocky relationship with the feisty Missourian from the start, and this new classification system was the last straw.[126] *Editor & Publisher,* the newspaper industry trade publication, termed the classification program "the most drastic peacetime censorship ever attempted in this country." Fearing that government employees would become energetic censors, the magazine predicted that "the magic words 'national defense' or 'national security' can be made to mean almost anything."[127]

President Truman tried to reassure journalists, pointing out that members of the press were overlooking language that said "information shall not be classified and withheld from the public on the ground that it affects the national security, unless it is in fact actually necessary to protect such information in the interests of national security." According to Truman, the executive order should "correct abuses which may have grown up by use of over-classification of information in the name of national security."[128] But Truman coupled attempts to mollify journalists with attacks on them for releasing information that he considered to be detrimental to the national security. Attitudes hardened on both sides, and the harsh adversarial relationship between the president and the press so common in later years began.

During these years, journalists were fighting a growing governmental tendency to withhold information. In one area in particular, such activity became increasingly irritating. Although journalists initially had not been eager to report news about atomic energy, that attitude began to change by the early 1950s.[129] By then, however, legislative barriers hampered coverage. The Atomic Energy Act of 1946, which established civilian control over nuclear research, severely restricted information available to the press and public. Reporters could find some solace in one section of the act that said, "the dissemination of scientific and technical information relating to atomic energy should be permitted and encouraged so as to provide that free interchange of ideas and criticisms which is essential to scientific progress." But the law defined restricted data as "all data concerning the manufacture or utilization of atomic weapons, the production of fissionable material, or the use of fissionable material in the production of power, but . . . not . . . any data which the Commission from time to time determines may be published without adversely affecting the common defense and security."[130] Such language put government censors fairly securely astride the channels of information about atomic energy.

Little opposition was voiced when the law was passed. The cold war was just getting under way, and journalists were anxious to prove their patriotism. In fact, in 1946, editors of the *Baltimore News-Post* reported to the FBI an individual who was trying to sell them photographs of materials that went into the bomb's construction.[131] By 1948, some journalists sought to convince their colleagues to demand greater access to atomic information. As if to prove the problems of atomic coverage, by 1950, American journalists had a full-blown case of censorship of atomic information on their hands. Gerald Piel, editor of the *Scientific American,* told ASNE members that the Atomic Energy Commission had forced him to stop a press run of a recent issue in order to prevent the distribution of a single paragraph in a story by Hans A. Bethe, a leading authority on atomic energy. Some 3,000 copies of the issue were destroyed, as were the plates containing the offensive information. According to Piel, the data had been declassified by the agency and had appeared elsewhere before being included in the *Scientific American* piece. Editors attending the 1950 ASNE session at which Piel told his tale of woe responded by creating a special subcommittee on atomic energy under the organization's standing committee on freedom of information. But no resolutions roundly condemning the government's actions were issued nor were there any lawsuits attempting to right the wrong done to the *Scientific American.*

Journalists had some hope for relief from the shroud of secrecy that surrounded atomic energy information when the Eisenhower administration, which was interested in the commercial development of nuclear power sources, initiated efforts to revise the Atomic Energy Act. The new law, passed in 1954, required "a continuous review of Restricted Data . . . in order to determine which information may be declassified and removed from the category of Restricted Data without undue risk to the common defense and security."[132]

Decisions about the release of information relating to the military use of atomic energy were to be made jointly by the Atomic Energy Commission and the Department of Defense, an arrangement that created an inherent bias against the release of information.

By 1955, members of Congress shared press concerns about increasing restrictions on the availability of information of all kinds, for they, too, were having problems obtaining data from the executive branch that they considered essential to their functioning as lawmakers. Congressional problems stemmed in large part from executive refusal to share records assumed necessary for probes into the Communist menace. Harry S. Truman's policy of withholding critical files from the House Committee on Un-American Activities was harshly criticized. And members of Congress were offended when Dwight D. Eisenhower refused to allow members of his administration to testify before Senator Joseph McCarthy's subcommittee that was investigating alleged Communist infiltration of the army in 1954. By 1957, the Eisenhower administration, facing a Congress dominated by Democrats, issued a memorandum listing several kinds of information that it considered protected from disclosure to Congress. Included was data about military and diplomatic matters, investigatory files and reports, and records incidental to public policy making.[133]

Soon, the House of Representatives set up a special subcommittee on government information. John E. Moss, Jr., Democrat of California, headed the subcommittee, which was to investigate "charges . . . that Government agencies have denied or withheld pertinent and timely information from those who are entitled to receive it." Complaints had come from journalists, researchers, and members of Congress. "In many cases there is no apparent excuse for agencies of the executive branch of government either to withhold such information or to refuse to communicate it when requested," said the committee's charter. Committee members were reminded that "an informed public makes the difference between mob rule and democratic government. If the pertinent and necessary information on governmental activities is denied to the public, the result is a weakening of the democratic process and the ultimate atrophy of our form of government."[134]

Over the years, Moss and his subcommittee did their best to rid the executive branch of the idea that it had the right to decide whether information should be made available to Congress and to the general public. Through a variety of public hearings and private negotiations, Moss regularly pried information out of executive hands, often embarrassing department officials for their overly restrictive policies. Eventually Moss became convinced that the executive branch would respond only to a legislatively mandated requirement that information be disclosed. His major contribution to American understanding of the operations of the nation's government was the Freedom of Information Act (FOIA), which was signed into law by Lyndon B. Johnson in 1966.[135] The act places an affirmative responsibility upon executive agencies to make information available to the public, but it also provides a number of rationales that agencies can cite for not releasing data. The process for obtaining the information most often is cumbersome and ineffective, offering the government considerable room to avoid disclosure. Over the years, the FOIA has been much debated, much litigated, and much amended in efforts to further limit the access that it provides to executive branch information. Despite the recurring problems, the law remains a milestone in the struggle to provide American citizens with information about their government necessary for informed decision making.

Another milestone in increased freedom of expression appeared during these dark years of repression as well. As usual in times of increased conservatism, many Americans became attracted to still another campaign to clean up literature and motion pictures. Once more the goal was to use these media to build good American values. The generation's moral purists launched their attack on several fronts only to find the U.S. Supreme Court invoking the First Amendment to protect two favorite targets of censorship: the movies and allegedly obscene literature. A third medium of expression, comic books, faced an outraged public for the first time in the 1950s.

The attack on comic books reached its peak in the mid-1950s and focused on the supposed connection between comic books and juvenile delinquency. New York City psychiatrist Fredric Wertham was largely responsible for rousing the nation's parents into a state of frenzy over the effect that comic books had on children. In numerous writings and speeches on the topic, Wertham convinced American parents that comic books provided a blueprint for a life of crime and delinquency. His complaints were much like those raised in Anthony Comstock's time about dime novels. Wertham's criticisms of comic books, however, achieved credibility because of his profession. He couched his findings in scientific terms and related them to children that he saw in mental health clinics; from these encounters, he generalized about the entire youthful population. The doctor's warnings led various cities and states to enact regulations against certain kinds of comic books. The U.S. Senate even looked into the relationship between comics and juvenile delinquency in an ongoing investigation of youthful crime.[136]

According to the Senate investigation, more than 30 million crime and horror comic books were printed every month. If only 50 percent of the books were sold each month, publishers would realize a gross annual profit of $18 million. These objectionable books accounted for about 20 percent of the total output of the comic book industry, which had been in existence only since 1935. By reading these comics, the Senate subcommittee on juvenile delinquency said, children were exposed to brutality and violence and were shown how to commit criminal offenses. In addition, the criminal life was glorified in comic books, making it seem worthy of emulation. While the Senate subcommittee rejected the notion of federal regulation of comic books "as being totally out of keeping with our basic American concepts of a free press operating in a free land for a free people," it saw nothing wrong in citizens' groups pressuring vendors and wholesalers who sold the offensive publications. The committee also endorsed an effective code of self-regulation for the industry, noting that an attempt to clean up the comics in 1948 failed because few publishers had cooperated in the effort.[137]

With the Senate hearings as impetus, comic-book publishers joined together to stave off further interference. The Comics Code Authority was given the power to inspect story lines, art work, and advertising to make sure that none of these violated the code, which was geared toward keeping details of crime and violence out of print. Some of the rules sounded much like those self-imposed on the movie industry in the 1930s. For instance, "inclusion of stories dealing with evil shall not be used or shall be published only where the intent is to illustrate a moral issue and in no case shall evil be presented alluringly, nor so as to injure the sensibilities of the reader." And "respect for parents, the moral code, and for honorable behavior shall be fostered."[138] As with the motion-picture code, participating publishers ostentatiously displayed the authority's seal. Distributors and wholesalers began refusing to handle any comic books without that seal. Wertham was delighted: twenty-four of the twenty-nine publishers producing crime- and violence-filled comics shortly went out of business.[139]

Civil libertarians were unhappy about the pressures being exerted on the comic-book industry. The American Civil Liberties Union, finding no agreement among experts as to the effect that comic books actually had on children, could see no reason to infringe constitutional protections. "Some persons have suggested that, as a general rule, censorship is wrong, but that it might be proper to censor comic books since only children's reading would be affected," said the ACLU. "If the problem existed in a vacuum, it could be effectively argued that children's reading material should be handled differently than adult material, because the youthful mind has not matured to the level where it can assimilate and wisely evaluate a complex of ideas." But censorship never exists in a vacuum, the ACLU contended. Allow it to begin, and stopping it might be very difficult. In addition, said the ACLU, many comic-book readers were adults, and "the ACLU is opposed to the prior censorship of reading material for adults, even if children may obtain access to such material, for we believe that the First Amendment flatly prohibits it. To condone pre-censorship for children is to risk abandonment of all reading material to the censor, since in one way or another youngsters are apt to obtain any book at some time."[140]

Self-regulatory codes, according to the ACLU, were dangerous and always should be opposed. "Collective adherence to a single set of principles in a code," the ACLU warned, "has the effect of limiting different points of views, because individual publishers—as well as writers—are fearful of departing from the accepted norm lest they be held up to scorn or attack and suffer economic loss." Such restrictions then reduce the number of ideas available in society, which, in turn, affects "the lifeblood of a free society." Despite the ACLU warnings about "the dangers of monopoly or uniformity of ideas," the comics code went forward.[141] With the comics code, the development of this medium was arrested. Comic-book publishers, instead of experimenting to find the medium's potential, opted for conformity and commercial success.

The motion-picture industry also had chosen conformity and commercial success. Safe and profitable films were the rule for several years, but by World War II, producers began to rebel against the restrictions that the Motion Picture Production Code imposed on their creativity. Howard Hughes was the first to contest the authority of the code office when he issued *The Outlaw* in 1943. The problem here was provocative footage and advertisements featuring Jane Russell. Because of Hughes's involvement with the war effort, he pulled the film but re-released it in 1946. This time he successfully defied the production code and earned more than $3 million for his act of mutiny.[142]

Hughes's success raised the question of how long other producers could be held in check. When the Supreme Court broke up the monopoly over the distribution and exhibition of films in 1948, the justices indirectly opened the way for greater freedom of expression on the screen.[143] And in 1952, the Supreme Court provided an even clearer answer when it overturned its 1915 ruling that had labeled movies as simply entertainment and found a limited First Amendment protection for motion pictures. The movie involved in the case was *The Miracle,* a foreign-language film by Roberto Rossellini that starred Anna Magnani. The story line was controversial, for it featured Magnani as a simple-minded goatherd who was raped by a man she identified as St. Joseph, her favorite saint. Most of the movie dealt with her pregnancy, her belief that she was carrying a divine child, and her mistreatment by other villagers. The Roman Catholic Church in the United States condemned the film and sought its banning. The New York State licensing commission obliged, barring the film from display on the grounds that it was sacrilegious. A unanimous Court overturned the state ruling and ordered that the film be shown without interference.[144]

The Court now found that "it cannot be doubted that motion pictures are a significant medium for the communication of ideas," said Justice Tom C. Clark, writing for the Court. Movies "may affect public attitudes and behavior in a variety of ways, ranging from direct espousal of a political or social doctrine to the subtle shaping of thought which characterizes all artistic expression. The importance of motion pictures as an organ of public opinion is not lessened by the fact that they are designed to entertain as well as to inform." Although some argued that "motion pictures possess a greater capacity for evil, particularly among the youth of a community than other modes of expression," Clark said, "it does not follow that motion pictures should be disqualified from First Amendment protection. If there be capacity for evil it may be relevant in determining the permissible scope of community control, but it does not authorize substantially unbridled censorship such as we have here."[145]

Just what sort of community control the Court would allow was unknown at the time of *The Miracle* decision. Motion-picture producers soon released even more films that were not cleared by the industry's code authorities. The Supreme Court continued to rule on movie-related cases and by 1965, finally decided that a well-defined censorship program with specific legal safeguards could withstand constitutional scrutiny.[146] By that time, however, producers paid little attention either to the motion-picture code or to licensing authorities. In 1968, the industry abandoned the code in favor of a rating system.[147] Now, instead of all movies being made to suit all audiences, which was the premise under which the production code operated, producers make their movies to meet the criteria of a certain classification. Although the ratings system has come under harsh criticism from time to time and has been revised periodically, it still stands. The compromise involved here probably ensures the greatest freedom of expression possible to a medium so dependent on audience support.

Faith in the audience to make wise reading or viewing decisions forms the crux of most opposition to efforts at censorship, while lack of confidence in Americans to make such choices governs most restrictive movements. In the 1950s, still another attempt to limit the nation's choices of adult reading occurred. The National Organization for Decent Literature (NODL), another Catholic-sponsored censorship group, hit its stride in the postwar era. Not content to pursue fringe literature, NODL representatives condemned critically acclaimed books by best-selling authors. Targets included the paperback versions of works by Ernest Hemingway, William Faulkner, John Dos Passos, George Orwell, and Emile Zola—often because the artwork on book covers was highly suggestive. Members would visit stores selling these books, inform the proprietors of their concerns, and offer to issue each store owner a certificate for display that attested to the fact that no inappropriate books were sold on the premises. Parishioners then were advised to patronize only stores posting such signs.[148]

Few of the books under attack had been involved in legal actions, so the only NODL charge against the volumes was that the books offended members' moral convictions. Through their techniques, the NODL affected the reading habits of far more than Catholics. By influencing merchants not to carry certain books, other people were stopped from purchasing them as well. A congressional committee investigating problems of "pornographic materials" during this time period noted that significant problems existed in connection with "pocket-size books, which originally started out as cheap reprints of standard works, [but] have largely degenerated into media for the dissemination of artful appeals to sensuality, immorality, filth, perversion, and degeneracy." The committee majority seemed to agree with "civil and religious organizations . . . that the same concerted action should be taken against moral filth as would be taken against material filth." Thus, the committee recommended a long list of legislation designed to stop the flow of "obscene, lewd, lascivious, or filthy" materials. A committee minority found the majority recommendations unacceptable, warning, "There is a distinction between what may broadly be classified as obscene and what falls within the realm of free thought and creative expression, which is perhaps the most basic and fundamental principle in the free way of life."[149]

Not only had the committee failed to recognize the difference between the obscene and the acceptable, but so, too, had the National Organization for Decent Literature. Many legal scholars believed that protection for literature in the United States would not be available until the Supreme Court finally entered the fray. In 1957, the justices handed down their first major decision on obscenity, which provided a fairly expansive protection for written materials. Although convictions in the cases were affirmed, Justice William Brennan, writing for five members of the Court, said, "the portrayal of sex, *e.g.,* in art, literature and scientific works, is not itself sufficient reason to deny material the constitutional protection of freedom of speech and press." A closer examination of the matter is necessary, Brennan said, arguing that "the standards for judging obscenity [must] safeguard the protection of freedom of speech and press for material which does not treat sex in a manner appealing to the prurient interest." Although refusing to grant constitutional protection to obscene materials, Brennan did give Supreme Court sanction to a liberal test: "Whether to the average person, applying contemporary community standards, the dominant theme of the material taken as a whole appeals to prurient interest."[150] Later Courts would expand and contract the test for obscenity, but none would abandon it completely. Now, a standard existed against which literature could be measured. The fact that a test existed, however, would not end efforts to restrict the availability of literature extrajudicially.

By the end of the postwar Communist scare, freedom of expression, which had spent much of the period in exile, was on the rebound. By the mid-to-late 1950s, many supporters of the right to think, believe, and speak freely regained confidence. External events lessened the level of fear in this country, and the censure of Joe McCarthy considerably lowered the level of strident rhetoric. By the turn of the decade, a new generation would begin taking control of the nation. Old fears and concerns would be discarded, and new concerns about social justice would move to the forefront. With this change came a new belief in freedom of expression and new experimentation to find the outer limits of national tolerance. The level of discourse in the next decade or so would reach new highs and new lows, break new records for loudness, and create new forms in which expression of opinion could be put forth. Once again, the nation would find its voice.

CHAPTER 8

★ ★ ★

Manning the Barricades:
Freedom of Expression
in the Vietnam Era

Although Americans indulge themselves in great paroxysms of fear from time to time, eventually they return to the rationality that the founding fathers expected of them. Such was the situation at the dawning of the 1960s. As with other periods of reaction to great repressive episodes, the 1960s opened the floodgates to new ideas. The nation's economic structure had been the primary target in the last period of free discussion during the 1930s; now, the country's social structure was under the microscope. Relations between races commanded attention as did American military involvement in a small Southeast Asian country known as Vietnam. Although discussions may have begun peacefully enough, few individuals in positions of power paid attention to concerns raised by calm, rational voices. By the end of the decade, discussions were conducted by bullhorns in the middle of congested demonstrations with law enforcement personnel ready to intervene on the slightest pretext. Civil discourse had disappeared, but the revolutionary ideas for change in American society remained.

Many scholars believe that the election of John F. Kennedy as president triggered the youthful idealism that later spilled into the streets. That evaluation is at least partially true, although Kennedy himself never led those seeking civil rights for blacks, nor did he support those who questioned American involvement in Vietnam. His rhetoric was inspiring, but in many respects, he deviated little from the presidents who preceded him. Internationally, for instance, he followed the old cold-war line. Domestically, he was cautious on race relations due to the need to preserve Southern Democratic support. Early civil rights leaders came from outside the government despite their reliance on the federal government for their final victories. Leaders of the antiwar movement initially came from longtime pacifists, many of whom had spent time in jail for their beliefs in World War II and the Korean War. The more youthful protesters generated their own leadership, which at times looked to Robert Kennedy or Eugene McCarthy for inspiration, but who more often drew upon their own idealism.

Kennedy's administration also is almost legendary for its good relationships with journalists. Never before had so many reporters had so much access to a president. Many journalists made their way into the president's inner circle; still more were on the White House social list. This closeness, however, led to compromises and accessions to presidential requests that journalists later came to regret. In a variety of international crises, ranging from the Bay of Pigs invasion in 1961 to the Cuban missile crisis of 1962 and the U.S. buildup in South Vietnam, journalists heeded presidential entreaties to tone stories down or to place information in the most patriotic light. Presidential manipulation of the press was continuing, but now it was being practiced by a charming chief executive that the reporters liked.[1]

The first major conflict between the president and the press came early in his administration. Kennedy had inherited an Eisenhower administration plan to send Cuban exiles back home to overthrow Fidel Castro. Journalists discovered the exiles training for the invasion and uncovered the connection that these individuals had with the Central Intelligence Agency (CIA). Stories about these activities dotted the nation's press in late March and early April 1961.[2] A *New York Times* story came perilously close to revealing invasion details, but after consultation within the newspaper, the story was toned down considerably and many specifics were deleted. The attack was a disaster, with most of the invading force either killed or captured. Part of the blame for the failure, Kennedy believed, rested with the American press. Reporters, he charged shortly after the failed invasion, should "re-examine their own responsibilities." During a cold war, which the president considered still existing, journalists needed to display the same caution they would bring to a declared, shooting war: "Every newspaper now asks itself with respect to every news story, 'Is it news?' All I suggest is that you add the question: 'Is it in the interest of national security?'"[3]

Due to world conditions, Kennedy said, the press should establish voluntary censorship measures to preserve national security. Leading journalists quickly met with the president to argue that government possessed sufficient machinery to keep vital information confidential without restricting the press.[4] Although suggesting a reversion to World War II–era standards on the publication of national security information, Kennedy sent conflicting signals. At a meeting with press leaders, for instance, he criticized various stories about the Cuban invasion that had appeared in the *New York Times,* while at the same time telling *Times* executive Turner Catledge, "If you had printed more about the operation you would have saved us from a colossal mistake." More than a year later, the president told *Times* publisher Orvil Dryfoos, "I wish you had run everything on Cuba . . . I am just sorry you didn't tell it at the time."[5]

Despite his comments, the president believed freedom of the press was subservient to the broader national interest. He reminded journalists of their role in times of crisis by revealing that his administration had a censorship plan already on the books should it ever be needed. As Edward A. McDermott, director of the Office of Emergency Planning, told members of Congress, "We consider that censorship is an indispensable part of war and that planning for it should keep pace with other war plans."[6] The problem, House members made clear to McDermott, was not having a code ready should the nation find itself involved again in war, but rather how the code would be used in gray areas when international tensions were high.

Press concerns were justified because President Kennedy intended to regulate what the press told the American people. When news from Vietnam started to include information that Kennedy thought would negatively affect American backing for his policy, the president campaigned for more positive coverage. He tried, for example, to have David Halberstam of the *New York Times* recalled from Saigon because Halberstam's stories revealed corruption within that regime and showed its dwindling base of support. The president felt that Halberstam and other reporters who were submitting similar material were simply too young and inexperienced for such an important chore and that they did not understand the problems their stories caused for national security. When told of the president's concerns, Arthur Hays Sulzberger, publisher of the *Times,* said that he thought Halberstam was doing a good job and that he intended to keep the reporter there. Sulzberger then cancelled plans to routinely rotate Halberstam home in order to avoid giving the appearance that the newspaper was caving in to presidential demands. Neil Sheehan, a reporter for United Press International, who likewise incurred presidential ire, found his ability to report significantly restricted as a result of presidential complaints.[7] In other instances where the president was concerned about too many leaks of sensitive information, he used the Federal Bureau of Investigation (FBI) to find out who was passing data to reporters.[8]

Just how far Kennedy could go in misleading the American people and in seeking journalistic cooperation in that deception was tested in the Cuban missile crisis of 1962. At least initially, Kennedy was able to put off members of the press who had information on the presence of Soviet missiles in Cuba. When he discovered that James Reston, Washington bureau chief for the *New York Times,* had the story, Kennedy personally called Reston and his publisher to request that the data not be published until the government announced its plans. The *Times* honored the request. About the same time, Arthur Sylvester, assistant secretary of defense for public affairs, released a statement saying that "the Pentagon has no information indicating the presence of offensive weapons in Cuba." Sylvester later justified this blatant lie by calling news generated by the government "part of the arsenal of weaponry that a President has." Press concerns about obtaining accurate information mounted during the missile crisis. No reporters were allowed on the ships maintaining the quarantine of Cuba, making journalists dependent on government sources of information, which were of dubious reliability. As Arthur Sylvester later told the journalists, "It's inherent in [the] government's right, if necessary, to lie to save itself when it's going up into a nuclear war. That seems to me basic—basic."[9]

Surely the Cuban missile crisis of 1962 was one of the most dangerous situations ever facing the American people. Whether that danger justified lying to the media and, through them, to the American people, however, is another matter. Although some journalists believed that the nation was so close to war in October 1962 that the government was justified in restricting information made available, many others argued that if the government was unprepared to tell the people the truth about a crisis, then the government should say nothing at all. In the latter instance, the government's credibility would be preserved, and members of the press would not feel manipulated. But the Kennedy administration could not bypass an opportunity to mold public opinion. As successive administrations became involved in similar news management activities, journalists became increasingly leery of official information. Many reporters felt used by the Kennedy administration and by the personable man who headed it. Never again, they vowed, would they be so taken in by a politician. The adversarial relationship between the president and the press, which had begun to take root during the Truman administration, blossomed during the Kennedy years. After his assassination, the reality of Kennedy's interactions with the press was lost in the mystical reverence that surrounded his memory. He became known for his openness rather than for his news management and for his charm rather than for his criticism. When journalists looked at the Johnson administration, they perceived a stark contrast even though the new president practiced most of Kennedy's techniques.

Perhaps one reason why recent presidents have become so eager to limit freedom of expression is that they suffered from an overabundance of discussion, much of which focused on problems in American life. Political leaders always have viewed campaigns to change the fundamental structure of society with less than equanimity, and their unhappiness now extended to the press because journalists spread the news of national discontent. A major reform campaign of the era was, of course, the civil rights movement. Although its goals were socially acceptable, many political leaders were less than tolerant of the means used to reach those goals. Arguing for civil rights in the formal setting of a courtroom was one thing; taking the cause into the streets was entirely different. But by the early 1960s the streets played a prominent role as blacks sought equal rights. And in most cases, the U.S. Supreme Court found the activities that blacks engaged in during these protests to be a form of expression protected by the First Amendment.

Although the civil rights movement in the streets is generally associated with Dr. Martin Luther King, Jr., and the Montgomery, Alabama, bus boycott of 1956, blacks began protesting with their feet years earlier. The first national demonstration on behalf of equal rights won its point without ever occurring, thus showing blacks how potent even threatened speech acts could be. The event in question was a march on Washington scheduled for July 1941. Using Coxey's Army and the Bonus Army as models, A. Philip Randolph, international president of the Brotherhood of Sleeping Car Porters, made plans to bring thousands of blacks to the nation's capital to pressure Franklin Roosevelt into making the growing defense industry provide better jobs and wages for black workers. The march was called off after Roosevelt established the Fair Employment Practice Committee, which essentially granted those requests. The notion of black people protesting in the shadow of the nation's Capitol would be reborn under Dr. King in 1963, and Randolph would be by King's side when the march that culminated with King's "I Have a Dream" speech occurred.[10]

Randolph never again was the sole initiator of a civil rights protest, but he made an invaluable contribution to organizers that followed. In 1943, he became attracted to satyagraha, the passive resistance or civil disobedience technique used so effectively by Mohandas Gandhi in India. Following the religious belief that love and truth would inevitably defeat violent oppression, persons who practiced passive resistance responded to their oppressors' brutality with love. In addition, they accepted punishment for noncooperation with unjust laws as part of their campaign to change society. Serving time in jail for violating unjust laws was simply another way to defeat the system. Through such behavior, they believed, the voices of the oppressed could be heard more distinctly than if they had argued hundreds of cases in courts of law.

Passive resistance and civil disobedience became integral parts of the civil rights movement. Nonviolence was first put on display in 1947, when a group of eight blacks and eight whites participated in the Journey of Reconciliation through the upper South. In 1946, the Supreme Court had found segregation on interstate buses unconstitutional.[11] In 1947, blacks and whites boarded the buses to test compliance with the ruling. Sponsored by the Congress of Racial Equality (CORE) and the Fellowship of Reconciliation (FOR), both pacifist groups, all participants were carefully trained in techniques of nonviolent protest. Plans for the journey were carefully made and set the pattern for future demonstrations. Attorneys for the National Association for the Advancement of Colored People (NAACP) in each community, for instance, were ready to defend any individual who was arrested; bail money was put aside. The first freedom riders failed to achieve one of their objectives, for their activities attracted little media attention. Although they faced some danger, the ride was less eventful than some of the later efforts to desegregate the South.[12]

Perhaps one reason why the 1947 effort received so little attention was that blacks had not yet been driven to the use of alternative and more symbolic forms of communication in their efforts to achieve equality. The push to integrate the nation's institutions had long been concentrated in the court system under the careful supervision of the conservative NAACP, whose leadership refused to use the streets for redress of grievances. As Southern states increased their persecution of the organization after *Brown v. Board of Education*[13] in 1954, however, the NAACP withdrew from continued active participation in desegregation efforts in order to fight Southern moves in court. Lawyers for the leading civil rights organization strongly believed that violating legally enacted laws, no matter how unjust they might be, was unwise.

Thus, while the cases banning or strictly limiting NAACP activities in the South were moving toward the Supreme Court, the mass movement whose leaders believed that the nation needed to be awakened to the evils of segregation appeared. These leaders also believed that few journalists or politicians paid attention to blacks who obeyed the rules and argued in courtrooms. Black men, women, and children in the streets making their points with their bodies and their lives presented a much more dramatic picture. This was a new form of communication, and one that could not be ignored. By the time the NAACP won Supreme Court approval to resume its work in the Deep South, strident rhetoric and physical confrontation were gaining national attention.

The new generation of civil rights leaders soon discovered that actions did indeed speak louder than words. A successful bus boycott in Baton Rouge, Louisiana, in 1953 inspired other blacks throughout the South to attack the hated institutions of segregation, but the Montgomery bus boycott launched the movement. The picture of Rosa Parks who was arrested for refusing to give her seat to a white man captured the nation's imagination. That view was so impressive that most news stories neglected to point out that Parks was a longtime civil rights activist whose actions were part of a calculated challenge to the city's segregated bus system. Blacks in Montgomery had long been unhappy with the way in which they were treated by the city-owned bus company. Following the typical Southern pattern, seating was divided by race, with the blacks allocated seats in the back of the bus. More blacks than whites rode public transportation, but blacks had to stand if all of the black-only seats were filled—even if vacant seats existed in the white-only section. In addition, blacks had to pay their fares at the front of the bus but could board only by the rear door. These grievances had led to talk of a possible bus boycott, but until Mrs. Parks refused to give up her seat, nothing had happened. Her action launched a yearlong effort that finally led to a Supreme Court declaration that the state's laws requiring the segregation of buses were unconstitutional.[14] The Montgomery bus boycott also gave the movement and the nation Dr. Martin Luther King, Jr., who, although he had only recently taken a position as a minister in the community, became the boycott's leader.[15]

Violent reactions to the boycott made the Montgomery campaign the nation's top news story. The boycott began in early December 1955; at the end of January 1956, Dr. King's home was bombed. Two nights later, dynamite was thrown on the lawn of the home of another boycott leader. In February 1956, Dr. King and more than 100 other blacks were indicted under an old Alabama law that forbade boycotts. The statute was one of several laws against the labor movement enacted in 1921. One of the statutes prevented picketing and was invalidated by the Supreme Court in the 1940 decision of *Thornhill v. Alabama*.[16] The civil rights activists hoped that the Court would come to a similar decision about the statute banning boycotts.[17] Those persons charged under the law, including King, surrendered to authorities. King was found guilty, fined $500, and sentenced to more than a year at hard labor. National support for the boycott poured in from both blacks and whites and from labor unions and peace organizations.[18]

In November 1956, the Supreme Court, in a per curiam, or unsigned, opinion upheld a lower court's decision that found Alabama's laws requiring the segregation of buses unconstitutional. A month later, the Montgomery bus system allowed blacks to sit anywhere they chose. The success of the Montgomery experience led to other boycotts, most of which were equally successful. In 1957, many of the black ministers who had provided the leadership for these boycotts met in Atlanta, Georgia, and formed the Southern Christian Leadership Conference (SCLC), with Dr. King as its head.

Supreme Court decisions forcing the integration of schools and other public facilities and the growth of the civil rights movement in the South stirred opposition. The Ku Klux Klan enjoyed a revival in the 1950s, but the most powerful opponents of integration shunned the discredited Klan and congregated in White Citizens Councils, which attracted members from the better elements of society. The White Citizens Councils attacked the growing black protest effort with high-sounding manifestos and legal, social, and physical pressures. Law enforcement officers harassed demonstrators and, at times, subjected them to physical violence. Protesters were arrested on the flimsiest of charges, which Southern courts routinely upheld.[19] Convictions appealed to federal courts showed mixed results because Southerners filled regional benches. Federal law enforcement officers were not quick in providing support. In fact, in later years, civil rights leaders would contend that FBI agents often stood around taking notes rather than aiding demonstrators.[20] President Dwight Eisenhower reluctantly sent federal troops into Little Rock, Arkansas, in 1957 to uphold a court order to desegregate the schools. And President Kennedy, at times, was maneuvered by the weight of public opinion into intervening in cases involving Dr. King or into sending federal agents to protect the rights of demonstrators. But he seldom seemed enthusiastic about such intervention.

Once Southern blacks had discovered the symbolic force of their actions little could stop them. In February 1960, a group of students at N.C. Agricultural and Technical College in Greensboro, North Carolina, entered the segregated lunch counter of a local Woolworth's store and began the first sit-in. Blacks in the South were more than welcome to spend their money at all counters of the region's department stores save one—the lunch counter. The students decided to test that resolve by quietly occupying seats at the lunch counter. The movement spread throughout the South. As one group of students would be arrested, another would take its place. The student protest, initiated without the guidance or approval of adult civil rights groups, galvanized another segment of the black population. By summer 1960, a number of Southern communities had integrated their lunch counters, and another civil rights organization had been born. The Student Nonviolent Coordinating Committee (SNCC) ran the youthful effort independently of any adult program. In another move vital for the development of freedom of expression in the decade, white college students from the North headed South to join the protests. Shortly, these white liberal students would form an organization of their own, the Students for a Democratic Society (SDS), which would be modeled loosely on SNCC.

The convictions of students for sitting-in at lunch counters in East Baton Rouge, Louisiana, provided the Supreme Court with an opportunity to rule on demonstration-related issues in 1961. The justices had been siding with NAACP efforts to overturn Southern restrictions on its operations, and now a unanimous Court overturned the convictions of the sit-in participants. Although several justices had differing reasons as to why the students should be freed, the concurrence of John Marshall Harlan II is of particular interest to any discussion of freedom of expression. "There was more to the conduct of those petitioners than a bare desire to remain at the 'white' lunch counter and their refusal of a police request to move from the counter," said Harlan. "We would surely have to be blind not to recognize that petitioners were sitting at these counters, where they knew they would not be served, in order to demonstrate that their race was being segregated in dining facilities in this part of the country. Such a demonstration, in the circumstances of these two cases, is as much a part of the 'free trade in ideas' as is verbal expression, more commonly thought of as 'speech.'" Earlier Court decisions justified this conclusion, Harlan said. "If the act of displaying a red flag as a symbol of opposition to organized government is a liberty encompassed within free speech as protected by the Fourteenth Amendment, the act of sitting at a privately owned lunch counter with the consent of the owner, as a demonstration of opposition to enforced segregation, is surely within the same range of protections."[21] In this particular case, the store owner had not ordered the youths to leave, thus allowing Harlan to categorize the sit-ins as symbolic speech, a label that would protect many future demonstrators.

Symbolism alone was insufficient to end segregation; generally it was combined with action as when the Congress of Racial Equality decided to attack Southern racism in 1961. A relatively small civil rights group established in 1942, CORE was primarily a Northern organization with a large number of liberal whites as members. Well known for its pacifist beliefs, CORE decided to follow the example set in 1947 by the Journey of Reconciliation and to test the integration of bus stations in the Deep South. Carefully integrated teams of CORE members boarded Greyhound and Trailways buses to see if companies were following Supreme Court orders to desegregate their facilities.[22] Target states were Alabama, Louisiana, and Mississippi, but the Freedom Riders did not make it out of Alabama. Intimidation and violence were anticipated, and the behavior of Southern law enforcement officials and private citizens exceeded the riders' worst expectations. Participants were so badly injured that CORE had to abandon the trip. SNCC members picked up the mission, but they, too, were beaten. Federal intervention was essential to protect the remaining Freedom Riders from further attack while they were taking refuge in the Reverend Ralph David Abernathy's church in Birmingham. Scenes of brutality shown on the evening news forced President Kennedy to send federal officers in to protect the blacks in exercising their legal rights. Southern governors called out the National Guard to protect the buses and to minimize further adverse publicity. Although the impact of such speech acts in the fight for integration was obvious, several more bloody encounters lay ahead.[23]

Kennedy administration officials, wanting no more bloody freedom rides, urged black leaders to concentrate on voter registration efforts, but civil rights leaders saw the problems of discrimination against blacks as far more extensive than the denial of the franchise. Although voter registration was part of their campaign, their overall goal was to destroy segregation in the South. Everywhere civil rights leaders looked, people were pleading with them to tackle their problems. Not all of the campaigns, however, were successful. The movement and Dr. King encountered their first real failure in Albany, Georgia, where law enforcement authorities reduced the newsworthiness of hundreds of arrests by almost eliminating the brutality involved in earlier encounters. In addition, city authorities went into the state courts to obtain an injunction against the city's blacks and any outsiders, ordering them not to disturb the community's peace.

Once again, as it had earlier in the century during labor disputes, the injunction smothered a protest. Even though the order had been issued by a federal district judge with strong ties to the white establishment, Dr. King decided to obey it. Some of his advisers had counseled him to practice civil disobedience and take the consequences, but he decided against that tactic here. The Albany campaign fell apart.

Other Southern communities copied the Albany injunction, and Dr. King's advisers continued to urge civil disobedience. The injunction and civil disobedience had their inevitable collision in Birmingham, Alabama, where Dr. King went to help a friend, the Reverend Fred Shuttlesworth, break the city's racial barriers. Plans included a boycott of the city's merchants in order to win a biracial commission to plan for the integration of the city's schools. Movement leaders frankly hoped to provoke the city fathers into acts of brutality that would lead to federal intervention. The possibility of white violence against the protesters was good because Eugene "Bull" Connor, the city's commissioner of public safety, was considered easy to provoke. Demonstrations began, and the city's black leaders went to Connor for a permit to parade through the city on Good Friday and Easter Sunday. Connor relied upon a broadly worded parade ordinance to refuse the permit. Said Connor in response to the black request, "You will not get a permit in Birmingham, Alabama to picket. I will picket you over to the city jail." Two days later in response to another request for a parade permit, Connor responded, "Under the provisions of the city code . . . a permit to picket . . . cannot be granted by me individually but is the responsibility of the entire commission."[24] Believing that the civil rights march likely would occur on schedule without a permit, the city fathers obtained an injunction from a state circuit court judge that barred individuals including King, Shuttlesworth, and Abernathy from engaging in activities designed to breach the peace of the city.

Once again the injunction was being used to stop the expression of dissident opinions. King was under strong pressure to obey the injunction, knowing full well that the Kennedy administration would be unwilling to support a protest that violated the law. And an injunction was the law until successfully challenged and overturned in court. In addition, funds for bail bonds were running low, and King was needed to raise money. But the Georgia experience still grated on him, and King intended to violate the injunction. "We had decided," he would later write, "that if an injunction was issued to thwart our demonstrations, it would be our duty to violate it." Experience had shown that "the injunction method has now become the leading instrument of the South to break the direct-action civil-rights drive and prevent Negro citizens and their white allies from engaging in peaceful assembly, a right guaranteed by the First Amendment."[25] King vowed to lead the Good Friday march, announcing, "I am prepared to go to jail and stay as long as necessary."[26]

Fifty-two demonstrators, including Dr. King, were arrested in Birmingham on that Good Friday afternoon. All except Dr. King were placed in regular jail cells; King was placed in solitary confinement. The leaders of the Birmingham marches faced both civil and criminal contempt charges, the former being the worst because an individual could be kept in prison indefinitely on such charges until he apologized for his actions and pledged not to further disobey the injunction. The same judge who had issued the injunction found the defendants, including King, guilty of criminal contempt only and sentenced them to the maximum five-day jail term allowable under law. He also lectured the defendants that the proper way to challenge an injunction was not by disobeying it but by appearing in court.

Birmingham demonstrations continued, with the civil rights leaders injecting a new factor into the marches—children. Youngsters from the city's black elementary and high schools marched downtown, and more than 1,000 of them were arrested. To this point, the campaign had been much like the free-speech fights of the Industrial Workers of the World earlier in the century. Civil rights leaders kept putting new demonstrators on the streets in the hopes of so overtaxing the jails and other facilities that city leaders would capitulate. Whether the technique would have worked is unknown, for Bull Connor intervened on the second day of student demonstrations. To prevent the young people from reaching the downtown area, he used the city's police dogs and fire hoses. The sight of children being attacked made grisly viewing on the evening news, and the federal government began pressuring Birmingham authorities to end the standoff. Eventually the city fathers agreed to set up a biracial committee, to integrate public accommodations, and to meet other black demands. Before the Birmingham incident was over, white supremacists bombed the church served by Dr. King's brother and the motel that had been used as Dr. King's headquarters. A riot ensued, and President Kennedy mobilized the National Guard to restore peace and to protect the agreement.

Events in Birmingham forced the Kennedy administration's hand and led to the introduction of broad civil rights legislation. The summer after Birmingham was marked by the great march on Washington, which probably was the high point of the American civil rights movement. More than 200,000 marchers descended on Washington on August 28 to encourage congressional action on the civil rights measure. Although the Kennedy administration feared that the demonstration might impede passage of the legislation, by July Kennedy obviously had determined to emulate Franklin Roosevelt's treatment of the Bonus Army in 1933. The president even termed the upcoming march "a peaceful assembly calling for the redress of grievances . . . in the great tradition."[27] Representatives from all civil rights organizations shared the platform on that day, which is most remembered for Dr. King's rhetoric: "I have a dream that one day. . . . all of God's children, black men and white men, Jews and Gentiles, Protestants and Catholics, will be able to join hands and sing in the words of the old Negro spiritual, 'Free at last! Free at last! Thank God almighty, we are free at last!'"[28]

Even as marchers listened to speeches near the Lincoln Memorial, small fissures were growing into major divisions within the civil rights movement. SNCC head John Lewis wanted to use his speech to issue a militant challenge to recalcitrant Southerners. He was dissuaded from marring the occasion with such rhetoric, but the fact that he even wanted to present his remarks showed that more militant leaders were gaining strength. The black power movement appeared, and the slogan "Freedom Now!" took root. Soon whites who had been active in several civil rights organizations were excluded from leadership positions and shortly were driven out altogether. Slowly the attention of the movement switched from integration in the South to economic equality in the North, and the great urban riots began.

Five major riots rocked the nation in 1965, twenty-one followed in 1966, and seventy-five in 1967. Some scholars argue that urban violence is a form of speech, a way in which disenfranchised and hopeless ghetto youths voice their cries for help.[29] Unfortunately, few whites could understand the language of injury and destruction, and support for the civil rights movement within the white community dissipated. The years, though, were ones of violence, and all speech acts became less tolerated as the decade drew to a close. Increased calls for respect for law and order and for a decrease in the volatility of American society replaced tolerance.

The inability to cope with increasingly disruptive speech and accompanying actions appeared even in the Supreme Court, which had long supported the black cause. In the early 1960s, the Court repeatedly rescued civil rights workers who were engaged in symbolic speech. In 1963, for instance, eight members of the Court overturned convictions of close to 200 young blacks who had assembled on the state house grounds in Columbia, South Carolina, to petition the legislature for a redress of grievances. Said Justice Potter Stewart for the majority, "The circumstances in this case reflect an exercise of these basic constitutional rights in their most pristine and classic form."[30]

And in 1964, the Court, determined to protect the access of blacks to American newspapers, provided the press with a new protection against libel suits brought by government officials. The cause of the action was a full-page editorial advertisement in the *New York Times* that criticized the actions of Montgomery, Alabama, officials in light of the protest there by Dr. King. The advertisement contained several factual errors, and L. B. Sullivan, the city's police commissioner, sued the newspaper and some of the signatories. As the justices unanimously decided to protect the *New York Times* and the advertisement's signatories, the Southern situation was clearly on the Court's mind. Justice William J. Brennan showed this attitude in his majority opinion: "We consider this case against the background of a profound national commitment to the principle that debate on public issues should be uninhibited, robust, and wide-open, and that it may well include vehement, caustic, and sometimes unpleasantly sharp attacks on government and public officials." A newspaper that provides space for such commentary should not be subjected to repeated libel suits from allegedly injured public officials. Consequently, said Brennan, "the constitutional guarantees require, we think, a federal rule that prohibits a public official from recovering damages for a defamatory falsehood relating to his official conduct unless he proves that the statement was made with 'actual malice'—that is, with knowledge that it was false or with reckless disregard of whether it was false or not."[31] From a desire to protect the access of blacks to editorial advertising and to shield newspapers that were trying to expose the mistreatment of blacks in the South, then, came the decision that effectively eliminated the crime of seditious libel. From that point on, public officials would have a much more difficult time winning libel actions based on news stories about their official activities.

But the *New York Times* decision may well have been the high-water mark of Court support for the speech activities of American blacks. Later in 1964, the Court overturned the conviction of several black students for engaging in a sit-in at a Baltimore, Maryland, restaurant, but three justices joined in a dissent by Hugo Black. The crux of Black's dissent was on other grounds, but he took time to attack directly the youths' contentions that freedom of expression was at stake. "The right to freedom of expression is a right to express views—not a right to force other people to supply a platform or a pulpit," Black said. "A great purpose of freedom of speech and press is to provide a forum for settlement of acrimonious disputes peaceably, without resort to intimidation, force, or violence. The experience of ages points to the inexorable fact that people are frequently stirred to violence when property which the law recognizes as theirs is forcibly invaded or occupied by others."[32] When action accompanied speech, Black believed that the speech no longer deserved absolute protection from government interference. Here the Court was dealing with "speech plus," a creation that first appeared in labor picketing cases in the 1940s, and the government had every right to regulate the action portion of the speech.

Black made a similar argument in a 1965 dissent in a case involving picketing near a courthouse in East Baton Rouge, Louisiana. Although the First Amendment removed "from government, state and federal, all power to restrict freedom of speech, press, and assembly *where people have a right to be for such purposes,*" Black said the amendment did not "grant a constitutional right to engage in the conduct of picketing or patrolling, whether on publicly owned streets or on privately owned property. . . . Picketing, though it may be utilized to communicate ideas, is not speech, and therefore is not of itself protected by the First Amendment."[33]

By 1967, Justice Black commanded a five-member majority of the Court as he upheld the convictions of blacks demonstrating at the jail in Tallahassee, Florida, to protest the incarceration of young people arrested for actions in other parts of the community. The question the Court had to answer, Black said, was whether the state statute "unconstitutionally deprives petitioners of their rights to freedom of speech, press, assembly or petition." The majority decided it did not. "The sheriff, as jail custodian, had power . . . to direct that this large crowd of people get off the grounds. There is not a shred of evidence in this record that this power was exercised . . . because the sheriff objected to what was being sung or said by the demonstrators or because he disagreed with the objectives of their protest."[34] The sheriff simply wanted the jail grounds vacated so that he could operate the facility properly, and the Supreme Court majority approved of his goal.

The changing attitudes on the Court did not bode well for Martin Luther King when the case involving his violation of the Birmingham injunction came up in 1967. In an atmosphere most likely poisoned by several years of urban riots, a five-member majority of the Court upheld the convictions for criminal contempt. The injunction, said the majority, likely was too broad and imprecise to withstand judicial review, but the court order had to be obeyed until overturned by another judicial body. "This Court," said Justice Stewart, "cannot hold that the petitioners were constitutionally free to ignore all the procedures of the law and carry their battle to the streets." Although "one may sympathize with the petitioners' impatient commitment to their cause," he said, "respect for judicial process is a small price to pay for the civilizing hand of law, which alone can give abiding meaning to constitutional freedom."[35]

Chief Justice Earl Warren led the dissenters, arguing that injunctions had long impeded freedom of expression. Pointing to their use in labor disputes, Warren noted, "the injunctions might later be dissolved, but in the meantime strikes would be crippled because the occasion on which concerted activity might have been effective had passed. Such injunctions, so long discredited as weapons against concerted labor activities, have now been given new life by this Court as weapons against the exercise of First Amendment freedoms." To Warren, there was "only one apparent reason why the city sought this injunction and why the court issued it: to make it possible to punish petitioners for contempt rather than for violating the [parade] ordinance, and thus to immunize the unconstitutional statute and its unconstitutional application from any attack. I regret that this strategy has been so successful."[36]

William O. Douglas was even more forceful in his support of civil rights marchers' rights to violate what they considered to be an unconstitutional law and an illegal injunction. "The rich can buy advertisements in newspapers, purchase radio or television time, and rent billboard space. Those less affluent are restricted to the use of handbills or petitions, or parades, or mass meetings," he said. So, to Douglas, the Court should be even more sympathetic to the concerns of individuals in the latter category. The communicative activity must go on regardless of permit or injunction, he argued, "for if a person must pursue his judicial remedy before he may speak, parade, or assemble, the occasion when protest is desired or needed will have become history and any later speech, parade, or assembly will be futile or pointless." He lectured his colleagues who upheld the conviction, saying that "one who reads this record will have, I think, the abiding conviction that these people were denied a permit solely because their skin was not the right color and their cause was not popular."[37] The Court majority, he implied, had abandoned its role as the protector of these individuals.

A similar approach was taken by Justice Brennan, also in dissent, who contended that the majority's decision to uphold the injunction was a reaction to the violent turn taken by the civil rights movement. "The Court today lets loose a devastatingly destructive weapon for infringement of freedoms jealously safeguarded not so much for the benefit of any given group of any given persuasion as for the benefit of all of us." To his colleagues on the bench and to the nation, he said, "We cannot permit fears of 'riots' and 'civil disobedience' generated by slogans like 'Black Power' to divert our attention from what is here at stake—not violence or the right of the State to control its streets and sidewalks, but the insulation from attack of *ex parte* orders and legislation upon which they are based even when patently impermissible prior restraints on the exercise of First Amendment rights."[38]

To show just how correct the dissenters were in their evaluation of the parade ordinance itself, two years later, in 1969, a unanimous Court overturned convictions for violating that law. Potter Stewart, who had written the decision upholding the contempt convictions for violating the injunction against parading in Birmingham, represented the views of six members of the Court as he declared the law itself unconstitutional. "Our decisions," he said, "have made clear that a person faced with such an unconstitutional licensing law may ignore it and engage with impunity in the exercise of the right of free expression."[39] The difference between the two cases was crucial for anyone seeking to use any form of speech act. An unconstitutional law forbidding expressive activity may be ignored with little or no difficulty, the Court said, because the First Amendment protected individuals ensnared by such a provision. If a court issued an injunction forbidding individuals to violate the unconstitutional law, however, the protesters faced an entirely different situation. Here, they must get the injunction dissolved before legally engaging in the constitutionally protected activity. If they violated the injunction, the protesters could legitimately be found guilty of contempt of court, and the U.S. Supreme Court would not overturn those convictions. With these decisions, the Court had indeed resurrected the injunction as a weapon to use against unpopular causes.

One of the most unpopular of all causes—the antiwar movement that rocked the nation during the Johnson and Nixon administrations—had its roots solidly in the civil rights movement. Many of the people participating in antiwar protests had been involved heavily in civil rights activities before most black organizations had purged their membership rolls of white liberals. The developing antiwar movement profited from this influx of experienced protesters. Even more important for the antiwar effort was the revival of activism on American university campuses. With the dawning of the new decade, liberalism once more was in fashion, and leftist factions composed of individuals who wanted even more radical changes in society reappeared. The New Left was a strange mixture of dissident ideas that had permeated American society for years. A bit of anarchism, a bit of socialism, a bit of communism, and a bit of purely American idealism were all wrapped up in a diverse movement to rid the nation of racism, of a hated war, and of other perceived evils.

Probably the most famous of the New Left organizations was the Students for a Democratic Society. The SDS evolved from the Student League for Industrial Democracy, a less-than-successful effort by the Socialist party to keep radicalism on campuses alive in the 1950s. In 1961, the SDS had some twenty chapters on college campuses and fewer than 600 members. In 1962, student radicals from around the country gathered to infuse new life and purpose into the organization. Tom Hayden was assigned the task of writing the organization's bible, the Port Huron Statement, which stressed the SDS's firm belief that all individuals should have an equal voice in decision making. The manifesto covered a variety of topics from politics and foreign policy to civil rights and disarmament. Running throughout the document was a strong criticism of the older generation.[40]

The campus world that the SDS sought to influence was permeated by youth who felt much the same way, although with different degrees of intensity and over different issues. Student involvement in a variety of social protests soon led a highly motivated core of young people to advocate revolutionary ideas for their universities and nation.[41] The SDS notion of participatory democracy became important to college students, even though the vast majority of them had little to do with the organization itself. SDS members believed that Americans of all ages—including college students—should help to make decisions that affected their lives. That idea could have been most revolutionary because the United States was established on the idea of representative government, with those persons elected to office making decisions based on their best judgment and being held responsible by their constituents only at set intervals. In addition, in a capitalist society, some individuals were automatically considered more important than others, and their views were given more consideration. At its heart, participatory democracy could mean an equal voice for all Americans, with decisions made at a great town meeting only after extended debate. How this goal was to be achieved was unclear, but the slogan "Let the People Decide" became the watchword for many youthful dissidents who sought to change their universities, communities, and nation.

Student involvement in issues considered outside their purview began even before the SDS embraced participatory democracy. Students at the University of California in Berkeley first brought the incipient youth movement to the attention of the federal government. Members of the House Committee on Un-American Activities were holding hearings in Berkeley in 1960 to investigate individuals with suspicious political affiliations. When a University of California student was called, Berkeley students showed up in large numbers. They were allowed into the hearing room in city hall for a morning session and disrupted the proceedings. That afternoon, committee personnel tried to allow only older persons who were thought to be more sympathetic to the committee's work to enter. The students who were excluded beat on the closed committee doors and sang "The Battle Hymn of the Republic." The few students who had managed to enter stood, sang "The Star Spangled Banner," recited the pledge of allegiance, and were removed from the chamber. The next day, more students showed up at the hearings, only to find even fewer seats available. The crowd, which filled much of city hall, was cleared by authorities using fire hoses. Students then picketed outside of the building while the hearings continued. From this episode, a hard core of activists developed on the Berkeley campus entirely separate from the SDS, whose Port Huron Statement was two years away.[42]

Despite the fact that Berkeley had a reputation for student activism, the university also had strict rules as to where this activity could occur. Information could be distributed on campus, but planning, recruiting, and fund-raising for off-campus activities was strictly forbidden on campus. As Chancellor Edward Strong explained, advocacy of all ideas affecting the wider community was

banned from the campus proper for fear its presence would indicate state
endorsement. Given the university's attitude, students traditionally set up card
tables on a small strip of land just outside one of the university's main gates to
promote their causes. Both students and administrators had assumed this free-
speech strip was owned by the city and was available for such activities. Just
before fall semester of 1964, however, university officials discovered they owned
that land and promptly stopped student advocacy close to campus. This set the
stage for what became known as the Free Speech Movement.

The university's action led liberals, conservatives, and radicals to agree to
picket, hold vigils, and conduct rallies to win a policy change. If necessary, some
students even planned to engage in civil disobedience. The students were met by
what they perceived to be an intransigent administration. Their goal became far
broader than just winning back access to the narrow strip of land outside the
gates; students now wanted the freedom to advocate causes on campus as long
as they did not interfere with normal university activities.

Demonstrations continued off and on throughout the semester. In early
December, the situation deteriorated. Students who had participated in earlier
demonstrations had received disciplinary letters from the university over
Thanksgiving vacation warning of possible expulsion. Leaders of the Free
Speech Movement called the letters another example of the university's unwillingness to understand campus problems. The university, they charged, had
become a factory that simply produced graduates rather than an institution in
which proper values were taught and respected. A massive rally on campus was
followed by a sit-in in the administration building, which, in turn, was followed
by the arrest of more than 750 people for trespassing. The students, in the tradition of civil disobedience, went limp as arresting officers tried to clear the
building and had to be carried out. Police spent some twelve hours emptying the
building, with students complaining that treatment of the demonstrators
became much rougher as time went on. Movement leaders called for a campus-
wide strike, and the governor sent state highway patrol officers to Berkeley. The
escalating response and counter-response evident at Berkeley established the formula for almost all future campus demonstrations. In most instances, the vast
majority of the students remained uninvolved in the protests until outside police
forces appeared and arrests, accompanied by what students considered to be
excessive force, occurred. After this intervention, the protest movement picked
up substantial support among middle-of-the-road and more conservative students who then felt that their rights could also be in jeopardy.

The Berkeley confrontation was defused when the university system's board
of regents promised to review campus rules. Although for the present existing
rules would be enforced, the regents asserted that they supported granting students all freedoms under the First Amendment that were consistent with the
educational goals of the university system. To the student protesters, any statement placing the board of regents behind the First Amendment was indeed a
victory. After a semester of disruption, Christmas vacation seemed to end the
Free Speech Movement on the Berkeley campus, at least for the moment.

Berkeley would never again be the same; indeed, no university in America would ever be the same. The Free Speech Movement energized students throughout the United States to seek a greater voice in their campus lives. The responsibility of a college environment to nurture student thought processes necessary for developing responsible citizens was little in evidence during these years. As the social consciences of students awakened, standard administrative procedures no longer were acceptable. Campus unrest spread. By 1970, some 30 percent of American colleges and universities had experienced some form of protest. Much of protest would be directed at the war in Vietnam and at university involvement in military research projects. With each new instance of campus unrest, the face of the American university system was permanently altered.

Although few officials responded positively to these campus uprisings, one body did pay heed. In 1970, the President's Commission on Campus Unrest, headed by William Scranton, the former governor of Pennsylvania, issued a report that carefully criticized the violence on the nation's college campuses but also succinctly identified the concerns that led to such unrest. Students were idealistically attempting to "remake America in its own image" through their protests, said the commission report. Although "most student protestors are neither violent nor extremist," a small minority did cause problems. "Perpetrators of violence must be identified, removed from the university as swiftly as possible, and prosecuted vigorously by the appropriate agencies of law enforcement." The commission believed that "too many students have acted irresponsibly and even dangerously in pursuing their stated goals and expressing their dissent." Conversely, "too many law enforcement officers have responded with unwarranted harshness and force in seeking to control disorder." A university should be "an open forum where speakers of every point of view can be heard. The area of permitted speech and conduct should be at least as broad as that protected by the First Amendment."[43] With greater tolerance on all sides and more freedom on campus to express varying views, commission members believed problems could be settled peacefully.

Commission members felt that, to a certain degree, reports of violence on campus had been blown out of proportion. Some 30 percent of the nation's colleges and universities had been touched by unrest in the 1960s, according to the commission's report. Only 5 percent of those protests had included violence of any kind, yet an entire generation was being tarred with the radical label.[44] Destructive incidents such as the takeover at Columbia University in 1968 and the bombing of the Army Mathematics Center at the University of Wisconsin in August 1970, where one person was killed, garnered much media attention. Other, calmer student protests failed to make headlines.

To a certain extent, the commission's calls for moderation by all parties were futile. By 1970, when the report was issued, the nation was locked in almost mortal combat between persons who opposed the direction pursued by the national government and persons who supported their government, right or wrong. Positions had hardened, and little room existed for compromise. The main source of unrest, of course, was the Vietnam War. By 1970, protest in the country focused almost solely on that issue. Through the years, opposition to the war had grown both in size and in volubility, and by 1970 few voices spoke in moderation. The lessons that the civil rights and the student movements had taught about how to reach the masses of Americans were not lost on the antiwar movement. These techniques were carefully honed by those opposed to the war in Vietnam. Before the movement had run its course, dramatic gestures were far more prevalent than speeches, and repression of dissident ideas was the order of the day.

The antecedents of the antiwar protests of the 1960s and 1970s rested firmly in the radical pacifist movement that emerged in the late 1950s. The dawning of the nuclear era at the end of World War II aroused substantial concerns about the ability of civilization to survive. Atomic scientists were among the first to band together in an attempt to control the development of this potent weapon of destruction. The Federation of Atomic Scientists, formed in November 1945, directly addressed the growing enthusiasm for atomic weapons. An Emergency Committee of Atomic Scientists, which included in its leadership individuals of the stature of Albert Einstein, promoted international control of atomic energy in an effort to neutralize the ability to develop weapons of war. American nuclear pacifists condemned both the United States and the Soviet Union for their participation in the arms race.[45]

As the cold war deepened, campaigns for international control of atomic energy and criticism of the United States for developing nuclear weapons became almost traitorous. The Emergency Committee of Atomic Scientists became inactive in January 1949 and disappeared completely in 1950. The Federation of Atomic Scientists continued its work, publishing its *Bulletin of the Atomic Scientists* that had as its cover the famous clock that showed how many minutes remained before nuclear holocaust destroyed the world. But the public had little tolerance for calls to curb atomic weapons research in the 1950s. Concern about spies led to intensive investigations into the loyalty of the scientific community, which dampened the ardor of antinuclear protesters even more.

In 1954, however, the situation changed. The first hydrogen bomb was exploded in the Pacific, and the world learned about fallout. Winds had carried the atomic particles to a fishing boat bearing twenty-three Japanese workers, and the health hazards posed by invisible materials became an immediate concern. To many antinuclear groups, the issue was simple: security or world health. Nature knew no national boundaries where fallout was concerned; the entire world was jeopardized by continued atomic testing and certainly would be destroyed by a war involving nuclear weapons. The Democrats used the issue as part of their unsuccessful 1956 presidential campaign. And in April 1957, Dr. Albert Schweitzer condemned further atomic testing as "a folly for which humanity would have to pay a terrible price." He called for the creation of a public opinion "informed of the dangers involved in going on with the tests and led by the reason which this information imposes" to force diplomats to stop the tests.[46] To this end, petitions circulated among university scientists calling for an international agreement to halt the testing of atomic weapons, and congressional committees began holding hearings on the fallout problem.

Two organizations evolved out of this increased concern about nuclear weapons: the Committee for Nonviolent Action (CNVA) and the Committee for a

Sane Nuclear Policy (SANE). The two groups followed substantially different approaches to the same problem. CNVA members were radical pacifists who believed in action rather than words. SANE, on the other hand, worked more through traditional channels. The direct-action phase of the antinuclear campaign actually began in 1955, before the two organizations were formed, when twenty-eight New York City pacifists were arrested for not participating in a city-wide civil defense alert. Under a city ordinance, traffic was to stop when the air raid sirens sounded, and everyone in the open was to take shelter for at least ten minutes. The pacifists refused to participate in such a charade and were denounced for endangering the lives of the entire city; one of their number was hospitalized for psychiatric evaluation. The protests continued during the annual air raid drills in New York and other cities. Each time the protest occurred, its participants were treated even more harshly by authorities, with longer and longer jail terms being meted out for their civil disobedience.

In 1957, on the twelfth anniversary of the Hiroshima bomb blast, pacifists staged their first protest at a nuclear weapons test area. A number of them purposefully entered the base grounds and were arrested. In 1958, four Quaker pacifists aboard a sailing ship invaded a nuclear test site in the Pacific. Albert Bigelow, skipper of the *Golden Rule*, had been a naval officer during World War II and had converted to the Quaker faith. His trip into the test site was only logical, he said. "I am going because it is time to do something about peace, not just talk about peace." In addition, he said he believed his potential sacrifice could make a difference: "I am going because however mistaken, unrighteous, and unrepentant governments may seem, I still believe all men are really good at heart, and that my act will speak to them. I am going in the hope of helping change the hearts and minds of men in government. If necessary I am willing to give my life to help change a policy of fear, force, and destruction to one of trust, kindness, and help."[47] When Bigelow and his crew were arrested and their boat was towed out of the test site, another ship, the *Phoenix*, moved into the same area. Also in 1958, CNVA members tried to stop the construction of a missile base in Cheyenne, Wyoming, with some activists sitting down in front of trucks hauling construction materials. In order to clear the roadway, demonstrators had to be dragged or carried away; one person was hit by a truck before he could be removed. By the turn of the decade, the era of radical confrontation on peace-related issues had arrived.

As the radical peace movement picked up supporters, it also found strong and determined opponents. Perhaps the event that most convinced the nation's Communist hunters to pursue these activists was a San Francisco-to-Moscow march that began in December 1960. After ten months, a group of American and European peace activists reached their destination. Along the way, they urged citizens of various nations to oppose militarism, refuse to join their nation's army, and demand a stop to the international arms race. These ideas obviously were Communistic, and Senator Thomas Dodd, Democrat of Connecticut, temporary chairman of the Senate Internal Security Subcommittee, began investigating the movement to promote an international test ban treaty.

SANE leaders were strongly anti-Communist in the mode of the Americans for Democratic Action and had taken a number of steps, including asking for an FBI investigation, to determine if subversives had infiltrated the organization. Although the FBI refused to help a private group, SANE leadership kept a sharp eye out for any disloyalty. CNVA leaders, on the other hand, tended to welcome all who would protest against the growing nuclear menace. Dodd continued his pursuit of SANE for months. His committee issued no report on the organization, and no connection was found between SANE and international communism. The damage, however, had been done. SANE lost members because of disillusionment over SANE's willingness to retreat in the face of congressional attacks. Some of SANE's major supporters, including Linus Pauling and A. J. Muste, left because of its failure to endorse the right of individuals to disagree with national policy. Campus SANE chapters also disintegrated, with many of their members shifting to the newly formed Students for a Democratic Society.

Despite such adverse reactions, SANE leaders continued their activities. In April 1961, they backed an effort that brought together some 25,000 Americans in an antiwar demonstration, the largest of its kind since the heyday of the peace movement in the 1930s. SANE continued to oppose activities that could lead to war, encouraging the U.S. government, for instance, to find alternatives to confrontation during times of international tension like the erection of the Berlin Wall and the Cuban Missile crisis. The organization's major goal, the signing of a test ban treaty between the United States and the Soviet Union, was finally achieved in July 1963. The idea that had once been denounced as communistic by some members of the Senate was ratified by vote of 80-19, the largest margin on record for arms control since the 1920s. Once again, an idea that had been considered revolutionary and dangerous had, through the continuous activity of its supporters, won the day. By 1963, a nuclear test ban was considered only logical; by the end of the 1980s, nuclear arms reductions would be well under way.

Even as the nuclear test ban protesters saw their goal within reach, another peace campaign was beginning. This crusade, however, would come close to tearing the nation apart. A Ban the Bomb rally held at the United Nations Plaza in New York City on Easter Sunday 1963 featured the first signs protesting American involvement in Vietnam. The peace movement, which was relatively small and badly splintered at the time, did not welcome efforts to dilute its effectiveness by bringing up a new issue, especially one that was contaminated by communism. How could loyal Americans advocate allowing a nation to fall under the heel of the godless Communists? And how could peace groups, who were so close to winning a test ban treaty, remain effective if they were identified with such an effort? The questions continued as the protest against the Vietnam War grew. And grow it did. The first major antiwar protests occurred in August 1963 in conjunction with the annual Hiroshima Day observances.[48]

By 1963, the war to preserve South Vietnam's independence had been in progress for eighteen years. The struggle had claimed its first American life in 1945. In 1954, in the midst of the cold war, the United States became the protector of the small Asian nation after the French, who had governed Vietnam as part of its colonial empire, abandoned the fight. The motivating force behind American intervention was the ever present domino theory—if the United States let just one nation, no matter how small or seemingly insignificant, fall into the hands of the Communists, other nations likewise would fall, and the United States would soon be fighting the Communists on the shores of California. Presidents Eisenhower and Kennedy quietly increased the American presence in South Vietnam, but despite infusions of money, materiel, and American military advisers, South Vietnam remained vulnerable. President Ngo Dinh Diem refused to make changes in his corrupt government, and as a Catholic, Diem refused to grant religious toleration to individuals adhering to the traditional Buddhist faith. The situation became more tense in the fall of 1963, when Diem and his brother, Ngo Dinh Nhu, head of the nation's secret police force, were assassinated in a coup that had U.S. support.

But the nation's attention was still diverted from the war. The assassination of John F. Kennedy provided the new president, Lyndon B. Johnson, with an extended honeymoon period. Johnson concentrated public attention on the civil rights movement and his war against poverty in the United States. Privately, Johnson fought the North Vietnamese. More military advisers were sent to South Vietnam, and the administration became harshly critical of the few voices in the Congress who protested. Outside the government, the antiwar movement became increasingly voluble. David Dellinger, a pacifist who had served time in jail during World War II for his views and who would be a defendant in the Chicago Seven trial, began pushing for American withdrawal. The Berrigan brothers, Catholic priests who would be defendants in other major legal cases resulting from war protests, began their activities. And Dr. Benjamin Spock, the famous pediatrician who would also figure prominently in later legal battles, lent his name to a "Declaration of Conscience" issued in support of draft resisters.

Opposition to escalating American involvement in the war was ineffective initially. In early August 1964, the Pentagon announced that an American destroyer off the coast of North Vietnam had been attacked by North Vietnamese patrol boats. No one was injured, and the ship sustained only slight damage, but President Johnson announced that further attacks would lead to harsh retaliatory measures. On August 4, another unprovoked attack supposedly occurred, and the president ordered an air strike against North Vietnam. Intent on building national support, Johnson went on television after 11:30 p.m. to tell the American people of his action; the next day his staff presented Congress with what became known as the Gulf of Tonkin Resolution, which empowered the president to take all steps necessary to protect American forces in the area. Congress ratified the resolution with little debate and by overwhelming margins. The vote in the House, for example, was 416 to 0, while senators supported the president by a margin of 88 to 2. Congress had essentially declared war on Vietnam without going through the constitutional formalities for doing so and without maintaining control over how the conflict would be waged. Through the Gulf of Tonkin Resolution, the president continued to increase American participation in the war and as a result, sparked an opposition to the war that intensified in direct proportion to each escalation that he made.

Despite the growing unrest, the American public supported President Johnson and Gulf of Tonkin Resolution and elected him to his own four-year term in office by an overwhelming majority in November 1964. His opponent, Barry Goldwater, had been unable to calm voters' fears about his alleged militarism. Johnson, on the other hand, had promised to pursue peace and to concentrate on domestic issues. Even as he spoke, the United States was becoming more deeply involved in Vietnam. Protests picked up in late 1964, with the War Resisters League, a pacifist organization of long and honorable lineage, calling for an immediate withdrawal of all American troops and a cessation of aid to Vietnam. Around Thanksgiving time, members of SANE marched in front of the White House to demand a negotiated peace settlement. And in December, the Students for a Democratic Society, which had been strongly involved in the civil rights and antipoverty campaigns, announced its opposition to increased American involvement in the war.

Although the SDS leadership was divided on what to say and how to say it, the executive committee enacted a simple resolution against American involvement: "SDS advocates that the U.S. get out of Vietnam for the following reasons: (a) the war hurts the Vietnamese people; (b) the war hurts the American people; (c) SDS is concerned about the Vietnamese and American people."[49] Anyone who supported that statement could join an antiwar march in Washington during spring vacation. The inability of the group to agree on such issues as whether the war should be ended through unilateral withdrawal or negotiation became inconsequential as the planned protest drew more and more supporters. But the plans also drew additional critics who were greatly concerned about the unwillingness of SDS members to exclude individuals with Communist affiliations from participating in the march. Once again the fear of communism was raised as a weapon against the revolutionary ideas being put forth by some of society's dissidents. Now, a number of peace groups and longtime radicals supported the SDS approach. Some 15,000 people showed up in Washington in spring 1965 to protest America's increasing involvement in Vietnam.

The protest, which proceeded without incident, catapulted the SDS to national prominence. Suddenly, the nation's news media, which had carefully avoided the burgeoning New Left in general and the student movement in particular, discovered the SDS. The new publicity brought a change in SDS goals. Broader-based social programs gave way to the antiwar effort. Although the SDS avoided assuming the leadership of the antiwar movement out of concern for its other activities, the group's other programs decreased in importance as opposition to the war grew. In addition, the spotlight that additional publicity cast on the organization brought in thousands of new members from the nation's college campuses. Media discovery of the organization proved something less than a blessing. Now, the SDS could be blamed if demonstrations got out of hand, and the SDS became a target of congressional investigatory committees. Both the House Committee on Un-American Activities and the Senate Internal Security Subcommittee probed the organization, and the U.S. Justice Department began exploring possible Communist influence in the antiwar movement.[50]

SDS leaders themselves triggered much of the infamy that hounded them. In addition to their refusal to purge known Communists from their ranks, Tom Hayden, an SDS founder, made his first trip to North Vietnam in 1965. When

Hayden returned, he became an all-out opponent of the war. He traveled the nation speaking and writing against the war, advocating civil disobedience, and urging the people to limit governmental authority to interfere with their lives— forcibly if necessary. Loyal Americans simply would not behave in such ways, reasoned war supporters. SDS leaders thus were not loyal Americans, and because SDS leaders were helping to plan antiwar activities, all those opposed to the war were disloyal. The logic involved here seems rather far-fetched, but in the early days of vociferous opposition to the war in Vietnam, charges of disloyalty based on such slender connections were common.

Initial protests against the war were rather calm compared with demonstrations in the latter part of the 1960s. Increased air attacks on North Vietnam and the dispatching of additional troops to the South brought about small protests, often on college campuses. Orderly picketing and demonstrations and the placement of carefully worded newspaper advertisements against the war were the most popular early weapons. Intellectual challenges to American involvement in Vietnam were often the foundation of these protests. One of the most popular antiwar activities on college campuses was the teach-in, which began in March 1965 on the campus of the University of Michigan in Ann Arbor.

University faculty members frustrated about the Johnson administration's increased bombing of North Vietnam became early and outspoken opponents of the war. Many of them had supported Johnson for president in 1964, believing that he would not enlarge the Vietnamese conflict. Feeling betrayed, they turned to research, writing, and teaching—the things that they knew best—to win additional opponents to the war. At first, the Michigan professors wanted to cancel classes for one day and replace them with sessions dealing with the historical, political, moral, and military background of American involvement in Vietnam. After they ran into trouble with that plan, the professors moved the teach-in to the evening, and some 3,000 students showed up to spend most of the night listening to lectures about the war and debating American policy.[51]

Teach-ins spread coast to coast as both professors and students sought information to counter the official administration line on American involvement, a point of view that many believed was being passed on to the American people uncritically by the news media. Although most of the sessions were critical of American involvement, Johnson administration representatives and spokesmen for the South Vietnamese government regularly were invited to attend. When pro-administration speakers did appear, the audience engaged in some heckling, which, of course, made news. Although news coverage was not quite what organizers wanted, the movement did garner media attention if only because the first teach-in occurred shortly after the Free Speech Movement at Berkeley. Journalists were not terribly sensitive to the issues rippling through the nation's college campuses, but they knew something newsworthy was beginning.

The Johnson administration sought to denigrate the teach-in movement whenever possible. In attempting to dismiss the movement shortly after it began, Secretary of State Dean Rusk commented in April 1965, "I sometimes wonder at the gullibility of educated men and the stubborn disregard of plain facts by men who are supposed to be helping our young to learn—especially to learn how to think."[52] Such comments only spurred organizers on. The worst encounter between the teach-in organizers and the Johnson administration involved one of the administration's academics, McGeorge Bundy. As a leading defender of the administration's policy in Southeast Asia, Bundy was invited to participate in a national teach-in scheduled for Washington in mid-May 1965. The academics hoped that the sheer power of their logical arguments would win policy changes. While Bundy initially had agreed to participate, he pulled out at the last moment, sending participants a sharply worded letter that criticized their motives and defended administration policies.

Although Bundy acknowledged that "members of the academic community and members of the Administration share a deep interest in the encouragement of such fair and open discussion," he added pointedly that some administration officials believed that such debate could cause problems for national policy because "it can give encouragement to the adversaries of our country." Acknowledging that "there is some ground for this argument, since . . . Communists have little understanding of the meaning of debate in a free society," Bundy gave opponents of the teach-ins added credence by noting that "the Chinese will continue to pretend, and perhaps in part believe, that American policy is weaker because 700 faculty members have made a protest against our policy in Vietnam."[53]

Even though the administration clearly was not pleased with the teach-in movement, Bundy and others did perfunctorily acknowledge the importance of free debate while pointing out the dangers that those discussions created for national policy. The Johnson administration, however, was not the only force keeping a wary eye on teach-ins. Eugene D. Genovese, a Marxist historian at Rutgers University, found himself in significant difficulty with state authorities over remarks that he made during the teach-in on his campus. After explaining his political philosophy, he said, "Unlike most of my distinguished colleagues here this morning, I do not fear or regret the impending Vietcong victory in Vietnam. I welcome it."[54]

Genovese was considered to be a capable and thought-provoking teacher and scholar, but his reputation did not protect him from an inquiry into his political views. The results of this investigation were far different from those expected from a similar body in the 1950s. While disagreeing with Genovese's political philosophy, the two New Jersey assembly members conducting the probe stressed that "the teacher has the privilege of freedom to search out and teach the truth and that he should be protected by the University and the State in the exercise of that freedom." The development of different views "is essential to freedom and our way of life. Full and frank discussion of current issues and the presentation of all legitimate points of view are to be encouraged." Nevertheless, the legislators noted that a college professor's freedom of speech was not unqualified. At the very least, statutes prevented advocacy of the overthrow of the government, and university policy barred presentation of personal beliefs in the classroom that were unrelated to his area of expertise.[55]

The Genovese matter became an issue in the state governor's race that year with former Vice President Richard M. Nixon entering the fray by seeking to limit the right of dissent during times of national crisis. "No one has questioned the right of Professor Genovese or anyone else to advocate any controversial issue in peacetime," Nixon said. "The question ... is whether a professor, employed by a state university, should have the right to use the prestige and forum of the university for advocating victory for an enemy of the United States in wartime." Foreshadowing his attitude toward dissent during his presidency, Nixon added, "Where the choice confronting us is between the lives of American men fighting to preserve the system which guarantees freedom of speech for all and the right of an individual to abuse that freedom, the lives of American fighting men must come first." To Genovese Nixon said, "we must never forget that if the war in Vietnam is lost and the victory for the Communists, which Professor Genovese says he 'welcomes,' becomes inevitable, the right of free speech will be extinguished throughout the world."[56] Regardless of Nixon's comments, the incumbent governor of New Jersey was reelected, and Eugene Genovese kept his job.

Ironically, teach-ins also raised concerns among some opponents of war who decided that calm and peaceful activities were not gaining the attention necessary to bring about change. As Bayard Rustin, a longtime pacifist and an organizer of the 1963 civil rights march on Washington, told a New York rally in June 1965, "We know that the Wagner Act which gave labor the right to organize and bargain collectively was empty until workers went into the streets. The civil rights movement has learned this lesson. This is a lesson that must be applied now to the peace movement as well. We must stop meeting indoors and go into the streets."[57] In addition, the media, whose attention was vital if the antiwar protest was to win a spot on the national agenda, paid little attention to calm protests and logical discussions. Todd Gitlin, an SDS activist, noted that "The media were giving lurid prominence to the wildest and most cacophonous rhetoric, and broadcasting the most militant, violent, bizarre, and discordant actions, and, within the boundaries of any action, the most violent segments. . . . Where a picket line might have been news in 1965, it took tear gas and bloodied heads to make headlines in 1968."[58]

By 1965, antiwar demonstrators searched for ways to win the nation's attention. Symbolic speech once again became an answer. Some protesters publicly burned their draft cards; others carried Vietcong flags; and some desecrated American flags. As scenes of war opponents defying the federal government by their actions became commonplace, members of Congress took exception and amended the conscription statute to make it possible to bring criminal charges against anyone who "forges, alters, knowingly destroys, knowingly mutilates, or in any manner changes any such [draft] certificate."[59] Persons who violated the law could be subjected to a fine of $10,000 or imprisonment for five years upon conviction. To Mendel Rivers, the powerful head of the House Armed Services Committee, the law was essential. "It is a straightforward clear answer to those who would make a mockery of our efforts in South Vietnam by engaging in the mass destruction of draft cards," Rivers said. "If it can be proved that a person knowingly destroyed or mutilated his draft card, then ... he can be sent to prison, where he belongs. This is the least we can do for our men in South Vietnam fighting to preserve freedom, while a vocal minority in this country thumb their noses at their own Government."[60]

The constitutionality of the law was tested quickly when David J. Miller, a pacifist and a member of the Catholic Worker movement, burned his draft card in front of a New York City induction center in October 1965. Miller had had a deferment while in college, but he returned his card after graduation, declaring that he had become a pacifist and would have nothing to do with the selective service system. After he refused to apply for conscientious objector status, he was ordered to report for induction. He refused, his classification was changed to 1-A, and he was sent a new draft card, which he carried for a few weeks until he burned it at the mass meeting. At his trial, his attorneys tried to argue that Congress, in enacting the provision against the destruction of draft cards, was, in reality, seeking to suppress freedom of expression. Miller, however, was convicted.[61]

Miller's argument made little headway with the court of appeals either. Although his attorney argued that "symbolic speech is protected by the First Amendment; burning a draft card in a public meeting is such symbolic speech; moreover, card-burning is a most dramatic form of communication, and there is a constitutional right to make one's speech as effective as possible," the appeals court rejected the notion. In upholding Miller's conviction, the court wrote of the new law that, "except to prohibit destruction of certificates, the statute does not prevent political dissent or criticism in any way. It is narrowly drawn to regulate a limited form of action. . . . [A]side from destroying certificates, appellant and others can protest against the draft, the military action in Vietnam and the statute itself in any terms they wish."[62]

Although the Supreme Court refused to review Miller's case, the justices did take on the case of David Paul O'Brien, who had been convicted of burning his draft card on the steps of the South Boston, Massachusetts, courthouse. O'Brien's case was different in that the appeals court found the statute forbidding the burning of draft cards unconstitutional. Seven members of the Court disagreed and reinstated the conviction. "We cannot accept the view that an apparently limitless variety of conduct can be labeled 'speech' whenever the person engaging in the conduct intends thereby to express an idea," said Chief Justice Earl Warren for the majority. Congress, he wrote, could constitutionally require all draft-aged individuals carry a valid card on their person at all times.[63] The Supreme Court ruling did not end the phenomenon. Burning those slips of paper still served as an ideal form of symbolic speech, and now that participants faced prison terms for their actions, media representatives were even more likely to record such protests.

Draft-card burnings almost inevitably led to further symbolic displays against the war. In early November 1965, for instance, Norman Morrison, a 32-year-old Quaker and father of three children, burned himself to death in front of the Pentagon, following in the footsteps of Buddhist monks who had practiced this form of protest in South Vietnam. Several days later, a second opponent of the war, Roger LaPorte, a member of the Catholic Worker movement, killed himself in a similar fashion near the United Nations building. Against this backdrop, participants in demonstrations were greeted by counterprotesters carrying placards saying, "Burn Yourself Instead of Your Card."[64]

When LBJ halted the bombing of North Vietnam and announced an effort to find a peaceful solution in late 1965, opponents of the war were hopeful. But the bombing resumed on January 31, 1966, and opposition picked up. J. William Fulbright, Democrat from Arkansas, announced that the Senate Foreign Relations Committee, which he chaired, would begin inquiring into American involvement in Southeast Asia. The senator also announced his regrets at having voted for the Gulf of Tonkin Resolution. Thus Fulbright indicated his opposition to the war, adding greatly to the social acceptability of such a stance. Although the senator was not terribly pleased about the direction that growing opposition to the war was taking, he said demonstrations were inevitable given the roadblocks to unbiased discussion of the war. "It is only when the Congress fails to challenge the Executive, when the opposition fails to oppose, when politicians join in a spurious consensus behind controversial policies," he said, "that the campuses and streets and public squares of America are likely to become the forums of a direct and disorderly democracy."[65]

Defending the nation's stance on the war became increasingly difficult in 1966. Pickets and hecklers regularly protested any prowar discussion in all but the most conservative locations. Protesters, for instance, blockaded the car carrying Secretary of Defense Robert McNamara at Harvard University, and his audience peppered McNamara with hostile questions and rudely responded to his comparison of antiwar protesters to fascist thugs who operated in Germany and Italy prior to World War II. The president himself publicly denounced demonstrators who relied on "storm trooper bullying, throwing yourself down in the road, smashing windows, rowdyism, and every time a person attempts to speak to drown him out" rather than pursuing "responsible dissent."[66]

Opposition to the war, however, continued to spread. A tax resistance movement picked up steam when numerous citizens, including folksinger Joan Baez, the troubadour of the antiwar movement, announced their refusal to pay federal income tax to support the war effort.[67] Tax refusal could trace its honorable lineage to Henry David Thoreau, who refused to pay his taxes as a protest against the Mexican War. In the Vietnam era, the movement's supporters argued that some 80 percent of the federal budget paid for past, present, and future wars. Although the government generally put a lien on the individual's bank account to obtain any money due, tax refusers did not consider this a defeat because "the refuser does not take his taxes to the collector; they must be seized." Even so, "many defaults are never followed up, while others are merely looked into and let alone. In tax refusal one acts firmly to forestall war, no matter what happens eventually." The group hoped that "refusal in itself might become powerful enough to change the course of history."[68] The tax refusal movement never became that successful; and other activities were needed. In spring 1966, activists staged their first raid on a draft board office and mutilated the records of individuals classified 1-A. And in fall 1966, voters delivered a decided rebuke to Johnson administration policies. Democrats lost forty-seven House seats, three

Senate seats, and eight governorships. For whatever reason, disagreement over government policies was growing.

Even individuals and groups with substantial positive connections with the Johnson administration began to voice strong concerns about the president's Vietnam policy. Civil rights organizations, for example, became increasingly vocal in their objections to the draft. Their argument was that black men were fighting the war while white men safely stayed home with student or other deferments. In early 1966, after the men charged with the murder of a Student Non-Violent Coordinating Committee volunteer in Tuskegee, Alabama, were acquitted, SNCC head Stokely Carmichael began advocating draft resistance as a way to frustrate the administration's policy of having blacks fight a colonial war against people of color in Southeast Asia.[69] The New Left picked up the idea and developed draft resistance to an art form.

An early victim of this increased interest in draft resistance was Julian Bond, SNCC director of public information, who was ousted from the seat that he had won in the Georgia House of Representatives. Bond, one of the first blacks elected to that legislative body, had, of course, endorsed the SNCC statement. Shortly after its issuance, he told a Georgia radio station, "I like to think of myself as a pacifist and one who opposes that war and any other war and eager and anxious to encourage people not to participate in it." He added, "I think it is sorta [sic] hypocritical for us to maintain that we are fighting for liberty in other places and we are not guaranteeing liberty to citizens inside the continental United States." Leaders of the Georgia legislature then denied him his seat because, in their opinion, he could not legitimately take the required oath to support the constitutions of the United States and the state of Georgia. As Victor Berger had done during the Red Scare, Bond ran for his vacated seat and won. Banned again, he sought the seat again, was elected, and was banned once more. This time, the U.S. Supreme Court stepped in and unanimously ordered Bond seated. The First Amendment "requires that legislators be given the widest latitude to express their views on issues of policy," said Chief Justice Earl Warren. "Just as erroneous statements must be protected to give freedom of expression the breathing space it needs to survive, so statements criticizing public policy and the implementation of it must be similarly protected."[70]

Incidents of individuals who refused induction increased. In at least some of the cases brought against resisters, individuals attempted to plead the Nuremberg defense, based on the charter used to adjudicate the guilt of individuals charged with war crimes at the end of World War II. The Nuremberg principles established as war crimes the "planning, preparation, initiation or waging of a war of aggression, or a war in violation of international treaties, agreements or assurances." Antiwar demonstrators claimed that American involvement in Vietnam violated the Kellogg-Briand Pact of 1928, which was concluded during an earlier pacifist movement and which had renounced war as an instrument of national policy. Such military actions also breached the principles of the United Nations Charter in which members pledged to respect the territorial integrity of other nations. According to the protesters, the Nuremberg principles made anyone participating "responsible for all acts performed by any persons in execution of such plan."[71]

As David Henry Mitchell III, one of the first to use the Nuremberg defense, told the court, "I was obliged and had a duty and responsibility, not just morally, but also legally . . . to refuse to cooperate with the draft which was engaged in . . . securing manpower for various criminal activities around the world."[72] The court in Mitchell's case was not moved by appeals to higher principles. None of the international treaties and agreements was seen as an appropriate reason for refusing to obey legitimate laws, said the judge. The jury found him guilty. Mitchell was sentenced to a term in jail at least the equivalent of the time served by someone who was drafted. The conviction was upheld on appeal, and the Supreme Court refused to review the decision. Other individuals resting their cases on the Nuremberg principles in the future would find them similarly wanting. Jury decisions, however, did not stop protesters from believing that they had a higher law on their side.

The discontent that was permeating American society as a whole during the mid-1960s reached into the U.S. military as well. In June 1966, for instance, three Army privates stationed at Fort Hood, Texas, refused to obey orders to go to Vietnam. The Fort Hood Three, as they became known, sought an injunction canceling their orders on the basis that they would be forced to commit acts that violated the Constitution and various laws and treaties of the United States. Their effort was unsuccessful, and the Fort Hood Three eventually were court-martialed for refusal to obey orders. Two of the defendants were sentenced to five years in prison; one was dishonorably discharged. The army had made its point that orders were to be obeyed, and no review tribunal overturned the decision.[73]

A similar fate befell Dr. Howard Levy, a dermatologist in the army medical corps, who refused to train medical aides to accompany special forces units in 1965–66. In addition to refusing to carry out his orders, Levy made numerous antiwar comments to enlisted personnel. At one time he said, "The United States is wrong in being involved in the Viet Nam War. I would refuse to go to Viet Nam if ordered to do so. I don't see why any colored soldier would go to Viet Nam." Black soldiers, he said, "should refuse to go to Viet Nam and if sent should refuse to fight because they are discriminated against and denied their freedom in the United States, and they are sacrificed and discriminated against in Viet Nam by being given all the hazardous duty and they are suffering the majority of casualties." Levy was court-martialed for conduct unbecoming an officer and for failure to obey orders. When the case reached the Supreme Court, Justice William Rehnquist, writing for five justices, upheld the conviction. "While the members of the military are not excluded from the protection granted by the First Amendment, the different character of the military community and of the military mission requires a different application of those protections," he said. "The fundamental necessity for obedience, and the consequent necessity for imposition of discipline, may render permissible within the military that which would be constitutionally impermissible outside it."[74]

Court-martial proceedings, dishonorable discharges, and prison terms did little to stop protest within the military against American involvement in Vietnam. By 1967, off-duty service personnel could visit coffeehouses around the world where peace issues were debated. A special underground press aimed directly at military personnel developed, and the more courageous military protesters organized on-post groups against the war. Before too long, the most famous of the military-related protest groups, the Vietnam Veterans Against the War, was organized. One unhappy side effect of discontent within the military over the Vietnam War, of course, was an increased number of incidents of violence against officers in Vietnam as well as increased drug use and growing insubordination. Violent reactions often have been the end products of ignoring or deprecating efforts to raise concerns in a more legitimate fashion. Although soldiers and civilians tried to communicate peacefully and forthrightly, almost all attempts were rejected in favor of maintaining close control on what military personnel could hear and say.[75]

Ignoring the growing antiwar movement became increasingly difficult. A Conference on Noncooperation in October 1966 produced the first major manifesto by pacifist groups against the draft. The statement ended by saying, "We urge and advocate that other young men join us in noncooperating with the Selective Service System."[76] The language placed the antiwar activists backing the statement squarely in violation of draft laws, which forbade, in no uncertain terms, efforts to discourage young men from fulfilling their military obligations. Soon, prosecutors would pursue older individuals for encouraging younger men to break the law.

Protests escalated in 1967. In February, some 2,500 members of the Women's Strike for Peace tried to enter the Pentagon to confront military officials responsible for sending their sons to Vietnam. Secretary of Defense McNamara allowed the middle-aged women to enter the Pentagon, but he refused to talk with them. On college campuses, students began to protest visits by certain job recruiters. Dow Chemical, manufacturer of napalm, which the students believed to be a particularly hideous weapon of war, was a favorite target. As the actions against Dow Chemical recruiters became more numerous, the techniques used to end them became harsher. Buildings were cleared with tear gas and Mace, and demonstrators were arrested, often rather violently. But actions continued against the manufacturer of napalm as did student protests against the draft, especially as changes in the deferment system popularized the belief that the government was trying to run their lives. Undergraduate deferments remained intact, but the 1967 version of the draft law limited deferments for graduate students and gave special preference only to individuals enrolled in fields that the military considered necessary.

Some 26.8 million men were considered of draft age between the Gulf of Tonkin Resolution in August 1964 through March 1973, when the last Americans left Vietnam. Of that number, almost 11 million men saw military service during those years; more than 15.4 million young men won exemptions of various kinds; and another 570,000 became draft offenders of some sort. During most of the war, winning exemptions was far from difficult. In fact, most middle-class white youths who made the effort stayed out of the service. For the first time in American history, draft counselors advised individuals how to avoid being drafted. In World War I, these persons would have been arrested for interfering with the war effort; in the Vietnam era, most of these counselors worked unmolested, arguing that they were simply interpreting the law for the young men who sought their assistance.[77]

Exemptions came readily to those men who remained in school, who were married, who had children, or who were in certain jobs. For a while, many young men made such choices on the assumption that they were freely picking a route that would avoid induction into the armed services. But in 1967, they learned that many of their decisions had been manipulated by draft officials, and their outrage intensified.

Details of the selective service system's plans to manipulate the lives of American young people emerged when a leftist publication printed a copy of a memorandum that described the "channeling" power of the draft in shaping the nation's future. According to the 1965 memorandum, "while the best known purpose of Selective Service is to procure manpower for the armed forces, a variety of related processes take place outside delivery of manpower. . . . Many of these may be put under the heading of 'channeling manpower.' Many young men would not have pursued a higher education if there had not been a program of student deferment." In addition, "many young scientists, engineers, tool and die makers, and other possessors of scarce skills would not remain in their jobs in the defense effort if it were not for a program of occupational deferments. Even though the salary of a teacher has historically been meager, many young men remain in that job, seeking the reward of a deferment."[78] Government manipulation of their lives through draft deferments only made the war more repugnant.

Although the draft tried to manipulate the lives of young American men, its basic inefficiency provided many opportunities for avoidance. The nation's selective service program was run by some 4,000 draft boards across the country. Administered by unpaid members of the community, draft boards often decided the fates of hundreds of young men in a single sitting. Petitions for exemptions from the draft for a variety of reasons, including those based on conscience, often were presented. If the ruling went against the petitioner, another document could be filed, and another and another. Often youths tied the draft machinery up to such an extent that they were bypassed simply to be rid of them and their paperwork. In addition, as the war and the draft progressed, men who were not granted the desired exemptions often found assistance in the courts.

For the first time in its history, the Supreme Court significantly broadened the meaning of the term conscientious objector. In 1965, for instance, the Court decided that the statutory requirement that a person believe in a "Supreme Being" before being granted conscientious objector status was designed to test "whether a given belief that is sincere and meaningful occupies a place in the life of its possessor parallel to that filled by the orthodox belief in God of one who clearly qualifies for the exemption."[79] When such a sincere belief, although not based on a religious faith, was held, the exemption was to be granted. The Court further underlined this interpretation in 1970, when a plurality found that provisions in the law banning individuals with political, sociological, or philosophical opinions against war from conscientious objector status should not be read "to exclude those who hold strong beliefs about our domestic and foreign affairs or even those whose conscientious objection to participation in all wars is founded to a substantial extent upon considerations of public policy."[80] The key, according to the Court, was the strength of the beliefs. Later in 1970, the justices decided that individuals who sought conscientious objector status must oppose all wars and not just that in Vietnam.[81] Even with this restriction, most American males, with the proper coaching, could obtain conscientious objector status. Some 172,000 men won that classification during the war years, and almost all did alternative service that amounted to two years at a low-paying job. The alternative service program, however, was poorly designed and supervised. Some 50,000 men left their assignments before the two years were up; only about 1,000 men were convicted for such violations.[82]

Draft-aged men unable or unwilling to seek conscientious objector status found other approaches to avoiding service available. Perhaps the most repugnant to American ideals were those tactics designed to ensure that individuals failed their pre-induction physicals. Substantial weight loss or gain could be a ticket out of danger, as could psychological problems or the wearing of braces. Other individuals took a more brutal approach by maiming themselves in order to become unsuitable for induction. A number of men evaded the draft by refusing to register initially, by refusing to show up for induction, and some, by leaving the country. Some 50,000 young men chose exile, most often in Canada or Sweden, rather than face the consequences of their opposition to what they considered to be an unjust war. Most of the 210,000 draft resisters did stay in the United States, but not all of them encountered judicial retribution for their activities. Indeed, their fates varied based on the personal inclinations of the judges involved. Jurists in some parts of the nation routinely handed out stiff prison sentences for such activities; elsewhere, probation was the norm.

White members of the middle class were most able to manipulate the draft. Blacks generally were more willing to remain loyal to their country. Civil rights leaders, for instance, usually advocated supporting government policies in Vietnam in order to retain federal favors. As the war continued, however, blacks became less willing to tolerate the drain that the war imposed on their communities. Some 20 percent of the draftees fighting in Vietnam were blacks, a total far out of proportion to their representation in the draft-aged population. SNCC was the first organization to take a strong stand against American involvement in the war, but it was becoming increasingly known for its radicalism. Before long, other black groups joined SNCC in opposing the war, especially as government estimates revealed that it cost some $30,000 to kill one enemy soldier, which was three times the amount that it cost to train blacks for good jobs. As civil rights leaders became convinced that money that was supposed to alleviate poverty in the United States was being spent in Southeast Asia, unrest grew.[83]

By February 1967, Dr. Martin Luther King, Jr., moved into outright opposition to the war. In April, Dr. King called for resistance to the draft. "As we counsel young men concerning military service," he said, "we must clarify for them our nation's role in Vietnam and challenge them with the alternative of conscientious objection. . . . Every man of humane convictions must decide on the protest that best suits his convictions, but we must *all* protest."[84] The administration responded with an all-out effort to pressure him into changing his stance. Other black leaders denounced King's position, and J. Edgar Hoover's FBI, which had been watching the civil rights leader for years, tried to undermine his credibility.[85] All efforts proved unsuccessful, and opposition to the war now was even more broadly based.

Students, civil rights activists, and longtime pacifists joined in planning a major antiwar protest in the spring of 1967, organized by an umbrella group known as the Spring Mobilization to End the War in Vietnam. Mobe leaders vowed to create an all-inclusive coalition of antiwar groups that would be so large that the government would be forced to hear its grievances. All-inclusive, of course, meant that Communists would participate. That decision pushed some of the more conservative groups such as SANE out of the coalition, for its members still refused to work with Communists.[86] The decision also opened the antiwar movement to even more governmental criticism, but plans for the march went on.

Accompanying the march was a mass meeting of draft-aged young men at Sheep's Meadow, New York, where some 175 youths engaged in a mass draft-card burning. Sponsors of the Spring Mobilization refused to back the draft-card burning as an official part of the march, but the young men conducted their protest at the same time. "The climate of anti-war opinion is changing," the organizers of the Sheep's Meadow action said. "In the last few months student governments, church groups, and other organizations have publicly expressed understanding and sympathy with the position of individuals who refuse to fight in Vietnam, who resist the draft. We are ready to put ourselves on the line for this position, and we expect that these people will come through with their support."[87]

Support for the broader antiwar position appeared in several cities around the country on that April day. Police officials estimated the total number of participants at around 125,000; organizers said perhaps 400,000 individuals had marched. Regardless of the actual number, turnout was substantial, and concern within the administration increased. Secretary of State Dean Rusk, appearing on "Meet the Press," sought to dismiss the marchers as unrepresentative of the American people and their sentiments on the war. Two hundred million Americans had not participated in any antiwar protest, he said, "and those who speak for the 200 million Americans are the President and the Congress." Although Rusk admitted that "we have in our constitutional system an opportunity for lawful and peaceful expression," he voiced his apprehension "that the authorities in Hanoi may misunderstand this sort of thing and that the net effect of these demonstrations will be to prolong the war and not to shorten it." After all, he said, "if we heard that 100,000 people were marching in Hanoi for peace, we would draw very important conclusions from it. Now we don't know whether Hanoi is sufficiently sophisticated to understand that . . . these demonstrations will not affect the conduct of the war."[88]

The success of the spring march gave rise to plans for a Stop the Draft Week for fall of 1967. Among its leaders was a new group of draft opponents known as "The Resistance," which was formed by David Harris, president of the student body at Stanford University. On April 15, the day of the spring march, Resistance leaders announced their plans to designate October 16, 1967, as the date for draft-aged men around the country to turn in their draft cards. "Resistance means that if the government is to continue its crimes against humanity, it must first deal with our opposition," said movement leaders. "We do not seek jail, but we do this because as individuals we know of no justifiable alternative and we believe that in time many other American men will also choose to resist the crimes done in their names."[89]

Such opposition to the war became of increasing concern to American military officials. Even General William Westmoreland, commander of American forces in Vietnam, complained, saying, "Despite staggering combat losses, he [the enemy] clings to the belief that he will defeat us. And through a clever combination of psychological and political warfare, both here and abroad, he has gained support which gives him hope that he can win politically that which he cannot accomplish militarily." American troops in Vietnam, Westmoreland said, "are dismayed . . . by recent unpatriotic acts here at home." The enemy "does not understand that American democracy is founded on debate, and he sees every protest as evidence of crumbling morale and diminishing resolve. Thus, discouraged by repeated military defeats but encouraged by what he believes to be popular opposition to our effort in Vietnam, he is determined to continue his aggression from the North. This, inevitably, will cost lives."[90]

President Johnson echoed Westmoreland's concerns in a speech on Vietnam given in late September 1967. The North Vietnamese, he said "still hope that the people of the United States will not see this struggle through to the very end." That hope is based on a fundamental misunderstanding of American democracy: "They mistake dissent for disloyalty. They mistake restlessness for a rejection of policy. They mistake a few committees for a country. They misjudge individual speeches for public policies." Antiwar activities caused problems, the president said. Americans "must not mislead the enemy. Let him not think that debate and dissent will produce wavering and withdrawal. For I can assure they won't. Let him not think that protests will produce surrender. Because they won't. Let him not think that he will wait us out. For he won't."[91]

Perhaps only SDS leaders believed Johnson's words when he said that protests would not change national policy in Vietnam. The organization, which was beginning its period of radicalization, opposed the fall 1967 effort, which included a march on the Pentagon. Their comments reflected, to a certain degree, the discouragement of many generations of protesters. "We feel," said a statement issued by the organization's national convention, "that these large demonstrations—which are just public expressions of belief—can have no significant effect on American policy in Vietnam. Further, they delude many participants into thinking that the 'democratic' process in America functions in a meaningful way. The U.S. government has the power to simply ignore demonstrators who threaten its interests." Large demonstrations, said the SDS, were not the best tool for bringing about change. In 1967 SDS members indicated their belief in such activities as "local demonstrations, referendums, or draft resistance."[92] By late 1968, a splinter group would advocate violence.

Ignoring the SDS withdrawal from Stop the Draft Week, planning continued. One part of the protest was the issuance of "A Call to Resist Illegitimate Authority," signed by more than 150 authors, professors, clergy, and others, including Dr. Benjamin Spock and Yale University chaplain William Sloane Coffin. The statement, released in August for signature, stressed that its adherents believed "that every free man has a legal right and a moral duty to exert every effort to end this war, to avoid collusion with it, and to encourage others to do the same." The greatest challenges, of course, rested on the young men who faced the draft. But this older group pledged its "support to those who undertake resistance to this war. We will raise funds to organize draft resistance unions, to supply legal defense and bail, to support families and otherwise aid resistance to the war in whatever ways may seem appropriate." Their pronouncement, they said, was "the sort of speech that under the First Amendment must be free, and that the actions we will undertake are as legal as is the war resistance of the young men themselves." But the signers recognized that courts might hold signers "liable to prosecution and severe punishment. In any case, we feel that we cannot shrink from fulfilling our responsibilities to the youth whom many of us teach, to the country whose freedom we cherish, and to the ancient traditions of religion and philosophy which we strive to preserve in this generation."[93]

The draft-card turn-in, which the Resistance advocated and the Call to Resist Illegitimate Authority supported, occurred on October 16. More than 250 draft cards were collected during a ceremony at a Boston church, where Michael Ferber, a demonstration organizer, said, "Each of our acts of returning our draft cards is our personal No; when we put them in a single container or set fire to them from a single candle we express the simple basis of our unity." But more was needed, Ferber said. "Let us make sure we are ready to work hard and long with each other in the months to come, working to make it difficult and politically dangerous for the government to prosecute us, working to help anyone and everyone to find ways of avoiding the draft, to help disrupt the workings of the draft and the armed forces until the war is over."[94]

Antiwar activists planned more than symbolic speech during Stop the Draft Week. Demonstrators, for instance, sought to close down the nation's second largest military induction center in Oakland, California. The 6,000 to 10,000 participants in the Oakland campaign hoped to avoid violence, if at all possible, with demonstrators dispersing if approached by authorities in order to regroup and to renew the attack on the induction center. The demonstrations in Oakland turned bloody before the week ended, and hundreds of protesters were arrested.

The Washington demonstration had two prongs. On October 20, the Reverend Coffin and Dr. Spock showed up at the Department of Justice to turn in more than 1,000 draft cards collected earlier in the week. In presenting the cards,

Coffin acknowledged that the older supporters of the draft resistance movement could not shield participants from the retribution of the government. In fact, he said, "we can only expose ourselves as they have done. The law of the land is clear. Section 12 of the National Selective Service Act declares that anyone 'who knowingly counsels, aids, or abets another to refuse or evade registration or service in the armed forces . . . shall be liable to imprisonment for not more than five years or a fine of ten thousand dollars or both.'" These older men challenged the government to prosecute them. "We hereby publicly counsel these young men to continue in their refusal to serve in the armed forces as long as the war in Vietnam continues," Coffin said, "and we pledge ourselves to aid and abet them in all the ways we can. This means that if they are now arrested for failing to comply with a law that violates their consciences, we too must be arrested, for in the sight of that law we are now as guilty as they."[95]

On October 21, some 50,000 protesters gathered at the Lincoln Memorial. Speakers told antiwar advocates that the days of peaceful protest were over. Basically agreeing with the SDS stance, movement leaders believed that government officials paid no attention to mass gatherings that provoked no violence. Civil disobedience and confrontation now became the movement's tactics, and a number of demonstrators proceeded to the Pentagon, where some protesters stormed the building. About twenty-five of them got inside, where they were caught, beaten, and arrested. Others stayed in the parking lot for the duration of their forty-eight-hour parade permit, and some were arrested when they refused to leave at the end of that period.

Government retaliation against the demonstrators was swift. Among the first to take action was General Lewis Hershey, head of the Selective Service Administration. He told local draft boards to review the files of individuals who had participated in demonstrations. Maintaining special deferments for these individuals was no longer in the national interest, he said, and the young men should be immediately reclassified 1-A and subjected to induction.[96] The power of the government to punish individuals who were exercising First Amendment rights was, of course, challenged in the courts. While reclassified individuals were awaiting their day in court, their cases were in the hands of a special unit of the U.S. Department of Justice, which had been set up in the wake of public outcry over General Hershey's orders. This special unit was assigned to determine which draft protesters to prosecute. In announcing the formation of the special unit, Justice Department officials quickly noted that "lawful protest activities, whether directed to the draft or other national issues, do not subject registrants to acceleration." In fact, "the lawful exercise of rights of free expression and peaceful assembly have incurred and will incur no penalty or other adverse action. These rights are guaranteed by the Constitution. They are vital to the preservation of free institutions, which our men in Vietnam are fighting to protect."[97] The Supreme Court agreed that the lawful exercise of First Amendment rights could not lead to automatic reclassification and blocked such treatment of demonstrators.[98]

Yet just what constituted lawful exercise of freedom of speech and assembly in the government's eyes was uncertain. Leaders of various Stop the Draft Week protests were picked up on a variety of charges. The masterminds of the escalated confrontation in front of the Oakland induction center were among the first swept up by law enforcement officials. Charges against the Oakland Seven, as they became popularly known, focused on conspiracy to break a variety of laws by distributing written material explaining how the demonstration would be organized and conducted, establishing a bail fund, teaching participants how to use wooden sticks as clubs, and bringing loudspeakers to the demonstration site. The prosecution and defense teams maneuvered for almost a year before the case went to court. Although the defendants did not take the stand on their own behalf, some forty-seven witnesses testified in an attempt to prove that no conspiracy existed. In some of the most liberal instructions ever given in an antiwar demonstration case, the judge told jurors that they could consider the beliefs of the defendants about the legality of the Vietnam War and the draft in reaching their decision. And the judge provided careful instructions that ensured that the jury understood that many of the defendants' actions were protected by the First Amendment. With such careful preparation, jurors brought in verdicts of not guilty, making the Oakland Seven case unique in the annals of major prosecutions for antiwar activists.[99]

Government officials also moved against five individuals involved in the distribution of "A Call to Resist Illegitimate Authority" and in the presentation of draft cards at the Justice Department during Stop the Draft Week. Known popularly as the Boston Five, defendants included Dr. Spock and the Reverend Coffin. Members of the Justice Department's special unit had made these men targets almost from the beginning. Not only were they prominent and well respected, but they had been very public in what they had done. Justice Department officials, in going after Spock, Coffin, and their codefendants, were sending a clear message to war protesters that the costs of their activities had just increased substantially.

The Boston Five defendants were charged with conspiracy to obstruct the draft in various ways. The conspiracy doctrine has a long and disreputable heritage in the annals of American efforts to suppress dissent. Conspiracy, for example, was the charge against many of the early labor organizers when all they really had done was join together in an attempt to better their working conditions. And conspiracy was the charge levied against the defendants in the Dennis case, when the government could not prove that the leaders of the Communist party actually had attempted to overthrow the government. Conspiracy charges offer many advantages to prosecutors. The defendants do not have to know one another nor have they had to actually made plans together in order to be so charged. Also, in a conspiracy trial, each defendant is responsible for the statements and actions of all other defendants, regardless of whether he knew or approved of them. The government does not have to pinpoint an exact time in which the crime was committed; nor is it necessary for prosecutors to name the exact place where it occurred. In the Spock case, prosecutors had a number of geographical locations to choose from as possible sites for prosecution. Prosecutors picked Boston because they felt they were more likely to obtain convictions there. And by choosing to charge the defendants with conspiracy, the government did not have to prove that they had successfully persuaded anyone to avoid induction. Their intent to limit enrollment in the armed services was sufficient.[100]

As with most American political trials, the Spock case showed the nation's judicial system at its worst. The defendants had hoped to use the trial as a show-case for their antiwar positions, but they found that almost impossible. The judge, who was clearly partial to the government, ruled against defense efforts to introduce the Nuremberg principles and questions about the constitutionality of fighting in Vietnam and the draft. Defense arguments then were limited to stress-ing the difficulty involved in proving a conspiracy among five individuals who either did not know one another or who barely were acquainted. Defense attor-neys also tried to cloak their clients' activities in the First Amendment.

The judge, however, gave minimal attention to First Amendment claims and instructed the jurors that the crime involved was "the counseling, which means advising a person to pursue a particular course of action; or aiding, which means assisting, helping, supporting another in the commission of a crime; or abetting, which means encouraging, inducing, inciting another to commit a crime, or a plan or conspiracy to do so by speech or conduct."[101] If the jurors were convinced that the Spock defendants had participated in such activities, then no First Amendment protection was possible, for Congress had a clear right to prevent these evils from occurring. The Boston Five stood little chance of winning. Still, the jury deliberated eight hours before finding four of the defendants guilty. As he sentenced the men, the judge labeled the actions of Spock, Coffin, and the other two convicted defendants as the equivalent of treason. All were given two-year jail terms; three of the men were given $5,000 fines; the youngest defendant was fined only $1,000.

The case was, of course, immediately appealed. As with almost every case brought against antiwar protesters, the convictions were overturned. Appeals judges sitting on the Spock case found "inseparable from the question of the suf-ficiency of the evidence to convict . . . the rights of the defendants, and others, under the First Amendment."[102] By the time the appeals court judges finished sorting out the activities involved, two of the defendants, including Spock, were acquitted. Two others, including Coffin, were ordered to face new trials on more specific charges. Although the appeals court decision likely dampened the joy that government attorneys felt after they had first obtained the convictions, the victory over freedom of expression still rested with the prosecution. Government attorneys had launched such a broad attack on the right of five individuals—leaders in the antiwar movement—to express themselves that they had tied a significant portion of the movement up in legal actions. Funding that might have helped sponsor other antiwar activities went for legal defense. And some indi-viduals who might have been tempted to challenge the government on issues related to Vietnam had become more timid for fear of facing legal prosecution. The ability of the government to intimidate the movement through threatened legal actions was immense, and government attorneys used that ability repeat-edly in future years.

Other attempts at intimidation occurred as well. Congress, in addition to launching investigations into various New Left organizations, sought to punish students who participated in disruptions on college campuses and to restore order to the academic world. The most obvious way to execute the congressional will was to cut off federal funding for any students or faculty members convicted for their participation in campus unrest. In July 1968, for instance, the appropriation act for the National Aeronautics and Space Administration, an agency providing research funding for graduate students and faculty members, forbade the use of these funds by any individual convicted of "(1) inciting a riot or civil disorder; (2) organizing, promoting, encouraging, or participating in a riot or civil disorder; (3) aiding or abetting any person in committing any offense specified . . . ; or (4) any offense determined by the Administrator of the National Aeronautics and Space Administration to have been committed in furtherance of, or while participating in, a riot or civil disorder."[103] Similar measures limited funding from other federal sources.[104]

Congressional efforts to curb antiwar unrest took other forms as well. In 1967, lawmakers amended a 1946 law that prohibited certain kinds of activities on the Capitol grounds to stiffen its provisions against antiwar demonstrations.[105] This prowar Congress would brook no invasions by the likes of a Coxey's Army or a Bonus Expeditionary Force. No protesters would present their petitions for redress of grievances in an unbecoming way. Attempts to insulate congressmen from their constituents were, of course, challenged in the courts. An effort to stop enforcement of the law failed in 1968.[106] On appeal, however, the court overturned the measure, saying, "The desire of Congress, if such there be, to function in the 'serenity' of a 'park-like setting' is fundamentally at odds with the principles of the First Amendment." Although the court was willing to admit that "some substantial governmental interests in the Capitol Grounds may warrant protection," it could find none that were "sufficiently substantial to override the fundamental right to petition 'in its classic form' and to justify a blanket prohibition of all assemblies, no matter how peaceful and orderly, anywhere on the Capitol Grounds."[107]

Appeals in the case were several years away, and lawmakers were heartened by the initial decision. Believing that they could quiet national dissent by a series of repressive laws, they again added to the statute books. During these years, members of Congress were convinced that much of the discontent in the nation was caused by a few agitators who went from state to state promoting unrest among previously peaceful citizens. By April 1968, members of Congress had enacted the Safe Streets Act, which included a provision punishing any individual who "travels in interstate or foreign commerce or uses any facility of interstate or foreign commerce, including, but not limited to, the mail, telegraph, radio, or television" to "incite a riot," or to "organize, promote, encourage, participate in, or carry on a riot," or to "commit any act of violence in furtherance of a riot," or to "aid or abet any person inciting or participating in or carrying on a riot or committing any act of violence in furtherance of a riot." Maximum punishment upon conviction was a fine of not more than $10,000 or imprisonment for not more than five years or both.[108] This act would be tested in the cauldron of the Democratic National Convention in Chicago.

The executive branch also was concerned about the effects that protests against the war had on foreign policy, but its fears were also more wide-ranging. Some of the nation's largest black communities had been wracked by violence in recent years. Just why the urban ghettoes were experiencing such unrest and what to do about it presented problems that seemed incapable of solution. Some members of Congress and of the Johnson administration firmly believed that militant activists—the Black Panthers, for instance, who had emerged from the wreckage of the nonviolent civil rights movement and from the needs of the inner city—were primary instigators of the escalating domestic violence. In addition, many political leaders still believed that the Communist party was in some way behind the unrest, even though the party was very small and the unrest was widespread. Some members of the New Left fostered this belief as they waved Vietcong flags in demonstrations and praised Che Guevara, the Cuban revolutionary leader who had been executed for his attempts to export the Communist revolution to Bolivia in 1967. Only Communists, said conservatives, would pick such heroes.

At the same time, the nation's college campuses, according to these conservative critics, were seething with unrest. Reverting to the long-held belief that bad ideas came from outsiders, many Americans decided that college students could not come up with revolutionary ideas on their own. Some sinister force was behind it all. In addition, the youthful counterculture was in full bloom. Although clean-cut young Americans could be seen at various protests, more often the demonstrators had long hair, wore clothes that looked as if they had come from a rag basket, and appeared as if they had not bathed in weeks. Drug use was on the upswing, and sexual promiscuity was increasingly prominent in some circles. "Make love, not war" became a favorite slogan. To the politicians in Washington, the flower children of the counterculture represented all that was wrong with a permissive society. From the ghettoes to the university campuses, political leaders believed that the nation was falling apart because of lax standards.

As Congress was passing a spate of repressive measures, the executive branch ordered the nation's main investigatory agencies to uncover the causes of the unrest and to put a stop to it. J. Edgar Hoover, who still headed the FBI, simply transferred his anti-Communist tactics to the New Left. COINTELPROs or Counter-Intelligence Programs designed to cause problems for New Left organizations were set up using models from the anti-Communist period.[109] Agents were told to instigate or to take advantage of "personal conflicts or animosities existing between New Left leaders." They also were to create the "impressions that certain New Left leaders are informants for the Bureau or other law enforcement agencies." Given CIA funding of certain student groups and the propensity of government agencies to set up networks of informers, these rumors would not be hard to start. Agents also could plant articles in student newspapers or the underground press to "show the depravity of New Left leaders and members," or they could write anonymous letters to "parents, neighbors and the parents' employers" about activists.[110]

Agents were also told to encourage hostile press coverage of New Left groups and to "be alert for opportunities to confuse and disrupt New Left activities by misinformation. For example, when events are planned, notification that the event has been cancelled or postponed could be sent to various individuals."[111] Thus, the FBI interfered with the activities of the New Left just as private police and government agents had undermined the labor and anarchist movements and the Communist party in earlier years. In addition, the bureau continued collecting dossiers on American citizens involved in activities that Hoover considered subversive. Thousands of files on American citizens who were exercising their right to disagree with a government policy were kept during these years.

FBI agents were not the only members of the nation's intelligence community that were turned loose on the general public at the time. The CIA, which was barred by law from conducting investigations within the United States, began work under a presidential order to discover whether antiwar groups were under the influence of hostile foreign governments. Military intelligence agents, again barred from becoming involved in civilian affairs, collected data on forces within the United States that allegedly were prepared to undermine its stability. College campuses were primary targets for military surveillance operations, with officers posing as students to infiltrate suspect groups and persuading administrators to help keep an eye on possibly disruptive students.

Proponents of the war also enlisted the Internal Revenue Service (IRS) to intimidate citizens who participated in unacceptable activities through long and intensive tax audits. Such selective enforcement successfully intimidated some dissidents. When combined with the increasing number of prosecutions for violations—real or alleged—of various statutes, the work by the FBI, CIA, military intelligence, and the IRS created a wide net of restraint designed to keep all but the most hardy from voicing their disapproval of the government's position in Vietnam. The government's best efforts, however, were less than effective, for the protest movement remained viable and, in fact, intensified during 1968.

A natural question is whether the government was overreacting when it began its wide range of repressive measures. Although accurately evaluating the real dangers of the period from a later perspective is difficult, sufficient evidence exists to justify some of the concerns voiced by administration leaders. The size and boldness of the antiwar demonstrations in late 1967 had raised significant apprehensions. The movement was reaching its tentacles deeper into the nation as well. A group called Business Executives Move for Vietnam Peace emerged in the winter of 1968. Comprised of some 1,600 business leaders across the country, the organization opposed the war on pragmatic grounds: it was not successful and hence should be abandoned. Increased support for the antiwar movement appeared in the halls of Congress. Senator Eugene McCarthy of Minnesota emerged early as a popular antiwar challenger to Lyndon Johnson for the Democratic presidential nomination. Amazingly, McCarthy, backed by an army of college-aged supporters, won 42 percent of the Democratic votes in the New Hampshire primary in early March 1968. Four days later, Senator Robert F. Kennedy of New York, heir to the legacy of his assassinated brother, entered the Democratic fray against Johnson. The chances for the movement to post electoral successes in 1968 had never seemed better.

In addition, external events conspired to build even greater fears within Americans who supported the war. On January 23, 1968, for instance, the U.S. intelligence ship *Pueblo* was captured off the coast of North Korea; in response, President Johnson mobilized some 15,000 reservists. On January 30–31, the North Vietnamese launched their Tet offensive into South Vietnam, which not only brought guerrillas into the heart of Saigon but found them briefly occupying the grounds of the American embassy. Historians fairly unanimously agree that the Tet offensive turned a large number of everyday Americans against the war. The reason for the change in opinion was fairly simple: media coverage convinced many viewers that the war simply could not be won.

Problems in reporting the Tet offensive only highlighted the difficulties involved in bringing news from Vietnam to the American people. Vietnam was the first television war; the medium had been in its infancy during the Korean conflict. Now, Americans had a chance to see firsthand just what war was like, for death and dying came directly into the nation's homes each evening. Not only did television reveal the bloody and less than gallant aspects of war, but the nature of the medium played up the fighting and obfuscated the diplomatic reasons behind it. Complicated explanations about containing communism simply did not fit well in short news segments; action did. As the war wore on, the increasingly bloody action captured the journalists' attention, much the way that the more violent demonstrations attracted more news coverage at home. Television reporters, of course, were not the only ones who presented such versions of the war at home, for print media journalists kept pace.[112]

Despite administration complaints, the press was somewhat schizophrenic about Vietnam. For quite some time, journalists reporting the U.S. government's view from Washington, D.C., backed administration actions. Correspondents based in Saigon, on the other hand, fairly quickly discovered that the South Vietnamese regime that American troops were fighting to preserve was autocratic, incompetent, corrupt, and repressive. These critical stories often were not well received by stateside editors, who toned them down. Thus, generally uncritical reporting continued through the Gulf of Tonkin Resolution, and the U.S. press rallied behind the president, as it had done so many times before. To American journalists working at home, foreign policy and national security issues simply were not subjects for debate. In addition, reporters still followed the professional ethic that kept them from evaluating information for their audience. This approach, which had allowed Senator Joseph R. McCarthy to win so much credibility a few years earlier, meant the press served as an uncritical conduit for the government's version of events in Vietnam and allowed government sources to feed the American people a highly managed version of the news from Southeast Asia. To journalists who still were steeped in the cold war mystique, the fate of the free world was at stake in the jungles of Vietnam.

Government information policies successfully kept the war on the back burner of American political life for quite some time. Details about U.S. involvement were hard to come by, and when data were released the language always framed American activities benignly. For instance, advisers, not troops, were sent. American officials worked hard to keep details of just what those advisers were doing once they reached South Vietnam from the general public. By December 1961, U.S. advisers were flying South Vietnamese troops into battle, going with them on ground missions, and helping with overall military planning. Reporters in South Vietnam were given little information as to what was going on, although they could tell from simple observation that American involvement was far more extensive than official sources led them to believe. Efforts to gather facts on the true nature of American involvement were blocked in Washington and in South Vietnam, where both the American and South Vietnamese representatives erected substantial roadblocks.

As American involvement grew, officials had increasing difficulty in managing the news. And as the disparity between the official version of events and what actually transpired grew, the press began, in May 1965, to talk about the "credibility gap," which referred to discrepancies between the official version of events and what was actually occurring in Southeast Asia. The growing number of stories about the way in which the Johnson administration was misleading the American public about the nation's commitment in Vietnam further fueled protests at home. The news stories and the protests, in turn, created problems for a national policy that counted heavily on convincing the North Vietnamese that the United States was firmly resolved to continue the conflict. As the American government searched for ways to halt the flow of adverse news stories, officials repeatedly considered imposing censorship on all correspondents reporting from the field. The system that they talked about would have been similar to that used in the two world wars. Unfortunately, censorship was out of the question unless the government wanted to admit that a state of war existed. In addition, any censorship program would have depended heavily on South Vietnamese cooperation, which was doubtful at best. Even without formal censorship, voluntary agreements with journalists not to release details of current or pending operations were negotiated with little difficulty. One problem with the agreed-upon approach, however, was that reporters stationed in Saigon could easily discover that official sources were slanting available information. Consequently, the credibility gap grew.

Despite growing protests about managed news, the press more often than not still supported the war. Complaints centered on the nature and quality of information provided by official sources. Early in the war, for example, American correspondents began to dispute official casualty figures. Military manipulation of data on dead and wounded can be traced at least to the American Civil War, and most likely even earlier, but the antiquity of the practice made it no more palatable to correspondents. Officials soon began claiming that details about casualties could provide the enemy with vital information about troop strength and position, leading them to disclose even less information. Soon the notion of keeping secrets from the enemy included the concealment of bombing raids and other missions. The amount of information being made available officially to the press decreased as the war continued. Still there were lines that journalists refused to cross. When Harrison Salisbury of the *New York Times* went to North Vietnam in December 1966 and sent back a series of stories on the impact of the war there, many of his colleagues denounced his work as being heavily tainted with propaganda. Even though journalists might disagree with the way in which the war was being conducted and reported, few were ready to make their medium serve the North Vietnamese.

Victory remained elusive, and protests against the war increased at home. Where American reportage would have gone without the Tet offensive is unknown, but Tet occurred, and with it came a substantial change in journalistic response to the war. From January 30–31, 1968, the North Vietnamese and their allies in the South, the National Liberation Front (Vietcong), carried out simultaneous attacks on more than one hundred cities and towns throughout South Vietnam. The attack was a complete surprise and led to some of the heaviest fighting of the war. When the battle showed that even the American Embassy in Saigon was not safe, reporters began to reevaluate their stances on the war. Back at home, public opinion polls as early as 1967 had begun to show that a plurality of American citizens believed that entering the war had been a mistake. The information that the press in South Vietnam sent back about Tet further convinced the nation, sweeping journalists along with the flow.

Editorializing against the war picked up substantially after Tet, with both print and broadcast journalists participating. The key statement against the war came from CBS Evening News anchor Walter Cronkite, who went to South Vietnam after Tet to evaluate the situation for himself. Upon his return, he used time on his news show to call for an end to the fighting. "It seems now more certain than ever that the bloody experience of Vietnam is to end in a stalemate," he said. "To say that we are closer to victory today is to believe, in the face of the evidence, the optimists who have been wrong in the past. To suggest we are on the edge of defeat is to yield to unreasonable pessimism. To say that we are mired in stalemate seems the only realistic, yet unsatisfactory, conclusion." The solution was clear to Cronkite: "The only rational way out then will be to negotiate, not as victors but as honorable people who lived up to their pledge to defend democracy, and did the best they could."[113] When Lyndon Johnson heard Cronkite's statement, he knew that he had lost the support of the American people. A little more than a month later, the president announced that he would not seek another term and would devote himself to seeking peace in Vietnam.

After Tet, protest against the war involved more and more mainstream people, even though radical activists still attracted most of the attention. Journalism reflected the split within the nation. Protest became an increasingly legitimate story to cover, and the government's pronouncements no longer were accepted uncritically. In the years of recrimination that followed, the press consistently has been blamed for stirring the people to revolt against government policy in Vietnam, adversely affecting diplomatic efforts, undercutting the morale of the troops in the field, and creating the hostile atmosphere to which the troops returned when the war ended. Journalistic behavior during the Vietnam War has become the main reason for limiting press coverage of later military operations.

This criticism of the press, however, misplaces the blame for the fate of the Vietnam War and its veterans. Journalists, as usual, were followers in the anti-Vietnam protests; they simply were swept along with the rest of the nation when the tide finally turned against the war. The American people were deciding that the war was wrong before journalistic opinion switched after the Tet offensive. Military officers blame the press for the loss of public support, arguing, for instance, that journalists failed to report that American and South Vietnamese soldiers turned the Tet attack into a substantial victory. If that fact had been reported, they claimed, Americans would have continued to support the war, the conflict would have ended differently, and the nation would have remained united. Such arguments ignore the fact that dissent was growing throughout the nation without great press encouragement before the Tet offensive and that press reports of a military victory after the major surprise attack likely would not have ended the protest. The arguments also ignore the distrust that official government policy on war-related information had created. Journalists simply no longer believed official news sources.

In fact, if there is a villain in the coverage of the Vietnam War, it is the government's information policy. From the beginning, official sources manipulated facts in order to downplay American involvement and to minimize potential political problems at home. Little or no effort was made through 1968 to build an honest and factual basis for public support of the Vietnam conflict.[114] Without governmental efforts to educate the public, Americans were left to accept the good motives of the government on faith. In light of stories about the use of antipersonnel bombs, napalm, and other defoliants to fight the war, such trust slowly evaporated. As antiwar forces continued to argue that the Vietnam conflict was a civil war in which Americans should not interfere, as American casualty figures mounted, and as the financial costs of continuing the conflict grew, support for the government position all but vanished. Whether governmental honesty would have created a different situation with regard to the war is an imponderable question of history. We do know that governmental dishonesty undeniably altered the course of American history. The nation continued to be wracked by protest, and the role of the press in America was forever changed. In the wake of the war, reporters have become far more critical of official versions of events, and the adversarial role of the press in its relationship to government increased substantially.

But the change in press attitude toward the Vietnam War did not lead to an end of the conflict. The war persisted until January 1973, when a peace pact was signed calling for withdrawal of American troops within sixty days. The five years that elapsed between the Tet offensive and the end of the conflict saw some of the largest demonstrations against any government policy in the nation's history and some of the harshest retaliatory measures on record. Even as the nation was trying to assess the Tet episode and its impact on the future of the war, a small group of war protesters escalated the level of protest.

Now moving into the headlines were the Berrigan brothers, Catholic priests by profession and antiwar protesters by conviction. On the night of May 17, 1968, seven men and two women entered the draft board offices at Cantonsville, Maryland, dumped the records of men classified 1-A into large mesh trash baskets, took them outside, and burned them. The Cantonsville raid was one of a series of attacks on the heart of the selective service system—the local draft board and its registry of all eligible young men within the community. Records were not computerized, and if files could be destroyed or defaced, local officials faced an arduous task in reconstituting them.[115]

Soon to be known as the Cantonsville Nine, the raiders clasped hands, prayed, and waited for the police to arrive. To make sure that the world understood what had occurred, reporters were notified before the raid, and a statement was issued about the group's motivations. "We are Catholic Christians who take our faith seriously," said the statement. "We used napalm because it burned people to death in Vietnam. . . . We destroyed these records because they exploit our young men and represent misplaced power concentrated in the hands of the ruling class. . . . We believe some property has no right to exist."[116] Among those arrested were Philip Berrigan, the leader of the raid, who was a member of the Order of St. Joseph, and his brother, Daniel, who was a member of the Society of Jesus, better known as the Jesuits.

The Berrigans were leaders of the New Catholic Left, an increasingly radical movement against the war. The church they represented reflected the nation's turmoil over Vietnam, for it was badly split over the proper attitude to take about the nation's involvement. Priests and nuns opposed to the way in which the war had abused both American citizens, through the draft and discriminatory racial practices, and residents of Vietnam decided to challenge the nation on whether conscience was more important than law and order. Both brothers had been active in antiwar protests for several years, and both had been arrested before.

National response to the Cantonsville raid was favorable. The peace talks that Lyndon Johnson had initiated were getting nowhere, and protesters pushed harder. In addition, the behavior of the Cantonsville Nine was being emulated elsewhere. In Milwaukee, Wisconsin, for instance, five Catholic priests and a Protestant minister removed more than 10,000 files of young men classified as 1-A from the city's draft office and set them afire with homemade napalm. The action created havoc with the city's processing of youth for the draft. The Ultra-Resistance, which was comprised of individuals willing to risk prison terms to jar the consciences of their fellow Americans on the war, had been born.[117] Governmental authorities became increasingly apprehensive.

When the Cantonsville Nine came to trial in October 1968, numerous demonstrations were held on their behalf. Maryland Governor Spiro Agnew, who was running for the vice presidency on the Nixon ticket, requested additional federal marshals to help control the crowds around the trial site. The defendants admitted that they had committed the acts in question and asked to explain their behavior to the jury. The judge granted permission, which the judge in the Spock case a month earlier had refused to do. The judge even allowed Daniel Berrigan to end the proceedings with the Lord's Prayer, in which the judge and prosecutor participated. Two hours later, all defendants were found guilty. Daniel Berrigan was given a three-year prison term; Philip was given three and a half years.

The defendants had never expected to be acquitted. In fact, they viewed their prison terms as proof of the depth of their beliefs. The appeals process allowed them to remain out of prison for most of 1969 and to further inspire for the fast-developing Ultra forces. The convictions were upheld on the circuit court level, where the judges dealt with the defendants' assertions that they were morally justified in breaking the law. "Faced with the stark reality of injustice, men of sensitive conscience and great intellect have sometimes found only one morally justified path, and that path led them inevitably into conflict with established authority and its laws," the court said, but a review of history, philosophy, and religion would find great disagreement "as to when, if at all, civil disobedience, whether by passive refusal to obey a law or by its active breach, is morally justified."[118]

Agreeing that civil disobedience "must be non-violent and the actor must accept the penalty for his action," the judges refused to overturn the convictions. Individuals must answer for their actions, said the court, for the United States was built on law not on anarchy: "To encourage individuals to make their own determinations as to which laws they will obey and which they will permit themselves as a matter of conscience to disobey is to invite chaos. No legal system could long survive if it gave every individual the option of disregarding with impunity any law which by his personal standard was judged morally untenable."[119]

Members of the Supreme Court refused to review the convictions, and the Catonsville defendants headed for jail. As the date for their surrender approached, they discussed the possibility of joining members of the Black Panthers and the Students for a Democratic Society underground. To them, such a stance would be similar to draft resistance. Only Daniel Berrigan eluded the FBI's grasp. During four months as a fugitive, Daniel Berrigan wrote for publication, spoke publicly, granted interviews on his antiwar beliefs, and became the only Catholic priest ever to make the FBI's Ten Most Wanted List. Finally, both the Berrigans were behind bars, and the morale of the Catholic radicals hit bottom.

While the Berrigans were heating up antiwar protests, students, many of them prompted by radical elements within the Students for a Democratic Society, staged disruptions on numerous American college campuses, the most violent of which occurred at Columbia University in New York City.[120] In addition, on April 26, 1968, the largest student protest in the nation's history occurred as more than one million high school and college students boycotted classes to show their disdain for the war. As spring faded into summer, the stakes of protest heightened considerably. On April 4, 1968, Dr. Martin Luther King, Jr., was assassinated in Memphis, where he was organizing a garbage workers' strike, and the nation's black communities erupted in agony and protest. With King's death, an increasingly powerful voice against the war was stilled. And on June 6, 1968, Senator Robert F. Kennedy died of wounds inflicted the night before as he celebrated his victory in the California presidential primary. The senator, who had entered the presidential race in March after Eugene McCarthy had proven that Lyndon Johnson might be beaten had taken a strong antiwar stance. With his death came the end of any real chance that an antiwar candidate could win the White House, and the movement was devastated.

Although badly bruised by the assassinations, the antiwar movement refused to abandon efforts to force the 1968 political conventions to reflect antiwar concerns in writing platforms and naming tickets. Most of the attention was focused on the Democratic National Convention, where protesters wanted to show their contempt for Lyndon Johnson and, if possible, to pull likely nominee Hubert H. Humphrey into the antiwar camp. The convention was set for Chicago, fiefdom of one of the last remaining big city bosses, Richard J. Daley. August 1968 was not an especially opportune time to bring any antiwar demonstration onto the mayor's turf. A strong law and order man, Daley had little sympathy for disruptive protest. In the face of black unrest after the King assassination, for example, Daley was reported to have ordered his police force to "shoot to kill arsonists, shoot to maim looters." He later toned the order down slightly but did nothing to change police behavior toward demonstrators.[121] A few days after the suppression of the black protest, white supporters of the civil rights cause marched to condemn police treatment of blacks. The Chicago police were colorblind in their suppression of protest; the white marchers were attacked by police officers as well. Later that spring, as marchers peacefully protested the war in other American cities, individuals trying to do the same thing in Chicago were met by police with clubs, Mace, and tear gas.[122] The price of protest in Chicago clearly was high.

As the convention approached, Mayor Daley worried over the image that his city would project to the nation. In light of past experiences, Daley became convinced that antiwar protesters would try to create havoc during the convention, and he prepared for the worst. The amphitheater in which the convention was to be held was ringed with barbed wire, and elaborate security precautions were put in place to make sure that only properly certified individuals could gain access to the building. All 12,000 members of the Chicago police force were ordered to work twelve-hour shifts during the convention, and between 5,000 and 6,000 members of the National Guard were mobilized. In addition, some 6,000 U.S. Army troops, armed with flamethrowers and bayonets, were moved to the Chicago suburbs. The city also was filled with FBI agents as well as members of military intelligence units and other federal, state, and local investigatory agencies, many of which successfully planted agents within the protesting groups.[123]

With the likelihood of violence increasing, plans for the Chicago protest became increasingly confused. David Dellinger, chairman of the National Mobilization Committee to End the War in Vietnam, was an avowed pacifist and strongly backed a peaceful demonstration, but he made a number of statements that indicated that action rather than peaceful protest was a top priority. Two other leading organizers of the Chicago protests, Tom Hayden and Rennie Davis of the Students for a Democratic Society, also sent out conflicting signals as to their intent for the demonstrations.

If anything, too many organizations contemplated protesting in Chicago. Reaching agreements on goals or activities became unlikely, and the possibility of peaceful dissent continually receded. This was especially true when the Youth International Party, or the Yippies, a countercultural movement headed by Abbie Hoffman and Jerry Rubin, threatened to put LSD in the city's water supplies, swim nude in Lake Michigan, stage a mass love-in, and burn the city to the ground. Although many members of the antiwar movement had become disheveled in appearance, cavalier in their disregard for social customs in morals and manners, likely to use drugs, and apt to employ language that was disgustingly frank and unpleasant, the Yippies were considered the worst offenders. A possible invasion by the dirtiest, most disreputable elements in society only bolstered Mayor Daley's determination to squelch dissent.

Although far reduced in numbers because of the city's repressive image, the protesters were a mixed bag—members of the radical fringe, representatives of the counterculture, average college students, and middle-class professionals. In addition, discontented youths from the surrounding area came in to swell the demonstrators' numbers. Protest organizers had hoped that tens of thousands of activists would show up in Chicago; perhaps ten thousand were present at the peak of the demonstrations on Wednesday, August 28. At least half of the participants came from Chicago and the surrounding area, and according to some estimates, police outnumbered the demonstrators by at least three to one. In addition, says Todd Gitlin, an organizer of the SDS who covered the convention as a reporter for leftist publications, the composition of the protesters had changed. Earlier demonstrations had run about fifty-fifty male-female; in Chicago, the males outnumbered the females by eight or ten to one, suggesting a greater possibility for violence. And the language used in Chicago changed dramatically from earlier demonstrations as well. Before Chicago, chants had focused on "Peace now" and "Hell no, we won't go." In Chicago, the language was "Pigs are whores" and "Pigs eat shit," with the term pig, of course, referring to police officers.[124]

Despite these new elements, the protesters sought to coordinate their activities and tried to get official permits for rallies, parades, and demonstrations. They especially wanted permission to sleep in some of the city's parks at night and to stage at least one march to the convention site. Under Mayor Daley's instructions, all requests for permits were refused. When the activists determined to proceed anyway, confrontation was inevitable.

While the protesters were beginning their activities in Chicago, the Democratic party started its convention. Badly divided on the war issue, a strong antiwar contingent argued for the inclusion of a peace plank in the party's platform. Under the language proposed, the party would have endorsed ending the bombing of North Vietnam, negotiating a mutual withdrawal of forces from South Vietnam, and encouraging the South Vietnamese government to talk with the National Liberation Front, the guerrilla organization that had been waging the civil war for years.[125] When forced to the floor of the convention, the peace plank lost by a vote of 1,567 to 1,041. After the vote was announced, the New York and California delegations rose to sing "We Shall Overcome," and the managers of the convention turned down the audience microphones and amplified music from the band hired by the party. Dissent within the convention obviously was not permitted.

To make sure that the best possible face was placed on the convention proceedings, officials limited press access to the amphitheater floor and restricted the number of minicameras that network newspeople were allowed to use. Gathering news on the convention floor soon became hazardous to the reporter's health. CBS correspondent Dan Rather, for instance, was pushed around by convention security forces and hit in both the stomach and back as he fell to the floor. His offense was attempting to interview a delegate who was being removed from the floor. When he got back on the air, he told Walter Cronkite, "I think we've got a bunch of thugs here."[126] Another CBS correspondent, Mike Wallace, was roughed up and arrested due to a misunderstanding with a police officer.

If dissent and coverage of dissent was not to be allowed within the convention itself, such activities were even less tolerated outside the hall. The initial encounter between demonstrators and police came on the first night of the convention. As police sought to clear Lincoln Park at 11 p.m., violence ensued. Over the next several days and nights, encounters between police and protesters increased. The conflicts were exceedingly brutal, with police using clubs and tear gas to subdue demonstrators who initially were unarmed but who later equipped themselves with bricks and stones. As the police continued efforts to end the protests, demonstrations spilled out of park areas and onto main streets where private property was damaged. Police were indiscriminate in their application of force, and innocent passers-by were assaulted as were persons trying to help injured protesters. Before the convention was over, police forces invaded the headquarters of Eugene McCarthy's supporters in the Hilton Hotel, dragging staff people out of bed and beating them for allegedly throwing beer cans from hotel windows on the police below. Demonstrators began to term Chicago "Czechago," a reference to the brutal way in which the Soviets had recently suppressed the Prague Spring effort to achieve democracy in Czechoslovakia.

Quite naturally, rhetoric heated up. After an encounter with police sent Rennie Davis to the hospital with a split skull, Hayden told the crowd that "if blood is going to flow, let it flow all over the city. If gas is going to be used—let that gas come down all over Chicago and not just over us in this park. That if the police are going to run wild let them run wild all over the city of Chicago and not over us in this park. That if we are going to be disrupted, and violated, let this whole stinking city be disrupted and violated." In addition, Hayden told his listeners, "I'll see you in the streets."[127] Although there is no evidence that Hayden's words prompted an immediate confrontation with police, they were later used against him as proof of his intention to foment a riot.

Before long, the nation's attention was turned as much to what was happening outside of the convention hall as within. Television cameras focused on increasingly nasty encounters between police and demonstrators; and the smell of tear gas invaded some of the leading convention hotels. Hippies and clean-cut demonstrators, young and old, black and white, male and female, rich and poor alike were targets of police action. On the convention floor, Senator Abraham Ribicoff of Connecticut went to the podium to term Mayor Daley's techniques for handling dissent "Gestapo tactics."[128] The mayor jumped to his feet, shook his fist in Ribicoff's direction, and cursed. A lip-reader later told the public that the mayor had shouted in Ribicoff's direction: "Fuck you you Jew son of a bitch you lousy motherfucker go home."[129] The level of discourse among the nation's leaders obviously was not significantly higher than that outside the convention hall.

Suppression of the protests outside of the convention hall became a major news story. Television cameras were trained on the activities outside almost as much as on the nomination process inside the hall. For their efforts, journalists became the targets of police brutality. Even if they identified themselves as reporters, the police were likely to take out their frustrations on the journalists, who, they thought, were spurring the protesters on to greater feats of violence and were giving Chicago a bad name across the nation. Correspondents said that police officers had removed their badges, name tags, and other identifying information before they plunged into the mêlée. Comments such as "Get the cameras" and "That doesn't mean a damn thing to me" were reported in response to the presentation of news credentials.[130]

Journalists were appalled by what they witnessed in Chicago, and they told their readers and viewers of their concerns. Perhaps even more than the Tet offensive, the confrontation in Chicago radicalized the American news media and pushed them into the arms of the anti-establishment demonstrators. Much to their amazement, journalists soon discovered that they were in the minority in their outrage over the way in which the demonstrators had been treated in Chicago. Many Americans, especially the ones who wrote or telegraphed or telephoned news outlets, supported Mayor Daley's actions. At CBS affiliates, the mail ran something like 11 to 1 in support of the mayor; at NBC, only about 1,000 of some 8,500 letters supported the protesters. Mayor Daley himself reported receiving 135,000 letters endorsing his actions.[131] And the mayor launched a massive public relations campaign to spruce up his image and that of his city. Daley accepted an invitation to be interviewed by Walter Cronkite, and during the twenty-three-minute session, he told the CBS news anchor that he had ordered police to protect the city from a wave of threatened political assassinations.

The American people believed the mayor. What Richard Nixon soon would call the silent majority had made itself heard in the aftermath of Chicago as a substantial number of Americans clearly indicated their unwillingness to allow the nation to continue in the state of upheaval that had dominated most of Lyndon Johnson's presidency. To a certain extent, these people were picking up on the rhetoric of another presidential candidate in 1968—George C. Wallace, the former governor of Alabama, who was running on the American Independence party ticket. The bluntly spoken candidate came down hard on long-haired students, anarchists, Communists, pot smokers, and dwellers on the fringes of society. "If anybody ever lies down in front of my car it will be the last car he ever lies down in front of in his life," Wallace said at one time. At another time, he suggested, "We ought to turn this country over to the police for two or three years and everything would be all right."[132] The major problem afflicting the United States was the fact that its young people did not respect the country that granted them such privileges. To Wallace, to Nixon, and to an increasing number of American citizens, the time had come to make sure that American young people understood just how grateful they should be to live in the United States.

Other analysts of the American scene came up with similar evaluations. Reuven Frank, president of NBC news, said after Chicago, "The average middle-class American has gone through many wrenching experiences. His tranquility has been shattered. He has been exposed to realities of war in a way no previous generation of Americans has had to face its wars. He has seen ghetto riots in his living room. He has watched with horror young people of good background expressing contempt for his dearest values in the way they dress and act and what they say." The time had come for changes in American society. One of the changes that middle America demanded was that television reduce its emphasis on protest. As CBS correspondent Eric Sevaried explained, "Over the years the pressure of public resentment against screaming militants, foul mouthed demonstrators, arsonists and looters had built up in the national boiler. With Chicago it exploded. The feelings that millions of people released were formed long before Chicago. Enough was enough: the police *must* be right. Therefore, the reporting *must* be wrong."[133] The great war against the press, which would flower in the next administration, was beginning.

Lyndon Johnson appointed the obligatory presidential commission to investigate the violence in Chicago. Headed by Chicago lawyer Daniel Walker, the commission determined that during the convention "the Chicago police were the targets of mounting provocation by both word and act. It took the form of obscene epithets, and of rocks, sticks, bathroom tiles and even human feces hurled at police by demonstrators." "Some of these acts," the commission report said, "had been planned; others were spontaneous or were themselves provoked by police action. Furthermore, the police had been put on edge by widely published threats of attempts to disrupt both the city and the Convention." Such was the provocation; "the nature of the response was unrestrained and indiscriminate police violence [occurred] on many occasions, particularly at night," the report said. "Newsmen and photographers were singled out for assault, and their equipment deliberately damaged. Fundamental police training was ignored; and officers, when on the scene, were often unable to control their men. As one police officer put it: 'What happened didn't have anything to do with police work.'"[134]

As the members of the Walker Commission concluded, "To read dispassionately the hundreds of statements describing at firsthand the events of Sunday and Monday nights is to become convinced of the presence of what can only be called a police riot." The nation cannot afford such behavior if it is to remain true to its fundamental beliefs and freedoms, commissioners agreed. "In principle at least," the report said, "most Americans acknowledge the right to dissent. And, in principle at least, most dissenters acknowledge the right of a city to protect its citizens and its property." The problem occurs when those rights come into conflict. "Convention week in Chicago," the commission said, "is what happens, and the challenge it brings is plain: to keep *peaceful assembly* from becoming a contradiction in terms."[135] But the nation no longer wanted to deal with these issues. Mayor Daley exemplified the attitude toward the Walker Commission's report when, three days after its release, he announced a 22 percent pay increase for experienced police and fire officers.[136]

Also quickly following the convention were the now obligatory indictments of protest ringleaders. The charge once again was conspiracy, with the defendants accused of violating portions of the Safe Streets Act of 1968 that made it a crime to cross state lines to foment riots. The prosecutors' net pulled in five of the organizers of the Chicago demonstrations: Dellinger, Hayden, Davis, Rubin, and Hoffman. The federal prosecutors also arrested Bobby Seale, a leader of the Black Panthers, in an effort to destroy that organization. Altogether eight defendants, known popularly as the Chicago Eight, faced yet another political trial following the Chicago convention. Calling themselves The Conspiracy, the Chicago Eight defendants, individuals with diverse interests and beliefs, were forced to make common cause against an enemy that they perceived to be every bit as dangerous as that enemy considered them.[137]

The Chicago Eight trial was one of the most difficult of the antiwar trials. Seale's lawyer fell ill and could not meet the date set by Judge Julius Hoffman for the trial to begin. Seale sought a postponement until his attorney could be present; the judge denied the request and appointed someone to represent the Black Panther leader. The designated attorney was unacceptable to Seale, who dismissed him and wanted to represent himself. Judge Hoffman refused to allow Seale to serve as his own attorney, and after repeated interruptions of the trial proceedings, had Seale bound and gagged in the courtroom. Eventually, Seale's case was severed from that of the other defendants, and the Chicago Eight became the Chicago Seven.

As the trial began, the remaining defendants decided to turn the proceedings into a morality play in which they would use outrageous behavior to make their views of the charges and of the trial known to the world. The behavior ran from the sublime to the ridiculous. Abbie Hoffman, who was no relation to the judge on the case, brought a National Liberation Front flag to the courtroom. David Dellinger tried to read the names of American soldiers killed in Vietnam into the court record. Daily the trial became even more of a political persecution because of the behavior of Judge Hoffman, who quickly aligned himself with the prosecution and ruled the courtroom with an iron hand.

Judge Hoffman, for instance, refused to allow attorneys to launch a defense based on the First Amendment. Defense counsel planned to contend that a recent Supreme Court ruling refined the clear and present danger test so greatly that speech advocating action was protected by the First Amendment unless immediate lawless action resulted.[138] Attorney William Kunstler and his colleagues argued that the antiriot provisions of the Safe Streets Act were unconstitutional because the defendants were charged with having made speeches months before the Chicago convention that allegedly incited violence at the convention. The government contended that speech issues were not involved and that the case revolved solely around the intentions of the defendants to foment a riot in Chicago. The judge agreed with the prosecution, and the trial went forward.

Most of the government's case came from undercover law enforcement officials who had infiltrated the antiwar movement. Jerry Rubin, for example, had picked up a long-haired, burly, dirty motorcycle gang member as a personal bodyguard while he was in Chicago. The gang member turned out to be an undercover police officer who testified that he had heard Bobby Seale telling the crowd, "The time for singing We Shall Overcome is past. Now is the time to act, to go buy a 357 magnum, a carbine and an automatic and kill the pigs. We've got to break up into small groups and create guerrilla warfare everywhere. We can no longer be arrested in large groups or be killed in large groups. We've got to break into small groups and surround the pigs."[139] The defense tried to get this testimony excluded on Fourth Amendment grounds, claiming illegal police surveillance. Judge Hoffman found no merit in the objections.

Nor would the judge allow the defendants to enter into evidence a document written by Hayden and Davis some four months before the convention that attested to their peaceful intentions. "The campaign should not plan violence and disruption against the Democratic National Convention," the document began. "Deliberately planned disruptions will drive away people who are worried about arrests or violence and thus sharply diminish the size and political effect of the mobilization." In fact, "little would be served except the political hopes of Johnson, Nixon and Wallace by a Chicago action that would be seen . . . as a gathering of 'every crackpot group, protest group and every disruptive, violent force in America that thinks it has a pipeline to absolute truth.'" The Chicago protests, in fact, "must demonstrate the opposite; that the government is the real source of crackpot thinking and violence. . . . We believe the demonstrations can be orderly and directed."[140]

For a moment, it seemed as if the trial would have to be repeated because the jurors reported themselves as deadlocked at eight-to-four in favor of conviction. The judge refused to release the jury, and eventually all defendants were acquitted of the conspiracy charges. But Dellinger, Hayden, Davis, Hoffman, and Rubin were found guilty of crossing state lines with the intent to incite a riot. Each of the five was sentenced to a maximum of five years in jail and given $5,000 fines. Defendants were also assessed the costs of the prosecution and were ordered to stay in jail until the costs and fines had been paid.

The convictions, quite naturally, were appealed, and in 1972, after the steam had both run out of the antiwar movement and the war itself, a court of appeals reversed all of the convictions and remanded some counts for retrial. The appeals court judges found numerous errors in the original trial including the prejudicial attitudes of both the judge and the prosecutor in the case. The appeals panel closely examined the question of whether the antiriot act was constitutional. The query was essential, explained the court, because "rioting, in history and by nature, almost invariably occurs as an expression of political, social, or economic reactions, if not ideas. The rioting assemblage is usually protesting the policies of a government, an employer, or some other institution, or the social fabric in general, as was probably the case in the riots of 1967 and 1968 which are the backdrop for this legislation." In addition, "a riot may well erupt out of an originally peaceful demonstration which many participants intended to maintain as such. Each participant is entitled to a careful distinction between responsibility for the lawful and constitutionally protected demonstration and responsibility for the activity for which the legislative body validly prescribes a penalty."[141]

"The first amendment is premised upon the value of unfettered speech," the judge said. "Constitutional protection is clearly not to be limited, therefore, to mild or innocuous presentation, and it is unrewarding to search for a formula describing punishable advocacy of violence in terms of fervor or vigor. The real question is whether particular speech is intended to and has such capacity to propel action that it is reasonable to treat such speech as action." The court determined that the law had been worded carefully enough to make individuals aware of the activities that were prohibited and to provide a sufficiently precise limitation on punishable activities. The law did present problems for the court, however, and the judges said, "we acknowledge the case is close" in holding the statute constitutional.[142] The Supreme Court refused to hear an appeal of the case, so the status of the antiriot act remained dependent upon the circuit court's ruling. The federal government did not reopen the case against the Chicago Seven after the appeals court decision. By this time, another trial would have exacerbated old wounds and perhaps rekindled a sputtering and dying protest movement.

The demonstrations in Chicago on which the trial was based formed both the high point and the low point of the antiwar protest movement in the United States. The violence that the activities provoked, even if accurately attributed to police rather than to demonstrators, rocked the great middle class out of its lethargy. Middle America found that it did not like the United States portrayed on their television screens. Attracting the greatest enmity was the behavior of the protesters. A great push for law and order began with the confrontation in Chicago. The escalating tenor of protest had offended too many people, most of whom, unfortunately, had been just as unwilling to listen to different ideas when voiced calmly as they were to tolerate the more violent exposition of revolutionary thoughts that had taken place in Chicago. Once again, it became popular to support the government, to take pride in the flag, to back the war in Vietnam.

A new president representing a different political party moved into the White House—not on the wings of a substantial mandate, but the call for change was clearly evident. Some political experts contend that Richard Nixon won the White House because many of the liberals opposed to the war in Vietnam boycotted the polls in November because they could find no sympathetic candidate for whom to cast their votes. Whatever the reason, the day Richard Nixon took possession of the Oval Office marked the start of an intense campaign to silence dissent in the United States. Disagreement with national policy, which had been the hallmark of most of the decade, no longer was acceptable. The only ideas that would be heard, if Richard Nixon had his way, would be those of his "silent majority." The dirty-bodied and foul-mouthed protesters who had captured center stage were to be returned to the holes from which they came. No longer, Nixon proclaimed, would society be forced to protect itself from such ill-mannered individuals and un-American ideas.

CHAPTER 9

★ ★ ★

Striking Back at Dissenters:
Freedom of Expression
in the Early Nixon Years

The Democratic National Convention was pivotal for the American experience with dissent. For almost a decade, the national scene had been dominated by the increasingly louder voices of citizens demanding redress of sundry grievances. When speech alone, either strident or peaceful, proved insufficient to bring about change, action had been added to force government to pay attention to the desires of a discontented minority. And when peaceful action in the form of marches and demonstrations proved unsuccessful, violent confrontation took center stage. The pattern was familiar. Government disregard of the peaceful petitioning for redress of grievances by citizens on this continent goes back at least to Bacon's Rebellion in 1676. Rather than listening to citizen concerns and trying to find mutually acceptable solutions, government often bloodily repressed individuals who boldly questioned official policy. Public reaction to such government actions varied little over time, as the main concern seemed to be restoring society to its former lawful condition as quickly as possible.

Despite the lessons of history, many Americans felt sure that the police violence against demonstrators at the Democratic National Convention would mobilize national support for the antiwar movement. Just the opposite was true. Increased demands for changes in American society indeed were heard after the convention. But the changes sought were regressive rather than progressive. The dominant urge was to return to the allegedly simpler earlier days in U.S. history when protesters did not regularly disrupt government and university life and when young people were respectful of their elders, wore short hair, and were clean in their personal attire, lifestyle, and language. The national nervous system had become so attenuated during the Kennedy and Johnson presidencies that tolerance no longer was possible. If a calmer society could be won only by quieting the voices of those people demanding an end to racism, poverty, and war, then such steps were necessary. The emerging silent majority, however, failed to realize that the problems that had sparked the protests would not disappear. Attempting to suppress dissent was even worse than ignoring it, and for a while, the nation was wracked with even more disruption, destruction, and bloodshed.

Serving as catalyst for much of this activity was Richard M. Nixon, who won the presidency in 1968 by a narrow margin in part because of his alleged secret plan to end the Vietnam War and in part because people believed he could stop the protests. He carefully played upon these concerns throughout his campaign. His acceptance speech at the Republican National Convention, for instance, set the tone for his attack on protesters: "As we look to America, we see cities enveloped in smoke and flame. We hear sirens in the night. We see Americans dying on distant battlefields abroad. We see Americans hating each other; fighting each other, killing each other at home. And as we see and hear these things, millions of Americans cry out in anguish: Did we come all this way for this? Did American boys die in Normandy and Korea and Valley Forge for this?" Nixon advised his audience to "listen to the answers to those questions. It is another voice, it is a quiet voice in the tumult of the shouting. It is the voice of the great majority of Americans, the forgotten Americans, the non-shouters, the non-demonstrators. The answer of course is no."[1]

In addition to telling Americans that most of them favored a calmer, more peaceful society, he pledged "an honorable end to the war in Vietnam."[2] He led the press and the nation to believe that he had a secret plan for ending the war quickly, although in truth he had no clear-cut program. Instead, he envisaged using a strategy employed by Dwight Eisenhower to halt the Korean conflict. Often called the "madman theory," Eisenhower simply threatened to increase American involvement in the war, perhaps to the point of using nuclear weapons against China, if negotiations did not end the fighting. Nixon's theory was similar. He planned to increase the use of American forces against the North Vietnamese and to issue an ultimatum demanding serious negotiations by November 1, 1969. If the North Vietnamese would not cooperate, he would devote even more U.S. military power to the conflict. Under this policy, American commitment and casualties grew, and Nixon ordered the secret bombing of Cambodia to show the North Vietnamese that a new and serious player had entered the game.[3]

His program's success rested on the administration's ability to keep the escalation secret and to convince the North Vietnamese that the nation supported the president. The mere existence of an antiwar movement endangered his strategy. Nixon was convinced, as Lyndon Johnson had been, that any dissent on war policy led the enemy to believe that the nation lacked the will to bring the conflict to a successful conclusion. Thus, as part of his strategy for winning the war in Vietnam, Nixon launched an offensive against dissidents at home.

Under his administration, for example, the Chicago Eight prosecution was begun. Other legal cases were started as well even though the grounds for proceeding at times were quite flimsy. Prosecutions of antiwar protesters, however, were popular with the people who made up juries. The government often obtained convictions of individuals whose outlandish actions and language had offended the sensibilities of jurors. Many of these convictions did not withstand the scrutiny of an appeals court charged with considering the impartiality of trials and the effect convictions had on First Amendment rights. To a certain extent, the Nixon administration was unconcerned about reversals of convictions upon appeal. By that time, several years had passed, and a segment of the antiwar movement had been fairly well disabled in the interim.

The Nixon White House also increased the use of the Federal Bureau of Investigation (FBI) and other intelligence-gathering agencies against antiwar dissenters. Earlier administrations had begun this practice, but Nixon demanded greater results. Both antiwar and black militant groups felt administrative pressure. The agencies resorted to tried and true countersubversive activities including the planting of both spies and *agents provocateurs,* disrupting meetings, and trying to create dissension. Electronic eavesdropping of all kinds and intensive surveillance also were popular. The first indication of the extent of government interference in the lives of dissidents came when an antiwar group broke into the FBI's Media, Pennsylvania, office in 1971 and stole about 1,000 official documents. The materials were selectively distributed to friendly journalists and congressmen who then made the damaging details public.[4] Fuller disclosure came in the post-Watergate era when both houses of Congress launched major investigations into the inappropriate uses of the nation's intelligence-gathering community during the Nixon administration.

Strangely enough, Nixon's concerns about dissent began while the organized antiwar movement was allowing his administration time to put his peace plan in place. Optimism increased as the president brought 25,000 troops home in late spring; by the end of 1969, 65,000 American military personnel had been withdrawn from Vietnam. With the removal of American ground troops, U.S. casualties went down, which further reduced protest in the early months of the administration. Antiwar advocates did not know, however, that in place of ground forces Nixon had escalated the air war and had begun dropping bombs on neutral Cambodia.

The quietness of the antiwar movement did not indicate a peaceful nation. The nation's campuses were still seething with unrest, which was a combination of protest against the draft, racism on campus, and the impersonal university system that, students thought, ignored their needs. Student response to such perceptions varied from university to university. At San Francisco State College, for instance, students effectively shut the school down for months because of administration unwillingness to meet black students' demands for more minority admissions and greater emphasis on courses of interest to minority students.[5] At other universities, students showed their displeasure with the establishment by their rudeness to dignitaries receiving honorary degrees. When presidential adviser Henry Kissinger received an honorary degree from Brown in June 1969, for example, more than two-thirds of the graduating class turned their backs on him.[6] Elsewhere students responded with violence. The President's Commission on Campus Unrest found that more than 8,000 campus-related bombings, attempted bombings, or bomb threats occurred between January 1, 1969 and April 15, 1970. Favorite targets were ROTC buildings and locations associated with war-related research. In addition, more than 4,000 people were arrested for participating in campus violence during the 1968–1969 academic year, with the total rising to about 7,200 during the following school year.[7]

To Richard Nixon the model to emulate in dealing with campus unrest clearly was California Governor Ronald Reagan, who in 1966 had campaigned against radicalism at the University of California at Berkeley. Once in office, Reagan engineered the firing of university system president Clark Kerr, who, many conservatives felt, had not been strong enough in the face of the Free Speech Movement. The governor continued to be outspoken, as when he labeled student plans for a Vietnam Commencement in 1967 during which they pledged not to serve in Vietnam "obscene." When campus radicals took over a piece of university land that had stood vacant for some time to establish a people's park, Reagan called in the National Guard. Violence, of course, ensued, and Berkeley was an occupied camp for more than two weeks.[8] Many of the nation's liberals were appalled at the governor's behavior; to the president and his growing constituency, Reagan had shown just the right amount of firmness and control.

Such an attitude was especially appreciated by blue-collar workers and members of the lower middle class who saw campus protesters as privileged children who were seeking to destroy the lifestyle that outsiders strove so hard to attain. The fear was similar to that of the middle and upper classes earlier in the century when faced with the revolutionary ideas put forth by anarchists and labor union members. Once again, the foundations of society were threatened; and once again, the solid core of the nation was called upon to repress individuals with dangerous notions. In addition, the silent majority of the late 1960s could identify with their ancestors' worries about the international ramifications of what was occurring on their streets. Students were rising in other parts of the world and threatening the existence of their nations as well, and an urban guerrilla movement was beginning international terroristic activities in some of the most presumably civilized spots on the globe. As the middle classes throughout the world became more intent on repressing the revolutionary thoughts, the youths raised the decibel level of communication. If words would not be heard, if parades and chants would not be noticed, perhaps bombs would win the attention of their elders.[9]

Americans focused their immediate fears on two urban guerrilla movements. One, the Weathermen, emerged as the result of a split within the ranks of the Students for a Democratic Society (SDS). The second, the Black Panthers, developed as the civil rights movement fragmented and urban black youths banded together. The Nixon administration made little effort to distinguish between violent and peaceful protest groups. To the White House, the intermixture of protesters and their goals served the administration's basic desire to suppress dissent. If violent groups could be confused with peaceful organizations and if all could be tainted with the drug abuse and free sex practiced by the counterculture, then their repression would be much easier.

The Black Panthers gave the Nixon administration a perfect opportunity to play on the nation's fears of black militancy, while the Weathermen allowed focusing attention on deviant behavior within the white, college-aged population. After the final orgy of destruction that rampaged through the urban ghettoes in the wake of the assassination of Dr. Martin Luther King, Jr., the hearts of the big cities quieted down. Rather than rejoicing at the calmness, federal officials feared that the United States now faced a spurt of urban guerrilla tactics from discontented blacks. The traditional civil rights movement led by Dr. King never had reached the problems of the inner cities, where issues were more economic than political. After King's death, leadership of the Southern Christian Leadership Conference passed to the Reverend Ralph David Abernathy, who lacked King's charisma and ability. Within months of Abernathy's ascension, King's movement essentially died in the muck of Resurrection City in Washington, D.C. Abernathy had brought King's long-planned Poor People's Campaign to the nation's capital to win support for economic improvements for blacks. The tens of thousands of expected participants failed to materialize, and the 2,500 or so who did come were virtually ignored.[10] To say the least, the timing for another civil rights demonstration was inopportune. Americans were still reeling from the violence that had followed King's assassination, and a mass showing of black strength was not welcomed on Capitol Hill. In addition, 1968 was an election year, and the nation's resources were increasingly being drained to support the war in Vietnam. The traditional civil rights movement was over.

In its place arose a movement even more frightening to the conservative white community. The roots of the Black Panther party can be traced, at least in part, to the racial pride movement started by Elijah Muhammad in the 1950s and spread throughout the northern ghettos by Malcolm X. The Black Muslims, as the Lost-Found Nation of Islam was popularly known, advocated racial separatism. Black was beautiful, and white was dangerous and deceitful. "Our *enemy* is the *white* man!" Malcolm X would say, as he stressed that Black Muslims wanted a separate society "where we can reform ourselves, lift up our moral standards, and try to be godly."[11] The black separatist movement fell on hard times when the personal peccadillos of Elijah Muhammad became known and as Malcolm X began to realize that some cooperation with the white community was necessary to change society. "If you attack [a man] because he is white, you give him no out," Malcolm said in early 1965. "He can't stop being white." Rather, he said, "We've got to give the man a chance. He probably won't take it, the snake. But we've got to give him a chance."[12] Where this new line of rhetoric would have taken him is unknown because in March 1965, Malcolm X was murdered, apparently by a dissident faction of Black Muslims, although some claim that the assassination was orchestrated by whites who found Malcolm too dangerous.

The black nationalism of Malcolm X and the Black Muslims soon merged with another strain of discontent to form the much feared Black Panther Party for Self-Defense. The panther emblem had first appeared in 1964, when blacks in Lowndes County, Alabama, used it to symbolize their new political party. The Lowndes County Freedom Organization put up a full slate of black contenders for office in this highly segregated community. All lost, but black pride was enhanced substantially by the effort. The panther emblem was then picked up by Huey Newton and Bobby Seale, two college-educated ghetto youths, as the symbol for the Black Panther party. The Panthers were started in October 1966 in response to what Newton and Seale perceived to be increasing police violence against blacks in Oakland, California. Blacks in that community armed themselves and shadowed police officers who patrolled the ghetto. With weapons ostentatiously in view, the Panthers' main goal was to take pictures of police violence against blacks in an attempt to force a change in behavior. But their rhetoric was that of revolution, and the white community soon decided that they must be eliminated as a power in the ghetto.[13]

Blacks who advocated violent change in society encountered great difficulty. In New York State, for instance, officials dusted off their criminal anarchy law, last used against Benjamin Gitlow in the 1920s, to prosecute William Epton, "a self-acknowledged Marxist and president of the Harlem 'club' of the Progressive Labor Movement." Epton was convicted for inciting the July 1964 Harlem riots. Just before the riots began, Epton had been pouring inflammatory words on a combustible situation. Epton spoke in the afternoon; the riot started in the evening. Even though the New York court agreed that there was "no evidence that the defendant or his alleged co-conspirators had any hand in causing the riots that began on the evening of July 18, 1964," the appellate judges concluded that he had violated the law. The jury, said the appeals court, had a "sufficient basis . . . to conclude that his words and actions created a 'clear and present danger'" that the state was justified in stopping.[14]

At one point Epton had told the crowd: "They [the cops] declared war on us and we should declare war on them and every time they kill one of us damn it, we'll kill one of them and we should start thinking that way right now." In another spot, he said, "We will not be fully free until we smash this state completely and totally. Destroy [it] and set up a new state of our own choosing and of our own liking. And in that process of making this state, we're going to have to kill a lot of these cops, a lot of these judges, and we'll have to go up against their army." In fact, he said, "we will take our freedom. We will take it by any means necessary . . . we know the beast that we are dealing with . . . we have to create a revolution in this country and we will create a new government that is run by the people."[15] Some critics of the decision claimed that the judges refused to place Epton's comments in context and that they rejected the fact that ghetto rhetoric was different from that used in other settings in order to win an audience.[16]

Differences in cultural contexts, however, made little difference to the American judicial system when it came to dealing with black radicals. Their rhetoric and their willingness to engage in violence to achieve their goals was simply too frightening. The Nixon administration provided a textbook example of that fear of black radicals, for, as Nixon took over, apprehension over the Black Panther party led to massive surveillance and harassment. To a large degree, Nixon was an ideal person to lead the charge against the Panthers, for under his supervision, government officials attacked many of the gains won by the more peaceful civil rights movement. The administration tried to win a moratorium on court-ordered busing to achieve integration, sought to defeat legislation to enforce the fair housing law and to extend the Voting Rights Act of 1965, and asked the U.S. Supreme Court to delay the integration of Mississippi public schools.[17] The administration's actions were well received by the conservative coalition the president was building, and thanks to concerns that the Panthers were Marxists who were trying to communize to the ghettos, the attack on them could be rationalized as a Communist issue rather than a racial one.

The logic of this treatment was explained in July 1969 by FBI Director J.

Edgar Hoover, who labeled the Black Panther party "the greatest threat to the internal security of the country." Because of their Marxist-Leninist background, Hoover said, "its members have perpetrated numerous assaults on police officers and have engaged in violent confrontations with police throughout the country. Leaders and representatives of the Black Panther party travel extensively all over the United States preaching their gospel of hate and violence not only to ghetto residents, but to students in colleges, universities and high schools as well."[18] Some of what the FBI director said was true, for party members did seek to convert blacks to their cause, and party members also were trained in the use of firearms. In general, they preferred to use the firearms defensively; shootouts did indeed occur, often upon the provocation of police officers devoted to demolishing the party. The Nixon administration sought indictments of party members on a variety of pretexts. Because the case against Bobby Seale for being an active planner of the Chicago demonstrations was extremely weak, his indictment under the antiriot provisions of the Safe Streets Act was one indication that the administration was serious. With Seale busy with the Chicago trial, the top Panther leadership was effectively out of commission. Huey Newton was serving time in jail for manslaughter, and Eldridge Cleaver had fled the country to avoid being returned to jail for violation of parole. Now the federal government turned to lower-level leadership, much the way previous administrations had attacked level after level of the Industrial Workers of the World and the Communist party.

In some instances, governmental attempts to suppress the Panthers met with resistance. In May 1969, for example, Charles Bates, the FBI special agent in charge of the San Francisco office, balked at instructions to launch a major offensive against the Panthers on the grounds that they were conspiring to overthrow the government with force and violence. "The Panthers right now are not many people and perhaps do not represent many people, as far as most of their actions are concerned," Bates told his superiors. "However, they do represent an idea, or a voice in the ghetto, and are often called upon by Negro residents, to come quell a disturbance in a playground or talk to someone alleging police brutality." An all-out effort against the Panthers could convey the impression that "the FBI is working against the aspirations of the Negro people," he said. Bates's superiors remained unmoved. His favorable mention of the Panthers' breakfast program for poor children brought the response that the activity was simply an effort "to create an image of civility, assume community control of Negroes, and to fill adolescent children with their insidious poison."[19] The San Francisco office, aware of the power of the Washington headquarters, joined a major offensive against this dangerous black organization.

Informers were found to tell the FBI of Panther plans. *Agents provocateurs* were planted to spur the group on to activities that would inflame white anxieties. Anonymous letters were sent to various factions to cause splits within the ranks. In many instances, they succeeded. The top Panther leadership was badly fractured as a result of government efforts to undermine the relationship between Huey Newton and Eldridge Cleaver. In other situations, the results were bloody. The worst violent incident occurred when a group of Chicago police, acting on intelligence provided by an FBI informer, raided an apartment where Fred Hampton, a leader of the Chicago Panthers, was sleeping. The informer had provided a floor plan of the apartment and had drugged the occupants before he left. Police fired nearly one hundred shots into the apartment; only one Panther shot was fired, apparently as a bodyguard fell to the floor dead. Hampton was shot three times, at least twice in the head from close range. Police justified the raid on grounds that the apartment was being used to store illegal weapons, even though the informer had told FBI agents that any weapons on the premises were legally registered. In reality, Hampton's major crime was his success in organizing disgruntled young black people.[20] The repression practiced against the Panthers proved to be only a warmup for the expansion of suppressive tendencies that soon affected a broader spectrum of the American people.

Giving the Nixon administration yet another opportunity to orchestrate the nation's fears into a great repressive symphony was the emergence of The Weathermen, a radical faction of the SDS that appeared after the group's summer 1969 national convention. This fanatical group believed that all peaceful measures had failed to change American society; the only alternative left was revolution. They swore to lead the attack, for, they contended, only American young people could change their society. "Young people have less stake in a society (no family, fewer debts, etc.), are more open to new ideas (they have not been brainwashed for so long or so well), and are therefore more able and willing to move in a revolutionary direction," explained the Weatherman manifesto, a document entitled "You Don't Need a Weatherman to Know Which Way the Wind Blows." After examining foreign and domestic problems, the manifesto declared, "The legitimacy of the State is called into question for the first time in at least 30 years, and the anti-authoritarianism which characterizes the youth rebellion turns into rejection of the State, a refusal to be socialized into American society. Kids used to try to beat the system from inside the army or from inside the schools; now they desert from the army and burn down the schools."[21]

Individuals advocating this complete rejection of American society had benefited from the best that society had to offer. Their families were financially well-off; they went to good schools; and they spent their time denouncing everything that others would so gladly have. Included in the crop of Weatherman leaders were Kathy Boudin, the daughter of a prominent left-wing lawyer who had defended many antiwar activists; Diana Oughton, daughter of an Illinois banker and Republican state legislator and great-granddaughter of the founder of the Boy Scouts of America; and Cathy Wilkerson, the daughter of a radio-station owner.[22] Their initial goal was to encourage working-class young people to join them in revolution. Thus Weathermen barged into blue-collar high schools in several cities trying to win recruits. When few high schoolers joined the Weathermen, the organization focused on bringing so much violence to American streets that the national government would quake in fear and immediately end the war in Vietnam.

The major Weather encounter occurred in Chicago in 1969, when several hundred young people gathered in Lincoln Park to launch "Four Days of Rage" aimed at punishing the city for its behavior during the Democratic National

Convention the year before. The demonstrators came equipped with medical kits, protective clothing, and appropriate weapons, including chains and clubs. About three hundred Weathermen faced off against some 2,000 Chicago police officers. The result was injured police officers, injured Weathermen, and the trashing of well-to-do sections of the city. Some 250 Weathermen were arrested during the affray, and bail bonds totalled $2.3 million.[23]

Much to the administration's delight, the Days of Rage occurred in Chicago just days before a far greater threat to Nixon's foreign policy plans. Although the October 15 Moratorium movement had no connection with the radical SDS faction, the administration suggested connections with radicals of various persuasions. The Moratorium was, perhaps, one of the most dangerous of all the protests against the war. Orchestrated by the people who had run Eugene McCarthy's presidential campaign, the Moratorium offered moderate opponents of the war a chance to show their opposition without doing anything too outlandish. They could wear a black armband, turn on their car headlights, honk their horns, or walk off of their jobs or out of their classrooms for just one day. Just how many Americans would participate in Moratorium Day was unknown. The Nixon administration tried to take the edge off the observance by announcing that Lewis Hershey, the much detested head of the Selective Service Administration, was leaving his post. When all else failed, Vice President Spiro Agnew began his campaign against the "effete corps of impudent snobs" that made up the demonstration, and the administration exerted pressure on the media to downplay Moratorium protests.[24]

Millions of Americans participated in Moratorium Day across the country. Although some critics said that the participants still came primarily from the upper middle classes, the protest was one of the most successful in the history of the antiwar movement. In the midst of triumph, however, came hints of future problems. In New York City, for instance, workers at the city's fire and police stations violated Mayor John Lindsay's orders that flags in the city be flown at half-mast for the day. In addition, some 200 wounded Vietnam veterans attending the fourth game of the World Series as guests of the New York Mets refused to allow the flag at the stadium to be lowered.[25] The lines were being drawn between those who opposed the war and those who opposed the protesters. The divisions would become clearer in just a few weeks.

The Moratorium was on October 15; antiwar protesters also had plans for a national Mobilization against the war on November 15, which called for gathering thousands of demonstrators in Washington, D.C. Nixon, who had been irate about the October 15 event because he felt that it undercut his plans to push the North Vietnamese into ending the war by November 1, was determined that the November 15 protest would fall far short of its anticipated goals. Mobilization organizers, for instance, wanted permission to parade down Pennsylvania Avenue and to pass in front of the White House, long the traditional parade route in the nation's capital. The Justice Department warned District officials against giving permission for such a march, contending that it had "reliable reports that a minority of those expected to come to Washington may be planning to foment violence or to stage confrontations which could cause personal and property damage not only to the peaceful participants of the planned demonstration but also to the citizens of the city."[26] Even as the Justice Department was working to hold down the activities of demonstrators, the FBI and other intelligence-gathering agencies took steps to undermine the fragile coalition organizing the demonstration.

Nixon still was not convinced that he had sufficiently neutralized the Mobilization. So, on November 3, Nixon told the American people his plans for the "Vietnamization" of the conflict in South Vietnam—for withdrawing American fighting forces and turning the responsibility for continuing the war over to the South Vietnamese. The address, better known as his "Silent Majority" speech, was aimed directly at picking up support from Americans such as the firefighters in New York City who would not allow the American flag to be lowered on Moratorium Day. "I recognize that some of my fellow Americans have reached different conclusions as to how peace should be achieved," he said. In addition, "honest and patriotic citizens disagree with the plan for peace I have chosen." Demonstrations had shown him the depth of these feelings but yielding to the demands of the minority was wrong. Although "one of the strengths of our free society is that any American has a right to reach that conclusion and to advocate that point of view," he said, "as President of the United States, I would be untrue to my oath of office to be dictated by the minority who hold that point of view and who try to impose it on the nation by mounting demonstrations in the street." Ignoring the fact that minority views in the past had, at times, been correct, Nixon displayed almost complete intolerance for the opinions of Americans opposed to his plan to end the war. "If a vocal minority, however fervent its cause, prevails over reason and the will of the majority, this nation has no future as a free society." In fact, Nixon told his audience, "North Vietnam cannot defeat or humiliate the United States. Only Americans can do that."[27]

The address commanded free air time on all three television networks. And as was customary, network news commentators and guest experts analyzed the speech after it had been delivered. On ABC, Frank Reynolds noted that the speech offered "no new initiative, no new proposal, no announcement of any more troop withdrawals. And in short, Mr. Nixon has taken a hard line not only against the North Vietnamese, but also against those in this country who oppose his policy." ABC's leading guest analyst was W. Averell Harriman, an elder statesman in the Democratic party who had served as President Johnson's chief negotiator at the Paris peace talks. CBS relied solely on its own commentators for discussion, but once again, the talk emphasized the lack of new initiatives in the speech. Eric Sevareid, the network's national correspondent, for example, noted that the president "is asking for trust to let him have flexibility and a free hand." Sevareid questioned whether the speech was sufficient to win the time Nixon needed: "I would think that on its face this speech would not draw the fangs of some of the leading critics, particularly here in the Capitol . . . who were ready, if there was something given them of a definite nature in this speech to cease their criticism and to support the President. I would doubt now that they would do anything but keep on with the attack." In addition, he said, "It may give a little more strength to that demonstration scheduled for the middle of the month." John Chancellor, anchoring the commentary on NBC, also noted that "the President used some hard language, apparently directed against the antiwar demonstrators who demonstrated last month and will demonstrate this month."[28]

The president had carefully prepared the speech and indeed had sought to appeal directly to the American people for support for his war policies. The commentary after the speech, the White House felt, not only negated the effect of the address but was disrespectful to the office of the president. Thus, the commentary led Nixon and his staff to decide that it was finally time to silence the media just as it planned to silence the demonstrators. For Richard Nixon, silencing the press was a much cherished goal. As a man long in the public eye, Nixon had had many unhappy experiences with the press. He felt that journalists had not properly covered his role in the Alger Hiss–Whittaker Chambers matter while he was a member of the House Committee on Un-American Activities. Nor did he appreciate the way in which the press reported his activities on behalf of the Nixon-Mundt bill, which later became the Internal Security Act of 1950.[29]

His first substantial media-related problem came during his campaign for vice president in 1952 when journalists disclosed the existence of a private political fund from which he could draw to meet expenses. The disclosure of this "slush fund" almost led Dwight Eisenhower to remove Nixon from the ticket. He was saved from political oblivion only because of a televised address in which he denied accepting illegal political gifts and claimed that the only gift that he had accepted and would not return was a dog named Checkers who had been given to his daughters. The Checkers speech kept Nixon on the ticket and launched both his national political career and his intense hatred of American journalists. That dislike intensified during the 1960 presidential campaign in which Nixon felt that press was decidedly biased toward his opponent, the personable and photogenic John F. Kennedy.

Nixon's relationship with the press hit one of its lows in 1962 after he lost the California governor's race. He blamed the press for his defeat even though 70 percent of the state's newspapers had endorsed his candidacy and the reporting of the race had been objective. As the press was waiting for Nixon's formal concession statement, the candidate suddenly appeared and launched a tirade against the way in which the press had covered not only the 1962 campaign but his entire political career. He directed most of his anger to the print media, noting, "I can only say thank God for television and radio for keeping the newspapers a little more honest." But he stressed that the way in which the press treated him was of no more concern to him. "You won't have Nixon to kick around anymore, because, gentlemen, this is my last press conference."[30]

These experiences formed the backdrop for the relationship between the Nixon administration and the press. Most of his staff members were determined to protect the president from reporters and to defend his policies from journalistic meddling. Some aides were ready to take action after the October 15 Moratorium because they felt the press had been far too respectful of the demonstrators who were, after all, undermining the president's policies. Jeb Stuart Magruder, one of the bright young men in the White House, for instance, wrote a memorandum to his superior, H. R. Haldeman, two days after the Moratorium that called for a reassessment of the administration's policies toward the press. "It is my opinion," he said, "this continual daily attempt to get to the media or to anti-Administration spokesmen because of specific things they have said is very unfruitful and wasteful of our time." "The real problem that faces the Administration," Magruder continued, "is to get to this unfair coverage in such a way that we make major impact on a basis which the networks-newspapers and Congress will react to and begin to look at things somewhat differently. It is my opinion that we should begin concentrated efforts in a number of major areas that will have much more impact on the media and other anti-Administration spokesmen and will do more good in the long run."[31]

His suggestions included having the Federal Communications Commission (FCC) monitor network coverage of the president. "If the monitoring system proves our point, we have then legitimate and legal rights to go to the networks, etc. and make official complaints from the FCC. This will have much more effect than a phone call" from White House personnel. The antitrust division of the Justice Department should be used as well, he contended, because "even the possible threat of anti-trust action I think would be effective in changing their views." The Internal Revenue Service (IRS) was another agency that could intimidate journalists into more appropriate behavior: "Just a threat of an IRS investigation will probably turn their approach." The administration could also begin to show favorites among the media in an effort to demonstrate the benefits of proper coverage. And finally, he suggested mobilizing the Republican National Committee for "major letter-writing efforts" to convince the media of grassroots support for the president.[32] Magruder's ideas—and more—eventually were implemented in the Nixon administration's ongoing battle with the press. The "silent majority" speech provided the pretext for that action.

Quickly taking the offensive, Dean Burch, new head of the FCC, made a clearly extralegal and intimidating call to the networks to demand transcripts of the commentaries that had followed the address. Burch, a conservative Republican partisan who had managed Barry Goldwater's 1964 presidential campaign, saw nothing wrong with manipulating the news media to obtain favorable coverage. Displaying a similar lack of regard for the chilling effects of his comments, Herbert Klein, director of the White House Office of Communication, told reporters on a Sunday morning talk show that continued press misbehavior would invite governmental intervention. The major weapon against the networks, however, was the vice president of the United States. Spiro T. Agnew had a talent for turning a vicious phrase right into the heart of his intended victim. Ten days after the president's "silent majority" speech, Agnew spoke before a group of Midwestern Republicans in Des Moines, Iowa. Usually such an appearance would merit press coverage only from local journalists, but this speech was carried over network television. An advance copy of the talk had been made available to television executives, almost daring them to ignore the vice president's comments.

Television network news operations were the targets of his prose that day. "No medium has a more profound influence over public opinion," Agnew said of television, but "nowhere in our system are there fewer checks on vast power." This reality should lead to greater responsibility by network broadcasters, the vice president contended, which he found profoundly lacking. Turning his attention to the president's speech on Vietnam, he said, "When the President completed his address—an address, incidentally, that he spent weeks in preparation of—his words and policies were subjected to instant analysis and querulous criticism. The audience of 70 million Americans gathered to hear the President of the United States was inherited by a small band of network commentators and self-appointed analysts, the majority of whom expressed in one way or another their hostility to what he had to say." Although the vice president accepted the notion that "every American has a right to disagree with the President of the United States and to express publicly that disagreement," he argued that "the President of the United States has a right to communicate directly with the people who elected him, and the people of this country have the right to make up their own minds and form their own opinions about a Presidential address without having a President's words and thoughts characterized through the prejudices of hostile critics before they can even be digested."[33]

Making matters even worse, said Agnew, was the fact that "a small group of men, numbering perhaps no more than a dozen anchormen, commentators and executive producers" decided what millions of Americans saw on network television. Such individuals "can elevate men from obscurity to national prominence within a week. They can reward some politicians with national exposure and ignore others," he said. Their actions could be most subtle. "A raised eyebrow, an inflection of the voice, a caustic remark dropped in the middle of a broadcast can raise doubts in a million minds about the veracity of a public official or the wisdom of a Government policy." Those individuals wielding such power were almost totally out of touch with the real America, he added. "To a man these commentators and producers live and work in the geographical and intellectual confines of Washington, D.C., or New York City, the latter of which [veteran journalist] James Reston terms the most unrepresentative community in the entire United States." From this, Agnew said, "we can deduce that these men read the same newspapers. They draw their political and social views from the same sources. Worse, they talk constantly to one another, thereby providing artificial reinforcement to their shared viewpoints." Their views, he stressed, were not the views of the majority of Americans. He denied asking for government censorship of the news media, but he questioned "whether a form of censorship already exists when the news that 40 million Americans receive each night is determined by a handful of men responsible only to their corporate employers and is filtered through a handful of commentators who admit to their set of biases."[34]

To the vice president, the network news operations were run by liberals who spread their ideas throughout the United States. Among these visions of American life so deceptively foisted off on the people of the United States was one that led American citizens—and representatives of foreign governments as well—to believe that dissent dominated the nation. "How many marches and demonstrations would we have if the marchers did not know that the ever-faithful TV cameras would be there to record their antics for the next news show?"[35] The American protest movement, to Spiro Agnew, was a creation of the mass media. Take away the cameras and the reporters, and the movement would fade away. Take away the "instant analysis and querulous criticism," and the nation would support presidential policies on Vietnam and other issues.

In reality, Agnew's denunciation of "instant analysis and querulous criticism" was totally inappropriate for the "silent majority" speech. Journalists had been given copies of the address several hours before the president went on the air, and national security adviser Henry Kissinger had provided a press briefing about the substance of the president's policy before the broadcast as well. To a substantial extent, the journalists' commentary reflected a national disappointment that the president had not announced a plan for ending the war. Response to Agnew's speech was immediate and strongly favorable. Networks and their affiliates received thousands of telephone calls, telegrams, and letters. Letters to the editor also flooded the nation's newspapers complaining about the bias present in television reporting. A goodly number of the favorable public responses generated by Agnew's speech had been encouraged by the White House, a fact then unknown to the nation's journalists. Taking the vice president's comments and the response to them at face value, the networks launched in-house evaluations of their commentary and coverage, most of which vindicated their policies. Still, the vice president's speech worked. Although the networks claimed to be unintimidated by his comments, their coverage of the Mobilization two days later was significantly different from that afforded the Moratorium in October.

Government officials had done their best to keep protesters from even reaching the nation's capital. Nevertheless, at least 250,000 people showed up for the November 15 Mobilization. Some estimates from marchers place the total somewhere between 500,000 and 700,000, which would make it the largest political demonstration in the nation's history. The largely peaceful gathering was virtually ignored by network news operations. Most Americans who relied on their television sets for information found the networks unwilling to interrupt weekend football games to provide coverage. Weekend news programs did, however, highlight a small group of demonstrators who headed for the Department of Justice to protest police violence against demonstrators around the country. The group was forcibly dispersed by the police using tear gas. The demonstrators had caused relatively little damage, which might not have occurred at all had the police not intervened; 114 protesters were arrested. Attorney General John Mitchell claimed that the work of police and the threat of bringing in federal troops had reduced the possible violence, and he said the scene from the Justice Department window "looked like the Russian revolution going on."[36]

Mitchell's analogy to the Russian Revolution was close to the view provided most Americans. Indeed, television cameras depicted the march as a major assault by unruly demonstrators on the seat of national law and order. The networks apparently were thoroughly intimidated by Agnew's speech and by the number of viewers who apparently approved of the vice president's remarks. Network executives believed that the nation was either tired of news of these demonstrations or unsympathetic to the demonstrators' goals. Although network news personnel might agree personally with antiwar protests, the medium was sensitive to the economic support of its audience and dependent on the government for licensing. Thus television executives intended to be far more careful in choosing information for the evening news. At least one network news executive already had picked up on the change in national mood. As early as March 1969, Av Westin, executive producer of ABC News, was telling his staff, "I think the time has come to shift some of our focus from the battlefield, or more specifically from American military involvement with the enemy, to themes and stories under the general heading 'We are on our way out of Viet Nam.'"[37] A similar move was under way at NBC News, where Robert J. Northshield, who was executive producer of the "Huntley-Brinkley Report" through 1968, noted that the emphasis in coverage there changed in early 1969 as well.[38] And in light of Agnew's criticism of the concentration of media anchors in New York and Washington, D.C., ABC News, despite its belief that its broadcasts were fair, put a news anchor in Chicago to represent "Middle America."[39]

Consequently, by the end of 1969, the American people, who relied on television for their news, were given the impression that the war had wound down several years before its actual ending and that the peace movement had all but disappeared from the national scene at the moment of its biggest success. Factual information, a key ingredient for intelligent participation in government, had fallen victim to the twin forces of economic and political pressure. Northshield acknowledged the cramped view of reality that television provided when he noted in 1972 that Nixon "*has* ended the war, because you don't see the war on the tube any more. So the war has ended, though we are bombing the hell out of these poor people, more than ever."[40] Reality, however, seemed to have little relationship to what appeared on the evening news. Television journalists could ill afford to take chances.

With the broadcast journalists brought into line, the Nixon administration turned its attention to print journalists. Here, the problem was somewhat different, for print journalists were always quick to wrap themselves in the First Amendment, a protection less available to broadcasters. In addition, print journalists had more time and space to make themselves obnoxious to the administration. Just as the Mobilization was getting under way, for instance, the *New York Times* broke the story of the My Lai massacre in which an American platoon under the command of Lt. William L. Calley, Jr., killed 567 Vietnamese men, women, and children on March 16, 1968. Military authorities had successfully suppressed the story for more than eighteen months. Richard Nixon wanted no more such disclosures.

Agnew was unleashed against the print outlets as well. This time, he claimed to be concerned about "the trend toward the monopolization of the great public information vehicles and the concentration of more and more power in fewer and fewer hands." His particular target was the Washington Post Company, which owned the largest newspaper in the nation's capital, as well as four major television stations, an all-news radio station, and *Newsweek* magazine, all of which, said the vice president, were "grinding out the same editorial line." "I'm not recommending the dismemberment of the Washington Post Company," he said, "I'm merely pointing out that the public should be aware that these four powerful voices harken to the same master."[41]

In addition, the vice president took on the *New York Times* for its willingness to grant too much credence to protesters. In response to Agnew's earlier denunciation of campus demonstrations, the *Times* had editorialized, "He [Agnew] lambasted the nation's youth in sweeping and ignorant generalizations, when it's clear to all perceptive observers that American youth today is far more imbued with idealism, a sense of service and a deep humanitarianism than any generalization in recent history, including particularly Mr. Agnew's generation."[42] Agnew scoffed at this depiction of American youth—"who march under the flags and portraits of dictators, who intimidate and harass university professors, who use gutter obscenities to shout down speakers with whom they disagree, who openly profess their belief in the efficacy of violence in a democratic society." He also criticized those youths who fled to Sweden or Canada to avoid the draft, noting, "they are not our heroes. Many of our heroes will not be coming home; some are coming back in hospital ships, without limbs or eyes, with scars they shall carry for the rest of their lives."[43] And yet the press ignored such facts.

"I'm not asking immunity from criticism," Agnew said. Politicians expected the press to comment on their words and actions, he said, but he was disturbed by what he perceived to be an effort by his "political and journalistic adversaries" to make sure "that I circumscribe my rhetorical freedom while they place no restriction on theirs." No longer, he promised, would the newspapers be immune from criticism. "When they go beyond fair comment and criticism they will be called upon to defend their statements and their positions just as we must defend ours. And when their criticism becomes excessive or unjust, we shall invite them down from their ivory towers to enjoy the rough and tumble of public debate." Despite his hard words, Agnew stressed, "I don't seek to intimidate the press, or the networks or anyone else from speaking out. But the time for blind acceptance of their opinions is past. And the time for naive belief in their neutrality is gone."[44]

Just what the Nixon administration meant by the vice president's comments soon became clear. About six weeks after Agnew's second speech, a new Florida corporation filed papers challenging the license of a television station owned by the Washington Post Company in Miami. Chances of the action being simply coincidental were miniscule, especially after it was revealed that the corporation was headed by a business partner of Bebe Rebozo, a close personal friend of the president. The Miami station had a sound reputation, especially in the area of public affairs programming, and the challenge soon was dropped. The failure to carry the effort through in no way minimized its effect, for the newspaper company now was on notice that although the administration might not be able to attack its print outlets, its lucrative broadcasting connections were indeed vulnerable. The newspaper company found another of its stations under attack in early 1970, after its Jacksonville television operation reported information that contributed to the rejection of Harold Carswell, a Nixon nominee to the Supreme Court.

President Nixon clearly approved of the efforts to quiet press critics. In a

December 9, 1969, press conference, for example, he talked about the vice president's attack on television commentary, saying, "The vice president does not clear his speeches with me. . . . However, I believe that he rendered a public service in talking in a very dignified and courageous way about a problem many Americans are concerned about, and that is the coverage of news media and in particular television news media of public figures."[45] In a less public forum, he approved additional assaults on the media. One of the most popular attacks in late 1969 and early 1970 was carried out by the Department of Justice, where federal prosecutors began issuing subpoenas for journalists' files, unused still photographs, and television news outtakes (unused footage) to use in prosecuting radical groups like the Weathermen and the Black Panthers.

One week in early 1970 showed print and broadcast journalists just how extensive this government subpoena threat could be. The first subpoena went to the Columbia Broadcasting System (CBS) for used and unused film relating to a news program on the Black Panther party that the government hoped would help to build a case against a Panther leader. A second subpoena followed immediately, asking CBS for all correspondence, notes, memoranda, and data on telephone calls connected with the program dating back to mid-1968. Then federal authorities subpoenaed the files of *Time, Life,* and *Newsweek* relating to the Weathermen. Following on the heels of that subpoena came one delivered to Earl Caldwell, a black *New York Times* reporter assigned to cover the Black Panther party at its home base in the San Francisco area. The latter subpoena demanded that he bring his notes and tape recordings of his interviews with Panther leaders to a federal grand jury session investigating party activities.

The subpoenas brought two fundamental principles into conflict. As citizens, reporters are obligated to tell authorities about possible criminal activities. But reporters providing such information jeopardized their ability to gather information about radical groups—exactly what the Nixon administration had in mind. Through pressure on network news officials, it had succeeded in removing the bloodiness of the Vietnam War and the activities of the nation's antiwar movement from the forefront of television news coverage. Now, if it could eliminate information about radical fringe organizations, another goal would be accomplished. As soon as the extent of the subpoena problem became known, members of the press began pushing the administration to stop using journalists to build its cases against radicals.

"The Department of Justice does not consider the press 'an investigative arm of the Government,'" Attorney General John Mitchell said in response to press complaints in August 1970.[46] Because of a rising clamor against serving journalists with subpoenas, the Justice Department under Mitchell promulgated guidelines designed ostensibly to reduce the number of subpoenas issued. Recognizing that "compulsory process . . . may have a limiting effect on the exercise of 1st Amendment rights," the department said it would attempt to negotiate with journalists for information before seeking subpoenas and pledged that no subpoenas would be issued without the attorney general's express approval. In granting these authorizations, the attorney general promised to evaluate the prosecution's belief that a crime had been committed and that the information sought was "essential to a successful investigation." In addition, the government "should have unsuccessfully attempted to obtain the information from alternative non-press sources." If the subpoena was authorized, the request "should normally be limited to the verification of published information," with "great caution . . . observed in requesting subpoena authorization . . . for unpublished information."[47] Despite the guidelines, the subpoenas continued, and reporters geared up for a Supreme Court confrontation on the issue.

Early 1970 marked the revelation of another effort by governmental authorities to undermine the ability of the press to inform the American people as well. In January, journalists discovered that four U.S. government agents had spent two weeks masquerading as legitimate reporters within the Saigon press corps. Initially, correspondents in South Vietnam and the United States considered the intrusion a mistake; within a few months, however, journalists discovered that federal, state, and local government agents had been masquerading as reporters at least since 1967. The reason was simple: journalists had access to radical groups that was unavailable to most government agents. By posing as reporters, these agents could infiltrate radical groups to gather information. In fact, a team of Army Security Agency officers was so successful with its fictitious Midwest Video News service that it obtained an exclusive interview with Yippie leader Abbie Hoffman, who thought he was talking to legitimate news reporters. Practicing journalists were incensed at the government's practices. "Reporters have a hard enough time getting information from groups such as militant black students, who are naturally suspicious of the establishment press," said Joel Havemann, a Chicago reporter who discovered a government agent posing as a reporter at a demonstration by black students. "If these groups begin to suspect that every reporter they talk to may be a policeman, our job will become impossible."[48]

Subpoenas and government agents posing as journalists were only two prongs of the administration's attack on the radical movement. When both of these efforts became public, the mainstream press launched loud and forceful protests against their continuation. The third prong of the attack, however, caused no outcry from the establishment press. The target here was the underground press, a collection of ragtag newspapers published in many major cities and devoted solely to news omitted from mainstream newspapers. High priorities for coverage, of course, were the radical community, campus demonstrations, and the antiwar movement. Interspersed among such stories were details about the counterculture so despised by middle-class Americans. The underground press talked of drug use—especially of marijuana and LSD—as if it were legal, discussed sex in the most blatant terms, and flavored most stories with more four-letter words than military veterans used. Little in them would merit a ringing defense from establishment journalists, and they received no such support despite plaintive cries from some civil libertarians that government infringement on the freedom of the underground press could serve as an opening wedge for similar action against mainline journalism.[49]

Underground newspapers burgeoned in the early sixties, as did the national protest movement; as the movement died out in the early seventies, so, too, did the underground press. Both deaths were, of course, aided by a healthy dose of governmental intervention. Underground press offices and workers were regularly watched by government agents; they and the people who sold the publications were harassed routinely; and their offices were often subjected to illegal searches and seizures. The goal in each attack was to silence an advocate for political and social change. But the government never brought charges against the underground press for its political views. Rather, charges focused on the newspaper offices being used to plan illegal activities, or on staff members using drugs on the premises, or on the newspaper carrying obscene materials.

Most of the harassment took place on the local level, where the underground press of the 1960s and 1970s became heir to intimidation tactics exerted against the abolitionist, German-American, and Socialist presses before them. Printing facilities became hard to find, and if someone agreed to print the newspaper, community pressure ended the contract. Office rents were raised for underground press newspapers. Advertising would be canceled. Important materials would be lost in shipping. Newsstands handling the newspapers would be coerced into removing them, and vendors selling the publications on street corners faced intimidation by local police for such offenses as littering. The editor of *The Daily Planet* in Miami, for instance, was arrested twenty-nine times in 1969–70 for selling obscene literature on the city's streets. He was acquitted in twenty-eight of those arrests, but he had to put up bail bonds of $93,000 during that time period.[50] As with the antiwar movement, arrests, bail bonds, and legal fees drove all but the most hardy out of business even though the underground press usually won its legal battles against government agencies.

Probably the most celebrated action against an underground press outlet involved the *Los Angeles Free Press* and its printing in 1969 of the names, addresses, and telephone numbers of eighty California narcotics officers, many of whom were working undercover. A source in the state attorney general's office offered the information to the *Free Press,* and its editors decided to print the list because they believed the undercover agents comprised a secret police force that jeopardized the further existence of a free society. The state charged the publisher and writer of the story with receiving stolen property, which was a felony. The newspaper and its editors also faced civil suits, as California authorities filed a $10 million action against the underground newspaper for obstruction of justice. In addition, some of the named agents filed a $15 million class-action suit on behalf of all of the named individuals for invasion of privacy. The trial attracted little attention in the mainline press. Bill Thomas, city editor of the *Los Angeles Times,* for instance, found nothing in the trial worth covering. After all, he said, "it has nothing to do with freedom of the press. For what they did they got what was coming to them."[51]

The *Free Press,* however, argued the case squarely on free-press grounds, claiming that if its editors were convicted for receipt of stolen property, all journalists in the country would stand in jeopardy every time they took documents from a source. In addition, they contended, American journalism would be irreparably damaged if the press was limited to detailing only the information that the owners of documents wanted released. The newspaper's attorney told the jury that "this prosecution is the most vicious, sneaky, pernicious back-door attack on a fundamental American freedom that I have ever seen or read."[52] Jury members refused to believe that publishing the names of undercover police officers was encompassed by freedom of the press, and after six days of deliberation, they found the newspaper officials guilty. The newspaper's editor and the reporter responsible for the story were fined a total of $6,000, and the corporation publishing the paper was fined another $500. Both individuals were put on probation for three years. The newspaper's appeal was joined by the *Los Angeles Times,* which finally became convinced that freedom of the press indeed was at stake, but the convictions were sustained. The *Free Press* settled the $10 million obstruction of justice suit by agreeing to pay the state $10,000—in monthly installments of $500. The invasion of privacy suit was settled for $43,000, which was payable in monthly installments of $2,000. The *Free Press* also agreed to publish an apology to the agents' families. The fines essentially bankrupted the newspaper, and the judgment stood as a precedent for use in later cases of unauthorized leaks.

Underground newspapers got in trouble with authorities intent on preserving law and order and cleaning up society in other ways as well. The Madison, Wisconsin, *Kaleidoscope,* for example, published a statement from the New Year's Gang, which claimed responsibility for the bombing of the Army Mathematics Research Center on the University of Wisconsin campus. When the editor of the newspaper was summoned before a grand jury to reveal the source of the document, he refused to testify and was jailed for contempt. In Dallas, police raided the office of the *Dallas Notes* twice—once because the newspaper allegedly was publishing obscene materials and once because of a report that marijuana was being used on the premises. As a result of the raids, two tons of newspaper issues were confiscated without any judicial determination that the material contained therein was obscene, and cameras and office equipment were taken.

Attorneys for the newspaper sought a restraining order against Dallas authorities that would have prohibited any further raids on the office unless and until a judge had declared that the newspaper had published obscene material. Both the federal district court and the court of appeals granted the injunction, but the Supreme Court vacated the order on the grounds that federal courts should not intervene in pending state criminal prosecutions. Justices William Brennan and Thurgood Marshall agreed with the five-member majority but noted that had the case come before them on more appropriate constitutional grounds, including allegations of prior restraint based on the removal of the office equipment, they likely would have decided differently. Justice William O. Douglas was vehement in his denunciation of the Court's decision, saying, "If this search-and-destroy technique can be employed against this Dallas newspaper, then it can be done against the New York Times, the Washington Post, the Seattle Post Intelligencer, the Yakima Herald-Republic, the Sacramento Bee, and all the rest of our newspapers."[53]

Underground newspapers were subjected to other forms of intimidation as well, including the denial of press passes that were necessary for reporters to visit crime scenes. A Twentieth Century Fund investigation of press problems in the late 1960s and early 1970s found this police practice reprehensible. Such discriminatory granting of press passes, the Fund report said, established "a double standard of treatment, one for the underground and one for the established press—a double standard that is inconsistent with the First Amendment's guarantee of freedom for all the press." What bothered Fund Task Force members even more was "the attitude of the established press toward official harassment of the underground press," which was "characterized by neglect." The Task Force found that many underground press complaints of abuse by police "were not mentioned in either the news or editorial columns of the established press. . . . [T]he underground press has been left largely to its own fragile devices by the more affluent elements of the news media."[54]

A quick review of journalistic support for dissident elements of society would show that the establishment press has almost never identified with dissenters. In 1972, when the Twentieth Century Fund made its investigation, Task Force members obviously hoped that the pressures brought against journalists by the Nixon administration would lead to a greater cohesion among representatives of the press and a greater willingness to repel all attempts to intimidate. But most American journalists were unwilling to share their treasured First Amendment protection with the disreputable, dirty, and disgusting underground press. They would have taken that stance even without the Nixon administration's efforts to stifle dissent. With the encouragement of the Nixon administration, placidity settled over much of the nation's news reporting.

In many respects, the administration's repression of dissent and encouragement of the presentation of a static picture of American life fit well with a growing desire to end the disruptions of the 1960s. Society had been rent by protests and marches and harsh language for too long; its collective nervous system was strained to the breaking point; and a period of quiet was essential. Because of this growing national desire, the president likely could have reached his goals without using intimidation, but Richard Nixon was never known for patience where the press was concerned. The president had a view of how America should appear and would brook no interference from protesters or journalists.

Although the antiwar movement had reached its high point with the protests in the fall of 1969, concern about its possible activities once warm weather came again in the spring haunted the executive branch. The administration even disregarded the fact that one of the most contentious elements of the war, the draft, had been discontinued in late 1969 when a lottery was instituted to fill future manpower needs. Still, Nixon was on edge. For one thing, the defendants in the Chicago Seven trial, who were out on bail, were touring the country speaking to crowds of adoring young people on college campuses. In addition, congressional elections loomed in the fall of 1970, and Richard Nixon did not relish the thought of additional antiwar spokesmen winning seats. In fact, he wanted to defeat some of the more prominent dovish senators and representatives and bring in a Congress more supportive of his plans to end the war.

Concerns about the violent nature of protest in America heated up again in March 1970, when an accidental bomb blast destroyed a town house in Greenwich Village. Three members of the Weathermen were killed in the explosion;

several others escaped. With the news, the public became convinced that the 300 or so disenchanted young people who made up the Weathermen intended to destroy the nation. The antiwar movement, to which the Weathermen errone-ously were tied, was tarnished still further. The connection was not so far-fetched in many people's minds. After all, had not the Weathermen said that the war was too much of an abstraction to the American people? To win support had they not said it was necessary to "bring the war home," "to turn New York into Saigon"?[55] The explosion provided the Nixon administration with the perfect excuse for increasing surveillance of left-wing militants. Such observation already had increased; now, the White House could announce it publicly and claim that the bomb blast had led to its initiation.

The antiwar movement struggled in spring 1970. The Moratorium commit-tee, which had enjoyed so much success the preceding October, found few sup-porters turning out for peace days in January, February, and March. Nor did a proposed fast for the Lenten season advocated by a group of clergy and lay peo-ple win many participants. An April 15 demonstration organized by several anti-war groups brought out 25,000, the largest turnout nationwide, in New York City. The movement clearly was at a low point. Under Nixon's expert guidance, the war was winding down, and through his pressure on the press, it was less an issue in newscasts and newspapers. The movement likely would have died at that point had the president not made a substantial miscalculation.

Because the North Vietnamese were proving recalcitrant at the bargaining table, the president decided to send American troops into Cambodia to obliter-ate enemy supply sources. The incursion by American ground forces into a neu-tral country destroyed the president's efforts to quiet protest; the nation's college campuses erupted in opposition. When asked his views of the demonstrations, President Nixon stressed his belief that most college students were studious and loyal Americans who would not participate in these activities. In the process of his discussion, he managed to further alienate American youth by his character-ization of their beliefs: "You know, you see these bums, you know, blowing up the campuses. Listen, the boys on the college campuses today are the luckiest people in the world, going to the greatest universities—and here they are burning up the books, storming around the issue. I mean—you name it. Get rid of the war and there'll be another issue."[56]

But the issue of the day—the Cambodian incursion—would not go away. Pro-tests spread not just geographically but to new groups that had not previously objected to the war. Whether the outcry would have simply exhausted itself in a few days without additional provocation is unknown. But the fuse soon was pro-vided that, when detonated, led to the closing of some 450 colleges and univer-sities for varying periods in May and to the calling out of the National Guard in at least twenty-four places around the country.[57] That trigger, of course, was what happened at Kent State University in Ohio.

The campus at Kent State had been the site of various minor disruptions in the two or three years prior to 1970, but essentially it was a middle-class school that remained rather quiet while protests rocked other campuses. With the Cam-bodian incursion, however, the largest demonstrations in the school's history occurred, and the governor called out the National Guard to maintain order. Governor James H. Rhodes, who had just become a senatorial candidate, vowed "to keep this university open at all costs. To close it down would be to play into the hands of all the dissident elements that are trying to do just that." The governor, seeing the turmoil as an election issue, loosed a stream of rhetoric designed to alienate most of the young people who were truly concerned about their government's actions. Demonstrations on the Kent State campus, he said, were not initiated or led by university students. Protest leaders, he said, "just move from one campus to the other and terrorize the community" leading good, middle-class Ohio students astray. "They're worse than the Brown Shirts and communist element and also the nightriders and the vigilantes. They're the worst type that we harbor in America." Indeed, said the governor, "I'll say 99-percent-plus of the students at Kent State want it open. They're here for an education."[58] And the governor was ready to keep the university open.

On Monday, May 4, 1970, Kent State students gathered to continue their protests. Few heard a radio announcement that said that outdoor gatherings and protests were banned by special order of the governor and that anyone participating in them would be arrested. The National Guard started to disperse the students. Tear gas canisters were lobbed into the crowd, and the students threw them back at the guardsmen. Rocks and other materials were also thrown at the guardsmen, although few found their mark. Nevertheless, a number of troops, believing that their tear gas was exhausted and that they were about to be overrun by students, dropped to their knees, readied their rifles, and fired. According to an audio tape made at the scene, the shooting lasted for thirteen seconds. When it was over, four students lay dead; nine others were severely wounded. All the dead had been registered at the university, and all had attended classes regularly. Of the four who were killed, only two were known to have participated in earlier demonstrations. At least some of the students were trying to get out of the way when bullets cut them down. According to pictures taken at the scene, the firing stopped only because a major beat his troops over the head with his swagger stick to gain their attention. Students were kept from rushing headlong on the guard position only by the intervention of several professors. Observers and participants generally agreed that no one involved in the demonstration had done anything that merited his or her being shot much less being killed.

The deaths at Kent State set the nation's campuses on fire. In many locations, the school year was abruptly shortened in order to end the disruptions by sending students home. Although the President's Commission on the Causes of Campus Unrest condemned both students and the authorities around the nation for allowing the situation to get so out of hand,[59] little was done by way of a permanent remedy. An attempt by Interior Secretary Walter Hickel to win greater presidential toleration for student concerns was unsuccessful as well. A letter written by Hickel and released to the press led to his eventual dismissal for lack of loyalty to the president.[60]

Richard Nixon believed protesters already had disrupted in his foreign policy plans too much. Now as a result of the Cambodian incursion, Congress finally repealed the Gulf of Tonkin resolution that had provided the president with authority to maintain troops in Indochina. Nixon ignored the repeal and continued to keep U.S. forces active in the Vietnam conflict. Congress tried to cut off funding for American activity in Cambodia as of July 1, the date President Nixon said the incursion should end. That measure failed, but Congress eventually enacted a measure designed to limit financing for ground troops absent a formal declaration of war. By that time, most U.S. participation was in the form of air strikes.

Although the antiwar movement, for all intents and purposes, collapsed as of late spring 1970, this fact does not mean that the nation approved of continuing the war. Indeed, public opinion polls indicated that more and more Americans wanted the war to end and that increasing numbers of respondents believed that getting in the war in the first place had been unwise. But Nixon was winding down the war, and the intensity of the protest movement simply could not be sustained. The major actions had been taken; the fire had burned out on the slopes of Blanket Hill at Kent State University. Except for a few isolated incidents, the organized movement ended. Richard Nixon, however, seemed unable to believe that, and he eagerly welcomed all new supporters. When a group of hard-hat workers in New York City attacked a small antiwar protest, he was so jubilant that he invited some of them to the White House a few days later for presidential congratulations. And he worked hard to stage events that would solidify his base of support. He went, for instance, to a Billy Graham rally in Knoxville, Tennessee, to show himself as unafraid to face the people. When a small group of demonstrators protested, cameras and microphones recorded not only the harshness of the comments addressed at the president of the United States but the vile language used in the presence of the nation's preeminent evangelist.

Through all of this, Nixon felt that he had not been adequately informed that protest was likely when news about the Cambodian incursion became public. Rather than blame his isolation from advisers with dissenting views for this lack of information, the president decided that the intelligence system obviously was faulty. As a result of presidential concern, a young White House adviser named Tom Huston devised a plan, which Nixon approved in July 1970, for the White House to play a more active role in the surveillance of the nation's dissidents. Almost nothing would be untouched in this far-reaching campaign to stop radical ideas and those persons who advocated them. Intelligence agencies from all parts of government would be given a virtual carte blanche to do whatever was necessary to stop dissent. Break-ins, wiretappings, and mail intercepts were just a few of the tactics proposed. Only the objections of FBI director J. Edgar Hoover blocked the plan's implementation. To keep the White House from developing a rival intelligence system, the FBI, CIA, National Security Agency, and Internal Revenue Service all stepped up their activities. In the end, the White House still wanted more information and established its own espionage team, the infamous Plumbers, to gather evidence against the nation's leading dissidents.

Intimidation of the press continued unabated as well. The efforts at times were blatant as when White House personnel tried to keep the networks from providing time to Nixon's opponents to respond to televised messages. Why the Nixon administration was so concerned about Democratic access to television is unclear, for the president clearly dominated the airwaves during his first eighteen months in office. Records show that the president appeared in prime-time viewing hours thirty-one times during that period, more times than Presidents Eisenhower, Kennedy, and Johnson in their entire terms.[61] The networks asked no questions as to whether Nixon's speeches were presidential or political and publicized his appearances ahead of time to guarantee a maximum audience. In addition, Nixon appeared on the airwaves in press conferences, which he moved from midday to evening hours, and in various events staged especially for television cameras. He completely dominated television, repeatedly reaching the American people without interference.

In 1970, as the two major political parties prepared for the fall congressional elections, the Democratic National Committee (DNC) challenged the president's unimpeded access to television. Many of Nixon's speeches were political in nature, said DNC Chairman Lawrence O'Brien, and the other side should be heard. When Nixon scheduled an appearance on April 30, 1970, to announce and defend the Cambodian incursion, the Democrats once more sought time to reply; only ABC agreed. The Democrats, convinced that escalation of the war was a partisan issue, filed papers with the Federal Communications Commission demanding that the networks be forced to sell them time to counter the president's free access to the American people. "Under the First Amendment to the Constitution and the Communications Act," said the DNC petition, "a broadcaster may not, as a general policy, refuse to sell time to responsible entities, such as DNC, for the solicitation of funds and for comment on public issues." Why, asked the DNC, "are the public airwaves—the most powerful communications media in our democracy—to be used to solicit funds for soap, brassieres, deodorants and mouthwashes, and not to solicit funds to enhance the exchange of ideas?"[62]

In challenging the decision of the networks not to sell time to the Democrats, the party alleged that the networks were not following FCC rules that required broadcasters who presented controversial ideas to adequately represent all sides of the issue. The Fairness Doctrine grew out of the desire by some broadcasters to editorialize on certain issues. At first the FCC decided that such commentary was inappropriate; later, editorializing was permitted, if responsible representatives of criticized positions were given time to respond. The doctrine, however, had not been applied to the selling of time, and many broadcasters traditionally refused to sell commercial time to individuals or groups that wanted to hawk ideas rather than merchandise. Until the Nixon era, that attitude had generally been accepted. Eventually, the complaints sparked a response from Frank Stanton, president of CBS, who called O'Brien to offer the party twenty-five minutes of free time. The show was to be the first in a series called "The Loyal Opposition." The program prepared by the party was harshly political in nature and drew immediate reaction from the Republican National Committee, which demanded time to respond to the Democratic presentation. The FCC, in hearing the Republicans' complaint, ordered the network to allow their response. At the same time, the Republican-dominated commission agreed to a compromise that required the networks to provide political opponents time to respond to presidential addresses, thus defusing one of the Democrats' complaints.

On the same day that they decided the presidential address issue, the FCC ruled that broadcasters did not have to sell time for marketing ideas. If the complainants could prove that broadcasters had not covered opposing views adequately, then a Fairness Doctrine issue might develop; until that point, however, the commission was unwilling to disturb a commercial system more attuned to peddling products than ideas. In so ruling, the FCC rejected attempts by both the DNC and an organization called the Business Executives' Move for Peace to purchase time for spot announcements. The two disgruntled parties took the issue into court. In March 1971, the federal court of appeals reversed the commission ruling, holding that arbitrary rules against selling time for persons who wanted to promote ideas violated the First Amendment.[63]

The case was appealed to the Supreme Court, where a majority of the justices overturned the lower court ruling and returned the airwaves safely to soda pop and soap powder. Justice William Brennan dissented, noting that "the principle at stake here . . . concerns the people's right to engage in and to hear vigorous public debate on the broadcast media." Unimpeded public access to the airwaves through editorial advertisements, Brennan said, was essential. "If the public is to be honestly and forthrightly apprised of opposing views on controversial issues, it is imperative that citizens be permitted at least *some* opportunity to speak directly for themselves as genuine advocates on issues that concern them." Freedom of speech, he said, "does not exist in the abstract. On the contrary, the right to speak can flourish only if it is allowed to operate in an effective forum— whether it be a public park, a schoolroom, a town meeting hall, a soapbox, or a radio and television frequency. For in the absence of an effective means of communication, the right to speak would ring hollow indeed." The Court traditionally had recognized this need, Brennan said, by ruling "that the First Amendment embodies, not only the abstract right to be free from censorship, but also the right of an individual to utilize an appropriate and effective medium for the expression of his views." Through the Court's decision, he contended, an important public forum for ideas had been closed to the American people.[64]

The Court's decision was handed down in 1973, three years after the issue was first raised. By that time, the president was bogged down in the growing Watergate scandal, and he was unable to profit from the Court's limiting his political opponents' access to the nation's dominant means of communication. While the case was just beginning to make its way through the system, the Nixon White House already had effectively implemented the desired restrictions. White House staff member Charles Colson, for instance, met with the heads of the networks in early fall to make sure that no more "Loyal Opposition" programming would undermine Republican election plans. He reported to H. R. Haldeman that "there was unanimous agreement that the President's right of access to TV should in no way be restrained. Both CBS and ABC agreed with me that on most occasions the President speaks as President and there is no obligation for presenting a contrasting view under the Fairness Doctrine."[65]

Despite Colson's apparent success with network executives and the expert staging of an election eve appearance in San Jose, California, where radicals picketed him and threw stones, bottles, and eggs in his direction, Nixon failed to increase his hold on Congress. In addition, the Democrats began sending Senator Edmund Muskie of Maine forth as their spokesman against the president. Calm and reserved, Muskie, who was emerging as the leading candidate for the party's 1972 presidential nomination, urged the nation to engage in reasoned debate on various issues. The president began worrying about his own reelection and took steps to further undercut his challengers.

Although opponents to his Vietnam policy already were reeling, the administration wanted to end all protest. A move by the South Vietnamese army, backed by American air power, into Laos in February 1971 seemed to spark little reaction. Or perhaps, little reaction was reported despite concerted efforts by antiwar leaders. The old question of whether a tree falling in the forest made any noise became increasingly pertinent. If a demonstration occurred but no journalists showed up, was it really a demonstration? Ignoring increasing problems in obtaining media attention, plans for protest continued. The incursion into Laos, for instance, led longtime protest groups to arrange a march on Washington for April. A newer organization scheduled a massive exercise in civil disobedience in Washington in May to bring government operations to a grinding halt if the war had not ended by then.

Of more immediate concern was the growing spotlight cast on the behavior of U.S. troops in Vietnam. In late January and early February, members of the fast-growing Vietnam Veterans Against the War (VVAW) highlighted atrocities committed by American troops. More than 100 veterans testified about incidents that they themselves had witnessed. Although a transcript of the hearings was entered into the *Congressional Record,* the nation heard little of the charges due, at least in part, to lack of media coverage. Undiscouraged, the veterans congregated in Washington for a demonstration in April that included returning combat medals awarded for their service in Vietnam. Veterans staged a candlelight march to the Capitol one night and threw their medals over a fence and onto the grounds as a gesture of supreme disgust. The increasing emphasis on war crimes was aggravated in March by the conviction of William Calley for premeditated murder at My Lai. The president played to the nation's unwillingness to believe that American troops could do such things and ordered Calley released from the stockade until he personally reviewed the conviction.

While he was freeing Calley from prison, Nixon was pursuing yet another set of antiwar foes in one of the last major political trials of the era. The primary target once again was Philip Berrigan, now one of the Harrisburg Seven. Six of the seven defendants indicted in January 1971 were Catholic priests or nuns. They were charged with conspiring to raid federal offices, to bomb government property, and to kidnap presidential adviser Henry Kissinger. According to the indictment, the conspirators planned to plant bombs in heating tunnels under the nation's capital with detonation scheduled for Washington's birthday. The kidnapping was set for about the same time; Kissinger was to be released in exchange for an immediate end of the war.[66]

Whether the conspiracy ever really existed is unclear. What is certain is that the government had in its possession copies of letters between Philip Berrigan and Sister Elizabeth McAlister in which the possibility of such actions was mentioned. The murky part of the equation is the role that Boyd F. Douglas, an inmate serving time with Berrigan, played in getting those ideas into the letters. Douglas, who was allowed to leave the prison on study release, served as courier between Berrigan and McAlister and as an informant for the FBI. Copies of the letters that he carried went first to bureau agents and then to the addressees. His testimony was pivotal to the government's case. But by 1972, when the Harrisburg Seven trial was held, jurors were increasingly suspicious of the role of government provocateurs in protesters' activities. With a good deal of the case based on Douglas's involvement, the jury deadlocked after seven days of deliberation on the major charges. Berrigan and McAlister were found guilty only of circumventing the prison's censorship system with their letters.

The indictment of the Harrisburg Seven did little to cool the ardor of individuals still dedicated to stopping the war. On April 24, some 500,000 people showed up in Washington to protest the continuation of the war, one of the largest one-day antiwar demonstrations on record and one of the most poorly reported. Large numbers turned out for similar activities around the country. Participants cut across the American scene, including college students, professionals, members of the clergy, and union members. They met peacefully, cleaned up their garbage, and went home. The next day some 150 Quakers, who had come to Washington on their own to protest the continuation of the war, were arrested when they tried to move their peace vigil from Lafayette Park, across from the White House, to the sidewalk in front of the president's home. The lines were being drawn for one of the last major antiwar demonstrations.

The following week, the People's Coalition showed up in Washington, and the White House was prepared. Some 5,000 city police, 1,500 National Guardsmen, 500 National Park Police, and 10,000 federal troops were ready to keep the city open.[67] A proclamation declaring a state of emergency in the city was ready for the president to sign if necessary. The May Day demonstrators, led by a group of young people known as the May Day Tribe, moved into the city on Monday, May 3, to close down access routes. Law enforcement officials greeted them; tear gas filled some streets of Washington, and a few encounters became violent. To some observers, the scene resembled General Douglas MacArthur's attack on the Bonus Army in 1932. By the end of the third day of demonstrations, some 12,000 people had been arrested for protest-related activities, the largest number ever charged in the history of the movement. As he watched law enforcement authorities at work, Attorney General John Mitchell compared the demonstrators to Hitler's brownshirts. The court system took a somewhat different view of the whole affair. The three judges hearing the cases proceeded slowly and released most detainees or set minimum bail. In the end, the demonstrators were victorious. In 1975, the courts decided that many of the arrests were illegal, and some 1,200 people arrested during the May Day protests were awarded monetary damages.[68]

Immediately after the arrests, many key members of the administration figured that their decisive action had effectively ended antiwar actions. And, indeed, actions after May 1971 became far fewer and less successful. Ironically, the movement was disappearing just as the U.S. Supreme Court became increasingly hospitable to its activities. In a series of cases decided in the late 1960s and early 1970s, the justices regularly protected the activities of antiwar protesters under the relatively new doctrine of symbolic speech. The idea that actions speak louder than words had been presented to the Court before. The flag salute cases before World War II definitely involved the use of speech acts rather than words to communicate their ideas as did many of the cases stemming from civil rights demonstrations. Although the speech acts involved in antiwar protests often were obnoxious and raucous, the justices regularly found them to be protected under the First Amendment.

All segments of American society were touched by the Court's interpretation of symbolic speech. The justices, for example, approved the efforts of schoolchildren to join in antiwar protests by a seven to two vote. John and Mary Beth Tinker and their friend, Christopher Eckhardt had run afoul of school administrators for wanting to wear black armbands to class as a silent protest against the war. The principal thought that the armbands would disrupt the educational process. First sending the young people home, he later suspended them. Justice Abe Fortas, writing for the majority, decided that wearing the armbands "was closely akin to 'pure speech' which, we have repeatedly held, is entitled to comprehensive protection under the First Amendment." Finding no proof that the students wearing the armbands had upset school operations, Fortas said that "the action of the school authorities appears to have been based upon an urgent wish to avoid the controversy which might result from the expression, even by the silent symbol of armbands, of opposition to this Nation's part in the conflagration in Vietnam."[69]

The school, Fortas said, was imposing content-based restrictions on the students because it allowed other political symbols, including the Iron Cross that symbolized the Nazi party, to be worn in school. For years, the Court had held that any restrictions on speech had to be content-neutral in order to pass judicial scrutiny. In other words, the regulations must apply equally to speech on all sides of the political spectrum. In addition, Fortas said, the Court had long held that students do not "shed their constitutional rights to freedom of speech or expression at the schoolhouse gate."[70] Young people must be allowed to have opinions on the Vietnam War and to express those opinions, by wearing a black armband if necessary. The Tinker children were ordered reinstated.

Black armbands proved to be the simplest symbol that the Court dealt with during this period; the most complex and emotionally upsetting symbol was the flag. To the president's men, and indeed, to all good patriots, the flag was honored above all other national symbols, as exemplified by the flag lapel pins they wore. The question was whether their ostentatious patriotism would affect the Supreme Court or whether the justices would look at the possibility that flag abuse conveyed a message. The Court ducked the issue of symbolic speech in the first flag case to come before it. A New York black man, Sidney Street, was charged with burning his forty-eight-star flag to protest the shooting of civil rights leader James Meredith in Mississippi in 1966. As he set fire to the flag, Street purportedly said, "If they let that happen to Meredith, we don't need an American flag." Later he reportedly told a gathering crowd, "We don't need no damn flag." He was convicted for violating a state law protecting the flag; a five-man majority reversed the conviction. Street, said Justice John Marshall Harlan II for the majority, may have been convicted for the language that he uttered about the flag rather than for burning it. If that was the case, the First Amendment barred punishment.[71]

The dissenters, who included Chief Justice Earl Warren and Justice Hugo Black, argued that the majority was reaching for a reason to overturn the conviction. Protecting the flag was well within the powers of state and federal government, they contended. "I believe that the States and the Federal Government do have the power to protect the flag from acts of desecration and disgrace," the chief justice maintained. Justice Black agreed, noting, "It passes my belief that anything in the Federal Constitution bars a State from making the deliberate burning of the American flag an offense. It is immaterial to me that words are spoken in connection with the burning. It is the *burning* of the flag that the State has set its face against."[72]

But the Court could not long avoid cases in which use of the flag was considered inappropriate. In 1974, as Richard Nixon's presidency was entering its final days, the justices ruled on two such cases. In both instances, a majority found fault with the statutes under which the convictions were obtained. A Massachusetts law, for instance, forbade treating the flag contemptuously, and Valarie Goguen was arrested for wearing a small cloth version of the flag on the seat of his trousers. Justice Lewis Powell, speaking for five members of the Court, found the state law too vague. Its provisions did not adequately warn Goguen that wearing a flag would be considered a crime. "Flag wearing in a day of relaxed clothing styles may be simply for adornment or a ploy to attract attention. It and many other current, careless uses of the flag nevertheless constitute unceremonial treatment that many people may view as contemptuous," Powell said. But, "in a time of widely varying attitudes and tastes for displaying something as ubiquitous as the United States flag or representations of it, it could hardly be the purpose of the Massachusetts Legislature to make criminal every informal use of the flag."[73]

To the three dissenters—Chief Justice Warren Burger and Justices Harry Blackmun and William Rehnquist—Massachusetts meant precisely what the law said—that it was illegal to treat the flag contemptuously. Goguen had done so and should be punished. The Goguen dissent began Rehnquist's career as a leading defender of the flag on the Court. Unable to find that Goguen was communicating any ideas by placing the flag on his trousers, Rehnquist refused to find the First Amendment relevant to his case. Goguen had not sewn just any piece of red, white, and blue cloth to the seat of his pants, Rehnquist said; what he had used was "the one visible manifestation of two hundred years of nationhood." The state had not "prohibited Goguen from wearing a sign sewn to the seat of his pants expressing in words his low opinion of the flag, of the country, or anything else. It has prohibited him from wearing there a particular symbol of extraordinary significance and content, for which significance and content

Goguen is in no wise responsible."[74] Because of its uniqueness as a representation of American values, Rehnquist would have allowed the state to protect the flag.

Rehnquist, however, was destined to remain in the minority on flag issues. Another five-member majority, this time through a per curiam decision, overturned the conviction of Harold Spence for attaching a peace symbol to his flag with removable tape in violation of a Washington State law. He then flew the flag upside down from his apartment window, which stood on private property, on May 10, 1970. He did so, he testified, to protest the Nixon administration's invasion of Cambodia and the killings at Kent State University just a few days before: "I felt there had been so much killing and that this was not what America stood for. I felt that the flag stood for America and I wanted people to know that I thought America stood for peace." This time, an anonymous opinion writer squarely addressed the communicative elements involved in the case. "To be sure, appellant [Spence] did not choose to articulate his views through printed or spoken words," the Court said. "But the nature of appellant's activity, combined with the factual context and environment in which it was undertaken, lead to the conclusion that he was engaged in a form of protected expression." Given when the event occurred, "it would have been difficult for the great majority of citizens to miss the drift of appellant's. . . . pointed expression of anguish . . . about the then-current domestic and foreign affairs of his government. An intent to convey a particularized message was present, and in the surrounding circumstances the likelihood was great that the message would be understood by those who viewed it." This clearly was "a case of prosecution for the expression of an idea through activity," and the conviction could not stand.[75]

Once again Rehnquist led the dissenters, arguing that protection of the flag was a sufficiently important governmental interest to outweigh any incidental burdens on free-speech rights. A state "could not require all citizens to own the flag or compel citizens to salute one," he said. Nor could it "punish criticism of the flag, or the principles for which it stands, any more than it could punish criticism of this country's policies or ideas." But Rehnquist found that this particular statute made no such demands. "Its operation does not depend upon whether the flag is used for communicative or noncommunicative purposes; upon whether a particular message is deemed commercial or political; upon whether the use of the flag is respectful or contemptuous; or upon whether any particular segment of the State's citizenry might applaud or oppose the intended message." Indeed, he said, "it simply withdraws a unique national symbol from the roster of materials that may be used as a background for communications." And, said Rehnquist, the state's decision was perfectly acceptable.[76]

Treatment of the flag was not the only cause of controversy during these years. The Court, for example, squarely faced at least two cases in which the language of the counterculture raised significant First Amendment issues. The first case involved Paul Robert Cohen and his black leather jacket on which he had emblazoned the words "Fuck the Draft." After wearing his jacket in the Los Angeles County Courthouse, Cohen was convicted of disturbing the peace through offensive behavior. Five members of the Court joined the opinion of Justice Harlan that declined to find the language obscene. "It cannot plausibly be maintained that this vulgar allusion to the Selective Service System would conjure up such psychic stimulation in anyone likely to be confronted with Cohen's crudely defaced jacket," he said. Nor could it be argued that an "individual actually or likely to be present could reasonably have regarded the words on appellant's jacket as a direct personal insult." The state also argued that the situation presented a captive audience scenario, in which the Court had allowed some infringement on free-speech activities because of the inability of the audience to escape a particular message. Harlan disagreed: "Those in the Los Angeles courthouse could effectively avoid further bombardment of their sensitivities simply by averting their eyes." The bottom line in the case, Harlan said, was that "the State has no right to cleanse public debate to the point where it is grammatically palatable to the most squeamish among us." Indeed, he said, "while the particular four-letter word being litigated here is perhaps more distasteful than most others of its genre, it is nevertheless often true that one man's vulgarity is another's lyric."[77]

Similar thinking led to the overturning of the conviction of Gregory Hess for disorderly conduct in Bloomington, Indiana. Hess had said, "We'll take the fucking street later" during an antiwar demonstration.[78] Although the justices disliked the language of the younger generation, they were unwilling to send an individual to jail simply for uttering foul language. Nor was the Court willing to allow an individual to be sent to prison for criticizing the president. Robert Watts, an 18-year-old attending a rally on the grounds of the Washington Monument in 1966, was arrested for saying, "They always holler at us to get an education. And now I have already received my draft classification as 1-A and I have got to report for my physical this Monday coming. I am not going. If they ever make me carry a rifle the first man I want to get in my sights is L.B.J." Members of the Army Counter Intelligence Corps reported the statement, and Watts was arrested under the 1917 Threats Against the President Act, which was designed to protect the chief executive from persons who would harm him. Five members of the Court in a per curiam decision found the language crude and offensive but not punishable under the law: "We do not believe that the kind of political hyperbole indulged in by petitioner fits within the statutory term."[79]

Justices also refused to condone an attack on a local unit of the Students for a Democratic Society. Writing for eight members of the Court, Lewis F. Powell found that Central Connecticut State College could not bar an SDS chapter from campus. Students forming the chapter pledged that they would follow college rules and that the chapter would be independent of the national organization. The college president rejected a campus committee's recommendation that official recognition be granted. With its application denied, the SDS chapter could not use campus facilities for meetings or communication, a problem that the Court found to greatly impinge upon the students' associational rights under the First Amendment. Without proof of disruption by the students seeking recognition on the Connecticut campus, the administrator had no right to ban the group from campus.[80]

The Supreme Court's refusal to support Richard Nixon's goal of suppressing dissent may well have been an indication that the president's campaign to create a placid, agreeable society was doomed. As if to confirm that possibility, the press, which many in the administration thought to be sufficiently cowed through past intimidation, suddenly posed new problems for the White House. Difficulties arose from both the print and the broadcast media, although most attention seemed to focus on the confrontation between the administration and the *New York Times* and the *Washington Post* over the publication of the Pentagon Papers. The broadcast assault on government occurred earlier in the year—February 23 to be precise—and involved the CBS documentary "The Selling of the Pentagon."[81]

Plans for the hour-long documentary grew out of a desire to show how government information programs manipulated national opinion. As correspondent Roger Mudd told his audience, "Nothing is more essential to a democracy than the free flow of information. Misinformation, distortion, propaganda all interrupt that flow. They make it impossible for people to know what their government is doing, which, in a democracy, is crucial." At the end of the documentary, Mudd said, "On this broadcast we have seen violence made glamorous, expensive weapons advertised as if they were automobiles, biased opinions presented as straight facts. Defending the country not just with arms but also with ideology, Pentagon propaganda insists on America's role as the cop on every beat in the world." The problems that such an operation caused were great, he said. "Not only the public but the press as well has been beguiled, including at times ourselves at CBS News. This propaganda barrage is the creation of a runaway bureaucracy that frustrates attempts to control it."[82]

In all, the presentation was a devastating portrayal of government control of the sources of information. The documentary was in the tradition of hard-hitting CBS programming on difficult problems, and it immediately attracted criticism. Obviously the program had touched a governmental nerve. The day after the broadcast, the primary challenge was launched by F. Edward Hébert, chairman of the House Armed Services Committee, who, although he had not seen the show, called it one of "the most misleading, damaging attacks on our people over there that I have ever heard of." After seeing a tape of the program, he termed it "the most horrible thing I've seen in years. The most—the greatest disservice to the military I've seen on television. . . . [A] splendid professional hatchet job."[83]

In response to the growing chorus of criticism, CBS announced a rebroadcast of the program—with a fifteen-minute segment added to give critics a chance to be heard. By this time, Vice President Agnew had jumped on the anti-CBS bandwagon, terming the documentary "a disreputable program" and noting "thank heaven we had the Pentagon during a couple of crucial times in our history. I think they defended the country a lot better than CBS is doing at the present time." Richard Salant, president of CBS News, appeared on the added segment to defend the program: "We are proud of 'The Selling of the Pentagon' and CBS News stands behind it. We are confident that when the passions die down, it will be recognized as a vital contribution to the people's right to know." The program's critics were not too happy with the rebroadcast and particularly thought it unfair when CBS used their hostile comments on tape rather than allowing them to make the statements live. From the network's perspective, the rebroadcast was quite successful because it won an audience of more than 14 million people, up from the 9.5 million viewers who had watched the original show a month earlier. Calls after the rebroadcast revealed a substantially favorable public reaction.[84]

CBS picked up a Peabody Award and an Emmy for the documentary, and the Pentagon announced changes in some of its public relations activities as a result of the broadcast. But beginning in April, the network had to face the realities unleashed by the broadcast. At that point, Representative Harley O. Staggers, Democrat of West Virginia and chairman of the House Interstate Commerce Committee, which had jurisdiction over broadcasting, had a subpoena issued by the committee's Special Subcommittee on Investigations, which he also chaired, asking CBS to turn over "outtakes"—or film not used in the broadcast—to committee investigators. CBS President Frank Stanton responded to the subcommittee subpoena that asked for "all film, workprints, outtakes, sound tape recordings, written scripts and/or transcripts" related to the documentary by saying, "We will comply with that part of the subpoena which calls for a film copy and written transcript of the material actually broadcast."[85] Print journalists would not turn their unpublished materials over to investigators, he said; broadcast journalists would behave no differently.

The committee refined its subpoena, but Stanton still refused. Staggers, in commenting on the request, stressed that as far as he was concerned the subpoena carried no First Amendment implications. He also carefully differentiated between newspaper journalists, who he believed would have the right to refuse the request, and broadcast journalists, who had fewer protections due in large part to the fact that the federal government regulated broadcasting. As the feud developed, the print media came out almost unanimously behind CBS, and much of the blame for the congressional attack was laid wrongly at the feet of the Nixon administration, which had steered clear of the controversy except for encouraging the condemnation of CBS by the vice president.

While the Nixon administration sought to extricate itself from this controversy, Representative Staggers continued his campaign against the network. Tempers frayed as CBS continued to defy the House subpoena by arguing that freedom of the press would be jeopardized if the House obtained the unused materials. One confrontation between Staggers and CBS President Stanton ended with the congressman telling the broadcaster: "This is the most powerful media we have in America today, and you talk about chilling effects. This runs chills up and down the spine of every person in America." Freedom of the press was one thing to Representative Staggers, but abuse of that freedom was another. "When there is untruth put over these networks they can control the land, and you know they can if we allow this to go on," he said. "Anything I say or you say can be distorted and made to be a fact and they can ruin every president, every member of this Congress, or anybody else if we allow this to go on. WE MUST HAVE THOSE OUTTAKES."[86]

Network officials continued to refuse to comply with the subpoena, and the subcommittee voted to ask that Stanton be held in contempt of Congress. The full committee followed suit. The issue then went before the House, where CBS faced an uphill battle because the full House rarely refused to cite an individual for contempt if the citation had been approved by one of its committees. CBS believed that Stanton would be found in contempt of Congress, and the network made plans to appeal to the courts. Members of the House, however, began to voice disapproval of Staggers's efforts; the Democratic leadership wanted to recommit the citation to committee, which would effectively kill it, rather than have it come to a vote. But Staggers would not be denied his vote. Personal honor was at stake for him and for his friend and colleague F. Edward Hébert. The chairman of the House Armed Services Committee defended his and Staggers's efforts against CBS. "They cry—'First Amendment.' I believe in the First Amendment and there is nobody in this room who can challenge my standing on that. They have had their First Amendment. They have had their chance to lie under the First Amendment. If it were not for the First Amendment, they could not have practiced the deceit that they have practiced. I am one of the victims of that deceit," Hébert told his colleagues. "I agree that the public has a right to know. How is the public going to know if we do not make them show what they have under the table and up their sleeves?" Despite the arguments of Staggers and Hébert, the sentiment of the House more accurately was reflected by a statement made by Emanuel Celler, the New York Democrat who headed the Judiciary Committee. "The First Amendment," Celler said, "towers over these proceedings like a colossus." Eventually, the House voted 226 to 181 to recommit the request for a contempt citation to committee, thus killing it.[87]

The decision to let CBS News off the hook came in the summer of 1971, just weeks after the Nixon administration had been dealt a defeat in its campaign against the press. The specter of the Supreme Court's decision in the Pentagon Papers case hung heavily over the House of Representatives as it debated the CBS subpoena. Many congressmen saw the attempt to review the editorial judgments of CBS journalists as something that would definitely fall before a Supreme Court determined to protect First Amendment privileges of the press. Just how resolved the Court was to protect the press, however, could well be disputed given the Pentagon Papers decision.

Publication of the Pentagon Papers, a history of American involvement in the Southeast Asian conflict through the Johnson administration in June 1971 triggered an important confrontation between the Nixon administration and the press. The encounter began with a decision by Secretary of Defense Robert McNamara in the waning days of his term to authorize a history of the nation's involvement in the war. Some thirty-five scholars worked on the study, all forty-seven volumes of which were immediately classified upon completion, even though much of the material included came from the public domain, including many newspaper articles. Several copies of the study wound up at the Rand Corporation, a think tank often used by the Defense Department, where Daniel Ellsberg was employed. One of the few people at Rand to read the entire forty-seven volume study, Ellsberg had had field experience in Vietnam and had started to work against the war in 1967. After having protested rather passively by signing antiwar letters, he now was ready to seek an end to the war himself. "Only Congress and the public, informed in time and organized in protest," he said, "could now dissuade the President from prolonging the American war in Vietnam."[88]

Ellsberg believed that the study stored at the Rand Corporation provided the perfect vehicle for informing the public. He and his colleague in disclosure, Anthony J. Russo, began photocopying the Pentagon Papers in the fall of 1969. They carefully cut off or concealed markings that would have revealed that the documents had been classified. The first set of the papers went to J. William Fulbright, the Arkansas Democrat who headed the Senate Foreign Relations Committee. An increasingly ardent foe of the war in Vietnam, Fulbright put the Ellsberg documents in a safe while he tried to obtain a copy of the study from the Pentagon. Secretary of Defense Melvin Laird refused the senator's request, citing the extreme sensitivity of the documents. Not wanting to get Ellsberg in trouble for providing the copies, Fulbright then kept the study locked up for months.

After several unsuccessful attempts to find someone who would publicize the study, Ellsberg finally gave the papers to Neal Sheehan, a reporter for the *New York Times* who had spent some time in Vietnam, in March 1971. Although Ellsberg gave Sheehan thousands of pages of documents, he withheld four volumes that pertained to diplomatic efforts to end the war and to obtain the release of prisoners of war. But the documents Sheehan received opened the door to a substantial and controversial story.

Mixed responses greeted Sheehan on his arrival at the *New York Times*'s Washington bureau with Ellsberg's papers. Key *Times* personnel wondered about the potential audience for the material. By spring 1971, the war was winding down, and few people were interested in reviving such a divisive issue. After reviewing some of the material, however, *Times* leadership decided to proceed with the story. Extra personnel were assigned to help process the documents, and the project was cloaked in secrecy. They spent weeks organizing the data and carefully screening the documents to delete those papers that might endanger national security. Constantly hanging over their heads was the fear that Ellsberg would take the documents to someone else if the *Times* waited too long to publish and the very real possibility that the federal government would act against the newspaper when it did publish. The *New York Times* was already involved in one major court encounter with the Department of Justice: reporter Earl Caldwell was fighting, with *Times* support, efforts to force him to testify before a grand jury about his contacts with the Black Panther party. Now, another confrontation loomed.

The series was ready for publication in mid-June 1971, almost three months after Sheehan had obtained the documents. The June 13 edition headlined the first installment of the story: "Vietnam Archive: Pentagon Study Traces 3 Decades of Growing U.S. Involvement." The page was dominated by a picture of the president's daughter, Tricia, who had gotten married the previous afternoon. One of the few administration leaders to move beyond the wedding story to the Pentagon Papers was Defense Secretary Laird, who was scheduled to appear on a Sunday talk show. He hurriedly called Attorney General John Mitchell to find out what he should say if the subject came up, which it did not. Mitchell had responded that Laird should reply that the government was looking into the matter, but the attorney general was not willing to disturb his weekend to begin the investigation.

As the second installment appeared on Monday, June 14, the government began its discussions on what to do. One problem facing the administration was that no one really knew what the papers contained. Although the study was historical and did not include material on the Nixon administration, the government was unwilling to stand by while so much classified information was being revealed. In addition, Henry Kissinger argued strongly that the publication could hurt secret negotiations with the North Vietnamese and could damage talks that were going on at that time to normalize relations with the People's Republic of China.

Administration personnel were not ready to act against the *Times* until Monday evening. At 7:30 p.m., Assistant Attorney General Robert Mardian called the *Times* to read a copy of a telegram that was en route from the attorney general. The information being published, the telegram said, "contains information relating to the national defense of the United States and bears a top-secret classification." Thus, publication was forbidden under the Espionage Act. "Moreover," Mitchell's telegram said, "further publication of information of this character will cause irreparable injury to the defense interests of the United States. Accordingly, I respectfully request that you publish no further information of this character and advise me that you have made arrangements for the return of these documents to the Department of Defense."[89]

After a heated discussion at the newspaper's headquarters and a call to publisher Arthur Ochs Sulzberger, who was in Europe at the time, the *Times* proceeded with publication on Tuesday. Its official response said, in part, "The *Times* must respectfully decline the request of the Attorney General, believing that it is in the interest of the people of this country to be informed of the material contained in this series of articles." The attorney general, said the *Times,* had made it clear that he intended to take the matter to court should the *Times* refuse to cease publication voluntarily. The newspaper did not fear such a recourse: "The *Times* will oppose any request for an injunction for the same reason that led us to publish the articles in the first place. We will of course abide by the final decision of the court." A third installment of the Pentagon Papers appeared on Tuesday, June 15. That same day, the government sought an injunction to stop the *Times* from further publication. The information already published, the petition said, had "prejudiced the defense interests of the United States." Continued publication would cause additional harm and "result in irreparable injury to the United States."[90] U.S. District Judge Murray I. Gurfein, who had been on the bench only a few days, issued the restraining order.[91].

For the first time in the nation's history, a newspaper had been prevented from publishing material. The national abhorrence for prior restraint had existed as long as the nation itself. Even though the writers of the Constitution and the Bill of Rights could not agree on just how much was included in the concept "freedom of the press," they generally accepted Sir William Blackstone's definition that, at the least, freedom of the press meant the absence of prior restraint. The Supreme Court had finally read that concept into constitutional law in 1931, when it outlawed prior restraint in *Near v. Minnesota.*[92] The Court in 1963 had reaffirmed its belief that "any system of prior restraints of expression comes to this Court bearing a heavy presumption against its constitutional validity."[93] And in May 1971, the Court again said that any governmental attempt to impose a prior restraint "carries a heavy burden of showing justification for the imposition of such a restraint."[94] Still, the administration hoped that the legal system would find that publication of the Pentagon Papers fell within one of the exceptions to the general prohibition against prior restraint allowed by Chief Justice Charles Evans Hughes in 1931. "No one," he wrote, "would question but that a government might prevent actual obstruction to its recruiting service or the publication of the sailing dates of transports or the number and location of troops."[95] Convincing a court that a historical document whose latest data was at least three years old would endanger current military operations offered a daunting challenge.

While the two parties were gearing up for a court contest in New York City, Daniel Ellsberg grew worried. He feared that a prolonged court contest would dissipate any antiwar momentum that the three days of publication might have engendered. After the television networks, who were watching "The Selling of the Pentagon" controversy run its course, refused to carry the story, Ellsberg made contact with the *Washington Post,* which had been scrambling to catch up with a leading competitor. The *Post* made plans to carry segments of the Papers beginning on the Friday after the injunction had stopped the *Times* from further publication. While the *Post* was at work, a former *New York Times* reporter revealed that Daniel Ellsberg had been the source of the documents. Now the antiwar scholar was being sought by both journalists, who wanted a piece of the action, and the FBI, which sought to stop his dissemination of classified documents. Ellsberg successfully evaded the authorities for two weeks—just enough time to continue distributing bits and pieces of the historical study to journalists around the country.

Actual *Post* publication came only after a heated protest from the newspaper's attorneys, who felt that the *Post* should wait until the restraining order against the *Times* had been lifted. As with the *New York Times,* the final decision was made by the publisher. Katharine Graham, knowing how the Nixon administration had attempted to intimidate the *Post* and its far-flung holdings in the past, gave her approval. The first edition of the *Post* containing the Pentagon Papers appeared on Friday, June 18. Late that afternoon, the *Post* received a telegram from the attorney general that was identical to the one sent to the *Times.* The *Post,* of course, refused to comply. About 5:15 that afternoon, government lawyers asked Judge Gerhard A. Gesell for a restraining order against the *Post* similar to that issued against the *Times.* Here, however, the judge affirmed the right of the *Post* to publish the materials.

Government attorneys hurried over to the appeals court, where a panel of judges was rounded up. The judges deliberated, and the *Post*'s Saturday edition went to press containing another installment of the Pentagon Papers. At 1:20 a.m., two of the three judges who had heard the appeal from Gesell's ruling voted to bar the *Post* from further publication—at least until the government had a chance to argue its case more fully. The matter was sent back to Gesell for further hearings. Strangely, the late editions of the Saturday *Washington Post* carried a story next to that day's installment of the Pentagon Papers saying that the newspaper had been restrained from further publication pending a full hearing. The order, the appeals judges decided, had come too late to stop a press run already well along. The Saturday story could appear; all others would be halted pending further hearings.

A week had passed. The *Times* had published information on events occurring in the Johnson administration. After three days of publishing, it had been restrained by the government. The nation's press had been without segments of the papers for two days, and then the *Post* began to present segments from its 4,000-plus pages of the study, which focused on the Eisenhower administration. After two days, it too was quieted. The matter was now in the courts; the administration could relax. Or could it? That proverbial loose cannon, Daniel Ellsberg, was still free with his copies of the study and with easy access to photocopying machines. Within days, more documents appeared in the *Boston Globe,* the Chicago *Sun-Times,* the *Los Angeles Times,* eleven newspapers within the Knight chain, the St. Louis *Post-Dispatch,* the *Christian Science Monitor,* and *Newsday.* Each newspaper dealt with a different aspect of the study. Government action against the offending newspapers was uneven at best. Some newspapers escaped even a threatening telephone call, while others were enjoined from further publication. This inconsistent action gave rise to the notion that the newspapers that were taken to court had been longtime opponents of the Nixon administration, while those newspapers that escaped federal injunctions basically were supporters who had strayed on this one particular issue.[96] As more newspapers published material from the study and were enjoined from further release of the data, the rush to overturn restraining orders ceased. Now, publications that were enjoined looked to the cases involving the *Times* and the *Post* to settle whether the government could indeed place a prior restraint on the nation's press.

While the case was moving through the court system, the Nixon White House dealt with another aspect of the problem. Almost immediately the president sent a memorandum to his top aide, H. R. Haldeman, saying, "We must take action within the White House to deal with the problem," which he defined as the *New York Times*'s "irresponsibility and recklessness in deliberately printing classified documents without regard to the national interest." His orders were simple: "Until further notice under *no circumstances* is anyone connected with the White House to give any interview to a member of the staff of the *New York Times* without my express permission." In addition, "under absolutely no circumstances is anyone on the White House staff on *any subject* to respond to an inquiry from the *New York Times* unless and until I give express permission (and I do not expect to give such permission in the foreseeable future)."[97] In addition, White House staff members argued that the administration needed "to explain why this [publication] injures national security and why secret documents must be secure. . . . We need to get across the feeling of disloyalty on the part of those who publish these papers."[98] Although the administration took great delight in liberal publications like the *Times* and the *Post* airing the mistakes of previous

Democratic administrations, officials still felt it important to protect the integrity of the classification system—and they also planned to make an example of Daniel Ellsberg.

Prosecuting Ellsberg took a back seat to hearings in federal district courtrooms in both Washington and New York on whether the newspapers could be permanently restrained from publishing the documents. Judge Murray Gurfein presided over a secret hearing into the government's request for a permanent injunction against the *New York Times*. At its conclusion, he ruled in favor of the *Times*. "The security of the Nation is not at the ramparts alone," he said. "Security also lies in the value of our free institutions. A cantankerous press, an obstinate press, an ubiquitous press must be suffered by those in authority in order to preserve the even greater values of freedom of expression and the right of the people to know," he said. "It is not merely the opinion of the editorial writer or of the columnist which is protected by the First Amendment. It is the free flow of information so that the public will be informed about the Government and its actions."[99]

Indeed, he said, "these are troubled times. There is no greater safety valve for discontent and cynicism about the affairs of Government than freedom of expression in any form. This has been the genius of our institutions throughout our history. It is one of the marked traits of our national life that distinguish us from other nations under different forms of government." The judge was unpersuaded by the government's arguments of irreparable damage to the nation's security. "No cogent reasons were advanced as to why these documents except in the general framework of embarrassment . . . would vitally affect the security of the Nation."[100] Although he had decided the case in the favor of the *Times*, he extended his temporary restraining order to allow the government an opportunity to appeal his ruling. The court of appeals in New York City extended the order.

While the *Times* was awaiting the next step in its case, the *Post* was back before Judge Gesell for a full-blown hearing, part of which, at the government's request, was held in secret. At the end of the day-long session, Gesell reaffirmed his original decision in favor of the *Post*. The government had not presented any "proof that there will be a definite break in diplomatic relations, that there will be an armed attack on the United States, that there will be an armed attack on an ally, that there will be a war, that there will be a compromise of military or defense plans, a compromise of intelligence operations, or a compromise of scientific and technological materials." Because of the failure of the government to make its case, publication must proceed. The First Amendment, he said, provides "no basis upon which the court may adjust it to accommodate the desires of foreign governments dealing with our diplomats, nor does the First Amendment guarantee our diplomats that they can be protected against either responsible or irresponsible reporting. . . . The First Amendment remains supreme."[101] Gesell stayed the order long enough for government attorneys to have the court of appeals extend the injunction.

Both newspapers faced the full benches of their respective courts of appeal on Tuesday, June 22, 1971. By that time, the *Times* had been restrained from further publication of the Pentagon Papers for a week. The court cases that ensued, like those hearings that had already passed, were strange events. Lawyers for neither the government nor the newspapers had read the study that they were arguing about; public and secret briefs were filed, with some of the newspapers' attorneys being denied access to the secret briefs because they had no security clearance; and parts of the hearings were held in secret to allow the government to make what it considered its most sensitive arguments. The two courts reached conflicting opinions. The appeals court in New York City maintained the restraining order against the *Times* and told Judge Gurfein to hold additional hearings on points raised by the government during the appellate argument.[102] The judges in Washington, D.C., however, found in favor of the *Post,* but they did extend the restraining order to allow for appeal to the Supreme Court.[103]

The *New York Times* entered its appeal to the U.S. Supreme Court on Thursday, June 24. That same day, the government appealed the decision of the District of Columbia appeals court. Friday, June 25, was to have been the final conference day of the year for the Court, and the justices were anxious to leave town for their summer recess, but the Court agreed to hold an extraordinary session on Saturday morning, June 26, to hear oral arguments in the first instance of government-imposed prior restraint in the nation's history. Justices Hugo Black, William O. Douglas, William J. Brennan, Jr., and Thurgood Marshall voted against reviewing the cases at all. They preferred simply allowing further publication. Two Nixon appointees—Chief Justice Warren Burger and Harry A. Blackmun—were joined by John Marshall Harlan II, Potter Stewart, and Byron R. White in voting to hear the case.

On June 30, 1971, five days after the case was presented, and a little more than two weeks after the *New York Times* had been enjoined from further publication, the Supreme Court ruled. Six justices joined in a per curiam decision that lifted the restraining orders against both newspapers and allowed them to resume publication. The three-paragraph order essentially said that the government had not met its substantial burden of proving that printing the materials would harm national security. Consequently, the prior restraint could not be sustained. All nine justices wrote individually to explain their views. The six-member majority was comprised of Black, Douglas, Brennan, Stewart, White, and Marshall. Dissenting were Chief Justice Burger and Justices Harlan and Blackmun.

Justices Black and Douglas joined in one another's opinions, stressing, as Black said, "every moment's continuance of the injunctions against these newspapers amounts to a flagrant, indefensible, and continuing violation of the First Amendment." Justice Douglas, after examining the Espionage Act and finding nothing within its provisions that would allow the prosecution of the newspapers for publishing the material in question, noted that "secrecy in government is fundamentally anti-democratic, perpetuating bureaucratic errors. Open debate and discussion of public issues are vital to our national health. On public questions," he said, "there should be 'uninhibited, robust, and wide-open' debate."[104]

These two members of the Court, however, were the only ones who broadly supported press freedom. Justice Brennan, for instance, a strong supporter of

First Amendment rights, began his concurrence by noting that "our judgments in the present cases may not be taken to indicate the propriety, in the future, of issuing temporary stays and restraining orders to block the publication of material sought to be suppressed by the Government." Although he was appalled at this first attempt at prior restraint in the history of the nation and although he stressed that the First Amendment "stands as an absolute bar to the imposition of judicial restraints in circumstances of the kind presented by these cases," he noted that the case turned on the inadequacy of the government's case. "The First Amendment," he said, "tolerates absolutely no prior judicial restraints of the press predicated upon surmise or conjecture that untoward consequences may result. . . . Unless and until the Government has clearly made out its case, the First Amendment commands that no injunction may issue."[105]

Support for the press's position became even less enthusiastic in Justice Stewart's concurrence. The executive branch of government, he said, had great constitutional powers to conduct national defense and international affairs without interference from either the congressional or judicial branches of government. The only real check on those powers, he said, "may lie in an enlightened citizenry—in an informed and critical public opinion which alone can here protect the values of democratic government." Even so, the presidential power in international affairs "require[s] both confidentiality and secrecy." The balancing of these two conflicting needs concerned Stewart, who criticized the tendency of government to make far too much information secret. "For when everything is classified, then nothing is classified, and the system becomes one to be disregarded by the cynical or the careless, and to be manipulated by those intent on self-protection or self-promotion. . . . The hallmark of a truly effective internal security system would be the maximum possible disclosure, recognizing that secrecy can best be preserved only when credibility is truly maintained." Since the executive had not chosen this approach, now the Court was being asked to perform a function that Stewart felt was not proper for the judiciary. Because he had to reach a decision, he concluded, "I am convinced that the Executive is correct with respect to some of the documents involved. But I cannot say that disclosure of any of them will surely result in direct, immediate, and irreparable damage to our Nation or its people." Stewart joined in the judgment of the Court to allow publication.[106]

Justice White reached a similar decision for much the same reasons. "I do not say that in no circumstances would the First Amendment permit an injunction against publishing information about government plans or operations," he said. "Nor, after examining the materials the Government characterizes as the most sensitive and destructive, can I deny that revelation of these documents will do substantial damage to public interests." Despite those beliefs, he added, "I nevertheless agree that the United States has not satisfied the very heavy burden that it must meet to warrant an injunction against publication in these cases." Just because he could not justify prior restraint, however, did not mean that Justice White was ready to let the press escape punishment. He advised the government that "failure by the Government to justify prior restraints does not measure its constitutional entitlement to a conviction for criminal publication. That the

Government mistakenly chose to proceed by injunction does not mean that it could not successfully proceed in another way." To White, prosecution under the Espionage Act for illegally publishing material harmful to the national defense was an excellent idea.[107]

The three dissenters made clear their disdain for the entire case. Each talked about the haste with which the cases were brought. The fact that the *New York Times* argued that the public's right to know was being sorely abridged by any continuation of the restraining order irritated the chief justice. *Times* journalists, Chief Justice Burger said, had taken months to sort through the papers involved in the study; now, they demanded that the court system decide complicated and important issues in days. He wanted the government to review the documents and to advise publishers on what material should or should not be revealed in the national interest. In addition, he noted that the newspapers had the responsibility, incumbent on all citizens, to report the receipt of stolen property to the appropriate authorities. And the Pentagon Papers, he stressed, certainly fell into the category of stolen property.

Even greater bluntness about the behavior of the press came from Justice Blackmun, who noted, "The First Amendment, after all, is only one part of an entire Constitution." In his view, "Each provision of the Constitution is important, and I cannot subscribe to a doctrine of unlimited absolutism for the First Amendment at the cost of downgrading other provisions." He predicted dire consequences as a result of publication—" 'the death of soldiers, the destruction of alliances, the greatly increased difficulty of negotiation with our enemies, the inability of our diplomats to negotiate,' . . . [the] prolongation of the war and . . . further delay in the freeing of United States prisoners"—all of which would be the press's responsibility. "I hope that damage has not already been done," he said. "If, however, damage has been done . . . then the Nation's people will know where the responsibility for these sad consequences rests."[108]

The Supreme Court's decision in favor of publication was six to three, but few of the justices in the majority favored anything close to an absolute bar to government-imposed prior restraint. Regardless of the realities here, the press generally was jubilant. The *New York Times* and *Washington Post* immediately began carrying additional material taken from the study. At the White House, press secretary Ronald Ziegler responded to questions about the president's reaction to the decision by saying, "There is really no need for him to issue a statement on this. The President's view on the First Amendment is well known."[109] The Pentagon told Congress that as soon as its officials had completed an official review of the papers, each member would be sent a complete set of the study.

Some journalists were less than ecstatic about the decision, feeling that two weeks of prior restraint and the Court's split decision could mean later problems. John S. Knight, head of the newspaper chain that had printed some of the papers, noted in the Detroit *Free Press* that jubilation should be restrained. "For the first time in our history except for wartime censorship," he said, "the Government prevented for 15 days publications of articles under the plea of national security. Therefore, the press in its euphoria may not be giving sufficient thought to the possibility that actually a precedent has been set for further restraints upon the right to publish."[110]

In the wake of victory the press did not think about how the president of the United States might respond to this rebuff delivered by the Supreme Court. For the first three years of his administration, Richard Nixon had worked assiduously to intimidate media representatives. In many ways, the Pentagon Papers case, although unplanned by his administration, could have been the crowning achievement of that campaign. Had the Supreme Court approved prior restraint in cases of national security, a White House capable of seeing the simplest activity in those terms would have been unrestrained in its censorship operations. But the Court rejected governmental suppression of the press, and Richard Nixon reacted. In fact, he reacted slightly in advance of the Court decision, almost as if he had known it was coming. When the White House finally found out that Daniel Ellsberg was the source of all those documents, the order went out to make him pay for his behavior. To accomplish this end, the administration unleashed its own enforcement agents, the Plumbers, upon him. With the Plumbers' break-in of the office of Ellsberg's psychiatrist, Richard Nixon stepped over the line from intimidation into illegal conduct. With that burglary, he set in motion the events that would lead to his resignation.

CHAPTER 10

Toppling a President:
Freedom of Expression
in the Age of Watergate

After the Pentagon Papers decision the White House may well have been likened to a medieval castle preparing for siege. Although the country was far quieter in 1971 than it had been for years, pockets of dissent still annoyed Richard Nixon, and the press, which had been faltering under his consistent barrage, had gotten its second wind thanks to the Supreme Court. No one could be trusted, and enemies were all around. Henry VIII's ability to have opponents of his current policies—political, religious, or matrimonial—beheaded must have seemed appealing. Equally attractive might have been the Stuart kings' Court of the Star Chamber that sentenced dissidents to long prison terms. Regardless of whether the president and his assistants consciously patterned their behavior after such past geniuses of repression, the White House began a campaign of intimidation and suppression that would have made earlier absolute monarchs proud. In doing so, however, the White House apparently forgot that the behavior of the Stuart kings led to the beheading of Charles I and a civil war that drove the royalists from power.

Two days before the Supreme Court granted the American press its dubious victory in the Pentagon Papers case, Justice Department attorneys won an indictment of Daniel Ellsberg for violating the Espionage Act and for converting government property—the documents that he had copied and distributed—to his own use. Many administration members hoped to tie him to Democratic presidential aspirants as well and thus to undermine political rivals. Ever hopeful, the administration also wanted to link Ellsberg with the remnants of the New Left movement. As the investigation of Ellsberg continued, the president became preoccupied with unauthorized disclosures of government information. Soon, the White House goal became one of stopping all information leaks. Appropriately enough, the administration set up a special unit called the Plumbers to stop all leaks. One of their first tasks was to uncover as much incriminating information about Ellsberg as possible, an assignment that eventually led them to break into the office of Ellsberg's psychiatrist, Dr. Lewis Fielding, in order to rifle his files.[1]

In late December, the government obtained a second indictment against Ellsberg and his accomplice, Anthony Russo. This one charged them with fifteen counts of conspiracy, conversion of government property, and espionage. If convicted on all counts, Russo faced 35 years in prison; Ellsberg's prison term could have been 115 years. The new indictment was obtained in Los Angeles, near the Rand Corporation headquarters. Ellsberg's attorneys immediately protested that the government was trying to move the trial away from Washington where most of the pertinent defense witnesses lived to a site where it felt more assured of gaining a conviction. Southern California, where the documents were copied, was the site of many defense-related industries and the retirement home of thousands of military personnel.

Pretrial concerns focused on issues never before litigated. For instance, what precisely was a "document . . . connected with the national defense" as listed in the Espionage Act?[2] In addition, the case was based on the notion that the government could own information, which Ellsberg's attorneys considered doubtful since no government information could be copyrighted. And because the heart of the government's case rested on Ellsberg's unauthorized dissemination of top-secret information, the classification system itself would finally be tested in court. Not only had document classification not existed in 1917 when the Espionage Act was written, but the system had been established by executive order rather than by congressional act. Besides, government officials regularly provided classified documents to selected members of the press, making a mockery of the impenetrable shield that the government contended existed around top-secret papers. Ellsberg's attorneys also planned to argue that none of Ellsberg's actions deprived the government of its property because he had left the original documents in government hands. The primary issue in the case, according to the Ellsberg defense, was the importance of freedom of speech in a world in which information vital to the functioning of a democracy had been shielded from public view via the abused classification system.

A jury was seated in summer 1972, but the case was postponed indefinitely when the government revealed that someone connected with the defense had had his telephone tapped. Defense attorneys demanded that the case be stopped while they went to court to find out more about the eavesdropping. When the Supreme Court refused to hear the issue, the trial finally began in January 1973. But by that time, Watergate had begun to unravel. In fact, the Ellsberg trial was proceeding at the same time that the burglars were being tried in Washington, and defense counsel tried to tie the case against Ellsberg and Russo to a general pattern of government misconduct that was being revealed almost daily.

By April, the trial essentially was over. On April 26, the prosecutor told Judge Matthew Byrne, Jr., that G. Gordon Liddy and E. Howard Hunt, two of the Plumbers, had broken into Dr. Fielding's office. About the same time, one of the president's right-hand men, John Ehrlichman, met secretly with the judge about the possibility of Byrne accepting a top-level government appointment, supposedly as head of the Federal Bureau of Investigation (FBI). The judge made both incidents public and ordered a wider investigation into government tampering with the case. He tried to continue the case, but when information that Ellsberg himself had been overheard in an illegal government wiretap of telephones at the home of one of Henry Kissinger's aides became public, Byrne dismissed all charges against Ellsberg and Russo.

Although Ellsberg escaped punishment, the fundamental question of whether provisions of the Espionage Act applied to such behavior remained unanswered. For all of the government's efforts to punish those involved in the Pentagon Papers affair, it had wound up with one Supreme Court decision in favor of freedom of the press and one district court judge dismissing charges because of governmental misconduct. Recourse to the court system had been disastrous for Nixon's campaign to solidify support and eliminate dissent, so the president continued his extralegal efforts.

Nixon had already taken a variety of steps against the press. Angered by the way in which journalists had reported the problems encountered by his nominees to the Supreme Court and by the emphasis placed on the Kent State killings, he had moved reporters out of his sight at the White House in 1970. Nixon ordered the White House swimming pool drained and covered in order to install new press facilities. The complex was badly needed, but it served the president more than the journalists. The new press headquarters were away from the heart of the White House, and journalists no longer could keep track of who was coming and going into the offices in the West Wing. Beginning about the same time, Nixon worked even harder to undercut the White House press corps, which he considered too liberal and unsympathetic. He began holding briefings for press and broadcast representatives from around the country rather than for the journalists assigned to the White House. In some instances, the out-of-towners came to Washington for the sessions; in other cases, the president went to them.[3]

To further shape the way in which the American people were told of his administration, Nixon, whose closest advisers came from advertising and public relations jobs, established one of the largest presidential public relations operations in the nation's history. As one step in the process, they restricted reporters' direct access to members of executive departments. Trying to get telephone calls through to longtime sources became almost impossible as secretaries, once they discovered that a journalist was on the line, routinely re-directed the call to the department's public information office. Fred Graham, who was covering the Justice Department for the *New York Times,* referred to the "chilling effect" of the policy. If Graham wanted to talk to a source and he knew the source also wanted to talk to him, "I have to give his secretary a phony name—a name that my source knows is me. When the secretary asks what my call is in reference to, I say 'personal.'"[4] That way, the call would get through, despite the president's best-laid plans to block access.

Nixon also made his displeasure with certain journalists known by excluding them from the pool assigned to travel with the president. And, through Ehrlichman, Nixon sought to rid himself of his most persistent questioner, Dan Rather, CBS News White House correspondent. Richard Salant, president of CBS News, reported that Ehrlichman, in the middle of a friendly conversation, "suddenly lit into Dan Rather and called him a hatchet man and told me how unhappy they were with him." According to Salant, "There were only two things I felt I ought to do, aside from telling him I thought Dan Rather was great. One was to make it public, and the other was to let Dan Rather know that he was now assured of being the White House correspondent as long as he ever wants to."[5]

About the same time that the administration began its Plumbers operation, it also established the so-called "enemies list" that carried names of individuals who had particularly displeased the president. The people on the list were targeted for both increased harassment by government agencies and efforts to undermine them personally and professionally. One of the first journalists to make the list was CBS news correspondent Daniel Schorr, who apparently offended the White House by pointing out that the president's rhetoric about helping Catholic parochial schools financially was just that—rhetoric. According to Nixon aide Charles Colson, Schorr was "a real media enemy."[6] Two days after the offending broadcast, orders went out from H. R. Haldeman, most likely with the approval of the president, for the FBI to launch a full-scale background investigation on Schorr. J. Edgar Hoover, who was nearing the end of both his tenure as FBI director and his life, sent a "special inquiry" to all field offices on August 19 instructing them to complete an investigation on Schorr "without fail" by August 23. The president wanted an "extremely expedite[d] investigation of Schorr," said the director's message. The news reporter, he said, "is being considered for presidential appointment, position not stated. Do not," he warned, "indicate White House interest to persons contacted."[7] The field investigation was so extensive that agents interviewed twenty-five people in various parts of the country in seven hours. Family, friends, and employers began calling Schorr asking what was going on.

As the scale of the inquiry became known, the investigation was called off, and the White House prepared the cover story that Schorr was being considered for a government appointment in the environmental area that had been filled while the inquiry was in progress. As Watergate unraveled over the next several years, the true reason behind the investigation was revealed. Angered by Schorr's reporting, the White House simply had decided to harass the journalist by subjecting him to FBI scrutiny. Questions remain, however, as to whether the Nixon administration intended to make the investigation quite so apparent or whether Hoover did that simply to embarrass the president. The investigation, Schorr concluded, affected his functioning as a journalist. Nixon's actions, Schorr said, "forced me to submit to a thousand jokes about whether my FBI 'shadow' was still with me, and whether it was safe to talk to me on the telephone. He made me worry about whether I was still perceived by the public as an objective reporter, and whether I might be a source of embarrassment to my own news organization in its conflicts with the government." The veteran correspondent concluded that "there are many kinds of 'chilling effects' on the exercise of press freedom. Whenever a president uses the powers entrusted to him to go after a reporter, there are bound to be some."[8]

Nixon and his staff saw their actions as justified. The liberal press blocked Nixon's efforts to set America on a conservative right path. To a large extent, confrontations between the president and the press had been ongoing since the days of George Washington. Franklin D. Roosevelt had honed the conflict to a fine point, but he had accused a conservative press of obstructing liberal goals. Whether the press had changed its political philosophy in the intervening years is beside the point; it suited the Nixon administration's purposes to term journalists liberal. If forced to rely on facts to support his charges, Nixon would have had a difficult time making the liberal label stick. Although studies tend to show practicing journalists are more liberal than many Americans, it is equally true that newspaper owners presented an overwhelmingly conservative face to the nation. Indeed, most newspaper owners were quite in tune with Richard Nixon's goals.[9] Exceptions existed, of course, and the president's ire focused on those exceptions, which he then magnified to the point that they represented the entire press community.

In addition, Nixon followed in the footsteps of his predecessors who believed that journalists should report only information approved by the administration. But he faced a generation of journalists who had become increasingly distrustful of government as a result of the news management techniques of the Kennedy and Johnson administrations. By Nixon's administration, journalists believed that the First Amendment required them to serve as the loyal opposition to any government in power, be it conservative or liberal. The more that political figures tried to manipulate the news, the more journalists believed that politicians were trying to hide something, and the harder the questioning, the more intense the investigation. Faced with a new enemy, Nixon took a page from Roosevelt's book and attempted to intimidate the press into changing its behavior. Nixon, with a far greater federal establishment at his command and with less self-confidence than FDR, went after the press with greater gusto than had his predecessor. Although journalists did not whither under the Roosevelt attack, they did indeed start to bend under the Nixon barrage.

Seemingly always insecure, Nixon was gearing up for the 1972 election campaign. With major items still on his foreign and domestic agendas, he planned to leave nothing to chance. His administration's attack on the press had been long and moderately successful. But he still had problems with some segments of the communications industry. As a leader of the more conservative wing of the Republican party, Nixon had a responsibility to a constituency that followed in the footsteps of Anthony Comstock. The president felt required to take a stand against forces in society that were once again leading American young people to perdition. The dangers this time were far more formidable than dirty literature or comic books. Now the fears were based on sexual promiscuity and drug use, in addition to the more traditional concerns about political radicalism. The president had already taken on political radicalism among young people and seemed to be winning that battle. The next step was to attack the promotion of illicit drug use.

In the 1960s and early 1970s, the popular drugs among American young people were marijuana and LSD, and by September 1970, Vice President Spiro Agnew was taking on the American music industry for recording songs with lyrics that, he said, promoted the drug culture. While noting some current music was good, Agnew warned that "in too many of the lyrics, the message of the drug culture is purveyed." Several songs earned specific denunciation. A 1960s Beatles hit, "With a Little Help from My Friends," he said, contained the wording "I get *by* with a little help from my friends, I get *high* with a little help from my friends." "Until it was pointed out to me," Agnew said, "I never realized that the 'friends' were assorted drugs with such nicknames as 'Mary Jane,' 'Speed,' and 'Benny.' But the double meaning of the message was clear to members of the drug culture—and many of those who are tempted to join." Even the titles of some songs should raise danger signals, Agnew contended, as he listed "The Acid Queen," "Eight Miles High," "Couldn't Get High," "Don't Step on the Grass, Sam," and "Stoned Woman" as objectionable.[10]

"I am sure," Agnew said, "that very few, if any, station managers in America would deliberately allow the use of their radio facilities to encourage the use of drugs." The vice president said that he believed "few parents would knowingly tolerate the blaring of a drug-approving message from phonographs in their homes. And few musicians intend their 'in-jokes' and double meanings to reach past the periphery of pot users. But the fact is that the stations do, the parents do, and the musicians do."[11] The vice president's rhetoric was insufficient to stop radio stations from playing such music, and so the next volley came from the Federal Communications Commission (FCC), which in March 1971 issued a public notice warning radio stations about potential adverse consequences of playing music advocating the use of drugs. If these lyrics are repeatedly heard, said the FCC majority, "it raises serious questions as to whether continued operation of the station is in the public interest. . . . In short, we expect broadcast licensees to ascertain, before broadcast, the words or lyrics of recorded musical or spoken selections played on their stations."[12]

To FCC Commissioner Nicholas Johnson, an appointee of Lyndon Johnson, the public notice was an attempt at outright censorship of "song lyrics that the majority disapproves of." In addition, Johnson said, "It is an attempt by a group of establishmentarians to determine what youth can say and hear; it is an unconstitutional action by a Federal agency aimed clearly at controlling the content of speech." The message, he contended, was plain: censor any lyrics that might promote the use of drugs or else face problems at license renewal time. The attack on song lyrics, he said, "is a thinly veiled political move. This Administration has, for reasons best known to the President, chosen to divert the American people's attention to 'the drug menace,' and away from problems like: the growing Southeast Asian war, racial prejudice, inflation, unemployment, hunger, poverty, education, growing urban blight, and so forth."[13]

The music that attracted the attention and dollars of American youth had been undergoing a dramatic change in the 1960s and early 1970s. Now music had a political focus, and the musicians of the era became the troubadours of various protest movements. Although Agnew and the FCC picked on lyrics that they viewed as promoting drug use, music that raised the social conscience also was suspect. Unable to touch songs with words focusing on social problems, the administration turned instead to lyrics that supposedly urged listeners to experiment with drugs. By the time the FCC was finished with this particular crusade, many radio stations had imposed outright bans on more than twenty songs that the U.S. Army, for some reason, said had drug-related lyrics. No federal agency connected with drug enforcement had labeled the lyrics as encouraging illegal actions. Artists affected included the Beatles, the Byrds, Jefferson Airplane, and the Grateful Dead. Even folksingers Peter, Paul, and Mary found their popular "Puff, the Magic Dragon" on the list of songs having drug-related lyrics.[14]

For radio station managers who did not want simply to ban songs just because conservative FCC members agreed with the U.S. Army's categorization, the problem became one of determining just what the commission wanted the stations to do. Few broadcasters could figure it out. Several stations asked for clarification from the commissioners and received a contradictory response. "Clearly," said the commission majority, "in a time when there is an epidemic of illegal drug use—when thousands of young lives are being destroyed by use of drugs like heroin, methedrine ('speed'), cocaine—the licensee should not be indifferent to the question of whether his facilities are being used to promote the illegal use of harmful drugs." On the other hand, said the commissioners, a licensee that took all records referring to drugs off the air went too far; the FCC did not promote censorship. "We trust that with the issuance of this opinion," said the commissioners, "such licensees will cease such grossly inappropriate policy and rather will make a judgment based on the particular record."[15]

Still dissatisfied with the FCC's explanation, one station tried to win approval of a policy based squarely on the First Amendment. Yale Broadcasting Company's management acknowledged that some of the songs were "controversial and not approved of by certain segments of the American populace" because they presented "unpopular political, cultural and social ideas" and referred "to the illegal use of drugs." But, it added, "the licensee believes that songs, including their lyrics, are protected forms of expression under the First Amendment, and deserve to be heard by our audience without interference. Moreover, it is the obligation of the licensee to be responsive to the First Amendment rights of its audience." While defending their right to play songs on First Amendment grounds, the station said it was aware "of the problems of drug abuse and will always attempt to present programming which responds to this issue of current and pressing public concern. Such programming is and will be in the form of news, spot announcements and specific programming directed to this issue."[16] The FCC refused to rule on Yale Broadcasting's approach to song lyrics, saying that it had said enough on the matter and that station management could base its actions on previous comments.

Unhappy with the FCC's inaction, Yale Broadcasting went into court. The federal appeals court upheld the FCC,[17] and the Supreme Court refused to hear the case. Two justices, William O. Douglas and William J. Brennan, would have set the case for oral argument. Sufficiently outraged at the Court's decision, Douglas wrote a dissent to the refusal to grant certiorari. The FCC's action, he said, constituted an impermissible invasion of First Amendment freedoms. If the FCC warning notice stood, the ramifications might be endless. "For now the regulation is applied to song lyrics," he said. "Next year it may apply to comedy programs, and the following year to news broadcasts." To Douglas, "Songs play no less a role in public debate, whether they eulogize the John Brown of the abolitionist movement, or the Joe Hill of the union movement, provide a rallying cry such as 'We Shall Overcome,' or express in music the values of the youthful 'counterculture.'" In all instances, "the Government cannot, consistent with the First Amendment, require a broadcaster to censor its music any more than it can require a newspaper to censor the stories of its reporters. Under our system the Government is not to decide what messages, spoken or in music, are of the proper 'social value' to reach the people."[18]

FCC officials, of course, won the day, and the Supreme Court's unwillingness to challenge the FCC's attempts to clean up the airwaves had far-reaching effects. In 1973, the same year that the Court refused to review the drug-lyrics issue, another odd case concerning the censorship of the airwaves began moving through the system. According to the story given out at the time, a father was riding in the car with his young son when the radio station they were listening to broadcast comedian George Carlin's "Filthy Words" monologue, which had been recorded before a live audience. Further research into the background of the complaint revealed that the father, John R. Douglas, was a conservative Republican who was a member of the national planning board for Morality in Media, and the son was a 15-year-old. The complaint against the Carlin monologue did not come in for six weeks, leading some skeptics to wonder whether the complainant had even heard the recording over the air.[19] In any event, the father asked the FCC to ban these recordings from the airwaves. In 1975, the commission ruled in the father's favor but did not impose formal sanctions on the station. Instead, the commission said its order would be "associated with the station's license file, and in the event that subsequent complaints are received, the Commission will then decide whether it should utilize any of the available sanctions it has been granted by Congress."[20]

Pacifica Foundation, which operated the offending radio station, believed that the commission's action had a chilling effect on its freedom and took the matter into court. In 1978, a closely divided Supreme Court gave its blessing to the FCC's actions. Even though the five majority justices failed to agree on one opinion, the message still was clear: bad language had no place on the American airwaves. In delivering the plurality opinion of the Court, Justice John Paul Stevens acknowledged that "the words of the Carlin monologue are unquestionably 'speech' within the meaning of the First Amendment" and that just because "society may find speech offensive is not a sufficient reason for suppressing it." But broadcasting was a different kind of speech and thus subject to regulation.[21]

"The broadcast media have established a uniquely pervasive presence in the lives of all Americans. Patently offensive, indecent material presented over the airwaves confronts the citizen, not only in public, but also in the privacy of the home, where the individual's right to be left alone plainly outweighs the First Amendment rights of the intruder," Stevens said. The radio station had broadcast a disclaimer before it carried the Carlin monologue, but that was insufficient, Stevens said. "Because the broadcast audience is constantly tuning in and out, prior warnings cannot completely protect the listener or viewer from unexpected program content. To say that one may avoid further offense by turning off the radio when he hears indecent language is like saying that the remedy for an assault is to run away after the first blow." In addition, "broadcasting is uniquely accessible to children, even those too young to read," Stevens said. "Pacifica's broadcast could have enlarged a child's vocabulary in an instant." Consequently, the FCC was justified in determining that indecent language was inappropriate over the airwaves during certain hours of the day.[22]

Justice William J. Brennan led the dissenters in charging that the majority had essentially decided that "the degree of protection the First Amendment affords protected speech varies with the social value ascribed to that speech by five Members of this Court." The decision, he complained, was another attempt by conservatives on the Court "to unstitch the warp and woof of First Amendment law in an effort to reshape its fabric to cover the patently wrong result the Court reaches in this case," which he found "dangerous as well as lamentable." Equally disturbing, he said, was the fact that the decision represented the "depressing inability to appreciate that in our land of cultural pluralism, there are many who think, act, and talk differently from the Members of this Court, and who do not share their fragile sensibilities."[23]

Although Nixon had left office by the time the Pacifica decision was handed down, that ruling and other opinions by the FCC in subsequent years restricting so-called morally offensive programming to even fewer hours have done much to remake the American airwaves in a way that Nixon and his conservative colleagues would find most attractive. Unfortunately, however, the FCC actions against songs containing lyrics that allegedly promoted drug use and against bad language on the air did not reach still another area of great concern for conservatives: obscenity. In this area, Nixon had a few problems, but again the Supreme Court provided the appropriate conservative solution.

Nixon's problems in the area of obscenity resulted from the work of the Commission on Obscenity and Pornography, established by Congress in 1967, which issued its report in 1970. Nixon had named only one commission member and had denounced its activities. The commission's report distressed a society that was increasingly concerned about sexual promiscuity. Indeed, the commission's recommendations would have made Anthony Comstock turn over in his grave. In fact, the very first sentence of recommendations read: "The Commission believes that much of the 'problem' regarding materials which depict explicit sexual activity stems from the inability or reluctance of people in our society to be open and direct in dealing with sexual matters." From there on, from the conservative perspective, everything was downhill. The commission, for instance, recommended launching a massive sex education campaign to tear away misperceptions about sex and begin an open discussion on issues surrounding obscenity and pornography. Even worse, it recommended that all legislation keeping sexual materials from consenting adults be repealed. "Extensive empirical investigation, both by the Commission and by others," the report said, "provides no evidence that exposure to or use of explicit sexual materials play a significant role in the causation of social or individual harms such as crime, delinquency, sexual or nonsexual deviancy or severe emotional disturbances." Noting that "society's attempts to legislate for adults in the area of obscenity have not been successful," the commission stressed that "public opinion in America does not support the imposition of legal prohibitions upon the right of adults to read or see explicit sexual materials."[24]

In addition, the commission's report noted that "adult obscenity laws deal in the realm of speech and communication. Americans deeply value the right of each individual to determine for himself what books he wishes to read and what pictures or films he wishes to see." Such beliefs "value and protect the right of writers, publishers, and booksellers to serve the diverse interests of the public" that cannot be infringed "unless a clear threat of harm makes that course imperative. Moreover, the possibility of the misuse of general obscenity statutes prohibiting distribution of books and films to adults constitutes a continuing threat to the free communication of ideas among Americans—one of the most important foundations of our liberties." While recognizing that many Americans feared "that the lawful distribution of explicit sexual materials to adults may have a deleterious effect upon the individual morality of American citizens and upon the moral climate in America as a whole," the commission said the majority of its members believed these fears flowed "from a belief that exposure to explicit materials may cause moral confusion which, in turn, may induce antisocial or criminal behavior." The commission reiterated its conclusion that no such connection existed. In fact, the commission majority hypothesized that "the open availability of increasingly explicit sexual materials" and "the ready availability of effective methods of contraception, changes of the role of women in our society, and the increased education and mobility of our citizens" had a greater effect on sexual morality than did sexually explicit materials.[25]

This permissiveness drove Nixon's sole commission appointee, Charles Keating, a Cincinnati lawyer who headed a private organization called "Citizens for Decent Literature," into court to force the commission to delay release of its report until he could draft a dissent.[26] In that dissent, Keating labeled the majority's recommendation's "shocking and anarchistic." "At a time when the spread of pornography has reached epidemic proportions in our country and when the moral fiber of our nation seems to be rapidly unravelling," he said, "the desperate need is for enlightened and intelligent control of the poisons which threaten us—not the declaration of moral bankruptcy inherent in the repeal of the laws which have been the defense of decent people against the pornographer for profit." The majority report violated all that Keating held dear, and he argued vehemently for the protection of decency and morality: "Far from needing repeal of legislation controlling pornography, what is called for is a return to law enforcement which permits the American to determine for himself the standards of acceptable morality and decency in his community. Our law enforcement in the area of obscenity has been emasculated by courts, seemingly divorced from the realities of our communities, determining from afar the standards of those communities."[27]

In large measure, Keating's dissent was prescient. The legal system had indeed made a jumble of obscenity law since the Supreme Court began ruling on obscenity cases in the 1950s. In its first decision on the matter, five justices had agreed that "implicit in the history of the First Amendment is the rejection of obscenity as utterly without redeeming social importance,"[28] thus placing obscenity outside protected speech. As the Court heard more cases, the justices became increasingly willing to protect more material. In 1966, the Court reached a high-water mark when a plurality held that in order to ban literature, the state must prove that "(a) the dominant theme of the material taken as a whole appeals to a prurient interest in sex; (b) the material is patently offensive because it affronts contemporary community standards relating to the description or representation of sexual matters; and (c) the material is utterly without redeeming social value."[29] The community standards applied here and in other cases, much to the dismay of Keating and other conservatives, were national standards. At the least, conservatives argued through Keating and others, local standards should be used in evaluating what is obscene.

By 1973, the Supreme Court, under the tutelage of Warren Burger, was ready to provide the limits on obscenity desired by Charles Keating and the Nixon administration. For one thing, the five-man majority established a new standard for judging obscenity. According to Chief Justice Burger, who wrote for the majority, the new guidelines for judging obscenity were: "(a) whether 'the average person, applying contemporary community standards' would find that the work, taken as a whole, appeals to the prurient interest . . . ; (b) whether the work depicts or describes, in a patently offensive way, sexual conduct specifically defined by the applicable state law; and (c) whether the work, taken as a whole, lacks serious literary, artistic, political, or scientific value." In terms of community standards, Burger said, "Under a National Constitution, fundamental First Amendment limitations on the powers of the States do not vary from community to community, but this does not mean that there are, or should or can be, fixed, uniform national standards of precisely what appeals to the 'prurient interest' or is 'patently offensive.'" Indeed, he said, "our Nation is simply too big and too diverse for this Court to reasonably expect that such standards could be articulated for all 50 States."[30]

With this ruling, the standard by which obscenity would be judged took a giant step backward. Now, there would be fifty sets of standards for evaluating obscenity, and as states began implementing these new guidelines, obscenity definitions would vary from community to community as lawmakers and judges decided that even states were too large to be considered homogeneous in their attitudes toward sexually explicit literature. Conservative communities could protect themselves while liberal areas could have access to such information. Liberals in conservative towns and conservatives in liberal communities would continue to protest that they were being discriminated against by this procedure. For the person trying to sell such materials, ascertaining the criteria that would be used should a case go to court became impossible, as predicted by the dissenters in the 1973 case. Another aspect of the conservative revolution being engineered by Richard Nixon was falling into place.

As the end of Nixon's first term in office approached, much of society had been remade to his specifications. Although the antiwar movement was not completely destroyed, it was basically silenced. The media still were causing a few problems here and there, but they, too, were substantially cowed. The effort to save society from moral degradation was moving along. As the president prepared to claim the presidential nomination and to run for a second term in 1972, everything indicated even greater changes ahead. But as 1972 progressed, the shadow of a "third-rate burglary attempt"[31] at Democratic National Headquar-

ters at the Watergate Hotel on June 17 spread across the land and began to interfere with the president's plans to redesign American life.

The election year began with concerted attacks on a somewhat new enemy
and with reminders of problems that old foes could cause. Investigative reporter
Jack Anderson started the year off badly for the president by publishing verbatim
notes of sessions of the Washington Special Action Group discussing the international crisis between India and Pakistan. The leak came from Defense Department sources and showed the administration's intense dislike for the Indians and
a decision to "tilt" toward the Pakistanis in the dispute. The executive branch
began an intensive search for the source of the leak and unleashed the Plumbers
on Anderson. They started a close surveillance of him and, most likely, tapped
his telephone. But the White House team handling leak control clearly knew no
bounds when it came to efforts to quiet speech that distressed the president. They
tried, for instance, to discredit Anderson, a practicing Mormon and father of
nine, by linking him to a homosexual affair and to embarrass him by inducing
him to take a hallucinogenic drug. When more leaks on other topics showed up
in Anderson's columns, his assistant Les Whitten was arrested on trumped-up
charges that were later dismissed. Although unsuccessful, the campaign against
Anderson showed that the White House was prepared to stop at nothing to
closely control the information provided to the American people.

By spring 1972, the Nixon administration was ready to take action against a
new enemy: public television. The national system of public television grew out
of repeated complaints, going back as far as the passage of the Communications
Act of 1934, that broadcasters served only majority interests. In 1967, the federal
government, through the Public Broadcasting Act, financed a national system
to help produce quality programming for public television stations.[32] Richard
Nixon disliked public television because he considered it a bastion for liberal,
antiwar, anti-establishment programming, and one of his goals was to bring it
under control.[33]

That hatred peaked as public television officials announced plans to have
Sander Vanocur and Robert MacNeil anchor a series of 1972 election specials.
The president especially disliked Vanocur, who as an NBC correspondent had
asked Dwight Eisenhower in 1960 to cite the major decisions in which Nixon
had participated as vice president. When the president asked for a week to think
about the question, Nixon believed his hopes to succeed Eisenhower in the
White House had been fatally wounded. The fact that the problem had been
caused by Eisenhower's inability to answer the question was lost on Nixon. Vanocur should not have asked the question in the first place, and if he had not been
so close to the Kennedys, Nixon fumed, he would not have raised the query.
Adding to the president's fury was a segment planned for the "Great American
Dream Machine," a magazine program that dealt with attempts by the FBI to
plant *agents provocateurs* in the peace movement. The segment was deleted
from the show before it was sent around the country, but it did air in New York
City. Although the piece received poor marks for its quality and content from
relatively unbiased observers, the administration was denounced for coercing
public television executives into pulling the story.

Nixon sought new ways to stop government financing of unacceptable public affairs programming. Publicly, the administration warned of significant policy questions involved in federal funding of public affairs programming on public television. Privately, White House staffers were far more direct: "No one participating in this exercise has been unclear as to the President's basic objective: To get the left-wing commentators who are cutting us up off public television at once, indeed yesterday if possible."[34]

In 1972, Congress passed, by overwhelming margins in both houses, a two-year, $155 million appropriation for public television. Richard Nixon vetoed the measure, raising a round of criticism that he was trying to control another medium of expression. Congress took no steps to override the veto and instead passed the one-year $45 million appropriation that the White House had recommended. The chairman of the Corporation for Public Broadcasting (CPB) resigned in protest, and a Republican majority took over the administrative arm of public television. With a limited budget, the public affairs division could not afford to do gavel-to-gavel coverage of the political conventions as planned. Instead, MacNeil and Vanocur anchored ninety-minute nightly summaries of the Democratic convention. When the Republican convention came around, funds miraculously appeared to allow gavel-to-gavel programming. MacNeil and Vanocur refused to participate in such apparently biased scheduling; Bill Moyers presided while MacNeil and Vanocur handled thirty-minute summaries of highlights. Although the expected criticism from outsiders occurred, the president was delighted, and his approval was all that really mattered.

As Republicans gained control of the Corporation for Public Broadcasting, the administration began to see public television as its own personal channel to the American people. White House personnel assumed that they would be told what CPB officials planned to broadcast beforehand and would have veto power over objectionable programs. Indeed, they were outraged when something appeared on the air that they disliked. When public television carried a speech by Democratic presidential candidate George McGovern, for instance, Charles Colson complained: "How did we miss the fact that National Educational Television ran the full McGovern speech to the Security Analysts in New York?" And, said Colson, "not only do they run it once, but they re-ran it a second time. Somewhere along the line we're not watching these things carefully enough. . . . The Corporation for Public Broadcasting also never made known to us that this had happened, so we . . . found out only by monitoring. They damn well, as a public corporation, had an obligation to tell us."[35] Implicit in Colson's words, of course, was the idea that the White House should have the final approval over the information that public television put before the American people.

After Richard Nixon's landslide victory in 1972, he named even more members to the Corporation for Public Broadcasting board. The independence of public television seemed doomed, but as in many other areas, Nixon went too far. The individual station licensees, already banded together loosely in the Public Broadcasting System, strengthened their connections and worked to free public broadcasting from government interference. Community backers of public television, many of whom were well connected politically, joined the campaign to save public television from administrative encroachments. The battle intensified as the CPB announced the programs that would not be funded for the upcoming season. Almost every public affairs show offered was on that list: William F. Buckley's "Firing Line," Tony Brown's "Black Journal," "Bill Moyers' Journal," "The Advocates," and "Washington Week in Review." The limited public television budget, the CPB had decided, would go to shows that could be repeated. Public affairs programs because of their timeliness could be shown only once.

A public outcry saved "The Advocates," which presented conservatives and liberals debating various issues, and "Black Journal," the only program pitched to a black audience. With the others still candidates for cancellation, opposition to the president's campaign against public television grew. But the tide turned only after White House assistant Patrick J. Buchanan, a sharp-tongued conservative, voiced the administration's views of these programs on an ABC talk show in early 1973. Going down the list of programs, he pulled out all stops in denouncing the programs. "If you look at public television," he told host Dick Cavett, "you will find you've got Sander Vanocur and Robert MacNeil, the first of whom, Sander Vanocur, is a notorious Kennedy sycophant, in my judgment, and Robert MacNeil, who is anti-administration. . . . 'Washington Week Review' is unbalanced against us. . . . You have 'Black Journal,' which is unbalanced against us." Such a line-up made the president's stance against public affairs programming funded by government money logical, Buchanan said.[36]

Buchanan's forceful defense of the political attack on public television sounded the death knell for administrative intervention. No longer could CPB officials argue the philosophical rightness of producing timeless programming. Now Congress began investigating administration meddling in the business of an independent corporation funded by the government. James R. Killian, former head of the Carnegie Commission that had long supported public television, was named head of the Corporation of Public Broadcasting, and under his direction, the board adopted a statement of principles that essentially denounced the administration's activities. "Just as an informed citizenry is essential to a functioning democracy, so public affairs programs are an essential ingredient of a healthy system of public broadcasting," the statement said. Given more money, public broadcasting would resume public affairs programming.[37]

Congress approved a total of $175 million for public broadcasting over two years. The measure was sent to the president, whose administration was facing hearings conducted by the Senate Select Committee on Presidential Campaign Activities, better known as the Watergate Committee. Nixon signed the appropriation bill without public protest. As a final blow to the president's campaign against public television, those stations carried daily, gavel-to-gavel coverage of the Watergate Committee hearings chaired by Senator Sam Ervin of North Carolina. Although commercial networks carried the hearings on a rotating basis, they often omitted segments of the proceedings for other programming. On public television, the whole sessions were shown during the day and repeated in the evening hours, drawing the largest audience in public television history.

Although the struggle over CPB's public affairs programming ended with a victory for the right to express views that differed from the administration's, other encounters provided mixed results. The Supreme Court, for instance, handed the administration major victories in its campaign to keep both media and protest movements in line. On the other hand, the justices sharply restricted the ability of administration officials to function in an area that the president's representatives considered to be critically important.

Both victory and defeat came in the area of antiwar protest. The administration's victory came when the Court began to contract its definition of a public forum and ruled that shopping centers or malls, which by 1972 were becoming the nation's preferred place for buying goods and services, were private property that could be kept free of proselytizing dissenters. For some thirty years, the Court had been steadily advancing the definition of a public forum. Access to public streets and parks, which constituted the first Court-endorsed public forum in 1939,[38] was essential for the dissemination of ideas because there potential recruits could be contacted with ease. In 1946, the Court extended the definition of a public forum to include a company town in which a business firm provided all of the services normally provided by a municipality and to which the public had general access. People could not be isolated from ideas just because they lived in towns owned by companies that wanted to keep the ideas out, said the Court. "The more an owner, for his advantage, opens up his property for use by the public in general," the Court had said, "the more do his rights become circumscribed by the statutory and constitutional rights of those who use it."[39] By 1968, the Court, in its first shopping center case, ruled that union members could picket a store with which they had a disagreement even if that store was located in a mall. Said Justice Thurgood Marshall for the Court at that time, "The State may not delegate the power, through the use of its trespass laws, wholly to exclude those members of the public wishing to exercise their First Amendment rights on the premises in a manner and for a purpose generally consonant with the use to which the property is actually put."[40]

The issue in 1968 was the right of labor union members with a dispute against a particular store in the mall to picket on the premises rather than being forced to public property on the outskirts of the mall where the protest would be far less effective. In 1972, however, the issue was the right of individuals opposed to the Vietnam War to distribute handbills in a shopping center. While admitting that the mall was generally open to the public and that its management had allowed certain groups including the American Legion and the Salvation Army to solicit funds within its boundaries, Justice Lewis F. Powell wrote for the majority that mall owners had the right to ban antiwar protesters from the premises. The distribution of handbills by five young people was quiet and orderly and was not accompanied by littering; only one person complained. But the center's security guards told the young people that they would have to move to the public sidewalks and streets surrounding the mall. "The handbilling by respondents in the malls of Lloyd Center had no relation to any purpose for which the center was built and being used," Powell wrote for five members of the Court. Although the general public was invited to the mall, that invitation was limited to individuals who wished to do business with the center's tenants. Persons who wanted to sell ideas were forced to use the streets and sidewalks around the mall. These rules did not unreasonably restrict protesters' rights, Powell said. After all, automobiles had to stop before entering or leaving the mall, providing plenty of opportunity for the distribution of handbills. "It must be remembered," Justice Powell said, "that the First and Fourteenth Amendments safeguard the rights of free speech and assembly by limitations on *state* action, not on action by the owner of private property used nondiscriminatorily for private purposes only."[41]

Thurgood Marshall, who had written the decision opening up shopping centers only four years earlier, was outraged. Lloyd Center served as the functional equivalent of a downtown business district, he said, and received many special favors from Portland city officials, which should have provided the state action necessary to force the mall to open itself to ideas that were unpopular with the management. In fact, the mall's management had conceded that if the young people had been protesting activities by one or more of the center's occupants, they would have been allowed to continue. But because they were advocating different ideas, they were barred. The distinctions drawn by the majority greatly irritated Marshall, who argued that "for many Portland citizens, Lloyd Center will so completely satisfy their wants that they will have no reason to go elsewhere for goods or services. If speech is to reach these people, it must reach them in Lloyd Center." In addition, "for many persons who do have easy access to television, radio, the major newspapers, and the other forms of mass media, the only way they can express themselves to a broad range of citizens on issues of general public concern is . . . to be permitted to speak in those areas in which most of their fellow citizens can found." That, to Marshall, was "the business district of a city or town or its functional equivalent." Unless the Court reverted to its earlier definitions of the public forum, "only the wealthy may find effective communications possible."[42]

The Court, however, did not return to its earlier vision of a public forum; in fact, if anything, the justices reduced the access of individuals without money to inexpensive means of communication, even when property was publicly owned. In 1984, for example, the Court decided that Los Angeles could forbid candidates for public office to nail campaign posters on public utility polls on the grounds that the signs constituted a visual blight. The fact that those signs also provided an important means of communication in an election campaign was ignored, as six members of the Court decided that a neat landscape was more important than election information.[43] The only real advance for public forum use came in 1980 when Justice William Rehnquist wrote for the Court in another shopping center case. This time, the Court upheld the right of Californians to dispense ideas in a mall because that state's supreme court had said that the state constitution opened private property for free-speech activities. A state may use its constitution to offer its citizens individual liberties that were more expansive than the U.S. Supreme Court was willing to find in the federal Constitution, he said.[44]

Although the Court refused to sanction efforts to use business property to express political views, the justices did protect individuals who wished to express dissident views elsewhere. Six members of the Court decided in 1972 that the

Fourth Amendment, which forbids illegal searches and seizures, blocked Nixon administration efforts to conduct electronic surveillance without court approval. The Department of Justice argued that the wiretaps were necessary "to gather intelligence information deemed necessary to protect the nation from attempts of domestic organizations to attack and subvert the existing structure of Government." The government also said that the Omnibus Crime Control and Safe Streets Act of 1968 allowed the president to institute wiretaps without court intervention when he believed that the nation's security was at stake. The Court disagreed.[45]

Governments may indeed protect themselves from individuals who would subvert them, Justice Lewis F. Powell said for the majority. "But a recognition of these elementary truths does not make the employment by Government of electronic surveillance a welcome development—even when employed with restraint and under judicial supervision," he said. "There is, understandably, a deep-seated uneasiness and apprehension that this capability will be used to intrude upon cherished privacy of law-abiding citizens." Recognizing that national security cases presented distinct problems not found in the investigation of other crimes, he noted that such cases also endanger constitutionally protected speech more. History "documents the tendency of Government—however benevolent and benign its motives—to view with suspicion those who most fervently dispute its policies." Because of this tendency, Powell said, "Fourth Amendment protections become the more necessary when the targets of official surveillance may be those suspected of unorthodoxy in their political beliefs. The danger to political dissent is acute where the Government attempts to act under so vague a concept as the power to protect 'domestic security.'" Courts must ensure that internal security concerns do not infringe on free speech. "The price of lawful public dissent must not be a dread of subjection to an unchecked surveillance power. Nor must the fear of unauthorized official eavesdropping deter vigorous citizen dissent and discussion of Government action in private conversation. For private dissent, no less than open public discourse, is essential to our free society."[46]

Although the Court would intervene to right specific wrongs, its members would not stop intelligence-gathering operations when complaints were more general. A week after the Court said that presidentially ordered electronic surveillance had to be supervised by the courts, the justices refused to stop the army from gathering information on civil disturbances and the people involved in them. Although the plaintiffs in the suit argued that such operations had a chilling effect on their freedom of speech, a Court majority accepted the army's contention that its files were built only on material found in the public domain and decided that no specific infringement of constitutional rights had been proven. The mere possibility of infringement of those rights, said Chief Justice Warren Burger for a five-member majority, was insufficient grounds to stop the army's efforts.[47]

Four members of the Court dissented, arguing that the army's intelligence-gathering operations did indeed infringe on First Amendment rights. William O. Douglas did not believe that the information in the army's files came from such benign sources as newspaper clippings. "The Army uses undercover agents to infiltrate these civilian groups and to reach into confidential files of students and other groups. The Army moves as a secret group among civilian audiences, using cameras and electronic ears for surveillance." Since the information gathered was widely distributed to other law enforcement agencies, Douglas perceived a distinct chill on freedom of expression. "Those who already walk submissively will say there is no cause for alarm. But submissiveness is not our heritage. The First Amendment was designed to allow rebellion to remain as our heritage. The Constitution was designed to keep government off the backs of the people. The Bill of Rights was added to keep the precincts of belief and expression, of the press, of political and social activities free from surveillance." According to Douglas, the Bill of Rights was designed "to allow men to be free and independent and to assert their rights against government. There can be no influence more paralyzing of that objective than Army surveillance. When an intelligence officer looks over every nonconformist's shoulder in the library, or walks invisibly by his side in a picket line, or infiltrates his club, the America once extolled as the voice of liberty heard around the world no longer is cast in the image which Jefferson and Madison designed."[48]

Indeed, Douglas had a valid point, for Thomas Jefferson and James Madison lived in a world of great fear similar to that experienced during the Nixon administration. Much of that apprehension had been generated by political forces, as in the Nixon administration, and Jefferson and Madison were outsiders who had to struggle to maintain their right to speak against entrenched power. As with the antiwar protesters of Nixon's time, Jefferson and Madison had different visions of America's future from those held by George Washington, John Adams, and Alexander Hamilton. The nation would have been far different had the two Virginians been successfully quieted by the Federalists. The fact that the nation not only survived the dissent of Jefferson and of Madison but had been enriched by it seemed lost on the Nixon administration, which warmly greeted one of the final pieces in its plan to suppress information about the nation's dissidents.

Perhaps the reporter's privilege case decided in June 1972 was the biggest blow of all against the media. The decision struck at the core of press operations: the ability of reporters, if necessary, to keep the sources of their information confidential. Journalists and sources had had such informal relationships for years, and at times, efforts to protect their sources had placed those journalists in jeopardy. John Nugent, for instance, was found in contempt of Congress for refusing to tell who gave him a copy of the Treaty of Guadalupe Hidalgo at the end of the Mexican War.[49] Because of the potential for trouble, the first so-called shield law, which allowed reporters to conceal the names of sources in certain instances, was enacted in Maryland at the end of the nineteenth century.[50] Few states followed Maryland's lead, and no such provision was found in federal laws. In 1915 the federal government tried to force a New York journalist to reveal the sources of his information about problems in the customs service. The journalist responded by taking the Fifth Amendment, arguing, in effect, that revealing the data might tend to incriminate him in some way.[51] In the late 1950s and early

1960s, more cases surfaced. In 1958, Marie Torre, a reporter for the *New York Herald Tribune,* went to jail for refusing to answer the questions of attorneys for Judy Garland who demanded to know who had made disparaging remarks that had hurt Miss Garland's career. When information went to the heart of a legal case, that court decided, reporters had no right to keep the names of sources confidential.[52] Thus, reporter's privilege had had a fairly long and fairly uncertain history in American jurisprudence. The fact that courts, at times, failed to find protection for journalists' sources in no way dissuaded the reporters from promising to keep the names of informants confidential.

The Nixon administration's assault on reporter's privilege was primarily directed at journalists who had won the confidence of dissident groups. Three cases were joined together for hearing by the Supreme Court in 1972. One involved a reporter who had interviewed drug users; the others involved journalists who had won the confidence of Black Panther leaders. In each instance, the reporter was asked by a grand jury to reveal the names of informants and other information that they had promised to keep confidential. In each case, the reporter claimed that such inquiries would dry up their sources and infringe on the First Amendment.

Five members of the Court found that a reporter's privilege simply did not exist and that journalists, as other citizens, must testify when asked to do so. Writing for the majority, Justice Byron R. White noted that "the First Amendment does not invalidate every incidental burdening of the press that may result from the enforcement of civil or criminal statutes." Consequently, "newsmen are not exempt from the normal duty of appearing before a grand jury and answering questions relevant to a criminal investigation." The Court's decision, White said, did not affect First Amendment rights. "This conclusion itself involves no restraint on what newspapers may publish or on the type or quality of information reporters may seek to acquire, nor does it threaten the vast bulk of confidential relationships between reporters and their sources," he said. "Only where news sources themselves are implicated in crime or possess information relevant to the grand jury's task need they or the reporter be concerned about grand jury subpoenas."[53]

To Justice White, sources wished to conceal their names to avoid criminal prosecution: "We cannot seriously entertain the notion that the First Amendment protects a newsman's agreement to conceal the criminal conduct of his source, or evidence thereof, on the theory that it is better to write about crime than to do something about it." He also rejected contentions that the flow of information would be cut off if reporters were compelled to testify before a grand jury. "The relationship of many informants to the press is a symbiotic one which is unlikely to be greatly inhibited by the threat of subpoena: quite often, such informants are members of a minority political or cultural group that relies heavily on the media to propagate its views, publicize its aims, and magnify its exposure to the public." Because of this fact, "we doubt if the informer who prefers anonymity but is sincerely interested in furnishing evidence of crime will always or very often be deterred by the prospect of dealing with those public authorities characteristically charged with the duty to protect the public interest as well as his."[54]

Justice William O. Douglas denounced the majority for restricting debate on essential national issues. He acknowledged that granting journalists immunity from testifying in court proceedings would allow them to bring unsettling information to the public, but Douglas said the press was to "explore and investigate events, inform the people of what is going on, and to expose the harmful as well as the good influences at work" and even to "bring anxiety or even fear to the bureaucracies, departments, or officials of government." He could see "no higher function performed under our constitutional regime."[55]

Although three other members of the Court agreed with Douglas, the Nixon administration had won the day. No longer would it be hampered by journalistic complaints that governmental subpoenas interfered with the First Amendment right to gather the news. The Supreme Court, the final arbiter of the Constitution, had decided by the slimmest of margins that the First Amendment provided no such protection. Journalists asked Congress for a federal shield law, but after months of hearings, the effort failed.[56] In the absence of a legally provided shield, reporters asked to testify had the option of revealing the desired information or of going to jail for contempt of court. A number of journalists chose jail,[57] but others pulled back from controversial stories. Each time a journalist debated whether a story was worth spending time in jail for, Richard Nixon won another victory over the press.

All of the credit for the increasing timidity of the American newspaper press, however, should not be laid at the doorstep of the Nixon administration. Much of the press's conservatism came once again from a growing concern about the financial bottom line. By the Nixon years, the face of American newspaper journalism had changed significantly. Although the number of daily newspapers in the nation had remained relatively stable at 1,749 since the end of World War II,[58] the newspaper world had changed dramatically by 1972. In 1972, for example, fewer than 4 percent of the nation's cities had competing newspapers, down from 15 percent in 1950 and from about 60 percent in 1910. Chain newspapers accounted for more than 60 percent of the nation's daily circulation in 1972, up from about 43 percent in 1950. The ten largest newspaper groups accounted for one-fourth of the annual revenue for the entire industry and for one-third of the total circulation.[59] Newspapers were buying newspapers and creating bigger and more profitable groups; larger groups were merging with smaller chains.

The newspaper business continued to be highly profitable and very attractive to potential buyers. Despite publishers' complaints about the inability of newspapers to make money, media critic Ben Bagdikian said that in 1971, the average return on sales for the newspapers listed on the stock exchange was 7.9 percent, making the newspaper industry the third most profitable in the United States.[60] And for the first time in the nation's history, Americans could see just how profitable the newspaper business was. Due to quirks in the federal inheritance tax laws, many family-held corporations became public corporations during the 1960s, and Securities and Exchange Commission requirements placed newspaper financial information on the public record. The income of many newspaper groups grew still more due to diversification. Many newspaper groups, for instance, were heavily involved in broadcasting. Known as cross-media operations because they operated both broadcasting and newspaper outlets, in 1972 chains controlled 36 percent of the daily newspapers, 25 percent of the television stations, 8.6 percent of the AM radio operations, and 9.5 percent of the FM radio stations in the country. A 1970 study showed that in 72 of the 1,500 American cities that had daily newspapers the newspaper publisher also controlled the community's broadcasting outlet.[61]

The ramifications of this economic power on freedom of expression were almost mind-boggling. In the communities where one person controlled both broadcasting and newspaper outlets, the opportunities for manipulating the information presented to the public were immense. Even if the publisher/licensee had no underhanded motives in mind, just the lack of competition could influence the amount and the nature of information provided. Such increased profit margins and stock market listings led to new problems for freedom of expression. When a newspaper group wished to convince investors to buy stock in its public corporation, its officers knew that the least bit of controversy could adversely affect stock values. When friends of Richard Nixon filed challenges to the licenses of two television stations owned by the *Washington Post,* that corporation's stock dropped on Wall Street.[62] Controversy obviously was not good for business, and newspaper publishers knew it. Many of them became even less willing to challenge the status quo.

In addition, publishers had won a special favor from Congress in 1970. In 1969, the Supreme Court had issued a ruling that stunned the business side of newspaper operations as much as the reporter's privilege decision would the news side. For a number of years, newspaper publishers around the country had been entering into joint operating agreements. These accords occurred in communities where two newspapers existed under different owners but where one of the two voices was actually or allegedly in danger of going out of business. To save the second voice, the newspapers entered into a unique agreement in which the weaker publication used the advertising, circulation, and production facilities of the stronger publication. Only the news operations remained separate. The Justice Department brought suit against one of these cooperative agreements, charging that joint operating contracts violated antitrust laws because they allowed price fixing for advertising and circulation, profit pooling, and market control. The Supreme Court agreed.[63]

Writing the majority opinion was that stalwart defender of First Amendment values William O. Douglas. His taking on the opinion seems as contradictory as Hugo Black writing the main opinion in the Associated Press antitrust case in 1945. But both men found the business practices of the press antithetical to the freedom of the press they saw guaranteed by the First Amendment. "Neither news gathering nor news dissemination is being regulated by the present decree," Douglas wrote. "It deals only with restraints on certain business or commercial practices. The restraints on competition with which the present decree deals comport neither with the antitrust laws nor with the First Amendment."[64] He then proceeded to quote Black's comment in the Associated Press case that "a command that the government itself shall not impede the free flow of ideas does not afford nongovernmental combinations a refuge if they impose restraints upon that constitutionally guaranteed freedom. Freedom to publish means freedom for all and not for some."[65] The newspapers involved in joint operating agreements were ordered to dissolve the arrangements that protected them from the challenges of doing business on their own and to resume full competition with one another.

Greatly distressed by the Court's ruling, representatives of twenty-two newspapers involved in these agreements besieged Congress for relief. Publications in such major cities as San Francisco, Miami, St. Louis, and Pittsburgh were entangled in the lobbying effort. Newspaper chains caught up in the controversy included Cox, Knight, Ridder, Hearst, and Scripps-Howard. The newspaper owners persuaded Congress to grant newspapers participating in joint operating agreements a special exemption from the antitrust laws. The Newspaper Preservation Act[66] was enacted by a vote of 64 to 13 in the Senate and 292 to 87 in the House.[67] Richard Nixon signed it without question, despite advice from his attorney general to the contrary. The president, however, knew what he was doing. The law required any further joint operating agreements to be approved by the attorney general. Any renewals or changes in the existing agreements also had to be filed with the Justice Department.[68] Now, newspaper publishers would be beholden to the White House.

But Richard Nixon had more than a legislative lever to use against the nation's press, for the American people again were questioning the quality of the nation's journalism. Journalists had been infected by the social changes of the 1960s and early 1970s and now were demanding the right to participate in life rather than just observe it. To a large part, they were simply returning to the practices of the nineteenth century, but to late-twentieth-century editors and publishers, journalists were rocking the foundations of a free and impartial press. In addition, some reporters were demanding the right to advocate certain points of view in their writing rather than simply serve as a conveyor belt for facts provided by sources.[69] To make matters even worse, some journalists were demanding a voice in running their newspapers.[70] If management ignored their demands, the reporters were likely to begin publishing a journalism review that would tell the whole world the sins of omission and commission that could be laid at the owner's feet.[71] To the nation's publishers, who found the changing American scene as appalling as most members of the Nixon White House, these developments were simply the last straw. Not only were newspapers being attacked regularly and, the publishers thought, unfairly by the nation's political leaders, but the publications were being attacked from within. In addition, the consumer movement had convinced the American people that, in the final analysis, the nation's newspapers were responsible to *them*.

The criticism being directed at American journalism during these years really was nothing new. Commentary about the way in which the newspaper press operated had become increasingly hostile since the turn of the century. For decades, journalists, politicians, and other interested parties had inspected the press and found it sorely wanting, generally because the publishers were more interested in making money than in serving the people who bought their publications. Suggestions for improvement had ranged from studying journalism in college to beginning professional organizations for journalists to passing laws to require newspapers to improve their performance. By the 1970s, the first two proposals had long been in effect with little impact on the quality of the product produced. Still the criticism continued, as did the suggestions for improvement. In 1967, for instance, A. H. Raskin, assistant editor of the editorial page for the *New York Times,* commented, "The credibility gap is not a White House exclusive; it also separates press and people. There is a disturbing skepticism among large groups of readers, including many of the best educated and most intellectually alive, about whether what they read in their newspapers is either true or relevant."[72] The term credibility gap had been coined by journalists to describe the discrepancy between the White House version of the Vietnam War and what others saw as factual. Now, the term was being applied with increasing regularity to reporting and reality.

What triggered the latest attack on the press is hard to pinpoint. Undoubtedly, the bad news that all forms of media had been bringing into American homes in the 1960s was a significant factor. The press had told of campus unrest, antiwar protests, and death and dying in Vietnam almost daily. And from time immemorial, the practice has always been to attack the messenger for the message. Critics from within the profession, however, were astonished when publishers of three major newspapers in New York City—the *Herald Tribune,* the *Journal-American,* and the *World-Telegram*—merged them into one super publication in 1966. The *World Journal Tribune* lasted about a year before it, too, folded. The crassness demonstrated in killing off so many newspapers jolted many critics into action. "In New York, as elsewhere, the ultimate loser," said press critic Bagdikian, "is the public, which has been exhibiting an historic thirst for information on public affairs that has been met by the typical American paper by a reduction in the amount of news it prints."[73]

From such criticism came calls for the newspaper industry to take corrective action. In his *New York Times* article, Raskin had called for the creation of "Departments of Internal Criticism to check on the fairness and adequacy of their coverage and comment." The department head, he said, "ought to be given enough independence in the paper to serve as an *ombudsman* for the readers, armed with authority to get something done about valid complaints and to propose methods for more effective performance of all the paper's services to the community, particularly the patrol it keeps on the frontiers of thought and action."[74] From this proposal and similar suggestions by others came the assignment at some American newspapers of an ombudsman, an insider with significant journalistic experience, to monitor newspaper performance. Ombudsmen would field complaints from the general public, write memos for use internally, and, at times, produce columns for publication. The first ombudsman went to work on the *Louisville Courier-Journal* shortly after Raskin's article appeared.[75]

But the appearance of the ombudsman was insufficient to stem the growing tide of criticism of the news media in general and the newspaper in particular. In 1969, a group of concerned citizens, most of whom were uninvolved with the media, formed Accuracy in Media, Inc. (AIM), an organization designed to monitor newspaper, radio, and television performance and to complain vociferously about the perceived misuse of those institutions. At first, AIM officials tried to obtain corrections and balance from the offending publication; when their efforts were rebuffed, as they generally were, AIM leaders then publicized their complaints in any forum possible. A favorite tactic was taking out full-page advertisements in an offending newspaper to highlight the publication's inadequacies. Primary targets were the *New York Times* and the *Washington Post,* the two newspapers that claimed a national audience.

Many journalists who felt the prick of AIM's criticism labeled the organization as a nongovernmental ally of the Nixon administration. For example, Charles Seib, managing editor of the *Washington Star-News,* charged that Abraham Kalish, the organization's executive secretary, was "for accuracy as long it's his kind of accuracy." Judging from the material that Kalish found fault with, Seib believed that Kalish "obviously represents a right-wing point of view." Kalish, who served as unpaid leader of the organization, countered that "most of the news media are liberal-oriented, and most of the complaints that come to us concern the liberal media." "I make a special effort to find conservative error," he said, "but we can't make up cases if they don't exist or if we don't get complaints."[76] And Kalish readily disputed any impression that "AIM is a kind of kooky, right-wing outfit that nit-picks, creates mountains out of molehills and is not really competent to judge the work of the professional in the news business." On the contrary, he said, "Accuracy in Media has a record of being extremely accurate. We scrupulously avoid wild charges and generalizations. We wish our critics could say the same. We are not right-wing kooks. We are in the center. Admittedly that puts us to the right of those that are left of center, but I see no reason why that should put us beyond the pale."[77]

Regardless of whether Kalish and his supporters considered themselves to be left, right, or in the center politically, their criticisms were unwanted by journalists who traditionally turned a deaf ear to comments from nonprofessionals. In fact, more often than not, journalists simply ignored all complaints about their work, citing the First Amendment as an absolute bar to all attempts by anyone—citizen or president—to tell the press how to do its job. By the 1970s, however, that standard position was not sitting well with longtime practicing journalists like Norman Isaacs, a past president of the American Society of Newspaper Editors: "Each time wise, thoughtful men had asked us as a profession to look into our standards and our practices we had taken refuge in the First Amendment." Criticism by Vice President Spiro Agnew was brushed off on such grounds, and public opinion polls that showed that a fair percentage of the American people believed that American newspapers did not deal fairly with political or social issues were ignored for the same reason. This behavior, Isaacs said in the fall of 1970, was no longer acceptable or wise. "We needed to be rebuilding faith in the American press; the shrugging off of inaccuracy and slanting in news columns was the most dangerous course we could follow."[78] He suggested that to protect the First Amendment privileges of the press, the newspaper industry must put its house in order.

The vehicle for improving the image of the newspaper press, Isaacs said, was a national news council that would hear complaints about media actions and give publicity to inappropriate behavior. The council, in his mind, would have no enforcement power and thus would not breach the protective barriers of the First Amendment, but it would, through publicity, be able to coerce the press into more reputable behavior. The idea of a national news council had been debated for some twenty years[79] and had been tried in various communities around the country.[80] But the press council idea had been substantially discredited because it had originated with a group of academics who knew nothing about the newspaper business. The intensity of criticism leveled at the press in the late 1960s and early 1970s, however, made the council idea somewhat more attractive—especially if it would stave off public and governmental criticisms and if it would be staffed by individuals closely tied to the communications industry.

Indeed, most segments of the mass communications field had come to believe that something had to be done to protect the press. Criticism was coming from all directions and all segments of society. Dr. W. Walter Menninger, a noted psychiatrist, for instance, suggested that journalists be licensed as doctors and lawyers are licensed to show that they met minimal standards.[81] And the Kerner Commission, which had been assigned by President Lyndon Johnson to look into the problem of racial disorders that had rocked American society, condemned press reportage of racial matters: "We have found a significant imbalance between what actually happened in our cities and what the newspaper, radio, and television coverage of the riots told us happened," the commission said. "Lacking other sources of information, we formed our original impressions and beliefs from what we saw on television, heard on the radio, and read in newspapers and magazines. We are deeply concerned that millions of other Americans, who must rely on the mass media, likewise formed incorrect impressions and judgments about what went on in many American cities." The American media failed society in yet another, perhaps more fundamental way, according to the Kerner report. "The news media have failed to analyze and report adequately on racial problems in the United States and, as a related matter, to meet the Negro's legitimate expectations in journalism. By and large, news organizations have failed to communicate to both their black and white audiences a sense of the problems America faces and the sources of potential solutions."[82]

Nor did journalists cover civil disorders themselves well. A special task force of the National Commission on the Causes and Prevention of Violence took journalists to task for their misbehavior at riot scenes. The media caused multiple problems whenever they showed up at the sites of civil disorders. They spread rumors; they provided live coverage that showed potential looters just where police were located; they drew people to the scene of the violence; and they focused on violent and emotional activities rather than trying to put events in perspective. In addition, the press contributed to conditions that caused unrest because of "the inability of new and different voices to gain routine and peaceful access to the centralized new media." The times, the task report said, called for new approaches to problems, and the media must lead the hunt for those new responses.[83]

American journalism was, as always, slow to respond to new challenges. In fact, journalistic failure to provide a realistic view of society and to equip Americans to make appropriate and necessary decisions prompted another challenge to the newspaper industry: the drive for a right of access to the press without the intervention or supervision of the owners. The access campaign began much the way that the privacy crusade began late in the nineteenth century—through an article in the *Harvard Law Review*. In 1967, George Washington University Law School professor Jerome A. Barron castigated the press for refusing to share a variety of ideas with the general public. Press indifference to new ideas "becomes critical when a comparatively few private hands are in a position to determine not only the content of information but its very availability, when the soap box yields to radio and the political pamphlet to the monopoly newspaper," he wrote. The problem takes on added dimensions when one realizes that "the mass communication industry is [not] pushing certain ideas and rejecting others but rather that it is using the free speech and press guarantees to avoid opinions instead of acting as a sounding board for their expression."[84]

Because the press refused to deal with controversial ideas, Barron said, new ways of communicating have been developed to "convey unorthodox, unpopular, and new ideas. Sit-ins and demonstrations" show "the inadequacy of old media as instruments to afford full and effective hearing for all points of view." New ways of communication lead to additional problems because "attention-getting devices so abound in the modern world that new ones soon become tiresome. The dissenter must look for ever more unsettling assaults on the mass mind if he is to have continuing impact." The continuing escalation of communication causes many problems, Barron continued. "It is a measure of the jaded and warped standards of the media that ideas which normally would never be granted a forum are given serious network coverage if they become sufficiently enmeshed in mass demonstration or riot and violence. Ideas are denied admission into media until they are first disseminated in a way that challenges and disrupts the social order. Then they may be discussed and given notice." Such a turn of events led Barron to ask, "Is it too bold to suggest that it is necessary to ensure access to the mass media for unorthodox ideas in order to make effective the guarantee against repression?" Barron argued that "nongoverning minorities in control of the means of communication should perhaps be inhibited from restraining free speech (by the denial of access to their media) even more than governing majorities are restrained by the first amendment." His goal was "an interpretation of the first amendment which focuses on the idea that restraining the hand of government is quite useless in assuring free speech if a restraint on access is effectively secured by private groups. A constitutional prohibition against governmental restrictions on expression is effective only if the Constitution ensures an adequate opportunity for discussion."[85]

The idea that newspapers could, in some way, be forced to allow dissident ideas into their columns caused great difficulty for press representatives who believed that they alone decided what ideas to present. The closest that they would come to recognizing any merits in the idea was in developing what they called an op-ed page, or a page opposite the editorial page, in which opinions differing from house views could be presented. The access movement, however, refused to die. The American Civil Liberties Union became one of its backers, and by 1972, a case involving a state law requiring newspapers to allow persons criticized in their columns space to respond entered the court system.

In the meantime, some newspaper publishers, with reluctance, got behind an idea put forth by the Twentieth Century Fund for a national press council. In 1972, the Fund issued a formal statement on establishing the council and announced plans for financing it. The fund task force, which included broadcast and print journalists as well as public figures, was not overly optimistic: "The national media council proposed here will not resolve all the problems facing the print and broadcast media, nor will it answer all of the criticisms voiced by the public and by the politicians." With cooperation from the media, the council "will, however, be an independent body to which the public can take its complaints about press coverage. It will act as a strong defender of press freedom. It will attempt to make the media accountable to the public and to lessen the tensions between the press and the government."[86]

Funding the council proved to be the easiest hurdle to surmount. The council made several false starts in picking a chairman and finally proved successful in meshing the person to the assignment when veteran journalist Norman E. Isaacs took over. Essentially, the council operated as a publicity agent, hearing complaints from individuals and responses from media, and airing its determination as to who was more in the right. The council had no enforcement power and depended on the good will of the media to make the hearings work and to publicize the council's findings. The key to its operations, then, was the cooperation of the media, and media reaction was mixed at best. The Associated Press, United Press International, CBS, *Time, Newsweek, Wall Street Journal,* and *Christian Science Monitor* were among those media outlets agreeing to cooperate with the new organization, with varying degrees of enthusiasm and differing extents of support. ABC, NBC, and the Los Angeles Times–Washington Post News Service adopted a wait-and-see attitude.[87]

Under such a cloud, the National News Council began operations. One of its first inquiries made journalists even more wary. In October 1973, shortly after the council began work, Richard Nixon charged the television networks once again with biased reporting, and the news council offered to investigate the president's accusations. The best council representatives could do was to meet with presidential press secretary Ronald Ziegler, who told members that the president was distressed about a wide variety of allegedly biased reporting by the media. With no specifics forthcoming, the council dropped its inquiry.[88] The possible investigation of the Nixon allegations was the most important item ever to reach the council's agenda. Most inquiries were far less momentous, and cooperation from the nation's media never was great. When the council's funds ran out in 1984, it quietly disappeared from the scene.

By the mid-1970s, the print media were well aware that accountability rested solely in their own hands. The public access case wound up before the Supreme Court in 1974, where a unanimous bench dealt the death blow to Jerome Barron's notion. The case involved a 1913 Florida statute that required newspapers that criticized a candidate for public office to give that candidate, free upon demand, space to answer the charges. Although Chief Justice Warren Burger acknowledged that the conditions under which the press operated in the 1970s were far different from those of the 1790s when the First Amendment was adopted, he found no reason to interfere in a newspaper's editorial decisions. Despite the difficulty that advocates of unpopular causes had in getting their views put before the public, Burger believed that forcing newspapers to print information would make them even less likely to touch controversial issues.[89] The fact that newspapers had ignored most controversial ideas through much of their history made little impression on a Court determined to uphold the constitutional barrier against the government making laws that affected freedom of the press.

Broadcasters, however, were in quite a different situation as Richard Nixon prepared to seek a second term. No one believed that the First Amendment prevented the government from interfering with what was broadcast into American homes. True, in recent years, broadcast journalists had won major battles over the right to refuse editorial advertisements and over the right to defy a congressional subpoena for material dealing with "The Selling of the Pentagon," but they had also suffered terribly under the repeated onslaughts of the Nixon administration. Worse still, they had lost major battles in the court system. The most costly challenge in terms of potential revenue involved the antismoking campaign of the mid- to late 1960s, when millions of dollars in advertising revenue were lost when cigarette advertising was banned from the airwaves.[90] And licensees also were reminded by a 1969 Supreme Court decision that they must allow individuals attacked on the airwaves free time to respond to that criticism.[91]

Because broadcasting was so different legally from newspaper publishing the Nixon administration's intimidation of the electronic media was much easier. And because of the amount of cross-ownership of media involved, owners of print outlets could be reached by threatening their broadcast licenses. At times rumblings would emanate from deep within the administration that sounded suspiciously like threats to license holders. For instance, the Justice Department started making sounds as if it was finally going to take action against newspapers holding broadcast licenses in the same community. The effort to make newspaper owners divest themselves of broadcast entanglements dated back to FDR, when his administration tried to strike at publishers' pocketbooks. At the request of the Justice Department, the FCC once again began to study the issue, thus seeming to allow the threat to remain on the back burner.[92] By 1975, however, the FCC issued orders banning the establishment of new cross-media arrangements in the same communities.[93] FCC officials based the order on the need to increase diversity within the communications business. By the time the FCC acted, the potential for monopolization of the broadcast industry by newspapers had substantially decreased. According to figures supplied by the American Newspaper Publishers Association (ANPA), newspapers owned 48 percent of the nation's television stations in 1948; in 1969, only 14 percent of the nation's television operations were run by newspapers. In 1975 the National Association of Broadcasters placed cross-ownership at 7 percent.[94] When the FCC finished redefining just what part of the cross-ownership problem it wished to address, only eight television and newspaper combinations and ten radio-newspaper combinations were singled out for imposed divestiture. Special exemptions brought the total down to seven television-newspaper combinations and eight radio-newspaper ownerships.

The ANPA, of course, challenged the ruling, arguing that the First Amendment rights of the newspapers were infringed by the order. The FCC was making newspaper owners second-class citizens by designing rules only for them, the publishers' organization said, as it viewed the divestiture order as part of the Nixon administration's plot to hurt political opponents. In response, the FCC pointed to the long history of Supreme Court support for regulation of the business side of the newspaper industry, which officials said was exactly what the divestiture order affected. In addition, FCC commissioners said the antitrust case against the Associated Press in 1945 supported the commission position that breaking up monopolies restricting the flow of diverse ideas did not violate the First Amendment.[95] The ANPA, quite naturally, rejected the FCC arguments and took the issue into the courts. In 1978, a unanimous Supreme Court upheld the FCC's divestiture order, with Justice Thurgood Marshall quoting approvingly from Hugo Black's decision in the Associated Press case thirty-three years before.[96] Although relatively few cross-ownership arrangements were affected by this order, the fear remained that Richard Nixon's vendetta against the press would continue to haunt newspapers with connections to broadcast operations.

Such concerns were not totally unfounded, given the scatter-gun approach that the Nixon administration took in attacking broadcast operations. If network news operations proved impervious to assault, then other areas might be more vulnerable. During these years, for example, the FCC began attacking profitable programming centers. Claiming to be reacting to pressure from viewers, FCC rules beginning in 1971 limited networks to only three hours of programming per night between the prime-time hours of 7 and 11 p.m. instead of the four hours that had been traditional. Although the rule affected only the top fifty markets in the country, all network affiliates would feel its impact because networks would not produce four hours of programming only for the less profitable outlets. The onslaught on network programming actually had begun in 1965, but the rule stemmed from what was perceived to be a Nixon FCC. The 7 to 8 p.m. time slot went back to local affiliates for allegedly improved programming, including first-run syndicated shows that the FCC claimed were routinely excluded while the networks controlled the full prime-time schedule of their affiliates.[97]

The attack against the networks continued in 1972, when the Justice Department filed suit against the networks for monopolizing prime-time entertainment production in order to increase profits. In the wake of the quiz-show scandals that had plagued the industry in the 1950s, the networks had assumed primary control of the programs that they showed. By the 1970s, networks often directly owned or had substantial investments in the production companies that provided the shows for nightly broadcast. The case was based on old statistics that showed significant network financial involvement in programming, a problem that had been remedied after the FCC ruled against these practices in the late 1960s. As with other actions against the networks, the issue had lain dormant until the Nixon administration revived it. In this instance, the networks entered into a consent decree with the Justice Department that drastically limited their financial involvement in the programming they used.[98] Although once again the action had begun under another administration, many observers believed that the administration was using the antitrust suit to keep networks in line during the upcoming election.

Preparations for the election campaign and for what the president and his staff assumed would be another four years in office continued apace. While Nixon and his associates maintained their attacks on broadcasting and print media and worked to eliminate all remnants of the antiwar movement, they took action on yet another subject dear to the president's heart. As with most presidents, Nixon was regularly annoyed by leaks of information to the press, but although others simply railed against unauthorized releases of information, Nixon decided to *do* something about them.

He began his campaign to protect government information with a seemingly innocuous revision of the nation's classification policy. His executive order began by reminding the public that "the interests of the United States and its citizens are best served by making information regarding the affairs of Government readily available to the public. This concept of an informed citizenry is reflected in the Freedom of Information Act and," he added somewhat disingenuously, "in the current public information policies of the executive branch." But, the executive order continued, some information was too sensitive for public distribution "because it bears directly on the effectiveness of our national defense and the conduct of our foreign relations" and thus "must be subject to some constraints for the security of our Nation and the safety of our people and our allies. To protect against actions hostile to the United States, of both an overt and covert nature, it is essential that such official information and material be given only limited dissemination." In fact, the order warned, "wrongful disclosure of such information or material is recognized in the Federal Criminal Code as providing a basis for prosecution."[99] His warnings given, Nixon's executive order then discussed the details of classifying and declassifying documents and explained a monitoring program that the White House established to supervise the entire process.

The executive order was put together in an attempt to circumvent congressional intervention in the process of classifying executive branch documents. The process, which had begun under the Truman administration, had always been carried out under the executive powers of the president.[100] In announcing his plan, Nixon claimed that it was designed to remove much of the secrecy from governmental operations. In his orders for declassification of information, for instance, top-secret information was to be downgraded and eventually released after ten years, unless officials could justify maintaining secrecy. In any event, after a document had been classified as secret for thirty years, it was to become public automatically. Despite the language of the document, the order was filled with enough loopholes to keep most information safely bottled up in the executive branch—just where Richard Nixon wanted it.

Appropriately enough, news of the president's planned order on classification policies leaked to the press a month or so before Nixon released it. Its contents worried the journalists, with the *Washington Post* predicting that the warning against unauthorized disclosure of information was in essence a suggestion that "legislation be enacted in imitation of the British Official Secrets Act which would impose criminal penalties not only on the government employee who divulges classified information but on the recipient of the information as well."[101] The Official Secrets Act of Great Britain, first enacted in 1911, protects all government information from disclosure in the press unless officially authorized. Journalists who publish information without permission face criminal penalties. The act consequently prevents almost all talk of governmental business in the press—unless officials decide that such discussion is appropriate.[102]

But did Richard Nixon intend to propose an American version of the Official Secrets Act? The answer became clearer in March 1973, when he sent Congress his Criminal Code Reform Act. Hidden away in text that tried to revive the death penalty and kill the insanity defense was a provision that would have made it a felony to have classified information in one's possession without authorization. Another section would allow the government to bring charges against any employee who "knowingly communicates such [classified] information to a person not authorized to receive it."[103] The legislative proposal was more than 600 pages long, but some members of Congress found the language dealing with the unauthorized release of information and denounced it. Senator Thomas Eagleton, Democrat of Missouri, for example, said that the provisions "when read together, authorize the jailing of newsmen for up to seven years for publishing information which has been classified—even where the newsman can show that the information was improperly classified, that it related to matters of waste or corruption, and that its disclosure clearly served the public interest."[104]

To Senator Edmund Muskie, Democrat of Maine, "on the surface, [the] language sounds reasonable, it does what existing law already does by insuring secrecy of data about our defense codes, about our electronic surveillance techniques, about military installations and weapons, about our atomic secrets and plans and operations which might aid our enemies." This information, he said, "is already kept secret by laws which punish its disclosure with intent to damage America and its security." But, he added, if the proposal became law, disclosure of information that was important for the people to know also could be blocked. "The only purpose behind further expansion of the secrecy laws," he said, "would be the effort to silence dissent within the government."[105]

Under the proposed legislation, journalists could be prosecuted if they did anything other than return classified information in their possession to the government. The proposal called for jail sentences of up to seven years and fines up to $50,000 for unauthorized publication. The 1973 measure was too complicated to be enacted in that term of Congress, and a new version of the bill had to be introduced in 1975. Known as S.1, this version of the criminal code revision was more than 700 pages long and was a good-faith effort to revise a criminal code that had grown up piecemeal over the nation's history. The proposal, once again, offered something for everyone: restoration of the death penalty, compensation for victims of crime, broadening of the federal government's ability to conduct wiretaps, liberalization of the marijuana laws, and punishment of reporters caught with certain government information in their possession.[106]

In the case of reporters, the offenses were even more broadly defined, and the punishments more severe than in the 1973 version. For instance, reporters could be prosecuted for receiving stolen property if they accepted a government document without official permission. They could be found guilty of a crime if they communicated national defense information that they were not supposed to have to someone unauthorized to receive it—in other words if they published it. If reporters published unclassified information relating to the national defense, they could be sent to jail for up to seven years and fined up to $100,000. In the latter instance, however, the reporter had to know that the information could damage the interests of the United States. And anyone who leaked classified information to a reporter could be charged with a crime, even if the person was no longer in government employ and if the document in question had been improperly classified.[107]

Such restrictions on the dissemination of government information were quickly denounced. The Reporters Committee on Freedom of the Press, a legal defense and research organization that promoted First Amendment freedoms, condemned the measure: "It is abundantly clear that the administration-supported S.1 is a crude and unconstitutional attempt to silence the type of aggressive news reporting which produced articles about the Pentagon Papers, the My Lai massacre, the Watergate coverup, the CIA domestic spying, the FBI domestic spying and other government misdeeds." This reporting, spokesman Jack Landau admitted, "has been embarrassing to the government and . . . has depended, in whole, or in part on government-compiled information and reports frequently supplied to the press by present or former government employes [*sic*] without authorization." If S.1 was enacted, Landau said, it "would severely restrict the current ability of the public to learn about government policy-making decisions, government reports and government crime by establishing . . . new types of criminal censorship." Under S.1, he said, "the only time a reporter would be legally free from the threat of a federal prosecution as the result of publishing government information is if the information came to him from a government handout—precisely the type of censorship system which the First Amendment was designed to eliminate."[108]

An amalgam of the Nixon-backed proposal and a criminal code revision package sponsored by members of Congress, S.1 sent a clear message to reporters. The administration was out to stop unauthorized leaks such as those that revealed the government's position in the India-Pakistan war, but Nixon wanted even more. He certainly wanted to make it impossible for any future Daniel Ellsbergs to find outlets for information taken from the government. Since the attempt to impose prior restraint on the *New York Times* and the *Washington Post* had failed miserably and the prosecution of Ellsberg himself was unsuccessful, some way had to be found to protect information harmful to government interests. One of Nixon's main targets became a new breed of government employee: the whistleblower.

The whistleblower was an extremely dangerous dissenter. Almost any employee could become sufficiently alarmed about a governmental action to release information to the press. This form of dissent flowered as protests of other kinds ran rampant throughout the country in the late 1960s and early 1970s. These individuals, men and women at all levels of government and industry, found within themselves the courage to risk their careers in order to point out situations dangerous to the public. Improper care of toxic wastes, problems with nuclear plant construction, and concealment of cost overruns at the Pentagon all were revealed by whistleblowers, individuals whom some scholars call ethical resisters.[109]

Nixon had been burned by these whistleblowers many times. In one instance that impeded his efforts to increase the surveillance of American citizens by government agencies, an army officer who had served in Army Intelligence wrote two articles for the *Washington Monthly* magazine in 1970 detailing abuses. In January 1970, Christopher Pyle, who had left the Army, wrote: "Today, the Army maintains files on the membership, ideology, programs, and practices of virtually every activist political group in the country."[110] Pyle called on the president and Congress to take action to stop these intrusions into American political life. The army pledged to stop its surveillance, but six months later, it still was continuing. Pyle took to print once more. "The Army still watches civilian politics," he said. "Despite over fifty congressional inquiries, the threat of House and Senate hearings, and a lawsuit by the American Civil Liberties Union, more than 1,000 plainclothes soldier-agents continue to monitor the political activities of law-abiding citizens."[111] This time, Congress refused to believe army promises and began the investigations it had only threatened after the first revelations. The surveillance procedures slowly were disbanded.

Thus one aspect of Richard Nixon's program to use the entire federal apparatus to suppress dissent had come to light because of the outrage of one former army officer. As that was happening, at least one member of the U.S. Supreme Court was bestowing his blessing on whistleblower Daniel Ellsberg and his allies, the *New York Times* and the *Washington Post.* Justice Hugo Black, in his concurring opinion in the Pentagon Papers case, noted, "Only a free and unrestrained press can effectively expose deception in government. And paramount among the responsibilities of a free press is the duty to prevent any part of the Government from deceiving the people and sending them off to distant lands to die of foreign fevers and foreign shot and shell." The two newspapers had fulfilled that function. "In my view," Black wrote, "far from deserving condemnation for their courageous reporting, the New York Times, the Washington Post, and other newspapers should be commended for serving the purpose that the Founding Fathers saw so clearly. In revealing the workings of government that led to the Vietnam war, the newspapers nobly did precisely that which the Founders hoped and trusted they would do."[112]

Whistleblowers would continue to play an important role in American society despite Richard Nixon's efforts to silence them. In most cases, they did so publicly, placing their names and reputations on the line. The most famous whistleblower of the entire Nixon administration remains anonymous. That person is, of course, "Deep Throat," the executive branch source that kept *Washington Post* reporters Bob Woodward and Carl Bernstein on the right track as they investigated the Watergate scandal. That relationship, which did much to bring about the downfall of the president, was developing in 1972 as Richard Nixon ran for reelection.

The 1972 campaign was unusual, with much of the strangeness being related to the "dirty tricks" perpetrated against opposition candidates by persons directed by White House insiders. Administration leaders soon targeted Edmund Muskie, Democratic senator from Maine, for attack. He was considered the most dangerous possible opponent for Nixon and had to be driven from the race, preferably before his campaign gained momentum. The goal was to cripple Muskie's candidacy before New Hampshire residents voted in the nation's first presidential primary. The dirty tricksters of the White House found a valuable ally in William Loeb, publisher of the right-wing *Manchester Union Leader*.

Probably the most damaging assault on Muskie came in the form of the so-called "Canuck Letter," which Loeb ran. Although the letter was later tied to Donald Segretti and his dirty tricks campaign, that connection was unknown at the time of publication. The author claimed that a Muskie aide had made derogatory comments about Americans of French-Canadian ancestry, who made up a substantial portion of the New Hampshire electorate. The letter appeared on February 24, 1972, two days before Muskie was due to campaign in the state. On February 25, Loeb published a reprise of a *Newsweek* piece that had run two months earlier that contained comments derogatory to the senator's wife. On February 26, Muskie talked to the press in New Hampshire from the back of a flatbed truck. In the midst of near-blizzard conditions, he attacked Loeb, calling him a "gutless coward," defended his wife, and broke down in tears.[113] His Lincolnesque image had been destroyed, and his hopes for the presidential nomination were doomed.

Reflecting on the problems that his campaign encountered, Muskie said later, "Our campaign was constantly plagued by leaks and disruptions and fabrications." But, he said, "we could never pinpoint who was doing it. . . . Somebody was out to ambush us. We assumed it was being done by Nixon people because that's the nature of this administration; they have no sensitivity to privacy or decency in politics. But we had no proof it was them."[114] The lack of decency and sensitivity that Muskie laid at the doorstep of the administration was underlined when information about the conviction of Senator Thomas Eagleton of Missouri, the Democratic candidate for vice president, for drunk driving and information about his having been hospitalized for treatment of depression was released to the press. Later the responsibility for gathering and releasing this information was placed squarely within the White House.[115] Once again the twisting of data by the president and his aides had corrupted the political system. By denying the American people true information about the candidates, and by manipulating the data that was available to discredit opponents, the Nixon White House had abridged the most fundamental First Amendment rights: the ability to engage in intelligent discussion on political issues, in this case debating the qualifications of rival candidates for the presidency.

In the meantime, Richard Nixon's campaign for the presidency was purring along untouched by the disasters that plagued his Democratic opponents. As the incumbent, Nixon refused to be drawn into the partisan fray. He seldom left the White House to campaign and sought to remain above the issues; when he did travel, he went only to lavishly staged political events. Dan Rather, the CBS White House correspondent, began ending his broadcasts by saying that he was "with the Nixon campaign at the White House."[116] George McGovern, the senator from South Dakota and the Democratic candidate for president, found himself jousting with dozens of Nixon surrogates around the country and unable to make contact with the other principal character in the election, Richard Nixon.

The press, McGovern said, did not do its job in the 1972 election. Because Nixon was unavailable for interrogation—and because the Nixon White House had so intimidated the press by election time—journalists concentrated all of their attention on McGovern. Every flaw in the Democrat's campaign—and there were many—was examined and made public. When he had an opportunity to address a group of International Press Service editors in October 1972, McGovern chastised the press for its behavior. "When a candidate issues press releases but holds no press conferences, it is up to the reporters to inform the country that he is hiding. When a candidate tells a lie to a handpicked crowd," he said, "it is up to reporters to tell the country the truth. And when a candidate will not give answers, it is up to the reporters to keep asking questions—or to keep reminding the people of what they would ask if the candidate would come within shouting distance."[117]

When one reporter, Cassie Mackin of NBC News, tried to behave that way, she found out how quickly the White House could respond. On September 28, 1972, Mackin discussed Nixon's attacks on McGovern's positions. She said that the Nixon campaign, so far, had consisted solely of "speeches before closed audiences—invited guests only." The press had little access to the president to find out what his comments meant. In addition, she said, "there is a serious question of whether President Nixon is setting up straw men by leaving the very strong impression that McGovern is making certain proposals which in fact he is not." After showing a film clip of the president talking about "some who believe" in certain things, Mackin continued, "the President obviously meant McGovern's proposed defense budget, but his criticism never specified how the McGovern plan would weaken the country. On welfare, the President accuses McGovern of wanting to give those on welfare more than those who work—which is not true. On tax reform, the President says McGovern has called for 'confiscation of wealth'—which is not true."[118] Mackin was not even off the air before critical comments from the White House came pouring in. One of three top-ranking officials who called almost immediately, Kenneth Clawson, charged that "she, in effect, called the President a liar."[119]

Clawson's call obviously was a result of a March 1972 suggestion by Patrick J. Buchanan to former Attorney General John Mitchell, who was running the Committee to Re-elect the President. Buchanan proposed monitoring election coverage—" 'clock[ing]' precisely the positive and negative coverage of presidential and vice presidential candidates on the networks." "If we are getting anything more than 'equal time,' this committee can remain silent," the memorandum said, but "if we get anything less than equal time . . . get on the horn to the network President and point this out, indicating that if it is not corrected, and equal time not provided, this will be made an issue in the campaign, and the subject of legislation in the coming Congress."[120]

Despite this tactic, the administration had decided to "let up on the pounding of the press" as part of Nixon's election strategy. Victor Gold, Vice President Agnew's press secretary, reported that strategists believed that "they had things going their way with McGovern" and that it was time to cool the rhetoric. The vice president, who had been the point man in many of the assaults on the press during Nixon's first term, was ordered to avoid attacking the media during the campaign. "We don't want you going out and being abrasive" was the word Gold said the vice president got. The fact that hostilities disappeared for a few months did not cloud the fact, Gold said, that the administration was "geared up for an all-out war against the media" as soon as the election was over.[121]

After several years of bludgeoning by the Nixon administration, few journalists tackled the president during the election. In fact, evaluations of the press coverage of the campaign showed that good journalism—and information upon which voters could make informed decisions—was at an all-time low. In previous national elections, for example, the networks had run prime-time documentaries on key issues; no such programming occurred in 1972. To avoid charges of bias, television and print journalists took to "twining" their stories—providing exactly the same amount of space or time to each candidate, regardless of whether the candidate had done or said anything worthy of attention. This practice was of particular benefit to Richard Nixon, who made few appearances during his run for a second term. In addition, few journalists touched the most controversial story of the campaign: the Watergate break-in. Media critic Ben H. Bagdikian said that of more than four hundred reporters working in Washington during the 1972 election year, fewer than fifteen worked full time on the Watergate story, and some of those journalists worked on the assignment for a very limited period of time. "The average Washington bureau," he said, "had no one working fulltime on the Watergate story." What was even worse, he said, was that "it is possible that more man-hours of investigative journalism were put into the 1962 rumor (never confirmed) that John F. Kennedy had been secretly married in 1947 than were assigned to investigate the Watergate Affair."[122]

Newspaper editorial endorsements tumbled on Nixon's head. Whereas 78 percent of the nation's daily newspapers had endorsed Nixon when he ran against John F. Kennedy in 1960, 80 percent backed him in 1968, when he ran against Hubert H. Humphrey.[123] In 1972, 93 percent of all daily newspapers endorsing a candidate backed Richard Nixon. In fact, whole newspaper chains supported the president regardless of the interests of their individual editors. The orders came from the top. Scripps-Howard Newspapers, for instance, sent out an editorial endorsing the president that was to be printed in all of its publications. The headline was to read: "We Choose Nixon Again."[124] Although experts harbor significant doubts as to the value of newspaper editorial endorsements, the fact that so many publishers, who were conservative in the first place, decided to back the incumbent president likely had some relationship to the president's campaign of intimidation. With a cowed journalistic establishment and a rival candidate who was undermined at every turn by his own ineptness and by the dirty tricks of White House operatives, Richard Nixon won a landslide victory. The president took 520 out of 537 electoral votes; only Massachusetts went into the Democratic column. Although Nixon was unable to bring Republican majorities into Congress with him, to a large extent, the executive branch had decided that it no longer needed to be bothered by Congress. With a second four-year term stretching out before him, Richard Nixon intended to consolidate his position and confirm his supremacy in the nation. One of his first goals, of course, was to silence the few remaining pockets of opposition.

Television networks remained a key target. Clay T. Whitehead, director of the president's Office of Telecommunications Policy, sounded the clarion call for the second term's campaign against the broadcasters in a December 18, 1972, speech. Apparently dissatisfied with the results of their intimidation offensive, the administration attacked the bonds between local affiliates and the three networks. Whitehead presented a wily scheme in his Indianapolis address. The three-year licensing period for local stations simply was too short, he said, and he offered to advocate a five-year license, a change that all local station owners would appreciate. In return, he strongly suggested that the local stations tell the networks that they did not like some of their programming. In fact, he implied that local stations, instead of running the liberal news programming the networks sent their way, should protest it.

"Excessive concentration of control over broadcasting is as bad when exercised from New York as when exercised from Washington," he said. Local stations "can no longer accept network standards of taste, violence, and decency in programming. If the programs or commercials glorify the use of drugs; if the programs are violent or sadistic; if the commercials are false or misleading, or simply intrusive and obnoxious; the stations must jump on the networks rather than wince as the Congress and the FCC are forced to do so." In the area of news, he said, local licensees "cannot abdicate responsibility for news judgments." They must stop the "ideological plugola" sent into the local communities. After all, "station licensees have final responsibility for news balance—whether the information comes from their own newsroom or from a distant network." With such an obligation resting on their shoulders, Whitehead said, licensees should not be surprised that "station managers and network officials who fail to act to correct imbalance of consistent bias from the networks—or who acquiesce by silence— can only be considered willing participants, to be held fully accountable by the broadcaster's community at license renewal time."[125]

Local licensees, who were far more conservative than network executives, did not need to be told twice that they should counter the liberal programming coming their way. In most cases, local affiliates already were upset about the tenor of network entertainment, news, and documentary programming. Frank Stanton, president of CBS, recalled feeling quite a bit of pressure from local affiliates after the Whitehead speech. At times, the man who had resisted a contempt citation from Congress in the "Selling of the Pentagon" said, "I used to think that this was [Charles] Colson shaking the tree." In November 1972, Stanton recalled, Colson called to complain about CBS coverage that he thought was biased against the president. In the course of the conversation, Colson warned Stanton about plans "to squeeze the networks economically."[126]

Other prime targets for suppression, of course, were remnants of the antiwar movement. By election day, 1972, Nixon had finished his campaign against the Berrigan brothers. Although the trial had not ended the way Nixon wanted it to, the Ultra-Resistance, typified by the two priests, was no longer a factor. He also had effectively silenced the Vietnam Veterans Against the War. Leaders of that group were indicted in 1972 for planning to sabotage the Republican National Convention in Miami by, among other things, shooting incendiary devices from slingshots and crossbows. The case was badly tainted by the presence of an *agent provocateur,*[127] and a jury acquitted the defendants in September 1973.[128]

Despite his opposition to the antiwar movements, Richard Nixon intended to be the peace candidate during the campaign. Although George McGovern, who had long been an opponent of the war, tried to assume that role, Nixon and his cronies tied the Democratic candidate to the radical fringe that they had been working so hard to discredit. To cement his position as the peace candidate, Nixon brought the final American ground troops in Vietnam home in August. To further underline his credentials, the president sent Henry Kissinger before the nation on October 26 to announce "peace is at hand." The agreement had not been finalized, and many details still remained to be worked out, but the president wanted the credit for stopping the war before the election. By December, the tentative agreement had fallen apart. Although the South Vietnamese were the cause of the breakdown, Nixon blamed North Vietnam. To force an agreement, he ordered a massive bombing of the North during the Christmas holidays. Some 36,000 tons of bombs fell on Hanoi and Haiphong over a period of twelve days beginning December 18, and the harbors were mined. The total tonnage of bombs dropped during that short period was more than the amount dropped from 1969 to 1971.[129]

Many in the nation were outraged by the bombing. Congress, which was away for the holidays, promised to take action when it returned. Much of the nation's press reported that the bombing was not confined to military targets and was damaging civilian areas and killing noncombatants. Conservatives strongly disputed such contentions, claiming that the press was being manipulated by enemies of the nation into presenting an untrue picture of the attacks.[130] Although peace talks reopened on January 8, and an agreement was announced on January 27, the legacy of the Christmas bombing would linger, especially for the press. Its reporting of that event would remain high on the conservatives' list of charges against the patriotism of journalists in later years.

As the Vietnam era receded into memory, the transgressions of the press would be recalled, and new generations of Americans would come to question the role of journalists in wartime. Surely, they would argue, the press had a responsibility to support American men and women in uniform and not to question the morality of the acts that they were performing under orders from their commander-in-chief. When easy responses to that contention were not forthcoming, the debate degenerated into emotional encounters in which facts were unnecessary. But the heated nature of the discussions proved once again that the role that the press should play in military conflicts was at best unclear. Once more the old adage about the military officer who would prefer to fight the war in secret and let the press know only who had won surfaced. In fact, in the 1980s, the military under Ronald Reagan would try this approach when it invaded Grenada. But the Grenada invasion was a brief encounter; the Vietnam War, which was the longest in the nation's history, could not be shielded from reporters. Although the peace agreement called for the withdrawal of all American troops within sixty days, it could not be forgotten that 57,000 Americans had lost their lives in that conflict and that perhaps $150 billion had been spent in a war that at best only delayed an inevitable solution.[131]

Even though Richard Nixon claimed credit for ending the war and Henry Kissinger shared the Nobel Peace Prize with the North Vietnamese negotiator, neither deserved the accolades sent their way. Instead, they should be sent to the thousands of people who staked their lives and their careers on their protests to end the war. For once in the nation's history, the American people had broken through the protective shell placed around the nation's foreign policy. Although dissenters had tried to change the course of many wars in the past, only those individuals who had problems with the creation of a national empire after the Spanish-American War had registered any amount of success. But in the Vietnam era, American dissenters made it perfectly clear through their marches, draft-card burnings, willingness to endure beatings, and jail terms that the war in Vietnam was unacceptable. Although many Americans would object to the tactics of the antiwar movement and to the heightened rhetoric surrounding it, a majority of them would come to accept, for whatever reason, the basic idea that continuing the fighting was unwise.

Perhaps the victory of the antiwar movement was what the Founding Fathers had in mind when they decided to protect freedom of speech, press, and assembly. If the founders had not exercised those freedoms, the nation never would have shaken off British rule. And many of their activities had been denounced by their contemporaries. They had taken to the streets, performed acts of violence, and mounted propaganda campaigns to engineer independence. Another group of protesters in the 1830s had launched the highly unpopular campaign to end slavery. In both cases, the protesters had interfered with the plans of sitting governments. And in both cases, the use of their expressive rights had brought about great changes in American society. The antiwar leaders of the 1960s and 1970s, no less than the early patriots and abolitionists, were telling the government that the people had a right to be heard.

Despite our heritage, American governments have seldom been willing to listen to the voice of the people on important issues such as war and peace. Letting the people know too much about what the government was doing or allowing them to express their opinions too forcefully simply was unwise. The only role that many government leaders assigned to the people was to elect leaders who then would go to Washington to behave as they, the leaders, saw best. The people were not to intervene in the process again until the next election. With the success of the antiwar movement fresh in the minds of succeeding administrations, efforts to prevent the people from intervening further in the plans of government would heighten. To accomplish this end, administrations would sharply reduce the availability of information on what they were doing, and future presidents would seek deliberately to mislead public opinion. Without information on which to base dissent, disagreement with government policies becomes more difficult. And when later presidents became adept at putting a benign face on their efforts to quash dissent before it had a chance to begin, those people who did find fault with presidential policies would be unable to find much support. Richard Nixon, whose administration laid the groundwork for later presidents, however, was unable to clothe in an innocuous light his actions against those persons who disagreed with him. He and his cohorts publicly attacked dissenters of all varieties with a sledgehammer; no one could harbor any doubts about his intentions. His substantial election victory, tainted though it was, gave him new incentives to proceed against any remaining enemies.

Nixon worked to make his second inaugural perfect. When some 100,000 protesters gathered in Washington to demonstrate against his taking the oath again, the press virtually ignored them. All the attention was on the pomp and pageantry befitting a coronation. Behind the façade was a growing concern about the Watergate situation. The trial of the men charged with trying to bug the Democratic National Headquarters in June 1972 began on January 8, 1973. Nixon loyalists offered a substantial financial settlement to get the men to go to jail without revealing their connections to the administration.

News of the Watergate break-in showed White House news suppression techniques at their height. When the White House viewed the first of a two-part story on Watergate on the CBS "Evening News" with Walter Cronkite in late October 1972, Charles Colson soon was on the telephone with network president Frank Stanton. The segment that attracted the White House's ire was a fourteen-minute piece that dealt with the implications of the break-in. According to Stanton, Colson "complained bitterly that CBS was devoting too much attention to Watergate in its news reporting." The CBS president said that he thought the presidential aide considered the segment unfair. "I reviewed that broadcast with him trying to show why I believe it to be eminently fair and balanced. As I was doing so, however, Colson interrupted me and said, in substance, that 'whether the report was fair or not, it should not have been broadcast at all.'" CBS carried the second part of the story but in a considerably shorter form. In answer to questions as to why the story was cut, Richard Salant, CBS News president, said, "I cut the second part because it repeated a section that we'd already run in a special report on Watergate in August. It was as simple as that." Individuals who worked on the news broadcast claimed that the cuts were ordered to avoid making the network seem anti-administration.[132]

The prime target of administration ire over Watergate reporting, of course, was the *Washington Post,* where Carl Bernstein and Bob Woodward, two reporters who would take their places in press folklore, were pursuing the president of the United States with a passion and a hunger unmatched by any of their colleagues. The responses to their work ranged from the vulgar to the Machiavellian and the petty. The vulgar came from John Mitchell, who, when told about plans the *Post* had to run a story about his controlling a secret reelection fund while he was still attorney general, responded, "All that crap, you're putting it in the paper? It's all been denied. [Newspaper publisher] Katie Graham's gonna get her tit caught in a big fat wringer if that's published. Good Christ! That's the most sickening thing I ever heard."[133] The scheming reaction came from the president, who, when talking to presidential aides H. R. Haldeman and John Dean, discussed the possibilities of launching another campaign against the *Washington Post's* television licenses. According to transcripts of White House conversations, Nixon had said, "The main, main thing is the *Post* is going to have damnable, damnable problems out of this one. They have a television station . . . and they're going to have to get it renewed." Traditionally, few competing applications had been filed for station licenses, but more recently, the FCC had been granting more challengers the licenses once held by others. Dean reminded the president of this increased activity against license holders, and Nixon responded, "and it's going to be God damn active here. . . . Well, the game has to be played awfully rough."[134] The petty incident came after the election when the administration barred *Washington Post* society reporter Dorothy McCardle, a 68-year-old grandmother who had covered social events at the White House during the terms of five presidents, from covering various activities including a Christmas party for the children of foreign diplomats.

For months, the *Washington Post* had hammered the administration with its news stories on the break-in. The biggest story, which tied members of the top echelons of the White House to financial misconduct and perversion of the electoral system, broke shortly before the election. Few newspapers picked up on the information, and voters almost totally ignored the derogatory data. Now, only the trial had to be negotiated before the Nixon administration would be free to finish remaking the nation. Things seemed to be going the administration's way when four of the accused men entered guilty pleas. After a sixteen-day trial, two others, Gordon Liddy and James McCord, were found guilty by a jury. Nothing had come out about the White House connection, and, the White House probably thought, nothing would. Administration leaders did not take into consideration the stubbornness of Chief Federal District Judge John J. Sirica, who was convinced that he had not received the full story in the trial. He threatened Liddy and McCord with long prison terms and held them under substantial bail in an attempt to break their silence.

On March 23, 1973, James McCord sent a letter to Sirica telling him that witnesses at the trial had committed perjury and that the defendants had been pressured to keep quiet. The convicted burglar wanted to meet with Sirica personally "since I cannot feel confident in talking with an FBI agent, in testifying before a grand jury whose U.S. Attorneys work for the Department of Justice, or in talking with other government representatives."[135] McCord fingered former attorney general and former head of the Committee to Re-elect the President John Mitchell as the person who had directed the break-in. Shortly thereafter, Acting FBI Director L. Patrick Gray admitted that he had destroyed evidence linked to the Watergate episode on the advice of presidential aides. By April 17, Nixon went before the White House press corps to announce that he had begun a major investigation into allegations that members of his administration were implicated in the break-in and its subsequent cover-up.

That day presidential Press Secretary Ron Ziegler also addressed the reporters. For months he had been condemning any and all coverage of the break-in. In October 1972, for instance, he had said, "I will not dignify with comment stories based on hearsay, character assassination, innuendo, or guilt by association. . . . The President is concerned about the techniques being applied . . . in the stories themselves." Later that month, he had labeled a *Washington Post* story as "shabby journalism . . . a blatant effort at character assassination." And on March 30, 1973, Ziegler had said, "As we have said before, nobody in the White House had any involvement or prior knowledge of that event [Watergate]. I repeat the statement today."[136] After the president's statement announcing the new White House investigation, the press badgered Ziegler unmercifully about whether his former statements were still valid. Finally, the press secretary said that the president's statement of that day "is the operative statement." He added, "The others are inoperative."[137]

The operative life of Nixon's April 17 statement was brief. By April 30, the president had fired his personal counsel John Dean and had accepted the resignations of top aides H. R. Haldeman and John Ehrlichman and Attorney General Richard Kleindienst. The president announced the resignations on national television, calling Haldeman and Ehrlichman "two of the finest public servants it has been my privilege to know." He said that he accepted the responsibility for the misdeeds of his subordinates, implying that he himself knew nothing of what had transpired. Nixon pledged himself to getting on with the business of governing the nation. The next day, Ron Ziegler met again with the press. This time, he had something special to say. After the recent revelations, he said, "I would apologize to the *Post,* and I would apologize to Mr. Woodward and Mr. Bernstein. . . . We would all have to say that mistakes were made in terms of comments. I was over enthusiastic in my comments about the *Post,* particularly if you look at them in the context of developments that have taken place. . . . When we are wrong, we are wrong, as we were in that case."[138]

From that point, the president became increasingly involved in the Watergate crisis, and his ability to control his critics dissipated. As the story unfolded, more and more reporters flocked to the investigation, whereas for months Woodward, Bernstein, and the *Washington Post* had been almost alone. The burglary and related matters revealed fundamental shortcomings in the press, for most big-name journalists working in Washington deprecated the *Post*'s efforts and believed the assignment of two unknown reporters to the task was ludicrous. Correspondents assigned to the White House, the Watergate crisis revealed, were next to useless when it came to uncovering real information in the nation's capital. They relied too much on presidential favors for access to information and took much of their news from official briefings rather than by gathering it on their own.[139]

Despite the president's efforts at damage control, the Watergate story increasingly overshadowed the American political scene. In summer 1973, for instance, the Senate Watergate hearings, chaired by Senator Sam Ervin, Democrat of North Carolina, dominated television screens; many former White House staff members testified. The president had blocked the appearance of current staff members on the grounds of executive privilege, but by summer 1973 so many of those persons involved in the scandal itself had left government service for one reason or another that even John Mitchell, John Ehrlichman, and H. R. Haldeman were susceptible to subpoena. One high point in the proceedings was the appearance of fired presidential counsel John Dean, who carefully detailed Nixon's efforts to suppress dissent. Probably the most important witness of all, although few would have anticipated that fact, was a lower echelon White House staffer named Alexander Butterfield. In the course of his testimony, Butterfield revealed that the president had had his own offices bugged and that almost all conversations held in those locations had been recorded.

In response, Nixon correctly argued that other presidents, including John Kennedy and Lyndon Johnson, had taped White House conversations. In fact, said the incumbent, he had had the Johnson taping system removed when he moved into the White House. But Lyndon Johnson had suggested that Nixon reinstall the recorders to provide information for use later in writing his memoirs.[140] After the system was put back in place, most White House personnel forgot about its existence, but the machine had captured many incriminating conversations. Thus, the Butterfield disclosure sparked almost a yearlong battle that ultimately brought down the president. Everyone wanted those tapes—the Senate committee, the courts, and the special prosecutor named to look into the whole matter. Polite requests followed by formal subpoenas piled up at the door of the White House, and the president claimed executive privilege. Conversations on the tapes, he maintained, pertained to confidential activities within the executive branch and could not be disclosed without adversely affecting governmental operations. Everyone seeking the tapes believed that on them they would find the so-called "smoking gun"—the evidence that would connect the president to a group of inept burglars.

Before the tape controversy came to a head, however, Nixon was buffeted by another crisis. On October 10, 1973, Vice President Spiro T. Agnew resigned in disgrace after pleading "no contest" to a charge of income tax evasion in connection with illegal payments from contractors that he had received while he was governor of Maryland. Agnew became only the second vice president in the nation's history to resign before his term expired; the first, John C. Calhoun, left over political differences with Andrew Jackson.

Never one to do anything quietly, the vice president let loose a barrage of criticism of the press as he left office. Journalists, he claimed, in an effort to seek retribution for his earlier criticism of them, had unconscionably circulated leaks from a grand jury investigation into his past behavior. "The attacks were increased by daily publication of the wildest rumor and speculation, much of it bearing no resemblance to the information being given the prosecutors," he said. "All this was done with full knowledge that it was prejudicial to my civil rights." To make matters worse, the vice president said, "the news media editorially deplored these violations of the traditional secrecy of such investigations but at the same time many of the most prestigious were ignoring their own counsel by publishing every leak they could get their hands on."[141] Journalists found themselves in a ticklish position in light of Agnew's comments. Many of them acknowledged that the only way that they could publish details of grand jury investigations was through news leaks. Grand jury proceedings, because they are one-sided, are kept confidential, and journalists usually honor such restrictions. Here reporters argued that Agnew's position in the government justified the use of any information made available. After all, the vice president was, in the words of the old cliché, a heartbeat away from the presidency. If questions existed about his honesty, the nation should know about them. The fact that these stories allowed the press to get even with a longtime nemesis most likely was not overlooked either.

Shortly after Agnew's departure, Nixon took an action that sealed his fate. Archibald Cox, the special prosecutor appointed to investigate the Watergate affair, had become increasingly obnoxious about the tapes. The president was tired of Cox's constant efforts to invade his domain, and on Saturday night, October 20, he ordered Attorney General Elliott Richardson to fire the special prosecutor. Richardson resigned rather than carry out the order as did his top assistant, William D. Ruckelshaus. Cox was finally fired by Solicitor General Robert Bork, third in line in the Justice Department. By October 23, the Saturday Night Massacre, as it had been dubbed by the press, led to the introduction of numerous resolutions for the impeachment of the president. The firestorm of protest prompted Nixon's agreement to release the most desired tapes and his announcement that a new special prosecutor would be appointed. The problem, he explained to his staff, was not the existence of a special prosecutor, but that "fucking Harvard professor" who filled the position.[142] A Texan, Leon Jaworski, was named to the post, and under his direction, most of the Watergate principals faced trial and were convicted for their misdeeds.

On October 26, six days after the Saturday Night Massacre, the president held a news conference. Although the White House press corps had not covered itself with glory during the early days of the Watergate investigation, its members were making up for lost time. Since the April 30 resignations, questioners were increasingly hostile. With all of the problems endured in October 1973, Nixon had had enough. His cool demeanor was shattered, and he lashed out at the journalists. "I have never seen such outrageous, vicious, distorted reporting in 27 years of public life," he said. "Don't get the impression that you arouse my anger," he said. "You see, one can only be angry with those he respects."[143] By late November, the president was in even greater trouble. Judge Sirica, who was screening the tapes, discovered an 18½-minute gap in a key section. Nixon's critics immediately charged that he purposely had deleted an incriminating conversation. The president, who was visiting Disney World in Florida, retorted, "I am not a crook."[144]

By March 1, 1974, a Washington grand jury had indicted seven former White House and campaign aides for conspiracy to obstruct justice. Included among them were H. R. Haldeman, John Ehrlichman, Charles Colson, and John Mitchell. A week later, another grand jury indicted others for conspiracy to break in to the office of Daniel Ellsberg's psychiatrist. Among the defendants in this case were Ehrlichman and Colson. About the same time, the House Judiciary Committee began hearings on bringing impeachment charges against the president.

Most of the details about the Watergate investigations and trials are outside the scope of this study, but one area definitely is pertinent. The Watergate investigation led to a major confrontation over the existence of executive privilege, or the right of a president to decide arbitrarily what information he will make available to Congress, the courts, and the American public. Problems with executive privilege date back to George Washington's desire to conceal information about an Indian massacre of American troops. Richard Nixon simply tried to carry the doctrine to the extreme. He had successfully relied upon executive privilege many times in the past, but when the White House tapes became the issue, that shield proved ineffective.

The problem caused by the tapes became larger and graver. The Senate Watergate committee, which had been rebuffed on earlier requests for tapes, asked for some 500 tapes and documents, and the president had responded that he would not provide the information requested. To agree, he said, would "unquestionably destroy any vestige of confidentiality of presidential communications, thereby irreparably impairing the constitutional functions of the office of the presidency."[145] The president also refused a request by Special Prosecutor Jaworski in April, again resting his stance on the need to protect the executive from the prying eyes of other branches of government. In addition, he said, all relevant materials had been submitted. A subpoena from the House Judiciary Committee for the tapes of forty-two conversations for use in its impeachment hearings also was refused. All parties were displeased by the president's responses and assessed their options.

Nixon tried to get around the subpoenas in late April by providing a 1,200-page edited transcript of the tapes. All that was taken out, said the president, was off-color language, and those deletions were noted by the insertion of "expletive deleted" in the appropriate places. None of the parties was satisfied with the edited transcripts, and the case headed into court again. The effort to obtain the tapes had been in and out of the courts for months with mixed results. To finally settle the matter, Jaworski appealed directly to the Supreme Court, and the justices met in extraordinary session in July 1974 to hear oral arguments in the case.

The question that Jaworski's petition put before the Court was whether the president's effort to preserve executive privilege should be allowed to stand in the face of the special prosecutor's need for evidence in a criminal trial. Under the arrangement suggested to the Court, a federal district court judge, most likely

Sirica, would review the tapes in secret to decide whether they contained any information pertinent to the case. Only if they did would the contents of the tapes be placed before the grand jury and eventually used in court. Chief Justice Warren Burger, himself a Nixon appointee and writing for a unanimous Court that contained two other Nixon appointees, ordered the president to turn the tapes over to the special prosecutor. "The President's need for complete candor and objectivity from advisers calls for great deference from the courts," he said, but "when the privilege depends solely on the broad, undifferentiated claim of public interest in the confidentiality of such conversations, a confrontation with other values arises." The president had not argued the necessity of protecting military, diplomatic, or sensitive national security secrets, Burger said, consequently, "we find it difficult to accept the argument that even the very important interest in confidentiality of Presidential communications is significantly diminished by production of such material for *in camera* [confidential] inspection with all the protection that a district court will be obliged to provide." If the president has such unrestricted powers to resist subpoenas for data involved in criminal proceedings, said the chief justice, the constitutional balance of powers among the branches of government would be badly impaired.[146]

With the battle for the tapes lost on July 24, Nixon turned them over. On July 27, the House Judiciary Committee approved two articles of impeachment. In one, Nixon was charged with obstructing justice; the other accused him of repeatedly violating his oath of office. Three days later, a third article charging him with an unconstitutional defiance of congressional subpoenas was approved. On August 9, 1974, a little more than two years after the Watergate break-in, Richard Nixon resigned his office and left the nation's capital in disgrace. But the problems of Nixon, the tapes, and executive privilege were far from over. The next question became one of who actually owned the tapes. Nixon had worked out an agreement with the director of the General Services Administration, which had custody of presidential documents, that would have allowed him to retain ownership of the tapes and other documents then on deposit in Washington, D.C., and eventually to destroy the tapes. Under terms of the agreement, the materials would be preserved for three years, just in case they were needed in additional criminal proceedings. After that, Nixon could do whatever he wanted to with the tapes. They were to be destroyed at Nixon's death or on September 1, 1984, whichever date came first.[147]

Although 1984 seemed an appropriate choice for a president who had tried to destroy the personal freedoms of thousands of Americans to obliterate all traces of his offenses, members of Congress felt differently about the tapes. In addition to the tapes being vital presidential documents that should be preserved, their very existence would stand forever as a memorial to the dangers of unrestricted presidential power. Congress quickly enacted the Presidential Recordings and Materials Preservation Act of 1974, which allowed Nixon to have access to the materials but forbade him to destroy any tapes without specific congressional approval.[148] As one would expect, the former president contested the act, and in 1977 the Supreme Court upheld its provisions. Chief Justice Warren Burger and Justice William Rehnquist dissented.[149] The dissenters saw the decision as a threat to the powers of future presidents, but the majority focused on the uniqueness of the situation presented by Nixon's resignation. For the time being at least, Richard Nixon's dominance over the U.S. government was ended.

His legacy lived on, however, as fallout from his presidency and the scandal that drove him from the Oval Office reverberated throughout the nation. Revelations about the widespread misuse of the nation's intelligence-gathering agencies to persecute political enemies that had surfaced during the Watergate investigations led to congressional inquiries. A Senate select committee looking into the way in which these operations had focused on domestic unrest during the Nixon presidency could not comprehend the mind-set that led to such a perversion of intelligence gathering: "We reject the view that the traditional American principles of justice and fair play have no place in our struggle against the enemies of freedom."[150]

To make matters worse, said the committee members, "our investigation has established that the targets of intelligence activity have ranged far beyond persons who could properly be characterized as enemies of freedom and have extended to a wide array of citizens engaging in lawful activity." The committee's inquiry found at least 300,000 names in Central Intelligence Agency files, at least 100,000 persons investigated by Army Intelligence officers, and at least 26,000 persons targeted for emergency detention by the FBI. Groups represented in various intelligence agency files ranged from the women's liberation movement and the National Association for the Advancement of Colored People to the John Birch Society and the Students for a Democratic Society. "Too many people have been spied upon by too many Government agencies and to[o] much information has been collected," the committee report said. In addition, the spying on Americans was indiscriminate. "The Government has often undertaken the secret surveillance of citizens on the basis of their political beliefs, even when those beliefs posed no threat of violence or illegal acts on behalf of a hostile foreign power." To accomplish these ends, government agents used secret informants, wiretaps, microphone bugs, illegal mail openings, and break-ins. Through these inquiries, the government collected "vast amounts of information about the personal lives, views, and associations of American citizens."[151]

Committee members could find little justification for this widespread prying into the lives of Americans, and they were appalled to discover that the investigations extended much further back in time than the Nixon administration. Such abuses were almost expected under his tutelage, but other presidents had been only somewhat less promiscuous in their misuse of the nation's intelligence-gathering apparatus. "Investigations of groups deemed potentially dangerous—and even of groups suspected of associating with potentially dangerous organizations—have continued for decades, despite the fact that those groups did not engage in unlawful activity." These investigations clearly invaded the area of a citizen's life guarded by the First Amendment, which "protects the Rights of American citizens to engage in free and open discussions, and to associate with persons of their choosing."[152]

The nation's intelligence-gathering agencies and the presidents who directed them obviously had a clouded vision of the true foundation of American greatness. "Free government depends upon the ability of all its citizens to speak their minds without fear of official sanction," the committee said. In comments as applicable to earlier experiences of the labor movement as to the dissent in the late 1960s and early 1970s, the committee noted, "the ability of ordinary people to be heard by their leaders means that they must be free to join in groups in order more effectively to express their grievances." In addition, the ability of all kinds of people to join together for such activities must be protected. "Constitutional safeguards are needed to protect the timid as well as the courageous, the weak as well as the strong. While many Americans have been willing to assert their beliefs in the face of possible governmental reprisals, no citizen should have to weigh his or her desire to express an opinion, or join a group, against the risk of having lawful speech or association used against him."[153]

Having a congressional committee make such a far-reaching statement about the right of individuals to dissent is admirable, but what would keep future presidents from abusing the nation's intelligence apparatus? Well, Congress tried setting up a watchdog committee to provide better supervision of the agencies, and members also enacted various pieces of legislation including a Privacy Act that placed restrictions on the ability of the government to keep files on American citizens involved in political activities.[154] In addition, individuals caught up in the agencies' net began fighting back. Using the Freedom of Information Act and the new Privacy Act, activists began to demand to see the government's files on them. Others sought to have the government destroy their records. Still others sought damages for agency violation of their civil rights. In the early 1980s, for example, a jury awarded a group of Washington, D.C., activists more than $700,000 in damages from FBI personnel and others who "violated their First Amendment rights to assemble for peaceable political protest, to associate with others to engage in political expression, and to speak on public issues free of unreasonable Government interference."[155]

Such success, however, was fleeting. By the 1980s, secrecy again was the byword in Washington, and Congress found itself investigating another White House abuse of power: the planning, on whatever level, of the Iran-contra affair that rocked the Reagan presidency. The abuse of intelligence agencies combined with secrecy in government seem to be never-ending problems, possibly untouchable by Congress until the majority of the American people pronounce this behavior unacceptable and back up their statements at the polls. The difficulty is that presidents, surrounded by the mystique of their office, find it easy to convince Americans that disclosing a variety of information would endanger national security and that complicated decisions about war and peace must be made by experts. Until Americans decide that they, by birthright and constitutional right, have the obligation to participate in discussions that shape the nation's future, even in matters of national security, the problem of governmental secrecy by presidential edict will continue.

The American people are perhaps the only force that can clean up another free-expression problem left over from the Nixon years as well. Watergate revealed the existence of large amounts of cash in the hands of Committee to Re-elect the President leaders that could be spent as deemed appropriate by committee officials. Thus, in addition to legitimate campaign activities, the money financed burglaries, dirty tricks, and other actions that undermined the political process. As a result of Watergate revelations, Congress was faced with the additional task of cleaning up the election process. The congressional goal was, in part, selfish. Campaign expenditures had gotten out of hand, and many candidates wanted to make it less expensive to seek office.[156] In addition, the American ideal of one man, one vote figured prominently in the endeavor. Each voter, according to this vision, had an equal opportunity to influence the government by his or her vote. Yet the undeniable fact was that some voters were more influential than others because they had great sums of money to use in advocating their points of view. Consequently, Congress decided to move into campaign reform.

Post-Watergate reforms struck at the core values protected by the First Amendment. The right to talk about the future of the nation is fundamental. Interestingly, however, the campaign reform movement brought about two diametrically opposed interpretations of how money and free speech were intermingled in the electoral process. One view held that money corrupted the process and that the true protection of political speech rested in the equalization of resources among candidates so that no candidate had an edge because he or she was a better fund raiser or came from a wealthy family. The opposing interpretation argued that money was vital to political speech and that individuals should be allowed to spend as much as they could raise and that their supporters should be allowed to spend without limit on their behalf as well. Money was necessary for effective political speech, the latter group contended, and individuals should be able to augment their speech as much as they could through the use of campaign funds. "Money talks" might be the appropriate aphorism to use to describe this latter vision of political speech, and the more money available, the more effective that talk.

Strangely enough, Congress had started its clean-up effort with the Federal Election Campaign Act of 1972.[157] The law placed limits on the amount that candidates for federal office could spend on advertising, which had become such an integral part of campaigning, and required full disclosure of expenditures and contributions. Richard Nixon signed the law in February 1972, and its provisions went into effect sixty days later. Presidential fund raisers used the time before the law's effective date to good advantage. More than $20 million of the $62 million raised for Nixon's reelection effort came in before disclosure of donors became mandatory. About $1.5 million of that money was given in cash, much of which was used to fund a variety of illegal activities. With the Watergate revelations fresh in their memories, members of Congress enacted substantial amendments to the law in 1974. The new regulations imposed limits on both contributions and expenditures, provided for mandatory disclosure of donations above a certain amount, and set up a firmer program for public financing of presidential elections.[158] The act was challenged immediately, and the Supreme Court used the First Amendment to undercut the ability of Congress to regulate the electoral process.[159]

The Court was so badly split on the issue that it delivered a 235-page per curiam opinion, in which five of the eight justices participating concurred or dissented in part. The majority opinion deftly sliced the campaign reform act to pieces. A fundamental requirement of the legislation was that both contributions that an individual made directly to a candidate and expenditures that a person made on his or her own to support a candidate were to be limited. The Court found that the governmental interest in preventing real or apparent corruption in political campaigns was sufficient enough to allow restrictions on contributions made directly to candidates. The limitation, the Court said, was narrowly drawn and left "persons free to engage in independent political expression, to associate actively through volunteering their services, and to assist to a limited but nonetheless substantial extent in supporting candidates and committees with financial resources."[160] Thus, the Court decided that the $1,000 limit on personal contributions to identified candidates during an election campaign was not an unreasonable restraint on freedom of political speech.

But when it came to expenditures in support of a candidate, the Court was of a different mind. The individual spending limit of $1,000 was ruled an unreasonable restraint on freedom of speech. The opinion noted that the law "would make it a federal criminal offense for a person or association to place a single one-quarter page advertisement 'relative to a clearly identified candidate' in a major metropolitan newspaper." This restriction, said the Court, "heavily burdens core First Amendment expression." After all, "advocacy of the election or defeat of candidates for federal office is no less entitled to protection under the First Amendment than the discussion of political policy generally or advocacy of the passage or defeat of legislation." The Court would not allow Congress to limit the speech of those individuals who had a great deal of money available to spend to support candidates. The fact that not all Americans could back candidates that way was, perhaps, unfortunate, but Congress could not attempt to equalize the power of different voices.[161]

The inability of the Court's majority to accept the congressional package irritated Justice Byron White, who could find no justification in limiting "the amounts an individual may give to a candidate or spend with his approval but fail[ing] to limit the amounts that could be spent on his behalf." The two activities—contributing and spending—were, to White, two sides of the same coin. In any event, White felt that the regulation of elections, including restrictions on the amount of money that could be spent to seek office, was entirely within the province of Congress and that the Court should not try to impose its opinions on an essentially political decision. The justice argued that Congress had a right to try to "restore and maintain public confidence in federal elections." In the light of Watergate, Congress could reasonably find that it was "critical to obviate or dispel the impression that federal elections are purely and simply a function of money, that federal offices are bought and sold or that political races are reserved for those who have the facility—and the stomach—for doing whatever it takes to bring together those interests, groups, and individuals that can raise or contribute large fortunes in order to prevail at the polls."[162]

White's arguments were of no avail, and congressional efforts to reform the electoral process were eviscerated. Congress continues to seek ways to reform the process—to restrict the amount of money that candidates can spend, to limit the influence of political action committees in elections, and to clean up the negative advertising that has become so typical of American office seeking. The measures have had little success. Additional court challenges seem to uphold the Nixonian principle of spending as much money as possible on elections,[163] with the net effect of accentuating the voices of those who have money to spend and diminishing the voices of those who lack it. The maxim that money talks in the political process still stands untouched.

In the long run, much of the Nixon legacy remains fairly untouched. Although the president was forced to resign in the face of a growing scandal brought on by his inability to tolerate even the slightest dissent, the nation is still strongly shaped by his prejudices. True, Congress took steps to reign in the nation's intelligence community, but oversight of the agencies has proved difficult because of a lack of trust between the parties. In addition, subsequent presidents, pushed by the development of international terrorism, have molded the intelligence community to suit their needs.

Dissenters may have looked upon the end of the war and the Nixon resignation as indications that their causes had triumphed, but the president's departure in 1974 also marked the loss of much of the nation's reforming spirit. Students, for instance, went back to their classrooms and became far more interested in grades and jobs than in causes. Rebels of the earlier period became upstanding members of the community, as the media in the 1980s would frequently report. Tom Hayden, a leading SDS organizer, for instance, would serve in the California state legislature. The end of the Vietnam War also marked the end of one overriding cause that could unite various factions. Causes would appear later but they would appeal to smaller groups of people—those opposed to the development of nuclear power, those against American actions in Central America, and those opposed to or favoring abortion. The mass movement may have disappeared with Richard Nixon.

The departing president also seemed to have won a victory over his archenemy, the press. Although Woodward, Bernstein, and the *Washington Post* gloried in acclaim—and the Pulitzer Prize—for pursuing the story that had toppled the president, the American people began to have second thoughts about an unrestrained news media. Within a short period of time, investigations such as that conducted by the *Washington Post* would be denounced as excesses of the press rather than as illustrative of its proper functioning. Readers and viewers grew impatient with constant reminders of problems in American life and less willing to pay attention. The influence of the media decreased, and under Ronald Reagan the manipulation of the media increased. Few defenders of journalists would emerge, while, in fact, many political and business leaders cheered problems encountered by journalists.

As far as Richard Nixon himself is concerned, after a few years of political ostracism, he found himself cast in the role as senior wise man in the Republican party, with his advice being sought on a variety of foreign policy issues, where his voice had been untainted by Watergate. But his beliefs changed little after his ouster. He still despised the press and thought little of the right of human beings to dissent against oppressive government policies. Nixon, for example, played a major role in encouraging George Bush to reopen channels of communication with the Chinese leadership after the massacre at Tiananmen Square in 1989. To Richard Nixon national policy always had been more important than political dissidents. Many of his successors would agree.

CHAPTER 11

★ ★ ★

Reaping the Whirlwind:
Freedom of Expression
in an Age of Reaction

Revelations of misconduct at the highest levels of government during the Watergate scandal led to attempts to reestablish the nation's value system. Richard Nixon left office under a dark cloud; Gerald Ford, who seemed far more open and accessible and much less intimidated by dissent, occupied the Oval Office. With the nation rescued from the clutches of Nixon and his men, Americans could rest assured that fundamental individual rights now were safeguarded. But had freedom of expression survived the Watergate scandal? Immediate signs were highly favorable. The press had been a major factor in saving the nation, and Bob Woodward and Carl Bernstein basked in all the glory that their Pulitzer Prize merited. Critics of the war could reflect on the effectiveness of their efforts. University administrative techniques remained forever changed after a decade of demonstrations. Indeed, life in the United States seemed to have been altered permanently.

Although immediate indications apparently favored a far more open society, those signs quickly disappeared. Americans of all ages were tired of the frenzy that had dominated their culture for a dozen years or more. Peace and quiet, money and morals, and law and order were the new orders of the day. As Americans sought safety in calmness, their society entered another period of extreme suppression of freedom of expression. A significant cause of the turmoil of the late 1960s and early 1970s, according to some critics, had been an excessive interference by the people in the processes of government. Journalists were blamed for part of the uproar because they had provided much of the information on which citizens had acted. To conservatives in government and business, the answer to the nation's problems after Watergate was much the same as it had been in earlier days: restrict the amount of information available to average citizens about governmental activities and thus limit their participation. Government and, indeed, society should be run by those people best equipped to make decisions and not by the masses. To deflect the energies of anyone who still might want to interfere, conservatives encouraged concern about a wide range of moral

430

issues in the hopes that Americans would occupy their time reforming society rather than meddling in government.

Much of this activity is associated with the Ronald Reagan presidency, but in fact, the seeds were planted during the Nixon administration. Reagan simply nurtured them into full bloom. In many respects, the presidencies of Gerald Ford and Jimmy Carter provided only an interlude before the age of reaction set in. Protecting a government from those it governs is fairly simple if you can keep the people both uninformed and afraid. In the years after Watergate, considerable effort was expended in both directions. To a large extent the secrecy that flowered during the Reagan years had been planted deep in American society. Even the Founding Fathers fell prey to the desire to keep their deliberations secret when they wrote the Constitution behind closed doors. Military leaders long had advocated concealing information from the American people, with some of the longest and loudest confrontations on censorship occurring during the Civil War. Franklin Roosevelt institutionalized government secrecy just prior to World War II when he issued an executive order authorizing the classification of documents. With the onset of the cold war, government secrecy took on a life of its own, which the Reagan administration enthusiastically nurtured. And the conservatives of the 1980s renewed American fears of international communism. Now, the president talked about the "evil empire" as represented by the Soviet Union and about the dangers that communism, backed by Cuba's Fidel Castro, posed for the entire Western hemisphere. Covert actions against such threats were right, logical, and patriotic, and taking the American people into the government's confidence simply was too risky.[1]

In 1982, the White House issued the new administration's executive order regarding the classification of documents. In one brief statement of about a dozen pages, the administration reversed a trend toward openness in government that had been in place since the Kennedy presidency. Previous presidents, including Richard Nixon, had sought to limit the number of individuals able to classify documents and to create an automatic review and declassification process. Jimmy Carter's executive order relating to national security information was weighted on the side of disclosure. The first paragraph of that order set the tone: "If there is reasonable doubt which designation is appropriate, or whether the information should be classified at all, the less restrictive designation should be used, or the information should not be classified." Carter required officials classifying a document for more than six years to sign the orders calling for prolonged withholding from public scrutiny. Overall, documents were to be reviewed and declassified in twenty years.[2]

The Reagan order presumed the appropriateness of secrecy rather than openness. "If there is reasonable doubt about the need to classify information, it shall be safeguarded as if it were classified pending a determination," the order said. "If there is a reasonable doubt about the appropriate level of classification, it shall be safeguarded at the higher level of classification pending a determination." Instead of setting goals for automatic release of documents, Reagan's order said, "information shall be classified as long as required by national security considerations." To make matters even worse, the order said that appropriate officials "may reclassify information previously declassified and disclosed" upon determination that "the information requires protection in the interest of national security." As far as the release of information was concerned, the executive order only promised that "information shall be declassified or downgraded as soon as national security considerations permit."[3] In an administration that saw almost everything in terms of national security, the order offered no definition of "national security." The magnitude of this endorsement of increased classification can be understood only in light of estimates that between 800,000 and a million documents are classified annually. Officials familiar with the process estimate that close to 90 percent of these documents could be made public without injuring the national security.[4]

Classifying documents was only one portion of the administration's overall offensive against openness in government. One of its most controversial attacks on freedom of expression came a year later, in 1983, when the president issued National Security Decision Directive 84 (NSDD 84), "Safeguarding National Security Information." Under its terms, "each agency of the Executive Branch that originates or handles classified information shall adopt internal procedures to safeguard against unlawful disclosures of classified information." At the minimum, each employee was to "sign a nondisclosure agreement as a condition of access." Employees with access to more sensitive information were required to agree to submit all books, articles, and speeches based on their governmental work for prepublication review by their employing agency. This latter category ensnared top officials at the State and Defense departments, National Security Council staff members, and key White House advisers, as well as senior members of the military and the foreign service. Any unauthorized disclosure of confidential information had to be reported, and the Federal Bureau of Investigation (FBI) would investigate "such matters as constitute potential violations of federal criminal law." In addition, government agencies dealing with classified information were told to "revise existing regulations and policies, as necessary, so that employees may be required to submit to polygraph examinations, when appropriate, in the course of investigations of unauthorized disclosures of classified information."[5]

The Nixon administration's attempt to punish individuals who leaked classified information to the public through revisions in the nation's criminal laws had failed. Now, the Reagan White House proposed to make it most uncomfortable for any government employee who dared to make confidential information public. Much of the administration's plan had been around for quite some time. Requiring employees to agree to a prepublication review of any material based on information obtained while in government employ was standard in the State and Defense departments, the Central Intelligence and National Security agencies, and the Atomic Energy Commission. In most cases, these agreements required that individuals obtain clearance for the rest of their lives, thus all but eliminating criticism of government after the employee left government service. In many cases, this review was required regardless of whether the employee dealt with classified material.[6] The rules were a brazen form of prior restraint, effectively sealing the lips of government employees. As a result, the regulations reduced the amount of information available for the processes of self-government. If past and present federal employees were forbidden to talk about what they had learned while so employed, a fruitful source of details about government operations would be forever silenced.

At first blush, these restrictions would seem to violate the employees' rights to freedom of expression. Indeed, some government employees have thought so, have written books or articles that were not approved, and then have gone to court to win the right to comment freely upon governmental policies and activities. Courts, however, have not been receptive to such claims. For instance, a court of appeals in 1972 forced Victor Marchetti to abide by the terms of an agreement with the CIA that required any writing that he did about the service to be passed first by agency censors. Marchetti had published a novel and at least one magazine article critical of CIA policies without agency clearance; now he was planning additional articles and had a book manuscript under way. Agency head Richard Helms, unsure of whether courts would enforce that agreement, initiated the court case in the hopes that if the agency lost Congress would enact better legislation to protect the nation's secrets.[7] But federal judges enforced the agency's agreement, finding that Marchetti's previous publications had drawn upon classified information seen while working at the agency and that the CIA could review all future works. "Citizens have the right to criticize the conduct of our foreign affairs," the court said, "but the Government also has the right and the duty to strive for internal secrecy about the conduct of governmental affairs in areas in which disclosure may reasonably be thought to be inconsistent with the national interest."[8]

Marchetti was not forced to work for the CIA or to sign the prepublication review agreement, which was a condition for his employment. But since he had done both voluntarily, the three-judge panel could find no reason to order the CIA to change its procedures despite the fact that the agreements were acknowledged to be prior restraints. While coming to this conclusion, the court seemed unable to appreciate the impact that its decision would have on Marchetti's speech, incongruously noting that Marchetti "retains the right to speak and write about the CIA and its operations, and to criticize it as any other citizen may."[9] But the restrictions that the court placed upon the contents of his speech severely curtailed his ability to criticize the agency and its practices.

To a large extent, the court ignored First Amendment issues in reaching its conclusion. In part this approach was encouraged by the CIA's framing the case in terms of contract law: Marchetti had signed an agreement, and the courts were to ensure that he met its terms. In part this approach was based on the judiciary's belief that the executive branch was best equipped to supervise intelligence-gathering operations. "There is a practical reason for avoidance of judicial review of secrecy classifications," the three-member panel said. "The significance of one item of information may frequently depend upon knowledge of many other items of information. What may seem trivial to the uninformed, may appear of great moment to one who has a broad view of the scene and may put the questioned item of information in its proper context." According to these judges, courts "are ill-equipped to become sufficiently steeped in foreign intelligence matters to serve effectively in the review of secrecy classifications."[10]

With their words, the judges accepted the "mosaic theory" of information release.[11] Since courts were incapable of knowing how pieces of information fit together, they should stay out of the matter altogether. When the book that Marchetti co-authored with a former State Department intelligence officer finally appeared in print, it had been badly mangled by CIA-ordered deletions. The agency had begun by demanding more than 300 excisions, with the number finally being reduced after lengthy court hearings. The book, *The CIA and the Cult of Intelligence,* appeared with blank spaces where the deleted material was to have been printed as a testimony to the CIA's power to restrict the speech of past and present employees.

The Supreme Court did not review the Marchetti case, but it came to a similar conclusion in a case involving another CIA employee. Here, Frank Snepp published a book about his experiences in Vietnam without submitting the manuscript for prepublication review. The 1977 book, *Decent Interval,* was an indictment of the American government's behavior as South Vietnam fell to the North. After working on the book covertly, the volume appeared in the nation's bookstores before the CIA could seek a court-ordered review. The agency refused to allow Snepp, who had been a valued member of the intelligence community, to get away with his behavior. The Supreme Court, in a per curiam opinion, upheld the CIA's right to review all of Snepp's writings for the rest of his life. "When a former agent relies on his own judgment about what information is detrimental, he may reveal information that the CIA—with its broader understanding of what may expose classified information and confidential sources—could have identified as harmful," the Court said.[12] Because Snepp had already published his book, the Court awarded the CIA any profits that he might make from it.

Justice John Paul Stevens dissented, noting that because Snepp's book contained no classified information, Snepp had not breached his agreement to protect confidential data. "The CIA has a vital interest in protecting certain types of information," Stevens said, while "the CIA employee has a countervailing interest in preserving a wide range of work opportunities (including work as an author) and in protecting his First Amendment rights. The public interest lies in a proper accommodation that will preserve the intelligence mission of the agency while not abridging the free flow of information." The majority decision, he said, created "a species of prior restraint on a citizen's right to criticize his government. Inherent in this prior restraint is the risk that the reviewing agency will misuse its authority to delay the publication of a critical work or to persuade an author to modify the contents of his work beyond the demands of secrecy."[13]

Although Justice Stevens found it hard to believe that the government wanted such an extensive say in what their employees wrote or said, he was wrong. The urge to suppress critical speech knew no political bounds. Marchetti had his problems under the Nixon administration, and Snepp ran afoul of the CIA during the Carter presidency. Under Ronald Reagan, the campaign to limit critical speech reached its peak. The Reagan administration, for instance, successfully concluded the case against former CIA agent Philip Agee, which had begun several years earlier. Agee, also disenchanted with agency policies, took out his unhappiness differently: he traveled around the world exposing CIA operatives. Under existing law, government officials could only lift his passport. That they did, and the U.S. Supreme Court upheld the action despite Agee's complaints that the CIA was stifling his freedom of speech.[14] The Court's decision failed to reach the heart of the issue: the ability of individuals with information about the identities of intelligence operatives to reveal that data without punishment. To plug that loophole, the Reagan administration urged Congress to enact what became known as the Intelligence Identities Protection Act of 1982. Under its terms, individuals who released such information without authorization could be charged with a felony and subjected to jail sentences and fines upon conviction.[15]

Legislative redress was only one approach to silencing the loose tongues of governmental employees. NSDD 84 was another manifestation of that desire to suppress. Before long, the president's efforts to restrict employee speech and to use polygraphs to ferret out leakers ran into strong congressional opposition. Amendments were appended to other legislation forcing the president to delay implementation of his order, and hearings were held into the use of lie detectors on government employees. In the face of such opposition, Reagan withdrew the order. He did not, however, recant his basic philosophy.

With Congress blocking implementation of NSDD 84, the administration simply used older prepublication review contracts throughout the government. Congressional objections, the administration reasoned, were based solely on terms of the proposed new contract; thus, the old ones could be used with impunity. Although Congress did not object, some members of the administration did. Jeane J. Kirkpatrick, former ambassador to the United Nations, for example, refused to sign the document. The form, she said, "went way beyond promising not to reveal classified information. It means you can't write anything about government. I'm interested in writing about foreign affairs. I said no."[16] The president let the matter drop in Kirkpatrick's case. His attempt to use lie detectors to stop the loss of government information was stymied by the opposition of Secretary of State George Shultz, who said, "The minute in this government I am told that I am not trusted is the day that I leave."[17] Once again the president backed off.

On another front, Ronald Reagan led a persistent attack on the Freedom of Information Act (FOIA), which was designed to broaden citizen access to the records of executive departments and regulatory agencies. Amending that law became an almost constant preoccupation of Reagan allies in Congress, who tried to provide greater protection for national security information and for data that businesses submitted to regulatory agencies. Major challenges to the act were successfully beaten back while niggling clarifications in language ate away at the heart of the principle that the people have a right to know about the activities of their government. Conservatives in both government and business had a great interest in diluting the pesky law. Through its provisions, for example, information about the army's involvement in the My Lai massacre, the CIA's role in the overthrow of Chilean president Salvador Allende, and the FBI's illegal surveillance of American citizens came to light. Businesses complained that competitors used FOIA provisions to force regulatory agencies to disclose trade secrets. The business complaints may have had some validity because between 50 and 60 percent of all requests for information under the act were business-related.[18] On the other hand, concealment of business data could hamper the nation's ability to determine the success of vital national policies including equal employment and environmental protection. Conservative government officials and business leaders, however, carefully ignored possible societal benefits from disclosure.

When frontal attacks on the Freedom of Information Act proved unsuccessful in Congress, the Reagan White House still made the law less effective.[19] Through Reagan's classification executive order, for instance, the administration pulled material already in the public domain back under its protective shield. Such labeling made it almost impossible for individuals to obtain some documents. In addition, citing the need for slashing the federal deficit, the number of employees assigned to process FOIA requests was decreased. Using the same grounds, government agencies began to limit fee waivers. Now requesters could anticipate hefty searching and copying fees for any FOIA request. The only way around a refusal to waive fees or an outright refusal to release documents was to take the matter into court, where a federal bench increasingly staffed by judges appointed by Ronald Reagan was less willing to interfere with executive branch decisions on FOIA matters.[20]

Thus, although unable to repeal the Freedom of Information Act, the president found considerable room for outfoxing congressional intent. And still he had other ways to decrease the amount of information made public. One of the most useful avenues was an act signed in the waning days of the Carter presidency designed to limit government intrusion into the lives of American citizens by reducing the number of reports that government kept on various subjects. The Paperwork Reduction Act of 1980 had admirable goals, including one that called for a 25 percent reduction in the amount of information collected by the government by 1983.[21] Coupling this act with the need to trim the federal budget, the Reagan administration began eliminating government publications. By 1984, more than 2,000 items were stricken from the list of government documents, with officials piously pointing to guides on buying a Christmas tree and cleaning a kitchen sink as examples of wasted effort and money. Less well publicized was the cancellation of *The Car Book,* which reported the results of auto safety and mileage tests conducted by the government; the automobile industry had objected to its continuation.[22] Other publications that helped consumers keep tabs on industry and maintain a watch on government likewise were eliminated under the guise of reducing governmental interference in the lives of the American people.[23]

Perhaps the high point of this effort to restrict access to information occurred in 1983 when U.S. armed forces invaded the small Caribbean island of Grenada. A coup had toppled the established leadership, a revolutionary military council had been installed, and deposed officials had been executed. President Reagan claimed that the lives of American students enrolled in a medical school on the island were endangered because Fidel Castro supported the revolt and that Cuban troops were on the island. The president's conclusions flew in the face of reality. Castro, for instance, denounced the coup, at least in part because his government had had close ties to the slain leaders. In addition, most of the Cubans on Grenada were construction workers, not soldiers. Refusing to believe Castro, Reagan decided the students had to be rescued, and he sent some 6,000 American troops to subdue a Grenadan military force of about 1,000, about 75 Cuban construction workers, and about 40 Cuban military advisers. Interestingly, the invasion occurred two days after a guerrilla attack in Beirut, Lebanon, destroyed the U.S. Marine Corps headquarters there and killed 241 men. More jaded observers saw the Grenadan action as designed to shift attention from the disaster in Beirut. If that was a reason behind the rapid intervention, the ploy worked, for the nation's focus quickly shifted to the Caribbean. At least part of the reason for the change, however, was unplanned, for a great deal of the comment about Operation Urgent Fury concentrated on the fact that, for the first time in American history, journalists were forbidden to accompany the nation's troops into battle.[24]

The decision to exclude journalists was made by the military and endorsed by civilian leaders. Such a move was not made in a vacuum, for U.S. military officials were simply following the precedent set during the Falklands War when British journalists were excluded from battle sites, leaving military officers with greater freedom to maneuver.[25] Unfortunately, the invading troops took longer than the one day their superiors thought would be necessary to subdue the island. As the operation ran into four days, government credibility became the issue, and reporters grew increasingly hostile.

Much of the anger directed at the military was richly deserved. Within hours after the president announced the invasion, more than 400 journalists were in Barbados, about 160 miles northeast of Grenada, and all of them were trying to get to the scene of the action. Four journalists who were on Grenada before the invasion occurred—three Americans and a Briton—were picked up by U.S. troops and taken to a U.S. ship where they were held virtually incommunicado for three days. They had stories, but the military refused to transmit them to the United States. When other reporters hired small boats or airplanes to take them to Grenada, the military made menacing moves that forced the journalists away from the island. For the first two days of the battle, the only news available to the American people on the confrontation came from government sources, complete with official videotape footage for the evening newscasts. By the third day of the invasion, military personnel took selected journalists on carefully supervised excursions around the island in an attempt to stifle critical commentary. The fifteen-member pool had been told that they would return to Barbados by 5 p.m. so that they could file their stories in time for the evening news. But President Reagan planned to address the nation on the invasion at 8 p.m., and the airplane carrying the journalists remained on the runway in Grenada—allegedly due to excessive air traffic in the area—until after his speech. Military officers had good reasons for restricting journalistic access to the island because as reporters obtained freer access to Grenada, they began filing stories that questioned official details. Their stories told of the inaccurate information and unproven opinions that had led to the invasion in the first place and of how a U.S. Navy plane had accidentally bombed a civilian mental hospital. Soon, the exclusion of the press and military performance became bigger stories than the rescue of the students.[26]

Realizing that excluding the press from the invasion had been a tactical error, General John W. Vessey, chairman of the Joint Chiefs of Staff, soon appointed a special panel to help set guidelines on "how in this modern age of the television camera, [with] instantaneous communications around the world, we can conduct military operations and protect the operation, protect our own people and still inform the American people."[27] The panel headed by Winant Sidle, a retired army major general who had been the chief military information officer during the Vietnam War, eventually recommended that planning for military operations in the future include arrangements for press coverage. Journalists involved in this coverage, however, must follow the military's rules. The procedures recommended, in fact, were much like those rules invoked during World War II and involved accrediting reporters, providing official briefings, and establishing ground rules. There would be no more Vietnams where journalists gathered their news unsupervised.

Although the recommendations of the Sidle Commission sounded good on paper and were greeted with great approval all around, they proved to be almost worthless. News media representatives trying to cover encounters between the United States and Libya in March and April 1986, for example, complained of inadequate access to the battle scene.[28] Similar complaints were raised about coverage of the U.S. Navy escort being provided for reflagged Kuwaiti tankers in the Persian Gulf in summer 1987.[29] And even greater complaints were heard in early 1990, after reporters trying to report on the Panama invasion were greatly restricted.[30] Journalists hypothesized that military limitations were designed to ensure that all operations were bathed in positive publicity.

The journalistic hypothesis was proven true faster than most reporters would have expected or hoped. In August 1990, less than a year after the secrecy-clothed Panama invasion, the United States and its allies went to the aid of Kuwait, which had been invaded by neighboring Iraq. After a buildup of several months, the air war started on January 16, 1991, and a brief ground war followed. From August 1990 through March 1991, American journalists practiced their profession under the strictest of rules. Information came primarily from official briefings that presented closely screened data that omitted anything that might endanger the operation's success. These daily briefings were held by civilian and military officials adept at handling the press. In fact, early in the operation, the services had a succession of people at the speaker's lectern—until they found just the right combination of official sources to explain the war to the American people.[31]

Only closely supervised pool reporters were allowed to visit with troops, and their military overseers made sure that conversations did not touch on any sensitive issues. If enterprising journalists did manage to find out anything that civilian and military officials did not want released, those officers simply deleted the material from written or broadcast copy. Censors also would change wording and shadings in the stories. For the first time since World War II, the copy of American reporters went back to the American people with the words "Cleared by American Censors" appended.

Why the news was so tightly controlled likely will be debated for years. One reason clearly stems from a pledge by President George Bush as the shooting war drew closer. "In our country, I know that there are fears of another Vietnam," he said. "Let me assure you, should military action be required, this will not be another Vietnam."[32] He was referring specifically to the fact that he did not intend to become involved in another long, drawn-out land war such as that in Vietnam. As the war progressed, however, "this will not be another Vietnam" also signified the unwillingness of military and civilian leaders to allow the press free reign as they had had in Vietnam. In fact, these leaders repeatedly referred to the Persian Gulf War as serving to erase the blot on the military's reputation that was placed there by the Vietnam War—and, they believed, in large part by the press.

Another reason for the tight control on news was, of course, the change in technology over the years. Vietnam had been the first televised war, and the military had not known how to handle the new medium. But the first televised war was far different from the first satellite war. In Vietnam, film still had to be shipped back to the United States for use; that meant a time delay of hours, if not days, before film went into the nation's living rooms. News from the Persian Gulf, however, came into homes and offices around the world immediately—including those of the enemy. The networks suspended programming for several days after the war broke out and regularly interrupted shows for the latest bulletins. Scud attacks on Israel and Saudi Arabia were popular special bulletins as Americans watched journalists, military personnel, and civilians don gas masks and take cover. Inaccurate information was commonplace as reporters told—incorrectly—of chemical warfare attacks.[33] And accurate information likewise was immediately revealed—telling Saddam Hussein, for example, exactly where in Israel his missiles had landed—until censors began limiting the transmission of such data. And, for the first time in our history, journalists provided a live view of the enemy's version of the war when Peter Arnett, a correspondent for the Cable News Network, reported regularly from the Iraqi capital.

Americans knew that the news was being censored on all sides; public opinion polls repeatedly proved that point. But those polls also proved another rather distressing point: Americans approved of the restrictions. A Times-Mirror poll, for instance, showed that at one point 79 percent of those questioned thought that military censorship was a good idea.[34] Such reactions thus put the press in a most difficult situation, and many critics felt that journalists generally handled themselves badly during the war. The American people, said these critics, were denied access to information that they needed to develop informed opinions about the war, and the press allowed itself to be manipulated by civilian and military officials by not protesting restrictions and doctored news.[35]

Not all journalists acquiesced silently to such restrictions. Walter Cronkite, onetime anchor of the "CBS Evening News," wrote in *Newsweek* early in the war, "With an arrogance foreign to the democratic system, the U.S. military in Saudi Arabia is trampling on the American people's right to know." He accused the military of "acting on a generally discredited Pentagon myth that the Vietnam War was lost because of the uncensored press coverage" and called for greater openness on the grounds that secrecy would encourage the American people to distrust military leaders.[36] Cronkite was also one of the witnesses appearing before a special hearing of the Senate Committee on Governmental Affairs that was looking into the Pentagon's rules. Also appearing was Sydney H. Schanberg, a correspondent for *Newsday,* who had spent years covering Indochina. Schanberg charged that "the caging of the press in the Gulf has nothing to do with military security, [that] it is an act of political security done out of fear that a free flow of information about the war could change public opinion." Censorship was designed to make the war "sound more like a choir-boys picnic than the grungy thing that it is," he said, as he noted that "swear words uttered by soldiers are being removed from stories by censors" and "when some pilots spent the evening before a major bombing run watching porno movies, that information was removed."[37]

Schanberg was one of a handful of media representatives challenging Pentagon restrictions in court. Plaintiffs in the case did not include the *New York Times* or the *Washington Post,* leading figures in earlier freedom of the press cases. Here the plaintiffs included a few individual journalists and magazines such as *The Nation, Harper's, The Progressive,* and *Mother Jones.* Through the case, the journalists claimed that "the press has a First Amendment right to unlimited access to a foreign arena in which American military forces are engaged." The Department of Defense (DOD) responded that "the First Amendment does not bar the government from restricting access to combat activities and that the regulations are narrowly tailored and necessitated by compelling national security concerns." The case, if brought to fruition, might have led to the first definitive statement on the rights of the press in covering a foreign war involving U.S. troops. The judge in the case, however, decided that the issue was moot. "The Persian Gulf war, like many recent U.S. military conflicts, was short and swift," he said. "As such, this court concludes that the controversy engendered by the . . . regulations did not 'last long enough for complete judicial review.'"[38] Thus the ability of the government to manipulate information about war continued unabated awaiting the possible challenge of another war.

The Reagan administration used information in other ways as well, at times lying outright to the world in order to achieve what the administration considered to be justifiable ends. Of course White House officials did not label their activities as lying. Instead, they used the euphemism "disinformation" and said they simply were trying to build up fear within their enemy's camp. Americans never would have become involved in such activities, the conservatives occupying the executive branch said, if it had not been for the Russians. After all, Communist defectors had long ago revealed that the Soviets were selectively spreading *dezinformatsiya* about the United States throughout the world; Americans were responding in kind. But the Reagan administration not only sought to affect enemies, it tried to convince the American people to back certain policies based almost wholly on manipulated data.[39]

Targets of the disinformation campaign were many. Fidel Castro and his Communist government in Cuba remained popular as the Reagan administration tried to link them to the international drug trade. Eastern Europeans in general and Bulgarians in particular were tied to a plot to assassinate Pope John Paul II that ended in his being wounded during a public appearance in Rome in 1982. Members of the renascent peace movement were tarnished as Communist dupes as they advocated an end to nuclear weapons and a general disarmament. But the disinformation campaign that blew up in the administration's face and brought the program to light involved an effort to destabilize the government of Libyan strong man Muammar Kaddafi in 1986.

Reporter Bob Woodward of Watergate fame had obtained a copy of a memorandum from national security adviser John Poindexter to President Reagan calling for a disinformation campaign against the Libyan leader. The United States had already attacked Libya once for its terrorist activities; now, the goal was to make "Kaddafi *think* that there is a high degree of internal opposition to him within Libya, that his key trusted aides are disloyal, that the U.S. is about to move against him militarily."[40] In order to make Kaddafi think that way, the government manipulated information so much that the American people came to the same conclusion. The *Wall Street Journal,* for instance, ran a story about alleged Kaddafi plans for more terrorist attacks, suggesting that the United States anticipated military retaliation.

That story was based on the government's disinformation campaign, which Poindexter defended, proclaiming that the government has the right to lie in order to protect national security. "The whole question comes down to: Is deception going to be a tool that the government can use in combatting a very significant national security problem, and I think that the answer . . . has to be yes," he told the *Los Angeles Times.* "We had no intent and did not plan or conspire to mislead the American press in any way," he added. Secretary of State George Shultz blamed the press for blowing the incident out of proportion. The media, Shultz said, could not resist reporting anything that the government wanted kept confidential. When they heard about the campaign against Kaddafi, they reported on it without asking whether it was true. Shultz's facile excuses won few converts among the nation's journalists. And within his own establishment, State Department spokesman Bernard Kalb, a former journalist who had specialized in reporting on foreign affairs, found himself at odds with the secretary. Kalb resigned after examining whether "as an American, as a spokesman, as a journalist . . . to enter a modest dissent."[41]

The Reagan administration was not the first to lie to the American people, nor was it the first to be caught. Dwight Eisenhower lied about the U-2 plane that the Soviets shot down over their territory; John Kennedy lied about the Bay of Pigs; Lyndon Johnson lied about the Vietnam buildup; Richard Nixon lied about Watergate; and Jimmy Carter lied about the plan to rescue the American hostages being held in Iran. In each of these instances, the lies were discovered, and the administrations involved offered few regrets for manipulating public opinion. Presidents seem to assume that an inherent right to lie accompanies them into the Oval Office. Such manipulation is easily justified on national security grounds. Disseminating factual information and allowing Americans to debate that information, which is supposedly their First Amendment right, simply is too dangerous, for the people still cannot be trusted to come to the right decisions.

Indeed, ignorance of government operations may be one of Ronald Reagan's greatest legacies. During his eight years as president, Reagan transformed a moderately open government into a predominantly closed one. His goal was to protect the American people from the great Red Menace, which topped the president's list of enemies until Mikhail Gorbachev assumed control in 1985 and boldly sought an adjustment in the Soviet Union's relationship with the United States. Even then, Reagan managed to maintain a fear of communism as a central theme of his administration; he simply switched to the Cuban brand that Fidel Castro was exporting throughout Central and South America. Capitalizing on these fears of Cuban communism, the president justified intervening in Central American affairs, including the backing of the contras, the so-called freedom fighters of Nicaragua. Other great Reagan enemies included Middle Eastern extremists such as the Ayatollah Ruhollah Khomeini of Iran, Yasser Arafat of the Palestine Liberation Organization, and Kaddafi. Indeed these great fears would lead to the major scandal of his administration, the Iran-contra affair, in which administration officials tried to obtain the release of American hostages held by Moslem extremists in Lebanon by selling arms to Iran and diverting part of the proceeds to support the contras in Nicaragua contrary to the express will of Congress. The fact that the Iran-contra affair became public knowledge is a tribute to the fact that Reagan had not been able to stop the flow of information completely.

American journalists could claim little credit for disclosing the Iran-contra scandal. In fact, during the Reagan years, American journalists were uncommonly docile. Part of this attitude had to do with the fact that Reagan was one of the best-managed presidents in American history. His White House aides understood journalists and their needs better than any before them. The most important thing, they knew, was to provide a videotape for the evening news in which Reagan's pleasing personality was spotlighted. White House aides kept the rest of the press corps inundated with government-approved information so that they would not seek their own news. The Washington press corps had always been more of an ally of the president than an adversary, despite journalistic myth to the contrary, and reporters maintained that role during the Reagan administration. The only time that the press truly played the adversary role was during the Vietnam and Watergate years; now it rested on both its laurels and its fears. The fear stemmed in part from the belief that the American people thought journalists too liberal and thus unfair to conservatives. Although much of this myth was invented by New Right politicians and based on faulty information, reporters still bent over backward trying to be fair to Ronald Reagan.[42]

Another factor behind the soft treatment granted Reagan was the fact that most journalists now worked for media conglomerates whose owners were solid Republicans as well as supporters and friends of the president. Although orders did not come down from the top saying that White House correspondents should treat the president gently, reporters knew how their employers felt, and they acted accordingly. In addition, journalists knew that locking horns with Ronald Reagan would be perceived differently from similar behavior with other politicians. Reagan was generally well liked by the American people, and his genial personality simply did not lend itself to rough treatment by the press corps. As a result—and despite what his publicists or his right-wing supporters might say—he was asked few hard questions, even when they were in order. He was not even challenged when his administration took steps that infringed upon the press's rights under the First Amendment. Certainly journalists at all levels protested loudly over the Grenada incident, but they were strangely quiet while other actions undercut freedom of expression.

With the help of increasingly conservative federal judges, many of whom Reagan had appointed, the administration made repeated attacks on the expressive freedoms of American citizens. The goal from the beginning apparently was a judicially approved official secrets act that would allow administration personnel to curtail dissemination of information even further without having to obtain the permission of Congress. Other presidents paved the way for restrictions on freedom of expression based on national security reasons. Richard Nixon, of course, tried but failed to stop the publication of the Pentagon Papers and to convict Daniel Ellsberg for giving the classified study to the media. After the Pentagon Papers incident, many Americans likely believed that no president would ever try to restrict publication of anything. Those who entertained such beliefs, however, could not have anticipated the Carter administration's response to an attempt by *The Progressive* magazine to reveal how the H-bomb was constructed. The case was fundamental to later Reagan administration efforts.

The whole matter started when freelance writer Howard Morland approached the magazine with an idea for an article. Morland, a former air force pilot, had become a strong foe of nuclear weaponry, a position the magazine shared. Morland, who had only a rudimentary scientific education, wanted to learn how to make a hydrogen bomb, so he visited libraries and spoke publicly with experts in the field. When his research revealed how easy it was to obtain the information, both the author and magazine editors believed they would have proven that details about the nation's thermonuclear program were shrouded in secrecy primarily to stifle informed debate. Americans, they believed, needed to know about nuclear weapons so that they could make intelligent decisions about their continued manufacture. Indeed, their plan worked better than any of the principals could have imagined. After six months of research, the article was completed, and Morland indeed had explained how to assemble a hydrogen bomb.[43]

Rather than publishing the material immediately, the editors of the magazine made a serious mistake. Concerned about the accuracy of scientific details—but not about the possibility of breaching any security regulations—they sent copies of the manuscript to various experts for comment. Many magazines follow this

procedure before publishing technical material, and so *Progressive* editors entertained no second thoughts about asking experts to review the piece before publication. One of these experts turned the manuscript over the Department of
Energy for comment. Even then, the manuscript likely would have been lost in
the department's bureaucracy had not the magazine's editors, becoming anxious
as the deadline for publication approached, sent another copy to department
officials for their comments. This time Morland's article captured the department's full attention.

Government attorneys asked a federal district court near the publication's
headquarters to stop the article from appearing in print. Barely eight years had
passed since the last request for a prior restraint against publication. The current
case, however, was quite different. In the Pentagon Papers affair, government
officials relied on vague references to the national security and on totally inapplicable sections of the Espionage Act to build a case against publication. But
here, federal attorneys accused the magazine's editors of violating a particular
federal statute. The Atomic Energy Act of 1954 specifically banned the distribution of "restricted data," which included "all data concerning: (1) design,
manufacture, or utilization of atomic weapons."[44] Under this provision, everything relating to nuclear weapons was automatically classified until it was purposefully removed from that category. Although Morland had used information
from a variety of sources, including documents that the government had declassified, the article in which he combined all of data fell under the so-called "born
secret" provisions of the act. It now was classified and would remain so until the
government decided otherwise, and as such, it could not be published. Since the
act had been written in the depths of the cold war and no one had ever challenged
its provisions before, magazine editors decided not to buckle under to government pressure. The material on which the article was based had come from the
public domain, and they could see no reason for the government to ban publication simply because the data had been assembled in a different form. American journalists were far from enthusiastic about the magazine's determination
to pursue the matter. As the *Los Angeles Times* said, "It is the wrong issue, at
the wrong time, in the wrong place."[45] The *Washington Post,* one of the primary
actors in the Pentagon Papers matter, was equally succinct in its evaluation.
Under a headline that read "John Mitchell's Dream Case," the *Post* termed the
Progressive case as "the one the Nixon administration was never lucky enough
to get: a real First Amendment loser."[46]

Few sided with the magazine as it went before Judge Robert Warren in March
1979. The judge had granted a temporary injunction against publication, and he
was more than willing to make the order permanent. In fact, he was so convinced
by the government's written arguments that he did not even hear witnesses on
the issue. While acknowledging the importance of First Amendment rights,
Warren noted that "First Amendment rights are not absolute. . . . not bound-
less." Agreeing with the magazine's attorneys that the article did not "provide a
'do-it yourself' guide" for building an H-bomb, he still had grave reservations.
"The article could possibly provide sufficient information to allow a medium
size[d] nation to move faster in developing a hydrogen weapon. It could provide

a ticket to by-pass blind alleys." Given the dangers that the article presented, Warren said, "this Court can find no plausible reason why the public needs to know the technical details about hydrogen bomb construction to carry on an informed debate on the issue."[47]

Granting that the case provided "a basic confrontation between the First Amendment right to freedom of the press and national security," Warren decided that national security was far more important. "In the short-run," he said, "one cannot enjoy freedom of speech, freedom to worship or freedom of the press unless one first enjoys the freedom to live." In fact, he said, "faced with a stark choice between upholding the right to continued life and the right to freedom of the press, most jurists would have no difficulty in opting for the chance to continue to breathe and function as they work to achieve perfect freedom of expression." Although the U.S. Supreme Court had established a stiff standard to meet in order to justify a prior restraint, Judge Warren determined that publication of details on manufacturing the H-bomb threatened "grave, direct, immediate and irreparable harm to the United States."[48]

As magazine attorneys prepared to appeal the case, several strange things happened. Government officials, for instance, found many of the more sensitive documents involved in the case indeed had been declassified and had been readily available at government libraries for several years. Officials reclassified many of the documents, claiming they had been declassified by mistake. While the appeal was pending, computer programmer Chuck Hansen made the matter moot. Hansen had the unusual hobby of collecting information about nuclear weaponry, and early in September, he sent letters to several newspapers showing what he said was a cross-section of a hydrogen bomb complete with details on how to trigger a thermonuclear explosion. One recipient, *The Daily Californian,* the student newspaper at the University of California at Berkeley, made plans to publish the letter but was enjoined from doing so. On September 16, the *Press Connection* in Madison, Wisconsin, published Hansen's letter. On the same day, the *Chicago Tribune* told the government that it planned to print portions of Hansen's letter, as if challenging the government to attempt to silence it.

On September 17, the Justice Department announced plans to seek dismissal of the restraining orders against *The Progressive* and the University of California newspaper because the material had now been printed. The Morland article finally appeared in the November 1979 issue of the magazine, six months after its intended publication date. In the issue containing the disputed article, *Progressive* editors said that they hoped to begin a debate "in which all of the nuclear policies pursued by our Government will be held up to public scrutiny and review." Although the editors hoped "that when Americans know the facts they will share our views," they had an even greater goal. "Most of all," they said, "we hope they will come to *know the facts.* We are willing to take our chances with the judgments of an *informed* people; that is called democracy. People who want to be ignorant and free, as Madison observed, want that which never was and never will be."[49]

In the wake of resolution of the *Progressive* case, newspaper editorial opinion modified somewhat. Although many editorialists were delighted that the government had dropped its case against the magazine, they were still convinced, with the *St. Petersburg Times*, that "No public good can come from wider dissemination of technical facts about the bomb. Americans can make informed decisions on such issues as nuclear energy and arms control without their morning paper publishing details of the H-bomb."[50] Other newspapers, however, joined with the *Detroit Free Press* in its assessment of the situation: "The threat of proliferation, this assault on the First Amendment reminds us, lies not just in the physical destruction that may someday occur from the spread of weapons technology, but in the police state psychology that develops as government strives to 'protect' us from accidents, disasters or terrorism."[51] According to the *Sacramento Bee,* a government victory would have caused "incalculable" damage "to the First Amendment and the public's right to know." As the government had prepared its appeal, its attorneys had argued that no technical data should have First Amendment protection. That doctrine, the newspaper noted, "would greatly have facilitated the censorship and suppression of everything from the specifications and effects of chemical pesticides to the conclusions of federal investigators about the causes of a particular aircraft accident." Court acceptance of that point, the newspaper said, would have meant "a judicially imposed official secrets act."[52]

Journalists had long believed that federal officials were so fascinated by the British Official Secrets Act that they wanted to have an American version. The British law ostensibly was enacted to protect national security matters, but over the years, various governments had enlarged its scope to the point where any activity touched by government remained confidential unless and until a properly delegated official released the data. English journalists are essentially reduced to telling the British people solely what the government wants known— unless, of course, they are willing to face criminal sanctions.[53] Few in American government circles fancy such an expansive official secrets act, but many are attracted to a version that would stop leaks of so-called national security information. But Congress has been reluctant to enact the necessary legislation, leaving the executive branch without much to rely on when it comes to restricting what it considers to be vital information. The classification system, for instance, does not have the force of law, so it could not be used to prosecute individuals who leak or print restricted data. The Atomic Energy Act was successful in blocking *The Progressive,* but once the information got out, the government did not prosecute those who printed it. The only weapon left to the government to stop the unauthorized release of information was the Espionage Act, and Ronald Reagan and his administration turned to this law in 1984 in an effort to win a judicially imposed official secrets act.

Presidents had awaited just the right case to use in experimenting with provisions of the Espionage Act. Richard Nixon had used it to prosecute Daniel Ellsberg, but that case fell apart due to governmental misconduct. Luckily for Ronald Reagan, the case that fell into his lap was relatively clear-cut. Samuel Loring Morison, an employee of the Naval Intelligence Support Center in Suitland, Maryland, had a security clearance that allowed him to work on Sensitive Compartmented Information, materials that were classified above top secret. His specialty, analyzing Soviet amphibious ships and mine warfare capabilities, gave him access to some of the nation's most sensitive intelligence data. Unfortunately for Morison, he was unhappy in his job. He longed to follow in the footsteps of his grandfather, Samuel Eliot Morison, a famous naval historian, and write about what he was analyzing daily. Thus Morison obtained permission from the Navy to edit the American section of *Jane's Fighting Ships,* a venerable British publication that reviews the world's navies. But Jane's was starting up a weekly publication, *Jane's Defence Weekly,* and Morison longed for a full-time position on the weekly's staff.[54]

To win a staff job, Morison had to convince *Jane's* just how valuable he would be. To do so, he sent the magazine classified information about an explosion at a Soviet shipyard and pictures of a Soviet nuclear-powered aircraft carrier then under construction. Complicating the situation was the fact that the pictures were taken by a top-secret spy satellite. Morison simply picked them up off a colleague's desk, clipped off classification markings on the margins, and sent them to *Jane's.* An investigation after the publication of the pictures led to Morison's doorstep. The FBI, for example, confiscated the ribbon off his typewriter at the office and discovered letters that he had written to the editor of *Jane's.* In addition, *Jane's,* abiding by Britain's Official Secrets Act and protecting its longtime friendship with the U.S. Navy, returned the pictures to the American government. FBI agents found Morison's fingerprints on the face of one of the prints. They arrested him as he was getting ready to take a vacation trip to London, where he planned to pursue the *Jane's* job in person.

Morison was charged with violating sections of the Espionage Act that were added to the World War I legislation at the height of the cold war. Specifically, he was accused of having lawful possession of certain national security information—data about the ship explosion—and "willfully communicat[ing] . . . the same to any person not entitled to receive it." In addition, he was said to have violated another provision designed to punish individuals who had "unauthorized possession of . . . photograph[s] . . . relating to the national defense, . . . which information the possessor has reason to believe could be used to the injury of the United States or to the advantage of any foreign nation."[55] In the charge related to sending photographs of the Soviet ship to *Jane's,* the government claimed that when *Jane's* printed the photographs, it revealed the capabilities of a super-secret U.S. spy satellite.

Accompanying the 1984 arrest was a concerted effort to portray Morison as a spy rather than as a person simply leaking information to the press. Considerable doubt existed as to whether the government could use the Espionage Act to punish individuals who leaked information to the press, but if federal attorneys could convince a judge that Morison's actions had jeopardized the nation's security, they had a better chance. In reality, federal attorneys were pursuing exactly the same devil in both scenarios. Their task was to end leaks—and if convicting a government employee who sent information to the press would accomplish that goal, then a conviction was both necessary and desirable. Morison was to be *the* test case on the applicability of the Espionage Act to individuals who passed information to the press rather than to foreign governments. Despite the fact that leaking was at the heart of the case, few press representatives endorsed Morison's effort to wrap his actions in the First Amendment. Federal authorities had been quite successful in cloaking his activities in crass materialism—after all, he had been paid by *Jane's* and was seeking full-time employment at the magazine. In addition, when he was first questioned, Morison had tried to place the blame on a fellow employee. And then, he was caught while trying to leave the country. Journalists, often forgetting the likes of Jay Near, prefer to have their First Amendment cases packaged in noble causes and personalities. Morison had no such image, and few journalists supported him during his 1985 trial.

Morison's lawyers tried to get the charges dismissed on the grounds that the statute violated basic First Amendment freedoms. They argued, for instance, that the law was unconstitutionally vague in that it did not give Morison proper notice that what he was doing would violate the law and that the statutory language did not apply to Morison because he gave information to the press rather than to a foreign government. District Court Judge Joseph H. Young turned back all efforts to have the indictment dismissed. To Young, a person could be charged for leaking data to the press just as easily as for passing it to a foreign government. On the latter point, he said, "The danger to the United States is just as great when this information is released to the press as when it is released to an agent of a foreign government." In fact, Young said, "the fear in releasing this type of information is that it gives other nations information concerning the intelligence gathering capabilities of the United States. That fear is realized whether the information is released to the world at large or whether it is released only to specific spies."[56]

When the trial began in October 1985, Judge Young was obviously on the side of the government. Morison's attorneys, for example, wanted at least two journalists to testify about the prevalence of information leaks in Washington, D.C., and about how high government officials regularly leaked classified data. The court ruled that in order for their testimony to be admitted, the journalists would have to reveal the sources of their data. They refused to do so and did not take the stand. In addition, Morison's attorneys wanted him to tell the court that he had no intention to harm the government when he gave the information to *Jane's,* which Young refused to allow. Motivation, he said, had nothing to do with the case. All the government had to do was to prove that Morison had violated regulations. After four hours of deliberation, the jury found Morison guilty. The judge sentenced him to two years in prison for espionage and theft of government property.

With the conviction, journalists became increasingly concerned. Despite Justice Department reassurances that the government would never use §793 of the Espionage Act against establishment journalists, they worried. The American Civil Liberties Union (ACLU), which had been trying to enlist the press in Morison's defense, played upon those fears. As Washington ACLU office head Morton Halperin said, "The danger is that you'll have a very hot story, you'll go to the White House, and there's a possibility that you'll hear the attorney general say, 'Well, if you print that story we'll indict you under 793, and if you don't believe it ask your attorneys about the Morison case." Many journalists, however, still believed that the government would never dare to use the Espionage Act against the establishment press. Still others, more in tune with the conservative feelings of the day, found it impossible to support a man whom they considered no better than a spy. Even so, thirty-one press-related organizations, including the conservative American Newspaper Publishers Association, whose president at the time was a former official spokesman for the Pentagon, filed a friend-of-the-court brief for Morison's appeal. At the heart of the carefully written document was a defense of individuals who leaked information to the press. The leaker, it said, was "engaged in activity at the core of the First Amendment's protection." Regardless of motivations, "the overall effect of public disclosures concerning the affairs of government is to enhance the people's ability to understand their government and to control their own destiny."[57]

The appeals court found no merit in Morison's contention that he was doing a public service by sending *Jane's* the material in question. The three-judge panel unanimously upheld the conviction. In a special concurrence, Judge J. Harvie Wilkinson III noted that the case had significant First Amendment overtones. "Criminal restraints on the disclosure of information threaten the ability of the press to scrutinize and report on government activity," he said. "There exists the tendency, even in a constitutional democracy, for government to withhold reports of disquieting developments and to manage news in a fashion most favorable to itself." Acknowledging James Madison's belief that a popular government needed to be based on widely disseminated information, he noted, "public debate . . . is diminished without access to unfiltered facts." Wilkinson stressed that "the First Amendment interest in informed popular debate does not simply vanish at the invocation of the words 'national security.' National security is public security, not government security from informed criticism. No decisions are more serious than those touching on peace and war; none are more certain to affect every member of society." Although the judge had difficulty placing Morison's actions in that category, he did admit that "the undeniable effect of the disclosure was to enhance public knowledge and interest in the projection of Soviet sea power such as that revealed in the satellite photos."[58]

Journalists were right to be concerned about the implications of Morison's conviction, Wilkinson said. The friend-of-the-court brief submitted by media representatives discussed stories on "illegal domestic surveillance by the CIA, design defects of the Abrams M-1 tank, Soviet arms control violations, and military procurement cost overruns" that had become public because of news leaks. The journalists contended that if their sources of information faced prosecution under the Espionage Act, " 'corruption, scandal, and incompetence in the defense establishment would be protected from scrutiny.' " Judge Wilkinson agreed that "investigative reporting is a critical component of the First Amendment's goal of accountability in government. To stifle it might leave the public interest prey to the manifold abuses of unexamined power." But he could not agree that upholding Morison's conviction would lead to that end: "Even if juries could ever be found that would convict those who truly expose governmental waste and misconduct, the political firestorm that would follow prosecution of one who exposed an administration's own ineptitude would make such prosecutions a rare and unrealistic prospect."[59]

The Supreme Court refused to hear his case, and Morison went off to jail. As he departed, some commentators began to argue that Reagan had succeeded where Woodrow Wilson had failed. Wilson, with a real war pending, had been unable to obtain legislation allowing him to censor the press. The Reagan administration, with the cold war disappearing before its eyes and the need for national security more in its mind than in actuality, won an official secrets act by judicial fiat. Although technically the Supreme Court's refusal to review the case meant that the ruling applied only to the five states covered by the Fourth District, many legal scholars felt that the Espionage Act now allowed the government to act against both employees and journalists who released information that the administration wanted kept secret. Others evaluating the case believed that Morison had only gotten what he deserved. He had signed a secrecy agreement; he had participated in routine briefings on what that agreement entailed; and he had deliberately violated the agreement—not to illuminate government deceit or mismanagement but to win a job on a publication that would be considered on the fringe of the journalistic establishment. To many in and out of the media, the First Amendment implications of his behavior were slight.

But what if a member of the mainline journalism establishment was threatened under the Espionage Act for printing materials deemed harmful to the national security? Would that lead to any different conclusions? Strangely enough, just such a situation presented itself as the Morison case was wending its way through the court system. In May 1986, CIA Director William J. Casey launched a campaign to keep details about secret intelligence communications out of the media through use of the Espionage Act. He announced his readiness to prosecute any journalist who released classified information "concerning the communication intelligence activities of the United States . . . [or information] obtained by the processes of communication intelligence from the communications of any foreign government."[60] Casey had at least two causes for concern. In one instance, journalists for the *Washington Post* and *Newsweek* had disclosed that secret communications monitoring devices had allowed the U.S. government to eavesdrop on conversations between Libyan officials in Tripoli and the Libyan People's Bureau in East Berlin prior to the April bombing of a Berlin discothèque in which two American servicemen were killed. The terrorist act served as the trigger for an American bombing raid on Libya. The problem with Casey's allegation was that President Reagan himself revealed details of the communications intercepts over national television as he justified American action against Libya.[61]

Casey's second cause for alarm raised even more significant questions for communications security and involved that perennial nemesis of government secrecy—Bob Woodward of the *Washington Post*. This time, Woodward's sources told him about American ability to monitor Soviet communications, and Woodward prepared a story based on the information. Because of the sensitivity of the data, *Post* editors negotiated with the government over what could be published and what had to be withheld. After months of negotiations, Casey simply told *Post* editors: "I'm not threatening you, but you've got to know that if you publish this, I would recommend that you be prosecuted under the intelligence statute."[62] The statute was, of course, the section of the Espionage Act that forbade the dissemination of information about communications capabilities. That section, like the one used against Morison, had never been used to prosecute leakers or members of the press before. What made Casey's threat extremely odd was that information about the nation's monitoring system was soon to be disclosed in a spy trial. Ronald Pelton, a one-time analyst for the National Security Agency (NSA), had been charged with espionage and conspiracy to commit espionage, with the allegations being based on his telling the Soviet Union about the monitoring program.

The Pelton trial was set to begin in May, and the CIA chief wanted to prevent reporting about the secrets that testimony would reveal. This strategy was underlined when Casey and Lt. General William E. Odom, NSA director, issued a joint warning to the press before the trial: "Those reporting on the trial should be cautioned against speculation and reporting details beyond the information actually released at trial. Such speculations and additional facts are not authorized disclosures and may cause substantial harm to the national security."[63] The kind of speculation that Casey disliked surfaced when NBC correspondent James Polk, reporting on the pending trial, said that Pelton "apparently gave away one of the NSA's most sensitive secrets—a project with the code name Ivy Bells—believed to be a top-secret eavesdropping program by American submarines inside Soviet harbors."[64] Casey said he would ask the Justice Department to look into a possible violation of the law by the NBC reporter. The Justice Department was reluctant to follow up on the request, and although future stories revealed even more information about the Ivy Bells project, no charges were brought.

Press representatives were irate over Casey's warnings. Lawrence K. Grossman, president of NBC News, for instance, said, "The notion that one cannot speculate, either the press or the public, without the authorization of the government is a repugnant notion." And CBS anchor Dan Rather said, "We try very hard not to tell Mr. Casey how to catch spies, and I hope he'll understand that we're not going to take it too seriously when he tells us how to cover trials." In fact, Rather added, "The only position for a journalist in this case must be one of respectful defiance."[65] Once again, a media-stimulated uproar led the administration to back down. While Casey said that journalists had become "hysterical" about his warning, White House officials said that the CIA chief had not chosen the correct word when he suggested that the press avoid speculation in its reports of the trial. Despite this conciliatory move, White House officials continued to caution journalists about going beyond information revealed in open court in their stories.[66]

The heads of the nation's security agencies also urged journalists to exercise restraint in reporting on intelligence information. Their reasoning was based largely on the mosaic principle—that the publication of additional details might provide a fuller picture than the nation's enemies already had. For example, they said, although the Soviet Union knew about the Ivy Bells project, it might not have all the data desired or it might not have completely trusted its source. With press corroboration, the Soviets would have a fuller understanding of just how valuable that information was. In addition, press reports could tell other less sophisticated adversaries important intelligence data. NSA director Odom explained this best when he said, " 'Yes, this little fact by itself is harmless to publish,' and the next little fact is harmless to publish." But, "somewhere down the road . . . the accumulation adds up to a rather considerable body of new information which was not in our interest to have out."[67] Despite agency concerns, the *Washington Post* published a tightly edited version of the Woodward story, the Pelton trial was reported on, and no prosecutions for violations of the Espionage Act were brought. But the threat was made, and whether a future administration will find it in its best interest to move against the press under the Espionage Act is a matter of conjecture.

A presidential desire to conceal information, however, is only one part of an administration's information program. Ronald Reagan indeed had complained about being "up to my keister" with unauthorized disclosures[68] and had authorized a far-reaching effort to restrict the amount of information available to the American people. But on the other side of the coin, the Reagan administration, by all accounts, was one of the most porous in the nation's history. A few top advisers controlled much of the administration's decision making, and they were more than willing to use the media to float trial balloons. Many other high-ranking officials were outside the chain of command and had no way to influence the process other than by leaking information to the press. In addition, inter- and intra-office rivalries were intense during the Reagan years, and all involved seemed willing to pass on information that could undercut a rival. Thus, news leaking became a high art form. In fact, Reagan and his colleagues had no problems with leaks—just as long as they were the ones releasing information. The administration's appetite for controlling information reached far beyond national borders, for it also wanted to limit data from foreign sources available to the American people. And with the help of a compliant court system, it largely succeeded.

For example, the Reagan administration revived the Foreign Agents Registration Act of 1938.[69] Under its provisions, individuals who circulated information produced by foreign governments had to register with American officials and clearly label the data as sponsored by a foreign state. Most often, this measure was applied to persons who represented unfriendly governments. In 1983, however, the Justice Department ordered the National Film Board of Canada to label three of its films being shown in the United States as political propaganda. The films were *If You Love This Planet,* which won an Academy Award for best documentary for its depiction of the aftereffects of nuclear war; *Acid Rain: Requiem or Recovery;* and *Acid from Heaven.* Canada had exported more than 400 films to the United States since 1947, and only once before had the Justice Department decided that one of its films was political propaganda.[70]

According to the law, the U.S. government could categorize a film as "political propaganda" if it might "influence . . . the public within the United States with reference to the political or public interests, policies, or relations of a foreign country or a foreign political party."[71] With the nation involved in an arms race with the Soviet Union, government officials certainly did not want citizens seeing a film that depicted the effects of nuclear war. Nor did officials want Americans to see the Canadian version of the acid rain problem since the United States and Canada were at odds over the issue. The order to label the films as political propaganda was not well received. California state senator Barry Keene went into federal court to stop the order. He charged that the labeling prevented him from finding "the best information available on matters of public importance, as a prelude to free and open debate." Individuals who wanted to use the films as a stimulus for discussion, he said, would have second thoughts when they discovered that they would be considered to be spreading foreign propaganda.[72] As a political figure, Keene said that he himself would be reluctant to show the labeled films because "his personal, political and professional reputation would suffer and his ability to obtain re-election and to practice his profession would be impaired."[73] In addition, members of the audience might be misled into discounting the validity of the arguments presented, he said. Keene's arguments persuaded a federal judge to issue the injunction against the labeling; the government objected, and the case went to the Supreme Court.

When the Supreme Court issued its decision in 1987, five justices found that the provisions of the Foreign Agents Registration Act imposed no restrictions on an affected individual's freedom of speech. Three members of the Court strenuously disagreed with the majority's definition of political propaganda. John Paul Stevens, writing for the majority, somewhat amazingly found the term "political propaganda," as used in the act, to have a neutral meaning. "The term 'political propaganda,'" he said, "does nothing to place regulated expressive materials 'beyond the pale of legitimate discourse.'" In fact, he said, "Congress did not prohibit, edit, or restrain the distribution of advocacy materials in an ostensible effort to protect the public from conversion, confusion, or deceit. To the contrary, Congress simply required the disseminators of such material to make additional disclosures that would better enable the public to evaluate the import of the propaganda." In addition, Stevens said, "the statutory definition of 'political propaganda' has been on the books for over four decades. We should presume that the people who have a sufficient understanding of the law to know that the term 'political propaganda' is used to describe the regulated category also know that the definition is a broad, neutral one rather than a pejorative one."[74]

Three dissenters attacked Stevens's understanding of the term "political propaganda." The majority, said Justice Harry Blackmun, reached its decision by "limiting its examination to the statutory definition of the term and by ignoring the realities of public reaction to the designation." If the Court had simply looked carefully at the legislative history of the act, the majority would have discovered that "Congress fully intended to discourage communications by foreign agents." As late as 1983, a Justice Department official had told Congress that "it is fair to say that the original act reflected a perceived close connection between political propaganda and subversion. It is this original focus . . . and therefore the pejorative connotations of the phrases 'foreign agent' and 'political propaganda' which has caused such misunderstanding over the years." Blackmun found such testimony convincing and chastised other members of the Court for their blindness.[75]

Blackmun's calls were ignored. Indeed, the Reagan administration and its conservative judges threw up repeated barriers to ideas advocated by foreigners and their governments. To restrict direct information about Cuba, for instance, the Reagan White House trotted out the Trading with the Enemy Act of World War I and its amendments. Under these provisions, most tourists were effectively banned from Cuba on the grounds that the American dollars that they spent on the island would help to shore up Castro's regime. The Supreme Court upheld the restriction.[76] In addition, the Reagan administration, more than any other on record, excluded foreigners who advocated politically unacceptable ideas from the United States.

Excluding politically undesirable aliens had been popular in the United States since the early twentieth century when immigration laws banned anarchists after President McKinley's assassination. New categories for exclusion were added over the years until the Immigration and Nationality (McCarran-Walter) Act of 1952 brought together all possible political reasons for keeping aliens from entering the United States. The law, for instance, allowed the government to prohibit the entry of persons advocating the Communist line. In addition, the legislation sanctioned the exclusion of individuals who "seek to enter the United States solely, principally, or incidentally to engage in activities which would be prejudicial to the public interest, or endanger the welfare, safety, or security of the United States."[77]

Some individuals excluded seemed somewhat logical given American foreign policy. For example, Hortensia Allende, widow of the assassinated Marxist president of Chile, was denied admittance to speak on the role of women in Latin America. She had been invited by Stanford University and the Archdiocese of San Francisco, but her Marxist connections and the possible implication of the CIA in the killing of her husband made her unwelcome. In other instances, the ban was based almost totally on the ideas being advocated. General Nino Pasti, a four-star general in the Italian Air Force who had served in top positions in the North Atlantic Treaty Organization, was kept out in 1983 because he wanted to attack the administration's plan to deploy Cruise missiles in Western Europe. The administration claimed that his ideas were suspect because he was associated with the World Peace Council, an organization that allegedly had Communist ties.[78]

The simple fact was that aliens had no right to enter the United States to speak on issues that any administration found reprehensible for whatever reason. The Supreme Court had concurred in the executive branch policy,[79] and foreigners with dissident ideas seemed faced with a lifelong ban from the United States. In 1977, however, Congress had begun to limit executive exclusion of aliens disagreeing with American policy. The world was endorsing greater freedom of movement, and the American exclusionary policy was contrary to international norms. Thus, Senator George McGovern, the former Democratic presidential candidate, proposed an amendment to the immigration law that required the admission of individuals who might otherwise be barred. As might be expected, the so-called McGovern Amendment allowed the administration to exclude individuals on national security rather than foreign policy grounds.[80] The loophole simply forced the government to switch the rationale on which exclusions were based and brought about no real change in policy until a federal court of appeals intervened. In a case involving a number of persons who had been refused admission to the United States, the court said that the government may exclude an alien who belongs to a proscribed organization "only if the reason for the threat to the 'public interest[,] . . . welfare, safety, or security' is *independent of* the fact of membership in or affiliation with the proscribed organization."[81]

As the court decision proved, the world was changing, and Congress continued to demand that the nation get in step as far as freedom of movement across international boundaries was concerned. In 1990, Congress permanently repealed the provisions of the McCarran-Walter Act that allowed for the exclusion of aliens on the basis of their political ideology.[82] The provisions had been lifted temporarily in 1987. The new law said that aliens are not to be "denied a visa or excluded from admission into the United States, subject to restrictions or conditions on entry into the United States, or subject to deportation because of any past, current, or expected beliefs, statements, or associations which, if engaged in by a United States citizen in the United States, would be protected under the Constitution of the United States."[83] This language would seem to allow aliens to freely enter this country to speak on issues in opposition to administration policy; only time will tell whether the nation's leaders can circumvent its provisions if they feel sufficiently threatened.

Fear is a powerful motivating factor, and when it is present, almost all other values are abandoned. One of the near fatalities during the Reagan years was academic freedom. For example, researchers working on projects funded by federal money found that their work was subjected to prepublication review in much the same way as that of other government employees. American scholars working in certain fields were discouraged from attending international meetings to present papers highlighting their work for fear that political or economic enemies would obtain access to vital research. If they insisted on attending, government officials were not above threatening prosecution on statutes that made it a crime to export certain technological data. Invitations to foreign scholars to attend American meetings were discouraged for similar reasons, and universities were informed that foreign nationals from particular countries should not be employed on sensitive projects. Indeed, some foreign nationals were excluded from selected classes. At one point, UCLA announced that one engineering class was available to American citizens only.[84] Scholars soon began to question whether American research and scholarship could flourish without cross-fertilization from foreigners working in similar fields. Such an exchange had long been considered essential for scientific progress, but the fears of the Reagan administration seemed to militate against these international relationships.

The Reagan paranoia reached into another citadel of freedom, the American library, as agents from the Federal Bureau of Investigation visited technical libraries around the country in 1987 to find out whether any foreigners were patrons. The material in the libraries was all in the public domain; no question about classification existed. But still the FBI feared hostile intelligence officers used libraries to obtain valuable information and to recruit espionage agents. Librarians retorted that libraries should be available to anyone who wanted to use them. When FBI agents seemed unwilling to accept that notion, leaders of the American Library Association turned to Congress for relief. Representative Don Edwards of California, a former FBI agent, introduced legislation to protect the First Amendment rights of library patrons. The bureau's campaign, Edwards said, "makes librarians into FBI informants, and threatens to bring suspicion on innocent persons." Indeed, he said, "the chilling effect of FBI agents asking librarians to report on users far outweighs any possible counterintelligence benefit."[85] Although the FBI refused to abandon its visits to libraries, it did agree to tone them down a bit. In the meantime, Congress debated proposals to end such practices but without resolution.

In each of the above instances, the Reagan administration contended that it was acting solely in the national interest. The protection of America for Americans, long a goal of the nation's conservatives, was foremost to Reaganites. In addition, the conservatives who came into power with Ronald Reagan advocated an increasingly elitist approach to government. The philosophy is probably as old as the nation itself, for few conservatives, from Alexander Hamilton on, have considered the masses capable of making wise decisions on national policy. The Reagan administration just went further in that direction than any other. And as in other conservative periods, the Reagan years were marked by an upsurge in the advocacy of patriotism as the reason for abdication of informed participation in government. And because the administration cloaked so many of its repressive activities in the aura of patriotism, opposition often was slow in developing.

Although super-patriots often have been active in American government, they had never enjoyed such prominence. Activities ranging from secrecy in government to suppression of dissident speech were wrapped in red, white, and blue bunting to an extent never before seen. In fact, the American flag became the key symbol of life in the United States. George Bush firmly took hold of Old Glory in his 1988 presidential campaign as he loudly questioned the patriotism of his opponent, Massachusetts Governor Michael Dukakis. The governor's mistake, it seems, was that he had vetoed a law that would have required the pledge of allegiance to be recited in Massachusetts schools. The law, Dukakis said, was clearly unconstitutional, and, based on a 1943 Supreme Court decision involving an attempt to force Jehovah's Witnesses' children to recite the pledge,[86] Dukakis was absolutely right. Bush, however, ignored the landmark decision and the great statement that it made about the true fundamentals of Americanism in favor of the inflammatory rhetoric that helped him win the White House.

The flag and President Bush's attitude toward it helped to set up one of the greatest challenges to the First Amendment in the history of the Bill of Rights. The episode started simply enough as a protest against the renomination of Ronald Reagan in 1984. At that point, members of the Youth International Party demonstrated in Dallas, the site of the Republican National Convention. By 1960s standards, their protests were tame. They entered a bank, threw deposit slips in the air and tossed around a bit of red paint; they knocked over trash cans; they spit on shoppers; and they burned an American flag, chanting as it burned, "America, the red, white, and blue, we spit on you."[87] It was this latter act that caused the problem. Gregory Johnson, one of the demonstrators, a self-proclaimed Communist revolutionary, was charged with violating the Texas flag statute, which made it a crime to desecrate the national or state flag. He was convicted by a Texas jury, and the case that rocked the First Amendment began its way to the Supreme Court.[88]

In June 1989, the Supreme Court, splitting five-to-four in its decision, found that burning the flag was a form of symbolic speech that could not be prevented by law. The decision was written by the ranking liberal on the Court, William Brennan, and was joined by two conservative Reagan appointees, Antonin Scalia and Anthony Kennedy, as well as by Thurgood Marshall and Harry Blackmun. Chief Justice William Rehnquist wrote the leading dissent, which was joined by Byron White, a Kennedy appointee, and Sandra Day O'Connor, a Reagan appointee. John Paul Stevens, a Ford appointee, dissented alone. Johnson, in burning the flag, Brennan said, was conveying an opinion, and consequently his action was protected by the First Amendment. "If there is a bedrock principle underlying the First Amendment," he wrote, "it is that the Government may not prohibit the expression of an idea simply because society finds the idea itself offensive or disagreeable." In addition, he said, the Court long had held that the government could not "compel conduct that would evince respect for the flag." The nation is not protected by sending individuals who burn the flag to jail, he said. In fact, "we can imagine no more appropriate response to burning a flag than waving one's own, no better way to counter a flag-burner's message than by saluting the flag that burns, no surer means of preserving the dignity even of the flag that burned than by—as one witness here did—according its remains a respectful burial." To Brennan and the Court's majority, "We do not consecrate the flag by punishing its desecration, for in doing so we dilute the freedom that this cherished emblem represents."[89]

The decision, said Justice Kennedy, may not be appreciated across the country, but "the hard fact is that sometimes we must make decisions we do not like. We make them because they are right, right in the sense that the law and the Constitution, as we see them, compel the result." Although he personally agreed "that the flag holds a lonely place of honor in an age when absolutes are distrusted and simple truths are burdened by unneeded apologetics," Kennedy could not find that "the Constitution gives us the right to rule as the dissenting members of this Court urge, however painful this judgment is to announce. . . . It is poignant but fundamental that the flag protects those who hold it in contempt."[90]

But the American flag, more than the national symbol of any other nation, has always been shrouded in mysticism, and many of the nation's super-patriots found the flag more representative of the United States than the Bill of Rights.

The Court had no sooner announced its decision than calls emerged to amend the Constitution to allow the punishment of persons who desecrated the flag. In essence, these guardians of the flag wished to put an asterisk next to the First Amendment in order to remove a certain kind of speech from its protection. Opponents of tampering with the Bill of Rights feared that other asterisks would follow and that soon the First Amendment would be riddled with so many exceptions that its protections would be worthless.

Although President Bush at first pledged to support the Court's decision as other presidents had done when they were personally offended by the justices' rulings, he changed his mind. Protecting the flag obviously was an important political issue, and as a politician who so clearly had placed the flag above the Constitution during his campaign for the presidency, Bush was unwilling to abandon the field. The issue was so volatile that congressional Democrats and Republicans vied to prove themselves the more patriotic. Democrats had learned from Dukakis's defeat that an ostentatious love of the flag played better with the American people than an abstract argument based the Constitution. Defending First Amendment principles plainly was an assignment only for politicians ready to end their careers. Consequently, the Senate showed its displeasure with the Court's ruling by voting 97–3 to condemn the ruling the day after it came down.[91]

Flashy resolutions condemning the Court's decision were insufficient to quiet growing public pressure for righting the wrong done to the flag. Vocal demands surfaced for amending the Constitution, and President Bush seized the initiative. Announcing his devotion to preserving the flag in front of the Iwo Jima monument at Arlington National Cemetery, the president suggested an amendment that read: "The Congress and the States shall have the power to prohibit the physical desecration of the flag of the United States."[92] Public support for the amendment ran high immediately after the Court's decision, but summer turned into fall as the houses of Congress held hearings on the proposal. And as the seasons turned, so, too, did national opinion. By September and October, fewer Americans favored amending the Constitution to protect the flag, but that change in opinion did not mean that the issue was dead.

Momentum grew for a content-neutral law to protect the flag as a substitute for a constitutional amendment. The goal was to write legislation that would punish all actions against the flag without evaluating the message that the action conveyed. Many members of Congress likened their effort to work in the 1960s when Congress made it a crime for draft-aged men to burn their draft cards. The Supreme Court upheld that legislation, contending that it was based on a compelling governmental interest in maintaining a pool of readily accessible men for the draft.[93] That decision was characterized by a neat bit of judicial legerdemain, for the law did indeed suppress expression. Burning draft cards was a potent way of displaying opinions about the war, and the law was enacted primarily to stop such dissent. But the Court had bowed to the wishes of Congress on this matter, and many in Congress hoped that a law protecting the flag would find a safe haven in the Court if all language that touched on expression was removed. The Texas statute that the justices struck down had forbidden desecration of the flag, which was defined as to "deface, damage, or otherwise physically mistreat in a way that the actor knows will seriously offend one or more persons likely to observe or discover his action."[94] Lawmakers sought a statute that just protected the physical integrity of the flag.

In large part, the push for the new statute was Democratic in origin; many Republicans still favored the constitutional amendment, arguing that nothing less could protect the flag. The statute passed by overwhelming majorities in both houses of Congress, with many members warning that the Supreme Court would find it, too, to be unconstitutional and that an amendment would be necessary. The law, as enacted in October 1989, said that anyone who "knowingly mutilates, defaces, physically defiles, burns, maintains on the floor or ground, or tramples upon any flag of the United States shall be fined under this title or imprisoned for not more than one year, or both." The law defined a "flag of the United States" as "any flag of the United States, or any part thereof, made of any substance, of any size, in a form that is commonly displayed." Congressional leaders wanted the law tested in the Supreme Court as soon as possible and thus included a provision that required immediate review should a lower court find the statute unconstitutional.[95]

The law went into effect at 12:01 a.m. October 28, 1989, and protesters around the country were ready. Flags of all sizes went up in smoke as dissidents announced their desire to stand upon the First Amendment. "We are burning the flag to say we will not stand by to see forced patriotism," said one Vietnam veteran who participated in a flag burning in Seattle, Washington. "Abridgement of the First Amendment right [of free speech] is the first infringement" on all other rights, he said.[96] Arrests followed, and within months, two federal district courts had declared the new flag protection statute unconstitutional.

The Supreme Court raised some eyebrows when it scheduled an expedited review of the new law, meaning that its decision would come down in June 1990—just before a congressional election campaign. When the decision was delivered, the same five-four split led to the same result: flag burning was a form of expression protected by the First Amendment. William J. Brennan, who again wrote for the majority, concluded his opinion by saying, "Punishing desecration of the flag dilutes the very freedom that makes this emblem so revered, and worth revering."[97] As expected, proposals to amend the Constitution to protect the flag were immediately introduced in Congress. Members of the House of Representatives voted on the proposed amendment on June 21, 1990, and it fell thirty-four votes short of the two-thirds needed to propose a constitutional amendment.[98] A few days later, the Senate took a symbolic vote, and the amendment fell nine votes short of the necessary two-thirds majority.[99] The issue of amending the Constitution to protect the flag was dead for the 101st Congress.

As the flag debate had proven, super-patriotism, which haunted the country earlier, had reappeared. Another example was the resurgence of the nativism that so obsessed certain segments of the nation earlier. The latest form of nativism included the traditional attempts to limit immigration, with Asians and Hispanics replacing Southern and Eastern Europeans as the causes for concern. But a somewhat different twist focused on the fundamental First Amendment right of these individuals to communicate. Conservatives worried about the slow assimilation of new immigrants into the American culture. As with immigrants of earlier periods, 1980s-era newcomers congregated together in communities that practiced the customs of their homeland and used the familiar language. These communities are highly insular in nature, say their critics, and keep immigrants from moving into the culture at large. One way to force them to become more like us, said the new nativists, is to take away their ability to function in society without using English. This theory gave birth to the notion that the United States should adopt English as its official language.

An amendment to the U.S. Constitution stating that "The English Language shall be the official language of the United States" was first introduced in Congress in 1981.[100] Although the federal amendment has made little progress, state constitutions in Arizona and California were amended to require English as the official language. Referenda in Florida and Colorado calling for similar statements passed, and numerous municipalities enacted regulations requiring the use of English. The measures touched on a variety of subjects ranging from attempts to end bilingual education in the schools, to stopping the preparation of ballots in more than one language, to requiring that signs carry messages only in English. The motivation, however, was generally the same: fear of how different people and different languages would affect the future growth and development of the United States.

In some parts of the country, broad general provisions about English being the official language were given additional weight by legislation that required government employees to use English in their jobs. Critics of such legislation said that thousands of people were being denied essential services under these laws and that the public could well be endangered if public safety workers were required to function in only one language. Slowly the measures began making their way into the court system. One of the first challenges involved the Arizona constitutional provision, which was attacked on First Amendment grounds.

Arizona's measure said, "[A]s the official language of this State, the English language is the language of the ballot, the public schools and all government functions and actions." Amendment provisions applied to all branches of government, all political subdivisions, all laws and programs, and "all government officials and employees during the performance of government business."[101] An insurance claims manager within the state's Department of Administration and a state senator joined to challenge the amendment as a violation of the First Amendment. In February 1990, a federal district judge found just such a violation. When read literally, said Paul Rosenblatt, the state amendment "would force Arizona governmental officers and employees whose use of a non-English language in the performance of their official duties is protected by the First Amendment . . . to either violate their sworn oaths to obey the state constitution, and thereby subject themselves to potential sanctions and private suits, or to curtail their free speech rights." These restrictions, Rosenblatt said, were far too expansive. Such governmentally required self-censorship violated the U.S. Constitution, and the amendment to the Arizona constitution could not stand.[102]

Such enthusiastic Americanism invaded numerous aspects of national life during the Reagan years. Differences of all kinds were feared. Many Americans saw peril everywhere. The Soviet Union remained the major evil well into Reagan's presidency. Joining the Russians on the list of formidable dangers was that vague category of individuals known as "terrorists." Here the nation faced real dangers, for wild-eyed fanatics hijacked airplanes, took hostages, and bombed places where Americans congregated overseas. But the Reagan administration often became too energetic in labeling its enemies. If a person or a cause could not easily be placed in the Communist category, the terrorist appellation would be used.[103] Once again, the United States had a federal administration that saw mortal enemies everywhere, and suppression became the order of the day.

The whole internal security apparatus that had fallen into disuse after the resignation of Richard Nixon was rejuvenated—with the general approval of Congress and the conservative community. Indeed, members of the House of Representatives had already tried unsuccessfully to resurrect the House Committee on Internal Security, better known by its old name, the House Committee on Un-American Activities. Some senators likewise tried to revive another terror of the cold war days, the Senate Internal Security Subcommittee; still other members of both houses proposed a joint committee on internal security. The Heritage Foundation, a conservative think tank, issued a 3,000-page report in November 1980 calling upon the new administration to take a harder line against dissenters and their organizations. "Individual liberties are secondary to the requirements of national security and internal civil order," the report said.[104] The administration agreed, and President Reagan issued an executive order in December 1981 that removed many restrictions on the domestic activities of intelligence-gathering agencies. The Central Intelligence Agency and military intelligence operations, for example, again were allowed to conduct counterintelligence activities within the nation's borders if the program was coordinated with the FBI,[105] and the FBI was allowed to resume supervision of dissident political activities.

Determining which dissident group most frightened the Reagan administration is difficult, but given its overall impact on the nation and the world, that honor most likely would go to the nuclear freeze movement. In many respects, freeze activity was a natural outgrowth of the antiwar movement in the 1960s and of earlier efforts to win a nuclear test ban treaty. This time, however, the goal was to end the international arms race and to eliminate the ever-present danger that human existence would be obliterated from the face of the earth. Spurred on by the Three Mile Island incident in which a nuclear power plant experienced a partial meltdown of its fuel supply, the freeze movement attracted a wide spectrum of Americans. Freeze proponents wanted both the United States and its NATO allies and the Soviet Union and its allies to stop the arms race in place— to freeze it—as a first step toward nuclear disarmament. The nations should agree to stop producing, testing, and deploying nuclear weapons, and all treaties should include firm ways to verify compliance. Disarmament was to follow.[106]

Despite the fact that nuclear freeze ideas seem perfectly reasonable now, the movement was considered almost treasonous at the outset. Ronald Reagan and his New Right constituency were firm believers in a strong military establishment. They believed that the United States had gotten soft, that it had lost its position of world leadership, and that it would regain its international status only through a strong military. The Soviet invasion of Afghanistan and the taking of hostages at the American embassy in Iran only confirmed those opinions. Thus under the administration's tutelage, the Defense Department budget grew substantially, and the United States stepped up the arms race. In light of these activities, the freeze movement grew even more determined to stop what its leaders perceived to be a mad rush toward nuclear annihilation.

The freeze movement largely was a peaceful one. Working within the political system was its strong point. Petitions with hundreds of thousands of signatures were gathered; freeze referenda were placed on state and local ballots; freeze laws were enacted around the country; politicians supporting an end to the nuclear arms race were supported. Doctors, lawyers, college professors, clergy, and politicians all climbed aboard the bandwagon. By 1982, Reagan and his colleagues, worried about the movement's success, sought to keep the movement from gaining further ground. They were ready, if necessary, to use the customary Communist label as a form of denunciation. When asked about the freeze movement that was sweeping Europe at the time, for instance, the president responded, "Oh, those demonstrations, these are all sponsored by a thing called the World Peace Council, which is bought and paid for by the Soviet Union."[107] Such offhanded comments were typical of the Reagan presidency, and the *New York Times* protested that "the charge that those who demonstrate opposition in vital issues of national security are either dupes of enemies or directly disloyal revives an ugly strain in the American political character." Even more sinister, said the *Times,* was the fact that "the purpose of such ugly defamation can only be to prevent debate, to abridge the rights of individuals and to cheat the nation of a rational choice of policies."[108]

The president's characterization of the international freeze movement did little to discourage Americans from supporting freeze proposals. In fact, Reagan's home state of California approved a freeze initiative that very year. Nor did the success of freeze activities do much to change the president's mind. Even though he claimed to believe that "the overwhelming majority of the people involved in that, I am sure, are sincere and well-intentioned," Reagan again connected the freeze movement to Communist subversion. "There was no question but that the Soviet Union saw an advantage in a peace movement built around the idea of a nuclear freeze, since they are out ahead [in the arms race]," he told a November 1982 press conference.[109] Despite the president's best efforts, the freeze movement continued to grow. In 1983, it picked up the support of the American Roman Catholic Church when the church's bishops issued a long pastoral letter that endorsed its fundamental moral principles.[110] Many of Reagan's contentions about its subversive nature were discredited when an FBI investigation could find no proof that the Soviets had infiltrated the movement.

As with most mass movements, the freeze campaign had its share of radicals who sought to win adherents by actions rather than words. In this case, they named themselves the Plowshares Movement from the biblical injunction to "beat swords into plowshares."[111] The first Plowshares action took place in 1980 when a group of eight protesters, including anti–Vietnam War activists Daniel and Philip Berrigan, entered a plant where nose cones for nuclear warheads were manufactured. They poured blood on documents, a reminder of earlier antiwar actions, and in the nature of the biblical passage from which they took their name, they hammered on two nose cones. They prayed, and they were arrested. The trials of the Plowshares Eight set the tone for trials of other radical dissenters during the Reagan years. In many of the antiwar trials of the 1960s and early 1970s, defendants were allowed to present evidence to justify their actions and were allowed to enter expert testimony to support that defense. No leeway was allowed here, and the defendants were convicted. Undaunted by the five- to ten-year prison terms meted out for burglary, conspiracy, and criminal mischief, others took up the Plowshares cause, and similar invasions of nuclear weapons plants followed.[112]

Soon radicalism became unnecessary to further the nuclear freeze movement. Ronald Reagan had decided that he wanted to be remembered as a man of peace who had moved the nation back from the precipice of nuclear disaster. The anti-Communist denunciations were gone, and Ronald Reagan began a series of historic actions that put many of the freeze goals into place as national policy. Once again, a dissenting group had weathered a ferocious storm of opposition only to find its ideas squarely in the mainstream of American political thought. The bad ideas that the freeze movement had advocated were not so bad after all, the president decided, and the stigma was gone.

Other ideas that interfered with foreign policy, however, did not fare as well. Especially vulnerable were individuals who opposed the president's policy on Central America. Many of these opponents were strong church people who lived in areas near the Mexican border. They were morally affronted both by the activities of right-wing death squads that rampaged through El Salvador and Guatemala and by the U.S. government's refusal to consider refugees from such terror as political refugees who merited asylum. Rather, the administration, which approved of the rightist activities in parts of Central America, rounded up the refugees and shipped them back to their homelands where they faced almost certain death from their political enemies. In addition, the government launched another round of red-baiting, charging that people who thought they were helping refugees were instead aiding Communists to obtain control in Central America. In response to what they considered to be the immoral and illegal activities of their government, a group of American church leaders set up the Sanctuary movement. Organizers contended that the government's actions violated legal principles that established the United States as a refuge for persons suffering from political persecution.[113]

This movement, too, was strongly based on biblical principles, for it revived the age-old religious tradition of sanctuary, of providing a place where individuals fleeing danger could go for safety. The movement started in March 1982, when members of a handful of churches in Arizona and California declared their churches to be places of refuge for persons fleeing Central America. Within four years, some 300 additional houses of worship joined the campaign. A new underground railroad, said to involve some 70,000 religious people of all faiths, helped move the refugees from vulnerable border spots in the Southwest to more secure locations in the central and eastern United States. The first arrests of Sanctuary workers occurred in 1984.

Defendants in the major trial of Sanctuary workers were caught by placing informers within the ranks of suspect organizations. Using evidence produced by these insiders, the government charged sixteen Sanctuary workers including two priests, three nuns, and one minister with conspiring with, encouraging, and aiding illegal aliens to enter the United States. In addition, they were charged with helping to conceal their whereabouts and moving them around the country. The trial followed the pattern encountered by Plowshares activists. In response to a government motion, the judge limited the kind of evidence the Sanctuary people could introduce. They could not talk about their religious convictions or the status of refugees and the laws that affected them; they could not introduce current events in El Salvador and Guatemala or U.S. foreign policy as factors in the case; nor could the defendants argue that the people that they were helping were fleeing persecution in their homelands. Although defense attorneys questioned the judge's impartiality, the trial went on, with the verdict virtually a foregone conclusion.

After an eighteen-week trial in Tuscon, Arizona, eight of the eleven Sanctuary workers were convicted. The jury had deliberated for forty-eight hours over nine days. The Immigration and Naturalization Service and the Justice Department, feeling that the trial had mortally wounded the Sanctuary movement, did not seek heavy sentences, in part for fear that long prison terms would only create martyrs. All those convicted eventually were given suspended sentences. Probation terms included a ban on associating with individuals who protected undocumented aliens. Throughout the whole episode, the government's goal once again was to make it clear that actions opposing national policy would bring extensive and expensive legal difficulties. Indeed, the trial had been expensive. In addition to lives and careers sorely disrupted by the arrests, trials, and fears of incarceration, the defense had cost some $1.2 million, most of which had been raised through direct mail solicitations and contributions from major Protestant denominations. When the government's costs were added in, the whole case had cost between $2 million and $3 million.[114]

On the day that the verdict was brought in, most of the Sanctuary defendants gathered with their supporters for a service in one of the churches that had been a refuge for Central Americans. Every member of the congregation received a copy of a "declaration of shared responsibility," which read, in part, "These defendants have now recommitted themselves to continue the ministry of Sanctuary for as long as persecution and death threaten refugees returned involuntarily from our shores to their homeland. This they have done in fidelity to the one God who long ago called an oppressed people out of bondage, and who today calls on all of us to love the sojourner among us because our ancestors were once refugees." The declaration concluded by stating, "I . . . share their faith and commitment, with a full knowledge that I also place myself in jeopardy. I have no choice. If they are guilty, so am I."[115] Most congregation members signed copies of the document. That weekend, more Central Americans took refuge in the church; within days, Sanctuary workers brought still more refugees across the border; and the movement continued. In 1987, the U.S. Supreme Court sided with at least some of the contentions made by Sanctuary workers when it ruled in an immigration case that the government was interpreting regulations on refugee status too rigidly.[116]

During the Reagan years a great deal of the dissent was firmly grounded in religious principles, both from the left and the right. The nuclear freeze movement, for instance, attracted persons from all faiths and benefited greatly from the pastoral letter written by Catholic bishops. The Sanctuary movement was firmly based in liberal religious communities. The more conservative religious groups also were active during these years. In large part, their work was motivated by groups such as the Moral Majority, Jerry Falwell's conservative lobbying group that sought to make a fundamentalist religious presence known throughout American society. Such groups usually sought to restore what they considered to be traditional American values. As with religious people who were active in Anthony Comstock's time, these individuals saw much that was wrong in American society and determined to fix it by bringing American life in line with biblical truths. To many Americans, the ideas put forth by the religious right also were revolutionary, and the conflicts between fundamentalists and other American groups that dotted the Reagan years were raucous and unsettling.

One of the most popular causes for religious fundamentalists was the anti-abortion campaign. Although long festering in American society, the abortion issue turned into a full-blown confrontation after the Supreme Court decided in 1973 that a woman had a constitutional right of privacy and could decide for herself, without state regulation, whether to have an abortion within the first two trimesters of pregnancy. The state could prohibit an abortion only during the last three months of pregnancy, and even then, the government was forbidden to interfere if an abortion was necessary to save the mother's life or health.[117] The decision represented a victory for abortion-rights activists and would not be allowed to stand uncontested. Earlier anti-abortion groups had fought the legalization of abortion, but with the decision, they were transformed into far more active organizations with a more diverse clientele.

For quite some time after the Supreme Court's abortion decision, anti-abortion activity was concentrated in mainstream organizations. The National Right to Life Committee (NRLC), the nation's largest such association, attracted men and women from the political left, center, and right and from all religious persuasions. For years, NRLC members worked through the political process to regulate abortions. Although they also practiced a variety of direct action techniques borrowed from the civil rights and antiwar movements of the 1960s, most were essentially peaceful. This phase of the movement disappeared in the wake of a 1983 Supreme Court decision that found various state and local regulations of abortion unconstitutional.[118] At about the same time, an effort to amend the Constitution to end constitutional protection for abortion failed in the Senate.[119]

As a result of these two setbacks and the increased emphasis on the family by New Right politicians, including Ronald Reagan, the character of the prolife movement changed dramatically. Although right-to-life groups had always argued that life began at conception and that abortion was murder, the religious and political conservatives who became active in the movement after 1983 accepted few limits on the kinds of activities that were appropriate to end the practice. Mainstream organizations such as the NRLC had been able to convince their followers that victory was available in the political sphere and that violence was counterproductive. But after years of work, these organizations had little progress to show, and new organizations sprang up to take their places, much the way the civil rights and antiwar movements had changed over time.

Domestic violence connected with the abortion debate escalated after 1983. According to prochoice statistics, 115 violent incidents occurred involving 46 clinics between 1977 and 1982. Between 1983 and March 1985, however, there were 319 violent acts against 238 clinics. By the end of 1985, 92 percent of the abortion clinics in the nation had reported some kind of harassment ranging from picketing to vandalism and worse.[120] At the most extreme end of the spectrum were those prolifers who advocated the use of arson and bombing to end abortion. Abortion, these activists claimed, was a crime, and they must do everything necessary to stop it. Such prolife radicals justified their actions on the grounds of necessity, exactly the same foundation that Plowshares and Sanctuary defendants assumed. While in the latter instance, this stance was rejected by conservatives, few conservative commentators opposed the stance taken by anti-abortion radicals.

Absolutely convinced that civil argument would not end abortion, radical prolifers became well known for their conduct at abortion clinics around the country where they tried to keep women from entering to have abortions. They blocked access to the doorways; they verbally challenged women trying to enter; they bothered patients after the fact; and they entered clinics and tried to disrupt activities. They also harassed persons who worked in the clinics, including the doctors who performed the abortions. Radical prolife groups sent threatening letters; they picketed personnel at home; and they made hostile telephone calls at all hours of the day and night. Such activities, they figured, were indeed worthwhile. Some 20 percent of the women who would have had abortions changed their minds as a result of prolife intervention. In addition, doctors and other workers at the clinics faced social ostracism; rents went up, and leases were lost on facilities; insurance costs skyrocketed; and more professionals reconsidered their roles in providing abortions.[121]

Despite the violence connected with these actions, the Reagan administration refused to intervene. While the nuclear freeze and Sanctuary movements were subjected to infiltration by government agents and eventual prosecution for their activities, radical prolifers were viewed with general approbation by the White House. When told that the radical right-to-life movement threatened internal security, the Reagan administration simply ignored the charges. Terrorists, the FBI said, wanted to bring down organized government, which was not the case with the radical prolife movement.

Only the Supreme Court seemed interested in curtailing the activities of radical prolifers, often at the expense of established First Amendment principles. In

1988, for example, four members of the Court joined in a decision by Sandra Day O'Connor that approved a Brookfield, Wisconsin, ordinance banning picketing in front of a private residence. The law was passed because anti-abortion radicals had been making life miserable for a physician who performed abortions and for his neighbors. Joining the majority decision were prolife supporters William Rehnquist, Antonin Scalia, and Anthony Kennedy, as well as Harry Blackmun, the author of the decision that gave constitutional sanction to abortions in the first place.[122]

The decision was controversial because it endorsed restrictions on activities normally permitted in the streets, which have long been considered a public forum. Before the ordinance took effect, "up to 40 sign-carrying, slogan-shouting protesters regularly converged on Dr. Victoria's home and, in addition to protesting, warned young children not to go near the house because Dr. Victoria was a 'baby killer.' Further, the throng repeatedly trespassed onto the Victorias' property and at least once blocked the exits to their home." In response, Brookfield enacted an ordinance that made it illegal to picket "before or about the residence or dwelling of any individual." While acknowledging that "the antipicketing ordinance operates at the core of the First Amendment by prohibiting appellees from engaging in picketing on an issue of public concern," Justice O'Connor found the "ban to be a limited one; only focused picketing taking place solely in front of a particular residence is prohibited." General marching through the residential neighborhood could continue, as could picketing that circled the residential block. Thus the doctor and his family could avoid the picketers' message while permitting the picketers to get their message across to the general public—if that was their goal.[123]

Justice O'Connor, in fact, doubted that the picketers wanted to speak to the general public, which generally was the desired audience for picketers. Instead, she said, "the picketing is narrowly directed at the household, not the public." These picketers "generally do not seek to disseminate a message to the general public, but to intrude upon the targeted resident, and to do so in an especially offensive way." In this case, O'Connor said, the picketers "subjected the doctor and his family to the presence of a relatively large group of protestors on their doorstep in an attempt to force the doctor to cease performing abortions. But the actual size of the group is irrelevant; even a solitary picket can invade residential privacy." The doctor and his family had no way to avoid the message, she said, and the community could stop such intrusions.[124]

Dissenters included abortion rights supporters William Brennan and Thurgood Marshall, whose devotion to the First Amendment clearly surpassed their concern for the message presented. Although Brennan agreed that "a crowd of protestors need not be permitted virtually to imprison a person in his or her own house merely because they shout slogans or carry signs," he added that "so long as the speech remains outside the home and does not unduly coerce the occupant, the government's heightened interest in protecting residential privacy is not implicated." He would have had little difficulty with the city's effort if it had been directed at limiting the number of pickets involved, the hours of picketing, or the noise level. These regulations would have been traditional time, place, and manner constraints, which the Court generally allowed when shown to be content neutral. "But to say that picketing may be substantially regulated is not to say that it may be prohibited in its entirety. Once size, time, volume, and the like have been controlled to ensure that the picket is no longer intrusive or coercive," Brennan said, "only the speech itself remains, conveyed perhaps by a lone, silent individual, walking back and forth with a sign." Although the target of such carefully regulated picketing might still feel uncomfortable, Brennan could find no reason to insulate him from those feelings.[125]

But as the abortion debate picked up, protecting the rights of radical anti-abortionists to demonstrate became more difficult. More communities enacted ordinances banning residential picketing after prolifers annoyed individuals who performed abortions. With these residential picketing restrictions, the communities forced confrontations at abortion clinics. But as time passed, communities also became concerned about the heightened abusiveness connected with picketing at the clinics. The focus of much of this apprehension soon concentrated on a new organization, Operation Rescue, which was formed in 1987 by born-again Christians. Operation Rescue attracted both Protestant fundamentalists and Roman Catholics to the battle against abortion. This group also took its name from scripture that called upon the faithful to rescue persons unjustly sentenced to death.[126] The group claimed to base its techniques on civil disobedience as advocated by Henry David Thoreau, Mohandas Gandhi, and Dr. Martin Luther King, Jr. Operation Rescue workers would congregate en masse and then move to keep patients from entering a designated abortion clinic. As the police moved in to arrest Operation Rescue members, the protesters went limp and had to be carried from the scene. Hundreds, perhaps thousands, of Operation Rescue workers across the country wound up in jail on trespassing and other charges.[127]

Judges around the country seemed to find Operation Rescue workers dangerous zealots as they agreed to requests to shield abortion clinics from Operation Rescue excesses. To provide such protection, the courts rejuvenated that time-honored vehicle for repressing undesirable speech, the injunction. In Atlanta, for instance, a Georgia judge banned Operation Rescue workers from going within 50 feet of the property line of any facility where abortions were performed. Operation Rescue workers, claiming that the order stopped them from "engaging in prayer, picketing, leafleting and other forms of peaceful expression on public forum streets and sidewalks," asked the U.S. Supreme Court to intervene to protect their First Amendment rights. In mid-May 1990, the Court, by a five-four vote, refused to order the injunction lifted.[128] A week later the Court refused an Operation Rescue appeal of an order keeping their members away from the doors of abortion clinics in New York.[129]

Another case involving abortion-related free-speech issues rocked the pro-choice movement as much as the Court's refusal to allow Operation Rescue activities to proceed uninhibited had distressed prolife supporters. Here the Court was asked to review regulations issued by the U.S. Department of Health and Human Services under Ronald Reagan and George Bush that prohibited family planning clinics that received federal funds from telling women about abortion as an alternative to an unwanted pregnancy.[130] When the ruling came down in late May 1991, the Court had split five-to-four in upholding the restrictions on the speech of clinic workers. Said Chief Justice William Rehnquist for the majority, "The Government can, without violating the Constitution, selectively fund a program to encourage certain activities it believes to be in the public interest, without at the same time funding an alternative program which seeks to deal with the same problem in another way." By doing so, Rehnquist said, the government has not imposed content-based restrictions on speech. Rather, "it has merely chosen to fund one activity to the exclusion of the other."[131]

Justice Harry Blackmun found the majority's reasoning specious at best. "Until today," he wrote, "the Court has never upheld viewpoint-based suppression of speech simply because that suppression was a condition upon the acceptance of public funds." Blackmun, who had written the decision that found a constitutional protection for the right of a woman to have an abortion, said, "It cannot seriously be disputed that the counseling and referral provisions at issue in the present cases constitute content-based regulation." And "whatever may be the Government's power to condition the receipt of its largess upon the relinquishment of constitutional rights, it surely does not extend to a condition that suppresses the recipient's cherished freedom of speech based solely upon the content or viewpoint of that speech."[132]

Much of the reaction to the Court's judgment in this case rested on concern that the justices soon would be restricting the right of women to have abortions. More fundamental to our study, however, is the impact that the logic displayed by the majority here could have on freedom of speech on other subjects throughout the country. As Walter E. Dellinger, a professor of law at Duke University, said in the wake of the decision, the ruling "is especially alarming in light of the growing role of government as subsidizer, landlord, employer and patron of the arts."[133] If the acceptance of government money can keep family planning professionals from talking with pregnant women about all legal options available, then accepting government funding for other projects could carry similar strings. If that happens, the government—or more particularly the president—could impose his or her political agenda in many areas while at the same time eliminating all dissent. The ramifications of such restrictions are almost impossible to comprehend. Official orthodoxy might well become the American approach to many divisive questions—so long as various institutions receive federal funding. Most immediately, such restrictions could become especially crucial in the area of federal funding for the arts as discussed below.

If the abortion cases are any indication, future free-expression cases may be quite different from those of the past because the religious fervor of participants often forces judges to pit clauses of the First Amendment against one another. Such a situation has already occurred in numerous cases involving parents who attacked books being used in the public schools for teaching values that allegedly undermine the Christian faith.[134] So far, decisions on the federal district court level in favor of the parents have been overturned on appeal,[135] but whether a more conservative judiciary will continue to promote a diverse and open school

system is, of course, unclear. In the meantime, challenges over the reading materials used in classrooms continue, as do disputes over what should be included
in school libraries.[136]

One basic question often focuses on whether the public schools should educate children for a multi-cultural world or whether the schools should avoid challenging fundamental values that some parents want to impart to their offspring.
Even more basic, perhaps, is the question of whose world view the schools should
present. This latter issue exceeds religious bounds, as civil rights groups have
attacked the portrayal of minorities, with a favorite target being *Huckleberry
Finn,* and as feminists have battled the depiction of women in books, including
the subservient role played by Jane in the introductory Dick and Jane readers.
Sex education, long a matter of controversy, has also been under attack from a
variety of perspectives.

Another of the most persistent challenges to the right of teachers to decide
what to teach has featured a continuation of the fight over evolution. The quarrel
was, of course, as old as Darwin's theory, but the issue continued to emerge in
new guises. One of the latest was a Louisiana law requiring that creation science
be taught in the public schools if evolution was taught. Lawmakers argued that
creationism was based as much on scientific theory as Darwinism and that students should be taught both—if they were taught either. The Supreme Court
found the Louisiana effort to insert the theory of creation into the curriculum a
violation of the Establishment Clause of the First Amendment.[137] But the arguments persisted as members of the Christian right, often backed by New Right
politicians, tried to bring the public school system more into line with fundamentalists ideals. One problem with this approach, of course, is that the public
schools serve an increasingly diverse audience, many of whom are not even
Christian.

Indeed, fundamentalist and evangelical Christians, joined by New Right politicians, probably had a sharper vision of America's future than any other 1980s
group. In addition, members of the conservative community, like the Communists during the popular front era in the 1930s, mastered the art of obfuscating
differences on certain issues in order to build coalitions designed to change society. Catholics and Protestant fundamentalists, for example, joined in the anti-
abortion campaign. Although motivated by different reasons, fundamentalists,
blacks, and women sought to purge schools of undesirable reading assignments.
Feminists and fundamentalists allied to rid the nation of pornography.[138] And
concerned parents joined together to purge entertainment of sex and violence
that could harm children.[139]

One of the more controversial of the clean-up campaigns of the 1980s
involved pornography. Some sexually explicit speech, the Supreme Court had
ruled, clearly stood outside the First Amendment. But obscenity was difficult to
isolate from protected speech, and all sexually explicit material was not necessarily obscene. That fact, however, has not stopped efforts to banish sexually
explicit material from American society.[140] Early in the 1980s, much of this effort
was directed by ardent feminists who believed that the portrayal of women in
pornography was a root cause of inequality between the sexes. Because such

materials featured women simply as sex objects or as persons to be beaten, battered, and abused, the feminists argued that women in the real world were subjected to physical abuse and to inequitable treatment at school, on the job, and at home. "Pornography doesn't just drop out of the sky, go into his head and stop there. Specifically, men rape, batter, prostitute, molest, and sexually harass women," explained Catharine A. MacKinnon, one of the leading feminist theorists on the relationship between pornography and the treatment of women. "Under conditions of inequality, they also hire, fire, promote, and grade women, decide how much or whether or not we are worth paying and for what, define and approve or disapprove of women in ways that count, that determine our lives."[141] Because the portrayals of women in pornography so conditioned men, equality between the sexes would come only with its elimination.

Some feminists took the tried-and-true approach of protesting at places where alleged pornography was sold, and targets often included publications such as *Playboy, Penthouse,* and *Hustler* magazines. Other protesters encouraged municipalities to pass ordinances outlawing the sale of pornographic materials.[142] Although such ordinances would regulate pornography, their defenders said the laws did not restrict speech. Instead, they contended, they were restricting offensive conduct that denied women their equal rights in society. Backers of the pornography legislation also claimed that the Supreme Court allowed shielding certain groups from the abuses of pornography in 1982 when the justices allowed states to regulate child pornography.[143]

The premise on which the law was based caused problems for judges asked to rule on its constitutionality. As the federal judge who heard the case based on the Indianapolis, Indiana, law said, the feminists and their supporters in government contended that "the production, dissemination, and use of sexually explicit words and pictures *is* the actual subordination of women and not an expression of ideas deserving of First Amendment protection."[144] Unable to accept these contentions, the district judge found the measure unconstitutional. Members of the appeals court panel agreed. "The ordinance discriminates on the ground of the content of the speech. Speech treating women in the approved way—in sexual encounters 'premised on equality' . . . —is lawful no matter how sexually explicit. Speech treating women in the disapproved way—as submissive in matters sexual or as enjoying humiliation—is unlawful no matter how significant the literary, artistic, or political qualities of the work taken as a whole," wrote the court. "The state may not ordain preferred viewpoints in this way. The Constitution forbids the state to declare one perspective right and silence opponents."[145] The effort to pass laws to protect women from the effects of pornography ended in 1986 when the Supreme Court affirmed the appeals court decision without opinion.[146]

The campaign against pornography, however, was far from over. Action shifted from the feminists to the Reagan administration and its conservative allies, and in 1986, the Attorney General's Commission on Pornography called for legislation to restrict sexually explicit materials. Whereas the President's Commission on Obscenity and Pornography in 1970 had recommended abolishing regulations on such materials because it found no connection between them and antisocial behavior, the 1986 report found such links. The task force's findings were immediately disputed by many social scientists whose work was quoted. The experts said that, in many cases, the commission had misused data in order to prove a direct tie between sexually explicit material and acts of sexual violence that did not truly exist.[147] One reason for the difference in findings between the two reports, said critics of the 1986 study, was that the latest commission was dominated by individuals with law enforcement backgrounds; the 1970 commission had many members with civil liberties interests. But commission members claimed that the difference rested in substantial societal changes since 1970 and said that in 1986, "we live in a society unquestionably pervaded by sexual explicitness. In virtually every medium, from books to magazines to newspapers to music to radio to network television to cable television, matters relating to sex are discussed, described, and depicted with a frankness and an explicitness of detail that has accelerated dramatically."[148]

To restrain any further emphasis on sexuality, the commission made ninety-two specific recommendations for increased activity at all levels of government against purveyors of these materials. The recommendations included proposals for laws calling for the forfeiture of any profits made through the violation of obscenity laws, much the way profits related to drug trafficking are forfeited. In addition, the commission suggested that "Congress should amend the Federal obscenity laws to eliminate the necessity of proving transportation in interstate commerce," which had been a requirement since Anthony Comstock's day. Instead, federal cases should be brought where "the distribution of the obscene material 'affects' interstate commerce." Task forces designed solely to investigate and prosecute obscenity offenses should be established on federal and state levels, and special attention should be paid to the alleged connection between the distribution of obscenity and pornography and organized crime.[149] State and local governments also should find ways to aid "those who suffer mental, physical, educational, or employment disabilities as a result of exposure or participation in the production of pornography." And state legislatures were encouraged to explore the possibility of "a civil remedy for harms attributed to pornography."[150]

Despite these wide-ranging recommendations, Attorney General Edwin Meese III denied any interest in censorship: "This department, as long as I am attorney general, is not going to engage in any censorship that violates the First Amendment."[151] Few in the publishing world, however, believed that the First Amendment would stop Meese from acting against materials that he considered pornographic or obscene. Little came of the recommendations under Meese, whose work as attorney general soon fell under the cloud of the Iran-contra scandal. Meese did, however, start a special unit within the Justice Department designed to attack pornographic materials. Started in 1986, the unit served primarily as a speech-writing force for Meese. Under Richard Thornburgh, who took over as attorney general after Meese's resignation, the unit has become more active. It now supervises Project PostPorn, a Justice Department effort aimed at forcing mail-order operations that sell sexually explicit—but not obscene—merchandise out of business. Techniques used to obtain the materials are quite similar to those practiced by Comstock, and the department hopes to bring these businesses into court in enough states that it will be financially impossible for them to defend all of the legal actions.[152] For the moment, any expansion of this attack has been blocked by a federal court order,[153] but existing cases seem to be going forward.[154]

Other efforts to clean up society, which began about the same time as the attorney general's commission was conducting its study, were far more fruitful. Probably the most successful campaign was launched in 1985 by a group of well-placed Washington wives, including Tipper Gore, wife of Tennessee Senator Albert Gore, and Susan Baker, wife of then–Secretary of the Treasury James Baker III, to reign in the growing explicitness of music lyrics.[155] The women created the Parents' Music Resource Center (PMRC), a lobbying group that started a campaign for self-regulation within the music industry. Their fears were based in part on studies that showed that young people listened to rock music for at least four hours every day. That music, critics contended, praised rape, incest, homosexuality, sadomasochism, bestiality, drug and alcohol use, and suicide.[156] Other critics claimed that the music promoted satanism. As with campaigns against dime novels and comic books in earlier days, once again critics called for action to protect American young people.

The recording industry, like the motion-picture industry before it, tried to find the least intrusive form of self-regulation necessary to satisfy PMRC demands. In August 1985, for instance, the Recording Industry Association of America, which represented about 80 percent of the nation's recording companies, announced plans to put labels on albums that contained "explicit lyrics." The music industry's proposal, however, was much less than the PMRC's goal of a uniform rating system applied across the industry with an outside body, perhaps somewhat like the old Hays Office, making the decisions.[157]

Few PMRC members believed recording industry disclaimers, and the "Washington wives," as they were pejoratively known, kept asking for more. And as with the movie industry before it, the recording industry soon found itself subjected to congressional hearings and other pressures designed to bring conformity.[158] Eventually, as with the movie industry, recording producers agreed to place warning labels on recordings or to provide printed lyrics for songs dealing with explicit sex, violence, or drug use. The label would read "Explicit Lyrics—Parental Advisory."[159] But once again, as with the movie industry, self-regulation was not successful. Labels were left off, printed too small, or done in jest; by 1987, PMRC was threatening additional action against the producers.[160] The threats took on added force as state legislatures considered bills that would require the labeling of recordings.

In response to pending legislation in twenty states, the recording industry and the Parents' Music Resource Center announced another agreement. Once again the industry promised to put "Explicit Lyrics—Parental Advisory" on LPs, cassettes, and compact disks that contained lyrics that focused on certain forms of sexual conduct, violence, or illegal drug and alcohol use. The idea was that parents would review song lyrics to decide whether they wanted their children to purchase or listen to such music. This agreement differed from the earlier one in that this time, the labels would be of like size with similar placement on all merchandise. Lyrics would be printed on the back of packaging, space permitting. In return for the agreement on labeling, state legislators withdrew pending legislation. This agreement, too, seems somewhat ineffectual, and the possibility for legislatively mandated labeling or court action to punish store owners who sell music containing objectionable lyrics continues.

In fact, after the recording industry announced its compliance with the latest PMRC demands, two events occurred that showed that the accord was considered in some quarters to be insufficient to stop the flow of objectionable music. Members of the Louisiana house, for instance, approved a mandatory labeling law that would prohibit the sale of songs containing lyrics that touch on "rape, incest, bestiality, sadomasochism, violent sex, prostitution, murder, satanism, suicide, ethnic intimidation, or the use of illegal drugs or alcohol" to an unmarried person under the age of 17.[161] And a federal judge in Florida found a 2 Live Crew album, "As Nasty As They Wanna Be," obscene and cleared the way for authorities to arrest shop owners who sold it in South Florida.[162]

In response to the increased pressure brought by the forces of censorship, some members of the recording industry have tried to develop a more effective response to attacks on their livelihood. Some are offering bonuses to individuals who show a voter's registration card upon purchasing a recording. Others are raising the equivalent of a music defense fund to help store operators who run afoul of censorship forces. Still others are adding a second label to their recordings that promises legal help if needed as a consequence of selling that particular item. Still others, unfortunately, are refusing to take on more controversial groups and lyrics in an effort to avoid the problem altogether.

Much of this reaction is due to the problems encountered by the rap-musicians 2 Live Crew. Rap music was different from contemporary rock music. In the latter, determining the words of controversial songs was very difficult to do; in the former, the words, which were spoken in cadence, were designed to be heard. The audience to which rap music appealed was primarily young, male, and black. The lyrics were, by most adult standards, appalling. Like rock music, these lyrics seethed with violence toward police officers,[163] women,[164] and other races, religions, and ethnic groups.[165] Performers contended that they were only depicting society as it really was—particularly for black young people in the inner cities to whom rap music was primarily directed.[166] Representatives of groups such as the American Civil Liberties Union found no reason to censor what the popular artists said, arguing that courts would not interpret the lyrics as advocating violence or crime.

But parents were concerned, and, through them, lawmakers maintained watch. Tipper Gore stressed that "words like 'bitch' and 'nigger' are dangerous. Racial and sexual epithets, whether screamed across a street or camouflaged by the rhythms of a song, turn people into objects less than human—easier to degrade, easier to violate, easier to destroy." She firmly believed that her crusade to end such song lyrics was vital.[167]

The 2 Live Crew imbroglio simply aggravated an already difficult situation. Before the confrontation over "As Nasty As They Wanna Be," 2 Live Crew was a moderately successful group. After this album was declared legally obscene by a federal district judge, the group's success grew substantially. "Nasty" sold many more copies, and the next album, "Banned in the U.S.A.," was a fantastic success.[168] The federal judge, in finding the recording obscene under Florida law, noted that "the evident goal of this particular recording is to reproduce the sexual act through musical lyrics. It is an appeal directed to 'dirty' thoughts and the loins, not to the intellect and the mind." In fact, he noted that the group had put out a clean version, "As Clean As They Wanna Be," and had discovered that sales of that recording were limited. Thus, their success rested on the explicit album, which he found "taken as a whole . . . legally obscene."[169]

A record-store owner convicted of selling the now obscene recording was fined $1,000 and court costs for his offense.[170] The group itself stood trial on obscenity charges in South Florida for a live performance in which they presented the nasty version of the lyrics in an adults-only show. After about two hours of deliberation, the jury found the performers not guilty on the obscenity charge. Jurors decided that lyrics were more comical than obscene.[171] One possible reason for the discrepancy in verdicts was the fact that the police recording of a live concert was hard to understand in court. Officers took the stand to read the offensive lyrics to the jury, which jurors found rather humorous. 2 Live Crew, however, is far from humorous. It and its counterparts are being blamed for a variety of ills in American society. Conservative columnist George F. Will, for instance, finds it ironic that "we legislate against smoking in restaurants; [but] singing 'Me So Horny' is a constitutional right." He says such music fosters social attitudes that led to the gang rape of a Central Park jogger in the spring of 1990.[172]

The correctness of Will's opinion is beyond the scope of this study. But similar concerns have energized various segments of society to try to repress such explicit song lyrics. A frontal attack on recordings seems unlikely to succeed, if only in part due to the fact that the Supreme Court has declared that "music, as a form of expression and communication, is protected under the First Amendment."[173] In addition, community standards are in effect when it comes to determining whether certain music may be suppressed because it is obscene. The vagaries of community standards may be seen in the 2 Live Crew incident where a federal judge, ruling without the aid of a jury, found that the recorded version of "As Nasty As They Wanna Be" offended the sensibilities of South Floridians as he understood them. A jury of South Floridians found the group itself not guilty of having presented an obscene concert.

Whether the lyrics of certain songs can be made obscene where minors are concerned, however, is another question. The Supreme Court has held that governments may enforce a different obscenity standard when it comes to minors,[174] but whether such steps would be taken is another matter. The effect of song lyrics on young people, however, obviously presents a serious problem to society. With music playing such an important part in the lives of young people, the crucial question is just how great a role it has in shaping their value systems. Research cited by the Parents' Music Resource Center supports that notion that song lyrics shape attitudes, but then earlier research also said that comic books corrupted readers' morals. At the heart of the issue is whether these concerns validate efforts to force the recording industry into self-regulation. And does the industry's agreement to label music constitute a form of self-censorship? Scholars and critics who have studied the effect of self-regulation on the motion-picture and comic-book industries report stunted growth as a result of the chill sent through the artistic reaches of those businesses. How the music industry will fare as the result of such challenges is unclear.

If difficulties arise in banning recordings such as those by 2 Live Crew from being produced or from being sold, government officials may have another way to limit the access of juveniles to such offensive materials. The Federal Communications Commission, spurred on by Congress and conservative groups such as the Reverend Donald E. Wildmon's American Family Association, has taken dead aim on indecency over the airwaves. Although the campaign has not yet attempted to limit the songs that may be played on the air, such a result is not inconceivable. Whether this action would directly affect recording sales is another matter because many of the more offensive songs simply are not played on the radio anyway. Their sales depend on a following independent of air play on either radio or television, but lack of such exposure could adversely affect the development of new groups and restrict the way in which the musical art form develops.

The decency-over-the-airwaves campaign is another one of those conservative-inspired, politically motivated efforts to clean up society. In fact, some critics say it was the direct result of conservative opposition to President Reagan's sending FCC chairman Mark Fowler's name to the Senate for confirmation to a second term. Wildmon complained that Fowler had done "nothing, zero, zilch" about the indecent programming that Wildmon believed was plaguing the airwaves.[175] The anti-Fowler campaign led to an accord between the FCC and various national decency organizations including the American Family Association, the National Federation of Decency, and Morality in Media. The latter groups agreed to send complaints about allegedly obscene materials to the FCC, and the commission promised to investigate.

FCC members had virtually abandoned the indecency field after the Pacifica decision in 1978.[176] Indecent programming was essentially defined as repeated use of the words found in George Carlin's monologue, and even those were not banned between 10 p.m. and 6 a.m. Such standards were too permissive for those watching the media and for the newly concerned members of the FCC. And, indeed, some radio broadcasters gave their critics reason to be concerned. On April 29, 1987, the FCC issued three opinions regarding allegedly indecent programming carried by three different radio stations. Its members found excerpts from a play dealing with the sexual fantasies of homosexuals,[177] a song played on a university radio station that focused on sexual intercourse,[178] and a sexually explicit talk show[179] unacceptable uses of the airwaves. Because the commission was changing its standards on such programming, commissioners magnanimously declined to take action against the three offending FM-radio licensees who had not had due warning of the new policy. Henceforward, however, things would be different.

Although the FCC would continue to use the Pacifica standard of whether "language or material that depicts or describes, in terms patently offensive as measured by contemporary community standards for the broadcast ... medium, sexual or excretory activities or organs," no longer would an FCC determination be based solely on the repetitive use of Carlin's seven "filthy" words. "In addition, although it remains that indecency will be actionable only when there is a reasonable risk that children are in the audience," the new FCC statement said, "the fact that an indecent transmission occurs after 10:00 p.m. and is preceded by a warning will not automatically insulate the transmission from enforcement action."[180]

Just what the new regulations meant in terms of programming was unclear, but to many individuals and groups who did not believe that the government had the right to choose the nation's listening material even if children were involved, the new approach to indecent transmissions was unacceptable. When asked to reconsider its position, the FCC reiterated its basic assumption that the government should help parents regulate what their children heard and noted that broadcasters might now be able to air programming of all sorts beginning at midnight. This, said the commission order, "is our current thinking as to when it is reasonable to expect that it is late enough to ensure that the risk of children in the audience is minimized and to rely on parents to exercise increased supervision over whatever children remain in the viewing and listening audience."[181] The results of the commission's reconsideration still were unacceptable to those who thought this bordered on censorship. Representatives of Action for Children's Television, the American Civil Liberties Union, and other interested parties filed suit. While the court did not agree that the FCC was meddling in purely private affairs, circuit court judges did say that the commission's standards needed to be more precise.[182]

With the court's decision, the matter went back to the commission—more or less. The FCC had already been influenced by conservative pressure groups to begin this campaign, and before it could engage in any reconsideration another force entered the fray: the Congress of the United States. Senator Jesse Helms, Republican of North Carolina, well known for his advocacy of morally correct causes, rose in the Senate on July 26, 1988, to propose an amendment to the FCC's budget. The language that Helms suggested was simple: "By January 31, 1989, the Commissioner[s] of the Federal Communications Commission shall promulgate regulations in accordance with Section 1464, Title 18, United States Code, to enforce the provisions of such Section on a 24 hour per day basis." Helms was highly critical of the so-called "safe harbor" granted broadcasters that would allow the use of questionable material between midnight and 6 a.m. "Garbage is garbage, no matter what the time of day or night may be," Helms said, and the government should no longer sanction its use.[183]

The law that Helms wanted enforced dated back to the Communications Act of 1934, which created the FCC. Language in section 326 created an impossible dilemma for commissioners and broadcasters. It said on the one had, "Nothing in this Act shall be understood or construed to give the Commission the power of censorship over the radio communications or signals transmitted by any radio station, and no regulation or condition shall be promulgated or fixed by the

Commission which shall interfere with the right of free speech by means of radio communication." Immediately after that emancipating sentence, however, the law said, "No person within the jurisdiction of the United States shall utter any obscene, indecent, or profane language by means of radio communication."[184] When the criminal code was revised in 1948, the last sentence was removed from the Communications Act and joined with other language referring to obscene materials.[185] The law clearly said what Jesse Helms said it did, and his amendment was added to the law establishing the commission's budget for the fiscal year ending September 30, 1989.[186]

From that point on, the fight over indecency on the airwaves intensified. On December 21, 1988, the FCC acquiesced to congressional wishes and adopted a rule to end all programming that could be considered indecent. The rule was scheduled to go into effect December 28.[187] Opponents of the rule rallied once more and on January 23, 1989, won a court order that stopped the FCC from implementing the twenty-four-hour ban until the court could consider its constitutionality.[188] Before that could happen, the U.S. Supreme Court issued a ruling in a "dial-a-porn" case in which it responded to similar congressional efforts to cleanse the telephone lines of sexually explicit messages. Here, the Court said that banning obscene telephone messages was permissible but that Congress had to be careful when it attempted to reach simply indecent communications. The approach that Congress had taken, the justices said, was too broad, and although its concern for children who had access to the telephone numbers was admirable, Congress should fashion a means to protect children that would not keep adults from having access to the messages if they so desired. "Sexual expression which is indecent but not obscene is protected by the First Amendment," the Court reminded Congress, and such communication only may be regulated "in order to promote a compelling interest" such as the protection of minors "if it [Congress] chooses the least restrictive means to further the articulated interest."[189]

Members of the Federal Communications Commission, considering themselves still under the requirements imposed by Congress, went back to the drawing board. On November 20, 1989, barely five months after the dial-a-porn decision, commissioners solicited public comment on whether banning indecent communication from the airwaves at all hours of the day was the least restrictive way to protect children. Although it allegedly was seeking public input as to whether the ban was necessary at all and whether the ban should be effective to protect all children under the age of seventeen rather than children under the age of twelve as was the practice in earlier decisions, the result of the inquiry was clearly in sight from the language of the FCC notice.[190]

Congress, the FCC said, clearly intended to protect children under the age of seventeen. In addition, states had statutes that protected those under seventeen from certain sexually oriented materials, and the Motion Picture Association of America barred young people under seventeen from certain of its releases under its rating system. Unless someone could come up with a good reason to lower the age, the FCC obviously was determined to use seventeen as the cutoff point. And, said the FCC, Congress was also correct in demanding a twenty-four-hour ban on indecent programming. Studies of listening habits revealed that the average number of teenagers tuning in to at least 15 minutes of radio programming between midnight and 6 a.m. was 716,000—certainly enough to warrant a total ban on indecent programming. But the question remained as to whether there was any way to allow indecent programming over the airwaves to reach consenting adults while stopping children from hearing it. Although the FCC had its own answer in mind, the commission asked for public comments.[191]

In August 1990, the commission announced that "no alternative to a 24-hour prohibition on indecent broadcasts would effectively serve this government interest" in protecting its children from sexually explicit material. The commission found no technological devices that would bar youthful access to such programming and apparently placed no trust in the ability of parents to set rules for their children and to enforce them. Only if a licensee could prove that "children in fact are not present in the broadcast audience in their market at the time the alleged indecent program was aired" could they escape retaliation by the FCC.[192]

The FCC's ruling led to a continuation of the court battle. Action for Children's Television (ACT), as lead party in the case, argued that parents rather than the government should be responsible for choosing the programming that their children heard or saw.[193] In May 1991, the court of appeals for the District of Columbia agreed with ACT and its fellow petitioners. The Federal Communications Commission, said the court, may not ban indecent material totally from the airwaves. "The fact that Congress itself mandated the total ban on broadcast indecency does not alter our view that . . . such a prohibition cannot withstand constitutional scrutiny," the panel said as it ordered the FCC to find a "safe harbor" for such broadcasts.[194]

The next likely step for those interested in cleansing the airwaves is to take the case before the U.S. Supreme Court, where the outcome is far from predictable because the High Court has become far more conservative in recent years. The special nature of broadcasting, which allows the government to regulate it, and its manner of infiltrating into the family home could entice the justices to agree with those who wish to restrict programming contents. If the Supreme Court sides with Congress and the FCC, the implications for contemporary music as well as for other programming would be immense, and a major form of communication for all members of society would be permanently cleansed of material that a certain segment of society finds unsuitable for children. Persons with sufficient money could, of course, attend live performances or purchase recordings of certain materials, but those without extra funding would be denied access to such information and entertainment. But perhaps that is just what those trying to purify society want—to keep almost all people of all ages from sexually explicit materials. If they succeed with over-the-air broadcasting,[195] the modern-day purity movement will have taken a major step toward achieving that goal.

With the attack on indecency in broadcasting well under way, leaders of the purity movement looked for new areas of society that needed cleansing. And they found just such a target in the National Endowment for the Arts (NEA). The United States does not have a long tradition of supporting the arts with public money as do other countries; the urge to censor that with which we disagree simply runs too deep to allow the leeway necessary for innovative artistic efforts at governmental expense. Only one earlier attempt was made to provide public funding for the arts. Efforts by the Works Progress Administration, which was part of Franklin Roosevelt's program to find jobs for unemployed artists, writers, and actors during the Depression, lasted only a few years. The material its members were turning out was considered socialistic by more conservative members of Congress, and the program ended.[196] There was no further involvement between artists and the government until the NEA was set up in 1965. The endowment had a relatively peaceful existence until 1989, when members of Congress discovered that federal funds had underwritten photographs by Robert Mapplethorpe and Andres Serrano, which were considered obscene by congressional conservatives.

The issue may not even have come to congressional attention without the aid of the widespread network of the Reverend Wildmon, a Methodist minister from Tupelo, Mississippi, who is determined to cleanse American society in the manner of Anthony Comstock. Wildmon's American Family Association, for instance, helped lead the campaign against the movie *The Last Temptation of Christ* and pressured sponsors of television shows to pull their advertising from programs that included too much sex or bad language. In April 1989, a member of his organization sent Wildmon a newspaper clipping complaining about the display of the Serrano photograph "Piss Christ," which featured a plastic crucifix partially submerged in a jar of urine. Outraged, Wildmon issued a press release condemning the National Endowment for the Arts for helping to finance the Serrano exhibit that included that particular picture and urged his supporters to tell Congress that they did not want their tax dollars spent for such blasphemous work.[197] One immediate result was a considerable uproar in Congress.

Congressional anger eventually focused on the Serrano photograph and on an exhibit of photographs by the late Robert Mapplethorpe, which critics labeled as pornographic and homoerotic. Among the latter photographs were those showing one man urinating into another's mouth, a man with a whip inserted in his anus, and the exposed genitals of an eight-year-old boy and a four-year-old girl. The NEA had given Serrano a $15,000 grant for his work; Mapplethorpe had a $30,000 NEA grant to finance his activities.[198]

By July 1989, the key player in the debate was Senator Jesse Helms, well known for his dislike of homosexuals. Helms attached an amendment to a bill funding the operations of the Interior Department, under which the NEA operates, to curtail the agency's freedom in granting money. Senate leaders were trying to push the funding bill through, and Helms threatened to make sure a copy of a catalog containing the Serrano picture was on every Senate desk if the amendment was not added. His amendment was accepted by the Democratic leadership, and it passed by a voice vote. The Helms proposal banned the use of federal money for "obscene and indecent" art or for any activity that "denigrates, debases or reviles a person, group or class of citizens on the basis of race, creed, sex, handicap, age or national origin." In addition, the amendment banned funding artwork that featured "sadomasochism, homoeroticism, the exploitation of children" and that "denigrates the objects or beliefs of the adherents of a particular religion or nonreligion." The amendment was so all-encompassing that voting against it was almost impossible. The Senate measure would have withheld $45,000 from the NEA budget for the next year as an indication of displeasure over the endowment's funding of Serrano and Mapplethorpe and would have barred the two agencies that provided their grants from receiving any NEA money for the next five years. As Helms said, "If someone wants to write ugly nasty things on the men's room wall, the taxpayers do not provide the crayons."[199]

Cries of outrage quickly came from the art community. Senators simply did not understand the rigorous review process involved in NEA grants, they said, and how money was awarded solely on artistic merit. In addition, senators did not appreciate the need for freedom from government intervention in order to maintain a viable artistic community in the United States. Government intervention in artistic projects was more appropriate for totalitarian nations than free ones, said the critics. Ted Potter, executive director of the Southeastern Center for Contemporary Art in Winston-Salem, North Carolina, which had funded Serrano, was particularly distressed. Those people who condemned Serrano's "Piss Christ" photograph did not understand that Serrano, a devout Roman Catholic, was unhappy about modern exploitation of religious feelings. "This was an artist generally presenting as a protest statement this critical and outrageous issue of religious abuse and exploitation," Potter said. "Fine protest art makes protest visible, and he's done that with this photograph."[200]

Congress refused to accept Helms's amendment in its final version of the law funding the NEA. Instead, it included language barring federal financing for work that was considered to be obscene or lacking serious artistic, literary, political, or scientific merit. In the latter phrasing, Congress borrowed phrasing from the U.S. Supreme Court's 1973 definition of obscenity.[201] The 1989 measure also set aside funds to study the way in which grants were awarded and to recommend improvements so that such incidents could not happen again.[202] Artists also had to agree not to violate the congressionally imposed restrictions. A federal judge eventually vetoed that arrangement, noting that "the chilling effect . . . arising from the NEA's vague certification requirement is unmistakably clear," especially since "the NEA occupies a dominant and influential role in the financial affairs of the art world in the United States."[203]

The battle over federal financing of the arts was far from over, however, despite the resolution of the 1989 skirmish. The NEA operates under a five-year congressionally granted charter, and its right to life was up for renewal in 1990. At the beginning of the 1990 struggle, the Bush administration seemed prepared to counter Helms. The president himself, when asked at a news conference about his attitudes on art censorship, said that he believed no federal official or agency "should be set up to censor what you write or what you paint or how you express yourself." Personally, he said, "I am deeply offended by some of the filth that I see into which federal money has gone, and some of the sacrilegious, blasphemous depictions that are portrayed by some to be art. And so, I will speak strongly out opposed to that." Just how firmly he opposed censorship was left open to question, for he added that he would try "to convince those who feel differently in terms of legislation that we will do everything in our power to stop pure blasphemy."[204] As the NEA funding debate continued, the administration pulled back from anything close to an unconditional endorsement of its renewal. Eventually, the 1990 legislation funding the NEA called for officials making grants to take into "consideration general standards of decency and respect for the diverse beliefs and values of the American public."[205] Neither side was satisfied with this compromise, and the battle promised to continue.

From this controversy over government funding of the arts comes a fundamental question of whether the government should support artists of any kind. The argument that the person who provides the money to carry out a project should have a say in what is done with that money has a certain degree of validity, especially since the Supreme Court has now approved limits on the speech of medical personnel in family planning clinics that receive federal funding. Also gaining credibility is the argument that funding artists is a luxury that the nation can ill afford in times of budget deficits and unmet social needs. A counterpoint is the fairly indisputable fact that if the nation wants to expose its people to art, the government likely will have to help underwrite the project. So great questions of national policy as well as fundamental free expression issues rest within the NEA controversy. Also open to question, apparently, is whether some of the artwork that has sparked the recent debate is indeed obscene. The director of the Contemporary Art Center in Cincinnati, Ohio, was arrested in April 1990 on obscenity charges for featuring Robert Mapplethorpe's photos, which, although criticized for their lack of taste, had not really been considered obscene in the judicial sense.[206] A jury later found him not guilty.[207]

Another key issue behind the debates in Congress and the Cincinnati arrest—and perhaps behind the debate over song lyrics and language used in television shows as well—is just what kind of society America should be. As the nation grows more diverse so, too, do its interests. Christian fundamentalists and their conservative political allies find the artwork and the lifestyles of other Americans unacceptable to their tastes and beliefs and, by extension, equally unacceptable for the United States. Others find the national image held by political conservatives and religious fundamentalists to be cramped, uncharitable, and un-American. American in the latter instance means a toleration and indeed a glorification of the differences among peoples and interests that have made the nation great. The question of whether diverse views—revolutionary or not—will be allowed to continue in the United States is a substantial one, and upon its resolution may rest the success or failure of the nation.

But resolving that question is most difficult especially when you reach topics that touch on racial and sexual harassment. When it comes to art, freedom seems relatively simple to grant; after all, you must make an effort to see a display of controversial photographs. No one forces you to look at them. The same is basically true of pornography; no one says that you must look at magazines or films that depict explicit sexual behavior. Song lyrics present a somewhat different problem, because they are more pervasive, coming at young people not only through their own music collections but through the radio and music videos on television. Parental counseling and, if necessary, intervention in purchasing and listening habits could replace regulatory schemes. One area where a buffer is not easily developed occurs when speech that features racial, sexual, or religious slurs is hurled directly at the individuals most likely to be injured by it. In recent years, this kind of speech has become an increasing problem.

Probably the most famous example of offensive speech directed at religious or ethnic groups in recent years involved the attempt made by the National Socialist Party of America, the American Nazi party, to march in Skokie, Illinois, a suburb of Chicago with a sizable Jewish population, including several thousand who had survived the Holocaust in Europe. When the Nazis first asked for permission to march, village leaders granted it, hoping for a quick and relatively trouble-free demonstration. The community soon was rocked by protests, and village officers reconsidered. Fearful of citizen unrest should the planned march occur, they tried to fend off the Nazi onslaught. First, they sought an injunction to ban the march, only to find that the state court system, after initially upholding the order, rejected it outright. The U.S. Supreme Court had intervened and ordered the state courts to reevaluate their position.[208]

When the injunction route failed, village officials tried enacting several ordinances that would have placed substantial obstacles in the path of Nazi marchers. The new laws: 1) required parades of a certain size to obtain at least $350,000 in liability insurance before a permit would be considered, 2) banned the dissemination of materials that would promote or incite racial or religious hatred, 3) refused to issue a parade permit to anyone who intended to disseminate such information, and 4) prohibited members of a political party to assemble in the streets of Skokie wearing military-style uniforms. Each ordinance was challenged in the courts and declared unconstitutional. The federal district court said that "it must be made clear from the outset that defendants [village officials] have no power to prevent plaintiffs from stating their political philosophy, including their opinions of black and Jewish people, however noxious and reprehensible that philosophy may be." The question involved, said the court, "is which danger is greater: the danger that allowing the government to punish 'unacceptable' ideas will lead to suppression of ideas that are merely uncomfortable to those in power; or the danger that permitting free debate on such unacceptable ideas will encourage their acceptance rather than discouraging them by revealing their pernicious quality." Supreme Court doctrine, said the district court, has established "that speech may be punished only when it actually causes some social harm which the government can legitimately prevent."[209] Such conditions did not exist here.

Nor could the court of appeals find any reason to sustain the Skokie effort, although the majority of the court found it necessary to note, "We would hopefully surprise no one by confessing personal views that NSPA's beliefs and goals are repugnant to the core values held generally by residents of this country, and, indeed, to much of what we cherish in civilization." But, "as judges sworn to defend the Constitution, however, we cannot decide this or any case on that basis. Ideological tyranny, no matter how worthy its motivation, is forbidden as much to appointed judges as to elected legislators."[210]

Although members of the court of appeals felt constrained to apologize for their decision, they, much as Justice Kennedy in the 1989 flag-burning case, did not follow their emotions. Constitutional principles were more important. The case, of course, was appealed to the Supreme Court, where only two members, Harry Blackmun and Byron White, voted to review the case. Blackmun questioned whether constitutional principles had been properly applied, and he wrote a dissent to the majority's denial of certiorari. The decision of the lower federal courts stood, and the Nazis were cleared to march in Skokie. But Blackmun believed that the case rested "upon critical, disturbing, and emotional facts, and [that] the issues cut down to the very heart of the First Amendment." He wanted a full hearing because he wondered "whether, in the context of the facts that this record appears to present, there is no limit whatsoever to the exercise of free speech."[211]

In the Skokie cases, no such limits were imposed. But the Nazis did not march in that predominantly Jewish community. Frank Collin, leader of the National Socialist party, had never really wanted to march there anyway. His goal was to demonstrate in Chicago, but that city, too, had imposed insurance and other barriers. While he fought those regulations in court, he had written to communities around Chicago seeking permission to march. Skokie was the only one to respond to his letter, with that response setting off months of legal action. About the same time that the last of the Skokie regulations was declared unconstitutional, the Chicago rules also were thrown out. The Nazi march occurred in downtown Chicago, where, for less than an hour, a handful of Nazis strutted, thousands of protesters jeered, and police kept the groups apart.

In the long run, however, there was a casualty or two from the Skokie affair. The major loser was the American Civil Liberties Union. Since its founding after World War I, the ACLU had become increasing supportive of disreputable people seeking to practice their First Amendment rights. The American Nazis were some of their best clients, and it was to the ACLU that Collin turned when Skokie attempted to exclude the party from its village limits. ACLU lawyers, many of them Jewish, were behind the lawsuits that led to the invalidation of Skokie regulations, but Jewish members, who provided strong ACLU financial support, withdrew in droves as a result. Aryeh Neier, ACLU executive director during this period, was a German Jew who had escaped to England in 1939. He well understood the horrors that the Nazis had created, but he also understood the value of free speech. "It is dangerous to let the Nazis have their way," he said, "but it is more dangerous by far to destroy the laws that deny anyone the power to silence Jews if Jews should need to cry out to each other and to the world for succor." He reminded his fellow Jews that "Jews have been persecuted too many times in history for anyone to assert that their sufferings are at an end. When the time comes for Jews to speak, to publish, and to march in behalf of their own safety, Illinois and the United States must not be allowed to interfere." Indeed it was for the Jews that he was protecting the Nazis. "The Nazis, I respond to those who ask how I, a Jew, can defend freedom for Nazis, must be free to speak because Jews must be free to speak and because I must be free to speak."[212]

Such an attitude requires fervent devotion to the values protected by the First Amendment, and as the 1980s drew to a close, more and more Americans began to wonder with Justice Blackmun whether "there is no limit whatsoever to the exercise of free speech."[213] The argument over racist speech and the harm that it can cause had been building for at least a decade. As one law review writer said, "Most people today know that certain words are offensive and only calculated to wound. No other use remains for such words as 'nigger,' 'wop,' 'spick,' or 'kike.'"[214] Most advocates of restrictions on racist speech realize that the major obstacle to such limits is the First Amendment. One argument used to circumvent that barrier is that such speech can be restricted because it does not communicate worthwhile ideas. In addition, advocates of these restrictions argue that such language is inherently harmful to the person at whom it is aimed and perpetuates racism and other ills in society.[215] These arguments, of course, imply that First Amendment protection is limited to speech deemed valuable by certain members of society. The problem here is that many of the revolutionary ideas that have benefited American life so greatly over the years have been denounced as harmful to certain groups. Quelling racist speech may well lead to efforts to quiet other offensive language as well.

The fight over racially harmful speech is spreading across the nation. The American Civil Liberties Union, strangely enough, may be one of its primary victims. Individual affiliates around the country have come out in support of restrictions on racist speech while the national organization continued its opposition to such codes. Ultimately, the ACLU issued a policy statement in the fall of 1990 that condemned the speech codes while affirming the right of universities to punish students for "acts of harassment, intimidation or invasion of privacy."[216] Such a policy drew the traditional line between unrestricted freedom of speech and an acceptable right to punish behavior. The battle over the campus codes has led Nadine Strossen, a New York Law School professor who took over as national ACLU president in 1991, to the belief that "the First Amendment is being embattled from all sides." She finds that "now we have minorities and feminists and the left allied with fundamentalists who believe some communitarian values take precedence" over the individual rights that the First Amendment has long been thought to protect. Restricting racist speech in society, she says, "is a politically easy solution to intractable underlying problems such as racism."[217]

The primary battleground in this particular free-speech fight has become college campuses, where administrators and students have taken offense over increasing incidents involving racist and sexist slurs. Targets were women, blacks, Asians, and homosexuals. Taunts could be shouted from passing cars, made face-to-face in social or academic settings, scrawled on dormitory doors, or placed in campus mailboxes. At times, they were accompanied by threats of physical violence. Obviously a product of growing feelings of frustration and futility on the part of various groups on campus, such language has led to calls for campus policies making such speech violate academic rules and merit various kinds of punishment.[218] Schools including Rutgers, the University of Wisconsin, and Stanford adopted policies to restrict such speech.[219] Other universities including Duke have tried to establish similar rules only to have them torn apart by resident experts on constitutional law.[220]

At least one case challenging such a policy has made it into the court system.

In September 1989, a federal district court in Michigan found that a University of Michigan policy designed to prevent speech criticizing individuals based on their "race, ethnicity, religion, sex, sexual orientation, creed, national origin, ancestry, age, marital status, handicap or Vietnam-era veteran status . . . however laudable . . . swept within its scope a significant amount of 'verbal conduct' or 'verbal behavior' which is unquestionably protected speech under the First Amendment." The court found the university's policy unacceptable because the judge could find "no evidence in the record that any officials at the University ever seriously attempted to reconcile their efforts to combat discrimination with the requirements of the First Amendment."[221]

Thus one university's attempt to prevent discrimination on campus by a policy designed to punish speech fell before the dictates of the First Amendment, but the university responded with a narrower code to replace the one that the judge found so offensive to First Amendment values. At least 200 of the nation's colleges and universities have adopted similar codes to regulate the speech of their students. University administrators all stress the need to protect minority students and to avoid confrontations among students when defending such codes. An example of the kind of unacceptable speech that is spreading across campuses, administrators point to a University of Wisconsin, Eau Claire, student who sent a computer message to an Iranian saying, "Death to all Arabs. Die, Islamic scum bags." The student was put on probation for that transgression.[222] And then there was the Brown University student who was expelled for shouting offensive language out of his dormitory window while he was drunk. Among the words used were "nigger," "faggot," and "Jew" combined with an obscenity. He was not directing his language at any particular person, but he lost his right to continue his studies at Brown anyway.[223]

Universities are grappling with the basic conflicts inherent in trying to restrict youthful exuberance and indiscretion, freedom of speech, and the desire to promote harmony on campus. University of Houston law professor Michael Olivas notes the problems caused by these campus codes but says, "These [minority] students are extremely vulnerable. . . . These comments humiliate and threaten. They don't have anything to do with free speech." Nadine Strossen, on the other hand, says that the campus codes "are undermining free speech, and they are doing nothing to stop racism and bigotry. . . . For university administrators, they are a cheap solution to a complex problem."[224] In addition, says Strossen, "We are never going to eliminate group hatred, oppression or bigotry by silencing its most crass expressions and forcing them to go underground."[225]

These problems likely will continue, and universities will continue to seek solutions. For students who feel that their First Amendment rights have been violated by the imposition of such codes, they may—in certain circumstances—resort to the court system for redress. If they are enrolled in a private college, however, that avenue is unavailable to them for no state action is involved in the repression of their speech. Representative Henry Hyde, Republican of Illinois, has introduced a bill in Congress to correct that problem; his measure would require private colleges to adhere to First Amendment principles,[226] but the measure faces tough sailing. Part of the problem that these speech codes raise, of course, is beyond the reach of university administrators because the difficulties rest deep within the hearts and souls of many Americans. Nothing that the government or the church or the school system has tried in the past has been able to root out this hard core of nativism. The problems on campus were but one of its many manifestations during the Reagan years. As with other episodes of intense nativism, this one, too, likely will pass, and a new period of toleration will follow. Some universities are attempting to speed that change along by sponsoring seminars and requiring classes that attempt to broaden both student tolerance and understanding of the contributions that other societies and people have made to world culture.[227] This approach has garnered increasing criticism. Universities, say some Americans, are trying to indoctrinate their students in liberal, "politically correct" views while stifling the free thought and debate of those who might disagree.[228]

Politically correct thinking, goes the argument, has been developed by radicals of the 1960s and 1970s who today are college professors. And in that role, these individuals are promoting the leftist ideas on politics, race, sex, and other matters that formed the core of their beliefs during their radical days. Critics point to literature courses where students must alternate between well-known white male authors and unknown women authors. Other universities require students to take courses that focus on issues relating to non-Western civilizations. Many traditionalists fear that sound educational values are being sacrificed in this effort to broaden students' horizons. And those traditionalists on campus often find that their right to criticize their institution's changing curriculum is substantially circumscribed.

To conservatives, political correctness is a disaster. President George Bush even weighed in in the battle against political correctness during a commencement address at the University of Michigan in May 1991. "Although the movement arises from the laudable desire to sweep away the debris of racism, sexism and hatred, it replaces old prejudices with new ones," said the president. "It declares certain topics off-limits, certain expressions off-limits, even certain gestures off-limits. What began as a cause for civility has soured into a cause of conflict and even censorship."[229]

While the political correctness movement may have desirable goals, said the president, "it replaces old prejudices with new ones," and its very existence was ironic as the bicentennial of the Bill of Rights approached. The president noted his concern over the fact that "neighbors who disagree no longer settle matters over a cup of coffee." Now, he said, "They hire lawyers and go to court. Political extremists roam the land, abusing the privilege of free speech, setting citizens against one another on the basis of their class or race." He called such behavior "bullying" and said, "it's not worthy of a great nation grounded in the values of tolerance and respect. Let us fight back against the boring politics of division and derision."[230]

To a certain extent, the problem of intolerant language on college campuses and the debate over what should be taught to today's college students symbolize the difficulties of an American society that has become increasingly fragmented. Under the Reagan and Bush administrations, rhetoric often has inflamed more than calmed, and acceptance of individual differences has all but disappeared. Rather than seeking to solve problems that such experiences have caused, the nation's leaders have pretended that the difficulties do not exist. In order for this fantasy to succeed, discussion of the nation's problems must disappear. Consequently, attacks on basic First Amendment rights have increased because freedom of expression forces the nation to deal with coarse, raucous, and unpleasant reality. Individuals practicing their rights under the First Amendment are likely to propose a bewildering assortment of revolutionary ideas for the remaking of society, and in recent years, few political leaders have wanted to be bothered with such ideas. The challenge for the future, then, may well be to persist until the national establishment not only recognizes the right of all Americans to speak their minds but listens to what these people have to say.

★★★

Epilogue

If William Shakespeare was right, and the past is a prologue to the future, what does the future hold for freedom of expression? With a new century looming for the Bill of Rights and the world, will the response to expressive activities be any different? Will the repressive nature of the Reagan years set the tone for the way in which society reacts to freedom of expression in the future? Or will that attitude, too, cycle out while a new era of tolerance is ushered in, as has been the tendency in the past? And if a new era of tolerance appears, how long will it last?

Trying to determine the future of freedom of expression from its recent past provides some dismal lessons indeed. The bicentennial year of the Bill of Rights, for instance, began with the nation at war. The lessons of Vietnam, Grenada, and Panama had been well learned, for journalistic access to information was tightly restricted, in part, said the authorities, because of the development of global communications systems that allowed the enemy immediate access to any data obtained by American reporters. Protests against such restrictions were few, and many Americans seemed to approve of keeping the press in check just as they seemed to disapprove of demonstrations against the war. The Persian Gulf War was an orgy of patriotism, and as the history of free expression tells us, speech is often repressed at such times.

The lessons from the history of freedom of expression detailed in the preceding pages are alternately uplifting and grim. The United States has lurched from periods when revolutionary ideas were soundly and, at times, violently repressed to times when the nation was rocked by the raucousness of uninhibited discussion. There seems to be little middle ground when it comes to freedom of expression. Either the cacophony of voices drowns out rational thought or the eeriness of silence threatens the smallest voice. Dissent is either a precious commodity or a dangerous substance, and dissenters are either national heroes or national goats. If we value freedom of expression and want it to stay around for a while, we must try to find out why Americans have such extreme attitudes.

Basically, dissenters have served as the conscience of the nation. Some exceptions may be found in the preceding history, but by in large, these people, whether they are labor organizers, anarchists, Communists, or Christian fundamentalists, were trying, to the best of their abilities, to point out what they perceived to be flaws in the national character on certain issues. By trying to force the nation to make changes in American life, these dissenters have taken on a most difficult task. People do not like to be told that they are imperfect, and Americans have long felt their society to be fairly close to the ideal. Such beliefs fly in the face of history, for society as it exists today in the United States is the product of change brought on by individuals who found the flaws and who had the courage to force the nation to acknowledge and remedy them. But presenting such revolutionary ideas never has been easy.

This reality makes one comment by Supreme Court Justice Antonin Scalia during oral arguments for the second flag-burning case unacceptable, even though he was trying to point out that flag burning was indeed communication. People who burn flags were sending a message, he told government attorneys defending the new law: "They're saying 'We hate the United States.'"[1] In reality, that is only part of the message that flag burners are sending. They are actually saying they hate the United States for the way it is treating its homeless, for the money it spends on armaments, for its abuse of minorities, or for whatever other cause paramount in their minds at the time. These protesters largely have been denied a voice in the chambers of government, where officials have systematically ignored the right of citizens to petition peacefully for a redress of grievances. That repressive tradition began with Bacon's Rebellion in 1676 and continues through today. Indeed, the failure of George III to hear the complaints of his subjects in the colonies led to revolution and independence, just as the unwillingness of Lyndon Johnson to listen to antiwar arguments led to years of national turmoil.

While most Americans agree that no government official listens to them, few try to draw attention to their concerns. As a result of years of Nixon intimidation and Reagan deprivation, many Americans have simply withdrawn from the political process as they find their efforts to participate stymied by the twin ogres of governmental bureaucracy and secrecy. Other Americans have turned to acting out their concerns to gain attention. From this latter group come flag burners and Operation Rescue workers. In the past, such dissenters have been responsible for ending British control of the United States, for stopping slavery, for ending segregation, and for stopping an unwise war in Southeast Asia. In such situations, their opponents might well have said that the protesters hated America when they really despised flawed national policies. From their complaints and willingness to place their property, reputations, and lives on the line has come a better America. Those who would quiet modern-day dissenters would do well to remember those results.

In fact, Americans can be proud that their heritage of free speech and their willingness to stand up against governmental wrongs has been accepted so widely throughout the world. The uprisings in China and in Eastern Europe in 1989 and 1990 were good old-fashioned American protest movements exported to other lands. What is ironic is that while Americans were cheering foreigners on in their efforts to topple communism, they were growing increasingly unwilling to allow dissent at home. When Rumanians, for example, defaced their flag and burned it to show their contempt for their government, Americans were filled with praise. When Gregory Johnson burned the American flag to show his distaste for the policies of Ronald Reagan, Americans were filled with revulsion.

But, say Americans, our problems are so much different from those faced by people in other countries. If we were fighting for democracy as were the Eastern Europeans, maybe flag burning would be acceptable. But, critics say, Americans are faced with overwhelming social problems, with homelessness, poverty, drug abuse, and AIDS topping an almost endless, depressing list. Those who would suppress uninhibited discussion of such issues argue that flag burning and intemperate speech will not provide the necessary answers. Indeed, they say, espousing deviant ideas likely will lead the nation into further chaos. Perhaps the problems are different in the United States, but many of these problems are directly related to the sense of alienation that runs deep in American society, an attitude fed by the exclusionary attitudes that Americans are so good at perpetuating. Dialogue will not cure AIDS or stop drug abuse or integrate Hispanics and Asians into the nation more quickly, but it might help to correct the root causes of some problems. Imprisonment and ostracism certainly have not provided the answers; discussion and understanding might.

During the Reagan years, a number of policies designed to restrict "offensive" activities have run afoul of the First Amendment. Perhaps that is one reason why conservatives have taken such a firm stand on the issue of flag burning. Somehow a chink in the First Amendment had to be found; somehow society had to be restored to a civility that First Amendment precedent simply would not allow. But almost every effort to curtail objectionable speech runs into problems. On college campuses, the effort is to curtail commentary critical of blacks, Jews, women, homosexuals. If such an effort succeeded, individuals such as Senator Jesse Helms, a well-known homophobic, would have difficulty speaking on campus. If such a policy were in place more widely in society, as some advocate, the word "nigger" would be outlawed, as perhaps it should be, but what would happen to the blacks who increasingly use the word to refer to one another? If society were purified to the extent that some reformers want, what would happen to books such as James Joyce's *Ulysses,* which once again might be banned because of its portrayal of sex? If music were restricted because of its effects on the listeners, what would become of songs such as "We Shall Overcome," which certainly has strong overtones of ethnic intimidation? The questions that the latest efforts to purify society raise are innumerable, and all of them go directly back to that pesky First Amendment.

Many of the difficulties experienced in society at large also may be connected to the Reagan administration's success in excluding the vast majority of the American people from the process of governing themselves. Once this occurs, Americans divert their attention into other parts of society where they feel they can make a difference. The New Right has capitalized on such a diversion of energy in order to try to bring American society back to what it considers to be the nation's conservative, religious roots. What the New Right forgets, however, is that the nation is far more heterogeneous than ever before, and fewer people are willing to have their fundamental value systems dictated by a small group of highly opinionated individuals. One answer to the turmoil in society may well be in opening up the marketplace for fuller discussion on more issues—both social and governmental. The court system has been doing well in keeping social issues open for debate. Now it needs to attack the curtain of secrecy that has been drawn so tightly around governmental operations.

The conservatives who sought to control the nation in the 1980s based their actions on a firm belief in the "original intent" of those who drafted the Constitution and the Bill of Rights. Society, they maintained, had gotten so far out of hand because the court system had been meddling in issues that the Founding Fathers never intended to be subjected to litigation. Stop abortion and return prayer and Bible reading to the public schools, they say, because the Founders certainly did not mean their words to sanction judicial intervention in such issues. If the conservative doctrine of original intent is applied to the First Amendment, most who espouse it would argue that only political speech, which lies at its very core, is protected. Quickly jumping over the implications of that admission, they focus on what the First Amendment would not protect, such as literary, artistic, or scientific expression. If the nation accepts the position that political speech was the primary beneficiary of the First Amendment, then the court system needs to become active in protecting such speech. Speech about government cannot be protected if the courts consistently uphold governmental efforts to conceal information or to keep ideas with which the current administration disagrees away from the American people.

One thing that an inspection of the speech and press of the 1780s and 1790s would reveal is that it was, above all else, intrusive, robust, and controversial. Information was provided to the American people, and they participated in making decisions for the government. The decisions may not have always been what the politicians in power wanted, but they allowed the people to speak and followed their wishes. John Adams, for instance, did not call out the militia to keep Thomas Jefferson from taking the presidency, even though Adams feared that Jefferson would reverse many of the Federalist's policies. Free speech and debate had led to the change in policies, as the American people had wished. In the 1980s, both the government and the people seem to have forgotten that intimate relationship. Instead, there were attacks on the First Amendment and on the principles for which freedom of expression has come to stand, simply because they are politically inexpedient or personally reprehensible for certain members of society. As the First Amendment celebrates its 200th birthday, it likewise stands in its greatest jeopardy. Now that the First Amendment has developed to the point where it provides a wide range of freedom, many in society and government want to cut it down to size—to their size, with each group ready to take a small chunk out of it. What will be left when the First Amendment is ready to celebrate its 300th birthday is up to the American people.

★ ★ ★

Notes

N.B.: Page citations of books that have been reprinted refer to the reprint edition unless specified otherwise.

Preface

1. Gitlow v. New York, 268 U.S. 652, 669, 673 (1925).

2. Alexander Hamilton, James Madison, and John Jay, *The Federalist Papers,* 2d ed., ed. Roy P. Fairfield (Garden City, N.Y.: Anchor Books, 1966), 263–64.

3. James Madison to W. T. Barry, 4 Aug. 1822, *Writings of James Madison,* ed. Galliard Hunt (New York: G. P. Putnam's Sons, 1910), 9:103.

4. See, for example, Leonard Levy, *Emergence of a Free Press* (New York: Oxford Univ. Press, 1985); David A. Anderson, "The Origins of the Press Clause," *UCLA Law Review* 30 (1983): 455–541; and Jeffery A. Smith, *Printers and Press Freedom: The Ideology of Early American Journalism* (New York: Oxford Univ. Press, 1988).

5. Among the few exceptions are Donna Lee Dickerson, *The Course of Tolerance: Freedom of the Press in Nineteenth Century America* (New York: Greenwood Press, 1990), and Timothy W. Gleason, *The Watchdog Concept: The Press and the Courts in Nineteenth Century America* (Ames: Iowa State Univ. Press, 1990).

6. See, for example, Zechariah Chafee, Jr., *Free Speech in the United States* (Cambridge, Mass.: Harvard Univ. Press, 1941; rpt., New York: Atheneum, 1969); Thomas I. Emerson, *The System of Freedom of Expression* (New York: Random House, 1970); Franklyn S. Haiman, *Speech and Law in a Free Society* (Chicago: Univ. of Chicago Press, 1981); and Harry Kalven, Jr., *A Worthy Tradition: Freedom of Speech in America,* ed. Jamie Kalven (New York: Harper & Row, 1988).

Chapter 1

1. Details about the labor movement in the latter quarter of the nineteenth century are taken from Sanford Cohen, *Labor in the United States,* 2d ed. (Columbus, Ohio: Charles E. Merrill Books, 1966), 59–82; Thomas R. Brooks, *Toil and Trouble: A History of American Labor* (New York: Delacorte Press, 1964), 38–83; Joseph G. Rayback, *A History of American Labor* (New York: Macmillan, 1959), 103–207; Albert A. Blum, *A History of the American Labor Movement* (Washington, D.C.: American Historical Association, 1972); Norman J. Ware, *The Labor Movement in the United States, 1860–1895* (New York: D. Appleton, 1929; rpt., Gloucester, Mass.: Peter Smith, 1959); and Robert

Justin Goldstein, *Political Repression in Modern America from 1870 to the Present* (Cambridge, Mass.: Schenkman, 1978), 1–60.

2. Cohen, 78.

3. See Lillian Symes and Travers Clement, *Rebel America: The Story of Social Revolt in the United States* (New York: Harper & Brothers, 1934), 99–177.

4. Quoted in ibid., 159 (emphasis included).

5. *Revenge Circular,* quoted in ibid., 172 (emphasis included).

6. *Albany Law Journal,* 15 May 1886, quoted in Henry David, *The History of the Haymarket Affair,* 2d ed. (New York: Russell & Russell, 1958), 217–18.

7. Quoted in ibid., 253–54.

8. *American State Trials,* ed. John Lawson (St. Louis, 1919), 12:264, quoted in ibid., 307.

9. *Advance and Labor Leaf,* 24 Sept. 1887, quoted in ibid., 375.

10. *Denver Labor Enquirer,* 22 Oct. 1887, quoted in ibid., 410.

11. See William O. Reichert, *Partisans of Freedom: A Study in American Anarchism* (Bowling Green, Ohio: Bowling Green Univ. Popular Press, 1976), 407–26; and Charles A. Madison, *Critics & Crusaders: A Century of American Protest* (New York: Henry Holt, 1947), 214–35.

12. See John D. Hicks, *The Populist Revolt: A History of the Farmers' Alliance and the People's Party* (Minneapolis: Univ. of Minnesota Press, 1931; rpt., Lincoln: Univ. of Nebraska Press, 1961).

13. Omaha Platform, July 1892, quoted in ibid., 439–40.

14. Lincoln *Farmers' Alliance,* 15 Feb. 1890, quoted in ibid., 404.

15. See Donald L. McMurry, *Coxey's Army: A Study of the Industrial Army Movement of 1894* (pub. by author, 1929; rpt., Seattle: Univ. of Washington Press Americana Library, 1968); and Malcolm O. Sillars, "The Rhetoric of the Petition in Boots," *Speech Monographs* 39 (1972):92–104.

16. See Felix Frankfurter and Nathan Greene, *The Labor Injunction* (New York: Macmillan, 1930; rpt., Gloucester, Mass.: Peter Smith, 1963), 47–81; and William E. Forbath, "The Shaping of the American Labor Movement," *Harvard Law Review* 102 (1989):1109–256.

17. See Almont Lindsey, *The Pullman Strike: The Story of a Unique Experiment and of a Great Labor Upheaval* (Chicago: Univ. of Chicago Press, 1942); and Daniel Novak, "The Pullman Strike Cases: Debs, Darrow and the Labor Injunction," in *American Political Trials,* ed. Michal R. Belknap (Westport, Conn.: Greenwood Press, 1981), 129–51.

18. In re Debs, 158 U.S. 564, 570, 572 (1895).

19. Ibid. at 597.

20. See Heywood Broun and Margaret Leech, *Anthony Comstock: Roundsman of the Lord* (New York: Albert & Charles Boni, 1927). See also Craig L. Fisher-LaMay, "Anthony Comstock: Victorian America, Sexuality and Free Speech" (Master's thesis, University of North Carolina at Chapel Hill, 1989); and Ralph K. Andrist, "Paladin of Purity," *American Heritage* (Oct. 1973), 4–7, 84–89. The purity crusades of the era are discussed in Paul S. Boyer, *Purity in Print: The Vice-Society Movement and Book Censorship in America* (New York: Charles Scribner's Sons, 1968); and David J. Pivar, *Purity Crusade: Sexual Morality and Social Control, 1868–1900* (Westport, Conn.: Greenwood Press, 1973).

21. Fisher-LaMay, 29.

22. Broun and Leech, 16.

23. See Felice Flanery Lewis, *Literature, Obscenity & Law* (Carbondale: Southern Illinois Univ. Press, 1976), 1–25.

24. These states were Vermont (1821), Connecticut (1834), Massachusetts (1835), Pennsylvania (1860), and New York (1868). Ibid., 7.

25. 5 Stat. 566 (1842).

26. 13 Stat. 507 (1865).

27. See Dorothy Ganfield Fowler, *Unmailable: Congress and the Post Office* (Athens: Univ. of Georgia Press, 1977), 55–57; and James C. N. Paul, "The Post Office and Non-Mailability of Obscenity: An Historical Note," *UCLA Law Review* 8 (1961):44–68.

28. 15 Stat. 196 (1868).

29. 17 Stat. 302 (1872).

30. Anthony Comstock, *Frauds Exposed,* quoted in Broun and Leech, 86.

31. *Congressional Globe,* 42d Cong., 3rd sess., 1 March 1873, Appendix, 168.

32. 17 Stat. 599 (1873).

33. 19 Stat. 90 (1876).

34. Queen v. Hicklin, 3 Q.B. 360, 371 (1868).

35. Quoted in Mary Ware Dennett, *Birth Control Laws: Shall We Keep Them, Change Them, or Abolish Them?* (New York: Frederick H. Hitchcock, 1926), 31–32.

36. See James Turner, *Without God, Without Creed: The Origins of Unbelief in America* (Baltimore, Md.: Johns Hopkins Univ. Press, 1985); Sidney Warren, *American Freethought, 1860–1914* (New York: Columbia Univ. Press, 1943); and Chris Wharton, "Speaking the Unspeakable: Birth Control Information and Freedom of Expression in Late 19th- and Early 20th-Century America" (Master's thesis, University of North Carolina at Chapel Hill, 1989).

37. Liberal League resolution quoted in Anthony Comstock, *Frauds Exposed; or, How the People Are Deceived and Robbed, and Youth Corrupted* (Montclair, N.J.: Patterson Smith, 1969), 402–3.

38. Ibid., 408–9 (emphasis included).

39. Liberal League petition quoted in Anthony Comstock, *Traps for the Young,* ed. Robert Bremner (Cambridge, Mass.: Belknap Press of Harvard Univ. Press, 1967), 188, 190.

40. Ibid., 192.

41. Ex parte Jackson, 96 U.S. 727, 732, 736, 733 (1878). See also In re Rapier, 143 U.S. 110 (1892), in which the Court upheld its earlier decision.

42. Comstock, *Traps for the Young,* 193.

43. House Report of the Committee on Revisions of the Laws, quoted in ibid., 195.

44. United States v. Bennett, 24 Fed. Cas. 1093, 1101 (1879).

45. Ezra H. Heywood, *Free Speech: Report of Ezra H. Heywood's Defense Before the United States Court in Boston, April 10, 11, and 12, 1883* (Princeton, Mass.: Co-operative Publishing, 1883), 22, 37–38 (emphasis included).

46. See Edmund Pearson, *Dime Novels; or, Following an Old Trail in Popular Literature* (Boston: Little, Brown, 1929); and Mary Noel, "Dime Novels," *American Heritage* (Feb. 1956), 50–55, 112–13.

47. Quoted in Broun and Leech, 224.

48. Andrist, 5.

49. Theodore Schroeder, *"Obscene" Literature and Constitutional Law: A Forensic Defense of Freedom of the Press* (New York: Privately printed, 1911), 25.

50. See Richard Hofstadter with Walter P. Metzger, *The Development of Academic Freedom in the United States* (New York: Columbia Univ. Press, 1955), 207–74.

51. Ibid., 413–67.

52. See Frank Luther Mott, *American Journalism,* 3rd ed. (New York: Macmillan, 1962), 411–612; Sidney Kobre, *The Development of American Journalism* (Dubuque,

Iowa: Wm. C. Brown, 1969), 349–547; Edwin Emery and Michael Emery, *The Press and America,* 5th ed. (Englewood Cliffs, N.J.: Prentice-Hall, 1984), 253–351; Willard G. Bleyer, *Main Currents in the History of American Journalism* (New York: Houghton Mifflin, 1927; rpt., New York: Da Capo Press, 1973), 322–88; Sidney Kobre, *The Yellow Press and Gilded Age Journalism* (Tallahassee: Florida State Univ. Press, 1964); and Michael Schudson, *Discovering the News: A Social History of American Newspapers* (New York: Basic Books, 1978), 61–120. See also J. Lincoln Steffens, "The Business of a Newspaper," *Scribner's* (Oct. 1897), 447–67.

53. *New York Evening Post,* quoted in Bleyer, 378.

54. See Ted C. Smythe, "The Reporter, 1880–1900," *Journalism History* 7 (1980):1–10.

55. Samuel D. Warren and Louis D. Brandeis, "The Right to Privacy," *Harvard Law Review* 4 (1890):195–96.

56. Henry B. Brown, "The Liberty of the Press," *American Law Review,* 34 (1900):334, 338.

57. Don R. Pember, *Privacy and the Press: The Law, the Mass Media and the First Amendment* (Seattle: Univ. of Washington Press, 1972), 16.

58. *New York Sun* quoted in the *Boston Morning Journal,* 9 April 1890, quoted in Pember, 37.

59. See Norman L. Rosenberg, *Protecting the Best Men: An Interpretive History of the Law of Libel* (Chapel Hill: Univ. of North Carolina Press, 1986), 178–206.

60. Storey v. Wallace, 60 Ill. 51, 57 (1871).

61. See Timothy W. Gleason, *The Watchdog Concept: The Press and the Courts in Nineteenth Century America* (Ames: Iowa State Univ. Press, 1990).

62. See Potter Stewart, "Or of the Press," *Hastings Law Journal* 26 (1975):631–37.

63. *New York Times,* 12 Dec. 1886, quoted in David Gordon, "The 1896 Maryland Shield Law: The American Roots of Evidentiary Privilege for Newsmen," *Journalism Monographs* No. 22 (Feb. 1972), 13.

64. See Jack R. Hart, "Horatio Alger in the Newsroom: Social Origins of American Editors," *Journalism Quarterly* 53 (1973):14–20.

65. See Edwin Emery, *History of the American Newspaper Publishers Association* (Minneapolis: Univ. of Minnesota Press, 1950; rpt., Westport, Conn.: Greenwood Press, 1970).

66. See Richard Burket Kielbowicz, "Origins of the Second-Class Mail Category and the Business of Policymaking, 1863–1879," *Journalism Monographs* No. 96 (April 1986); and Richard B. Kielbowicz, "The Growing Interaction of the Federal Bureaucracy and the Press: The Case of a Postal Rule, 1879–1917," *American Journalism* 4 (1987):5–18.

67. See Peter R. Knights, "The Press Association War of 1866–1867," *Journalism Monographs* No. 6 (Dec. 1967); Kobre, *The Yellow Press,* 295–304; and Victor Rosewater, *History of Cooperative News-Gathering in the United States* (New York: D. Appleton, 1930), 266–77.

68. Inter-Ocean Publishing Co. v. Associated Press, 184 Ill. 438, 453 (1900).

69. Kobre, *The Yellow Press,* 305–7.

70. John Hay to Theodore Roosevelt, 27 July 1898, in William R. Thayer, *The Life and Letters of John Hay* (Boston, 1915), 2:337, quoted in Harold U. Faulkner, *Politics, Reform and Expansion* (New York: Harper & Brothers, 1959; rpt., Harper Torchbooks, 1963), 248.

71. See Marcus M. Wilkerson, *Public Opinion and the Spanish-American War: A Study in War Propaganda* (Baton Rouge: Louisiana State Univ. Press, 1932); and Joseph E. Wisan, *The Cuban Crisis as Reflected in the New York Press (1895–1898)* (New York: Columbia Univ. Press, 1934). See also Kobre, *The Yellow Press,* 279–94.

72. See Mary S. Mander, "Pen and Sword: Problems of Reporting the Spanish-American War," *Journalism History* 9 (1982):2–9, 28.

73. Charles H. Brown, "Press Censorship in the Spanish-American War," *Journalism Quarterly* 42 (1965):581.

74. Wisan, 222–24; and Wilkerson, 10–12.

75. *New York Evening Post,* 15 March 1895, quoted in Wisan, 73.

76. Quoted in Wilkerson, 92.

77. See Robert C. Hilderbrand, *Power and the People: Executive Management of Public Opinion in Foreign Affairs, 1897–1921* (Chapel Hill: Univ. of North Carolina Press, 1981), 7–29.

78. For a discussion of how a nonsensational newspaper publisher covered the Cuban situation, see Benedict Karl Zobrist, "How Victor Lawson's Newspapers Covered the Cuban War of 1898," *Journalism Quarterly* 38 (1961):323–31.

79. *New York Sun,* 2 May 1898, quoted in Brown, 583.

80. See Robert L. Beisner, *Twelve Against Empire: The Anti-Imperialists, 1898–1900* (New York: McGraw-Hill, 1968); Daniel B. Schirmer, *Republic or Empire: American Resistance to the Philippine War* (Cambridge, Mass.: Schenkman, 1972); Fred H. Harrington, "The Anti-Imperialist Movement in the United States, 1898–1900," *Mississippi Valley Historical Review* 22 (1935):211–30; and Samuel Eliot Morison, Frederick Merk, and Frank Freidel, *Dissent in Three Wars* (Massachusetts Historical Society, 1970; rpt., Cambridge, Mass.: Harvard Univ. Press, 1970), 65–95.

81. See Harrington, 234–35; and Schirmer, 149–59.

82. *Springfield Republican,* quoted in *Literary Digest,* 13 May 1899, 541, quoted in Harrington, 225.

83. Edward Lawrence Godkin, *Reflections and Comments, 1865–1895* (New York: Charles Scribner's Sons, 1896), 4–8, quoted in Beisner, 74.

84. See Margaret A. Blanchard, "Finley Peter Dunne," *Dictionary of Literary Biography,* ed. Perry J. Ashley (Detroit, Mich.: Gale Research, 1983), 23:95–110.

85. Mark Twain, speaking at the Lotos Club, 23 March 1901, in *After Dinner Speeches at the Lotos Club,* ed. John Elderkin et al. (New York, 1911), 14–15, quoted in Morison, Merk, and Freidel, 95.

Chapter 2

1. *New York Times,* 8 Sept. 1901, quoted in Linda Cobb-Reiley, "The Meaning of Freedom of Speech and of the Press in the Progressive Era: Historical Roots of Modern First Amendment Theory" (Ph.D. diss., University of Utah, 1986), 55. See also Sidney Fine, "Anarchism and the Assassination of McKinley," *American Historical Review* 60 (1955):777–99.

2. Carlos F. MacDonald, "The Trial, Execution, Autopsy, and Mental Status of Leon F. Czolgosz, Alias Fred Nieman, The Assassin of President McKinley," *The American Journal of Insanity* 58 (1902):384, quoted in Don Sneed, "A Newspaper Analysis of the 'Trials' of William McKinley's Assassin" (Paper presented at the Annual Meeting of the American Journalism Historians Association, Las Vegas, Nev., Oct. 1985), 5.

3. *Washington Post,* 11 Sept. 1901, quoted in Sneed, 10.

4. People v. Most, 171 N.Y. Rep. 423, 430 (1902).

5. *New York Times,* 7 Sept. 1901, quoted in Cobb-Reiley, "The Meaning of Freedom of Speech," 87.

6. *New York Journal,* 4 Feb. 1901, quoted in Frank Luther Mott, *American Journalism,* 3rd ed. (New York: Macmillan, 1962), 541.

7. *New York Evening Journal,* 10 April 1901, quoted in ibid.

8. See Bernell E. Tripp, "The Decline of Yellow Journalism, 1901–1917" (Paper presented at the Annual Meeting of the American Journalism Historians Association, Charleston, S.C., Oct. 1988).

9. 32 Stat. 1221–22 (1903).

10. Clevenger-Gilbert, *Criminal Law and Practice of New York . . . As Amended to End of Legislative Session of 1948* (Albany, N.Y., 1948), Penal Law, Art. 14, sec. 160–64, quoted in Fine, 793.

11. Quoted in Fine, 797.

12. Turner v. Williams, Brief and Argument of Appellant, 49, quoted in David M. Rabban, "The First Amendment in Its Forgotten Years," *Yale Law Review* 90 (1981):537.

13. Turner v. Williams, 194 U.S. 279, 294 (1904).

14. See Melvyn Dubofsky, *We Shall Be All: A History of the Industrial Workers of the World,* 2d ed. (Urbana: Univ. of Illinois Press, 1988), 19–87.

15. See ibid. and Paul F. Brissenden, *The IWW: A Study of American Syndicalism,* 2d ed. (New York: Columbia Univ. Press, 1920; rpt., New York: Russell & Russell, 1957). See also William Preston, Jr., *Aliens and Dissenters: Federal Suppression of Radicals, 1903–1933* (Cambridge, Mass.: Harvard Univ. Press, 1963; rpt., New York: Harper Torchbooks, 1966).

16. Preston, 36.

17. Quoted in Brissenden, 92.

18. Quoted in ibid., 227.

19. 208 U.S. 161 (1908).

20. 30 Stat. 428 (1898).

21. 208 U.S. at 172.

22. 26 Stat. 209 (1890).

23. 208 U.S. 274 (1908).

24. *Literary Digest,* 4 April 1908, quoted in Robert J. Goldstein, "The Anarchist Scare of 1908," *American Studies* 15 (1974):67.

25. Quoted in Goldstein, 70.

26. Senate Committee on the Judiciary, *Transmission through the Mails of Anarchistic Publications: Message from the President of the United States,* 60th Cong., 1st sess., Document 426, 1.

27. 35 Stat. 416 (1908).

28. Gompers v. Buck's Stove & Range Co., 221 U.S. 418, 421 (1911). See Barry F. Helfand, "Labor and the Courts: The Common-Law Doctrine of Criminal Conspiracy and Its Application in the Buck's Stove Case," *Labor History* 18 (1977):91–114.

29. Ibid. at 437, 439.

30. See Senate *Final Report and Testimony Submitted to Congress by the Commission on Industrial Relations,* 64th Cong., 1st sess., 1916, document 415.

31. Ibid., 64.

32. Ibid., 65.

33. Ibid., 66–67.

34. Ibid., 98–99.

35. 38 Stat. 731, 738 (1914).

36. Quoted in David A. Shannon, *The Socialist Party of America* (New York: Macmillan, 1955), 72.

37. Max Eastman, "Is the Truth Obscene?," *The Masses,* March 1915, p. 1, quoted in Lynne Masel-Walters, "For the 'Poor Mute Mothers'? Margaret Sanger and *The Woman Rebel,*" *Journalism History* 11 (1984):4. See also David M. Kennedy, *Birth Con-*

trol in America: The Career of Margaret Sanger (New Haven, Conn.: Yale Univ. Press, 1970), 1–35.

38. See Timothy N. Walters and Lynne Masel-Walters, "The Conspiracy of Silence: Media Coverage of Syphilis, 1906–1938" (Paper presented to the History Division, Association for Education in Journalism and Mass Communication Annual Meeting, Washington, D.C., Aug. 1989).

39. See Ruth A. Inglis, *Freedom of the Movies: A Report on Self-Regulation from the Commission on Freedom of the Press* (Chicago: Univ. of Chicago Press, 1947); Richard S. Randall, *Censorship of the Movies: The Social and Political Control of a Mass Medium* (Madison: Univ. of Wisconsin Press, 1970), 9–32; Robert Stanley, *The Celluloid Empire* (New York: Hastings House, 1978), 174–230; and Charles Matthew Feldman, *The National Board of Censorship (Review) of Motion Pictures: 1909–1922* (New York: Arno Press, 1977).

40. Quoted in *Moving Picture World*, 20 April 1907, p. 101, quoted in Feldman, 3.

41. Block v. Chicago, 239 Ill. 251 (1909).

42. Feldman, 64–65.

43. Stanley, 177.

44. 37 Stat. 240 (1912).

45. 38 Stat. 151 (1913).

46. Mutual Film Corp. v. Ohio Industrial Commission, 236 U.S. 230, 241 (1915).

47. Ibid. at 243–44.

48. See Thomas R. Cripps, "The Reaction of the Negro to the Motion Picture Birth of a Nation," *Historian* 25 (1962/63):344–62.

49. D. W. Griffith, "The Rise and Fall of Free Speech in America," quoted in Harry Geduld, *Focus on D. W. Griffith* (Englewood Cliffs, N.J.: Prentice Hall, 1971), 43–45, quoted in Nickieann Fleener-Marzec, *D. W. Griffith's The Birth of a Nation: Controversy, Suppression and the First Amendment As It Applies to Filmic Expression, 1915–1973* (New York: Arno Press, 1980), 374–75.

50. See Richard Hofstadter, *The Age of Reform* (New York: Vintage Books, 1955).

51. See Margaret A. Blanchard, "Press Criticism and National Reform Movements: The Progressive and New Deal Eras," *Journalism History* 5 (1978):33–37, 54–55.

52. Hamilton Holt, *Commercialism and Journalism* (Boston: Houghton Mifflin, 1909), 98.

53. Will Irwin, "The Editor and the News," *Collier's*, 1 April 1911, p. 18. The series has been collected and reproduced under the title *The American Newspaper* (Ames: Iowa State Univ. Press, 1969).

54. Will Irwin, "The Foe From Within," in ibid., 1 July 1911, p. 30.

55. Will Irwin, "The Voice of A Generation," in ibid., 29 July 1911, p. 15.

56. See Linda Lawson, "Advertisements Masquerading as News in Turn-of-the-Century American Periodicals," *American Journalism* 5 (1988):81–96.

57. 37 Stat. 243 (1912).

58. Lewis Publishing Co. v. Morgan, 229 U.S. 288, 298 (1913) (emphasis included).

59. Ibid. at 313–14.

60. See Edwin Emery, *History of the American Newspaper Publishers Association* (Minneapolis: Univ. of Minnesota Press, 1950; rpt., Westport, Conn.: Greenwood Press, 1970), 110–18.

61. James Edward Rogers, *The American Newspaper* (Chicago: Univ. of Chicago Press, 1909), 38, 199.

62. Samuel Hopkins Adams, "The Great American Fraud," *Collier's*, 7 Oct. 1905, quoted in Arthur and Lila Weinberg, *The Muckrakers* (New York: Simon and Shuster, 1961; rpt., New York: Capricorn Books, 1961), 178.

63. [Mark Sullivan], "The Patent Medicine Conspiracy Against Freedom of the Press," *Collier's,* 4 Nov. 1905, rpt. in ibid., 179–94.

64. See Daniel Pope, *The Making of Modern Advertising* (New York: Basic Books, 1983), 185–226.

65. See Robert C. Hilderbrand, *Power and the People: Executive Management of Public Opinion in Foreign Affairs, 1897–1921* (Chapel Hill: Univ. of North Carolina Press, 1981), 52–71; and George Juergens, *News from the White House: The Presidential-Press Relationship in the Progressive Era* (Chicago: Univ. of Chicago Press, 1981), 1–90.

66. See Clyde Peirce, *The Roosevelt Panama Libel Cases* (New York: Greenwich Book Publishers, 1959); John Lofton, *The Press as Guardian of the First Amendment* (Columbia: Univ. of South Carolina Press, 1980), 146–68; and Norman L. Rosenberg, *Protecting the Best Men: An Interpretive History of the Law of Libel* (Chapel Hill: Univ. of North Carolina Press, 1986), 194–95.

67. *Indianapolis News,* 7 Dec. 1908, quoted in Peirce, 58–59.

68. *New York World,* 8 Dec. 1908, quoted in ibid., 61.

69. Quoted in Lofton, 155–56.

70. President Roosevelt to Congress, 15 Dec. 1908, quoted in Peirce, 77–78.

71. *New York World,* 16 Dec. 1908, quoted in ibid., 81–82.

72. United States v. Smith, 173 F. 227, 229–30 (D.Ind. 1909).

73. Quoted in W. A. Swanberg, *Pulitzer* (New York: Charles Scribner's Sons, 1967), 437.

74. United States v. Press Publishing Co., 219 U.S. 1 (1911).

75. *New York World,* 4 Jan. 1911, quoted in Lofton, 167.

76. See Margaret A. Blanchard, "Filling in the Void: Speech and Press in State Courts Prior to *Gitlow,*" in *The First Amendment Reconsidered,* ed. Bill F. Chamberlin and Charlene Brown (New York: Longman, 1982), 14–59; David M. Rabban, "The First Amendment in Its Forgotten Years," *Yale Law Journal* 90 (1981):514–95; Alexis J. Johnson, "The Formative Period of First Amendment Theory," *American Journal of Legal History* 24 (1980):56–75; Michael T. Gibson, "The Supreme Court and Freedom of Expression from 1791 to 1917," *Fordham Law Review* 55 (1986):263–333; Henry J. Abraham, *Freedom and the Court: Civil Rights and Liberties in the United States,* 4th ed. (New York: Oxford Univ. Press, 1982), 28–91; Margaret A. Blanchard, "The Institutional Press and Its First Amendment Privileges," *Supreme Court Review* (1978), 252–59; Timothy W. Gleason, *The Watchdog Concept: The Press and the Courts in Nineteenth-Century America* (Ames: Iowa State Univ. Press, 1990); and Linda Cobb-Reiley, "No Longer an Empty Box With Beautiful Words on It: First Amendment Legal Scholarship in the Progressive Years" (Paper presented at the Annual Meeting of the American Journalism Historians Association, Charleston, S.C., Oct. 1988).

77. Barron v. Baltimore, 32 U.S. (7 Peters) 243, 250 (1833).

78. See Timothy W. Gleason, "19th-Century Legal Practice and Freedom of the Press: An Introduction to an Unfamiliar Terrain," *Journalism History* 14 (1987):26–33.

79. William Blackstone, *Commentaries on the Laws of England* (Boston: T. B. Wait and Sons, 1818), 4:151–52 (emphasis included).

80. James Kent, *Commentaries on American Law,* 5th ed. (New York: printed for the author, 1844), 2:17.

81. Joseph Story, *Commentaries on the Constitution of the United States,* (Boston: Hilliard, Gray, 1833; rpt., Durham, N.C.: Carolina Academic Press, 1987), 2:597–98.

82. See M. Glenn Abernathy, *The Right of Assembly and Association,* 2d ed. (Columbia: Univ. of South Carolina Press, 1981).

83. Commonwealth v. Davis, 162 Mass. 510, 511 (1895).

84. Frazee's Case, 30 N.W. 72, 75 (1886).

85. Near v. Minnesota, 283 U.S. 697 (1931).

86. Roth v. United States, 354 U.S. 476 (1957).

87. New York Times v. Sullivan, 376 U.S. 254 (1964).

88. Branzburg v. Hayes, 408 U.S. 665 (1972).

89. Gibson, 270, n24.

90. *Constitution,* amend. XIV, sec. 1.

91. Rep. John A. Bingham of Ohio and Sen. Jacob Howard of Michigan argued during debates over ratification of the amendment that they believed *Barron v. Baltimore* to be wrongly decided and that, in their opinion, the Fourteenth Amendment would rectify that error by making the Bill of Rights fully applicable to the states. Abraham, 39.

92. Slaughterhouse Cases, 84 U.S. (16 Wall.) 36 (1873).

93. United States v. Cruikshank, 92 U.S. 542 (1876).

94. Ex parte Jackson, 96 U.S. 727 (1878).

95. Davis v. Beason, 133 U.S. 333 (1890).

96. Ex parte Curtis, 106 U.S. 371 (1882).

97. 205 U.S. 454 (1907).

98. 4 Stat. 488 (1831).

99. See Lofton, 62–78.

100. 205 U.S. at 465.

101. See Nye v. United States, 313 U.S. 28 (1941); Bridges v. California, 314 U.S. 252 (1941); and Pennekamp v. Florida, 328 U.S. 331 (1946).

102. See also Henry Schofield, "Freedom of the Press in the United States," *Proceedings of the Ninth Annual Meeting of the American Sociological Society* (1914), 67–116.

103. Thomas M. Cooley, *A Treatise on the Law of Torts,* 2d ed. (Chicago: Callaghan, 1888), 256.

104. Thomas M. Cooley, *A Treatise on the Constitutional Limitations Which Rest upon the Legislative Power of the States of the American Union* (Boston: Little, Brown, 1871), 497, 499–500.

105. Theodore Schroeder, *Free Speech for Radicals,* enlarged ed. (New York, 1916; rpt., New York: Burt Franklin, 1969), 42, 100.

106. Ibid., 107–8.

107. Thomas Jefferson to James Madison, 30 Jan. 1787, *The Writings of Thomas Jefferson,* ed. Paul L. Ford (New York: G. P. Putnam's Sons, 1894), 4:362–63.

108. Thomas Jefferson to William Stephens Smith, 13 Nov. 1787, in ibid., 4:467.

109. Schroeder, *Free Speech for Radicals,* 20.

110. Ernst Freund, *The Police Power: Public Power and Constitutional Rights* (Chicago: Callaghan, 1904), 509–11.

Chapter 3

1. Woodrow Wilson, Address to Congress, 19 Aug. 1914, in *Selected Literary and Political Papers and Addresses of Woodrow Wilson* (New York: Grosset and Dunlap, 1928), 2:71–72.

2. See Arthur S. Link, *Woodrow Wilson and the Progressive Era, 1910–1917* (New York: Harper & Row, 1954; Harper Torchbooks, 1963), 145–282.

3. John L. Heaton, *Cobb of "The World"* (New York: E. P. Dutton, 1924), 267–69, quoted in Robert C. Hilderbrand, *Power and the People: Executive Management of Public Opinion in Foreign Affairs, 1897–1921* (Chapel Hill: Univ. of North Carolina Press, 1981), 142.

4. See Donald Johnson, *The Challenge to American Freedom: World War I and the Rise of the American Civil Liberties Union* (Lexington: Univ. of Kentucky Press for the Mississippi Valley Historical Association, 1963); George Juergens, *News from the White House: The Presidential-Press Relationship in the Progressive Era* (Chicago: Univ. of Chicago Press, 1981), 126–72; Paul L. Murphy, *World War I and the Origin of Civil Liberties in the United States* (New York: W. W. Norton, 1979); H. C. Peterson and Gilbert C. Fite, *Opponents of War, 1917–1918* (Madison: Univ. of Wisconsin Press, 1957); and Harry N. Scheiber, *The Wilson Administration and Civil Liberties* (Ithaca, N.Y.: Cornell Univ. Press, 1960).

5. See John A. Thompson, *Reformers and War: American Progressive Publicists and the First World War* (Cambridge, Eng.: Cambridge Univ. Press, 1987); Charles De Benedetti, *The Peace Reform in American History* (Bloomington: Indiana Univ. Press, 1980), 79–107; *The Power of the People: Active Nonviolence in the United States,* eds. Robert Cooney and Helen Michalowski (Culver City, Calif.: Peace Press, 1977), 38–55; Charles Chatfield, *For Peace and Justice: Pacifism in America, 1914–1941* (Knoxville: Univ. of Tennessee Press, 1971), 15–41; Johnson, *The Challenge to American Freedom,* 1–25; Blanche Wiesen Cook, "Democracy in Wartime: Antimilitarism in England and the United States, 1914–1918," *American Studies* 13 (1972):51–68; and David S. Patterson, "An Interpretation of the American Peace Movement, 1898–1914," *American Studies* 13 (1972):31–49.

6. Link, 166–67.

7. Flag Day Address, 14 June 1917, *The Papers of Woodrow Wilson,* ed. Arthur S. Link (Princeton, N.J.: Princeton Univ. Press, 1983), 42:502–4.

8. New York *Gaelic-American,* 23 May 1914, quoted in Mick Mulcrone, "On the Razor's Edge: The Irish-American Press on the Eve of World War One" (Paper presented to the History Division, Association for Education in Journalism and Mass Communication Annual Convention, Washington, D.C., Aug. 1989), 12.

9. Third Annual Address to Congress, 7 Dec. 1915, *The Public Papers of Woodrow Wilson: The New Democracy, 1913–1917,* eds. Ray Stannard Baker and William E. Dodd (New York: Harper & Brothers, 1926), 3:423.

10. *New York Times,* 27 June 1916, quoted in Frederick C. Luebke, *Bonds of Loyalty: German-Americans and World War I* (DeKalb: Northern Illinois Univ. Press, 1974), 174.

11. See David A. Shannon, *The Socialist Party of America* (New York: Macmillan, 1955), 81–125.

12. See Melvyn Dubofsky, *We Shall Be All: A History of the Industrial Workers of the World,* 2d ed. (Urbana: Univ. of Illinois Press, 1988), 349–75.

13. 39 Stat. 919 (1917).

14. *Report of the Attorney General, 1918,* 56, 26 quoted in Scheiber, 14.

15. Paul P. Van Riper, *History of the United States Civil Service* (Evanston, 1958), 226, quoted in Scheiber, 15.

16. *Congressional Record,* 65th Cong., Special sess., (2 April 1917), 104, quoted in Scheiber, 17–18.

17. 40 Stat. 219 (1917).

18. Ibid., 230–31.

19. 40 Stat. 425–26 (1917).

20. *Report of the Attorney General of the United States, 1918,* 18, quoted in Zechariah Chafee, Jr., *Free Speech in the United States* (Cambridge, Mass.: Harvard Univ. Press, 1941; rpt., New York: Atheneum, 1969), 40.

21. 40 Stat. 553–54 (1918).

22. *Congressional Record,* 65th Cong., 2d sess., 9 April 1918, 4826, quoted in Murphy, *World War I and Civil Liberties,* 82.

23. Committee on Public Information, *Official Bulletin,* 16 April 1918, quoted in Murphy, 83.

24. *Congressional Record,* 65th Cong., 2d sess., 4 May 1918, 6050–51, quoted in Murphy.

25. 40 Stat. 1012 (1918).

26. *Congressional Record,* Proposed Espionage Act, 65th Cong., 1st sess., 2 April 1917, 766. See Thomas F. Carroll, "Freedom of Speech and of the Press in War Time: The Espionage Act," *Michigan Law Review* 17 (1919):621–65.

27. Woodrow Wilson to Arthur Brisbane, in Ray Stannard Baker, *Woodrow Wilson, Life and Letters: War Leader* (New York: Doubleday, Doran, 1939), 7:36, quoted in Chafee, 38.

28. *New York Times,* 13 April 1917, quoted in John Lofton, *The Press as Guardian of the First Amendment* (Columbia: Univ. of South Carolina Press, 1980), 172.

29. *Congressional Record,* 65th Cong., 1st sess., 18 April 1917, 781.

30. Ibid., 784–85.

31. Ibid., 789–90.

32. Ibid., 19 April 1917, 835, 837.

33. Ibid., 837.

34. Resolutions on War and Militarism: Majority Report [better known as the St. Louis Platform], *International Socialist Review* 17 (1917):672.

35. Peterson and Fite, 31.

36. Irwin St. John Tucker, "The Price We Pay," quoted in Pierce v. United States, 252 U.S. 239, 256–57 (1920).

37. Brief for the United States, Schenck v. United States, in *Landmark Briefs and Arguments of the Supreme Court of the United States: Constitutional Law,* eds. Philip B. Kurland and Gerhard Casper (Arlington, Va.: University Publishers of America, 1975), 18:1028–31. See Jeremy Cohen, *Congress Shall Make No Law: Oliver Wendell Holmes, the First Amendment and Judicial Decision Making* (Ames: Univ. of Iowa Press, 1989).

38. David Karsner, *Debs* (New York: Boni and Liveright, 1919), 23–24, quoted in Frederick C. Giffin, *Six Who Protested: Radical Opposition to the First World War* (Port Washington, N.Y.: Kennikat Press, 1977), 40–41.

39. *Mother Earth,* June 1917, 111, quoted in Giffin, 105.

40. *Mother Earth,* July 1917, 160–61, quoted in Giffin, 112.

41. "The Finished Mystery," 247, quoted in Rutherford v. United States, 258 F. 855, 864 (2d Cir. 1919).

42. See Peterson and Fite, 121–38; Johnson, 26–54; and Stephen M. Kohn, *Jailed for Peace: The History of the American Draft Law Violators, 1658–1985* (Westport, Conn.: Greenwood Press, 1986), 25–43.

43. See Dubofsky, 349–444; Peterson and Fite, *passim;* William Preston, Jr., *Aliens and Dissenters: Federal Suppression of Radicals, 1903–1933* (Cambridge, Mass.: Harvard Univ. Press, 1963; rpt., New York: Harper Torchbooks, 1966), 88–151; Philip Taft, "The Federal Trials of the IWW," *Labor History* 3 (1962):57–91; Robert E. Ficken, "The Wobbly Horrors: Pacific Northwest Lumbermen and the Industrial Workers of the World, 1917–1918," *Labor History* 24 (1983):325–41; and Johnson, 85–118.

44. Quoted in Giffin, 131. Thirty-five of the defendants received five-year terms; thirty-three, ten-year sentences, and fifteen, twenty-year terms. Haywood, while out of jail pending appeal, fled the country and spent the rest of his life in the Soviet Union.

45. See Robert L. Morlan, *Political Prairie Fire: The Nonpartisan League, 1915–1922* (Minneapolis: Univ. of Minnesota Press, 1955).

46. War Resolutions, *Leader,* 14 June 1917, quoted in ibid., 136–37.

47. Gilbert v. Minnesota, 254 U.S. 325, 327 (1920).

48. Inspector's memoranda from Post Office Archives, 2 May 1918, quoted in Johnson, *The Challenge to American Freedom,* 74.

49. See Haig A. Bosmajian, "The Abrogation of the Suffragists' First Amendment Rights," *Western Speech* 38 (1974):218–32.

50. *New York Times,* 19 Aug. 1917, quoted in ibid., 223.

51. *Congressional Record,* 65th Cong., 1st sess., 18 Aug. 1917, 6145, quoted in ibid.

52. See Luebke; and Carl Wittke, *The German American Press in America* (Lexington: Univ. of Kentucky Press, 1957).

53. See Frank L. Grubbs, Jr., *The Struggle for Labor Loyalty: Gompers, the A.F. of L., and the Pacifists, 1917–1920* (Durham, N.C.: Duke Univ. Press, 1968).

54. See Thomas R. Brooks, *Toil and Trouble: A History of American Labor* (New York: Delacorte, 1964), 132–44.

55. See Carol S. Gruber, *Mars and Minerva: World War I and the Uses of Higher Learning in America* (Baton Rouge: Louisiana State Univ. Press, 1975), and Richard Hofstadter with Walter P. Metzger, *The Development of Academic Freedom in the United States* (New York: Columbia Univ. Press, 1955), 468–506.

56. *The Nation,* 1 June 1918, p. 639, quoted in Hofstadter with Metzger, 497.

57. Commencement Address, 6 June 1917, quoted in Hofstadter with Metzger, 499.

58. See 20 Stat. 359 (1879).

59. Burleson memoranda, quoted in Donald Johnson, "Wilson, Burleson, and Censorship in the First World War," *Journal of Southern History* 28 (1962):48.

60. See Dorothy Ganfield Fowler, *Unmailable: Congress and the Post Office* (Athens: Univ. of Georgia Press, 1977), 109–25; Juergens, *News from the White House,* 195–204; Peterson and Fite, *passim;* and Murphy, 71–132.

61. Albert Burleson to John H. Bankhead, 21 Aug. 1917, quoted in Johnson, "Wilson, Burleson, and Censorship," 50.

62. *Literary Digest,* 6 Oct. 1917, 12, quoted in Johnson, "Wilson, Burleson, and Censorship," 51–52.

63. Oswald Garrison Villard, *Fighting Years: Memoirs of a Liberal Editor* (New York: Doubleday, Page, 1939), 327, quoted in Juergens, 201.

64. Quoted in Harold M. Hyman, *To Try Men's Souls: Loyalty Tests in American History* (Berkeley: Univ. of California Press, 1959), 272.

65. See Joan M. Jensen, *The Price of Vigilance* (Chicago: Rand McNally, 1968).

66. Justice Department Circular, May 1918, quoted in Hyman, 276.

67. Robert D. Ward, "The Origin and Activities of the National Security League, 1914–1919," *Mississippi Valley Historical Review* 47 (1960):51–65.

68. See Luebke, 3–26, for details about the lynching of Robert Prager in Collinsville, Illinois.

69. *New York Times,* 27 July 1918, quoted in Peterson and Fite, 206.

70. See George Creel, *How We Advertised America* (New York: Harper & Row, 1920); James R. Mock and Cedric Larson, *Words That Won the War* (Princeton, N.J.: Princeton Univ. Press, 1939); and Stephen Vaughn, *Holding Fast the Inner Lines: Democracy, Nationalism, and the Committee on Public Information* (Chapel Hill: Univ. of North Carolina Press, 1980).

71. *New York Times,* 6 June 1917, quoted in Lofton, 174.

72. *New York Tribune,* 11 April 1918, quoted in ibid., 181.

73. See Robert C. Hilderbrand, *Power and the People: Executive Management of Public Opinion in Foreign Affairs, 1897–1921* (Chapel Hill: Univ. of North Carolina Press, 1981), 142–64; Stephen Vaughn, "First Amendment Liberties and the Committee on Public Information," *American Journal of Legal History* 23 (1979):95–119; and Juergens, 168–90.

74. "Preliminary Statement to the Press of the United States," 28 May 1917, quoted in Vaughn, "First Amendment Liberties," 107.

75. See James R. Mock, *Censorship 1917* (Princeton, N.J.: Princeton Univ. Press, 1941).

76. See Phillip Knightley, *The First Casualty* (New York: Harcourt Brace Jovanovich, 1975; rpt., Harvest Books, 1976); and Cedric Larson, "Censorship of Army News During the World War, 1917–1918," *Journalism Quarterly* 17 (1940):313–23.

77. Fourteen Points, 8 Jan. 1918, quoted in *Papers of Woodrow Wilson,* 45:536.

78. See Juergens, 205–47; Hilderbrand, 164–97; Reginald Coggeshall, "Was There Censorship at the Paris Peace Conference?," *Journalism Quarterly* 16 (1939):125–35; Reginald Coggeshall, "Paris Peace Conference Sources of News, 1919," *Journalism Quarterly* 17 (1940):1–10; Reginald Coggeshall, "Peace Conference Publicity: Lessons of 1919," *Journalism Quarterly* 19 (1942):1–11; Reginald Coggeshall, " 'Violations of Confidence' at the Paris Peace Conference," *Journalism Quarterly* 22 (1945):115–23, 150; James D. Startt, "Early Press Reaction to Wilson's League Proposal," *Journalism Quarterly* 39 (1962):301–8; and James D. Startt, "Wilson's Trip to Paris: Profile of Press Response," *Journalism Quarterly* 46 (1969):737–42.

79. See Margaret A. Blanchard, *Exporting the First Amendment: The Press-Government Crusade of 1945–1952* (New York: Longman, 1986), 8–11.

80. 249 U.S. 47, 52 (1919).

81. 249 U.S. 204 (1919).

82. Debs v. United States, 249 U.S. 211 (1919).

83. 250 U.S. 616 (1919).

84. See Richard Polenberg, *Fighting Faiths: The Abrams Case, the Supreme Court, and Free Speech* (New York: Viking, 1987).

85. See ibid.; Gerald Gunther, "Learned Hand and the Origins of Modern First Amendment Doctrine: Some Fragments of History," *Stanford Law Review* 27 (1975):719–73; Fred D. Ragan, "Justice Oliver Wendell Holmes, Jr., Zechariah Chafee, Jr., and the Clear and Present Danger Test for Free Speech: The First Year, 1919," *Journal of American History* 58 (1971):39–43; and David S. Bogen, "The Free Speech Metamorphosis of Mr. Justice Holmes," *Hofstra Law Review* 11 (1982):97–189.

86. 250 U.S. at 630.

87. 251 U.S. 466, 479 (1920).

88. Ibid. at 495.

89. 252 U.S. 239, 269, 273 (1920).

90. Gilbert v. Minnesota, 254 U.S. 325, 343 (1920).

91. 255 U.S. 407, 423 (1921).

Chapter 4

1. See Robert K. Murray, *Red Scare: A Study of National Hysteria, 1919–1920* (Minneapolis: Univ. of Minnesota Press, 1955; rpt., New York: McGraw-Hill, 1964); Paul L. Murphy, *The Meaning of Freedom of Speech: First Amendment Freedoms from Wilson to FDR* (Westport, Conn.: Greenwood Press, 1972); Donald Johnson, *The Challenge to American Freedoms: World War I and the Rise of the American Civil Liberties Union* (Lexington: Univ. of Kentucky Press for the Mississippi Valley Historical Association, 1963); William Preston, Jr., *Aliens and Dissenters: Federal Suppression of Radicals, 1903–1933* (Cambridge, Mass.: Harvard Univ. Press, 1963; rpt., New York: Harper Torchbooks, 1966); William Anthony Gengarelly, "Resistance Spokesmen: Opponents of the Red Scare, 1919–1921" (Ph.D. diss., Boston University, 1972); Robert Justin Goldstein, *Political Repression in Modern America from 1870 to the Present* (Cambridge,

Mass.: Schenkman, 1978), 137–63; and Stanley Coben, "A Study in Nativism: The American Red Scare of 1919–20," *Political Science Quarterly* 79 (1964):52–75.

2. Murray, 53, 56.

3. See Stanley Coben, *A. Mitchell Palmer: Politician* (New York: Columbia Univ. Press, 1963), 196–245.

4. Frank J. Donner, *The Age of Surveillance: The Aims and Methods of America's Political Intelligence System* (New York: Alfred A. Knopf, 1980), 30–51.

5. Quoted in Murray, 133.

6. *Congressional Record,* 66th Cong., 1st sess., 17 Oct. 1919, 7063.

7. 40 Stat. 1012 (1918).

8. Coben, *A. Mitchell Palmer,* 217–45.

9. *Congressional Record,* 66th Cong., 1st sess., 3 Nov. 1919, 7881.

10. House Committee on the Judiciary, Subcommittee on Internal Security, *Sedition, Syndicalism, Sabotage, and Anarchy, Hearings on H. R. 10210, 10235, 10379, 10614, 10616, 10650, and 11089,* 66th Cong., 2d sess. (1919), 32–33.

11. Quoted in Edward J. Muzik, "Victor L. Berger: Congress and the Red Scare," *Wisconsin Magazine of History* 47 (1964):313.

12. Berger v. United States, 255 U.S. 22 (1921).

13. Quoted in Arthur Garfield Hays, *Trial by Prejudice* (New York: Covici, Friede, 1933), 260, quoted in Murray, 184.

14. *New York Times,* 5 Jan. 1920, quoted in John Lofton, *The Press as Guardian of the First Amendment* (Columbia: Univ. of South Carolina Press, 1980), 201.

15. *Washington Post,* 4 Jan. 1920, quoted in ibid.

16. *St. Louis Post-Dispatch,* 4 Jan. 1920, quoted in ibid., 202.

17. *San Francisco Examiner,* 6 Jan. 1920, quoted in ibid., 203 (emphasis included).

18. See Donald L. Smith, *Zechariah Chafee, Jr.: Defender of Liberty and Law* (Cambridge, Mass.: Harvard Univ. Press, 1986), 36–57.

19. Decision of Louis F. Post, Assistant Secretary of Labor, In Re Thomas Truss, 10 April 1920, quoted in R. G. Brown, Zechariah Chafee, Jr., et al., *To the American People: Report upon the Illegal Practices of the United States Department of Justice* (Washington, D.C.: National Popular Government League, 1920; rpt., New York: Arno Press, 1969), 62.

20. H.R. 11430 [the Graham Bill], quoted in *Congressional Record,* 66th Cong., 2d sess., 29 Jan. 1920, 2210.

21. Ibid.

22. *Congressional Record,* 66th Cong., 2d sess., 20 Jan. 1920, 1774.

23. Ibid.

24. Ibid., (10 Jan. 1920), 1322.

25. *Journal of the Assembly of the State of New York,* 143rd sess., 1:21, quoted in Thomas E. Vadney, "The Politics of Repression, a Case Study of the Red Scare in New York," *New York History* 49 (1968):57.

26. See Vadney, 56–75; and Melvin I. Urofsky, "A Note on the Expulsion of the Five Socialists," *New York History* 47 (1966):41–49.

27. New York Legislative Document, 143rd sess., No. 35, 11:335, quoted in Vadney, 66.

28. *To the American People,* 8.

29. Colyer v. Skeffington, 265 F. 17, 43 (D.Mass. 1920).

30. 41 Stat. 593 (1920).

31. 40 Stat. 1009 (1920).

32. 42 Stat. 5 (1921).

33. 43 Stat. 153 (1924).

34. See Harold Josephson, "Political Justice During the Red Scare: The Trial of Benjamin Gitlow," in *American Political Trials,* ed. Michal R. Belknap (Westport, Conn.: Greenwood Press, 1981), 153–75.

35. Gitlow v. New York, 268 U.S. 652, 666 (1925).

36. Ibid. at 669.

37. Ibid. at 673.

38. See Lisa Rubens, "The Patrician Radical: Charlotte Anita Whitney," *California History* 65 (1986):158–71, 226–27.

39. Whitney v. California, 274 U.S. 357, 375 (1927).

40. Ibid. at 375, 377, 376.

41. See H. C. Peterson and Gilbert C. Fite, *Opponents of War, 1917–1918* (Madison: Univ. of Wisconsin Press, 1957), 148–56; and Donald Johnson, *The Challenge to American Freedoms: World War I and the Rise of the American Civil Liberties Union* (Lexington: Univ. of Kentucky Press for the Mississippi Valley Historical Association, 1963), 176–93.

42. See Norman Hapgood, *Professional Patriots* (New York: Albert & Charles Boni, 1928).

43. See Kenneth B. O'Brien, Jr., "Education, Americanization and the Supreme Court: The 1920's," *American Quarterly* 13 (1961):161–71.

44. Meyer v. Nebraska, 262 U.S. 390, 401 (1923).

45. Pierce v. Society of Sisters, 268 U.S. 510 (1925).

46. See L. Sprague de Camp, *The Great Monkey Trial* (Garden City, N.Y.: Doubleday, 1968); Edward J. Larson, *Trial and Error: The American Controversy over Creation and Evolution* (New York: Oxford Univ. Press, 1985); Edward Caudill, "The Roots of Bias: An Empiricist Press and Coverage of the Scopes Trial," *Journalism Monographs,* No. 114, July 1989; and Marvin N. Olasky, "When World Views Collide: Journalists and the Great Monkey Trial," *American Journalism* 4 (1987):133–46.

47. Quoted in de Camp, 2. Tennessee's law actually was the third in the nation. Oklahoma enacted its statute in 1923, with Florida soon following. Larson, 54.

48. Quoted in de Camp, 257.

49. Epperson v. Arkansas, 393 U.S. 97 (1968).

50. See David Williams, "The Bureau of Investigation and Its Critics, 1919–1921: The Origins of Federal Political Surveillance," *Journal of American History* 68 (1981):560–79.

51. Quoted in Max Lowenthal, *The Federal Bureau of Investigation* (New York: William Sloane Associates, 1950), 298, quoted in Robert Justin Goldstein, *Political Repression in Modern America from 1870 to the Present* (Cambridge, Mass.: Schenkman, 1978), 176.

52. See Irving Bernstein, *The Lean Years: A History of the American Worker, 1920–1933* (Boston: Houghton Mifflin, 1960).

53. 38 Stat. 731 (1914).

54. Duplex Printing Press Company v. Deering, 254 U.S. 443, 474 (1921). See Stanley I. Kutler, "Labor, the Clayton Act, and the Supreme Court," *Labor History* 3 (1962):19–38; and John E. Semonche, *Charting the Future: The Supreme Court Responds to a Changing Society, 1890–1920* (Westport, Conn.: Greenwood Press, 1978), *passim.*

55. American Steel Foundries v. Tri-City Central Trades Council, 257 U.S. 184, 193–94 (1921) (emphasis included).

56. 38 Stat. 738 (1914).

57. 257 U.S. at 205.

58. Ibid. at 209.

59. Truax v. Corrigan, 257 U.S. 312, 328, 340 (1921).

60. Felix Frankfurter and James M. Landis, "Power of Congress Over Procedure in Criminal Contempts in 'Inferior' Federal Courts—A Study in Separation of Powers," *Harvard Law Review* 37 (1924):1107.

61. See Murphy, *The Meaning of Freedom of Speech*, 159–63.

62. Quoted in "Smothering a Strike by Injunction," *Literary Digest*, 16 Sept. 1922, p. 8.

63. "Trifling with Freedom," *Editor & Publisher*, 9 Sept. 1922, p. 26, quoted in Murphy, *The Meaning of Freedom of Speech*, 160–61.

64. *The Editor and His People: Editorials by William Allen White*, ed. Helen Ogden Mahin (New York: Macmillan, 1924), 349.

65. 44 Stat. 577 (1926).

66. See Felice Flanery Lewis, *Literature, Obscenity & Law* (Carbondale: Southern Illinois Univ. Press, 1976), 67–71; and Paul S. Boyer, *Purity in Print: The Vice-Society Movement and Book Censorship in America* (New York: Charles Scribner's Sons, 1968), 23–52.

67. 46 Stat. 688 (1930).

68. United States v. One Book Called "Ulysses," 5 F.Supp. 182 (S.D.N.Y. 1933); United States v. One Book Entitled Ulysses, 72 F.2d 705 (2d Cir. 1934).

69. See Mary Ware Dennett, *Who's Obscene?* (New York: Vanguard Press, 1930).

70. Ibid., 40–41.

71. Indictment quoted in ibid., 46.

72. United States v. Dennett, 39 F.2d 564, 569 (2d Cir. 1930).

73. See David M. Kennedy, *Birth Control in America: The Career of Margaret Sanger* (New Haven, Conn.: Yale Univ. Press, 1970), 218–71.

74. In *Eisenstadt v. Baird*, 405 U.S. 438 (1972), the Supreme Court confirmed the right of a person in a nonmedical field to distribute contraceptives and contraceptive information to unmarried individuals despite a state law to the contrary. Justice William O. Douglas, in concurring with the decision, noted that handing out material was an extension of Baird's First Amendment right to lecture on the topic. In *Carey v. Population Services International*, 431 U.S. 678 (1977), the Court found state prohibitions on the advertisement or display of contraceptive information unconstitutional under the First Amendment. The state's argument that some persons who saw the advertisements might find them offensive was insufficient to override the First Amendment's protection of freedom of expression. And in *Bolger v. Youngs Drug Products Corp.*, 463 U.S. 60 (1983), the Court upheld the right of the drug products firm to send unsolicited mass mailings that included informational pamphlets dealing with contraceptives, venereal disease, and family planning. In the latter case, the Court specifically found sections of the Comstock Act to be violations of First Amendment rights.

75. See Raymond Moley, *The Hays Office* (New York: Bobbs-Merrill, 1945); Ben Yagoda, "Hollywood Cleans Up Its Act: The Curious Career of the Hays Office," *American Heritage* (Feb. 1980), 12–21; Robert Stanley, *The Celluloid Empire: A History of the American Movie Industry* (New York: Hastings House, 1978), 174–230; Richard S. Randall, *Censorship of the Movies: The Social and Political Control of a Mass Medium* (Madison: Univ. of Wisconsin Press, 1970); and Ruth A. Inglis, *Freedom of the Movies: A Report on Self-Regulation from the Commission on Freedom of the Press* (Chicago: Univ. of Chicago Press, 1947), 62–171.

76. Yagoda, 15.

77. Inglis, 83–84.

78. Ibid., 114–16.

79. See Christopher H. Sterling and John M. Kittross, *Stay Tuned: A Concise History of American Broadcasting* (Belmont, Calif.: Wadsworth, 1978); Sydney W. Head, *Broadcasting in America* (Boston: Houghton Mifflin, 1956); Lucas A. Powe, Jr., *American Broadcasting and the First Amendment* (Berkeley: Univ. of California Press, 1987); Philip T. Rosen, *The Modern Stentors: Radio Broadcasters and the Federal Government* (Westport, Conn.: Greenwood Press, 1980); Louise Margaret Benjamin, "Radio Regulation in the 1920s: Free Speech Issues in the Development of Radio and the Radio Act of 1927" (Ph.D. diss., University of Iowa, 1985); Catherine L. Covert, " 'Loss and Change': Radio and the Shock to Sensibility in American Life, 1919–1924" (Paper presented at the Qualitative Studies Division, Association for Education in Journalism Annual Convention, Athens, Ohio, July 1982); and Daniel J. Czitrom, *Media and the American Mind* (Chapel Hill: Univ. of North Carolina Press, 1982), 60–88.

80. 36 Stat. 629 (1910).

81. 37 Stat. 302 (1912).

82. See Daniel E. Garvey, "Secretary Hoover and the Quest for Broadcast Regulation," *Journalism History* 3 (1976):66–70, 85; Benjamin, "Radio Regulation in the 1920s," 180–233; Edward F. Sarno, Jr., "The National Radio Conferences," *Journal of Broadcasting* 13 (1969):189–202; and Louise M. Benjamin, "Herbert Hoover, Issues of Free Speech, and Radio Regulation in the 1920s," *Free Speech Yearbook 1987*, 28–39.

83. Hoover v. Intercity Radio Co., 286 F. 1003 (C.A.D.C. 1923).

84. Telegram to E. E. Plummer, managing editor of *Radio Digest*, 10 March 1924, quoted in Benjamin, "Herbert Hoover, Issues of Free Speech," 30.

85. Radio talk by Secretary of Commerce and Labor Herbert Hoover, 26 March 1924, quoted in ibid.

86. Louise M. Benjamin, "Campaign Policies, Broadcasters, and the Presidential Election of 1924" (Paper presented to the History Division, Association for Education in Journalism and Mass Communication Annual Convention, San Antonio, Texas, Aug. 1987).

87. Address by Secretary of Commerce and Labor Herbert Hoover, 12 Nov. 1925, quoted in Benjamin, "Radio Regulation in the 1920s," 426–27.

88. United States v. Zenith Radio Corporation, 12 F.2d 614 (N.D.Ill. 1926).

89. Department of Commerce and Labor Press Release on the Zenith Case, 20 April 1926, quoted in Marvin R. Bensman, "The Zenith-WJAZ Case and the Chaos of 1926–27," *Journal of Broadcasting* 14 (1970):430.

90. 44 Stat. 1162 (1927).

91. See Donald G. Godfrey, "Senator Dill and the 1927 Radio Act," *Journal of Broadcasting* 23 (1979):477–89.

92. See David H. Ostroff, "Equal Time: Origins of Section 18 of the Radio Act of 1927," *Journal of Broadcasting* 24 (1980):367–79.

93. 44 Stat. 1170.

94. Ibid., 1166. See Frederick W. Ford, "The Meaning of the 'Public Interest, Convenience or Necessity,'" *Journal of Broadcasting* 5 (1961):205–18.

95. See Robert W. McChesney, "Free Speech and Democracy: The Debate in the American Legal Community over the Meaning of Free Expression on Radio, 1926–1939" (Paper presented to the Special Research Session on the History of Freedom of Expression, Sponsored by the Law and History Divisions, Association for Education in Journalism and Mass Communication Annual Convention, San Antonio, Texas, Aug. 1987).

96. Federal Radio Commission, Third Annual Report, 32 (1929), quoted in Powe, 108.

97. McChesney, "Free Speech and Democracy," 8–10.

98. See Alfred McClung Lee, *The Daily Newspaper in America* (New York: Macmillan, 1947), *passim;* Frank Luther Mott, *American Journalism,* 3rd ed. (New York: Macmillan, 1962), 635–50, 712–18; Edwin Emery and Michael Emery, *The Press in America,* 5th ed. (Englewood Cliffs, N.J.: Prentice-Hall, 1984), 371–422; and Jean Folkerts and Dwight L. Teeter, Jr., *Voices of a Nation* (New York: Macmillan, 1989), 376–79.

99. Lee, 173.

100. Ibid., 749.

101. Silas Bent, *Ballyhoo* (New York: Boni and Liveright, 1927), 208.

102. Ibid., 260.

103. Emery and Emery, 399.

104. Lee, 215–16.

105. International News Service v. Associated Press, 248 U.S. 215 (1918). See also Lee, 553–56.

106. Walter Lippmann and Charles Merz, "A Test of the News," *New Republic,* 4 Aug. 1920, pp. 1–42.

107. Quoted in Simon M. Bessie, *Jazz Journalism: The Story of the Tabloid Newspaper Era* (New York: Dutton, 1938), 19.

108. Jim Bishop, "The War of the Tabloids," *Playboy,* Jan. 1968, p. 164.

109. Ibid., 255.

110. Upton Sinclair, *The Brass Check* (Pasadena, Calif.: Published by the author, 1920), 42, 201.

111. Walter Lippmann, *Liberty and the News* (New York: Harcourt, Brace and Howe, 1920), 47, 75–76.

112. See Harvey Saalberg, "The Canons of Journalism: A 50-Year Perspective," *Journalism Quarterly* 50 (1973):731–34.

113. *Problems of Journalism,* Proceedings of the First Annual Meeting of the American Society of Newspaper Editors (1923), 40.

114. Canons of Journalism, quoted in Alice Fox Pitts, *Read All About It! Fifty Years of the American Society of Newspaper Editors* (Easton, Pa.: American Society of Newspaper Editors, 1974), 361.

Chapter 5

1. See Donald J. Liso, *The President and Protest: Hoover, Conspiracy, and the Bonus Riot* (Columbia: Univ. of Missouri Press, 1974).

2. Ibid., 230.

3. Roger Daniels, *The Bonus March: An Episode of the Great Depression* (Westport, Conn.: Greenwood, 1971), 211–41.

4. See Alan Brinkley, *Voices of Protest: Huey Long, Father Coughlin, and the Great Depression* (New York: Alfred A. Knopf, 1982); David H. Bennett, *Demagogues in the Depression: American Radicals and the Union Party, 1932–1936* (New Brunswick, N.J.: Rutgers Univ. Press, 1969); and Geoffrey S. Smith, *To Save a Nation: American Countersubversives, the New Deal, and the Coming of World War II* (New York: Basic Books, 1973), 11–52.

5. See James P. Shenton, "The Coughlin Movement and the New Deal," *Political Science Quarterly* 73 (1958):352–73.

6. Many of the myths about the behavior of Jewish individuals were based on a forged document entitled the *Protocols of the Elders of Zion.* This book was written by members of the czar's secret police in the late nineteenth century in an attempt to blame

Jewish citizens of Russia for all of that nation's social problems. The *Protocols* claimed that the Jews formed an international conspiracy designed to topple as many gentile governments as possible. The *Protocols,* which had been proven to be forgeries, were circulated fairly widely in the United States in the 1920s, providing "evidence" for anti-Semites to use in their campaigns. See Robert Singerman, "The American Career of the *Protocols of the Elders of Zion,*" *American Jewish History* 71 (1981):48–78.

7. See Leo P. Ribuffo, *The Old Christian Right: The Protestant Far Right from the Great Depression to the Cold War* (Philadelphia: Temple Univ. Press, 1983), 25–177; Smith, 53–86; and John M. Werly, "The Millenarian Right: William Dudley Pelley and the Silver Legion of America," *South Atlantic Quarterly* 71 (1972):410–23.

8. Quoted in Ribuffo, *The Old Christian Right,* 64 (emphasis included).

9. See Morris Schonbach, *Native American Fascism During the 1930s and 1940s: A Study of Its Roots, Its Growth and Its Decline* (New York: Garland, 1985); Sander A. Diamond, *The Nazi Movement in the United States, 1924–1941* (Ithaca, N.Y.: Cornell Univ. Press, 1974); and Smith, 87–100.

10. Joint Resolution 363, quoted in Schonbach, 373.

11. Schonbach, 372.

12. See Walter Goodman, *The Committee: The Extraordinary Career of the House Committee on Un-American Activities* (New York: Farrar, Straus and Giroux, 1968), 2–23; and August Raymond Ogden, *The Dies Committee: A Study of the Special House Committee for the Investigation of Un-American Activities, 1938–1944* (Washington, D.C.: Catholic Univ. of America Press, 1945), 38–46.

13. 52 Stat. 631 (1938).

14. State Department statement, quoted in Schonbach, 397.

15. 53 Stat. 1148–49 (1939).

16. 54 Stat. 1201 (1940).

17. 54 Stat. 670–71 (1940).

18. Quoted in Ribuffo, 183.

19. Frank J. Donner, *The Age of Surveillance: The Aims and Methods of America's Political Intelligence System* (New York: Alfred A. Knopf, 1980), 53–78; Kenneth O'Reilly, "A New Deal for the FBI: The Roosevelt Administration, Crime Control, and National Security," *Journal of American History* 69 (1982):638–58; and Athan G. Theoharis, "The FBI's Stretching of Presidential Directives, 1936–1953," *Political Science Quarterly* 91 (1976–77):649–72.

20. See Harvey Klehr, *The Heyday of American Communism: The Depression Decade* (New York: Basic Books, 1984).

21. Ogden, 25–30.

22. House Special Committee on Communist Activities in the United States, *Investigation of Communist Propaganda,* 71st Cong., 3rd sess., 1931, Report 2290, pp. 96–97, quoted in ibid., 29.

23. Stromberg v. California, 283 U.S. 359, 369 (1931).

24. See Larry Ceplair and Steven Englund, *The Inquisition in Hollywood: Politics in the Film Community, 1930–1960* (Berkeley: Univ. of California Press, 1983; Anchor Press, 1983), 1–128.

25. Klehr, 366.

26. See Samuel Walker, *In Defense of American Liberties: A History of the ACLU* (New York: Oxford Univ. Press, 1990), 127–33. Ernst's conversion to the anti-Communist cause was complete. After his death, evidence emerged that he carried on a regular correspondence with J. Edgar Hoover, much of which related to ACLU attempts to defend Communists during the cold war. Due in part to Ernst's efforts, the organization

provided little assistance to party members at that time. See Harrison E. Salisbury, "The Strange Correspondence of Morris Ernst and John Edgar Hoover, 1939–1964," *The Nation,* 1 Dec. 1984, pp. 575–89.

27. Quoted in *The Trial of Elizabeth Gurley Flynn by the American Civil Liberties Union,* ed. Corliss Lamont (New York: Modern Reader Paperbacks, 1968), 22. Miss Flynn was reinstated posthumously in 1976 as the result of a campaign on her behalf by Corliss Lamont. Walker, 133.

28. Goodman, 24–88.

29. Earl Latham, *The Communist Controversy in Washington: From the New Deal to McCarthy* (Cambridge, Mass.: Harvard Univ. Press, 1966), 149–50.

30. See Irving Bernstein, *The Lean Years: A History of the American Worker, 1920– 1933* (Boston: Houghton Mifflin, 1960), 358–90.

31. 47 Stat. 70 (1932).

32. 48 Stat. 198–99 (1933).

33. See Irving Bernstein, *Turbulent Years: A History of the American Worker, 1933– 1941* (Boston: Houghton Mifflin, 1969), 16–91.

34. Schechter v. United States, 295 U.S. 495 (1935).

35. 49 Stat. 449–50 (1935).

36. See Jerold S. Auerbach, *Labor and Liberty: The La Follette Committee and the New Deal* (Indianapolis: Bobbs-Merrill, 1966).

37. Quoted in ibid., 63.

38. National Labor Relations Board v. Jones and Laughlin Steel Corporation, 301 U.S. 1 (1937).

39. Hague v. CIO, 307 U.S. 496, 515 (1939).

40. 310 U.S. 88, 102–3 (1940). The Court had departed from Chief Justice William Howard Taft's hatred of picketing in 1937 when it upheld the right of a state to pass legislation permitting picketing during a labor dispute. The justices did not base that decision on First Amendment grounds. See Senn v. Tile Layers Protective Union, 301 U.S. 468 (1937).

41. The Court later would use the notion that discussion of labor disputes must be allowed to invalidate the conviction of a CIO officer for speaking about unions without first obtaining a permit from state authorities. The Texas law was designed to license individuals who were organizing workers into a union; the speaker merely was visiting to stir the organizers on to greater success. See Thomas v. Collins, 323 U.S. 516 (1944).

42. See Milk Wagon Drivers Union v. Meadowmoor Dairies, 312 U.S. 287 (1941).

43. See Bakery & Pastery Drivers v. Wohl, 315 U.S. 769 (1942).

44. See Charles DeBenedetti, *The Peace Reform in American History* (Bloomington: Indiana Univ. Press, 1980), 108–37; and Charles Chatfield, *For Peace and Justice: Pacifism in America, 1914–1941* (Knoxville: Univ. of Tennessee Press, 1971).

45. United States v. Schwimmer, 279 U.S. 644, 654–55 (1929).

46. United States v. Macintosh, 283 U.S. 605 (1931).

47. Hamilton v. Regents of the University of California, 293 U.S. 245, 262–63 (1934).

48. Ludlow Referendum Amendment, quoted in Ernest C. Bolt, Jr., *Ballots Before Bullets: The War Referendum Approach to Peace in America, 1914–1941* (Charlottesville: Univ. of Virginia Press, 1977), 155.

49. See Eileen Eagan, *Class, Culture, and the Classroom: The Student Peace Movement of the 1930s* (Philadelphia: Temple Univ. Press, 1981).

50. Reprinted in ibid., 60–61.

51. See Robert J. Comerford, "The American Liberty League" (Ph.D. diss., St. John's University, 1967); and George Wolfskill, *The Revolt of the Conservatives: A History of the American Liberty League, 1934–1940* (Boston: Houghton Mifflin, 1962).

52. "Statement of Principles and Purposes," quoted in Comerford, 21.

53. Quoted in Wolfskill, 224.

54. See Stephen Ponder, "Federal News Management in the Progressive Era: Gifford Pinchot and the Conservation Crusade," *Journalism History* 13 (1986):42–48.

55. See James L. McCamy, *Government Publicity: Its Practice in Federal Administration* (Chicago: Univ. of Chicago Press, 1938); Richard W. Steele, *Propaganda in an Open Society: The Roosevelt Administration and the Media, 1933–1941* (Westport, Conn.: Greenwood Press, 1985); and Betty Houchin Winfield, "The New Deal Publicity Operation: Foundation for the Modern Presidency," *Journalism Quarterly* 61 (1984):40–48, 218.

56. See Edwin Emery, *History of the American Newspaper Publishers Association* (Minneapolis: Univ. of Minnesota Press, 1950; rpt., Westport, Conn.: Greenwood Press, 1970), 218–46.

57. Act of April 20, 1925, ch. 285, 1925 Minn. Laws 358, quoted in Paul L. Murphy, "*Near v. Minnesota* in the Context of Historical Developments," *Minnesota Law Review* 66 (1981):136.

58. See Murphy, "*Near v. Minnesota,*" 95–160; John E. Hartmann, "The Minnesota GAG LAW and the Fourteenth Amendment," *Minnesota History* 37 (1960):161–73; Reed L. Carpenter, "John L. Morrison and the Origins of the Minnesota Gag Law," *Journalism History* 9 (1982):16–17, 25–28; and Fred Friendly, *Minnesota Rag* (New York: Random House, 1981; Vintage Books, 1982).

59. Near v. Minnesota, 283 U.S. 697, 720 (1931).

60. Ibid. at 716.

61. The ANPA's effort to find First Amendment protection for advertising was particularly unsuccessful. In addition to Congress being unwilling to accept the idea, the Supreme Court specifically barred advertising from such protection in 1942. See Valentine v. Chrestensen, 316 U.S. 52 (1942). By 1975, however, the tide of opinion had turned on the Supreme Court, and justices were well on their way toward developing the commercial speech doctrine in which advertisements were brought under the protection of the First Amendment in a limited way. See Bigelow v. Virginia, 421 U.S. 809 (1975).

62. See Graham J. White, *FDR and the Press* (Chicago: Univ. of Chicago Press, 1979).

63. See Margaret A. Blanchard, "Freedom of the Press and the Newspaper Code: June 1933–February 1934," *Journalism Quarterly* 54 (1977):40–49.

64. Journalists had long considered themselves professionals even though their salaries did not reflect that standing. The average wage in 1929 was $30 a week, the amount paid to clerks. Since 1914, a reporter's pay had gone up 30 percent while the cost of living had increased 50 percent. Reporters still worked six-day weeks for ten to twelve hours a day for their wages; persons working in mechanical positions on newspapers had five-day, forty-hour weeks. For details of the unionization effort, see Daniel J. Leab, *A Union of Individuals, 1933–36* (New York: Columbia Univ. Press, 1970).

65. Draft Code of the American Newspaper Publishers Association, quoted in Blanchard, "Freedom of the Press and the Newspaper Code," 43.

66. Executive Order Approving Code of Fair Competition for the Daily Newspaper Publishing Business, quoted in ibid., 48.

67. George Seldes, *Freedom of the Press* (Indianapolis: Bobbs-Merrill, 1935), xv. See Margaret A. Blanchard, "Press Criticism and National Reform Movements: The Progressive Era and the New Deal," *Journalism History* 5 (1978):33–37, 54–55.

68. Harold L. Ickes, *America's House of Lords* (New York: Harcourt, Brace, 1939), viii, 162–63.

69. Morris L. Ernst, *The First Freedom* (New York: Macmillan, 1946), 249–60.

70. See J. Edward Gerald, *The Press and the Constitution, 1931–1947* (Minneapolis: Univ. of Minnesota Press, 1948; rpt., Gloucester, Mass.: Peter Smith, 1968), 72–99.

71. Associated Press v. National Labor Relations Board, 301 U.S. 103 (1937).

72. Ibid. at 132–33. See Timothy W. Gleason, "Legal Advocacy and the First Amendment: Elisha Hanson's Attempt to Create First Amendment Protection for the Business of the Press," *American Journalism* 3 (1986):195–205.

73. 52 Stat. 1060 (1938).

74. Oklahoma Press Publishing v. Walling, 327 U.S. 186, 192, 194 (1946).

75. See Margaret A. Blanchard, "The Associated Press Antitrust Suit: A Philosophical Clash over Ownership of First Amendment Rights," *Business History Review* 61 (1987):43–85, and William F. Swindler, "The AP Anti-Trust Case in Historical Perspective," *Journalism Quarterly* 23 (1946):40–57.

76. Associated Press v. United States, 326 U.S. 1, 7, 20 (1945).

77. Ibid. at 20.

78. Alexander Hamilton, James Madison, and John Jay, *The Federalist Papers,* 2d ed., ed. Roy P. Fairfield (Garden City, N.J.: Anchor Books, 1966), 263–64.

79. See Robert W. McChesney, "Free Speech and Democracy: The Debate in the American Legal Community over the Meaning of Free Expression on Radio, 1926–1939" (Paper presented to the Research Session on the History of Freedom of Expression, History and Law Divisions, Association for Education in Journalism and Mass Communication Annual Convention, San Antonio, Texas, Aug. 1987).

80. See Robert W. McChesney, "Crusade Against Mammon: Father Harney, WLWL and the Debate over Radio in the 1930s," *Journalism History* 14 (1987):118–30; Robert W. McChesney, "Constant Retreat: The American Civil Liberties Union and the Debate over the Meaning of Free Speech for Radio Broadcasting in the 1930s," *Free Speech Yearbook 1987,* 40–59; Robert W. McChesney, "Franklin Roosevelt, His Administration, and the Communications Act of 1934," *American Journalism* 5 (1988):204–29; Robert W. McChesney, "Enemies of the Status Quo: The National Committee on Education by Radio and the Debate over the Control and Structure of American Broadcasting in the Early 1930s" (Paper presented to the History Division, Association for Education in Journalism and Mass Communication Annual Convention, San Antonio, Texas, Aug. 1987); and McChesney, "Free Speech and Democracy."

81. 51 Stat. 1064 (1934).

82. *1934 NCER Proceedings,* quoted in McChesney, "Enemies of the Status Quo," 23.

83. Bethuel M. Webster, Jr., "Notes on the Policy of the Administration With Reference to the Control of Communications," *Air Law Review* 5 (1934):107–31, quoted in McChesney, "Free Speech and Democracy," 30.

84. Louis G. Caldwell, "Freedom of Speech and Radio Broadcasting," *Annals of the American Academy of Political and Social Science,* Jan. 1935, quoted in ibid., 36.

85. Minna F. Kassner and Lucien Zacharoff, *Radio Is Censored!* (New York: American Civil Liberties Union, 1936), quoted in ibid., 40.

86. Broadcast programming came under scrutiny again in the 1960s, as an activist FCC began decrying the lack of quality in television programming. FCC Chairman Newton Minow, in fact, talked of the "vast wasteland" when he spoke of broadcast offerings. In addition, in the 1970s, minority interests challenged license holders who were not adequately representing the needs of all the community. When the FCC began awarding licenses to these challengers in order to increase broadcasting diversity, its policy was attacked in court. In 1990, the Supreme Court, in a five-four vote, upheld the FCC's efforts to increase the presence of minority interests and views on the airwaves. See Metro Broadcasting v. Federal Communications Commission, 110 S.Ct. 2997 (1990).

87. Quoted in Joon-Mann Kang, "Franklin D. Roosevelt and James L. Fly: The Politics of Broadcast Regulation, 1941–1944," *Journal of American Culture* 10 (1987):23.

88. Franklin Roosevelt to James L. Fly, 3 Dec. 1940, quoted in Erik Barnouw, *The Golden Web* (New York: Oxford Univ. Press, 1968), 170.

89. Kang, 25–27.

90. Federal Communications Commission, *Report on Chain Broadcasting,* 92, quoted in Barnouw, 171.

91. National Broadcasting Co. v. United States, 319 U.S. 190, 226–27 (1943).

92. See Raymond Moley, *The Hays Office* (New York: Bobbs-Merrill, 1945); Robert Stanley, *The Celluloid Empire* (New York: Hastings House, 1978), 174–230; Ruth A. Inglis, *Freedom of the Movies: A Report on Self-Regulation from the Commission on Freedom of the Press* (Chicago: Univ. of Chicago Press, 1947), 97–125; Richard S. Randall, *Censorship of the Movies: The Social and Political Control of a Medium* (Madison: Univ. of Wisconsin Press, 1970); and Ben Yagoda, "Hollywood Cleans Up Its Act: The Curious Career of the Hays Office," *American Heritage* (Feb. 1980), 12–21. The popularized version of the twelve separate studies on the effects of movies sponsored by the Payne Fund is Henry James Forman, *Our Movie Made Children* (New York: Macmillan, 1933).

93. *New York Times,* 2 Oct. 1933, quoted in Richard Corliss, "The Legion of Decency," *Film Comment* 4 (1968):26.

94. Quoted in Yagoda, 19.

95. See Simon N. Whitney, "Antitrust Policies and the Motion Picture Industry," in *The American Movie Industry: The Business of Motion Pictures,* ed. Gorham Kindem (Carbondale: Southern Illinois Univ. Press, 1982), 161–204; and Zechariah Chafee, Jr., *Government and Mass Communications: A Report from the Commission on Freedom of the Press* (Chicago: Univ. of Chicago Press, 1947; rpt., Hamden, Conn.: Archon Books, 1965), 537–677.

96. See United States v. First National Pictures, Inc., 282 U.S. 4 (1930); Paramount Famous Lasky Corp. v. United States, 282 U.S. 30 (1930); Interstate Circuit, Inc. v. United States, 306 U.S. 208 (1939); and United States v. Crescent Amusement Co., 323 U.S. 173 (1944).

97. United States v. Paramount Pictures, 334 U.S. 131 (1948).

98. Mutual Film Corp. v. Industrial Commission of Ohio, 236 U.S. 230 (1915).

99. 334 U.S. at 166.

100. Gitlow v. New York, 268 U.S. 652 (1925).

101. Stromberg v. California, 283 U.S. 359 (1931).

102. Near v. Minnesota, 282 U.S. 697 (1931).

103. De Jonge v. Oregon, 299 U.S. 353 (1937).

104. See William E. Leuchtenburg, *Franklin Roosevelt and the New Deal* (New York: Harper Torchbooks, 1963), 231–38.

105. Palko v. Connecticut, 302 U.S. 319, 325–27 (1937).

106. See Henry J. Abraham, *Freedom and the Court: Civil Rights and Liberties in the United States,* 4th ed. (New York: Oxford Univ. Press, 1982), 8–27.

107. United States v. Carolene Products Co., 304 U.S. 144, 152 (1938).

Chapter 6

1. Justus D. Doenecke, "Non-interventionism of the Left: The Keep America Out of War Congress, 1938–41," *Journal of Contemporary History* 12 (1977):221–36.

2. Wayne S. Cole, *America First: The Battle Against Intervention, 1940–1941* (Madison: Univ. of Wisconsin Press, 1953).

3. R. Douglas Stuart, Jr., to W. S. Hart, 13 March 1941, quoted in ibid., 113.

4. Philip La Follette, "With Malice Toward None," radio address, 12 Feb. 1941, quoted in ibid., 113–14 (emphasis included).

5. See Richard W. Steele, "Franklin D. Roosevelt and His Foreign Policy Critics," *Political Science Quarterly* 94 (1979):15–32.

6. Annual message to Congress, 6 Jan. 1941, in *The Public Papers and Addresses of Franklin D. Roosevelt*, comp. Samuel I. Rosenman (New York: Macmillan, 1941), 9:670.

7. Athan Theoharis, "The FBI and the American Legion Contact Program," *Political Science Quarterly* 100 (1985):273–78.

8. Francis Biddle, "The Power of Democracy: It Can Meet All Conditions," *Vital Speeches,* 15 Oct. 1941, p. 9, quoted in Patrick S. Washburn, *A Question of Sedition: The Federal Government's Investigation of the Black Press during World War II* (New York: Oxford Univ. Press, 1986), 51.

9. Cabell Phillips, "No Witch Hunts," *New York Times Magazine,* 21 Sept. 1941, p. 8, quoted in ibid., 51.

10. Francis Biddle, *In Brief Authority* (Garden City, N.Y.: Doubleday, 1962), 211.

11. Ibid., 235, 238.

12. Quoted in Mark Lincoln Chadwin, *The Hawks of World War II* (Chapel Hill: Univ. of North Carolina Press, 1968), 150–51.

13. See Jacobus tenBroek, Edward N. Barnhart, and Floyd W. Matson, *Prejudice, War and the Constitution* (Berkeley: Univ. of California Press, 1954).

14. Germany and Italy declared war on the United States a few days later.

15. See Lawrence S. Wittner, *Rebels Against War: The American Peace Movement, 1941–1960* (New York: Columbia Univ. Press, 1969), 34–124; Stephen M. Kohn, *Jailed for Peace: The History of the American Draft Law Violators, 1658–1985* (Westport, Conn.: Greenwood Press, 1986), 45–62; Charles DeBenedetti, *The Peace Reform in American History* (Bloomington: Indiana Univ. Press, 1980), 138–64; and Glen Zeitzer, "The American Peace Movement During the Second World War" (Ph.D. diss., Bryn Mawr College, 1978).

16. "Our Way in the Midst of War," Fellowship of Reconciliation Executive Board Statement, 9 Dec. 1941, quoted in Glen Zeitzer, "The Fellowship of Reconciliation on the Eve of the Second World War: A Peace Organization Prepares," *Peace & Change* 3 (1975):50.

17. 54 Stat. 889 (1940).

18. American Civil Liberties Union, *Conscience and the War: A Report on the Treatment of Conscientious Objectors in World War II* (New York: American Civil Liberties Union, 1943), 25, quoted in Wittner, 74.

19. Hoover memorandum, 8 June 1942, quoted in Richard W. Steele, "American Popular Opinion and War Against Germany: The Issue of Negotiated Peace, 1942," *Journal of American History* 65 (1978):715.

20. See David R. Manwaring, *Render Unto Caesar: The Flag Salute Controversy* (Chicago: Univ. of Chicago Press, 1962); and Irving J. Dilliard, "The Flag Salute Cases," in *Quarrels That Have Shaped the Constitution,* ed. John A. Garraty (New York: Harper & Row, 1962; Harper Torchbooks, 1975), 222–42.

21. See William Shepard McAninch, "A Catalyst for the Evolution of Constitutional Law: Jehovah's Witnesses in the Supreme Court," *Cincinnati Law Review* 55 (1987):997–1077; Richard C. C. Kim, "The Constitutional Legacy of the Jehovah's Witnesses," *Southwestern Social Science Quarterly* 45 (1964):125–34; and John E. Mulder and Marvin Comisky, "Jehovah's Witnesses Mold Constitutional Law," *Bill of Rights Review* 2 (1942):262–68.

22. Lovell v. City of Griffin, 303 U.S. 444, 448, 451 (1938).

23. Schneider v. State, 308 U.S. 147, 164 (1939).

24. Cantwell v. Connecticut, 310 U.S. 296, 310 (1940).

25. Minersville School District v. Gobitis, 310 U.S. 586, 595–96 (1940).

26. Ibid. at 601, 604.

27. Cox v. New Hampshire, 312 U.S. 569, 574 (1941).

28. Chaplinsky v. New Hampshire, 315 U.S. 568, 569 (1942).

29. Ibid. at 571–72.

30. Jones v. Opelika, 316 U.S. 584, 608, 610 (1942).

31. Ibid. at 623–24.

32. See American Civil Liberties Union, *The Persecution of the Jehovah's Witnesses* (New York: American Civil Liberties Union, 1941).

33. Jamison v. Texas, 318 U.S. 413, 415–16 (1943).

34. Largent v. Texas, 318 U.S. 418, 422 (1943).

35. Jones v. Opelika, 319 U.S. 103 (1943).

36. Murdock v. Pennsylvania, 319 U.S. 105, 111 (1943).

37. Ibid. at 115–16.

38. Martin v. Struthers, 319 U.S. 141, 156 (1943).

39. Douglas v. Jeannette, 319 U.S. 157, 166, 168–69 (1949).

40. Ibid. at 178–81.

41. The Court overturned the conviction of a Witness adult caught in another flag-salute case on the same day. See Taylor v. Mississippi, 319 U.S. 583 (1943).

42. West Virginia State Board of Education v. Barnette, 319 U.S. 624, 632 (1943).

43. Ibid. at 641–42.

44. See Lee Finkle, "The Conservative Aims of Militant Rhetoric: Black Protest during World War II," *Journal of American History* 60 (1973):692–713; Washburn, *A Question of Sedition;* Patrick S. Washburn, "The Pittsburgh *Courier's* Double V Campaign in 1942," *American Journalism* 3 (1986):73–86; and Patrick S. Washburn, "J. Edgar Hoover and the Black Press in World War II," *Journalism History* 13 (1986):26–33.

45. Washburn, "J. Edgar Hoover and the Black Press," 28–29.

46. *Amsterdam Star-News,* 20 Feb. 1943, quoted in ibid., 30.

47. 40 Stat. 217 (1917).

48. 54 Stat. 670 (1940).

49. United States v. Pelley, 132 F.2d 170, 174–75 (7th Cir. 1942).

50. Ibid. at 176–77.

51. Dunne v. United States, 138 F.2d 137, 142, 145 (8th Cir. 1943). See Thomas L. Pahl, "G-String Conspiracy, Political Reprisal or Armed Revolt?" The Minneapolis Trotskyite Trial," *Labor History* 8 (1967):30–51.

52. Dunne v. United States, 320 U.S. 790 (1943).

53. See Leo P. Ribuffo, "*United States v. McWilliams:* The Roosevelt Administration and the Far Right," *American Political Trials,* ed. Michal R. Belknap (Westport, Conn.: Greenwood Press, 1981), 201–32; Patrick S. Washburn, "FDR Versus His Own Attorney General: The Struggle over Sedition, 1941–42," *Journalism Quarterly* 62 (1985):717–24; and Leo P. Ribuffo, *The Old Christian Right: The Protestant Far Right from the Great Depression to the Cold War* (Philadelphia: Temple Univ. Press, 1983), 178–224.

54. Biddle, 236–38.

55. Maximilian St.-George and Lawrence Dennis, *A Trial on Trial: The Great Sedition Trial of 1944* (New York: National Civil Rights Committee, 1944), 119.

56. Hartzel v. United States, 322 U.S. 680, 689 (1944).

57. Ibid. at 683.

58. Keegan v. United States, 325 U.S. 478 (1945).

59. Viereck v. United States, 318 U.S. 236 (1943).

60. Baumgartner v. United States, 322 U.S. 665 (1945).

61. Ibid. at 673–74.

62. Knauer v. United States, 328 U.S. 654, 658 (1946).

63. *Constitution,* art. III, sec. 3.

64. Gillars v. United States, 182 F.2d 962, 968 (D.C. Cir. 1950).

65. Ibid. at 971.

66. D'Aquino v. United States, 192 F.2d 338, 352 (9th Cir. 1951). See Stanley I. Kutler, *The American Inquisition: Justice and Injustice in the Cold War* (New York: Hill and Wang, 1982), 3–32.

67. Ezra Pound broadcast, 26 May 1942, quoted in Charles Norman, *The Case of Ezra Pound* (New York: Funk and Wagnalls, 1968), 51.

68. Quoted in ibid., 64.

69. See Kutler, 59–88.

70. Post Office Department press release, 8 June 1942, quoted in Washburn, *A Question of Sedition,* 121.

71. See Arthur F. McClure, *The Truman Administration and the Problems of Postwar Labor, 1945–1948* (Rutherford, N.J.: Farleigh Dickinson Univ. Press, 1969), 23–34; and Sanford Cohen, *Labor in the United States,* 2d ed. (Columbus, Ohio: Charles E. Merrill, 1966), 115–44.

72. 57 Stat. 163 (1943).

73. Thornhill v. Alabama, 310 U.S. 88 (1940).

74. Milk Wagon Drivers Union of Chicago, Local 753 v. Meadowmoor Dairies, 312 U.S. 287, 293 (1941).

75. See Carpenters & Joiners Union of America, Local No. 213 v. Ritter's Cafe, 315 U.S. 722 (1942); and Bakery & Pastry Drivers and Helpers Local 802 v. Wohl, 315 U.S. 769 (1942).

76. See Hosoon Chang, "Labor Picketing and the First Amendment: Union Members' Right to Picket, Public Opinion and the U.S. Supreme Court" (Master's thesis, Univ. of North Carolina at Chapel Hill, 1990).

77. See Maurice Isserman, *Which Side Were You On? The American Communist Party During the Second World War* (Middletown, Conn.: Wesleyan Univ. Press, 1982).

78. Quoted in ibid., 131.

79. Schneiderman v. United States, 320 U.S. 118, 119 (1943).

80. Ibid. at 136, 139.

81. Ibid. at 172.

82. See Kutler, 118–51.

83. Bridges v. Wixon, 326 U.S. 135, 145 (1945).

84. Ibid. at 157, 166.

85. See Richard W. Steele, "Preparing the Public for War: Efforts to Establish a National Propaganda Agency, 1940–41," *American Historical Review* 75 (1970):1640–53; and Robert L. Bishop and LaMar S. Mackay, "Mysterious Silence, Lyrical Scream: Government Information in World War II," *Journalism Monographs,* No. 19, May 1971.

86. Quoted in Theodore F. Koop, *Weapon of Silence* (Chicago: Univ. of Chicago Press, 1946), 20.

87. Quoted in ibid., 163.

88. George Creel, the World War I censor, doubted the efficacy of such a program and argued against its implementation in any future war. See George Creel, "The Plight of the Last Censor," *Collier's,* 24 May 1941, p. 13, 34–36.

89. Quoted in Koop, 168.

90. Quoted in ibid.

91. See Jim A. Richstad, "The Press Under Martial Law: The Hawaiian Experience," *Journalism Monographs* No. 17 (Nov. 1970).

92. Phillip Knightley, *The First Casualty* (New York: Harcourt Brace Jovanovich, 1975; Harvest Books, 1976), 269–302. After the war, everyone found out that 5 battleships had been sunk and 3 were damaged in the attack, that 3 cruisers and 3 destroyers had been hit badly, that 200 airplanes had been destroyed, and that 2,344 men had been killed.

93. Elmer Davis, "Report to the President," ed. Ronald T. Farrar, *Journalism Monographs* No. 7 (Aug. 1968), 15–16.

94. Quoted in Richard W. Steele, "News of the 'Good War': World War II News Management," *Journalism Quarterly* 62 (1985):710.

95. Davis, 16.

96. Koop, 191–204.

97. Biddle, 325–43.

98. Davis, 18–19.

99. See Dina Goren, "Communication Intelligence and the Freedom of the Press: The *Chicago Tribune*'s Battle of Midway Dispatch and the Breaking of the Japanese Naval Code," *Journal of Contemporary History* 16 (1981):663–90; Larry J. Frank, "The United States Navy v. the *Chicago Tribune*," *Historian* 42 (1980):284–303; and Jim Martin, "Did the *Tribune* Spill the (Navy) Beans?" (Paper presented at the Annual Meeting of the American Journalism Historians Association, Atlanta, Ga., Oct. 1989).

100. *Chicago Tribune,* 7 June 1942, quoted in Frank, 284.

101. *Chicago Tribune,* 9 Aug. 1942, quoted in Goren, 684.

102. See Knightley, 269–333.

103. Reuters, 25 April 1944, quoted in ibid., 315.

104. Drew Middleton to Phillip Knightley, 1 Nov. 1972, quoted in ibid., 315–16.

105. See Patrick S. Washburn, "The Office of Censorship's Attempt to Control Press Coverage of the Atomic Bomb during World War II," *Journalism Monographs,* No. 120, April 1990; Koop, 272–84; and Christine Michele Kridler, "Silence at Ground Zero: Secrecy and the Atomic Bomb and the Postwar Effects of Censorship, 1939–1955" (Honors essay, School of Journalism, University of North Carolina at Chapel Hill, 1989), 15–32.

106. Koop, 274–75.

107. Ibid., 176–88.

108. Ibid., 43.

109. See Clayton R. Koppes and Gregory D. Black, *Hollywood Goes to War: How Politics, Profits, and Propaganda Shaped World War II Movies* (New York: Free Press, 1987).

110. "Government Information Manual for the Motion Picture Industry," quoted in ibid., 66.

111. Davis, 40.

112. See Allan M. Winkler, *The Politics of Propaganda: The Office of War Information, 1942–1945* (New Haven, Conn.: Yale Univ. Press, 1978).

113. Quoted in Sydney Weinberg, "What to Tell America: The Writers' Quarrel in the Office of War Information," *Journal of American History* 55 (1968):87.

114. Davis, 51.

115. See Margaret A. Blanchard, *Exporting the First Amendment: The Press-Government Crusade of 1945–1952* (New York: Longman, 1986).

Chapter 7

1. See Walter Goodman, *The Committee: The Extraordinary Career of the House Committee on Un-American Activities* (New York: Farrar, Straus and Giroux, 1968), 118–66.

2. United States v. Lovett, 328 U.S. 303 (1945).

3. See Earl Latham, *The Communist Controversy in Washington: From the New Deal to McCarthy* (Cambridge, Mass.: Harvard Univ. Press, 1966), 203–16; and John S. Service, *The Amerasia Papers: Some Problems in the History of US-China Relations*, China Research Monographs, No. 7 (Berkeley: Univ. of California Center for Chinese Studies, 1971).

4. *Almanac of American History*, ed. Arthur M. Schlesinger, Jr. (New York: Bison Books, 1983), 514.

5. Executive Order 9806, Establishing the President's Temporary Commission on Employee Loyalty, 25 Nov. 1946, 11 *Fed. Reg.* 13863. See Eleanor Bontecou, *The Federal Loyalty-Security Program* (Ithaca, N.Y.: Cornell Univ. Press, 1953), 1–34, and Alan D. Harper, *The Politics of Loyalty: The White House and the Communist Issue, 1946–1952* (Westport, Conn.: Greenwood Press, 1969), 20–59.

6. Quoted in Harper, 35.

7. Executive Order 9835, Prescribing Procedures for the Administration of an Employees Loyalty Program in the Executive Branch of the Government, 21 March 1947, 12 *Fed. Reg.* 1935, 1938.

8. Bontecou, 157–204.

9. Ibid., 357.

10. See Alexis de Tocqueville, *Democracy in America* (New York: Schocken, 1961), 1:216–26, 2:138–44; and Arthur M. Schlesinger, "Biography of a Nation of Joiners," *American Historical Review* 50 (1944):1–25.

11. Statement of the Loyalty Review Board, 17 Dec. 1947, quoted in Bontecou, 206.

12. Bontecou, 145.

13. Quoted in Alan Barth, *The Loyalty of Free Men* (New York: Viking, 1951), 36.

14. See Larry Ceplair and Steven Englund, *The Inquisition in Hollywood: Politics and the Film Community, 1930–1960* (Berkeley: Univ. of California Press, 1983).

15. Waldorf Statement, 3 Dec. 1947, quoted in ibid., 455.

16. Ibid.

17. Quoted in ibid., 331n.

18. Lawson v. United States, 175 F.2d 49, 53 (D.C. Cir. 1949).

19. The argument that the First Amendment should protect political beliefs and associations was presented to an appeals court in 1948, but the judges ruled that legislative committees could indeed inquire into such matters without offending the Bill of Rights. See Barsky v. United States, 167 F.2d 241 (D.C. Cir. 1948). When the Supreme Court refused to review the ruling, many observers assumed that the justices agreed that the First Amendment would not protect witnesses from legislative interrogation. The Court began to cast doubts on that interpretation in 1953, and by 1957, it had indicated that congressional investigations could indeed affect protected rights. Congress may investigate only those subjects about which it may make laws, and the First Amendment forbids legislative interference with expressive rights. See United States v. Rumely, 345 U.S. 41 (1953), and Watkins v. United States, 354 U.S. 178 (1957). See also Thomas I. Emerson, *The System of Freedom of Expression* (New York: Random House, 1970; Vintage, 1971), 247–81.

20. House Special Committee on Un-American Activities, *Investigation of Un-American Activities and Propaganda*, Report No. 2, 76th Cong., 1st sess., *Congressional Record* (1939), 13, quoted in Barth, 55.

21. House Special Committee on Un-American Activities, *Investigation of Un-American Propaganda Activities in the United States,* Report No. 1476, 76th Cong., 3rd sess. (1940), 24, quoted in ibid.

22. See James Caldwell Foster, *The Union Politic: The CIO Political Action Committee* (Columbia: Univ. of Missouri Press, 1975), 3–48.

23. See Arthur F. McClure, *The Truman Administration and the Problems of Postwar Labor, 1945–1948* (Rutherford, N.J.: Fairleigh Dickinson Univ. Press, 1969), 45–66; and R. Alton Lee, *Truman and Taft-Hartley: A Question of Mandate* (Lexington: Univ. of Kentucky Press, 1966), 1–21.

24. See Harvey A. Levenstein, *Communism, Anticommunism, and the CIO* (Westport, Conn.: Greenwood Press, 1981).

25. 61 Stat. 136 (1947).

26. This belief grew out of a 1941 Supreme Court case in which the speech activities of an employer, viewed in the context of that employer's total behavior, were deemed to be coercive against employees trying to set up an independent union. "The employer," said the Court, "is as free now as ever to take any side it may choose on this controversial issue." But, the justices added, "if the total activities of an employer restrain or coerce his employees in their free choice, then those employees are entitled to the protection of the [National Labor Relations] Act. And in determining whether a course of conduct amounts to restraint or coercion, pressure exerted vocally by the employer may no more be disregarded than pressure exerted in other ways." National Labor Relations Board v. Virginia Electric Power, 314 U.S. 469, 477 (1941). To counter this decision, employers won section 8(c) of the Taft-Hartley Act, which said, "the expressing of any views, argument, or opinion, or the dissemination thereof, whether in written, printed, graphic, or visual form, shall not constitute or be evidence of an unfair labor practice under any of the provisions of this Act, if such expression contains no threat of reprisal or force or promise of benefit." 61 Stat. 142 (1947). See Harry A. Millis and Emily Clark Brown, *From the Wagner Act to Taft-Hartley: A Study of National Labor Policy and Labor Relations* (Chicago: Univ. of Chicago Press, 1950), 95–128, and Walter L. Daykin, Anthony V. Sinicropi, and Michael W. Whitehill, "Free Speech Rights Under the Labor Management Relations Act," *Center for Labor and Management Monographs Series,* No. 7 (Iowa City: Univ. of Iowa Press, 1967).

27. Although this provision has been litigated, the Supreme Court has not reached the question of whether it infringed on the unions' constitutionally protected freedom of expression on electoral issues. In 1948, the Court decided that a union's use of its newspaper to endorse candidates did not violate the statute. See United States v. Congress of Industrial Organizations, 335 U.S. 106 (1948). In 1957, the Court decided to allow a case to go forth against a union for sponsoring a commercial television broadcast designed to win votes for certain congressional candidates. See United States v. United Auto Workers, 352 U.S. 567 (1957). In both cases, minority justices sought to reach the constitutional issue in the belief that restrictions on the expenditure of money to endorse candidates violated the First Amendment and went to the heart of the right of American citizens to participate in political speech.

28. 73 Stat. 522, 536–37 (1959).

29. See Mary Sperling McAuliffe, *Crisis on the Left: Cold War Politics and American Liberals, 1947–1954* (Amherst: Univ. of Massachusetts Press, 1976); and Steven M. Gillon, *Politics and Vision: The ADA and American Liberalism, 1947–1985* (New York: Oxford Univ. Press, 1987).

30. See Peter L. Steinberg, *The Great "Red Menace": United States Prosecution of American Communists, 1947–1952* (Westport, Conn.: Greenwood Press, 1984), 59–85.

See also Maurice Isserman, *If I Had a Hammer . . . : The Death of the Old Left and the Birth of the New Left* (New York: Basic Books, 1987), 1–34.

31. See Michal R. Belknap, *Cold War Political Justice: The Smith Act, the Communist Party, and American Civil Liberties* (Westport, Conn.: Greenwood Press, 1977), and Don R. Pember, "The Smith Act as a Restraint on the Press," *Journalism Monographs,* No. 10, May 1969.

32. See Norman D. Markowitz, *The Rise and Fall of the People's Century: Henry A. Wallace and American Liberalism, 1941–1948* (New York: Free Press, 1973).

33. Ibid., 271.

34. *Wheeling Intelligencer,* 10 Feb. 1950, quoted in Robert Griffith, *The Politics of Fear: Joseph R. McCarthy and the Senate,* 2d ed. (Amherst: Univ. of Massachusetts Press, 1987), 49.

35. Thomas C. Reeves, *The Life and Times of Joe McCarthy* (New York: Stein and Day, 1982), 224.

36. Griffith, 50–51.

37. Edwin R. Bayley, *Joe McCarthy and the Press* (Madison: Univ. of Wisconsin Press, 1981), 77. See also Daniel W. Pfaff, "The St. Louis Post-Dispatch Debate over Communism, 1940–1945," *Mass Comm Review* 16 (1989):52–62, and Dozier C. Cade, "Witch-Hunting, 1952: The Role of the Press," *Journalism Quarterly* 29 (1952):396–407.

38. Senate Committee on Foreign Relations, *State Department Employee Loyalty Investigation, Report,* 81st Cong., 2d sess., 1950, p. 167.

39. *Congressional Record,* 81st Cong., 2d sess., 1 June 1950, 7894.

40. Ibid.

41. The signers were Smith, Charles W. Tobey of New Hampshire, George D. Aiken of Vermont, Wayne L. Morse of Oregon, Irving M. Ives of New York, Edward J. Thye of Minnesota, and Robert C. Hendrickson of New Jersey.

42. See Ronald J. Caridi, *The Korean War and American Politics: The Republican Party as a Case Study* (Philadelphia: Univ. of Pennsylvania Press, 1968).

43. 64 Stat. 987 (1950).

44. See William R. Tanner, "The Passage of the Internal Security Act of 1950" (Ph.D. diss., University of Kansas, 1971).

45. 64 Stat. 987, 989.

46. Ibid., 989–90.

47. Ibid., 996.

48. Ibid., 1021.

49. See McAuliffe, 75–88. The Emergency Detention Act was in effect through 1971. See Richard Longaker, "Emergency Detention: The Generation Gap, 1950–1971," *Western Political Quarterly* 27 (1974):395–408.

50. Harry S. Truman, "Veto of the Internal Security Bill," 22 Sept. 1950, *Public Papers of the Presidents of the United States: Harry Truman, 1950* (Washington, D.C.: Government Printing Office, 1965), 645, 646–47, 649–50.

51. Ibid., 650.

52. Gitlow v. New York, 268 U.S. 652 (1925), and Whitney v. California, 274 U.S. 357 (1927).

53. Stromberg v. California, 283 U.S. 359 (1931); DeJonge v. Oregon, 299 U.S. 353 (1937); Herndon v. Lowry, 301 U.S. 242 (1937); and Schneiderman v. United States, 320 U.S. 118 (1943).

54. 339 U.S. 382, 393 (1950).

55. Ibid. at 394, 399.

56. Dennis v. United States, 341 U.S. 494, 509 (1951).

57. Ibid. at 579, 581.

58. Ibid. at 582–83, 588, 591 (emphasis included).

59. See John E. Mueller, *War, Presidents and Public Opinion* (New York: John Wiley & Sons, 1973); Hugh Garland Wood, "American Reaction to Limited War in Asia: Korea and Vietnam, 1950–1968" (Ph.D. diss., University of Colorado, 1974); and Philip D. Caine, "The United States in Korea and Vietnam: A Study in Public Opinion," *Air University Review* 20 (1968):44–55. See also Matthew E. Mantell, "Opposition to the Korean War: A Study in American Dissent" (Ph.D. diss., New York University, 1973); and Zelle Andrews Larson, "An Unbroken Witness: Conscientious Objection to War, 1948–1953" (Ph.D. diss., University of Hawaii, 1975).

60. Organization flier, quoted in Mantell, 168.

61. See Phillip Knightley, *The First Casualty* (New York: Harcourt Brace Jovanovich, 1975; Harvest Books, 1976), 336–56; and Thomas J. Cleary, Jr., "Aid and Comfort to the Enemy," *Military Review* 48 (1965):51–55.

62. Marguerite Higgins, *The Report of a Woman Combat Correspondent* (New York: Doubleday, 1951), 96–97, quoted in Knightley, 337.

63. See Ellen W. Schrecker, *No Ivory Tower: McCarthyism and the Universities* (New York: Oxford Univ. Press, 1986); and Lionel S. Lewis, *Cold War on Campus: A Study of the Politics of Organizational Control* (New Brunswick, N.J.: Transaction Books, 1988).

64. House Committee on the Judiciary, Subcommittee on Internal Security, *Subversive Influence in the Educational Process,* 83rd Cong., 1st sess., 1953, pp. 28–29, quoted in Lewis, 13–14.

65. Adler v. Board of Education of the City of New York, 342 U.S. 485, 493 (1952).

66. Ibid. at 508–10.

67. Sweezy v. New Hampshire, 354 U.S. 234, 250 (1957).

68. John Cogley, *Report on Blacklisting: Movies* (New York: Fund for the Republic, 1956; rpt., New York: Arno Press, 1972), 92–117; and Ceplair and Englund, 361–97.

69. See John Cogley, *Report on Blacklisting: Radio-Television* (New York: Fund for the Republic, 1956; rpt., New York: Arno Press, 1971); and Merle Miller, *The Judges and the Judged* (Garden City, N.Y.: Doubleday, 1952; rpt., New York: Arno Press, 1971). See also David Caute, *The Great Fear: The Anti-Communist Purge Under Truman and Eisenhower* (New York: Simon and Schuster, 1978; Touchstone, 1979), 521–38, and Pama A. Mitchell, "The Response of the Broadcasting and Advertising Trade Press to Television Blacklisting Practices, 1950–1956," *Mass Comm Review* 16 (1989):63–69.

70. Jean Muir, who played the mother on "The Aldrich Family," a television program sponsored by General Foods, was the first person fired for her political activities after the publication of *Red Channels.* Muir came to the attention of *Red Channels* publishers when a left-wing newspaper in New York City carried a publicity release announcing her role in the television show. *Red Channels* listed Muir as belonging to nine suspect organizations. She denied any connections with four of the groups and said that her relationship with the other five was innocent. She had resigned from one group when she discovered it was a Communist front, and she had sent a letter of congratulations to the Moscow Art Theatre on its fiftieth anniversary in honor of the Stanislavsky method of acting. She was a member of the Southern Conference for Human Welfare, a civil rights group whose members included Eleanor Roosevelt. *Red Channels* offered no independent proof of her disloyalty, yet her mere listing was sufficient to cost her her job. Miller, 35–46.

71. Most individuals seeking rehabilitation went through one of the clearance procedures. Few tried taking the list-making agencies to court in order to clear their names. One who did so was John Henry Faulk, who sued the operators of Aware, Inc., for libel for having included his name in one of their news bulletins. Faulk was unemployed for

more than six years as a result of the listing. A jury brought in a verdict of $3.5 million for Faulk against Aware, Inc., and its owners. Although the sum was reduced substantially, Faulk had won perhaps the only legal victory against cold war blacklisters. See Louis Nizer, *The Jury Returns* (New York: Doubleday, 1966), 237–467.

72. See Bayley, 143–45.

73. "Wechsler Implores ASNE to Speak Out Eloquently," *Editor & Publisher,* 9 May 1953, p. 7.

74. "ASNE Report," *Editor & Publisher,* 15 Aug. 1953, p. 34.

75. Ralph H. Johnson and Michael Altman, "Communists in the Press: A Senate Witch-Hunt of the 1950s Revisited," *Journalism Quarterly* 55 (1978):488.

76. "N.Y. Times, News Explain Firing of Barnet, Gordon," *Editor & Publisher,* 23 July 1955, p. 7.

77. *New York Post,* quoted in James Aronson, *The Press and the Cold War* (Boston: Beacon Press, 1973), 147.

78. *New York Herald-Tribune,* 10 Jan. 1956, quoted in ibid., 148.

79. *Wall Street Journal,* 9 Jan. 1956, quoted in ibid., 149–50.

80. Russell v. United States, 369 U.S. 749, 776–77 (1962).

81. Quoted in Griffith, 270.

82. Quoted in ibid., 274.

83. Quoted in Fred Friendly, *Due to Circumstances Beyond Our Control . . .* (New York: Vintage, 1968), 41.

84. 68 Stat. 775 (1954).

85. McAuliffe, 130–45.

86. 66 Stat. 163 (1952).

87. Warren's career as a liberal interpreter of law may well have been limited to the Supreme Court. As a California politician, his earlier experiences, including those with communism, often were quite different. See Edward R. Long, "Earl Warren and the Politics of Anti-Communism," *Pacific Historical Review* 51 (1982):51–70.

88. Joint Anti-Fascist Refugee Committee v. McGrath, 341 U.S. 123, 139 (1951).

89. Communist Party v. Subversive Activities Control Board, 351 U.S. 115 (1956).

90. Communist Party v. Subversive Activities Control Board, 267 U.S. 1 (1961).

91. Ibid. at 147–48.

92. Albertson v. Subversive Activities Control Board, 382 U.S. 70 (1965).

93. United States v. Robel, 389 U.S. 258, 264–66 (1967).

94. See Stanley I. Kutler, *The American Inquisition: Justice and Injustice in the Cold War* (New York: Hill and Wang, 1982), 89–117; and Alan Rogers, "Passports and Politics: The Courts and the Cold War," *The Historian* 47 (1985):497–511.

95. Kent v. Dulles, 357 U.S. 116 (1958).

96. Aptheker v. Secretary of State, 378 U.S. 500, 520 (1964).

97. Kleindienst v. Mandel, 408 U.S. 753, 768 (1972).

98. Ibid. at 772, 780.

99. Yates v. United States, 354 U.S. 298 (1957).

100. Service v. Dulles, 354 U.S. 363 (1957).

101. Watkins v. United States, 354 U.S. 178, 200 (1957).

102. Sweezy v. New Hampshire, 354 U.S. 234 (1957).

103. See Walter F. Murphy, *Congress and the Court: A Case Study in the American Political Process* (Chicago: Univ. of Chicago Press, 1962).

104. Scales v. United States, 367 U.S. 203 (1961).

105. Communist Party of Indiana v. Whitcomb, 414 U.S. 441 (1974).

106. Belknap, 185–210. See also Steinberg, 261–87.

107. Caute, 111–38.

108. Lerner v. Casey, 357 U.S. 468 (1958).

109. J. Robert Oppenheimer, one of the leading scientists on the Manhattan Project, had his security clearance suspended by the Atomic Energy Commission in 1953–54 because he was allegedly a security risk. Oppenheimer, who had been serving as a consultant on atomic projects, fell under suspicion because of numerous contacts with present or former Communists, including his wife. Even more fundamental to the revocation of his clearance was his opposition to the development of the hydrogen bomb. See Charles C. Alexander, *Holding the Line: The Eisenhower Era, 1952–1961* (Bloomington: Indiana Univ. Press, 1975), 56–57. In 1963, Oppenheimer was awarded the Fermi Prize of $50,000 by the Atomic Energy Commission for his contributions to the development of nuclear energy.

110. Caute, 181.

111. Flemming v. Nestor, 363 U.S. 603 (1960).

112. See Aldon D. Morris, *The Origins of the Civil Rights Movement* (New York: Free Press, 1984), 17–39; and American Jewish Congress, *Assault upon Freedom of Association: A Study of the Southern Attack on the National Association for the Advancement of Colored People* (New York: American Jewish Congress, 1957).

113. Quoted in American Jewish Congress, 14, 21.

114. Morris, 33.

115. National Association for the Advancement of Colored People v. Alabama, 357 U.S. 449, 460 (1958).

116. Ibid. at 462–63.

117. Shelton v. Tucker, 364 U.S. 479, 485–87 (1960).

118. National Association of Colored People v. Button, 371 U.S. 415, 429, 431 (1963).

119. Gibson v. Florida Legislative Investigating Committee, 372 U.S. 539, 548, 556–57 (1963).

120. There is some evidence that Southerners used federal investigatory committees to intimidate whites who sought to promote integration in the South as well. See John A. Salmond, " 'The Great Southern Commie Hunt': Aubrey Williams, the Southern Conference Educational Fund, and the Internal Security Subcommittee," *South Atlantic Quarterly* 77 (1978):433–52. For cases that raise that point see Braden v. United States, 365 U.S. 431 (1961), and Dombrowski v. Pfister, 380 U.S. 479 (1965).

121. 1 Stat. 68 (1789).

122. 60 Stat. 238 (1946).

123. Executive Order 10290, Establishing Minimum Standards for the Classification, Transmission, and Handling by Departments and Agencies of the Executive Branch, of Official Information which Requires Safeguarding in the Interest of the Security of the United States, 24 Sept. 1951, quoted in 3 *Code of Federal Regulations* 789. See David Wise, *The Politics of Lying: Government Deception, Secrecy, and Power* (New York: Vintage, 1973), 79–127; and Jean Stevens, "Classification: Threat to Democracy," *Freedom of Information Center Report No. 270*, School of Journalism, Univ. of Missouri at Columbia, Oct. 1971.

124. Ibid., 789–90.

125. Executive Order 10501, Safeguarding Official Information in the Interests of the Defense of the United States, 5 Nov. 1953, quoted in 18 *Federal Register* 7049.

126. See Margaret A. Blanchard, "Americans First, Newspapermen Second? The Conflict Between Patriotism and Freedom of the Press during the Cold War, 1945–1952" (Ph.D. diss., University of North Carolina at Chapel Hill, 1981), 308–37.

127. "Blackout," *Editor & Publisher,* 29 Sept. 1951, p. 38.

128. "When Mr. Truman Sounded Off on Responsibilities of the Press," *Editor & Publisher,* 13 Oct. 1951, p. 62.

129. See Blanchard, 366–76, and Christine Michele Kridler, "Silence at Ground Zero: Secrecy and the Atomic Bomb and the Postwar Effects of Censorship, 1939–1955" (Honors thesis, School of Journalism, University of North Carolina at Chapel Hill, 1989), 33–67.

130. 60 Stat. 766 (1946).

131. "Baltimore Daily Praised for A-Bomb Coup," *Editor & Publisher,* 19 Oct. 1946, p. 12.

132. 68 Stat. 941 (1954).

133. Norman Dorsen and John H. F. Shattuck, "Executive Privilege: The President Won't Tell," *None of Your Business: Government Secrecy in America,* ed. Norman Dorsen and Stephen Gillers (New York: Viking, 1974), 32.

134. Subcommittee charter, quoted in Robert O. Blanchard, "The Moss Committee and a Federal Public Records Law, 1955–1965" (Ph.D. diss., Syracuse University, 1966), 55–56.

135. 88 Stat. 250 (1966).

136. See J. P. Williams, "Why Superheroes Never Bleed: The Effects of Self-Censorship on the Comic Book Industry," *Free Speech Yearbook 1987,* 60–69. Wertham's argument is presented in Fredric Wertham, *Seduction of the Innocent* (New York: Rinehart, 1953).

137. Senate Committee on the Judiciary, Subcommittee on Juvenile Delinquency, *Comic Books and Juvenile Delinquency,* 84th Cong., 1st sess. (1955), 2–3, 23.

138. Ibid., 37.

139. Williams, 65.

140. American Civil Liberties Union, *Censorship of Comic Books: A Statement in Opposition on Civil Liberties Grounds* (New York: American Civil Liberties Union, 1955), 4–5.

141. Ibid., 7–8.

142. Robert Stanley, *The Celluloid Empire: A History of the American Movie Industry* (New York: Hastings House, 1978), 198–202.

143. United States v. Paramount Pictures, 334 U.S. 131 (1948).

144. Burstyn v. Wilson, 343 U.S. 495 (1952).

145. Ibid. at 501–2.

146. See Kingsley International Pictures Corp. v. Board of Regents, 360 U.S. 684 (1959); Times Film Corp. v. Chicago, 365 U.S. 43 (1961); and Freedman v. Maryland, 380 U.S. 51 (1965).

147. See Suzanne Yeager, "G-GP-R-X: Forced Self Regulation?," *Freedom of Information Center Report No. 257,* School of Journalism, Univ. of Missouri at Columbia, Feb. 1971; and Suzanne Yeager, "G-GP-R-X: Exercise in Ambiguity," *Freedom of Information Center Report No. 258,* School of Journalism, Univ. of Missouri at Columbia, March 1971.

148. John Fischer, "The Editor's Easy Chair: The Harm Good People Do," *Harper's,* Oct. 1956, pp. 14, 16–18, 20. See also William B. Lockhart and Robert C. McClure, "Literature, the Law of Obscenity, and the Constitution," *Minnesota Law Review* 38 (1954):302–12; and Paul Blanshard, *The Right to Read: The Battle Against Censorship* (Boston: Beacon Press, 1955), 168–201. For the other side of the NODL story, see John Courtney Murray, "The Bad Arguments Intelligent Men Make," *America,* 3 Nov. 1956, pp. 120–23.

149. House Select Committee on Current Pornographic Materials, *Pornographic Materials,* 82nd Cong., 2d sess. (1952), 3, 116, 121.

150. Roth v. United States, 354 U.S. 476, 487–89 (1957).

Chapter 8

1. See Montague Kern, Patricia Levering, and Ralph B. Levering, *The Kennedy Crisis: The Press, the Presidency, and Foreign Policy* (Chapel Hill: Univ. of North Carolina Press, 1983).

2. See Dom Bonafede, "The Press in the Cuban Fiasco," *Nieman Reports,* July 1961, pp. 5–6; Ben H. Bagdikian, "Press Independence and the Cuban Crisis," *Columbia Journalism Review,* Winter 1963, pp. 5–11; and Neal D. Houghton, "The Cuban Invasion of 1961 and the U.S. Press, in Retrospect," *Journalism Quarterly* 42 (1965):422–32.

3. Quoted in E. Clifton Daniel, "Bay of Pigs: More Than Just a Military Fiasco," in Walter M. Brasch and Dana R. Ulloth, *The Press and the State: Sociohistorical and Contemporary Studies* (Lanham, Md.: Univ. Press of America, 1986), 428.

4. Miles Beardsley Johnson, *The Government Secrecy Controversy: A Dispute Involving the Government and the Press in the Eisenhower, Kennedy, and Johnson Administrations* (New York: Vantage, 1967), 64–65.

5. Quoted in Daniel, 429.

6. House Subcommittee of the Committee on Government Operations, *Government Information Plans and Policies,* 88th Cong., 1st sess. (5 June 1963), 176–77.

7. Kern, Levering, and Levering, 141–91.

8. See Hanson W. Baldwin, "Managed News: Our Peacetime Censorship," *Atlantic Monthly,* April 1963, pp. 53–59.

9. Quoted in David Wise, *The Politics of Lying: Government Deception, Secrecy, and Power* (New York: Vintage, 1973), 56.

10. See Herbert Garfinkel, *When Negroes March: The March on Washington Movement in the Organizational Politics for FEPC* (Glencoe, Ill.: Free Press, 1959).

11. Morgan v. Virginia, 328 U.S. 373 (1946).

12. See Thomas R. Brooks, *Walls Come Tumbling Down: A History of the Civil Rights Movement, 1940–1970* (Englewood Cliffs, N.J.: Prentice-Hall, 1974); Aldon D. Morris, *The Origins of the Civil Rights Movement* (New York: Free Press, 1984); and Robert Weisbrot, *Freedom Bound: A History of America's Civil Rights Movement* (New York: Norton, 1990).

13. 349 U.S. 294 (1954).

14. Gayle v. Browder, 352 U.S. 903 (1956).

15. Morris, 17–76.

16. 310 U.S. 88 (1940).

17. See Randall Kennedy, "Martin Luther King's Constitution: A Legal History of the Montgomery Bus Boycott," *Yale Law Journal* 98 (1989):999–1067.

18. Brooks, 95–119.

19. See Francis M. Wilhoit, *The Politics of Massive Resistance* (New York: George Braziller, 1973).

20. See Kenneth O'Reilly, *"Racial Matters": The FBI's Secret File on Black America, 1960–1972* (New York: Free Press, 1989).

21. Garner v. Louisiana, 368 U.S. 157, 201–2 (1961).

22. Boynton v. Virginia, 364 U.S. 454 (1960).

23. See Catherine A. Barnes, *Journey from Jim Crow: The Desegregation of Southern Transit* (New York: Columbia Univ. Press, 1983), 157–75.

24. Quoted in Alan F. Westin and Barry Mahoney, "Martin Luther King, Jr., and the Supreme Court: On Protest and the First Amendment," *Civil Liberties Review,* Dec. 1976/Jan. 1977, p. 20. The entire article focuses on the Birmingham incident.

25. Martin Luther King, Jr., *Why We Can't Wait* (New York: American Library, 1963), 70, quoted in Morris, 261.

26. Quoted in Westin and Mahoney, 21.

27. *Public Papers of the Presidents of the United States: John F. Kennedy, 1963,* 572, quoted in Weisbrot, 83.

28. Stephen B. Oates, *Let the Trumpet Sound: The Life of Martin Luther King, Jr.* (New York: Harper & Row, 1982), 261–62, quoted in Weisbrot, 82–83.

29. See Robert M. Fogelson, *Violence as Protest: A Study of Riots and Ghettos* (Garden City, N.Y.: Doubleday, 1971).

30. Edwards v. South Carolina, 372 U.S. 229, 235 (1963).

31. New York Times v. Sullivan, 376 U.S. 254, 270, 279–80 (1964). See W. Wat Hopkins, *Actual Malice: Twenty-five Years after Times v. Sullivan* (New York: Praeger, 1989), 11–24.

32. Bell v. Maryland, 378 U.S. 226, 345–46 (1964).

33. Cox v. Louisiana, 379 U.S. 559, 578 (1965) (emphasis included).

34. Adderley v. Florida, 385 U.S. 39, 46–47 (1966).

35. Walker v. Birmingham, 388 U.S. 307, 321 (1967).

36. Ibid. at 331, 334.

37. Ibid. at 335–37.

38. Ibid. at 349.

39. Shuttlesworth v. Birmingham, 394 U.S. 147, 151 (1969).

40. See James Miller, *"Democracy Is in the Streets": From Port Huron to the Siege of Chicago* (New York: Simon and Schuster, 1987).

41. See Philip G. Altbach, *Student Politics in America: A Historical Analysis* (New York: McGraw-Hill, 1973).

42. See Max Heirich, *The Spiral of Conflict: Berkeley 1964* (New York: Columbia Univ. Press, 1971).

43. *Report of the President's Commission on Campus Unrest* (Washington, D.C.: Government Printing Office, 1970), 5, 7–8, 12.

44. Ibid., 45.

45. See Milton S. Katz, *Ban the Bomb: A History of SANE, the Committee for a Sane Nuclear Policy, 1957–1985* (New York: Greenwood Press, 1986); Maurice Isserman, *If I Had a Hammer . . . : The Death of the Old Left and the Birth of the New Left* (New York: Basic Books, 1987), 125–67; Lawrence S. Wittner, *Rebels Against War: The American Peace Movement, 1941–1960* (New York: Columbia Univ. Press, 1969), 240–75; *The Power of the People: Active Nonviolence in the United States,* eds. Robert Cooney and Helen Michalowski (Culver City, Calif.: Peace Press, 1977), 124–49; Susan Caudill, "Publicity as an Instrument of Reform" (Paper presented to the Public Relations Division, Association for Education in Journalism and Mass Communication, Washington, D.C., Aug. 1989); and Christine Michele Kridler, "Silence at Ground Zero: Secrecy and the Atomic Bomb and the Postwar Effects of Censorship, 1939–1955" (Undergraduate honors essay, School of Journalism, University of North Carolina at Chapel Hill, 1989).

46. *New York Times,* 24 April 1957.

47. Quoted in *Civil Disobedience in America,* ed. David R. Weber (Ithaca, N.Y.: Cornell Univ. Press, 1978), 259.

48. See Nancy Zaroulis and Gerald Sullivan, *Who Spoke Up? American Protest Against the War in Vietnam, 1963–1975* (Garden City, N.Y.: Doubleday, 1984); and Thomas Powers, *The War at Home: Vietnam and the American People, 1964–1968* (New York: Grossman, 1973).

49. SDS statement of December 1964, quoted in Todd Gitlin, *The Sixties: Years of Hope, Days of Rage* (New York: Bantam, 1987), 181.

50. See Todd Gitlin, *The Whole World Is Watching: Mass Media in the Making & Unmaking of the New Left* (Berkeley: Univ. of California Press, 1980), and Miller, 218–59.

51. See *Teach-ins: U.S.A.,* eds. Louis Menashe and Ronald Radosh (New York: Praeger, 1967).

52. Quoted in ibid., 118.

53. Quoted in ibid., 154.

54. Speech of Dr. Eugene D. Genovese, Rutgers Teach-In, 23 April 1965, quoted in ibid., 225.

55. Report to the New Jersey General Assembly, 28 June 1965, quoted in ibid., 232.

56. *New York Times,* 17 Oct. 1965, quoted in ibid., 234–35.

57. *Village Voice,* 24 June 1965, quoted in Powers, 71.

58. Gitlin, *The Whole World Is Watching,* 182.

59. 79 Stat. 586 (1965).

60. *Congressional Record,* 89th Cong., 1st sess., 10 Aug. 1965, 19871.

61. See John F. and Rosemary S. Bannan, *Law, Morality and Vietnam: The Peace Militants and the Courts* (Bloomington: Indiana Univ. Press, 1974), 40–62.

62. United States v. Miller, 367 F.2d 72, 78–79 (2d Cir. 1966).

63. United States v. O'Brien, 391 U.S. 367, 376 (1966).

64. Michael Ferber and Staughton Lynd, *The Resistance* (Boston: Beacon Press, 1971), 24.

65. *New York Times,* 22 April 1966, quoted in Powers, 117.

66. Quoted in Hugh T. Lovin, "The Lyndon Johnson Administrations and the Federal War on Subversion in the 1960s," *Presidential Studies Quarterly* 17 (1987):566.

67. By 1972, some 1,700 Americans refused to pay all or part of their income tax as a protest against the Vietnam War. Few, if any, suffered substantial punishment for their efforts as long as the Internal Revenue Service could obtain payment through liens on their bank accounts. Failure to pay taxes could have led to a $10,000 fine and one year in prison upon conviction, but although the government prosecuted other forms of protest, individuals who chose this method escaped arrest so long as the IRS got its money. Other approaches, such as claiming an increased number of dependents, were less successful. The most popular tax protest seemed to be withholding payment of a 10 percent excise tax attached to telephone bills. More than 56,000 Americans practiced this form of protest in 1971, with the IRS taking steps to recover the funds. See "The War Tax Protesters," *Time,* 19 June 1972, p. 71.

68. *Handbook on the Nonpayment of War Taxes* (New York: War Resisters League, 1966), quoted in *Conscience in America: A Documentary History of Conscientious Objection in America, 1757–1967,* ed. Lillian Schissel (New York: E. P. Dutton, 1968), 400.

69. See Milton Viorst, *Fire in the Streets: America in the 1960s* (New York: Simon and Schuster, 1979), 343–79.

70. Bond v. Floyd, 385 U.S. 116, 121, 136 (1966).

71. Nuremberg principles, art. VI, quoted in Bannan and Bannan, 13.

72. Court transcript, 1001–2, quoted in ibid., 32.

73. See David Cortright, *Soldiers in Revolt: The American Military Today* (Garden

City, N.Y.: Anchor Press/Doubleday, 1975); and Cathy Packer, *Freedom of Expression in the American Military: A Communication Modeling Analysis* (New York: Praeger, 1989).

74. Parker v. Levy, 417 U.S. 733, 736–37, 758 (1974).

75. Several attempts at legitimate communication with the military on antiwar matters reached the Supreme Court, where only one was granted the high court's blessing. In *Flower v. United States,* 407 U.S. 197 (1972), the Court found that John Thomas Flower could distribute his antiwar leaflets on a street within Fort Sam Houston because the military post was open to the general public. In *Greer v. Spock,* 424 U.S. 828 (1976), however, the Supreme Court found that when a base was closed to the public, the base commander could limit individuals allowed access to its personnel. The Supreme Court, by a six-member majority, refused constitutional challenges to the right of members of Congress to hold commissions in the military reserves. The Reservists Committee to Stop the War argued that such commissions violated a constitutional provision against members of Congress holding any other government office and that because of congressional connections with the military, the reservists committee had difficulty convincing members of Congress to oppose the war. See Schlesinger v. Reservists Committee to Stop the War, 418 U.S. 208 (1974). Finally, five members of the Court refused to stop an effort by the Senate Internal Security Subcommittee to obtain the bank records of the United States Servicemen's Fund, Inc., which was a primary sponsor of the coffeehouse movement for military personnel. See James O. Eastland v. United States Servicemen's Fund, 421 U.S. 491 (1975).

76. "Saying 'NO' to Military Conscription, for Draft-Agers Who Have Shunned, or Broken Their Ties to, the System," Oct. 1966, quoted in Ferber and Lynd, 50.

77. See Lawrence M. Baskir and William A. Strauss, *Chance and Circumstance: The Draft, the War and the Vietnam Generation* (New York: Alfred A. Knopf, 1978).

78. "Channeling," *Ramparts,* Dec. 1967, p. 34.

79. United States v. Seeger, 380 U.S. 163, 166 (1965).

80. Welsh v. United States, 398 U.S. 333, 342 (1970).

81. Gillette v. United States, 401 U.S. 437 (1971).

82. Baskir and Strauss, 41.

83. See Weisbrot, 246–52.

84. Quoted in *Conscience in America,* 435 (emphasis included).

85. Dr. King had been under surveillance by the FBI for years, allegedly because one of his friends and advisers had ties with the Communist party. This pretext was all J. Edgar Hoover needed to have his agents follow the civil rights leader, bug his motel rooms, tap his telephones, plant an informer in his organization, and send information relating to his alleged extramarital affairs to his wife. See O'Reilly, 125–55; and David J. Garrow, *The FBI and Martin Luther King, Jr.* (New York: W. W. Norton, 1981; rpt., New York: Penguin, 1983).

86. SANE did not abandon the antiwar effort. With other groups that were unable to join with Communists, it formed a group known as Negotiations Now!, which was designed to force the government to settle its differences with North Vietnam. Although many SANE members considered this approach to be middle-of-the-road, Norman Cousins, a longtime leader of the movement, withdrew his support because he considered it too leftist. Dr. Benjamin Spock, another SANE leader, withdrew because he considered the approach too conservative. See Katz, 93–125.

87. Quoted in Ferber and Lynd, 72–73.

88. Department of State Bulletin, 10 April 1967, quoted in Powers, 184.

89. "We Refuse—October 16," Resistance leaflet, quoted in Ferber and Lynd, 90.

90. *New York Times,* 25 April 1967, quoted in Powers, 195.

91. Quoted in Kathleen J. Turner, *Lyndon Johnson's Dual War: Vietnam and the Press* (Chicago: Univ. of Chicago Press, 1985), 196–97.

92. Statement of 1967 SDS National Convention, quoted in Ferber and Lynd, 129.

93. "A Call to Resist Illegitimate Authority," Aug. 1967, quoted in United States v. Spock, 416 F.2d 165, 192–93 (1st Cir. 1969).

94. Michael Ferber speech, 16 Oct. 1967, quoted in Jessica Mitford, *The Trial of Dr. Spock* (New York: Alfred A. Knopf, 1969), 28–29.

95. William Sloane Coffin speech, 20 Oct. 1967, quoted in ibid., 41.

96. *New York Times,* 9 Nov. 1967.

97. Justice Department statement quoted in Mitford, 56.

98. See Oestereich v. Selective Service System, 393 U.S. 233 (1968); Gutknecht v. United States, 396 U.S. 295 (1970); and Breen v. Selective Service Board, 396 U.S. 460 (1970).

99. Bannan and Bannan, 107–23.

100. See Mitford, 61–72.

101. Transcript of trial, 35–36, quoted in Bannan and Bannan, 121.

102. 416 F.2d at 169.

103. 82 Stat. 283 (1968).

104. See 82 Stat. 995 (1968); 82 Stat. 1062 (1968).

105. 81 Stat. 275 (1967).

106. Jeannette Rankin Brigade v. Chief of Capitol Police, 278 F.Supp. 233 (D.C.D.C. 1968).

107. Jeannette Rankin Brigade v. Chief of Capitol Police, 342 F.Supp. 575, 585 (D.C.D.C. 1972).

108. 82 Stat. 75–76 (1968).

109. See Athan Theoharis, *Spying on Americans: Political Surveillance from Hoover to the Huston Plan* (Philadelphia: Temple Univ. Press, 1978); and Frank J. Donner, *The Age of Surveillance: The Aims and Methods of America's Political Intelligence System* (New York: Alfred A. Knopf, 1980).

110. FBI memorandum to field offices, July 1968, quoted in Geoffrey Rips, *The Campaign Against the Underground Press* (San Francisco: City Lights Books, 1981), 61–62.

111. Quoted in ibid., 62–63.

112. See Daniel C. Hallin, *The "Uncensored War": The Media and Vietnam* (New York: Oxford Univ. Press, 1986); Kathleen J. Turner, *Lyndon Johnson's Dual War: Vietnam and the Press* (Chicago: Univ. of Chicago Press, 1985); William M. Hammond, *Public Affairs: The Military and the Media, 1962–1968,* United States Army in Vietnam Series (Washington, D.C.: Center of Military History, United States Army, 1988); Dale Minor, *The Information War* (New York: Hawthorn Books, 1970); Martin F. Herz assisted by Leslie Rider, *The Prestige Press and the Christmas Bombing, 1972: Images and Reality in Vietnam* (Washington, D.C.: Ethics and Public Policy Center, 1980); Michael J. Arlen, *Living-Room War* (New York: Viking, 1969); and Bob Brewin and Sydney Shaw, *Vietnam on Trial: Westmoreland vs. CBS* (New York: Atheneum, 1987).

113. Walter Cronkite, statement of 27 Feb. 1968, quoted in Brewin and Shaw, 42.

114. Hammond, in his official history of the military public affairs policy effort in Vietnam, points out that knowing manipulation rather than honesty was the premise used by the government in the conflict and that many of the problems of public attitude toward the war could be attributed directly to that policy.

115. See Richard Curtis, *The Berrigan Brothers* (New York: Hawthorn Books, 1974).

116. Quoted in ibid., 4.

117. See Francine Du Plessix Gray, "The Ultra-Resistance," in *Trials of the Resistance* (New York: Random House, 1970), 125–61.

118. United States v. Moylan, 417 F.2d 1002, 1008 (4th Cir. 1969).

119. Ibid. at 1009.

120. See Jerry L. Avorn, *Up Against the Ivy Wall: A History of the Columbia Crisis* (New York: Atheneum, 1969).

121. Quoted in William Small, *To Kill a Messenger: Television News and the Real World* (New York: Hastings House, 1970), 204.

122. Gitlin, *The Sixties,* 321.

123. Ibid., 323.

124. Ibid., 324–25, 327, 332.

125. Quoted in David Caute, *The Year of the Barricades: A Journey Through 1968* (New York: Harper & Row, 1988; Perennial Library, 1988), 296.

126. Quoted in Small, *To Kill a Messenger,* 207.

127. Quoted in United States v. Dellinger, 472 F.2d 340, 399 (7th Cir. 1972).

128. Quoted in Caute, 322.

129. Quoted in Gitlin, *The Sixties,* 334.

130. Quoted in Small, *To Kill a Messenger,* 205.

131. Ibid., 210.

132. Quoted in Caute, 293.

133. Quoted in Small, *To Kill a Messenger,* 215–16 (emphasis included).

134. Daniel Walker, *Rights in Conflict* (New York: Signet Books, 1968), xix.

135. Ibid., xxii, xiv (emphasis included).

136. Caute, 323.

137. See Jason Epstein, *The Great Conspiracy Trial* (New York: Random House, 1970).

138. Brandenburg v. Ohio, 395 U.S. 444 (1969).

139. Quoted in Epstein, 77.

140. Quoted in ibid., 386.

141. 472 F.2d at 359.

142. Ibid. at 360, 362.

Chapter 9

1. Quoted in Kathleen Jamieson, *Packaging the Presidency* (New York: Oxford Univ. Press, 1984), 229–30.

2. Quoted in Joe McGinnis, *The Selling of the President 1968* (New York: Trident, 1969), 90.

3. See Melvin Small, *Johnson, Nixon, and the Doves* (New Brunswick, N.J.: Rutgers Univ. Press, 1988), 129–224; and Nancy Zaroulis and Gerald Sullivan, *Who Spoke Up? American Protest Against the War in Vietnam, 1963–75* (Garden City, N.Y.: Doubleday, 1984), 175–423.

4. See Frank J. Donner, *The Age of Surveillance: The Aims and Methods of America's Political Intelligence System* (New York: Alfred A. Knopf, 1980); and Athan Theoharis, *Spying on Americans: Political Surveillance from Hoover to the Huston Plan* (Philadelphia: Temple Univ. Press, 1978).

5. William H. Orrick, Jr., *Shut It Down! A College in Crisis: San Francisco State College, October, 1968–April, 1969,* A Report to the National Commission the Causes and Prevention of Violence (Washington, D.C.: Government Printing Office, 1969).

6. Small, *Johnson, Nixon, and the Doves,* 176.

7. *Report of the President's Commission on Campus Unrest* (Washington, D.C.: Government Printing Office, 1970), 38–39.

8. See W. J. Rorabaugh, *Berkeley at War: The 1960s* (New York: Oxford Univ. Press, 1989).

9. See David Caute, *The Year of the Barricades: A Journey Through 1968* (New York: Harper & Row, 1988).

10. See Robert Weisbrot, *Freedom Bound: A History of America's Civil Rights Movement* (New York: W. W. Norton, 1990), 272–75.

11. Malcolm X quoted in Alex Haley, *The Autobiography of Malcolm X* (New York: Ballantine, 1973), 251, 246, quoted in Weisbrot, 173 (emphasis included).

12. Malcolm X, *Malcolm X Speaks,* ed. George Breitman (New York: Grove, 1965), 213, quoted in ibid., 177.

13. See John T. Elliff, *Crime, Dissent, and the Attorney General: The Justice Department in the 1960's* (Beverly Hills, Calif.: Sage, 1971), 82–152.

14. People v. Epton, 227 N.E.2d 829, 832, 835 (N.Y. App. 1967).

15. Ibid. at 832.

16. See Paul Harris, "Black Power Advocacy: Criminal Anarchy or Free Speech," *California Law Review* 56 (1968):702–55.

17. Kenneth O'Reilly, *"Racial Matters": The FBI's Secret File on Black America, 1960–1972* (New York: Free Press, 1989), 294.

18. *New York Times,* 16 July 1969, quoted in Elliff, 127.

19. FBI memoranda, quoted in O'Reilly, 302.

20. See O'Reilly, 293–324; and Ward Churchill and Jim Vander Wall, *Agents of Repression: The FBI's Secret Wars against the Black Panther Party and the American Indian Movement* (Boston: South End Press, 1988), 63–99.

21. "You Don't Need a Weatherman to Know Which Way the Wind Blows," quoted in *Weatherman,* ed. Harold Jacobs (Berkeley, Calif.: Ramparts, 1970), 70.

22. Todd Gitlin, *The Sixties: Years of Hope, Days of Rage* (New York: Bantam, 1987), 385.

23. Ibid., 393–94.

24. Small, *Johnson, Nixon, and the Doves,* 183–84.

25. William B. Hixson, Jr., "Nixon, the War and the Opposition: The First Year," *Journal of American Culture* 4 (1981):77.

26. Quoted in Elliff, 214.

27. Richard M. Nixon, "A Vietnam Plan: The Silent Majority," *Vital Speeches,* 15 Nov. 1969, p. 69.

28. Quoted in James Keogh, *President Nixon and the Press* (New York: Funk & Wagnalls, 1972), 171, 183–84, 186–88.

29. See William E. Porter, *Assault on the Media: The Nixon Years* (Ann Arbor: Univ. of Michigan Press, 1976); Joseph C. Spear, *Presidents and the Press: The Nixon Legacy* (Cambridge, Mass.: MIT Press, 1984); and Fred Powledge, *The Engineering of Restraint: The Nixon Administration and the Press,* (Washington, D.C.: Public Affairs Press, 1971).

30. *New York Times,* 8 Nov. 1962, quoted in Spear, 55–56.

31. White House Memorandum, 17 Oct. 1969, quoted in ibid., 113.

32. Quoted in John Tebbel and Sarah Miles Watts, *The Press and the Presidency* (New York: Oxford Univ. Press, 1985), 507–8.

33. Spiro T. Agnew, "Television News Coverage," *Vital Speeches,* 1 Dec. 1969, pp. 98–99.

34. Ibid., 99–100

35. Ibid., 100.

36. Quoted in Elliff, 219.

37. Av Westin, *News-Watch: How TV Decides the News* (New York: Simon and Schuster, 1982), 96.

38. Godfrey Hodgson, *America in Our Time* (New York: Random House, 1976; Vintage, 1978), 378.

39. Westin, 147.

40. Quoted in Hodgson, 378 (emphasis included).

41. Spiro T. Agnew, "The Newspaper Monopoly," *Vital Speeches,* 15 Dec. 1969, p. 134.

42. *New York Times,* quoted in ibid., 135.

43. Agnew, "The Newspaper Monopoly," 135.

44. Ibid., 135–36.

45. Arthur Woodstone, *Nixon's Head* (New York: St. Martin's, 1972), 141n, quoted in Spear, 116.

46. Quoted in Fred P. Graham, "Background Paper," in Twentieth Century Fund, *Press Freedoms Under Pressure* (New York: Twentieth Century Fund, 1972), 61.

47. Justice Department Guidelines for Subpoenas, 10 Aug. 1970, quoted in *Congressional Quarterly,* 1 Jan. 1972, p. 6.

48. Joel Havemann, *Chicago Journalism Review,* April 1971, quoted in Graham, 94.

49. See Laurence Leamer, *The Paper Revolutionaries: The Rise of the Underground Press* (New York: Simon and Schuster, 1972); and Geoffrey Rips, *The Campaign Against the Underground Press* (San Francisco: City Lights Books, 1981). See also Angus Mackenzie, "Sabotaging the Dissident Press," *Columbia Journalism Review,* March/April 1981, pp. 57, 59–60, 62–63.

50. Rips, 85.

51. Quoted in Leamer, 129.

52. Quoted in ibid.

53. Dyson v. Stein, 401 U.S. 200, 206 (1971). Douglas was correct in his prediction that if not stopped here, more newspaper offices would be searched. When local authorities searched the offices of *The Stanford Daily,* the student publication at Stanford University, they were looking for photographs and negatives relating to a demonstration in which several police officers were injured. The goal was to identify the students who had hurt the officers. Although a federal district court and a court of appeals agreed with the students' contention that the search violated the First Amendment, the Supreme Court disagreed. In 1978, five justices approved of the search of the newspaper's offices even though police had no proof that any staff members were involved in a crime. See Zurcher v. The Stanford Daily, 463 U.S. 547 (1978). After this decision, other journalists' offices were searched, and mainline journalists petitioned Congress for legislative protection, which was provided in late 1980. See Donald M. Gillmor, Jerome A. Barron, Todd F. Simon and Herbert A. Terry, *Mass Communications Law,* 5th ed. (St. Paul, Minn.: West Publishing, 1990), 393.

54. *Press Freedoms Under Pressure,* 36.

55. Quoted in Gitlin, 403.

56. Quoted in James A. Michener, *Kent State: What Happened and Why* (New York: Random House, 1971), 252n.

57. Small, *Johnson, Nixon, and the Doves,* 202.

58. Quoted in Michener, 250–51.

59. *Report of the President's Commission on Campus Unrest,* 2.

60. *New York Times,* 7 May 1970.

61. Newton Minow, John Bartlow Martin, and Lee M. Mitchell, *Presidential Television*, A Twentieth Century Fund Report (New York: Basic Books, 1973), 56.

62. Request for a Declaratory Ruling Concerning Access to Time on Broadcasting Stations from the Democratic National Committee to the FCC, 19 May 1970, pp. 1, 19, quoted in Fred W. Friendly, *The Good Guys, the Bad Guys and the First Amendment: Free Speech vs. Fairness in Broadcasting* (New York: Random House, 1976), 125, 122. Friendly discusses the Democratic National Committee challenge to the networks in 121–41.

63. Business Executives Move for Peace v. FCC, 450 F.2d 642 (D.C. Cir. 1971).

64. CBS v. Democratic National Committee, 412 U.S. 94, 172, 189–90, 193 (1973) (emphasis included).

65. Charles Colson to H. R. Haldeman, 25 Sept. 1970, quoted in Friendly, 131.

66. See William O'Rourke, *The Harrisburg 7 and the New Catholic Left* (New York: Thomas Y. Crowell, 1972).

67. Zaroulis and Sullivan, 361.

68. Small, *Johnson, Nixon, and the Doves,* 218.

69. Tinker v. Des Moines Independent Community School District, 393 U.S. 503, 505–6, 510 (1969).

70. Ibid. at 506.

71. Street v. New York, 394 U.S. 576, 579 (1969).

72. Ibid. at 605, 610 (emphasis included).

73. Smith v. Goguen, 415 U.S. 566, 574 (1974).

74. Ibid. at 603.

75. Spence v. Washington, 418 U.S. 405, 408–11 (1974).

76. Ibid. at 422–23.

77. Cohen v. California, 403 U.S. 15, 20–21, 25 (1971).

78. Hess v. Indiana, 414 U.S. 105 (1973).

79. Watts v. United States, 394 U.S. 705, 706, 708 (1969).

80. Healy v. James, 408 U.S. 169 (1972).

81. See William J. Small, *Political Power and the Press* (New York: W. W. Norton, 1972), 298–380.

82. Quoted in ibid., 303, 310.

83. Quoted in ibid., 313.

84. Quoted in ibid., 323, 329–30.

85. Quoted in ibid., 347.

86. Quoted in ibid., 357 (emphasis included).

87. Quoted in ibid., 370–71, 373.

88. Quoted in Peter Schrag, *Test of Loyalty: Daniel Ellsberg and the Rituals of Secret Government* (New York: Simon and Schuster, 1974), 41.

89. Quoted in Sanford J. Ungar, *The Papers & the Papers* (New York: E. P. Dutton, 1972), 120.

90. Quoted in ibid., 122, 124.

91. United States v. New York Times, 328 F.Supp. 324 (S.D.N.Y. 1971).

92. 283 U.S. 697 (1931).

93. Bantam Books, Inc. v. Sullivan, 372 U.S. 58, 70 (1963).

94. Organization for a Better Austin v. Keefe, 402 U.S. 415, 419 (1971).

95. 283 U.S. at 716.

96. See Jules Witcover, "Two Weeks that Shook the Press," *Columbia Journalism Review,* Sept./Oct. 1971, pp. 7–15.

97. Richard Nixon to H. R. Haldeman, 15 June 1971, quoted in *From: The President:*

Richard Nixon's Secret Files, ed. Bruce Oudes (New York: Harper & Row, 1989), 270–71 (emphasis included).

98. H. R. Haldeman Action Paper, 15 June 1971, quoted in ibid., 271–72.

99. 328 F.Supp. at 331.

100. Ibid. at 331, 330.

101. Quoted in Ungar, 173.

102. United States v. New York Times, 444 F.2d 544 (2d Cir. 1971).

103. United States v. Washington Post, 446 F.2d 1327 (D.C. Cir. 1971).

104. New York Times v. United States, 403 U.S. 713, 715, 724 (1971).

105. Ibid. at 724–27.

106. Ibid. at 728–30.

107. Ibid. at 731, 733.

108. Ibid. at 761, 763.

109. Quoted in Ungar, 252.

110. *Detroit Free Press,* quoted in *St. Louis Post-Dispatch,* 16 July 1971, quoted in John Lofton, *The Press as Guardian of the First Amendment* (Columbia: Univ. of South Carolina Press, 1980), 260.

Chapter 10

1. See Peter Schrag, *Test of Loyalty: Daniel Ellsberg and the Rituals of Secret Government* (New York: Simon and Schuster, 1974).

2. 40 Stat. 218 (1917).

3. See Fred Powledge, *The Engineering of Restraint: The Nixon Administration and the Press* (Washington, D.C.: Public Affairs Press, 1971); William E. Porter, *Assault on the Media: The Nixon Years* (Ann Arbor: Univ. of Michigan Press, 1976); and Joseph C. Spear, *Presidents and the Press: The Nixon Legacy* (Cambridge, Mass.: MIT Press, 1984).

4. Quoted in Powledge, 17.

5. Quoted in ibid., 25.

6. Thomas Whiteside, "Annals of Television: Shaking the Tree," *New Yorker,* 17 March 1975, p. 48.

7. Daniel Schorr, "The FBI and Me," *Columbia Journalism Review,* Nov./Dec. 1974, p. 10.

8. Ibid., 14.

9. See Ben H. Bagdikian, "The Politics of American Newspapers," *Columbia Journalism Review,* March/April 1972, pp. 8–13.

10. Spiro T. Agnew, Speech before the Nevada Republican Dinner, Las Vegas, Nev., 14 Sept. 1970, quoted in John R. Coyne, Jr., *The Impudent Snobs: Agnew v. the Intellectual Establishment* (New Rochelle, N.Y.: Arlington House, 1972), 371–72 (emphasis included).

11. Ibid., 372.

12. In Re Licensee Responsibility to Review Records before Their Broadcast, 28 F.C.C.2d 409 (1971).

13. Ibid., 412, 414.

14. Lucas A. Powe, Jr., *American Broadcasting and the First Amendment* (Berkeley: Univ. of California Press, 1987), 176–82.

15. In the matter of Licensee Responsibility to Review Records before Their Broadcast, 31 F.C.C.2d 377, 378, 380 (1971).

16. In the matter of Licensee Responsibility to Review Records before Their Broadcast, 31 F.C.C.2d 385, 389 (1971).

17. Yale Broadcasting Co. v. Federal Communications Commission, 478 F.2d 594 (D.C. Cir. 1973).

18. Yale Broadcasting Co. v. Federal Communications Commission, 414 U.S. 914, 916–18 (1973).

19. Powe, 186.

20. Declaratory Order, 21 Feb. 1975, 56 F.C.C.2d 94, 99 (1975).

21. Federal Communications Commission v. Pacifica Foundation, 438 U.S. 726, 744–45 (1978).

22. Ibid. at 748–49.

23. Ibid. at 762–63, 775.

24. *Report of the Commission on Obscenity and Pornography* (New York: Bantam, 1970), 53, 58–59.

25. Ibid., 60–61.

26. "Pornography: Odd Man In," *Newsweek,* 21 Sept. 1970, p. 44. In the late 1980s, Charles Keating would be a leading figure in the nation's savings and loan scandal.

27. *Report of the Commission on Obscenity and Pornography,* 580, 622–23.

28. Roth v. United States, 354 U.S. 476, 484 (1957).

29. Memoirs v. Massachusetts, 383 U.S. 413, 418 (1966).

30. Miller v. California, 413 U.S. 15, 24, 30 (1973).

31. Presidential Press Secretary Ronald Ziegler, quoted in Carl Bernstein and Bob Woodward, *All the President's Men* (New York: Simon and Schuster, 1974), 26.

32. 81 Stat. 365 (1967).

33. See David M. Stone, *Nixon and the Politics of Public Television* (New York: Garland, 1985).

34. Jon Rose, White House staff member, Nov. 1971, quoted ibid., 80.

35. Charles Colson memorandum to the White House Communications Office, quoted in ibid., 197.

36. Transcript of Dick Cavett Show, *Hearings Before the Senate Subcommittee on Communications of the Committee on Commerce,* 93rd Cong., 1st sess. (1973), 8.

37. CPB board minutes, 9 May 1973, quoted in Stone, 284.

38. Hague v. CIO, 307 U.S. 496 (1939).

39. Marsh v. Alabama, 326 U.S. 501, 506 (1946).

40. Amalgamated Food Employees Union v. Logan Valley Plaza, 391 U.S. 308, 319–20 (1968).

41. Lloyd Corp. v. Tanner, 407 U.S. 551, 564, 566–67 (1972) (emphasis included).

42. Ibid. at 580–81, 586.

43. City Council v. Taxpayers for Vincent, 466 U.S. 789 (1984).

44. PruneYard Shopping Center v. Robins, 447 U.S. 74 (1980).

45. United States v. United States District Court for the Eastern District of Michigan, 407 U.S. 297, 300 (1972).

46. Ibid. at 312–14.

47. Laird v. Tatum, 408 U.S. 1 (1972).

48. Ibid. at 25, 28–29.

49. See Everette E. Dennis, "Stolen Peace Treaties and the Press: Two Case Studies," *Journalism History* 2 (1975):6–14.

50. See David Gordon, "The 1896 Maryland Shield Law: The American Roots of Evidentiary Privilege for Newsmen," *Journalism Monographs* No. 22 (Feb. 1972).

51. See Margaret A. Blanchard, "The Fifth-Amendment Privilege of Newsman George Burdick," *Journalism Quarterly* 55 (1978):39–46, 67.

52. See Thomas B. Gilliam, "Newsmen's Sources and the Law," *Freedom of Infor-*

mation Center Report No. 259, School of Journalism, Univ. of Missouri at Columbia, March 1971.

53. Branzburg v. Hayes, 408 U.S. 665, 682, 685, 691 (1972).

54. Ibid. at 692, 694–95.

55. Ibid. at 721.

56. See Fred P. Graham and Jack C. Landau, "The Federal Shield Law We Need," *Columbia Journalism Review,* March/April 1973, pp. 26–35.

57. See Peggy Slasman, "Reporter's Privilege," *Freedom of Information Center Report No. 464,* School of Journalism, Univ. of Missouri at Columbia, Oct. 1982.

58. Ben H. Bagdikian, "The Myth of Newspaper Poverty," *Columbia Journalism Review,* March/April 1973, p. 20.

59. Robert L. Bishop, "The Rush to Chain Ownership," *Columbia Journalism Review,* Nov./Dec. 1972, p. 10.

60. Bagdikian, "The Myth of Newspaper Poverty," 21.

61. Bishop, 10, 15.

62. Bagdikian, "The Myth of Newspaper Poverty," 24.

63. Citizen Publishing Company v. United States, 394 U.S. 131 (1969).

64. Ibid. at 139.

65. Associated Press v. United States, 326 U.S. 1, 20 (1945).

66. 84 Stat. 466 (1970).

67. See Joe Lewels, Jr., "The Newspaper Preservation Act," *Freedom of Information Center Report No. 254,* School of Journalism, Univ. of Missouri at Columbia, Jan. 1971; and Paul M. Keep, "Newspaper Preservation Act Update," *Freedom of Information Center Report No. 456,* School of Journalism, Univ. of Missouri at Columbia, May 1982.

68. 84 Stat. 467. The Newspaper Preservation Act continues to be controversial. In the 1989 term, the Supreme Court heard arguments in a case brought against a joint operating agreement in Detroit. The *Detroit News,* which is a member of the Gannett chain, and the *Detroit Free Press,* which is part of the Knight-Ridder chain, claimed to fall under the law's provisions and created such an arrangement. A group calling itself Michigan Citizens for an Independent Press challenged Attorney General Edwin Meese's approval of the cooperative operation. The agreement was upheld in the lower courts, and an evenly split Supreme Court affirmed the lower court rulings. The Michigan Citizens group argued that neither newspaper was in imminent danger of failure. For background on the Michigan case, see Robbie Steel, "Joint Operating Agreements in the Newspaper Industry: A Threat to First Amendment Freedoms," *University of Pennsylvania Law Review* 138 (1989):275–315.

69. See Everette E. Dennis and William L. Rivers, *Other Voices: The New Journalism in America* (San Francisco: Canfield Press, 1974).

70. See Edwin Diamond, " 'Reporter Power' Takes Root," *Columbia Journalism Review,* Summer 1970, pp. 12–18.

71. See Claude-Jean Bertrand, "A Look at Journalism Reviews," *Freedom of Information Center Report No. 0019,* School of Journalism, Univ. of Missouri at Columbia, Sept. 1978.

72. A. H. Raskin, "What's Wrong With American Newspapers?," *New York Times Magazine,* 11 June 1967, p. 28.

73. Ben H. Bagdikian, "The American Newspaper: It's Just Bad News," *Esquire,* March 1967, p. 124.

74. Raskin, 84 (emphasis included).

75. See Donald T. Mogavero, "The American Press Ombudsman," *Freedom of Information Center Report No. 427,* School of Journalism, Univ. of Missouri at Columbia, Sept. 1980.

76. *Wall Street Journal,* 1 May 1973.

77. Reed J. Irvine, " 'AIM' Corrects Errors in Report," *Freedom of Information Center Report No. 0018,* School of Journalism, Univ. of Missouri at Columbia, Dec. 1975, p. 4. For additional background on AIM see James Cary, "Ready, AIM, Fire!—Accuracy in Media," *Seminar Quarterly,* Dec. 1972, pp. 13–19.

78. Norman E. Isaacs, "Why We Lack a National Press Council," *Columbia Journalism Review,* Fall 1970, p. 21.

79. Commission on Freedom of the Press, *A Free and Responsible Press* (Chicago: Univ. of Chicago Press, 1947). See Margaret A. Blanchard, "The Hutchins Commission, the Press and the Responsibility Concept," *Journalism Monographs* No. 49 (May 1977); and Jerilyn S. McIntyre, "The Hutchins Commission's Search for a Moral Framework," *Journalism History* 6 (1979):54–57, 63.

80. See Donald E. Brignolo, "Community Press Councils," *Freedom of Information Center Report No. 217,* School of Journalism, Univ. of Missouri at Columbia, March 1969.

81. Isaacs, 22.

82. *The Kerner Report: The 1968 Report of the National Advisory Commission on Civil Disorders* (New York: Pantheon, 1988), 363, 366.

83. David L. Lange, Robert K. Baker, and Sandra J. Ball, *Violence and the Media: A Staff Report to the National Commission on the Causes and Prevention of Violence* (Washington, D.C.: Government Printing Office, 1969), 152.

84. Jerome A. Barron, "Access to the Press—A New First Amendment Right," *Harvard Law Review* 80 (1967):1643, 1646.

85. Ibid., 1647, 1650, 1649, 1656.

86. Twentieth Century Fund, *A Free and Responsive Press* (New York: Twentieth Century Fund, 1972), 8–9.

87. See Amanda W. Nunamaker, "The National News Council: A Study of Its Concept and Development, 1972–1977" (Ph.D. diss., George Peabody College for Teachers, 1977).

88. National News Council, *In the Public Interest: A Report by the National News Council, 1973–1975* (New York: National News Council, 1975), 23–32.

89. Miami Herald v. Tornillo, 418 U.S. 241, 257 (1974).

90. See Fred Friendly, *The Good Guys, the Bad Guys and the First Amendment: Free Speech vs. Fairness in Broadcasting* (New York: Random House, 1975), 103–20. The battle over cigarette advertising continues. Dr. Louis W. Sullivan, secretary of health and human services, for instance, has attacked cigarette manufacturer sponsorship of sporting events, claiming that this is a way to slip advertising for the product in where a regular commercial is forbidden. See "Sullivan: Bush's Aide Makes Waves," *Newsweek,* 5 March 1990, p. 19. In response to such efforts to limit or eliminate all forms of cigarette advertising, the industry responds that they are selling a legal product and thus their speech in favor of that product is protected by the First Amendment under the commercial speech doctrine in which the Supreme Court has found limited protection for advertising. See *Virginia Pharmacy Board v. Virginia Consumer Council,* 425 U.S. 748 (1976).

91. Red Lion v. FCC, 395 U.S. 367 (1969).

92. See Stephen R. Barnett, "The FCC's Nonbattle Against Media Monopoly," *Columbia Journalism Review,* Jan./Feb. 1973, pp. 43–50.

93. Second Report and Order on Multiple Ownership of Standard, FM, and Television Broadcast Stations, 50 FCC2d 1046, Appendix F, 1099–1106 (1975).

94. Ibid., 1061.

95. Memorandum Opinion and Order Relating to Multiple Ownership of Standard, FM and Television Broadcast Stations, 53 FCC2d 589 (1975).

96. Federal Communications Commission v. National Citizens Committee for Broadcasting, 436 U.S. 775 (1978).

97. See Report and Order: Amendment to the Commission's Rules and Regulations with Respect to Competition and Responsibility in Network Television Broadcasting, 23 F.C.C.2d 382 (1970); Memorandum Opinion and Order on Network Television Broadcasting, 25 F.C.C.2d 318 (1970); Second Report and Order on Network Television Broadcasting, 50 F.C.C.2d 829 (1975).

98. See, for example, United States v. National Broadcasting Company, 1978-1 Trade Cases (1977).

99. Executive Order 11652, Classification and Declassification of National Security Information and Material, 8 March 1972, quoted in 3 C.F.R. 678.

100. The president's power to set up a classification system without legal sanction from Congress was upheld by the Supreme Court in *Environmental Protection Agency v. Mink,* 410 U.S. 73 (1973). Members of Congress wanted to see copies of materials sent to the president on underground nuclear testing at Amchitka Island, Alaska. When Nixon refused to provide the data, they brought suit under the Freedom of Information Act. The Court found that Congress in writing the first exemption to the act had allowed the president to protect information "specifically required by Executive order to be kept secret in the interest of the national defense or foreign policy." 410 U.S. at 81. That, the Court said, was tacit congressional recognition of the right of the president so to classify documents.

101. *Washington Post,* 22 Feb. 1972, quoted in Darryl W. Levings and Patricia Murphy, "A U.S. 'Official Secrets Act'?," *Freedom of Information Center Report No. 311,* School of Journalism, Univ. of Missouri at Columbia, Sept. 1973, p. 1.

102. See Jonathan Aitken, *Officially Secret* (London: Weidenfeld and Nicolson, 1971).

103. Senate Committee on the Judiciary, Subcommittee on Criminal Laws and Procedures, *Reform of the Federal Criminal Laws,* 93rd Cong., 1st sess. (16 April 1973), 5:4903.

104. Senator Thomas Eagleton, speech at the University of Missouri School of Journalism, 6 April 1973, quoted in Levings and Murphy, 3.

105. Senator Edmund S. Muskie, speech at Frostburg State College, 1 April 1973, quoted in ibid., 3.

106. See Senate Committee on the Judiciary, Subcommittee on Criminal Laws and Procedures, *S. 1: The "Criminal Justice Reform Act of 1975,"* 94th Cong., 1st sess. (1975), 11–37.

107. Roger Simon, "S.1: A Menace to the Press," *Quill,* July–Aug. 1975, pp. 19–20. See also Benno C. Schmidt, Jr., and Harold Edgar, "S.1: Would the New Bill Amount to an Official Secrets Law—And Could It Work?" *Columbia Journalism Review,* March/ April 1976, pp. 18–21; Thomas Kasle, "S.1: The Tangled Web," *Freedom of Information Center Report No. 369,* School of Journalism, Univ. of Missouri at Columbia, March 1977; Thomas Powers, "Nixon's Revenge?," *Commonweal,* 13 Feb. 1976, pp. 111–14; and Stephen Gillers, " 'Blueprint for Tyranny': Congress Overhauls the Laws," *The Nation,* 14 Feb. 1976, pp. 172–77.

108. Quoted in Simon, 20.

109. See Myron Peretz Glazer and Penina Migdal Glazer, *The Whistleblowers: Exposing Corruption in Government and Industry* (New York: Basic Books, 1989).

110. Christopher Pyle, "CONUS Intelligence: The Army Watches Civilian Politics," *Washington Monthly,* Jan. 1970, quoted in Charles Peters and Taylor Branch, *Blowing the Whistle: Dissent in the Public Interest* (New York: Praeger, 1972), 44.

111. Christopher Pyle, "CONUS Revisited: The Army Covers Up," *Washington Monthly,* July 1970, quoted in ibid., 59.

112. New York Times v. United States, 403 U.S. 713, 717 (1971).

113. Bernstein and Woodward, *All the President's Men,* 127n.

114. Quoted in ibid., 148.

115. Ibid., 133, 316. The question of whether information about personal health and driving records should be part of the presidential campaign is one that likely never will be answered satisfactorily. In part, such data does relate to the competency and reliability of the potential candidate. But some of it also is a gross invasion of privacy, particularly in the case of medical problems that were in the past. Such questions would rise again as the press ferreted out details of potential candidate Gary Hart's romantic adventures in the 1980s.

116. Quoted in Jules Witcover, "The Trials of a One-Candidate Campaign," *Columbia Journalism Review,* Jan./Feb. 1973, p. 26.

117. Quoted in ibid., 25.

118. Quoted in "Fairness and Balance in the Evening News," *Columbia Journalism Review,* Jan./Feb. 1973, p. 22.

119. Quoted in Ben H. Bagdikian, "The Fruits of Agnewism," *Columbia Journalism Review,* Jan./Feb. 1973, p. 21.

120. Quoted in Whiteside, 60.

121. Quoted in ibid.

122. Bagdikian, "The Fruits of Agnewism," 12–13.

123. Bagdikian, "The Politics of American Newspapers," 9.

124. Bagdikian, "The Fruits of Agnewism," 11.

125. Clay T. Whitehead, "Broadcasters and the Networks," *Vital Speeches,* 1 Feb. 1973, pp. 230–31.

126. Quoted in Whiteside, 75–76.

127. See Frank Donner, "The Confession of an FBI Informer," *Harper's,* Dec. 1972, pp. 54–65.

128. See "The Gainesville Eight," *Time,* 20 Aug. 1973, p. 46; "Judgment on Conspiracy," *Time,* 10 Sept. 1973, p. 12.

129. Melvin Small, *Johnson, Nixon, and the Doves* (New Brunswick, N.J.: Rutgers Univ. Press, 1988), 222–23. See also Nancy Zaroulis and Gerald Sullivan, *Who Spoke Up? American Protest Against the War in Vietnam, 1963–1975* (Garden City, N.Y.: Doubleday, 1984), 377–99.

130. See Martin F. Herz assisted by Leslie Rider, *The Prestige Press and the Christmas Bombing, 1972: Images and Reality in Vietnam* (Washington, D.C.: Ethics and Public Policy Center, 1980).

131. Robert H. Ferrell, "Emerging as a World Power," *The Almanac of American History,* ed. Arthur M. Schlesinger, Jr. (Greenwich, Conn.: Bison Books, 1983), 509.

132. Whiteside, 60–61.

133. Quoted in Bernstein and Woodward, *All the President's Men,* 105.

134. Quoted in Whiteside, 62.

135. Quoted in Bernstein and Woodward, *All the President's Men,* 275–76.

136. "Watergate: Words to Remember," *Columbia Journalism Review,* July/Aug. 1973, p. 19.

137. Quoted in Bernstein and Woodward, *All the President's Men,* 292.

138. Quoted in ibid., 311.

139. See Jules Witcover, "How Well Does the White House Press Perform?," *Columbia Journalism Review,* Nov./Dec. 1973, pp. 39–43.

140. John Edward Tyler, "Access to Presidential Materials," *Freedom of Information Center Report No. 346,* School of Journalism, Univ. of Missouri at Columbia, Nov. 1975, p. 2.

141. Quoted in "Agnew: Condemned by Leak?," *Columbia Journalism Review,* Nov./ Dec. 1973, p. 2.

142. Quoted in Bob Woodward and Carl Bernstein, *The Final Days* (New York: Simon and Schuster, 1976), 74.

143. Quoted in Porter, 185.

144. Quoted in Bernstein and Woodward, *All the President's Men,* 334.

145. Quoted in *The Almanac of American History,* 598.

146. United States v. Nixon, 418 U.S. 683, 706 (1974).

147. Tyler, 5.

148. 88 Stat. 1695 (1974).

149. Nixon v. Administrator of General Services, 433 U.S. 425 (1977).

150. Senate Select Committee to Study Governmental Operations with Respect to Intelligence Activities, *Final Report* (Washington: Government Printing Office, 1976), 2:1.

151. Ibid., 1, 6–7, 5.

152. Ibid., 5, 17.

153. Ibid., 290–91.

154. 88 Stat. 1896 (1974). See Richard Ehlke, "The Privacy Act after a Decade," *John Marshall Law Review* 18 (1985):829–46.

155. Hobson v. Wilson, 737 F.2d 1, 13 (D.C. Cir. 1984).

156. In 1960, John F. Kennedy and Richard Nixon spent about $25 million in the race for the presidency; about $175 million was spent in all elections that year. In 1972, the candidates for president spent $105 million, while other election spending was estimated at $250 million. Fred W. Friendly and Martha J. H. Elliott, *The Constitution: That Delicate Balance* (New York: Random House, 1984), 91–92.

157. 86 Stat. 3 (1972).

158. 88 Stat. 1263 (1974).

159. Buckley v. Valeo, 424 U.S. 1 (1976). See Friendly and Elliott, 91–107.

160. 424 U.S. at 28.

161. Ibid. at 40, 48.

162. Ibid. at 261, 265.

163. See, for example, Federal Election Commission v. National Conservative Political Action Committee, 470 U.S. 480 (1985).

Chapter 11

1. See Donna A. Demac, *Keeping America Uninformed: Government Secrecy in the 1980's* (New York: Pilgrim Press, 1984); and *Freedom at Risk: Secrecy, Censorship, and Repression in the 1980s,* ed. Richard O. Curry (Philadelphia: Temple Univ. Press, 1988).

2. Executive Order 12065, National Security Information, 28 June 1978, 3 *C.F.R.* 190, 191 (1979). See Roy Appleton III, "Official Secrecy: Rising or Demising?," *Freedom of Information Center Report No. 426,* School of Journalism, Univ. of Missouri at Columbia, Sept. 1980; and Karen M. Brown, "Government Classification: An Overview," *Freedom of Information Center Report No. 469,* School of Journalism, Univ. of Missouri at Columbia, Jan. 1983.

3. Executive Order 12356, National Security Information, 2 April 1982, 3 *C.F.R.* 167, 169–71 (1983).

4. Donna O'Neal, "Fighting Back: Congress Challenges Reagan's Information Pol-

icy," *Freedom of Information Center Report No. 498,* School of Journalism, Univ. of Missouri at Columbia, Sept. 1984, p. 4.

5. National Security Decision Directive 84, "Safeguarding National Security Information," 11 March 1983, reprinted in 9 Media Law Reporter 1759–60 (1983).

6. See Michael L. Warden, "Prepublication Review of Government Employee Speech: A Case Study of the Department of Defense and United States Air Force Security/Policy Review Programs" (Paper presented to the History Division, Association for Education in Journalism and Mass Communication Annual Convention, Portland, Ore., July 1988).

7. See Glenn J. Ruffenach, "The CIA and Censorship," *Freedom of Information Center Report No. 430,* School of Journalism, Univ. of Missouri at Columbia, Nov. 1980; and Jack Hitt, "Warning: CIA Censors at Work," *Columbia Journalism Review,* July/Aug. 1984, pp. 44, 46.

8. United States v. Marchetti, 466 F.2d 1309, 1315 (4th Cir. 1972).

9. Ibid. at 1317.

10. Ibid. at 1318.

11. See Michael L. Warden, "Tilting the Balance Toward Secrecy: 'Mosaic' Theory and Release of Information under the Freedom of Information Act" (Paper presented to the Law Division, Association for Education in Journalism and Mass Communication Annual Convention, Washington, D.C., Aug. 1989).

12. Snepp v. United States, 444 U.S. 507, 512 (1980).

13. Ibid. at 520, 526.

14. Haig v. Agee, 453 U.S. 280 (1981).

15. 96 Stat. 122 (1982).

16. Quoted in Angus Mackenzie, "Fit To Be Tied," *Quill,* July/Aug. 1985, p. 13.

17. *New York Times,* 21 Dec. 1985, quoted in Steven L. Katz, *Government Secrecy: Decisions Without Democracy* (Washington, D.C.: People for the American Way, 1987), 28.

18. Peter Hernon and Charles R. McClure, *Federal Information Policies in the 1980's: Conflicts and Issues* (Norwood, N.J.: Ablex Publishing, 1984), 65.

19. See Diana M. T. K. Autin, "The Reagan Administration and the Freedom of Information Act," in *Freedom at Risk,* 69–85.

20. See Central Intelligence Agency v. Sims, 471 U.S. 159 (1985).

21. 94 Stat. 2818 (1980).

22. O'Neal, 5.

23. See Donna A. Demac, "Office of Management and Budget: The Hidden Power," in *Freedom at Risk,* 103–16.

24. See Peter Braestrup, *Battle Lines: Report of the Twentieth Century Fund Task Force on the Military and the Media* (New York: Priority Press, 1985), 83–109; Elizabeth Hannan, "Censorship during the Invasion of Grenada: The Press, the Public and the Pentagon" (Paper presented to the International Division, Association for Education in Journalism and Mass Communication Annual Convention, Portland, Ore., July 1988); and Michael L. Warden, "The Military and the Media in Conflict: The Sidle Panel and the U.S. Invasion of Grenada" (Paper presented to the Mass Communication and Society Division, Association for Education in Journalism and Mass Communication Annual Convention, Portland, Ore., July 1988).

25. Phillip Knightley, "The Falklands: How Britannia Ruled the News," *Columbia Journalism Review,* Sept./Oct. 1982, pp. 51–53.

26. "Coverage Efforts Thwarted," *News Media & the Law,* Jan./Feb. 1984, p. 6; and Lyle Denniston, "Planning for Future Grenadas," *Quill,* Jan. 1984, pp. 10–13.

27. General John W. Vessey, "Meet the Press," 6 Nov. 1983, transcript, 3, quoted in Warden, "The Military and the Media in Conflict," 13.

28. "Battle Coverage Restrictions Debated," *News Media & the Law,* Summer 1986, p. 23.

29. "Pool Stories Delayed, Censored," *News Media & the Law,* Fall 1987, pp. 3–4.

30. [Raleigh, N.C.] *News and Observer,* 25 Jan. 1990 [hereafter cited as *News and Observer*].

31. Richard Zoglin, "It Was a Public Relations Rout Too," *Time,* 11 March 1991, pp. 56–57.

32. " 'No Vietnam,'" *Newsweek,* 10 Dec. 1990, pp. 24–25.

33. Howard Rosenberg, "TV and the Gulf War," *Quill,* March 1991, pp. 17–18.

34. "The People, The Press and the War in the Gulf," *Quill,* March 1991, p. 16.

35. See, for example, Lewis H. Lapham, "Trained Seals and Sitting Ducks," *Harper's Magazine,* May 1991, pp. 10–15.

36. Walter Cronkite, "What Is There to Hide?" *Newsweek,* 25 Feb. 1991, p. 43.

37. Testimony of Sidney Schanberg, Hearing before the Senate Committee on Governmental Affairs on Pentagon Rules on Media Access to the Persian Gulf War, 20 Feb. 1991, typescript copy, pp. 2, 6–7.

38. Nation Magazine v. U.S. Department of Defense, 762 F. Supp. 1558, 1561, 1569 (SDNY 1991).

39. See William Preston, Jr., and Ellen Ray, "Disinformation and Mass Deception: Democracy as a Cover Story," in *Freedom at Risk,* 203–23.

40. "A Bodyguard of Lies," *Newsweek,* 13 Oct. 1986, pp. 43–44, 46 (emphasis included).

41. Quoted in "White House 'Disinforms' Media, Public," *News Media & the Law,* Winter 1987, p. 7.

42. See Mark Hertsgaard, *On Bended Knee: The Press and the Reagan Presidency* (New York: Farrar, Straus & Giroux, 1988; rpt., New York: Schocken, 1989); Peter Stoler, *The War Against the Press: Politics, Pressure and Intimidation in the 80's* (New York: Dodd, Mead, 1986); Anthony Lewis, "The Intimidated Press," *New York Review of Books,* 19 Jan. 1989, pp. 26–28; C. T. Hanson, "Gunsmoke and Sleeping Dogs: The Prez's Press at Midterm," *Columbia Journalism Review,* May/June 1983, pp. 27–35; Jonathan Evan Maslow and Ana Arana, "Operation El Salvador," *Columbia Journalism Review,* May/June 1981, pp. 52–58; Herbert J. Gans, "Are U.S. Journalists Dangerously Liberal?," *Columbia Journalism Review,* Nov./Dec. 1985, pp. 29–33; Dan Hallin, "The Myth of the Adversary Press," *Quill,* Nov. 1983, pp. 31–32, 34–36; Scott Armstrong, "Iran-Contra: Was the Press Any Match for All the President's Men?," *Columbia Journalism Review,* May/June 1990, pp. 27–35.

43. See Bruce M. Swain, "*The Progressive,* the Bomb and the Papers," *Journalism Monographs,* No. 76, May 1982; Robert Friedman, "The United States v. The Progressive," *Columbia Journalism Review,* July/Aug. 1979, pp. 27–35; A. DeVolpi, G. E. Marsh, T. A. Postol, and G. S. Stanford, *Born Secret: The H-Bomb, the Progressive Case and National Security* (New York: Pergamon, 1981); and Nick Wreden, "Prior Restraint and the Progressive," *Freedom of Information Center Report No. 446,* School of Journalism, Univ. of Missouri at Columbia, Oct. 1981.

44. 68 Stat. 924 (1954).

45. *Los Angeles Times,* 13 March 1979.

46. Quoted in Friedman, 31.

47. United States v. The Progressive, 467 F.Supp. 990, 992–94 (W.D.Wis. 1979).

48. Ibid. at 995–96.

49. "The 'Secret' Revealed," *The Progressive,* Nov. 1979, p. 8 (emphasis included).

50. *St. Petersburg Times,* 19 Sept. 1979.

51. *Detroit Free Press,* 19 Sept. 1979.

52. *Sacramento Bee,* 24 Sept. 1979.

53. See Clark R. Mollenhoff, "Britain's Blindfolded Press," *Quill,* July/Aug. 1986, pp. 24–28.

54. See Philip Weiss, "The Quiet Coup," *Harper's Magazine,* Sept. 1989, pp. 54–65.

55. 64 Stat. 1004 (1950).

56. United States v. Morison, 604 F.Supp. 655, 660 (D.Md. 1985).

57. Quoted in Weiss, 62–63.

58. United States v. Morison, 844 F.2d 1057, 1081 (4th Cir. 1988).

59. Ibid. at 1084.

60. 65 Stat. 719 (1951).

61. See Jay Peterzell, "Can the CIA Spook the Press?," *Columbia Journalism Review,* Sept./Oct. 1986, pp. 29–34; "CIA Head Threatens Espionage Charges," *News Media & the Law,* Summer 1986, pp. 4–6; and "A Crackdown on Leaks," *Newsweek,* 19 May 1986, p. 66.

62. Quoted in "CIA Head Threatens," 5.

63. Quoted in ibid.

64. Quoted in Peterzell, 30.

65. Quoted in "CIA Head Threatens," 5.

66. *News and Observer,* 31 May 1986.

67. Ibid., 1 June 1986.

68. "A Crackdown on Leaks," 66.

69. 52 Stat. 631 (1938).

70. "Canada Film Orders Spark Lawsuits, Bill," *News Media & the Law,* Jan./Feb. 1984, p. 8.

71. 56 Stat. 250–51 (1942).

72. "Canada Film Orders," 8.

73. "Labeling Canadian Films 'Propaganda' Does Not Infringe Freedom of Speech," *News Media & the Law,* Summer 1987, p. 15.

74. Meese v. Keene, 481 U.S. 465, 480, 483 (1987).

75. Ibid. at 486, 488.

76. Regan v. Wald, 468 U.S. 222 (1984).

77. 66 Stat. 184 (1952).

78. See Burt Neuborne and Steven R. Shapiro, "The Nylon Curtain: America's National Border and the Free Flow of Ideas," *William and Mary Law Review* 26 (1985):719–77; and Steven R. Shapiro, "Ideological Exclusions: Closing the Border to Political Dissidents," *Harvard Law Review* 100 (1987):930–45.

79. Kleindienst v. Mandel, 408 U.S. 753 (1972).

80. 92 Stat. 970 (1978).

81. Abourezk v. Reagan, 785 F.2d 1043, 1058 (D.C. Cir. 1986) (emphasis included).

82. 104 Stat. 30 (1990).

83. 101 Stat. 1399–400 (1987).

84. John Shattuck, "Federal Restrictions on the Free Flow of Academic Information and Ideas," in *Freedom at Risk,* 54–55.

85. Quoted in Gene Lanier, "Libraries Invaded by the FBI," *Free Speech Yearbook 1987,* 69–70.

86. West Virginia State Board of Education v. Barnette, 319 U.S. 624 (1943).

87. Texas v. Johnson, 109 S.Ct. 2533, 2536 (1989).

88. See Karen Markin, "Land of the Free or Home of Obeisance: The Supreme Court and Compelled Respect for the Flag" (Seminar paper, School of Journalism, Univ. of North Carolina at Chapel Hill, 1990).

89. 109 S.Ct. at 2544–45, 2547–48.

90. Ibid. at 2548.

91. Senate Resolution 151, 101st Cong., 1st sess., *Congressional Record* (22 June 1989), S7189. See Randall Chase, "The Flag and Free Speech: A Burning Issue in the U.S. Congress" (Seminar paper, School of Journalism, Univ. of North Carolina at Chapel Hill, 1990).

92. Senate, Proposed Amendment to Protect the American Flag, 101st Cong., 1st sess., *Congressional Record* (17 October 1989), S13503.

93. United States v. O'Brien, 391 U.S. 367 (1968).

94. Texas Penal Code Ann., Sec. 42.09, quoted in Chase, 1.

95. 103 Stat. 777 (1989).

96. Quoted in *Durham* [N.C.] *Morning Herald,* 29 Oct. 1989.

97. United States v. Eichman, 110 S.Ct. 2405, 2410 (1990).

98. The actual vote was 254 in favor of the amendment to 177 against. *News and Observer,* 22 June 1990.

99. The actual vote was 58 for and 42 against. *Durham Morning Herald,* 27 June 1990.

100. Quoted in Joseph Leibowicz, "The Proposed English Language Amendment: Shield or Sword?," *Yale Law & Policy Review* 3 (1985):520.

101. *Arizona Constitution,* amend. XXVIII, 1, sec. 1–3, quoted in Yniguez v. Mofford, 730 F.Supp. 309, 317 (D.Ariz. 1990).

102. Ibid. at 314.

103. See Michael Ratner and Eleanor Stein, "The New Conspiracy Trial: Patterns in Federal Prosecution," in *Freedom at Risk,* 289–300.

104. Quoted in Athan Theoharis, "Conservative Politics and Surveillance: The Cold War, the Reagan Administration and the FBI," in *Freedom at Risk,* 265. See also Geoffrey R. Stone, "The Reagan Administration, the First Amendment, and FBI Domestic Security Investigations," in *Freedom at Risk,* 272–88.

105. Executive Order 12333, United States Intelligence Activities, 4 Dec. 1981, 3 *C.F.R.* 200.

106. See Pam Solo, *From Protest to Policy: Beyond the Freeze to Common Security* (Cambridge, Mass.: Ballinger, 1988).

107. Quoted in ibid., 94.

108. *New York Times,* 6 Oct. 1982, quoted in ibid., 96.

109. Ronald Reagan news conference, 12 Nov. 1982, quoted in ibid., 99.

110. "The Bishops Call a 'Halt,'" *Newsweek,* 16 May 1983, p. 26.

111. Isaiah 2:4.

112. *Swords into Plowshares: Nonviolent Direct Action for Disarmament,* eds. Arthur J. Laffin and Anne Montgomery (San Francisco: Harper & Row, 1987), 32–45.

113. See Michael McConnell and Renny Golden, "The Sanctuary Movement," in *Freedom at Risk,* 301–14.

114. Ann Crittenden, *Sanctuary: A Story of American Conscience and the Law in Collision* (New York: Weidenfeld & Nicholson, 1988), 327–28.

115. Quoted in ibid., 329.

116. Immigration and Naturalization Service v. Cardoza-Fonseca, 480 U.S. 421 (1987).

117. Roe v. Wade, 410 U.S. 113 (1973).

118. City of Akron v. Akron Center for Reproductive Health, 462 U.S. 415 (1983).

119. See Faye D. Ginsburg, *Contested Lives: The Abortion Debate in an American Community* (Berkeley: Univ. of California Press, 1989), 43–57.

120. Ibid., 50.

121. Ibid., 51. See also Michele Kort, "Domestic Terrorism: On the Front Line in an Abortion Clinic," *Ms.,* May 1987, pp. 48–53.

122. Frisby v. Schultz, 487 U.S. 474 (1988).

123. Ibid. at 494, 477, 479, 483.

124. Ibid. at 486–87.

125. Ibid. at 493–94.

126. Proverbs 24:11.

127. See Garry Wills, " 'Save the Babies,'" *Time,* 1 May 1989, pp. 26–28; Peg Tyre, "Holy War: On the Anti-Abortion Front Lines with Operation Rescue," *New York,* 24 April 1989, pp. 49–51; and Joseph M. Connors, "Operation Rescue," *America,* 29 April 1989, pp. 400–402, 406.

128. *News and Observer,* 15 May 1990.

129. *Durham Morning Herald,* 22 May 1990.

130. For a discussion of this controversy see Carole I. Chervin, "The Title X Family Planning Gag Rule: Can the Government Buy Up Constitutional Rights?," *Stanford Law Review* 41 (1989):401–34.

131. Rust v. Sullivan, 111 S. Ct. 1759, 1772 (1991).

132. Ibid. at 1780, 1781.

133. *News and Observer,* 25 May 1991.

134. "Tilting at 'Secular Humanism,'" *Time,* 28 July 1986, p. 68.

135. Mozert v. Hawkins County Board of Education, 579 F.Supp. 1051 (E.D.Tenn. 1984), 582 F.Supp. 201 (E.D.Tenn. 1984), 765 F.2d 75 (6th Cir. 1985), 647 F.Supp. 1194 (E.D.Tenn. 1986), 827 F.2d 1058 (6th Cir. 1987); and Smith v. Board of School Commissioners of Mobile County, 655 F.Supp. 939 (S.D.Ala. 1987), 827 F.2d 684 (11th Cir. 1978).

136. See, for example, Board of Education v. Pico, 457 U.S. 853 (1982).

137. Edwards v. Aguillard, 482 U.S. 578 (1987).

138. See Donald E. Wildmon, *The Case Against Pornography* (Wheaton, Ill.: Victor Books, 1986).

139. See Margaret A. Blanchard, "The American Urge to Censor: Freedom of Expression versus The Desire to Sanitize Society, from Anthony Comstock to 2 Line Crew," *William and Mary Law Review* (Spring 1992).

140. See Anne W. Nunamaker and Maurine H. Beasley, "Women, the First Amendment and Pornography: An Historical Perspective," *Studies in Communications* 4 (1990):101–18.

141. Catharine A. MacKinnon, "Pornography, Civil Rights, and Speech," *Harvard Civil Rights-Civil Liberties Law Review* 20 (1985):51–52.

142. See Donald Alexander Downs, *The New Politics of Pornography* (Chicago: Univ. of Chicago Press, 1989).

143. New York v. Ferber, 458 U.S. 747 (1982).

144. American Booksellers Association, Inc. v. Hudnut, 598 F.Supp. 1316, 1330 (S.D.Ind. 1984) (emphasis included).

145. American Booksellers Association, Inc. v. Hudnut, 771 F.2d 323, 325 (7th Cir. 1985).

146. Hudnut v. American Booksellers Association, Inc., 475 U.S. 1001 (1986).

147. *News and Observer,* 18 May 1986.

148. *Final Report of the Attorney General's Commission on Pornography* (Nashville, Tenn.: Rutledge Hill Press, 1986), 24.

149. Federal and state prosecutors have moved against sexually explicit materials in this context since the Meese Commission report was published. The Supreme Court has found no First Amendment impediment to the use of racketeering laws to punish distributors of obscenity. See Fort Wayne Books Inc. v. Indiana, 109 S.Ct. 916 (1989).

150. *Final Report of the Attorney General's Commission,* 77, 82.

151. *News and Observer,* 10 July 1986.

152. *Legal Times,* 18 June 1990.

153. *Legal Times,* 30 July 1990. See PHE, Inc. v. United States Department of Justice, 743 F.Supp. 15 (D.D.C. 1990).

154. See Bob Cohn, "The Trials of Adam & Eve," *Newsweek,* 7 Jan. 1991, p. 48.

155. The background of the fight against more modern music is discussed in Linda Martin and Kerry Segrave, *Anti-Rock: The Opposition to Rock 'n' Roll* (Hamden, Conn.: Archon Books, 1988).

156. Peggy Mann, "How Shock Rock Harms Our Kids," *Reader's Digest,* July 1988, pp. 101–5.

157. *Variety,* 14 Aug. 1985.

158. Ibid., 18 and 25 Sept. 1985.

159. Ibid., 6 Nov. 1985.

160. Ibid., 17 Dec. 1986, 17 June 1987.

161. *News and Observer,* 26 May 1990.

162. Skyywalker Records Inc. v. Navarro, 739 F.Supp. 578 (1990).

163. N.W.A., or Niggas with Attitude, a black rap group, ran afoul of the FBI with the song "F– Tha Police."

164. One of the top groups, Guns 'N' Roses, got in trouble for a song called "Used to Love Her," in which they chanted, "I used to love her but I had to kill her." Quoted in "The Rap Attitude," *Newsweek,* 19 March 1990, p. 58.

165. Public Enemy advocated blatant anti-Semitism: "So-called chosen, frozen." Quoted in ibid., 57.

166. For a discussion of music censorship as a racial issue, see Amanda Fox Spence, "Music Censorship in America: Will the Beat Go On?" (Honors essay, School of Journalism and Mass Communication, University of North Carolina at Chapel Hill, 1991).

167. *News and Observer,* 10 Jan. 1990.

168. "Gone Platinum," *Newsweek,* 30 July 1990, p. 57.

169. 739 F.Supp. at 591, 596.

170. *Durham Morning Herald,* 13 Dec. 1990.

171. Ibid., 21 Oct. 1990.

172. George F. Will, "America's Slide into the Sewer," *Newsweek,* 30 July 1990, p. 64.

173. Ward v. Rock Against Racism, 109 S.Ct. 2746, 2753 (1989).

174. Ginsberg v. New York, 390 U.S. 629 (1968).

175. *Wall Street Journal,* 4 Dec. 1986, quoted in John Crigler and William J. Byrnes, "Decency Redux: The Curious History of the New FCC Broadcast Indecency Policy," *Catholic University Law Review* 38 (1989):344. Wildmon's concerns about the quality of television broadcasting are detailed in Donald E. Wildmon, *The Home Invaders* (Wheaton, Ill.: Victor Books, 1985).

176. FCC v. Pacifica Foundation, 438 U.S. 726 (1978).

177. Station KPFK-FM in Los Angeles, another station licensed by the Pacifica Foundation, contended that the sections of the play, "The Jerker," carried over the air were an important part of a discussion on AIDS and were included within a program called "I Am Are You?" ("IMRU"), which was aimed at the area's homosexual community. The lan-

guage found offensive included: "I'll give you the gentlest fuck west of the Mississippi" and "We cuddled and played around a bit before he started working on my ass." The dialogue came from a conversation between two men. In the Matter of Pacifica Foundation, 2 F.C.C. Rcd 2698, 2700 (1987).

178. The objectionable song, played over KCSB-FM, in Santa Barbara, California, was "Makin' Bacon." See In the Matter of the Regents of The University of California, 2 F.C.C. Rcd 2703 (1987).

179. The show, hosted by Howard Stern, in Philadelphia, Pennsylvania, was carried during the morning hours and focused on sexually explicit dialogue between the host and those who called in. One excerpt that the FCC found offensive was:

STERN: "God, my testicles are like down to the floor. Boy, Susan, you could really have a party with these. I'm telling you honey."

RAY: "Use them like Bocci balls."

Quoted in In the Matter of Infinity Broadcasting Corporation of Pennsylvania, 2 F.C.C. Rcd 2705, 2706 (1987).

180. New Indecency Enforcement Standards, 62 Rad. Reg. (P&F) 1218 (1987).

181. In the Matter of Infinity Broadcasting Corporation of Pennsylvania, 3 F.C.C. Rcd 930, 937, n.47 (1987).

182. Action for Children's Television v. FCC, 852 F.2d 1332 (1988).

183. *Congressional Record,* 100th Cong., 2d sess., 26 July 1988, S9911–12.

184. 51 Stat. 1091 (1934).

185. 18 U.S.C. §1464 (1982).

186. 102 Stat. 2228 (1988).

187. 47 C.F.R. §73.3999 (1988).

188. Order, Action for Children's Television v. FCC, No. 88–1916, (D.C. Cir. filed 23 Jan. 1989), cited in Crigler and Byrnes, 331.

189. Sable Communications of California v. FCC, 109 S.Ct. 2829, 2836 (1989).

190. Notice of Inquiry, 4 F.C.C. Rcd 8358 (1989).

191. Ibid. at 6360–64.

192. In the Matter of Enforcement of Prohibitions Against Broadcast Indecency in 18 U.S.C. §1464, 5 F.C.C. Rcd 5297 (1990).

193. Telephone interview with Peggy Charren, president, Action for Children's Television, 22 March 1991.

194. Action for Children's Television v. Federal Communications Commission, 932 F.2d 1504, 1509 (D.C. Cir. 1991).

195. Persons concerned about the decency of material going into American homes also have attacked cable television programming. Most of the controversy here has focused on state and local attempts to regulate content. Because of the voluntary nature of cable subscriptions, such efforts have fallen before the First Amendment. Cases include Community Television of Utah, Inc. v. Roy City, 555 F.Supp. 1164 (D.C.Utah 1982) and Cruz v. Ferre, 755 F.2d 1415 (11th Cir. 1985).

196. William E. Leuchtenburg, *Franklin Roosevelt and the New Deal, 1932–1940* (New York: Harper Torchbooks, 1963), 126–28.

197. *Durham Morning Herald,* 3 Sept. 1989.

198. Ibid., 1 April 1990.

199. *News and Observer,* 28 July 1989.

200. *Durham Morning Herald,* 28 July 1989.

201. Miller v. California, 413 U.S. 15 (1973).

202. *Durham Morning Herald,* 30 Sept. 1989.

203. Bella Lewitzky Dance Foundation v. Frohnmayer, 754 F.Supp. 774, 783 (C.D.Cal. 1991).

204. *Durham Morning Herald,* 24 March 1990.

205. *News and Observer,* 28 Oct. 1990.

206. *Durham Morning Herald,* 8 April 1990.

207. "Mixed Signals on Obscenity," *Newsweek,* 15 Oct. 1990, p. 74.

208. National Socialist Party of America v. Village of Skokie, 432 U.S. 43 (1977); Village of Skokie v. National Socialist Party of America, 366 N.E.2d 347 (Ill. App. 1977); 373 N.E.2d 21 (Ill. Sup.Ct. 1978). General background on the Skokie incident is taken from Aryeh Neier, *Defending My Enemy: American Nazis, the Skokie Case, and the Risks of Freedom* (New York: E. P. Dutton, 1979); and Samuel Walker, *In Defense of American Liberties: A History of the ACLU* (New York: Oxford Univ. Press, 1990), 323–40. Neier was executive director of the ACLU during the Skokie incident.

209. Collin v. Smith, 447 F.Supp. 676, 686, 688 (N.D.Ill. 1978).

210. Collin v. Smith, 578 F.2d 1197, 1200 (7th Cir. 1978).

211. Smith v. Collin, 439 U.S. 916, 919 (1978).

212. Neier, 7.

213. 439 U.S. at 919.

214. Richard Delgado, "Words That Wound: A Tort Action for Racial Insults, Epithets, and Name-Calling," *Harvard Civil Rights-Civil Liberties Law Review* 17 (1982):14.

215. See, for instance, R. George Wright, "Racist Speech and the First Amendment," *Mississippi College Law Review* 9 (1988):1–28; and Mari J. Matsuda, "Public Response to Racist Speech: Considering the Victim's Story," *Michigan Law Review* 87 (1989):2320–81.

216. *Los Angeles Times,* 12 Feb. 1991.

217. *New York Times,* 29 June 1990.

218. Nancy Gibbs, "Bigots in the Ivory Tower," *Time,* 7 May 1990, pp. 104–6.

219. *News and Observer,* 22 May 1989, 9 July 1989.

220. *Durham Morning Herald,* 11 May 1989.

221. Doe v. University of Michigan, 721 F.Supp. 852, 853, 868 (E.D.Mich. 1989).

222. *Chicago Tribune,* 18 March 1991.

223. *New York Times,* 12 Feb. 1991.

224. *Los Angeles Times,* 12 Feb. 1991.

225. *Chicago Tribune,* 18 March 1991.

226. *Wall Street Journal,* 1 May 1991.

227. *Durham Morning Herald,* 21 May 1990.

228. "Taking Offense," *Newsweek,* 24 Dec. 1990, pp. 48–54; and William A. Henry III, "Upside Down in the Groves of Academe," *Time,* 1 April 1991, pp. 66–68.

229. [Durham, N.C.] *Herald-Sun,* 5 May 1991.

230. *News and Observer,* 5 May 1991.

Epilogue

1. *New York Times,* 15 May 1990.

Index